Critical Thinking Handbook:

4th – 6th Grades

A Guide for Remodelling Lesson Plans
in
Language Arts, Social Studies, & Science

by
Richard Paul, A. J. A. Binker, Karen Jensen, and Heidi Kreklau

Foundation for Critical Thinking
Sonoma State University
Rohnert Park, CA 94928
707-664-2940
© 1990

Acknowledgements
We wish to acknowledge the many helpful suggestions
and criticisms of Marla Charbonneau, Ken Adamson,
Roxane Wilkinson, Chris Vetrano, and Trish Taylor.
They are, of course, not responsible for any errors, mis-
takes, or misconceptions.

Price: $18.00
ISBN 0-944583-01-6
Library of Congress Catalog Card Number: 87-72836

Contents

6 Remodelling Social Studies Lessons

7 Remodelling Science Lessons

8 Remodelling Lessons in Other Subjects

Part II: Achieving the Deeper Understandings

9 Thinking Critically About Teaching: From Didactic to Critical Teaching

Appendices
Resources for Teaching Critical Thinking

Introduction

The Design of the Book

This handbook has one basic objective: to demonstrate that it is possible and practical to integrate instruction for critical thinking into the teaching of all subjects. We focus on language arts, social studies, and science, but we believe that the range of sample *before* and *after* lessons we provide will prove to any open-minded person that teaching so as to cultivate the critical thinking of students is eminently *practical.* We also believe that it should be given the highest priority, for it is *necessary* if we genuinely want to prepare our students for the real world which awaits them personally, politically, and vocationally.

Of course, to say that it is practical is not to say that it is simple and easy. To teach for critical thinking requires that teachers themselves think critically, and very often teachers have not been encouraged to do so. Furthermore, sometimes they do not feel competent to do so. Every teacher interested in fostering critical thinking must be prepared to undergo an evolutionary process over an extended period of time. Mistakes will be made along the way. Many didactic teaching habits have to be broken down, to be replaced by ones more like coaching than lecturing. In any case, there are many dimensions of critical thinking, and one needs to be patient to come to terms with them. Of course, since critical thinking is essential in the life of adults as well as children, teachers will find many uses for their emerging critical thinking abilities in their everyday life outside the classroom: as a consumer, citizen, lover, and person.

We have divided this handbook into two parts: "Putting Critical Thinking into Instruction," and "Achieving the Deeper Understandings." We have put a good deal of the theory of critical thinking instruction in "Part Two" because most teachers like to get a good look at application before they spend much time on theory. In a way this makes good sense. Why learn a theory if you're not happy with what the theory makes possible? On the other hand, it is sometimes hard to understand and appreciate the application if one is not clear about the theory that underlies it. *How* and *why* are often deeply intertwined. We hope therefore that the reader will move back and forth between parts one and two, as needed. It would probably be a good idea to thumb through the book as a whole, familiarizing yourself with what's there, so that when you run into a problem you will be apt to remember sections of the book that are likely to shed light upon it. For example, notice that the glossary of critical thinking terms may be of use if you run across a term in critical thinking whose use and importance is not perfectly clear to you. In fact, reading randomly in the glossary is a good way to stimulate your sense of what critical thinking is.

Each of the chapters makes the transition from a didactic paradigm of education to a critical one a little easier. This chapter provides an introduction to critical thinking and its importance for education, an introduction to lesson remodelling, and some suggestions for using this book. Chapter 2, "Global Strategies", begins to delve more deeply into what education for critical thought requires of teachers. Chapter 3 describes the thirty-five remodelling strategies, explains their importance, and suggests how to teach for them. The rest of "Part One" consists primarily of remodelled lessons. The three main subject areas are introduced with chapters describing the relationship between the subject and critical thought, and some frequently encountered flaws in textbook approaches.

"Part II: Achieving the Deeper Understandings", opens with a comparison of didactic and critical views on education. Its purpose is to help teachers grasp the educational big picture, and distinguish what education is and is not. It includes common features of texts that impede critical thought. Chapter 9 outlines the changes in curriculum required by a shift toward education for critical thought. Chapter 10 and 11 provide practical ideas for facilitating staff development in critical thinking. Chapter 12, "What Critical Thinking Means to Me", consists of short writings on critical thinking by Greensboro teachers after a workshop on critical thinking. In chapter 13 we consider the problem of defining critical thinking, and examine several definitions. Chapter 14 is an analytic glossary of words and phrases key to critical thinking and education.

Why Critical Thinking Is Essential to Education

If we consider some of the many complaints of classroom teachers concerning their pupils and then contrast them with what we look for in the ideal student, we will recognize that the fundamental missing element in schooling today is *thinking students* or, more precisely, *critically thinking* students.

Here are some of the many complaints we hear from teachers:

✓ "Most students aren't motivated; they don't want to study or work. They look for chances to goof off, clown around, or disrupt class. They'd rather talk about music, clothes, cars, ..."

✓ "Students forget what they've learned. We have to keep going over the same points, reminding them of what they've learned, rather than building on past learning. Each class begins at square one."

✓ "Most students are obsessed with grades and don't care about learning."

✓ "They're impatient. They want clear simple answers and they want them fast."

✓ "They make the same mistakes over and over again. They don't learn to correct their own mistakes."

✓ "They don't use what they've learned."

✓ "They need to be told every little thing. They don't even try to figure things out. They want us to do all of their thinking for them."

✓ "When I ask if there are questions they don't have any; but they haven't understood the lesson."

✓ "When assigned position papers, many students just write facts. The rest simply state and repeat their feelings."

✓ "They hate to read. (It's boring.)"

✓ "They hate to write. (It's too hard.)"

✓ "Instead of explaining or developing their ideas, they just repeat themselves."

✓ "They can't seem to stay on topic for long without going off on tangents."

The kind of students teachers would like to have are equally easy to describe:

✓ Students who are motivated to learn, get excited by ideas, don't need to be reprimanded, and pay attention by choice.

✓ Students who remember what they learned yesterday, last month, last year; who don't have to be reminded over and over again what was covered before.

✓ Students who see grades as a by-product of learning; who put learning on a par with grades.

✓ Students who recognize that they can't completely understand everything at once, who are willing to delve; who are unsatisfied with pat answers.

✓ Students who learn from their mistakes, correct themselves.

✓ Students who *use* what they've learned.

✓ Students who can and will try to figure things out for themselves and don't expect me to do all of the thinking.

✓ Students who recognize when they don't understand something and can ask questions for clarification.

✓ Students who can get beyond the facts and the surface to explore deeper meaning; students who respond thoughtfully and go beyond knee-jerk reactions and first impressions.

✓ Students who like to read and talk about what they've read.

✓ Students who recognize the need to write in order to develop their ideas.

✓ Students who know the difference between explaining themselves and repeating themselves.

✓ Students who can and do stick to the point.

If we look closely at how teaching is typically structured, we will see that at the root of it are conceptions of knowledge, learning, and teaching that unwittingly take the motivation to *think* away from students. In most classes most of the time, teachers are talking and actively engaged, while students are listening passively. Most teachers' utterances are statements, not questions. When teachers ask questions, they typically wait only a couple of seconds before they answer their own questions. Knowledge is taken to be equivalent to recall, so that when students can repeat what the teacher or text said, they are thought to have knowledge. Attempt is continually made to reduce the complex to the simple, giving students formulas, procedures, short cuts, and algorithms to memorize and practice in hopes that understanding will emerge at the same time.

Schoenfeld reports on an experiment in which elementary students were asked questions like this: "There are 26 sheep and 10 goats on a ship. How old is the captain?" 76 of the 97 students "solved" the problem by adding, subtracting, multiplying or dividing. (Schoenfeld, 1989.) They felt they were expected to do so as quickly and "correctly" as possible. They did *not* feel they were expected to *make sense of* the problem. Instruction and practice had not emphasized *understanding* the problem.

Schoenfeld cites many similar cases, including a study that demonstrated that students tend to approach "word problems" in math by using the key word algorithm, that is, when reading problems like, "John had eight apples. He gave three to Mary. How many does John have left?", they look for the words like 'left' to tell them what operation to perform. As Schoenfeld puts it, "... the situation was so extreme that many students chose to subtract in a problem that began 'Mr. Left ...'." (Schoenfeld, 1982.) Giving students such short cuts as indicator words, though it seems to make learning easier, actually interferes with learning in a deeper sense. Students are, in effect, taught that problems can be solved by circling data and going through steps practiced before ("I'm supposed to do this, then this, then this."); that they shouldn't slow down and think things through. They have had much more practice going through the steps than they have at thinking things through.

This tendency toward robotic, mindless responses becomes obsessive in many students. Hence, in their minds, history class becomes a place where they hear names, dates, events, and judgments about them, and then try to repeat what they have heard on tests. Literature becomes uninteresting stories to remember along with what the teacher said is important about them, such as foreshadowing.

Consider how students are generally taught factual detail. Students are continually presented with easily retainable facts (for example, foreign countries' main exports), and merely expected to reiterate them. They do not clearly understand *why* they should remember these facts. These collections of facts become merely sets of words in their heads, with no meaning, significance, or use. They *can* have meaning to students, can become *intelligible* to students, when they tell students something important, something students need to know. If students are trying to understand a country's economic problems, it may become important to know its chief exports. In such a context, that fact isn't just sitting there in the student's head as a bunch of words, it has meaning. It has a place in a broader picture; it has consequences; it helps that student understand that country's problem. It is *context*, not the mere fact itself, that gives it meaning, that makes it intelligible.

Values and principles tend to be treated as though they were facts. They are stated, and students are expected to reiterate them. This sort of process does not produce *understanding*. Principles (such as, "Write clearly!" and, "Stick to the point!") have their meaning and their justification in their application, in their *use*. I may know that I'm supposed to stick to the point, but this principle is little more than words to me if I don't know *how* to stick to the point, if I don't learn how to recognize *for myself* when I'm focused and when I stray. I can only learn how by practice, by *thinking* — by trying, sometimes succeeding, sometimes failing, by seeing for myself when I succeeded, when I failed, and by *understanding* the differences between the successes and failures.

A critical model of education reverses these patterns at every point. Students are continually asked to think about what they learn, to try to apply their new ideas, to compare their own ideas with those in their textbooks, to actively discuss what they are learning in small groups.

The underlying assumption in present education is that knowledge consists of bits of information, concepts, and skills which students can learn through lecture and rote memorization. Educators assume that students automatically replace ignorance with knowledge, misconception with truth. This assumption is unjustified.

One main consequence of this idea is that being told something, however clear the explanation, does not guarantee understanding. If you tell me something that contradicts or is incompatible with my present system of beliefs, I'm unlikely to replace my whole belief system with that new idea. I will often distort what you've said so that it fits my belief system. I may simply "tack it on" to my beliefs, ignoring the incompatibility between old and new, bouncing back and forth between them, sometimes using one, sometimes the other, willy-nilly; or I may simply fail to take it in at all. To really learn the new idea, I have to struggle through the problems the idea creates for me, *build* a new mental structure or system of beliefs. This process requires me to make my present beliefs explicit (figure out what I really think), and slowly reshape the old system into a new body of thought. Hence, to understand the new idea, concept, or principle, I have to think my way through to it, internalize it. One way to achieve this is through extended discussion, talking and listening to others as they internalize new knowledge. Consider how this conception of learning works.

When I state my thoughts aloud, I think again about what I'm saying, realize, perhaps, that my thinking is not clear. I may think of a new example; I may put the point in a slightly better way, or different way, and thus come to see new sense in it. When I have to convince others (such as classmates), I have to try to give convincing reasons for thinking as I do. The people I'm talking to respond: they understand some parts of what I've said better than others, forcing me to rephrase my point and so think it through again in a slightly different way, with the result that I understand it more clearly. My audience says things in response that had never occurred to me; they ask questions, raise objections, and so on. As I answer, I find myself saying things I hadn't realized I believed. Sometimes I say things I know are wrong, and so I have to change my original idea somewhat. My audience may suggest new examples, or expand on my ideas in a new way. In short, while I'm discussing things with my classmates *I am learning.* By listening to me, reacting, and hearing my replies, my classmates are learning. We're all thinking things through together. As a group, we know more, can figure out more, and have more and better ideas than any one of us has individually. Having done our own thinking and developed our own views, we understand more deeply; what we learn becomes part of us rather than mere words which we will soon forget.

This is at the heart of education for critical thought. Students learn to think by practicing thinking, learn to learn by practicing learning, learn to judge by practicing judging and by assessing those judgments. In this way, students come to use more of the full power of their minds.

When teachers begin to integrate critical thinking into their instructional practice, they have experiences like the following (taken from *The Greensboro Plan: Infusing Reasoning and Writing into the K-12 Curriculum*):

Beth:

I teach North Carolina History and 8th grade English, and I am always trying to bridge the gap and use an interdisciplinary approach. What critical thinking helps me do is go beyond the textbook and find things we can really discuss using the Socratic method — to go beyond just the facts and try to analyze the situation — to put ourselves in the other person's shoes — to look at a lot of different components.

Here is an article on slavery which I have copied and brought with me to show how you do not have to rewrite all your lesson plans to infuse critical thinking into your curriculum. Instead, you go further and bring in other things to enhance what you're teaching and give opportunities for discussion. This article is about slavery and slave trading. I have the students become one of the slaves on the ship and write a diary about how it would feel to be a slave. Later on in English, students write an essay on whether or not the ship captains should have been tried as criminals. This asks students to look at ideas from different viewpoints. For a final activity, I asked students to assume that they were a member of the English Parliament of 1807 and to write a persuasive essay on whether or not slavery should be banned and why.

Mandy:

Since I have taken part in this project, I have become a much more critical thinker. That's helped me tremendously in my classroom.

I always explain to my students how all our subjects are overlapping; this helps them in real life. One revised science lesson we used this year was building a rain forest in our room in a terrarium. We turned it into a vivarium by adding an anole, a small lizard.

The students decided they wanted to write a book about the anole, and the first thing they wanted to do was go to the library to *copy* information. Instead of this, we brainstormed to find out what we already knew and what we could learn just by observation. All my students became motivators for others while we worked with words.

After the pre-writing exercises, I took them to the media center for research. Again, they wanted to fall into the trap of copying from the encyclopedia. But I allowed them only to write down words — single words or maybe a phrase, rather than copying down sentences. It was difficult for them — it was difficult for me too.

They came back from the media center with ideas rather than with things they had copied. We talked about the ideas and categorized — and then I told them to write down ideas in their own words. It was amazing what happened! If I had given this assignment a year ago, a description of the anole would be only a few sentences long. My students this year wrote pages — they really did — and they were excited. This was their work; this was their description; it was not *World Book's* description. And it made it much more real to them — and of course more real to me, too.

In the first example, notice how students had to grapple again and again with the concept of slavery from different angles: What was it like? In what ways were different people partly responsible? What do I think of it? How can I convince others to agree with me? Each time students explored the issue, they were learning and using facts, probing and clarifying values, using principles, and each time they were putting these pieces together.

The second example above illustrates the difference between passive recall and active thought. Students first publicly shared their original beliefs, ideas, and suggestions. Then, when they consulted resources, they wrote only the barest bones of the information, and were thus forced to *reconstruct* the new knowledge. Furthermore, though this process was more difficult, the students wrote more and were more pleased with the results.

Finally, consider two more experiences of teaching students to learn deeply.

Sylvia

My involvement in the Reasoning and Writing project came about because I believe the following: *1)* students are faced with an explosion of information; *2)* given a limited time in which to learn, students must choose *what* information they need and learn *how* to acquire it; *3)* to make intelligent choices, students must exercise good judgment; *4)* successful living in today's world requires high order thinking and reasoning skills; *5)* writing can be used as a tool to improve thinking and reasoning skills in all curriculum areas ....

I have incorporated two new ideas this year: Socratic questioning and writing to aid concept development. I have worked primarily with one class, using questioning techniques to encourage students to think critically. The results have been encouraging: class discussions became more animated, students offered ideas freely, criticism was constructive, helpful, and resulted in better ideas. I believe that the entire class benefitted.

One high school teacher tried to focus on critical thinking in a sophomore English class. This teacher designed small group and paired discussions only to have the students complain, "You're supposed to use the grammar book. You're supposed to start on the first page and give us the sentences to do and then check them and then we do the next sentence ...."

The students insisted that "doing the sentences" was the top priority. One of the students said, in defense of this method, "We learned about prepositions." However, when the instructor asked the class *what* they had learned about prepositions, the class went silent. When asked, "Do you remember what prepositions are? Can you name some?" nobody could. Though this teacher continued her emphasis on critical thinking, she also gave students "sentences to do" for part of the class time. After the fourth day, no students objected when she neglected to assign more sentences. On their final exam, these students were asked, "Why is it better for a school to teach you how to find answers than to teach you the answers?" Among their responses were the following:

- ✓ So you can get in the habit of doing it yourself and not depend on someone else.
- ✓ When you teach people the answer, they will never try to find the answer thereself. They will look for somebody to give them the answer instead of looking for it because they don't know how to find it.
- ✓ When you get a job, they will expect you to find the answers yourself.
- ✓ Because it makes you feel good about yourself when you can look up something by yourself and get the answer correct. You feel more independent in school.
- ✓ School is not going to be with you all your life.
- ✓ So you can learn how to find the answers to *your* problems because one day you're going to have to find the answers yourself. Nobody is going to be able to give you the answers.
- ✓ Because it won't help you to know the answers and not know what they mean.
- ✓ Because in the future there won't be a teacher to hold your hand or to tell you everything you should know. You should learn on your own.

As you consider the rest of the material in this book, we ask you to apply these basic ideas to each facet of the task of incorporating critical thought into instructional practice. Just as students must struggle through a process of restructuring their thought to incorporate new facts, skills, and principles, so must teachers grapple with the problems of restructuring their conceptions of education and learn to apply the principles underlying it. We encourage you to work your way through our ideas — reading, explaining, listening, questioning, writing, applying, assessing — figuring out what you think about what we say.

Our Concept of Critical Thinking

Our basic concept of critical thinking is, at root, simple. We could define it as the art of taking charge of your own mind. Its value is also at root simple: if we can take charge of our own minds, we can take charge of our lives; we can improve them, bringing them under our self command and direction. Of course, this requires that we learn self-discipline and the art of self-examination. This involves becoming interested in how our minds work, how we can monitor, fine tune, and modify their operations for the better. It involves getting into the habit of reflectively examining our impulsive and accustomed ways of thinking and acting in every dimension of our lives.

All that we do, we do on the basis of some motivations or reasons. But we rarely examine our motivations to see if they make sense. We rarely scrutinize our reasons critically to see if they are rationally justified. As consumers we sometimes buy things impulsively and uncritically, without stopping to determine whether we really need what we are inclined to buy or whether we can afford it or whether it's good for our health or whether the price is competitive. As parents we often respond to our children impulsively and uncritically, without stopping to determine whether our actions are consistent with how we want to act as parents or whether we are contributing to their self esteem or whether we are discouraging them from thinking or from taking responsibility for their own behavior.

As citizens, too often we vote impulsively and uncritically, without taking the time to familiarize ourselves with the relevant issues and positions, without thinking about the long-run implications of what is being proposed, without paying attention to how politicians manipulate us by flattery or vague and empty promises. As friends, too often we become the victims of our own infantile needs, "getting involved" with people who bring out the worst in us or who stimulate us to act in ways that we have been trying to change. As husbands or wives, too often we think only of our own desires and points of view, uncritically ignoring the needs and perspectives of our mates, assuming that what we want and what we think is clearly justified and true, and that when they disagree with us they are being unreasonable and unfair.

As patients, too often we allow ourselves to become passive and uncritical in our health care, not establishing good habits of eating and exercise, not questioning what our doctor says, not designing or following good plans for our own well-ness. As teachers, too often we allow ourselves to uncritically teach as we have been taught, giving assignments that students can mindlessly do, inadvertently discouraging their initiative and independence, missing opportunities to cultivate their self-discipline and thoughtfulness.

It is quite possible, and unfortunately quite "natural", to live an unexamined life, to live in a more or less automated, uncritical way. It is possible to live, in other words, without really taking charge of the persons we are becoming, without developing, or acting upon, the skills and insights we are capable of. However, if we allow ourselves to become unreflective persons, or rather, to the extent that we do, we are likely to do injury to ourselves and others, and to miss many opportunities to make our own lives, and the lives of others, fuller, happier, and more productive.

On this view, as you can see, critical thinking is an eminently practical goal and value. It is focused on an ancient Greek ideal of "living an examined life". It is based on the skills, the insights, and the values essential to that end. It is a way of going about living and learning that empowers us and our students in quite practical ways. When taken seriously, it can transform every dimension of school life: how we formulate and promulgate rules, how we relate to our students, how we encourage them to relate to each other, how we cultivate their reading, writing, speaking, and listening, what we model for them in and outside the classroom, and how we do each of these things.

Of course, we are likely to make critical thinking a basic value in school only insofar as we make it a basic value in our lives. Therefore, to become adept at teaching so as to foster critical thinking, we must become committed to thinking critically and reflectively about our own lives and the lives of those around us. We must become active, daily, practitioners of critical thought. We must regularly model for our students what it is to reflectively examine, critically assess, and effectively improve the way we live.

Introduction to Remodelling: Components of Remodels and Their Functions

The basic idea behind lesson plan remodelling as a strategy for staff development in critical thinking is simple. Every practicing teacher works daily with lesson plans of one kind or another. To remodel lesson plans is to critique one or more lesson plans and formulate one or more new lesson plans based on that critical process. To help teachers generalize from specific remodelling moves, and so facilitate their grasp of strong sense critical thinking and how it can be taught, we have devised a list of teaching strategies. Each strategy highlights an aspect of critical thought. Each use of it illustrates how that aspect can be encouraged in students. In the chapter, "Strategies", we explain the thirty-five strategies illustrated in the remodels. Each strategy has two main parts: the "principle" and the "application". The principle links the strategy to the idea of strong sense critical thinking. In the application, we explain some ways the aspect of critical thought can be encouraged.

Complete remodelled lessons have three major components: an "Original Lesson", or statement of the "Standard Approach" (which describes the topic and how it is covered, including questions and activities); the "Critique" (which describes the significance of the topic and its value for the educated thinker, evaluates the original, and provides a general idea of how the lesson can be remodelled); and the "Remodelled Lesson" (which describes the new lesson, gives questions to be posed to students and student activities, and cites the critical thinking strategies by number). The strategy number generally follows the questions or activities it represents. When an entire remodel or section develops one dimension of critical thought in depth, the number appears at the top of the remodel or section. Complete remodel sets also include a list of "Objectives" which integrate the objectives of the original with the critical thinking goals; and the list of critical thinking "Strategies" applied in the remodel (listed in order of first appearance). Note the functions of these parts in the example below. Each component can serve some purpose for both the writer and the reader.

Advertising

Objectives of the remodelled lesson
The students will:
- practice listening critically by analyzing and evaluating T.V. commercials
- exercise fairmindedness by considering advertisements from a variety of perspectives
- analyze and evaluate the arguments given in ads
- practice using critical vocabulary to analyze and evaluate ads
- clarify key words
- distinguish relevant from irrelevant facts in ads
- examine assumptions in ads
- develop insight into egocentricity by exploring the ways in which ads appeal to unconscious desires

Standard Approach ──────────

> Very few texts actually address the issue of advertising. Those that do touch upon indicators to watch for which signal the use of some sort of reasoning — such indicators as "if ... then", "because", "since", "either ... or", and "therefore". Students are to decide if the reasoning presented is logical or illogical. Some lessons on ads focus on finding and decoding the factual information regarding sales. Students are often asked to write their own ads.

Critique

We chose this lesson for its subject: advertising. Ads are a natural tie-in to critical thinking, since many are designed to persuade the audience that it needs or wants a product. Ads provide innumerable clear-cut examples of irrelevance, distortion, suppressed evidence, and vague uses of language. Analysis of ads can teach students critical thinking micro-skills and show their use in context. Practice in analyzing and evaluating ads can help students develop the ability to listen critically. The standard approach, however, is not done in a way which best achieves these results.

Such lessons often focus more on writing ads than critiquing them. They tend to treat neutral and advertising language as basically equivalent in meaning, though different in effect, rather than pointing out how differences in effect arise from differences in meaning. They down-play the emptiness, irrelevance, repetition, questionable claims, and distortion of language in most ads. Their examples bear little resemblance to real ads. By rarely addressing ads aimed at students, texts minimize useful transfer.

Since most students are exposed to more television commercials than other ads, we recommend that students discuss real commercials aimed at them. We also provide suggestions for using ads to practice use of critical vocabulary and to discuss the visual and audio aspects of commercials.

Strategies used to remodel

S–22 listening critically: the art of silent dialogue
S–9   developing confidence in reason
S–14 clarifying and analyzing the meanings of words or phrases
S–16 evaluating the credibility of sources of information
S–3   exercising fairmindedness
S–31 distinguishing relevant from irrelevant facts
S–18 analyzing or evaluating arguments, interpretations, beliefs, or theories
S–35 exploring implications and consequences
S–30 examining or evaluating assumptions
S–28 thinking precisely about thinking: using critical vocabulary
S–2   developing insight into egocentricity or sociocentricity
S–29 noting significant similarities and differences

Remodelled Lesson Plan S–22

Due to the number of ads to which students are exposed, and their degree of influence, we recommend that the class spend as much time as possible on the subject. As students learn to approach ads thoughtfully and analytically and practice applying critical insight to their lives, they develop faith in their reasoning powers and their ability to see through attempts to irrationally manipulate them. **S–9**

To focus on ads and language, begin by having students give complete descriptions of what is said in a variety of television commercials. Put the quotes on the board. For each commercial, the class can evaluate the arguments presented in ads by discussing the following questions: What ideas does it give you about the product (or service) and owning or using it? Does it give reasons for buying the product? If so, what reasons? Are they good reasons? What are the key words? Do they have a clear meaning? What? **S–14** What other words could have been chosen? Who made this ad? Why? Do they have reason to distort evidence about the worth of the product? **S–16** How might someone who wasn't trying to sell the product describe it? How might a competitor describe it? **S–3** What would you need to know in order to make a wise decision about whether to buy it? Does the commercial address these points? **S–31** Why or why not? Has anyone here had experience with the product? What? **S–18**

The teacher interested in developing students' critical vocabulary can have students practice while critiquing ads. Use questions like the following: What does the ad *imply?* **S–35** Does the ad make, or lead the audience to make, any *assumptions?* Are the *assumptions* true, *questionable,* or false? **S–30** Does the ad contain an *argument?* If so, what is the *conclusion?* Is the *conclusion* stated or *implied?* Does the ad misuse any *concepts* or ideas? To judge the product, what facts are *relevant?* Are the *relevant* facts presented? **S–31** Does it make any *irrelevant* claims? **S–28**

When the commercials have been discussed, have students group them by the nature of the ads (repetition, positive but empty language, etc.) or by the appeals made (to the desires to have fun, be popular, seem older, etc.) Have students fill out the groups by naming similar commercials not previously discussed. Students could discuss why these appeals are made. "How do ads work? Why do they work? Do they work on you? On whom? Why? What are slogans for? Jingles? Why are running stories and continuing characters used? Why are the various techniques effective?" **S–2**

The class could also compare different ads for the same product, aimed at different audiences (e.g., fast food ads aimed at children, and at adults). "How do these two differ? Why? To whom is each addressed? Why are they different?" **S–29** The class could compare ads for different brands of the same or similar products; compare ads to what can be read on ingredients labels; or design and conduct blind taste tests. **S–18**

To gain further insight into listening critically, the class could also discuss aspects of the ads other than use of language. "What does the ad show? What effect is it designed to achieve? How? Why? What is the music like? Why is it used? Do the actors and announcers use their tone of voice to persuade? Facial expression? How? Are these things relevant to judging or understanding the product?" **S–22**

The teacher may also have the class critique ads for any stereotyping (e.g., sexual stereotyping). **S–2**

For further practice, if a VCR is available, watch and discuss taped commercials. Students could jot notes on critical points and share their insights.

The "Standard Approach" (or "Original Lesson") describes how the subject is treated. As a summary, it provides focus for the critique and remodel. Teachers who share their work can better follow the remodel when the original is clearly described. The critical thinking infused is better highlighted — for both the writer and the reader — when the original is available for contrast with the remodel.

The "Critique" generally begins by explaining the use of having students study the subject, the role such study has in the life of the critical thinker, and how critical thinking applies to the topic. It then provides a critique of the original from the point of view of education for critical thinking. Given the reasons for studying the topic, and the role such study should have for the critical thinker, the ways the original fosters and fails to foster such understanding is explicated.

Thus, the analysis of the significance of the topic provides a focus for and basis of the evaluation. The evaluation, then, mentions parts of the original that can be kept, and parts that should be changed or dropped, and *why*. The critique often includes a general statement suggesting what must be added to raise deeper issues and develop insight into the material. In short, the critique *justifies* the changes made to produce the remodel.

The "Remodelled Lesson" then follows, based on the analysis and evaluation of the topic and its treatment in the original. It reflects the reasoning given in the critique. It includes teacher questions and student activities designed to overcome the problems in the original. Citing the strategy numbers helps make the critical thinking infused explicit, and offers cross-referencing for others to better see what is being done in the new lesson and why. Readers of the remodel can refer to the strategy descriptions given in the "Strategy" chapter, if the function of the strategy is unclear to them. Furthermore, citing the strategy provides a check for the writer, who, during the writing and revision process, can evaluate the questions and activities to make sure that they do in fact engage the students in that particular dimension of critical thought.

The list of "Strategies used to remodel" helps readers who want to better understand a particular strategy, or want ideas for applying it, to easily find examples. As the readers read the "Remodelled Plan", they can easily refer to this list for the names of the strategies cited.

The "Objectives" provide an opportunity for writers of remodels to summarize their work, and show the readers how the strategies apply to the content, that is, to show the relationship between the content and critical thought. Writing objectives, looking at what you've written, and making the goals explicit as a list of what students will do, helps the writer ensure that the remodel does achieve the goals as stated. If not, the goals should be added to the remodel or dropped from the objectives. (Does the activity as described *really* have students carefully and fairmindedly evaluate these assumptions?) Objectives can also show relationships between the strategies as they apply to that lesson; they make explicit that, in this case, this one strategy is (or these three strategies are) used in the service of this main strategy. For example, "Students will practice dialogical thinking by considering evidence and assumptions from multiple perspectives." Reading through the objectives of other people's remodels can make it easier to find ideas in them to use in one's own work. When confronted with a particular remodelling problem, reading the objectives of other remodels is an easy way of finding out which remodels can provide help or inspiration.

The finished form of the complete "remodel sets" and the separation and order of their elements is not intended to suggest the precise order in which the elements are developed or written. Generally, the three major components are begun in rough form: an initial statement of key parts of the original and their functions, its most obvious strengths and weaknesses, and provisional revisions are usually jotted down first.

The writer can then step back and evaluate these rough ideas and begin to analyze the situation more deeply. Does my critique really get at the heart of the matter? Is the evaluation fair, accurately stated, and properly justified? Does my remodel really address the flaws I've identified? Could I add something to take the lesson more deeply into the subject? Am I missing a good opportunity to encourage careful, honest thought? Are the main points of the remodel explained or justified by what I've said in the critique?

The remodeller may also want to review pertinent strategies, skim other remodels for ideas, and share their work with colleagues for comments before beginning a final rewrite. When the three main components are in relatively finished form, the writer can list the strategies used. The final version of the "objectives" is usually written last and checked to ensure that it reflects the remodel.

Although going through an extended process like this may seem like a lot of unnecessary work, and you needn't write up every instance of infusing critical thinking in polished form, we encourage you to put at least some of your work in this form for the following reasons:

- First impressions and initial ideas about what to do may be misleading and are rarely as valuable for either students or colleagues as a finished product which has been carefully evaluated and revised.

- The evaluation, revision, double-checking, and analysis provide crucial opportunities for teachers to develop the ability to engage in careful critical thought.

- Having to organize one's ideas and express them clearly helps the writer to more thoroughly probe those ideas, and discover other ideas.

- An extended process creates a finished product which is clearer and more helpful to colleagues with whom it is shared, than rough notes and scattered ideas would be.

- The objectives most worthwhile to pursue in the remodel will rarely be apparent until after the analysis and critique of the original lesson plan and the development of a remodelled lesson.

- Revision after further analysis can correct such mistakes as failing to include crucial points, or covering the material in a superficial or tangential way. It's remarkably easy to blast a critique for missing an important opportunity for developing critical thought, but then neglect to take advantage of the opportunity oneself. It's easy to miss the main point, purpose, or context of a topic, principle, or skill, when first considering it. It's easy to write fabulous-sounding objectives and then fail to fulfill them.

We therefore recommend a more extended process of producing remodels, with the elements given above, whether done in that order or not. (For example, the first step might be to confer with colleagues. With some lessons, one might have to review some strategies, remodels, or the subject introduction before being able to come up with remodel ideas.) Whatever process you use, we strongly encourage you to gain some experience in the careful and complete analysis and evaluation required to produce well written, complete remodel sets.

How to Use this Book

You may choose to read this book as you would any other book, but if you do, you will probably miss a good deal of the benefit that can be derived from it. There are no algorithms or recipes for understanding or teaching critical thinking. Although we separate aspects of critical thinking, the global concept of the truly reasonable person is behind each aspect, and each aspect relates both to it and to the other dimensions. Thus, to develop critical thought, one must continually move back and forth between the global ideal of the rational and fairminded thinker and the details describing such a thinker. Similarly, although we separate the aspects of staff development for integrating critical thinking into instruction (understanding the concept, critiquing present practice, formulating remodels), teachers must continually move back and forth between these activities.

If you are a fourth, fifth, or sixth grade teacher and you want to improve your ability to teach for critical thinking, this book can help you develop the ability to remodel your own lesson plans. Your own teaching strategies will progressively increase as your repertoire of critical thinking strategies grows. As you begin, try to develop a baseline sense of your present understanding of critical thinking and of your ability to critique and redesign lesson plans. The critiques and remodels that follow, and the principles and strategies that precede them, may provide an immediate catalyst for you to take your lesson plans and redesign them. But the longer critiques and remodels here might seem intimidating. Some of the strategies may seem unclear or confusing, and you may bog down as soon as you attempt to redesign your own lessons. Keep in mind that in some of our remodels, we put as many ideas as we could, in order to provide as many examples and varieties of applications as possible. Thus, some of the remodelled plans are longer and more elaborate than you might initially be willing to produce or teach. The purpose of this book is not to simply give you lesson ideas, but to encourage you to develop your own.

We therefore suggest alternative approaches and ways of conceiving the process:

- Read through the strategies and a couple of remodels, then write critiques and remodels of your own. After you have attempted a critique and remodel, read our critique and remodel of a similar lesson. By using this procedure, you will soon get a sense of the difficulties in the critique-remodel process. You will also have initiated the process of developing your own skills in this important activity.

- Another way of testing your understanding of the critical insights is to read the principle section of a strategy, and write your own application section.

- You could review a remodel of ours and find places where strategies were used but not cited and places where particular moves could be characterized by more than one strategy.

- You may want to take several strategies and write about their interrelationships.

- Or you might take a subject or topic and list significant questions about it. Share and discuss your lists with colleagues.

- If, when reviewing a remodel, you find a particular strategy confusing, review the principle and application in the strategy chapter. If, when reading the strategy chapter, you feel confused, review the critiques and remodels of the lessons listed below it. If you are still confused, do not use the strategy. Review it periodically until it becomes clear.

- When remodelling your own lessons, you will probably find that sometimes you can make more drastic changes or even completely rewrite a lesson, while at other times you may make only minor adjustments. Some of your remodels may make use of many strategies, say, two or more affective strategies, and a macro-ability requiring the coordinated use of several micro-skills. For other remodels, you may use only one strategy. It is better to use one clearly understood strategy than to attempt to use more than you clearly understand.

- You may want to begin remodelling by using only one or two strategies clearest to you. After remodelling some lessons, you will likely find yourself spontaneously using those strategies. You could then reread the strategy chapter and begin infusing additional strategies with which you feel comfortable. Thus, as the number of strategies you regularly use grows, your teaching can evolve at the pace most comfortable to you.

- If students don't grasp a critical idea or skill when you introduce it, don't give up. Critical insight must be developed over time. For instance, suppose the first attempt to get students to fairmindedly consider each other's views fails. It is likely that students are not in the habit of seriously considering each other's positions, and hence may not listen carefully to each other. If you make restating opposing views a routine part of discussion, students will eventually learn to prepare themselves by listening more carefully.

- Although the main purpose of this book is to help you remodel lesson plans, we have not limited our suggestions to the remodelling process. We strongly urge you to apply the insights embedded in the strategies to all aspects of the classroom (including discussions, conflicts, and untraditional lessons such as movies). You may also use our remodels or sections of them. Though many of our lessons are too long for one class period, we did not suggest where to break them up, nor did we provide follow-up questions. If you do experiment with any of our remodels, you will probably have to remodel them somewhat to take your students and text into account.

- We urge you to apply your growing critical insight to the task of analyzing and clarifying your concept of education and the educated person. Of each subject you teach, ask yourself what is most basic and crucial for an educated person to know or to be able to do. Highlight those aspects and teach them in a way that most fosters in-depth and useful understanding.

- Texts often have the same features — whether problems or opportunities for critical thought — occurring over and over again. Hence, remodelling a couple of lessons from a text can give you a basic structure to use many times over the course of the year.

- When comparing your work to ours, keep in mind that this is a flexible process; our remodel is not the only right one. Any changes which promote fairminded critical thought are improvements.

However you use what follows in this book, your understanding of the insights behind the strategies will determine the effectiveness of the remodels. Despite the detail with which we have delineated the strategies, they should not be translated into mechanistic, step-by-step procedures. Keep the goal of the well-educated, fairminded critical thinker continually in mind. Thinking critically involves insightful critical judgments at each step along the way. It is never done by recipe.

Diagram 1

Three Modes of Mental Organization
(expressed in exclusive categories for purposes of theoretical clarity)

The Uncritical Person	The Self-Serving Critical Person (weak sense)	The Fairminded Critical Person (strong sense)
See Naive Nancy p. 24	See Selfish Sam p. 24	See Fairminded Fran p. 25

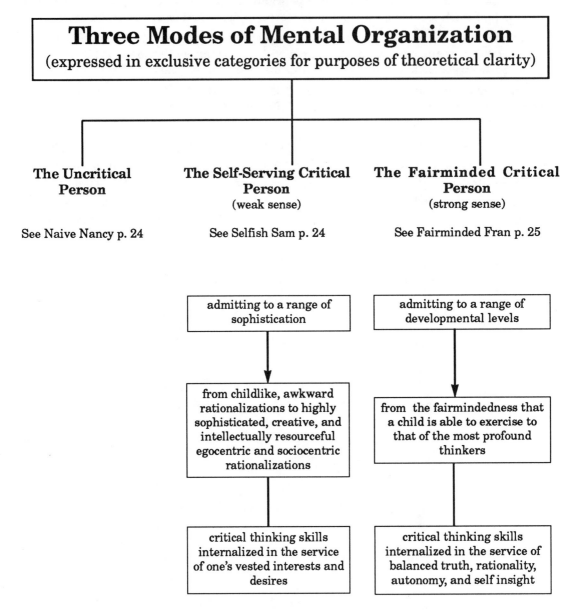

admitting to a range of sophistication	admitting to a range of developmental levels
from childlike, awkward rationalizations to highly sophisticated, creative, and intellectually resourceful egocentric and sociocentric rationalizations	from the fairmindedness that a child is able to exercise to that of the most profound thinkers
critical thinking skills internalized in the service of one's vested interests and desires	critical thinking skills internalized in the service of balanced truth, rationality, autonomy, and self insight

---

Note

Children enter school as fundamentally non-culpable, uncritical and self-serving thinkers. The educational task is to help them to become, as soon as possible and as fully as possible, responsible, fairminded, critical thinkers, empowered by intellectual skills and rational passions. Most people are some combination of the above three types; the proportions are the significant determinant of which of the three characterizations is most appropriate. For example, it is a common pattern for people to be capable of fairminded critical thought only when their vested interests or ego-attachments are not involved, hence the legal practice of excluding judges or jury members who can be shown to have such interests.

Diagram 2

Critical Thinking Lesson Plan Remodelling

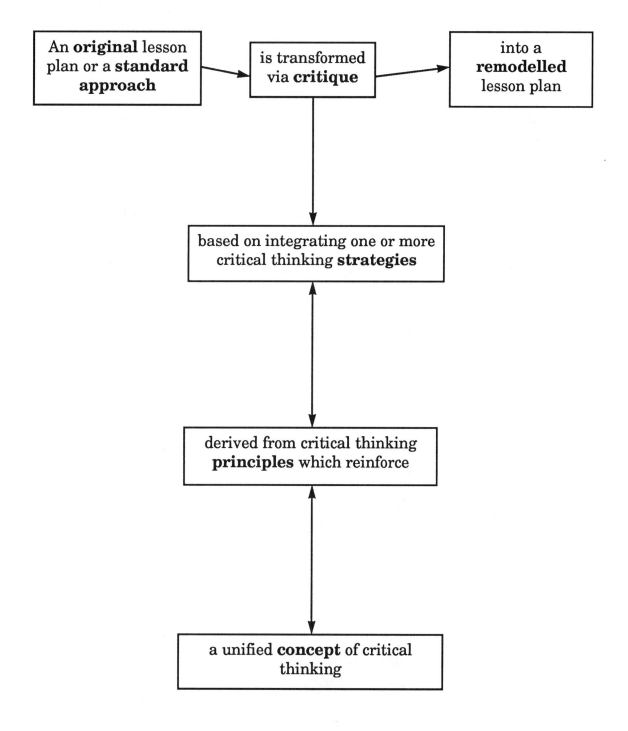

An **original** lesson plan or a **standard approach** — is transformed via **critique** — into a **remodelled** lesson plan

based on integrating one or more critical thinking **strategies**

derived from critical thinking **principles** which reinforce

a unified **concept** of critical thinking

Diagram 3

The Perfections and Imperfections of Thought

clear	vs	unclear
precise	vs	imprecise
specific	vs	vague
accurate	vs	inaccurate
relevant	vs	irrelevant
consistent	vs	inconsistent
logical	vs	illogical
deep	vs	superficial
complete	vs	incomplete
significant	vs	trivial
adequate (for purpose)	vs	inadequate
fair	vs	biased or one-sided

There are qualities of thought we should encourage whenever possible. We call these standards "perfections" of thought. We should continually help students become aware of them, to examine their own thinking to see whether it is clear or unclear, specific or vague, accurate or inaccurate,... We should use these standards explicitly in giving students feedback in each and every subject matter domain.

2 Making Critical Thinking Intuitive: Using Drama, Examples, and Images

Teaching For Intuitive Understanding

The meaning of "intuitive" we are using in this chapter makes no reference to a mysterious power of the mind, but rather to the phenomenon of "quick and ready insight" (Webster's New Collegiate Dictionary). This sense of the word is connected to the everyday fact that we can learn concepts at various levels of depth. When, for example, we memorize an abstract definition of a word and do not learn how to apply it effectively in a wide variety of situations, we end up *without* an intuitive foundation for our understanding. We lack the insight, in other words, into how, when, and why it applies. Children may know that the word 'democracy' means "a government in which the people rule", but may not be able to tell whether they are behaving "democratically" on the playground. They may know what the word 'cruel' means, but they may not recognize that they are being cruel in mocking a handicapped student. Helping students to develop critical thinking intuitions is, then, helping them gain the practical insights necessary for a quick and ready application of concepts to cases in a large array of circumstances.

We want critical thinking principles to be "intuitive" to our students in the sense that we want those principles ready and available in their minds for immediate translation into their everyday thought and experience. We base this goal on the assumption that concepts and ideas are truly understood only when we can effectively and insightfully use them in a wide range of circumstances, only when we have mastered their use to the point of spontaneous application. (See chart on the next page.)

Unfortunately much of what we originally learned in school as children was abstract and unconnected to everyday life and experience. And, since it is natural to teach as one was taught, our own students are probably doing precisely what we previously did: "learning" in an abstract way, learning, in other words, to perform for grades and approval, not to gain knowledge, skill, and insight, not to transform their behavior in the "real" world.

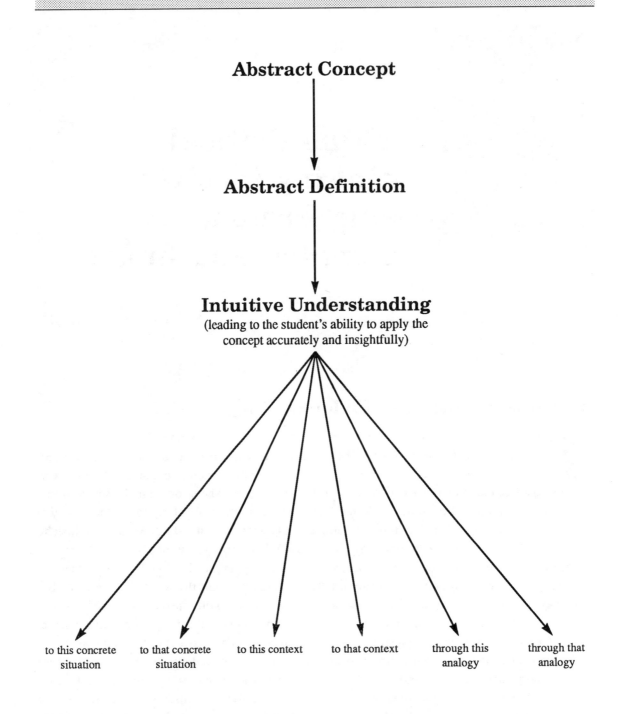

Abstract Concept

Abstract Definition

Intuitive Understanding
(leading to the student's ability to apply the
concept accurately and insightfully)

| to this concrete situation | to that concrete situation | to this context | to that context | through this analogy | through that analogy |

*Intuitive Understanding Enables Us
to Insightfully Bridge the Gap
Between Abstract Concept & Concrete Application*

This, then, is probably the fundamental reason why so much school learning is not effectively transferred to real life. It lacks the *intuitive* basis, the *insights*, for the translation. When we were students, our own teachers rarely took pains to ensure that we intuitively understood the basic concepts we were learning. Hence their teaching did not model for us teaching that fosters intuitive learning. As a result we are rarely sufficiently aware of the similar effect of our own teaching. As long as students are performing in certain standard ways, we often uncritically assume they "understand", that they are building a basis for using what they learn, that they will eventually be able to take what they learn and put it to use in the everyday world. This assumption is rarely justified.

As a first step toward preparing to help our students develop intuitive understandings of critical thinking concepts, we must make sure that the basic concepts that underlie critical thinking are intuitive to us. To help our students internalize the understandings essential to critical thought, we must ourselves gain practice in translating those same understandings into the context of our own lives. We must, in other words, internalize the basic concepts and principles of critical thinking so deeply that we habitually use them in all of the various dimensions of our own lives: as parents, consumers, teachers, and citizens, so that when we teach we teach in a way that helps our students translate all fundamental and root concepts and principles into the circumstances of their own day-to-day life. (See chart on the next page.)

Both we and our students, in other words, need to develop full-fledged *critical thinking intuitions*. This is, of course, a matter of long-term development. Neither we nor they can develop deep intuitions overnight. Nevertheless, from the beginning we must proceed with a sense of what we are aiming at. We must begin with an initial sense of what it is to develop intuitions. Then we must progressively deepen that sense as we explore a variety of ways of fostering critical thinking intuitions. The primary goal of this chapter is to lay a foundation for this understanding. All of the rest of the handbook will provide further examples to build upon as to the nature and importance of "intuitive" teaching.

To accomplish this end, we shall take a couple of the most fundamental distinctions that underlie critical thinking and illustrate how they can be made intuitive to children. At the same time, we will illustrate how these concepts can become more intuitive to us as teachers. Of course, we shall not attempt to cover all of the important distinctions but merely to illustrate the process of teaching for intuitive understanding. As you read, the kinds of essential "translations" required to help students ground basic concepts in basic insights should become progressively clearer.

We shall assume that you will pursue analogous strategies for the various other basic concepts in critical thinking on your own. Remember, the aim is an on-going commitment to the process of fostering an intuitive basis for all the principles of critical thinking, a commitment to the process of engaging students continually in translating back and forth between the abstract and the concrete, the general and the particular, the academic and the "real".

Using Dramatization to Foster Critical Thinking Intuitions

The Power of the Dramatic

The world that is most real to us is the world of actual persons dreaming, hoping, planning, acting out their lives, facing conflicts and problems, struggling to find happiness, success, and meaning. Abstract concepts become much more meaningful to us when we relate them directly to a dramatized world. That is why novels, plays, television programs and movies typically have much more appeal to and impact on us than abstract treatises do. One reason for this is that there is a

Abstract Concept
(e.g., the concept of democracy)

We might have our students look up the word in a dictionary where they will find abstract characterizations (like "rule by the people")

Building Intuitive Understanding
(We might lead a class discussion Socratically focused on questions like "What does it mean to say that the people rule?", "What does it mean to say that the people decide?", "What if the people don't consider the issues, have they still decided?" "What if they don't get accurate information, are they still deciding?" "In what sorts of situations in your life is democratic decision-making used?" "When is non-democratic decision-making used?", "Is it sometimes better not to decide things democratically?"

Leading To
students' starting to apply the concept of democracy seriously to their daily lives.

| Let's see, I guess there are a lot of decisions that are not *made* democratically. | At home we never vote on what to do. It seems like Dad decides some things and Mom decides others. | At school we don't decide many things democratically. The teacher makes most of the decisions. | We try to make decisions democratically in the playground, but usually some of the kids seem to do most of the deciding | Maybe democracy is not always a good way to decide things or maybe we need to change the way we do some things. |

direct relationship between stories and experiences. We learn about the world principally through our experiences of it and our experiences, from the beginning, are "story-like" in character.

When we talk about ourselves we tell others the story of our lives, as it were. Furthermore, most of our real beliefs are embodied in our actions and in what our actions "mean" to us. A powerful way to make the abstract more intuitive, is, therefore, to use stories and dramatized characters for that purpose. In this section, we will illustrate this point by the use of three fictional characters to illustrate three abstract concepts.

Uncritical, Selfish, and Fairminded Critical Thinkers

The distinctions between uncritical thinking and critical thinking, on the one hand, and between selfish and fairminded critical thinking on the other hand, underlie our whole approach to critical thinking. It highlights the danger of focusing on critical thinking skills alone, independent of critical thinking values. It continually calls to our attention the need to attend to the intellectual and moral standards our students are forming as a result of the way we are cultivating their learning.

A basic, though abstract, explanation for the differences between uncritical, selfish critical, and fairminded critical persons is given in the following brief characterizations:

1) *Uncritical persons* are those who have not developed intellectual skills, persons who are naive, conformist, easily manipulated, often inflexible, easily confused, typically unclear, narrowminded, and consistently ineffective in their use of language. They may have a good heart but they are not able to skillfully analyze the problems they face so as to effectively protect their own interests.

2) *Selfish critical persons* are skilled thinkers who do not genuinely accept the values of critical thinking, persons who use the intellectual skills of critical thinking selectively and self-deceptively to foster and serve their vested interests (at the expense of truth). They are typically able to identify flaws in the reasoning of others and refute them and to back up their own claims with plausible reasons, but they have not learned how to reason empathically within points of view with which they disagree.

3) *Fairminded critical persons* are skilled thinkers who do accept and honor the values of critical thinking, persons who use the intellectual skills of critical thinking to accurately reconstruct the strongest versions of points of view in conflict with their own and to question deeply their own framework of thought. They try to find and correct flaws in their own reasoning and to be scrupulously fair to those with whom they disagree.

This is fine as far as it goes, but how are we to make these abstractions more real to our students? And how are we and our students to see the significance of these distinctions in the everyday world?

It may seem to us that these theoretical discriminations are much beyond the grasp of our students. But whether they are or are not, is not a matter of the distinctions themselves, but of the way they are introduced to students. In fact, it is important for children to begin to grasp these differences as soon as possible. Let us now examine how we might use dramatization as a strategy for making these critical thinking concepts more intuitive.

Naive Nancy, Selfish Sam, and Fairminded Fran

One of the ways to aid students in developing critical thinking intuitions is to create characters whose dramatic personalities illustrate abstract distinctions. For example, we have created three imaginary children whose characters and personalities illustrate the contrast between the uncritical thinker, the selfish critical thinker, and the fairminded critical thinker. We can get some insight into the distinction by imagining what each of these characters might say about themselves if they had a clear sense of the person they were becoming and a willingness to be candid and forthright. Children who were actually developing these contrasting behavior patterns and traits would probably not, of course, have the insight suggested by these hypothetical self-descriptions.

First meet Naive Nancy. Here is what she might say of herself (if she could clearly see how she uses thinking to deal with the world):

Naive Nancy

"I don't need to think! I understand everything without thinking. I just do whatever occurs to me to do. I believe most of what I hear. I believe most of what I see on TV. I don't see why I should question either. And I don't need to waste a lot of time trying to figure things out. Why should I, when someone will figure things out for me if I wait long enough. It's a lot easier to say "I can't!" than to do a lot of work. My parents and my teachers take care of me when I can't take care of myself. The other day I was having trouble with my math homework and started to cry, so my father did it for me. My parents give me a lot of help. It's easier that way. I do what I'm told, keep my mouth shut, and go along with whatever my friends decide. I don't like to make waves. Thinking gets you into trouble."

Next meet Selfish Sam. Here is what he might say (if he could clearly see how he uses thinking to deal with the world):

Selfish Sam

"I think a lot! It helps me trick people and get what I want. I believe whatever I want to believe, whatever gets me what I want. I question anyone who asks me to do what I don't want to do. I figure out how to get around my parents. I figure out how to get other kids to do what I want them to do. I even figure out how to avoid thinking if I want. Sometimes I say "I can't!" when I know I could but don't want to. You can get what you want from people if you know how to manipulate them. Just the other night, I got to stay up till 11:00 by arguing with my mother about bedtime! It helps to tell people what they want to hear. Of course, sometimes what they want to hear isn't true, but that doesn't matter because you only get into trouble when you tell people what they don't want to hear. You can always trick people if you know how. Guess what, you can even trick yourself if you know how."

Next meet Fairminded Fran. Here is what she might say (if she could clearly see how she uses thinking to deal with the world):

Fairminded Fran

"I think a lot. It helps me to learn. It helps me to figure things out. I want to understand my parents and my playmates. In fact, I even want to understand myself and why I do things. Sometimes I do things that I don't understand. It's not easy trying to understand everyone and everything. Lots of people say one thing and do another. You can't always believe what people say. You can't believe a lot of what you see on TV. People often say things not because they mean them but because they want things and are trying to please you. I would like to make the world a better place. I want to make it better for everyone, not just for me and my friends. To understand other people you have to look at things as they do. You have to understand their situation and what you would feel like if you were them. You have to put yourself in their shoes. The other night I got mad at my sister because she wanted to watch a TV program that was on at the same time my favorite show was on. I didn't want to let her until I realized that she needed to watch her program to do some homework for school. I knew then that it wouldn't be fair of me to insist on my show, since she did have to do her homework for school. It isn't easy to be fair. It's a lot easier to be selfish and just think about yourself. But if I don't think about others, why should they think about me? I want to be fair to others because I expect everyone to be fair to me."

You may have noticed that we had each imaginary child introduce him or herself in terms of their attitudes toward thinking, how they go about thinking, and what they aim to achieve through their thinking. Each of these dimensions of character are important.

Naive Nancy does not see much reason to think at all. She takes things as they come. She believes

what she hears. She usually goes along with whatever her peers say. She intends no harm but also assumes that no one else is going to harm her. She is a ready victim for more sophisticated manipulators: adults or children. Naive Nancy will make a good student only insofar as thought is not required. She will literally, and thoughtlessly, do what she is told. She doesn't question or try to understand her own motives. She will make mistakes because she doesn't know how to listen closely and monitor what she hears for accuracy of interpretation. Wherever mindless obedience succeeds, she will get by. What is more, much of the time her innocent "helplessness" will enable her to get others to do things for her. Rather than try to think her way through a difficulty, she is learning to say "I can't do it!" after the first or second try. She is finding out that she can usually get by without much thinking. Her innocent likeability and perpetual "incompetence" is both her strength and her (ultimate) downfall. Her only real thinking skills are in the art of being helpless, in enticing others to do her thinking for her.

Selfish Sam contrasts well with Naive Nancy. Sam values thinking. And the more he does it, the more he values it. But only in a special sense. He thinks to gain advantage, to get what he wants, to successfully put his desires above the rights and needs of others. To put it briefly, Sam

is discovering the power of con-artistry. Sam is discovering that you can best get what you want by focusing clearly on your own desires, figuring out what is standing in the way of your interests, and manipulating others into acting in your interest. Selfish Sam is becoming an egocentric problem solver. He defines his problems so as to center them around getting what he wants for himself. Sometimes this means figuring out how to get out of work. But unlike Nancy, Sam is learning the power of figuring things out for himself. He is also learning how to impress both adults and kids by what he can do. Eventually Sam will come to appreciate the power there is in groups, the advantages one gains by becoming a leader and exercising control over others. He will use his thought to win others to his side, to defeat his "enemies" (whoever he doesn't like), and extend his power and advantage over others. It isn't that he doesn't care at all about others, but rather that he cares only about those

who serve him, those who are members of *his* group. Eventually, Sam could become an effective promoter of a vested interest, an excellent sales person, a politician, or a lawyer ... any job that can "successfully" be performed without a well developed sense of fairmindedness.

Fairminded Fran contrasts well with both Nancy and Sam. Like Sam, Fran is learning the power of thought. She is learning the value of figuring things out for herself. Unlike Nancy, she is not learning the art of "helplessness" because she is experiencing the pleasure and deep satisfac-

tion that comes from successfully figuring things out for herself. She is discovering that she has a mind and can use it to solve problems, protect herself, do difficult jobs, learn complicated things, express herself well, and get along with others. But that is not all she's learning. She is also learning that other people have minds, other people have desires and needs, other people have rights, and other people have a different way of looking at things. She is learning how to enter into the thinking of others, how to see things from other people's point of view, how to learn from other people's perspective. She is beginning to notice the need to protect herself from the "Sam's" of the world. She is learning to test for herself what people say. She is learning to protect her interests without violating the rights of others.

Fran's thinking is beginning to develop a richness that Sam's will never develop (as long as he thinks selfishly), for she is learning how much one can learn from others. Eventually, Fran will gain many insights from the art of thinking within the perspective of others that she is developing. Fran's early thinking is laying the foundation for later breadth of vision. Fran's ability to think for herself in a skilled and fairminded way will enable her to pursue any career goal that she later takes on. She will be highly valued by those who value justice and fairplay. But she will also be treated with suspicion by the "true believers", by the people whose first allegiance is to a special group, to "our side". Those given to *group think* will come to recognize that you can't depend on Nancy to always support the "right" side (our side). She sometimes agrees with the enemy, the opposition, the "other guys".

By introducing these characters, we can help make a basic distinction in critical thinking more alive and vivid to our students. We can breathe life into these important ideas and help our students build mental bridges between the abstract and the concrete, between the theoretical and the practical. There are, of course, a variety of ways that we might use these characters. We could, for example, develop stories about their adventures together, stories in which their interactions in a variety of situations further illuminate their contrasting modes of thinking and judging. We might make pictures and visuals which gave illustrated commentary from each of the characters about how to behave and act in various situations. We might have discussions with our students about which of these characters they thought they were most like *and why,* or what they liked or did not like about each of these characters. We could also ask if they ever acted like Naive Nancy or Selfish Sam, and then to explain, if some said yes, what it is that they did and why.

How many ways we find to make use of these dramatizations of contrasting modes of thinking entirely depends on the limits of our own imaginations. The important point is this: students learn deeply only those things they translate into their own experience and which make deep contact with their emerging values.

If you now review the above abstract definitions of the terms uncritical, selfishly critical, and fairmindedly critical and compare what you learned from Nancy, Sam, and Fran, you will have a basis for recognizing the importance of critical thinking intuitions. Students who gain an intuitive grasp of the differences among Nancy, Sam, and Fran will have the insights necessary to recognizing similar patterns of behavior in themselves and others.

Now let's turn our attention to another important distinction in critical thinking and experiment with a somewhat different process of making ideas more intuitive.

Exemplification: Understanding Abstract Concepts Through Vivid Everyday Examples

The Power of Examples

Everything in the natural world is concrete and particular. Whatever is abstract must ultimately translate, therefore, into what is concrete and particular. Giving examples, is a powerful way to help students learn. Furthermore, one of the best ways to assess student learning is to determine the extent to which they can give examples of what they are learning. In this section, we will illustrate how examples can be used to make abstract concepts intuitive. We will focus on two: inference and assumption.

Inferences and Assumptions

Learning to distinguish inferences from assumptions is another important distinction in critical thinking. It is therefore a good place to develop basic intuitions. In this case, we will not begin by developing characters who illustrate the concepts, we will instead explore alternative ways to make them vivid and practical, first to you the teacher, through a wide variety of everyday examples intelligible to adults. Then I will turn my attention more and more to the process by which we can help make these concepts more vivid to children. As before let us begin with a couple of abstract and general explanations of the concepts:

Inference: An inference is a step of the mind, an intellectual act by which one concludes that something is so in light of something else's being so, or seeming to be so. If you come at me with a knife in your hand, I would probably *infer* that you mean to do me harm. Inferences can be strong or weak, justified or unjustified.

Assumption: An assumption is something we take for granted or presuppose. All human thought and experience is based on assumptions. Assumptions can be unjustified or justified, depending upon whether we do or do not have good reasons for what we are assuming. For example, I heard a scratch at the door. I got up to let the cat in. I *assumed* that only the cat makes that noise, and that he makes it only when he wants to be let in.

We humans have no trouble actually making assumptions and inferences, for we make them, not only every day of our lives, we make them every moment of everyday of our lives (at least, every *waking* moment of our lives). Assumptions and inferences permeate our lives precisely because we cannot act without them. Our lives are conducted almost exclusively on the basis of the judgments, the interpretations, and the beliefs we form. Each is the result of the mind's ability to come to conclusions, to give meanings to what we experience, in short, to *make inferences.* And the inferences we make depend on what we take for granted, what we *assume,* as we attempt to make sense of what is going on around us.

Put a human in any situation and he or she starts to give it some meaning or other. People automatically make inferences to gain a basis for understanding and action. So quickly and automatically do we make inferences that we do not, without training, learn to notice them as such. We see dark clouds and infer rain. We hear the door slam and infer someone has arrived. We see a frowning face and infer the person is angry. Our friend is late and we infer she is being inconsiderate. We meet a tall boy and infer he is good at basketball, an Asian and infer he will be good at math. We read a book, and infer what the various sentences and paragraphs, indeed what the whole book, is saying. We listen to what people say, and make a continual series of inferences as to what they mean. As we write we make inferences as to what others will make of what we are writing. We make inferences as to the clarity of what we are saying, as to what needs further explanation, as to what needs exemplification or illustration.

Many of our inferences are justified and reasonable. But many are not. One of the most important critical thinking skills is the skill of noticing and reconstructing the inferences we make, so that the various ways in which we inferentially shape our experiences become more and more apparent to us. This skill, this sensitivity or ability, enables us to separate our experiences into analyzed parts. We learn to distinguish the raw data of our experience from our interpretations of those data (from, in other words, the inferences we are making about them). Eventually we realize that the inferences we make are heavily influenced by our point of view and the assumptions we have come to make about people and situations. This puts us in the position of being able to broaden the scope of our outlook, to see situations from more than one point of view, to become more openminded. (See chart on the following page.)

Abstract Concept
(e.g., the concept of inference)

Abstract Definition
(e.g., "to conclude or decide from something known or assumed; to derive by reasoning; to draw as a conclusion")

Building Intuitive Understanding
("Let's see, we're always having to make sense of what we experience, so that means, I guess, we have to draw conclusions about everything we give meaning to. In fact, that means that whenever I am making sense of *anything,* I must be making *inferences* about it, even though I never seem to notice myself doing this. I guess my mind works very quickly and silently and I often am unaware of what it is doing.")

Leading To
the ability to apply the concept accurately and insightfully to cases.

"When Jack was late and I decided he was being irresponsible, *that* was an inference"

"When my car didn't start and I concluded that the battery was dead, *that* was an inference"

"When I was about to put my red sweater on but decided it clashed with my brown pants, *that* was an inference"

"When Frank walked by without saying anything to me and I concluded that he was angry with me, *that* was an inference"

"Whenever I read a book and decide what it means, that must be the result of a whole lot of inferences"

Often, of course, different people make different inferences because they bring to situations a different point of view. They see the data differently. Or, to put it another way, they have different assumptions about what they see. For example, if two people see a man lying in a gutter, one might infer, "There's a drunken bum". The other might infer, "There's a man in need of help." These inferences are based on different assumptions about the conditions under which people end up in gutters and these assumptions are connected to the point of view about people that each has formed. The first person assumes: "Only drunks are to be found in gutters". The second person assumes: "People lying in the gutter are in need of help". The first person may have developed the point of view that people are fundamentally responsible for what happens to them and ought to be able to take care of themselves. The second may have developed the point of view that the problems people have are often caused by forces and events beyond their control.

In any case, as soon as possible, we want to help our students begin to notice the inferences they are making, the assumptions they are basing those inferences on, and the point of view about the world they are developing. To help our students do this we need to give them clear examples of simple cases, and lots and lots of practice analyzing and reconstructing them. For example, we could reconstruct the above inferences in the following way:

Person One

SITUATION: "A man is lying in the gutter."
ASSUMPTION: "Only bums lie in gutters."
INFERENCE: "That man's a bum."

Person Two

SITUATION: "A man is lying in the gutter."
ASSUMPTION: "Anyone lying in the gutter is in need of help."
INFERENCE: "That man is in need of help."

Our goal of sensitizing students to the inferences they make and to the assumptions that underlie their thinking enables them to begin to gain command over their thinking. Because all human thinking is inferential in nature, our command of our thinking depends on command of the inferences embedded in it and thus of the assumptions that underlie it.

Consider the way in which we plan and think our way through everyday events. We think of ourselves as washing up, eating our breakfast, getting ready for work, arriving on time, sitting down at our desk, making plans for lunch, paying bills, engaging in small talk, etc. Another way to put this is to say that we are continually interpreting our actions, giving them meanings, *making inferences* about what is going on in our lives. And this is to say that we must choose among a variety of possible meanings. For example, are we "relaxing" or "wasting time"? Am I being "determined" or "stubborn", or worse, "pig-headed". Am I "joining" a conversation or "butting in"? Is someone "laughing with me" or "laughing at me"? Am I "helping a friend" or "being taken advantage of"? Every time we interpret our actions, every time we give them a meaning, we are making one or more inferences on the basis of one or more assumptions.

As humans we continually make assumptions about ourselves, our jobs, our mates, our children, about the world in general. We take some things for granted, simply because we can't always be questioning everything. Sometimes we take the wrong things for granted. For example, I run off to the store (assuming that I have enough money with me) and arrive to find that I have left my money at home. I assume that I have enough gas in the car only to find that I have run out. I assume that an item marked-down in price is a good buy only to find that it was "marked up" before it was "marked down". I assume that it will not, or that it will, rain. I assume that my car will start when I turn on the key and press the starter. I assume that I mean well in my dealings with others. We make hundreds of assumptions without knowing it, that is, without thinking about it. Most of them are quite sound and justifiable. Some however are not.

The question then becomes: "How can we teach young children to begin to recognize the inferences they are making, the assumptions they are basing those inferences on, and the point of view, the perspective on the world that they are beginning to form?".

It seems to me that there are many ways to foster children's awareness of their inferences and assumptions. For one thing, all disciplined subject matter thinking requires that we learn to make correct assumptions about the content of what we are studying and that we become practiced in making justifiable inferences. For example, in doing math we make mathematical assumptions and mathematical inferences; in doing science we make scientific assumptions and scientific inferences; in constructing historical accounts we make historical assumptions and historical inferences.

Every subject we teach provides us with opportunities for facilitating student recognition of inferences and assumptions. When students mis-read a mathematical problem, for example, they make the wrong inferences about it, usually as the result of having made false assumptions about it. The difficulty for us is usually not because there aren't many opportunities to foster these skills and recognitions. It is usually because we ourselves are not practiced in this very art, hence we miss most of the opportunities inherent in the everyday classroom.

Here is one place to start. We can give students exercises which they can do in groups which help both them and us become more aware of inferences, assumptions, and points of view lurking behind them. We could start by asking the class collectively to identify common inferences. For example:

If it was 12:00 noon, what might you infer? .... (It's time for lunch.)

If there were black clouds in the sky? .... (It's probably going to rain.)

If Jack comes to school with a bump on his head? .... (He probably got hit.)

If there are webs in the corners of the ceiling? .... (Spiders made them.)

If Jill is in the 8th grade? .... (She is probably 13 or 14 years old.)

After some exercise of this sort, you could then switch to practice in small groups of the same sort. When you felt that the students were developing an intuitive grasp of inferences, you could then orchestrate some practice with assumptions, helping the students to see how the inferences they make are a result of the assumptions they bring to situations. For example:

If it was 12:00 noon and you inferred it was time for lunch, what did you assume?
(That everyone eats lunch at 12:00 noon.)

If there are black clouds in the sky and you infer that it's probably going to rain, what did you assume?
(That it usually rains whenever there are black clouds in the sky.)

If Jack comes to school with a bump on his head and you infer that he must have been hit, what did you assume?

(That the only time you develop a bump on the head is when you are hit.)

You could continue this exercise until students began to develop some skill in identifying the assumptions that accounted for their inferences. You could ask the students in each case to consider whether the assumptions made in each case was justified and why. For example, are we justified in assuming that everyone eats lunch at 12:00? Are we justified in assuming that it usually rains when there are black clouds in the sky? Are we justified in assuming that bumps on the head are only caused by blows?

The point would not be to get everyone to agree on which assumptions were justified but to begin to show students that we all make many assumptions as we go about our daily life and that we ought to be able to recognize and question them. As students develop these critical intuitions, they begin to notice more and more inferences made by themselves and others. They begin to recognize more and more what they and others are taking for granted. They begin to recognize more and more how their points of view shape their experiences.

Visualization: Using Visuals to Make Critical Thinking Principles More Intuitive

One of the most powerful ways to make abstractions more intuitive is through the process of visualization and imagination. We are sensual beings. Our senses play a powerful role in our learning. The power of sight, for example, sometimes enables us to grasp in a moment what would be very difficult otherwise — "A picture is worth a thousand words." (and there is no sense more powerful than sight).

Of course we must be careful in using images and pictures to represent abstract ideas. For one thing, pictures require interpretation and one picture can always be interpreted many ways. To put the point in other words, different people give different meanings to the same image or picture. We don't simply "see" what is there. We "read into", that is, make inferences about, what we see.

So though it is important to develop visuals that help our students develop critical intuition, we must be ever watchful of the interpretations that accompany visualization. We must be careful to distinguish, for example, "intuition" from "stereotype", simplification from oversimplification.

One principle of critical thinking in the strong sense is the principle of fairness to the views of others (See **S-3** in the Strategy Chapter). We have already dramatized this principle of thought in the character of Fairminded Fran, but suppose we try to use a visual to re-inforce the concept. Consider what we might use. We might try a representation of the scales of justice (see figure 1, next page).

Some discussion would be necessary before the students could begin to use this image in a fruitful way. Since the scales appear tipped in favor of "Justice for Ourselves", a Socratic discussion would be necessary to facilitate the students' recognition of our common tendency to be more sensitive to injustice toward ourselves than we are of injustice toward others, especially if we happen to be the perpetrators of the injustice.

We might introduce a second image of the scales (see figure 2, next page).

We might have the students discuss the implications of the two different drawings. This would help make both images more intelligible. Our discussion should result in the students giving

figure 1

figure 2

examples of experiences of their own, both of the sort in which others failed to treat them justly and in which they failed to treat others justly. Sibling rivalries are a fruitful area to discuss here, for at the bottom of them is often a perceived sense of unequal treatment. Through a discussion rich in examples which we should draw out from the students, the visual would begin to link up with vivid experiences, strengthening both the meaningfulness of the visual and the perceived implications of the experiences. This combination of visual and analyzed experiences is an excellent way to build critical thinking intuitions.

Or consider the following image.

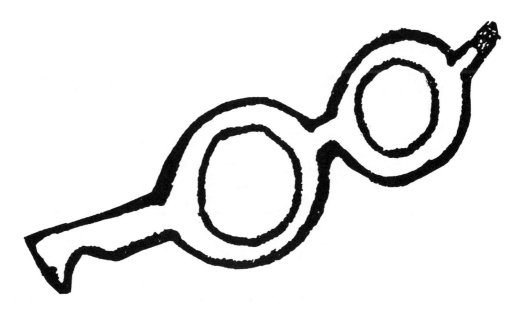

WE ALL SEE THE WORLD DIFFERENTLY

figure 3

We can use this to show students the need for insight into egocentricity as well as reciprocity. We could develop the analogy between different kinds of glasses and how we each develop a unique way of looking at the world, a unique point of view. We might also use an image of a mountain with different observers seeing different parts of it. Or we might use the parable of the six blind men examining different parts of an elephant, each of them coming to different conclusions about the shape of the elephant as a result. Or we might have the class discuss the folk adage of looking at the world through rose colored glasses. We could foster some sense of the importance of reciprocity by helping the students to begin to recognize the importance of seeing the world through the eyes (in this case, "glasses") of others. Whatever analogies and images we use, of course, it will be essential to translate them into clear examples and concrete experiences meaningful to our students.

Or consider this image of the statue of liberty. Though we can be sure that the image will engender common associations among most children raised in the United States, we cannot assume that the associations are based on an intuitive grasp of the principles of human rights and freedoms articulated in the Bill of Rights of the Constitution.

figure 4

The same would hold for virtually any other "patriotic" image or symbol, such as the flag, the White House, George Washington crossing the Delaware, Abraham Lincoln reading by the light of the fire in a one room cabin. In other words, just as pictures and images can be used to make an abstract idea more concrete and intuitive, so also can they be used to obfuscate or obscure fundamental meanings and principles. Using an image as a tool for fostering critical intuitions must be understood to involve not only the grounding of abstract concepts in vivid case-by-case applications, but also the critique of associations that so often lead to a systematic misinterpretation of relevant ideals, concepts, and principles.

After all, what does the Statue of Liberty stand for? What does it imply? Were these implications true in all the days of our national past? And are they still true today? Today, for example, West Germany is the only country in the world that provides universal refuge to all children of every nationality who need shelter and protection. It provides free food, shelter and education to all such children. The U.S. does not. Does this mean that we have abandoned the ideal that the Statue of Liberty stands for? Student discussion of these questions helps develop insight into the deeper meanings that underlie traditional ideals of the United States and the problems involved in living in accord with those ideals.

Imagination as a Form of Visualization

Critical thinking requires an extensive use of the student's imagination. Whenever we think about abstract meanings, whenever we try to understand or assess a statement or belief, whenever we attempt to predict a consequence, or determine the implications of an action, we need to use our imaginations effectively. Most students are not practiced in this use of their imaginations. They often find it difficult to conjure up circumstances that exemplify abstract meanings.

For example, suppose we ask students to describe a circumstance in which some person was behaving in an unquestionably honest way. Most students find it difficult to imagine a case when called upon to do so. Very few would say something like: "Well, if I found your wallet on the playground and nobody knew I found it, but I still returned it to you — that would be being honest." They recognize the case when *someone else* thinks it up, but they often have difficulty in thinking them up, imagining them, on their own.

One of the reasons for this deficiency is the failure at all levels of education to teach in a way that fosters intuitive learning. If we focused attention, as we should, on the ability of students to move back and forth comfortably and insightfully between the abstract and the concrete, they would soon develop and discipline their imaginations so as to be able to generate cases that exemplify abstractions. All students have, as a matter of fact, experienced hundreds of situations that exemplify any number of important abstract truths and principles. But they are virtually never asked to dig into their experience to find examples, to imagine cases, which illustrate this or that principle, this or that abstract concept.

The result is an undisciplined and underdeveloped imagination combined with vague, indeed muddled, concepts and principles. They are left with experiences that are blind, experiences from which they learn few truths, ideas that are empty, that they cannot relate perceptively to their experience. What is missing is the intuitive synthesis between concept and percept, between idea and experience, between image and reality.

Conclusion

Some people erroneously believe that critical thinking and intuitive thinking are incompatible opposites. If one means by intuitive thinking a form of inexplicable, non-rational thought, the claim is correct, for critical thinking is always both intelligible and rational. But if one means by intuition the process by which one translates the abstract into the concrete, based on insight into the principles upon the basis of which one is thinking, then not only are critical and intuitive thinking not incompatible, they are necessarily conjoined. Solid critical thinking always requires fundamental insights, fundamental intuitions, to guide it.

If this is true, then teachers committed to fostering the critical thinking of their students must interest themselves in the means by which critical thinking intuitions are formed and developed. The dramatic, the concrete, and the highly visual and imaginative, are crucial instrumentalities for this purpose. Properly used they inevitably foster reflective intuition and insight. Whatever we are teaching, we should therefore continually ask ourselves, "What are the intuitions and insights essential to this mode of knowledge and thought?" and "How can I most effectively foster them with these students?"

3 Global Strategies: Socratic Questioning & Role-Playing

I. The Role of the Teacher

A teacher committed to teaching for critical thinking must think beyond compartmentalized subject matter, teaching toward ends and objectives that transcend subject matter classification. To teach for critical thinking is, first of all, to create an environment in the class and in the school that is conducive to critical thinking. It is to help make the classroom and school environment a mini-critical society, a place where the values of critical thinking (truth, open-mindedness, empathy, autonomy, rationality, and self-criticism) are encouraged and rewarded. In such an environment, students learn to believe in the power of their own minds to identify and solve problems. They learn to believe in the efficacy of their own thinking. Thinking for themselves is not something they fear. Authorities are not those who tell them the "right" answers, but those who encourage and help them to figure out answers for themselves, who encourage them to discover the powerful resources of their own minds.

The teacher is much more a questioner than a preacher in this model. The teacher learns how to ask questions that probe meanings, that request reasons and evidence, that facilitate elaboration, that keep discussions from becoming confusing, that provide incentive for listening to what others have to say, that lead to fruitful comparisons and contrasts, that highlight contradictions and inconsistencies, and that elicit implications and consequences. Teachers committed to critical thinking realize that the primary purpose of all education is to teach students how to learn. Since there are more details than can be taught and no way to predict which the student will use, teachers emphasize thinking about basic issues and problems. Thus, details are learned as a necessary part of the process of settling such questions, and so are functional and relevant.

The teacher who teaches students how to learn and think about many basic issues gives them knowledge they can use the rest of their lives. This teacher realizes that subject matter divisions are arbitrary and are a matter of convenience, that the most important problems of everyday life rarely fall neatly into subject matter divisions, that understanding a situation fully usually requires a synthesis of knowledge and insight from several subjects. An in-depth understanding of one subject requires an understanding of others. (One cannot answer questions in history, for example, without asking and answering related questions in psychology, sociology, etc.) Students must discover the value of knowledge, evidence, and reasoning by finding significant payoffs in dealing with their everyday life problems outside of school. Recognizing the universal problems we all face, the teacher should encourage each student to find personal solutions through self-reflective experiences and thought processes:

> Who am I? What is the world really like? What are my parents, my friends, and other people like? How have I become the way I am? What should I believe in? Why should I believe in it? What real options do I have? Who are my real friends? Whom should I trust? Who are my enemies? Need they be my enemies? How did the world become the way it is? How do people become the way they are? Are there any really bad people in the world? Are there any really good people in the world? What is good and bad? What is right and wrong? How should I decide? How can I decide what is fair and what is unfair? How can I be fair to others? Do I have to be fair to my enemies? How should I live my life? What rights do I have? What responsibilities?

The teacher who believes in personal freedom and thinking for oneself does not spoon-feed students with predigested answers to those questions. Nor should students be encouraged to believe that the answers to them are arbitrary and a matter of sheer opinion. Raising probing questions whenever they are natural to a subject under discussion, the teacher realizes that, in finding the way to answers, the student forges an overall perspective into which subject matter discoveries will be fit. Neither the discussion nor the student should be forced to conclusions that do not seem reasonable to the student.

Thus, such teachers reflect upon the subjects they teach, asking themselves, "What ideas and skills are the most basic and crucial in this subject? What do practitioners in this field do? How do they think? Why should students be familiar with this subject? What use does a well-educated person and citizen of a republic make of this subject? How can these uses be made apparent to and real for my students? Where do the various subject areas overlap? How should the tools and insights of each subject inform one's understanding of the others? Of one's place in the world?"

The teacher committed to teaching for critical thinking realizes that the child has two sources of belief: beliefs that the child forms as a result of personal experience, inward thinking, and interaction with peers and environment; and beliefs that the child learns through instruction by adults. The first could be called "real" or "operational" beliefs. They are what define the child's real world, the foundation for action, the source of acted-upon values. They are a result of the child making sense of or figuring out the world. They are heavily influenced by what has been called "pleasure-principle thinking". They are in large measure egocentric, unreflective, and unarticulated.

People believe in many things for egocentric, irrational reasons: because others hold the belief, because certain desires may be justified by the belief, because they feel more comfortable with the belief, because they are rewarded for the belief, because they ego-identify with the belief, because others reject them for not acting on the belief, because the belief helps to justify feelings of like or dislike toward others.

Students, of course, also have spontaneously formed reasonable beliefs. Some of those are inconsistent with the expressed beliefs of parents and teachers. As a result of this contradiction with authority, students rarely raise these beliefs to what Piaget calls "conscious realization".

Students have also developed their own theories about psychology, sociology, science, language, and so on, covering most subjects. The totality of these real beliefs is unsynthesized and contains many contradictions which students will discover only if encouraged to freely express them in an atmosphere that is mutually supportive and student-centered.

The other source of belief, didactic instruction from adult authority figures, is an authority's interpretation of reality, not the students'. The students learn to verbalize it but do not synthesize it with operational belief. Therefore, they rarely recognize contradictions between these two belief systems. A student's own theories and beliefs are not necessarily replaced with the knowledge offered in school.

The teacher concerned with this problem, then, provides an environment wherein students can discover and explore their beliefs. Such teachers refrain from rushing students who are struggling to express their beliefs, allow time for thoughtful discussion, refuse to allow anyone to attack students for their beliefs, reward students for questioning their own beliefs, and support students when they consider many points of view.

Unless the teacher provides conditions in which students can discover operational beliefs through reflective thinking, these two systems of beliefs will exist in separate dimensions of their lives. The first will control their deeds, especially private deeds; the second will control their words, especially public words. The first will be used when acting for themselves; the second when performing for others. Neither, in a sense, will be taken seriously. Neither will be subjected to rational scrutiny: the first because it isn't openly expressed and challenged verbally; the second because it is not tested in the crucible of action and practical decision-making. This dichotomy, when embedded in an individual's life, creates a barrier to living an "examined life". Students lack the wherewithal to explore contradictions, double standards, and hypocrisies. They will use critical thinking skills, if at all, as weapons in a struggle to protect themselves from exposure, and to lay bare the contradictions of the "other", the "enemy". When they integrate critical thinking skills into this dichotomous thinking, they become self-serving, not fairminded, critical thinkers.

The role of the teacher could be summarized as follows:

- help break big questions or tasks into smaller, more manageable parts
- create meaningful contexts in which learning is valued by the students
- help students clarify their thoughts by rephrasing or asking questions
- pose thought-provoking questions
- help keep the discussion focussed
- encourage students to explain things to each other
- help students find what they need to know by suggesting and showing students how to use resources
- ensure that students do justice to each view, that no views are cut off, ignored, or unfairly dismissed

II. Socratic Questioning: Wondering Aloud About Meaning and Truth

Introduction

Socratic discussion, wherein students' thought is elicited and probed, allows students to develop and evaluate their thinking by making it explicit. By encouraging students to slow their thinking down and elaborate on it, Socratic discussion gives students the opportunity to develop and test their ideas — the beliefs they have spontaneously formed and those they learn in school. Thus, students can synthesize their beliefs into a more coherent and better-developed perspective.

Socratic questioning requires teachers to take seriously and wonder about what students say and think: what they mean, its significance to them, its relationship to other beliefs, how it can be tested, to what extent and in what way it is true or makes sense. Teachers who wonder about the meaning and truth of students' statements can translate that curiosity into probing questions. By wondering aloud, teachers simultaneously convey interest in and respect for student thought, and model analytical moves for students. Fruitful Socratic discussion infects students with the same curiosity about the meaning of and truth of what they think, hear, and read and gives students the clear message that they are expected to think and to take everyone else's beliefs seriously.

Socratic questioning is based on the idea that all thinking has a logic or structure, that any one statement only partially reveals the thinking underlying it, expressing no more than a tiny piece of the system of interconnected beliefs of which it is a part. Its purpose is to expose the logic of someone's thought. Use of Socratic questioning presupposes the following points: All thinking has assumptions; makes claims or creates meaning; has implications and consequences; focuses on some things and throws others into the background; uses some concepts or ideas and not others; is defined by purposes, issues, or problems; uses or explains some facts and not others; is relatively clear or unclear; is relatively deep or superficial; is relatively critical or uncritical; is relatively elaborated or undeveloped; is relatively monological or multi-logical. Critical thinking is thinking done with an effective, self-monitoring awareness of these points.

Socratic instruction can take many forms. Socratic questions can come from the teacher or from students. They can be used in a large group discussion, in small groups, one-to-one, or even with oneself. They can have different purposes. What each form has in common is that someone's thought is developed as a result of the probing, stimulating questions asked. It requires questioners to "try on" others' beliefs, to imagine what it would mean to accept them, and to wonder what it would be like to believe otherwise. If a student says that people are selfish, the teacher may wonder aloud as to what it means to say that, how the student explains acts others call altruistic, what sort of example that student would accept as an unselfish act, or what the student thinks it means to say that an act or person was unselfish. The discussion which follows should help clarify the concepts of selfish and unselfish behavior, identify the kind of evidence required to determine whether or not someone is or is not acting selfishly, and explore the consequences of accepting or rejecting the original generalization. Such a discussion enables students to examine their own views on such concepts as generosity, motivation, obligation, human nature, and right and wrong.

Some people erroneously believe that holding a Socratic discussion is like conducting a chaotic free-for-all. In fact, Socratic discussion has distinctive goals and distinctive ways to achieve them. Indeed, any discussion — any thinking — guided by Socratic questioning is structured.

The discussion, the thinking, is structured to take student thought from the unclear to the clear, from the unreasoned to the reasoned, from the implicit to the explicit, from the unexamined to the examined, from the inconsistent to the consistent, from the unarticulated to the articulated. To learn how to participate in it, one has to learn how to listen carefully to what others say, to look for reasons and evidence, to recognize and reflect upon assumptions, to discover implications and consequences, to seek examples, analogies, and objections, to seek to discover, in short, what is really known and to distinguish it from what is merely believed.

Socratic Questioning

- raises basic issues
- probes beneath the surface of things
- pursues problematic areas of thought
- helps students to discover the *structure* of their own thought
- helps students develop sensitivity to clarity, accuracy, and relevance
- helps students arrive at judgment through their own reasoning
- helps students note claims, evidence, conclusions, questions-at-issue, assumptions, implications, consequences, concepts, interpretations, points of view — the elements of thought

---

Three Kinds of Socratic Discussion

We can loosely categorize three general forms of Socratic questioning and distinguish three basic kinds of preparation for each: the spontaneous, the exploratory, and the focused.

Spontaneous or unplanned

Every teacher's teaching should be imbued with the Socratic spirit. We should always keep our curiosity and wondering alive. If we do, there will be many occasions in which we will spontaneously ask students questions about what they mean and explore with them how we might find out if something is true. If one student says that a given angle will be the same as another angle in a geometrical figure, we may spontaneously wonder how we might go about proving or disproving that. If one student says Americans love freedom, we may spontaneously wonder about exactly what that means (Does that mean, for example, that we love freedom more than other people do? How could we find out?). If in a science class a student says that most space is empty, we may be spontaneously moved to raise some question on the spot as to what that might mean and how we might find out.

Such spontaneous discussions provide models of listening critically as well as exploring the beliefs expressed. If something said seems questionable, misleading, or false, Socratic questioning provides a way of helping students to become self-correcting, rather than relying on correction by the teacher. Spontaneous Socratic discussion can prove especially useful when students become interested in a topic, when they raise an important issue, when they are on the brink of grasping or integrating a new insight, when discussion becomes bogged down or confused or hostile. Socratic questioning provides specific moves which can fruitfully take advantage of the interest, effectively approach the issue, aid integration and expansion of the insight, move a troubled discussion forward, clarify or sort through what appears confusing, and diffuse frustration or anger.

Although by definition there can be no pre-planning for a particular spontaneous discussion, teachers can prepare themselves by becoming familiar and comfortable with generic Socratic questions, and developing the art of raising probing follow-up questions and giving encouraging and helpful responses. Ask for examples, evidence, or reasons, propose counter-examples, ask the rest of the class if they agree with a point made, suggest parallel or analogous cases, ask for a paraphrase of opposing views, rephrase student responses clearly and succinctly. These are among the most common moves.

Translating Wonderings into Questions

- If you see little or no relevance in a student comment, you may think, "I wonder why this student mentioned that now?" and ask, "What connection do you see between our discussion and your point that ...?" or "I'm not sure why you mentioned that now. Could you explain how it's related to this discussion?" or "What made you think of that?" Either the point is germane, and you can clarify the connection, or only marginally related, and you can rephrase it and say "A new issue has been raised." That new issue can be pursued then, tactfully postponed, or can generate an assignment.

- If a student says something vague or general, you may think, "I wonder about the role of that belief in this student's life, the consequences of that belief, how the student perceives the consequences, or if there are any practical consequences at all". You may ask, "How does that belief affect how you act? What, for example, do you do or refrain from doing because you believe that?" You might have several students respond and compare their understandings, or suggest an alternative view and have students compare its consequences.

To summarize: Because we begin to wonder more and more about meaning and truth, and so think aloud in front of our students by means of questions, Socratic exchanges will occur at many unplanned moments in our instruction. However, in addition to these unplanned wonderings we can also design or plan out at least two distinct kinds of Socratic discussion: one that explores a wide range of issues and one that focuses on one particular issue.

Exploratory

What we here call *exploratory* Socratic questioning is appropriate when teachers want to find out what students know or think and to probe into student thinking on a variety of issues. For example, you could use it to assess student thinking on a subject at the beginning of a semester or unit. You could use it to see what students value, or to uncover problematic areas or potential biases, or find out where your students are clearest and fuzziest in their thinking. You could use it to discover areas or issues of interest or controversy, or to find out where and how students have integrated school material into their belief systems. Such discussions can serve as preparation in a general way for later study or analysis of a topic, as an introduction, as review, to see what students understood from their study of a unit or topic before they take a test, to suggest where they should focus study for test, as a basis for or guide to future assignments, or to prepare for an assignment. Or, again, you might have students take (or pick) an issue raised in discussion and give their own views, or have students form groups to discuss the issue or topic.

With this type of Socratic questioning, we raise and explore a broad range of interrelated issues and concepts, not just one. It requires minimal pre-planning or pre-thinking. It has a relatively loose order or structure. You can prepare by having some general questions ready to raise when appropriate by considering the topic or issue, related issues and key concepts. You can also prepare by predicting students' likeliest responses and preparing some follow-up questions. Remember, however, that once students' thought is stimulated there is no predicting exactly where discussion will go.

What follows are some suggestions and possible topics for Socratic discussions:

• "What is social studies?" If students have difficulty, ask, "When you've studied social studies, what have you studied/talked about?" If students list topics, put them on the board. Then have students discuss the items and try to group them. "Do these topics have something in common? Are there differences between these topics?" Encourage students to discuss details they know about the topics. If, instead of listing topics, they give a general answer or definition, or if they are able to give a statement about what the topics listed have in common, suggest examples that fit the definition but are not social studies. For example, if a student says, "It's about people," mention medicine. Have them modify or improve their definition. "How is social studies like and unlike other subjects? What basic questions does the subject address? How does it address them? Why study social studies? Is it important? Why or why not? How can we use what we learn in social studies? What are the most important ideas you've learned from this subject?"

> • When, if ever, is violence justified? Why are people as violent as they are? What effects does violence have? Can violence be lessened or stopped?
> • What is a friend? What is good about having a friend? Being a friend? When is it hard to be a friend?
> • What is education? Why learn?
> • What is most important?
> • What is right and wrong? Why be good? What is a good person?
> • What is the difference between living and non-living things?
> • Of what sorts of things is the universe made?
> • What is language?
> • What are the similarities and differences between humans and animals?

There may be occasions when you are unsure whether to call a discussion exploratory or focused. Which you call it is not important. What is important is what happens in the discussion. For example, consider this group of questions:

> • What does 'vote' mean?
>> How do people decide whom to elect? How should they decide? How could people predict how a potential leader is likely to act? If you don't know about issues or the candidates should you vote?
>> Is voting important? Why or why not? What are elections supposed to produce? How? What does that require? What does that tell us about voting?
>> Why are elections considered a good idea? Why is democracy considered good? What does belief in democracy assume about human nature?
>> How do people become candidates?
>> Why does the press emphasize how much money candidates have? How does having lots of money help candidates win?
>> Why do people give money to candidates? Why do companies?

These questions could be the list generated as possible questions for an exploratory discussion. Which of them are actually used would depend on how students respond. For a focused discussion, these questions and more could be used in an order which takes students from ideas with which they are most familiar to those with which they are least familiar.

Focused

Much of the time you will approach your instruction with specific areas and issues to cover. This is the time for focused Socratic questioning. To really probe an issue or concept in depth, to have students clarify, sort, analyze and evaluate thoughts and perspectives, distinguish the known from the unknown, synthesize relevant factors and knowledge, students can engage in an extended and focused discussion. This type of discussion offers students the chance to pursue perspectives to their most basic assumptions and through their furthest implications and consequences. These discussions give students experience in engaging in an extended, ordered, and integrated discussion in which they discover, develop, and share ideas and insights. It requires pre-planning or thinking through possible perspectives on the issue, grounds for conclusions, problematic concepts, implications, and consequences. You can further prepare by reflecting on those subjects relevant to the issue: their methods, standards, basic distinctions and concepts, and interrelationships — points of overlap or possible conflict. It is also helpful to be prepared by considering likeliest student answers. This is the type of Socratic questioning most often used in the lesson remodels themselves. Though we can't provide the crucial follow-up questions, we illustrate pre-planning for focused Socratic questioning in numerous remodels.

All three types of Socratic discussion require development of the art of questioning. They require the teacher to develop familiarity with a wide variety of intellectual moves and sensitivity to when to ask which kinds of questions, though there is rarely one best question at any particular time.

Some Suggestions for Using Socratic Discussion

- Have an initial exploratory discussion about a complex issue in which students break it down into simpler parts. Students can then choose the aspects they want to explore or research. Then have an issue-specific discussion where students share, analyze, evaluate, and synthesize their work.

- The class could have a "fishbowl" discussion. One third of the class, sitting in a circle, discusses a topic. The rest of the class, in a circle around the others, listens, takes notes, and later discusses the discussion.

- Assign an essay asking students to respond to a point of interest made in a discussion.

- Have students write summaries of their discussions immediately afterwards. They could also add new thoughts or examples, provide further clarification, etc. They could later share these notes.

A Taxonomy of Socratic Questions

It is helpful to recognize, in light of the universal features in the logic of human thought, that there are identifiable categories of questions for the adept Socratic questioner to dip into: questions of clarification, questions that probe assumptions, questions that probe reasons and evidence, questions about viewpoints or perspectives, questions that probe implications and consequences, and questions about the question. Here are some examples of generic questions in each of these categories.

Questions of Clarification

- What do you mean by _____?
- What is your main point?
- How does _____ relate to ___?
- Could you put that another way?
- What do you think is the main issue here?
- Is your basic point _____ or _____?
- Let me see if I understand you; do you mean _____ or _____?
- How does this relate to our discussion/ problem/ issue?
- What do you think John meant by his remark? What did you take John to mean?
- Jane, would you summarize in your own words what Richard has said? ... Richard, is that what you meant?

- Could you give me an example?
- Would this be an example: _____?
- Could you explain that further?
- Would you say more about that?
- Why do you say that?

Questions that Probe Assumptions

- What are you assuming?
- What is Karen assuming?
- What could we assume instead?
- You seem to be assuming _____. Do I understand you correctly?
- All of your reasoning depends on the idea that ___. Why have you based your reasoning on _____ rather than _____?
- You seem to be assuming ___. How would you justify taking this for granted?
- Is it always the case? Why do you think the assumption holds here?

Questions that Probe Reasons, Evidence, and Causes

- What would be an example?
- What are your reasons for saying that?
- What other information do we need to know?
- Could you explain your reasons to us?
- Is that good evidence for believing that?
- Are those reasons adequate?
- Is there reason to doubt that evidence?
- Who is in a position to know if that is the case?
- What would you say to someone who said ___?
- What do you think the cause is?
- By what reasoning did you come to that conclusion?
- How could we go about finding out whether that is true?
- Can someone else give evidence to support that response?

- How do you know?
- Why did you say that?
- Why do you think that is true?
- What led you to that belief?
- Do you have any evidence for that?
- How does that apply to this case?
- What difference does that make?
- What would convince you otherwise?
- What accounts for that?
- How did this come about?

Questions About Viewpoints or Perspectives

- You seem to be approaching this issue from _____ perspective. Why have you chosen this rather than that perspective?
- How would other groups/types of people respond? Why? What would influence them?
- How could you answer the objection that _____ would make?
- Can/did anyone see this another way?
- What would someone who disagrees say?
- What is an alternative?
- How are Ken's and Roxanne's ideas alike? Different?

Questions that Probe Implications and Consequences

- What are you implying by that?
- When you say _____, are you implying _____?
- But if that happened, what else would also happen as a result? Why?

- What effect would that have?
- Would that necessarily happen or only probably happen?
- What is an alternative?
- If this and this are the case, then what else must be true?

Questions About the Question

- How can we find out?
- How could someone settle this question?
- Is the question clear? Do we understand it?
- Is this question easy or hard to answer? Why?
- Would _____ put the question differently?
- Does this question ask us to evaluate something?
- Do we all agree that this is the question?
- Is this the same issue as _____?
- Can we break this question down at all?
- How would _____ put the issue?
- What does this question assume?
- Why is this question important?
- Do we need facts to answer this?
- To answer this question, what other questions would we have to answer first?
- I'm not sure I understand how you are interpreting the main question at issue.

There are Four Directions in which Thought Can Be Pursued

There is another way to classify, and so arrange in our minds, questions we can ask to help stimulate student thought. This second taxonomy emphasizes "four directions in which thought can be pursued". For some of our readers this additional way of thinking about the kinds of questions that help students develop and discipline their thought may make the categories above more *intuitive*. As you examine the diagram below, you will see that all of the categories above except two are accentuated.

This diagram, and the classifications implicit in it, helps accentuate the following important facts about thinking. All thinking has a history in the lives of particular persons. All thinking depends upon a substructure of reasons, evidence, and assumptions. All thinking leads us in some direction or other (has implications and consequences). And all thinking stands in relation to other possible ways to think (there is never just one way to think about something). This classificatory scheme highlights, therefore, four ways we can help students come to terms with their thought:

✔ We can help students reflect on how they have come to think the way they do on a given subject. (In doing this, we are helping them look into the *history* of their thinking on that subject, helping them find the source or origin of their thinking in their biographies.)

✔ We can help students reflect on how they do support or might support their thinking (in doing this, we are helping them to express the reasons, evidence, and assumptions that underlie what they think.)

✔ We can help students reflect on what "follows from" their thinking, what implications and consequences their thinking generates. (In doing this, we are helping them to realize that all thinking entails or involves "effects" or "results" that we are obliged to consider.)

✔ We can help students reflect on how it is that people with points of view different from theirs' might raise legitimate objections or propose alternative ways to think that they should take into account. (In doing this, we are helping them to think more broadly, more comprehensively, more fairmindedly).

One disadvantage of this four-fold classification is that it does not highlight the important categories of "questions of clarification" and "questioning the question", so, if we find this four-fold classification helpful, we should take pains not to forget these categories.

Socratic Discussion
There are *four directions* in which thought can be pursued.

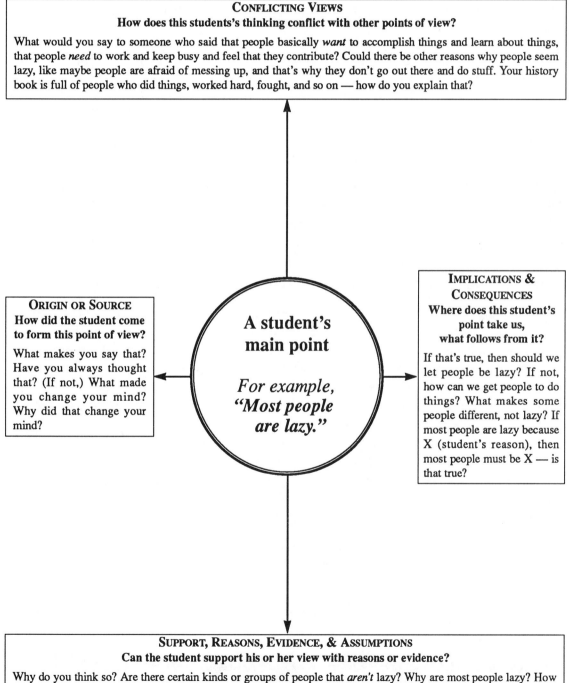

CONFLICTING VIEWS
How does this students's thinking conflict with other points of view?

What would you say to someone who said that people basically *want* to accomplish things and learn about things, that people *need* to work and keep busy and feel that they contribute? Could there be other reasons why people seem lazy, like maybe people are afraid of messing up, and that's why they don't go out there and do stuff. Your history book is full of people who did things, worked hard, fought, and so on — how do you explain that?

ORIGIN OR SOURCE
How did the student come to form this point of view?

What makes you say that? Have you always thought that? (If not,) What made you change your mind? Why did that change your mind?

A student's main point

For example, "Most people are lazy."

IMPLICATIONS & CONSEQUENCES
Where does this student's point take us, what follows from it?

If that's true, then should we let people be lazy? If not, how can we get people to do things? What makes some people different, not lazy? If most people are lazy because X (student's reason), then most people must be X — is that true?

SUPPORT, REASONS, EVIDENCE, & ASSUMPTIONS
Can the student support his or her view with reasons or evidence?

Why do you think so? Are there certain kinds or groups of people that *aren't* lazy? Why are most people lazy? How do you know? How could we find out if that might be so? Do people chose to be lazy, or decide that it doesn't matter if they are lazy, or are they just that way naturally? Do you think most people think of themselves as lazy? Why?

Wondering (And Wondering About Your Wonderings)

As a blossoming critical thinker, you will find yourself wondering in many directions. You will often, however, be unsure about how many of these wonderings to share with your students. You certainly don't want to overwhelm them. Neither do you want to confuse them or lead them in too many directions at once. So when do you make the wonderings explicit in the form of a question and when do you keep them in the privacy of your mind?

There is no pat formula or procedure for answering these questions, though there are some principles:

- *Test and find out*. There is nothing wrong with some of your questions misfiring. You won't always be able to predict what questions will stimulate students thought. So you must engage in some trial-and-error questioning.
- *Tie in to student experience and perceived needs*. You may think of numerous examples of ways students can apply what they learn, and formulate questions relating academic material to students' lives.
- *Don't give up too soon*. If students don't respond to a question, wait. If they still don't respond, you could rephrase the question or break it down into simpler questions.

The teacher must use care and caution in introducing students to Socratic questioning. The level of the questions should match the level of the students' thought. It should not be assumed that students will be fully successful with it, except over time. Nevertheless, properly used, it can be introduced in some form or other at virtually any grade level.

Transcript of a 4ᵗʰ Grade Socratic Discussion

The following is a transcript of a 4ᵗʰ grade exploratory Socratic discussion. The discussion leader was with these particular students for the first time. The purpose was to determine the status of the children's thinking on some of the abstract questions whose answers tend to define our broadest thinking. The students were eager to respond and often seemed to articulate responses that reflected potential insights into the character of the human mind, the forces that shape us, the influence of parents and peer group, the nature of morality and of ethnocentric bias. The insights are disjointed, of course, but the questions that elicited them and the responses that articulated them could be used as the basis of future discussions or simple assignments with these students.

While reading the transcript which follows, you may want to formulate questions that could have been asked but weren't: student responses that could have been followed up, or other directions the discussion could have taken. Other ways to approach the manuscript would include explaining the function of each question or categorizing the questions.

Transcript

➤ *How does your mind work?*
Where's your mind? **(A Foundational Question)**

Student: In your head. (numerous students point to their heads)

➤ *Does your mind do anything?* **(Question of Clarification)**

Student: It helps you remember and think.

Student: It helps, like, if you want to move your legs. It sends a message down to them.

Student: This side of your mind controls this side of your body and that side controls this other side.

Student: When you touch a hot oven it tells you whether to cry or say ouch!

➤ *Does it tell you when to be sad and when to be happy?*
How does your mind know when to be happy and when to be sad?
(Clarification and Probing Implications)

Student: When you're hurt it tells you to be sad.

Student: If something is happening around you is sad.

Student: If there is lightning and you are scared.

Student: If you get something you want.

Student: It makes your body operate. It's like a machine that operates your body.

➤ *Does it ever happen that two people are in the same circumstance but one is happy and the other is sad? Even though they are in exactly the same circumstance?*
(Exploring Viewpoints or Perspectives)

Student: You get the same toy. One person might like it. The other gets the same toy and he doesn't like the toy.

➤ *Why do you think that some people come to like some things and some people seem to like different things?*
(Exploring Viewpoints or Perspectives)

Student: Cause everybody is not the same. Everybody has different minds and is built different, made different.

Student: They have different personalities?

➤ *Where does personality come from?* **(Probing the Cause)**

Student: When you start doing stuff and you find that you like some stuff best.

➤ *Are you born with a personality or do you develop it as you grow up?* **(Probing the Cause)**

Student: You develop it as you grow up.

➤ *What makes you develop one rather than another?* **(Probing the Cause)**

Student: Like, your parents or something.

➤ *How can your parent's personality get into you?* **(Probing the Cause)**

Student: Because you're always around them and then the way they act, if they think they are good and they want you to act the same way, then they'll sort of teach you and you'll do it.

Student: Like, if you are in a tradition. They want you to carry on something that their parents started.

➤ *Does your mind come to think at all the way the children around you think? Can you think of any examples where the way you think is like the way children around you think? Do you think you behave like other American kids?*
(Exploring Viewpoints or Perspectives)

Student: Yes.

➤ *What would make you behave more like kids around you than like Eskimo kids?*
(Exploring Viewpoints or Perspectives)

Student: Because you're around them.

Student: Like, Eskimo kids probably don't even know what the word 'jump-rope' is. American kids know what it is.

➤ *And are there things that the Eskimo kids know that you don't know about?*
(Exploring Viewpoints or Perspectives)

Student: Yes.

Student: And also we don't have to dress like them or act like them, and they have to know when a storm is coming so they won't get trapped outside.

➤ *O.K., so if I understand you then, parents have some influence on how you behave and the kids around you have some influence on how you behave.... Do you have some influence on how you behave? Do you choose the kind of person you're going to be at all?*
(Probing Causes)

Student: Yes.

➤ *How do you do that do you think?* **(Probing Reasons and Causes)**

Student: Well if someone says to jump off a five-story building, you won't say O.K. You wouldn't want to do that ...

➤ *Do you ever sit around and say, "Let's see shall I be a smart person or a dumb one?"*
(Probing Implications)

Student: Yes.

➤ *But how do you decide?* **(Probing Causes)**

Student: Your grades.

➤ *But I thought your teacher decided your grades. How do you decide?* **(Probing Causes)**

Student: If you don't do your homework you get bad grades and become a dumb person but if you study real hard you'll get good grades.

➤ *So you decide that, right?* **(Probing Causes)**

Student: And if you like something at school, like computers, you work hard and you can get a good job when you grow up. But if you don't like anything at school you don't work hard.

Student: You can't just decide you want to be smart, you have to work for it.

Student: You got to work to be smart just like you got to work to get your allowance.

➤ *What about being good and being bad, do you decide whether you're good or you're bad? How many people have decided to be bad? (3 students raise their hands) [To first student:] Why have you decided to be bad?*
(Probing Causes)

Student: Well, I don't know. Sometimes I think I've been bad too long and I want to go to school and have a better reputation, but sometimes I feel like just making trouble and who cares.

➤ *Let's see, is there a difference between who you are and your reputation?*
What's your reputation? That's a pretty big word. What's your reputation?
(Clarification)

Student: The way you act. If you had a bad reputation people wouldn't like to be around you and if you had a good reputation, people would like to be around you and be your friend.

➤ *Well, but I'm not sure of the difference between who you are and who people think you are. Could you be a good person and people think you bad? Is that possible?*
(Clarifying and Probing Implications)

Student: Yeah, because you could try to be good. I mean, a lot of people think this one person's really smart, but this other person doesn't have nice clothes, but she tries really hard and people don't want to be around her.

➤ *So sometimes people think somebody is real good and they're not and sometimes people think that somebody is real bad and they're not. Like if you were a crook, would you let everyone know you're a crook?*
(Probing Implications)

Students: [Chorus] NO!

➤ *So some people are really good at hiding what they are really like. Some people might have a good reputation and be bad; some people might have a bad reputation and be good.*
(Clarification)

Student: Like, everyone might think you were good, but you might be going on dope or something.

Student: Does reputation mean that if you have a good reputation you want to keep it just like that? Do you always want to be good for the rest of your life?

➤ *I'm not sure ...* **(Clarification)**

Student: So if you have a good reputation you try to be good all the time and don't mess up and don't do nothing?

➤ *Suppose somebody is trying to be good just to get a good reputation — why are they trying to be good?* **(Probing Causes)**

Student: So they can get something they want and they don't want other people to have?

Student: They might be shy and just want to be left alone.

Student: You can't tell a book by how it's covered.

➤ *Yes, some people are concerned more with their cover than their book. Now let me ask you another question. So, if its true that we all have a mind and our mind helps us to figure out the world, and we are influenced by our parents and the people around us, and sometimes we choose to do good things and sometimes we choose to do bad things, sometimes people say things about us and so forth and so on ... Let me ask you: Are there some bad people in this world?* **(Probing Causes)**

Student: Yeah.

Student: Terrorists and stuff.

Student: Night-stalker.

Student: The TWA hijackers.

Student: Robbers.

Student: Rapers.

Student: Bums.

> ➤ *Bums, are they bad?* **(Clarification)**

Student: Well, sometimes.

Student: The Klu Klux Klan.

Student: The Bums ... not really cause they might not look good but you can't judge them by how they look. They might be really nice and everything.

> ➤ *O.K., so they might have a bad reputation but be good, after you care to know them. There might be good bums and bad bums.* **(Clarification)**

Student: Libyan guys and Machine gun Kelly.

> ➤ *Let me ask you, do the bad people think they're bad?* **(Exploring Perspectives)**

Student: A lot of them don't think they're bad, but they are. They might be sick in the head.

> ➤ *Yes, some people are sick in their heads.* **(Clarification)**

Student: A lot of them (bad guys) don't think they're bad.

> ➤ *Why did you say Libyan people?* **(Probing Reasons)**

Student: Cause they have a lot o' terrorists and hate us and bomb us ...

> ➤ *If they hate us do they think we are bad or good?* **(Probing Implications)**

Student: They think we are bad.

> ➤ *And we think they are bad? And who is right?* **(Exploring Perspectives)**

Student: Usually both of them.

Student: None of us are really bad!

Student: Really, I don't know why our people and their people are fighting. Two wrongs don't make a right.

Student: It's like if there was a line between two countries, and they were both against each other, if a person from the first country crosses over the line, they'd be considered the bad guy. And if a person from the second country crossed over the line, he'd be considered the bad guy.

> ➤ *So it can depend on which country you're from who you consider right or wrong, is that right?* **(Exploring Perspectives)**

Student: Like a robber might steal things to support his family. He's doing good to his family but actually bad to another person.

> ➤ *And in his mind do you think he is doing something good or bad?* **(Exploring Perspectives and Implications)**

Student: It depends what his mind is like. He might think he is doing good for his family or he might think he is doing bad for the other person.

Student: It's like the underground railroad a long time ago. Some people thought it was bad and some people thought it was good.

➤ *But if lots of people think something is right and lots of people think something is wrong, how are you supposed to figure out the difference between right and wrong?* **(Probing Causes)**

Student: Go by what you think!

➤ *But how do you figure out what to think?* **(Probing Causes)**

Student: Lots of people go by other people.

➤ *But somebody has to decide for themselves, don't they?* **(Probing Implications)**

Student: Use your mind?

➤ *Yes, let's see, suppose I told you: "You are going to have a new classmate. Her name is Sally and she's bad." Now, you could either believe me or what could you do?*
(Probing Consequences)

Student: You could try to meet her and decide whether she was bad or good.

➤ *Suppose she came and said to you: "I'm going to give you a toy so you'll like me." And she gave you things so you would like her, but she also beat up on some other people, would you like her because she gave you things?* **(Probing Consequences)**

Student: No, because she said I'll give you this so you'll like me. She wouldn't be very nice.

➤ *So why should you like people?* **(Probing Reasons)**

Student: Because they act nice to you.

➤ *Only to you?* **(Probing Implications)**

Student: To everybody!

Student: I wouldn't care what they gave me. I'd see what they're like inside.

➤ *But how do you find out what's on the inside of a person?* **(Probing Causes and Reasons)**

Student: You could ask, but I would try to judge myself.

Socratic questioning is flexible. The questions asked at any given point will depend on what the students say, what ideas the teacher wants to pursue, and what questions occur to the teacher. Generally, Socratic questions raise basic issues, probe beneath the surface of things, and pursue problematic areas of thought.

The above discussion could have gone in a number of different directions. For instance, rather than focussing on the mind's relationship to emotions, the teacher could have pursued the concept 'mind' by asking for more examples of its functions, and having students analyze them. The teacher could have followed up the response of the student who asked, "Does reputation mean that if you have a good reputation you want to keep it just like that?" He might, for instance, have asked the student why she asked that, and asked the other students what they thought of the idea. Such a discussion may have developed into a dialogical exchange about reputation, different degrees of goodness, or reasons for being bad. Or the concept 'bad people' could have been pursued and clarified by asking students why the examples they gave were examples of bad people. Students may then have been able to suggest tentative generalizations which could have been tested and probed through further questioning. Rather than exploring the influence of perspective on evaluation, the teacher might have probed the idea, expressed by one student, that no one is "really bad". The student could have been asked to explain the remark, and other students could have been asked for their responses to the idea. In these cases and others, the teacher has a choice between any number of equally thought provoking questions. No one question is the 'right' question.

III. Role Playing and Reconstructing Opposing Views

A fundamental danger for human thought is narrowness. We do not naturally and spontaneously open our minds to the insights of those who think differently from us. We have a natural tendency to use our native intelligence and our cognitive skills to protect and maintain our system of beliefs rather than to modify and expand it, especially when ideas are suggested that have their origin in a very different way of thinking. We can never become fairminded unless we learn how to enter sympathetically into the thinking of others, to reason from their perspectives and eventually to try seeing things as they see them.

Learning how to accurately reconstruct the thinking of others and how to role play their thinking (once reconstructed) are fundamental goals of critical thinking instruction. Very little work has yet been done in giving students opportunities to role play the reasoning of others, so it is not now clear to what extent or in what forms role playing to enhance critical reciprocity is possible.

But imagine some possible experiments. Students could brainstorm two lists, one list of their reasons for being allowed to stay up late and one for the reasons their parents might give forbidding it. A role play might be devised in which two students would pretend that they were parents and were asked, in that role, to give their reasons why their children should not be allowed to stay up late. It would be interesting to see how accurately the students could reconstruct the reasoning of their parents. They will probably find this challenging and should be encouraged to be as clear as possible in their reasons. Socratically questioning them would reveal more about their thinking. Then one might experiment with a discussion between a student playing "parent" and another student playing "daughter" or "son". The class might subsequently discuss what the best reasons were on each side of the dispute and who seemed to have the stronger argument.

History lessons might also provide opportunities for initial role playing experiences. For instance, students could role play discussions between Northerners and Southerners on disputed questions of the Civil War period, or between a member of the British royalty and a colonist concerning the events that led up to the Boston Tea Party.

An interesting follow-up exercise might be to have the students, either in pairs or singly, compose a dialogue on a given issue or on a chosen one. Remind them to brainstorm lists of reasons for both sides of the issue, being sure to focus on the side they don't hold. Then have them write a short dialogue expressing the opposing viewpoints. Some of the pairs of students could present their dialogues to the class.

IV. Teaching the Distinction Between Fact, Opinion, and Reasoned Judgment

Many texts claim to foster critical thinking by teaching students to divide all statements into facts and opinions. When they do so, students fail to grasp the significance of dialogical thinking and reasoned judgment. When an issue is fundamentally a matter of fact (for example, "What is the weight of this block of wood?" or "What are the dimensions of this figure?"), there is no reason to argue about the answer; one should carry out the process that yields the correct answer. Sometimes this might require following complex procedures. In any case, weighing and measuring, the processes needed for the questions above, are not typically matters of debate.

On the other hand, questions that raise matters of mere opinion, such as, "What sweater do you like better?" "What is your favorite color?" or "Where would you like to spend your vacation?" do not have any one correct answer since they ask us merely to express our personal *preferences.*

But most of the important issues we face in our lives are not exclusively matters of fact or matters of preference. Many require a new element: that we reason our way to conclusions while we take the reasoned perspectives of others into account. As teachers, we should be clear in encouraging students to distinguish these three different situations: the ones that call for facts alone, the ones that call for preference alone, and the ones that call for reasoned judgment. When, as members of a jury, we are called upon to come to a judgment of innocence or guilt, we do not settle questions of pure fact, and we are certainly not expected to express our subjective preferences.

Students definitely need to learn procedures for gathering facts, and they doubtless need to have opportunities to express their preferences, but their most important need is to develop their capacities for reasoned judgment. They need to know how to come to conclusions of their own based on evidence and reasoning of their own within the framework of their own perspectives. Their values and preferences will, of course, play a role in their perspectives and reasoning, but their perspectives should not be a matter of pure opinion or sheer preference. I should not believe in things or people just because I *want* to. I should have good reasons for my beliefs, except, of course, where it makes sense to have pure preferences. It does make sense to prefer butterscotch to chocolate pudding, but it does not make sense to prefer taking advantage of people rather than respecting their rights. Over time, students need to distinguish fact, opinion, and reasoned judgment, since they will never be good thinkers if they commonly confuse them as most students now do. (See the section on Text Treatment of Critical Thinking in "Thinking Critically about Teaching: From Didactic to Critical Teaching".)

In passing, be sure not to confuse this distinction with that of convergent and divergent questions. Questions of opinion and questions of reasoned judgment are both divergent, but the first does not involve the question of truth or accuracy (because it calls for expression of preference), while the second does (since reasoned judgment can be more or less reasonable, more or less prejudiced, more or less justified).

We have put this distinction into the "Global Strategies" chapter to underscore its importance as a pervasive emphasis in all instruction. In any event, we should always keep in mind global, as well as more specific, strategies for fostering critical thinking. When we habitually reflect on our role as teachers, play the role of Socratic questioner, seek opportunities to have students reconstruct and role play the thinking of others, and habitually encourage students to distinguish preference from reasoned judgment, we will discover new possibilities for critical thinking instruction and will develop global insights that help guide us in understanding and applying the strategies illustrated more specifically in the lesson remodels that follow.

Strategy List: 35 Dimensions of Critical Thought

A.   Affective Strategies

S-1   thinking independently
S-2   developing insight into egocentricity or sociocentricity
S-3   exercising fairmindedness
S-4   exploring thoughts underlying feelings and feelings underlying thoughts
S-5   developing intellectual humility and suspending judgment
S-6   developing intellectual courage
S-7   developing intellectual good faith or integrity
S-8   developing intellectual perseverance
S-9   developing confidence in reason

B.   Cognitive Strategies — Macro-Abilities

S-10 refining generalizations and avoiding oversimplifications
S-11 comparing analogous situations: transferring insights to new contexts
S-12 developing one's perspective: creating or exploring beliefs, arguments, or theories
S-13 clarifying issues, conclusions, or beliefs
S-14 clarifying and analyzing the meanings of words or phrases
S-15 developing criteria for evaluation: clarifying values and standards
S-16 evaluating the credibility of sources of information
S-17 questioning deeply: raising and pursuing root or significant questions
S-18 analyzing or evaluating arguments, interpretations, beliefs, or theories
S-19 generating or assessing solutions
S-20 analyzing or evaluating actions or policies
S-21 reading critically: clarifying or critiquing texts
S-22 listening critically: the art of silent dialogue
S-23 making interdisciplinary connections
S-24 practicing Socratic discussion: clarifying and questioning beliefs, theories, or perspectives
S-25 reasoning dialogically: comparing perspectives, interpretations, or theories
S-26 reasoning dialectically: evaluating perspectives, interpretations, or theories

C.   Cognitive Strategies — Micro-Skills

S-27 comparing and contrasting ideals with actual practice
S-28 thinking precisely about thinking: using critical vocabulary
S-29 noting significant similarities and differences
S-30 examining or evaluating assumptions
S-31 distinguishing relevant from irrelevant facts
S-32 making plausible inferences, predictions, or interpretations
S-33 evaluating evidence and alleged facts
S-34 recognizing contradictions
S-35 exploring implications and consequences

Strategies

Introduction

The purpose of this chapter is to illustrate how the concept of the autonomous, precise, fairminded thinker can be translated into classroom activities and discussions. We have broken the global concept of critical thinking down into 35 aspects or instructional strategies. Each strategy section has three parts. The "principle" provides the theory of critical thinking on which the strategy is based and links the strategy to the ideal of the fairminded critical thinker. We could have labeled it "What the Critical Thinker Does, and Why". We included it because we are convinced that one cannot do or teach critical thinking well without understanding why one should honor principles of critical thought, and to help overcome the tendency in education to treat insights and skills in isolation from each other. The "application" provides examples of when and how the strategy can be used in the classroom. Our lists of possible questions are often larger and more detailed here than in the remodels, and sometimes our remarks are general. We tried to provide some idea of when the principle could apply, to describe ways texts and some standard instructional practices can undermine or interfere with students learning the principle, and some initial suggestions to further illustrate and clarify the principle and get you started developing your own techniques for teaching it. Each strategy description concludes with a list of lesson plans in which we use the strategy for reference. If you aren't sure you understand the principle and how it can be taught, or want more examples of teaching it, or want to see it taught in context, you could look up some of the lessons and read a use of the strategy and (in many cases) justification for that use.

Here is an example. The thirteenth strategy on our list, **S–13,** is called "Clarifying Issues, Conclusions, or Beliefs". The principle that underlies it is briefly characterized as follows:

Principle: The more completely, clearly, and accurately an issue or statement is formulated, the easier and more helpful the discussion of its settlement or verification. Given a clear statement of an issue, and prior to evaluating conclusions or solutions, it is important to recognize what is required to settle it. And before we can agree or disagree with a claim, we must understand it clearly. It makes no sense to say "I don't know what you mean, but I deny it, whatever it is." Critical thinkers recognize problematic claims, concepts, and standards of evaluation, making sure that understanding precedes judgment. They routinely distinguish facts from interpretations, opinions, judgments, or theories. They can then raise those questions most appropriate to understanding and evaluating each.

Following it is an explanation of some of the ways we might teach for it:

Application: Teachers should encourage students to slow down and reflect before coming to conclusions. When discussing an issue, the teacher can ask students first, *"Is the issue clear? What do you need to know to settle it? What would someone who disagreed with you say?"* Students should be encouraged to continually reformulate the issue in light of new information. They should be encouraged to see how the first statement of the issue or problem is rarely best (that is, most accurate, clear, and complete) and that they are in a better position to settle a question *after* they have developed as clear a formulation as possible.

When discussing an issue, teachers can have students discuss such questions as, *"Do we understand the issue? Do we know how to settle it? Have we stated it fairly? (Does our formulation assume one answer is correct? Would everyone involved accept this as a fair and accurate statement of the issue?) Are the words clear? Do we have to analyze any concepts? Do we know when the key words and phrases apply and don't apply? Do we clearly understand how they apply to this case? Does this question ask something about facts? About the meanings of words? Are we evaluating anything? What? Why? What criteria should we use in the evaluation? What facts are relevant? How can we get the evidence we need? How would the facts be gathered? What would researchers have to do to conduct such a study? What problems would they face? How could those obstacles be surmounted?"*

When a statement is unclear, the class can discuss such questions as, *"How can we know whether or not this is true? What would it be like for this claim to be true? False? Do we clearly understand the difference? What evidence would count for it? Against it? Are any concepts (words or phrases) unclear? What does it assume? What does it imply? What does its opposite imply? Is there a clearer way to say this? Is there a more accurate way to say this? Can it be rephrased? Do the different ways of putting it say the same thing? Why would someone agree? Disagree?"*

This strategy provides a way of remodelling lessons that focus on "Fact/ Opinion," or which have vague passages of text.

To encourage students to distinguish fact from interpretation, the teacher could use questions like the following: *Does this description stick to the facts, or is reasoning or response included? Is this something that can be directly seen, or would you have to interpret what you saw to arrive at this statement? Is this how anyone would describe the situation, or would someone else see it differently? What alternative descriptions or explanations are there?* Students could then examine the assumptions, inferences, and theories underlying the alternatives.

Immediately after this we provide a list of lesson plans in which the strategy is used.

The reader should keep in mind the connection between the principles and applications on the one hand, and the character traits of a fairminded critical thinker on the other. Our aim, is not a set of disjointed skills, but an integrated, committed, thinking person. The strategies and lessons should be used to illuminate each other. If puzzled by a remodel (ours or your own), see the strategies. If puzzled by a strategy, see the originals and our critiques and remodels for clarification. All of the pieces of the remodelling process — understanding what critical thinking is and why one should do it; breaking the concept into teachable components; inventing ways to help students learn and practice critical thought; evaluating lessons; and improving them — all fit together. These activities are interdependent. (You're going to get very tired of that word before you're through.) Figuring out how to teach a particular principle helps you better understand what critical thinking is (and isn't). Analyzing and evaluating a lesson helps you see how critical thinking applies to particular situations. Clarifying the global concept of critical thinking helps you keep your focus on its most important features, and suggests ways of understanding and teaching specific principles and skills.

The strategies listed below are divided into three categories — one for the affective and two for the cognitive. This of course is not to imply that the cognitive dimension of critical thinking should be given twice as much emphasis. Indeed, the affective dimension is every bit as important to critical thinking. No one learns to think critically who is not motivated to do so. In any case, whatever dimension is emphasized, the other dimension should be integrated. We want students to continually use their emerging critical thinking skills and abilities in keeping with the critical spirit, and the critical spirit can be nurtured only when actually practicing critical thinking in some (cognitive) way. One cannot develop one's fairmindedness, for example, without actually thinking fairmindedly. One cannot develop one's intellectual independence without actually thinking independently. This is true of all the essential critical thinking traits, values, or dispositions. They are developmentally embedded in thinking itself. In teaching for critical thinking in a strong sense, the affective dimension of thinking is fully as important as the cognitive.

Furthermore, just as the cognitive and affective dimensions are interdependent and intertwined, so also are the various individual strategies. For purposes of learning, we articulate separate principles and applications. In the beginning, the connections between them may be obscure. Nevertheless, eventually we begin to discover how progress with any one principle leads inevitably to other principles. To see this, let us look first at the individual strategies in the affective dimension.

The Interdependence of Traits of Mind

Affective strategies are interdependent because the intellectual traits they imply develop best in concert with each other. Consider intellectual humility. To become aware of the limits of our knowledge, we need the courage to face our own prejudices and ignorance. To discover our own prejudices in turn, we often must empathize with and reason within points of view toward which we are hostile. To achieve this end, we must typically persevere over a period of time, for learning to empathically enter a point of view against which we are biased takes time and significant effort. That effort will not seem justified unless we have the confidence in reason to believe we will not be "tainted" or "taken in" by whatever is false or misleading in the opposing viewpoint. Furthermore, merely believing we can survive serious consideration of an "alien" point of view is not enough to motivate most of us to consider them seriously. We must also be motivated by an intellectual sense of justice. We must recognize an intellectual responsibility to be fair to views we oppose. We must feel obliged to hear them in their strongest form to ensure that we are not condemning them out of ignorance or bias on our part. At this point, we come full circle back to where we began: the need for intellectual humility.

Or, to begin at another point, consider intellectual good faith or integrity. Intellectual integrity is clearly a difficult trait to develop. We are often motivated, generally without admitting to or being aware of this motivation, to set up inconsistent intellectual standards. Our egocentric or sociocentric tendencies make us ready to believe positive information about those we like, and negative information about those we dislike. We are likewise strongly inclined to believe what serves to justify our vested interest or validate our strongest desires. Hence, all humans have some innate mental tendencies to operate with double standards, which of course is paradigmatic of intellectual bad faith. Such modes of thinking often correlate quite well with getting ahead in the world, maximizing our power or advantage, and getting more of what we want.

Nevertheless, it is difficult to operate explicitly or overtly with a double standard. We therefore need to avoid looking at the evidence too closely. We need to avoid scrutinizing our own inferences and interpretations too carefully. At this point, a certain amount of intellectual arrogance is quite useful. I may assume, for example, that I know just what you're going to say (before you say it), precisely what you are really after (before the evidence demonstrates it), and what actually is going on (before I have studied the situation carefully). My intellectual arrogance may make it easier for me to avoid noticing the unjustifiable discrepancy between the standards I apply to you and the standards I apply to myself. Of course, if I don't have to empathize with you, that too makes it easier to avoid seeing my duplicity. I am also better positioned if I lack a keen need to be fair to your point of view. A little background fear of what I might discover if I seriously considered the consistency of my own judgments can be quite useful as well. In this case, my lack of intellectual integrity is supported by my lack of intellectual humility, empathy, and fairmindedness.

Going in the other direction, it will be difficult to use a double standard if I feel a responsibility to be fair to your point of view, see that this responsibility requires me to view things from your perspective empathically, and do so with some humility, recognizing I could be wrong, and you right. The more I dislike you personally, or feel wronged in the past by you or by others who share your way of thinking, the more pronounced in my character the trait of intellectual integrity and good faith must be to compel me to be fair.

Distinguishing Macro-Abilities From Micro-Skills

Our reason for dividing cognitive strategies into macro-abilities and micro-skills is not to create a hard and fast line between the most elementary skills of critical thinking (the micro-skills) and the process of orchestrating those elementary skills, but rather to provide teachers with a way of thinking about two levels of learning. We use these two levels in most complex abilities. For intuitive examples, consider what is involved in learning to play the piano, learning to play good tennis, mastering ballet, or becoming a surgeon. In each of these areas, there is a level of skill learning which focuses on the most elementary of moves. For example, learning to practice the most elementary ballet positions at the bar, learning to play scales on the piano, or learning to hit various tennis strokes on the backboard. One must often return to this micro-level to ensure that one keeps the fundamentals well in hand. Nevertheless, dancing ballet is not practicing at the bar. Playing the piano is not simply playing scales. And hitting tennis balls against a backboard is not playing tennis. One must move to the macro level for the real thing. So, too, in critical thinking. Students have to learn the fundamentals: What an assumption is, what an implication is, what an inference and conclusion are, what it is to isolate an issue, what it is to offer reasons or evidence in support of what one says, how to identify a contradiction or a vague sentence.

But thinking critically in any actual situation is typically doing something more complex and holistic than this. Rarely in thinking critically do we do just one elementary thing. Usually we have to integrate or make use of a variety of elementary critical thinking skills. For example, when we are reading (a macro-ability) we have to make use of a variety of critical thinking micro-skills, and we have to use them in concert with each other. We might begin by reflecting on the implications of a story or book title. We might then begin to read the preface or introduction and start to identify some of the basic issues or objectives the book or story is focused on. As we proceed, we might begin to identify particular sentences that seem vague to us. We might consider various interpretations of them. As we move along, we would doubtless dip into our own experience for possible examples of what the author is saying. Or we might begin to notice assumptions the author is making. We would be making all of these individual moves as part of one integrated activity: the attempt to make sense of, to follow, what we are reading. As always, the whole is greater than and more important than the parts. We do not read to practice our critical thinking micro-skills; we use our critical thinking micro-skills in order to read, or better, in order to read clearly, precisely, and accurately.

Standard instruction and many approaches to teaching critical thinking or thinking skills often fail here. They over-emphasize drill in micro-skills and neglect their *use*. Being able to find assumptions only when someone tells you to is of little value. Articulating and evaluating assumptions helps one only if one does it when appropriate. This requires thinkers to notice for themselves when a problematic or questionable assumption is made, fairmindedly articulate it, rationally and fairmindedly judge it, and take that judgment into account appropriately. These abilities cannot be taught through drill. They must be developed and practiced *in the context* of some reasoning. Keep this principle of interdependence in mind as you read through the various strategies.

Have We Left Out Any Important Strategies?

As you begin to use the principles of critical thinking we have formulated in your teaching, you may wonder whether our list is complete. You may wonder, in other words, whether we may have left out any important critical thinking principles. The answer to this is "Yes and no." "No" in the sense that all of the important critical thinking principles are at least implicit in the ones we have formulated. "Yes" in the sense that some of what is merely implicit might properly be made explicit.

To exemplify this point, consider these insightful suggestions which we recently received from Rex Dalzell from New Zealand.

With respect to your list of strategies, I would like to suggest, with due intellectual humility, that the list could be usefully expanded by the addition of a further four strategies as follows:

Affective Strategies
Developing Intellectual Curiosity
In the affective area, I believe the development of an attitude of intellectual curiosity is of prime importance. Although there are elements of this dimension in other characteristics (e.g., independence of thought,

intellectual perseverance, etc.), and while the whole notion of critical thinking implies the presence of this attribute, it seems to me sufficiently important to warrant an explicit category of its own.

Critical thinkers need to be curious about their environment, they need to seek explanations of apparent discrepancies and they need to speculate as to possible causes of these discrepancies. In short, they need to be predisposed to wonder about the world around them. This sense of wonder, this intellectual curiosity that seeks explanations and proffers solutions, is something that can be and needs to be encouraged and developed. For this reason I believe it would be helpful to include it as a separate stand-alone category in any over-all schema.

Developing Social Sensitivity

In addition to developing insight into egocentricity and sociocentricity so that desirable levels of self-awareness are achieved it is also necessary, I believe, for critical thinkers to develop a high level of social sensitivity. By this I mean that critical thinkers need to become sensitive to the social situation they find themselves in so that they can judge effectively when it is and when it is not appropriate to exercise, at least overtly, their critical thinking skills. It is my experience that with some critical thinkers, particularly the "born again, evangelical" variety, they are quite insensitive to the social milieu in which they find themselves. Without due regard for the sensitivity of the situation, they launch forth with their battery of critical thinking skills and often destroy any possibility of a productive outcome.

In addition to being able to recognize the limits of their knowledge and being able to suspend judgment, critical thinkers also need to know when to put their skills into operation and when and how to articulate the results. Listing social sensitivity as a separate category would, I believe, be useful in helping critical thinkers develop this skill.

Cognitive Strategies: Macro-Abilities

Observing Critically

In addition to reading critically and listening critically, I believe it is very important for critical thinkers to learn how to observe critically. Intellectual curiosity is a necessary but not sufficient condition for critical observation to occur. Critical thinkers need to "see" as well as "look at" what is in their environment. They need to be trained to see the details of their surroundings, physical as well as social, and to accurately recall just exactly what they have seen. Most, if not all, of the micro-cognitive skills depend on this critical observation as a basis for productive application. As with intellectual curiosity and social sensitivity it seems to me that critical observation is a skill that merits recognition in its own right.

Expressing Precisely

While precision is an integral feature of all critical thinking and is highlighted by such macro skills as clarifying issues, conclusions, or beliefs, clarifying and analyzing the meanings of words and phrases, the overall emphasis is on precision of analysis rather than on precision of expression. While precision of expression is implied in many of the listed skills — how else for example, could one engage successfully in Socratic discussion or reasoned dialogue or dialectic without such precision? — it seems to me that it would be helpful to list it as a separate skill. If critical thinkers are not able to express themselves with precision then their overall effectiveness is greatly reduced.

You may decide to add these four principles to your personal list, even though we received them too late to incorporate them formally in this volume. In any case, it would be quite instructive to try to fill out these descriptions and write an "application section" for each of them. Keep this awareness alive as you begin to work out your own unique application of critical thinking principles.

Strategy List: 35 Dimensions of Critical Thought

In the chapter "Making Critical Thinking Intuitive" we introduced three hypothetical characters whose way of thinking illustrated the distinction between uncritical thinking (Naive Nancy), weak sense critical thinking (Selfish Sam), and strong sense critical thinking (Fairminded Fran). Before you examine our more formal explanations of the 35 dimensions of critical thinking you might find it useful to examine the following summaries as they might be expressed by Fairminded Fran. It is our hope that students will begin to think in these ways as we foster their thinking and encourage them to become not only skilled but fairminded as well.

As They Might Be Explained by Fairminded Fran

A. Affective Strategies

S-1 **thinking independently:** "I try to do my own thinking, to figure things out for myself. It's good to listen to others to find out what they're thinking, but you must always use your own thinking to decide who to believe and what to do."

S-2 **developing insight into egocentricity or sociocentricity:** "If I don't watch myself, I pay too much attention to what I want, and go along too quickly with what my friends say. I have to remember that everyone usually puts what they want first and believes what their friends believe. Just because I or my friends think something doesn't make it so"

S-3 **exercising fairmindedness:** "Whenever I disagree with someone I should try to look at things from their point of view. Maybe if I see why someone disagrees with me, I will find a reason to agree with at least part of what they are saying."

S-4 **exploring thoughts underlying feelings and feelings underlying thoughts:** "When I get angry or sad, I should think about why. Maybe I could change the way I am looking at things and then not be so angry or so sad after all."

S-5 **developing intellectual humility and suspending judgment:** "I shouldn't say things that I don't really know are true. Lots of things that people say aren't true. Even TV and books are sometimes wrong. I should always be willing to ask 'How do *you* know that? How do *I* know that?'"

S-6 **developing intellectual courage:** "I should be ready to speak up for what I think is right, even if it is not popular with my friends or the kids I am with. I should be courteous but I should not be afraid to think differently."

S-7 **developing intellectual good faith or integrity:** "I should be careful to practice what I preach. It is no good saying I believe in something if I don't really act on it."

S-8 **developing intellectual perseverance:** "It isn't always easy to solve problems. Sometimes you have to think for a long, long time to do it. Even though my mind gets tired, I must not give up too easily."

S-9 **developing confidence in reason:** "I know my head can figure things out, if I am willing to think logically, look for evidence, and accept only good reasons for things."

B. Cognitive Strategies — Macro-Abilities

S-10 **refining generalizations and avoiding oversimplifications:** "It's wrong to say 'everyone' when you only mean 'most' or 'no one' when you only mean 'just a few'. It's nice to make things simple, but not so simple that they're not true."

S-11 **comparing analogous situations: transferring insights to new contexts:** "Lots of things are like other things. Being lost in the city may be in some ways like being lost in your life. May be in both cases you need a map!"

S-12 **developing one's perspective: creating or exploring beliefs, arguments, or theories:** "It takes time to figure out what you really think, sometimes years! I should be ready to listen to what other people think and why. Then my own ideas can grow and grow."

S-13 **clarifying issues, conclusions, or beliefs:** "Often what people say is not as clear as they think. You should always be ready to say 'What do you mean?' or 'Could you explain that to me?'"

S-14 **clarifying and analyzing the meanings of words or phrases:** "Words are funny. Sometimes it sounds like you know them when you don't. Yesterday when my teacher asked me what 'democracy' meant, I thought I knew, but I found I couldn't explain it."

S-15 **developing criteria for evaluation: clarifying values and standards:** "If we are going to judge something as good or bad, we need a way to do it. But often we decide that something is good or bad and really don't know why we said so. People are funny!"

S-16 **evaluating the credibility of sources of information:** "We learn lots of things from other people, and from books and TV. But sometimes what we learn isn't so. We need to question what we hear people say and what we see on TV. Do they really know? Maybe and maybe not!"

S-17 **questioning deeply: raising and pursuing root or significant questions:** "My teacher often asks us questions that sound easy but aren't. The other day she asked us what a country is and it took us a lot of time to figure it out. I guess sometimes simple things aren't so simple."

S-18 **analyzing or evaluating arguments, interpretations, beliefs, or theories:** "The other day my brother and I argued about who should do the dishes. Finally we decided that we should do them together."

S-19 **generating or assessing solutions:** "It's interesting to try to solve problems. Sometimes there are even different ways to get the same job done."

S-20 **analyzing or evaluating actions or policies:** "I get mad when I am not allowed to do what my brother is allowed to do. My parents say it is because he is older than me, but sometimes I am not allowed to do what he was when he was my age That's not fair!"

S-21 **reading critically: clarifying or critiquing texts:** "When I read I try to figure out exactly what is being said. Reading is like being a detective. You have to ask questions and look carefully for answers."

S-22 **listening critically: the art of silent dialogue:** "When I listen to someone I ask myself whether I could repeat what they are saying and whether I could explain it to someone else. Sometimes I ask myself, 'Did anything like this ever happen to me?' This helps me see if I'm listening carefully."

S-23 making interdisciplinary connections: "I am finding out how I can use what I learn in one subject while I'm working on another. Lots of ideas work in different places."

S-24 practicing Socratic discussion: clarifying and questioning beliefs, theories, or perspectives: "I am finding out that you learn a lot more if you ask a lot of questions. I am also learning that there are different kinds of questions and that you can find out different things by asking them."

S-25 reasoning dialogically: comparing perspectives, interpretations, or theories: "It helps to talk to other kids when you are trying to learn. Sometimes they have good ideas, and sometimes it helps you to try to explain things to the other kids."

S-26 reasoning dialectically: evaluating perspectives, interpretations, or theories: "It even helps to talk to other kids who think differently from you. Sometimes they know things you don't and sometimes you find out that you need to think more before you make up your mind."

C. Cognitive Strategies — Micro-Skills

S-27 comparing and contrasting ideals with actual practice: "Lots of things we say we believe in, but then we don't do it. We say that everyone is equal but we don't give then an equal chance. We need to fix things so that we mean what we say and say what we mean."

S-28 thinking precisely about thinking: using critical vocabulary: "There are special words you can learn to help you talk about what goes on in your head. For example, inferences happen when you learn some things and decide other things because of that. Assumptions happen when you believe things without thinking about them. I try to watch my inferences and assumptions."

S-29 noting significant similarities and differences: "Sometimes it is important to see how alike things are that are different. Sometimes it is important to see how different things are that are alike. I always try now to see how things are both alike and different."

S-30 examining or evaluating assumptions:: "To do a good job of thinking you have to pay attention to what you believe without thinking. Sometimes we go along with stuff without thinking about it. When you do, watch out! You probably missed something important!"

S-31 distinguishing relevant from irrelevant facts: "It may be true but is it related? We often forget to ask this. To figure things out you must stick to the point and not get other things mixed in."

S-32 making plausible inferences, predictions, or interpretations: "I sometimes decide things that aren't true. Then I have to stop and think about why I did that. I try to be more careful next time. Things often seem to be one way at the moment and then turn out to be different."

S-33 evaluating evidence and alleged facts: "Detectives and police look carefully for evidence so they can find out who really did it. We need to find out evidence too, when we read and write and talk. We should try to find evidence before we decide who is right and wrong."

S-34 recognizing contradictions: "Sometimes kids say one thing today and another thing tomorrow. Sometimes parents and teachers do too. That's confusing. You should decide what you really mean and then stick to it and not go back and forth and back and forth."

S-35 exploring implications and consequences: "When things happen, other things happen because of them. If you say something mean to someone, they may feel bad for a long, long time. It's important to see that, otherwise we won't notice all the things we are making happen."

How Would Naive Nancy and Selfish Sam Understand the Strategies ?

It should be clear that Naive Nancy and Selfish Sam would give different explanations of the 35 dimensions of critical thought. Nancy would deceive herself into thinking that she was thinking critically when she was not. Furthermore, most of her understandings would be so abstract that she would not be able to apply the principles to her experience. Selfish Sam would emphasize the usefulness of the various dimensions of critical thinking for getting what he wants, for protecting himself, and for using others to his advantage. However, he would show little interest in the principles that focus on fairmindedness, intellectual humility, and integrity.

S-1 Thinking Independently

Principle: Critical thinking is autonomous thinking, thinking for oneself. Many of our beliefs are acquired at an early age, when we have a strong tendency to form beliefs for irrational reasons (because we want to believe, because we are rewarded for believing). Critical thinkers use critical skills and insights to reveal and eradicate beliefs to which they cannot rationally assent. In formulating new beliefs, critical thinkers do not passively accept the beliefs of others; rather, they analyze issues themselves, reject unjustified authorities, and recognize the contributions of justified authorities. They thoughtfully form principles of thought and action; they do not mindlessly accept those presented to them. Nor are they unduly influenced by the language of another. If they find that a set of categories or distinctions is more appropriate than that suggested by another, they will use it. Recognizing that categories serve human purposes, they use those categories which best serve their purpose at the time. They are not limited by accepted ways of doing things. They evaluate both goals and how to achieve them. They do not accept as true, or reject as false, beliefs they do not understand. They are not easily manipulated.

Independent thinkers strive to incorporate all known relevant knowledge and insight into their thought and behavior. They strive to determine for themselves when information is relevant, when to apply a concept, or when to make use of a skill. They are self-monitoring: they catch their own mistakes; they don't need to be told what to do every step of the way.

Application: A critical education respects the autonomy of the student. It appeals to rationality. Students should be encouraged to discover information and use their knowledge, skills and insights to think for themselves. Merely giving students "facts" or telling them "the right way" to solve a problem interferes with students' critiquing and modifying pre-existing beliefs with new knowledge.

Rather than having students discuss only those ideas mentioned in their texts, the teacher can have them brainstorm ideas and argue among themselves, for instance, about problems and solutions.

Before reading a section of text that refers to a map, chart, time-line, or graph, students could examine and discuss it.

Students could develop their own categories instead of being provided with them. "Types of Literature" lessons could be remodelled so that students group and discuss writings they have read, entertaining different ways to classify them. Students can classify animals before reading zoological classification systems in their texts.

Rather than asking students to place objects into pre-existing categories, for instance, the teacher can encourage students to form their own categories. Students can then discuss the reasons they had for forming each category. When different students have used different sets of categories to form groups, the teacher can ask such questions as: *When would this set of categories be most useful? When would that set be best? Why would someone else make different groupings?*

In math, instead of following directions in their texts, students can be given a task to perform or problem to solve in small groups. The class can then discuss their solutions and then compare them to what is in their text.

When a text tries to do too much of the students' thinking for them, it can be examined in depth. *"Why does the text tell you about this? Why do the authors think this (concept, skill, procedure, step) is worth knowing? Why does the text tell you to do this? What would happen if you didn't?"*

When giving written assignments, those assignments should provide many opportunities for the student to exercise independent judgment: in gathering and assembling information, in analyzing and synthesizing it, and in formulating and evaluating conclusions. Have students discuss how to organize their points in essays.

In science, students could put their own headings on charts or graphs they make, or decide what kind of graph would be most illuminating. Students can design their own experiments rather than follow directions in their texts.

Students could review material themselves, rather than relying on their texts for summaries and review questions. The teacher could routinely ask students, *"What are the most important points covered in the passage (chapter, story, etc.)?"* as a discussion beginner. The class could brainstorm about what they learned when studying a lesson, unit, or story. Only after they have exhausted their memories can the teacher try to elicit any crucial points neglected.

When discussing specific countries and periods of history, have students look at and discuss some combination of political, population distribution, physical, historical, linguistic, or land use maps before reading their texts. *"What can we tell about this country by looking at this map? What areas does it have? What kind of climate? Where do most of the people live? Why do you think they might live there? Where is the land easier to live on? Could that be why so many people live there? What languages do they speak? Who else in the world speaks that language? What can we infer from the fact that these people speak the same language as those over there? Were they in contact with each other at some point? What countries surround this country? What do we know about those countries? Judging by the physical map, would there have been much travel between this country and that, or would travel have been hard?"* After students have made educated guesses, the class could discuss how they could verify their predictions. Groups of students could be assigned specific points to research. After studying their texts and hearing the results of the research, students could review the points made in this discussion, distinguishing things they were able to figure out from what they didn't know and what they were wrong about, so that the next time their predictions can be better qualified.

Lesson plans in which the strategy is used

S-2 Developing Insight Into Egocentricity or Sociocentricity

Principle: Egocentricity is the confusion of immediate perception with reality. It manifests itself as an inability or unwillingness to consider others' points of view, to accept ideas or facts which would conflict with gratification of desire. In the extreme, it is characterized by a need to be right about everything, a lack of interest in consistency and clarity, an all or nothing attitude ("I am 100% right; you are 100% wrong."), and a lack of self-consciousness of one's own thought processes. The egocentric individual is more concerned with the *appearance* of truth, fairness, and fairmindedness, than with actually *being* correct, fair, or fairminded. Egocentricity is the opposite of critical thought.

As people are socialized, egocentricity partly evolves into sociocentricity. Egocentric identification extends to groups. The individual goes from *"I am right!"* to *"We are* right!" To put this another way, people find that they can often best satisfy their egocentric desires through a group. "Group think" results when people egocentrically attach themselves to a group. One can see this in both children and adults: My daddy is better than your daddy! My school (religion, country, race, etc.) is better than yours.

If egocentricity and sociocentricity are the disease, self-awareness is the cure. In cases in which their own egocentric commitments are not supported, few people accept another's egocentric reasoning. Most can identify the sociocentricity of members of opposing groups. Yet when we are thinking egocentrically or sociocentrically, it seems right to us (at least at the time). Our belief in our own rightness is easier to maintain because we suppress the faults in our thinking. We automatically hide our egocentricity from ourselves. We fail to notice when our behavior contradicts our self-image. We base our reasoning on false assumptions we are unaware of making. We fail to make relevant distinctions of which we are otherwise aware, and able to make (when making such distinctions does not prevent us from getting what we want). We deny or conveniently "forget" facts inconsistent with our conclusions. We often misunderstand or distort what others say.

The solution, then, is to reflect on our reasoning and behavior; to make our assumptions explicit, critique them, and, when they are false, stop making them; to apply the same concepts in the same ways to ourselves and others; to consider every relevant fact, and to make our conclusions consistent with the evidence; and to listen carefully and openmindedly to those with whom we disagree. We can change egocentric tendencies when we see them for what they are: irrational and unjust. Therefore, the development of students' awareness of their egocentric and sociocentric patterns of thought is a crucial part of education in critical thinking.

Application: Although everyone has egocentric, sociocentric, and critical (or fairminded) tendencies to some extent, the purpose of education in critical thinking is to help students move away from egocentricity and sociocentricity, toward increasingly critical thought. Texts usually neglect obstacles to rationality, content to point out or have students point out irrationality and injustice. We recommend that students repeatedly discuss *why* people think irrationally and act unfairly.

The teacher can facilitate discussions of egocentric or sociocentric thought and behavior whenever such discussions seem relevant. Such discussions can be used as a basis for having students think about their own egocentric or sociocentric tendencies. The class can discuss conditions under which people are most likely to be egocentric and how egocentricity interferes with our ability to think and listen. By discussing what people think (and how they think) when they are being egocentric and sociocentric, students can begin to recognize common patterns of egocentric thought. The class can discuss some of the common false assumptions we all make at times (e.g., "Anyone who disapproves of anything I do is wrong or unfair. I have a right to have everything I want. Truth is what I want it to be. Different is bad. Our group (country, school, language, etc.) is better than any other.") Teachers can also have students point out the contradictions of egocentric attitudes. ("When I use something of yours without permission, it is 'borrowing'; when you use something of mine, it is 'stealing.' Taking something without asking is O.K. Taking something without asking is wrong.") Sometimes story characters illustrate egocentricity.

The most real and immediate form of sociocentricity students experience is in the mini-society of their peers. Student attitudes present a microcosm of the patterns which exist on a larger scale in societies. All of your students share some attitudes which are sociocentric. Furthermore, students divide themselves into "subcultures" or cliques, each of which is narrower than the school-wide "culture". Honest and realistic exploration of these phenomena allows students to clarify and evaluate the ways in which "group think" limits them.

Often texts attempt to discourage sociocentricity by encouraging tolerance — asking students to agree that people whose ways are different are not necessarily wrong. Yet, by keeping discussion general and not introducing specific advantages of different ways, students are left with a vague sense that they should be tolerant, rather than a clear sense that others have ways worth knowing about and learning from.

Some texts inadvertently foster sociocentricity by giving only the U.S. or European side of issues, treating rationalizations as truth, or presenting some groups in a distinctly negative light. The teacher could encourage students to recognize sociocentric bias, reconstruct and consider other views of current and historical issues, and discuss how to avoid thinking sociocentrically.

Texts include many subtle forms of sociocentricity, displaying a narrowly European or American perspective in word choice. For example, a society might be described as "isolated" rather than "isolated from contact with Europeans."

Before beginning study of another culture, the teacher could elicit students' ideas of that group, including stereotypes and misconceptions. Ask, *"What are these people like? What do you think of when you think of them? How have you seen them portrayed in movies and on T.V.?"* After study, students could evaluate these ideas in light of what they have learned, and why they had them. *"Remember what you said about these people before we studied them? Which of our original believes were false or misleading? Why did we think that way? Where did we get these ideas? How do people come to think they know what other people are like before they know anything about them? What false beliefs might other people have about us? Why?"*

Lesson plans in which the strategy is used

S-3 Exercising Fairmindedness

Principle: To think critically about issues, we must be able to consider the strengths and weaknesses of opposing points of view; to imaginatively put ourselves in the place of others in order to genuinely understand them; to overcome our egocentric tendency to identify truth with our immediate perceptions or long-standing thought or belief. This trait correlates with the ability to reconstruct accurately the viewpoints and reasoning of others and to reason from premises, assumptions, and ideas other than our own. This trait also correlates with the willingness to remember occasions when we were wrong in the past despite an intense conviction that we were right, as well as the ability to imagine our being similarly deceived in a case at hand. Critical thinkers realize the unfairness of judging unfamiliar ideas until they fully understand them.

The world consists of many societies and peoples with many different points of view and ways of thinking. In order to develop as reasonable persons we need to enter into and think within the frameworks and ideas of different peoples and societies. We cannot truly understand the world if we think about it only from one viewpoint, as Americans, as Italians, or as Soviets.

Furthermore, critical thinkers recognize that their behavior affects others, and so consider their behavior from the perspective of those others.

Application: The teacher can encourage students to show reciprocity when disputes arise or when the class is discussing issues, evaluating the reasoning of story characters, or discussing people from other cultures.

When disputes naturally arise in the course of the day, the teacher can ask students to state one another's positions. Students should be given an opportunity to correct any misunderstanding of their positions. The teacher can then ask students to explain why their fellow student might see the issue differently than they do. *"What is Sue angry about? Why does that make her mad? Sue, is that right?"*

Students can be encouraged to consider evidence and reasons for positions they disagree with, as well as those with which they agree. For example, have students consider positions from their parents' or siblings' points of view. *"Why doesn't your mother want you to ...? Why does she think it's bad for you (wrong, etc.)? What does she think will happen?"*

Rather then always having students argue their points of view, call on a student who doesn't have a position on the issue under discussion — that is still thinking things through. Help that student clarify the uncertainty. *"What makes sense about what each side said? What seems wrong? What aren't you sure about?"*

Although texts often have students consider a subject or issue from a second point of view, discussion is brief, rather than extended, and no attempt is made to have students integrate insights gained by considering multiple perspectives. If students write a dialogue about an issue from opposing points of view, or contrast a story character's reasoning with an opposing point of view, or role play discussions, the teacher can have them directly compare and evaluate different perspectives.

When the class is discussing different cultures the teacher can encourage students to consider *why* people choose to do things differently or why other people think their ways are best. For example, ask, *"What would be some advantages to arranged marriages? Why might some people prefer that system to ours? What problems would it solve or lessen?"*

Students can be reminded of, and analyze, times that many members of a group or the class contributed something toward finding or figuring out an answer, solving a problem, or understanding a complex situation.

The class can discuss how hard it sometimes can be to be fairminded.

Lesson plans in which the strategy is used

S-4 Exploring Thoughts Underlying Feelings and Feelings Underlying Thoughts

Principle: Although it is common to separate thought and feeling as though they were independent opposing forces in the human mind, the truth is that virtually all human feelings are based on some level of thought and virtually all thought generative of some level of feeling. To think with self-understanding and insight, we must come to terms with the intimate connections between thought and feeling, reason and emotion. Critical thinkers realize that their feelings are their response (but not

67

the only possible, or even necessarily the most reasonable response) to a situation. They know that their feelings would be different if they had a different understanding or interpretation of that situation. They recognize that thoughts and feelings, far from being different kinds of "things", are two aspects of their responses. Uncritical thinkers see little or no relationship between their feelings and their thoughts, and so escape responsibility for their thoughts, feelings, and actions. Their own feelings often seem unintelligible to them.

When we feel sad or depressed, it is often because we are interpreting our situation in an overly negative or pessimistic light. We may be forgetting to consider positive aspects of our life. We can better understand our feelings by asking ourselves "How have I come to feel this way? How am I looking at the situation? To what conclusion have I come? What is my evidence? What assumptions am I making? What inferences am I making? Are they sound inferences? Are there other possible ways to interpret this situation?" We can learn to seek patterns in our assumptions, and so begin to see the unity behind our separate emotions. Understanding oneself is the first step toward self-control and self-improvement. This self-understanding requires that we understand our feelings and emotions in relation to our thoughts, ideas, and interpretations of the world.

Application: Whenever a class discusses someone's feelings (such as that of a character in a story), the teacher can ask students to consider what the person might be thinking to have that feeling in that situation. *"Why does he feel this way? How is he interpreting his situation? What led him to that conclusion? Would you have felt the same if you had been in his circumstances? Why or why not? What accounts for the difference? What could he have thought instead? Then how might he have felt?"*

This strategy can be used in the service of developing an intellectual sense of justice and courage. Students can discuss the thoughts underlying passionate commitment to personal or social change. *"Why was she willing to do this? Was she scared? What else did she feel that helped her ignore her fears? Why? How did she look at things that helped her endure and stick with it?"*

Students can discuss reasons for greed, fear, apathy, and other negative or hampering feelings. *"Why are people greedy? What thoughts underlie greed? Why do people feel they need more money? What does less money mean to them? Why? What assumptions underlie these attitudes? To what further thoughts do these attitudes lead?"*

When discussing a case of mixed feelings, the teacher could ask, *"What was he feeling? What else? (Encourage multiple responses.) What led to this feeling? That one? Are these beliefs consistent or contradictory? How could someone have contradictory responses to one situation? Is there a way he could reconcile these contradictions?"*

Students can also generalize about thoughts behind various emotions: behind fear, thoughts like — "This is dangerous. I may be harmed;" behind anger, thoughts like — "This is not right, not fair;" behind indifference, thoughts like — "This does not matter, no one can do anything about this;" behind relief, thoughts like — "Things are better now. This won't bother me anymore."

Lesson plans in which the strategy is used

S-5 Developing Intellectual Humility and Suspending Judgment

Principle: Critical thinkers recognize the limits of their knowledge. They are sensitive to circumstances in which their native egocentrism is likely to function self-deceptively; they are sensitive to bias, prejudice, and limitations of their views. Intellectual humility is based on the recognition that one ought not claim more than one actually knows. It does not imply spinelessness or submissiveness. It implies the lack of intellectual pretentiousness, arrogance, or conceit. It implies insight into the foundations of one's beliefs: knowing what evidence one has, how one has come to believe, what further evidence one might look for or examine.

Thus, critical thinkers distinguish what they know from what they don't know. They are not afraid of saying "I don't know" when they are not in a position to be sure. They can make this distinction because they habitually ask themselves, "How could one know whether or not this is true?" To say "In this case I must suspend judgment until I find out x and y," does not make them anxious or uncomfortable. They are willing to rethink conclusions in the light of new knowledge. They qualify their claims appropriately.

Application: Texts and testing methods inadvertently foster intellectual arrogance. Most text writing says, "Here's the way it is. Here's what we know. Remember this, and you'll know it, too." Behind student learning, there is often little more thought than "It's true because my textbook said it's true." This often generalizes to, "It's true because I read it somewhere."

Teachers can take advantage of any situation in which students are not in a position to know, to encourage the habit of exploring the basis for their beliefs. When materials call on students to make claims for which they have insufficient evidence, we suggest the teacher encourage students to remember what is said in the materials but also to suspend judgment as to its truth. The teacher might first ask for the evidence or reasons for the claim and have students probe its strength. Students can be encouraged to explain what they would need to learn in order to be more certain. You might have students consider how reasonable people respond to gossip or the news on T.V. They hear what is said, remember what they have heard, but do not automatically believe it.

In exposing students to concepts within a field, we can help students to see how all concepts depend on other, more basic concepts and how each field of knowledge is based on fundamental assumptions which need to be examined, understood, and justified. We can help students to discover experiences in their own lives which help support or justify what a text says. We should always be willing to entertain student doubts about what a text says.

We can model intellectual humility by demonstrating a willingness to admit limits in our own knowledge and in human knowledge generally. Routinely qualify statements: "I believe," "I'm pretty sure that," "I doubt," "I suspect," "Perhaps," "I'm told," "It seems," etc. This trait can be encouraged by frequent discussion in which ideas new to the students are explored for evidence and support.

Students should discuss such experiences as getting a bad first impression, then learning they were wrong; feeling certain of something, then later changing their minds; thinking they knew something, then realizing they didn't understand it; thinking they had the best or only answer or solution, then hearing a better one.

The teacher can have students brainstorm questions they have *after* study of a topic. Students could keep question logs during the course of research projects, periodically recording their unanswered questions. Thus, they can come to see for themselves that even when they have learned what is always expected of them, there is more to learn.

Lesson plans in which the strategy is used

S-6 Developing Intellectual Courage

Principle: To think independently and fairly, one must feel the need to face and fairly deal with unpopular ideas, beliefs, or viewpoints. The courage to do so arises from the recognition that ideas considered dangerous or absurd are sometimes rationally justified (in whole or in part) and that conclusions or beliefs inculcated in us are sometimes false or misleading. If we are to determine for ourselves which is which, we must not passively and uncritically accept what we have "learned". We need courage to admit the truth in some ideas considered dangerous and absurd, and the distortion or falsity in some ideas strongly held in our social group. It will take courage to be true to our own thinking, for honestly questioning our deeply held beliefs can be difficult and sometimes frightening, and the penalties for non-conformity are often severe.

Application: Intellectual courage is fostered through a consistently openminded atmosphere. Students should be encouraged to honestly consider or doubt any belief. Students who disagree with or doubt their peers or text should be given support. The teacher should raise probing questions regarding unpopular ideas which students have hitherto been discouraged from considering. The teacher should model intellectual courage by playing devil's advocate. *Why does this idea bother you?*

Texts often seem to suggest that standing up for one's beliefs is fairly easy; they ignore the difficulty of "doing the right thing." Students could discuss such questions as these: *"Why is it hard to go against the crowd? If everyone around you is sure of something, why is it hard to question it or disagree? When is it good to do so? When might you hesitate? When should you hesitate? Is it hard to question your own beliefs? Why?*

Students who have been habitually praised for uncritically accepting others' claims may feel the rug pulled out from under them for a while when expected to think for themselves. Students should be emotionally supported in these circumstances and encouraged to express the natural hesitancy, discomfort, or anxiety they may experience so they may work their way through these feelings. A willingness to consider unpopular beliefs develops by degrees. Teachers should exercise discretion beginning first with mildly unpopular rather than with extremely unpopular beliefs.

If, during the course of the year, an idea or suggestion which at first sounded "crazy" was proven valuable, students can later be reminded of it, and discuss it at length, and compare it to other events. *"How did this idea seem at first? Why? What made you change your mind about it? Have you had other similar experiences? Why did those ideas seem crazy or stupid at first?"*

Lesson plans in which the strategy is used

S-7 Developing Intellectual Good Faith or Integrity

Principle: Critical thinkers recognize the need to be true to their own thought, to be consistent in the intellectual standards they apply, to hold themselves to the same rigorous standards of evidence and proof to which they hold others, to practice what they advocate for others, and to honestly admit discrepancies and inconsistencies in their own thought and action. They believe most strongly what has been justified by their own thought and analyzed experience. They have a commitment to bringing the self they are and the self they want to be together. People in general are often inconsistent in their application of standards once their ego is involved positively or negatively. When people like us, we tend to over-estimate their positive characteristics; when they dislike us, we tend to underrate them.

Application: Texts often inadvertently encourage the mental split between "school belief" and "real life" belief and between verbal or public belief and belief that guides action. There is an old saying to the effect that "They are good prophets who follow their own teachings." And sometimes parents say, "Do as I say, not as I do." There is often a lack of integrity in human life. Hypocrisy and inconsistency are common. As educators, we need to highlight the difficulties of being consistent in an often inconsistent world.

As teachers, we need to be sensitive to our own inconsistencies in the application of rules and standards, and we need to help students to explore their own. Peer groups often pressure students to judge in-group members less critically than out-group members. Students need opportunities to honestly assess their own participation in such phenomena.

Texts often preach. They unrealistically present moral perfection as easy when it is often not. They ask general and loaded questions ("Do you listen to other views? Is it important to treat others fairly?") to which students are likely to simply respond with a "Yes!" Such questions should be remodelled and the "dark side" explored. For example, ask, *"When have you found it difficult to listen to others?"* or *"Why are people often unfair?"*

Language Arts texts sometimes have students roundly criticize characters without taking into account the difficulties of living up to worthy ideals. Students should be encouraged to give more realistic assessments. *"Would you have done otherwise? Would it have been easy? Why or why not? Why do so few people do this?"*

Social studies texts are harsher judges of other societies than of ours. Students should evaluate their texts' consistency in evaluation. The teacher may have to help students to recognize this problem.

When evaluating or developing criteria for evaluation, have students assess both themselves and others, noting their tendency to favor themselves.

Lesson plans in which the strategy is used

S-8 Developing Intellectual Perseverance

Principle: Becoming a more critical thinker is not easy. It takes time and effort. Critical thinking is reflective and recursive; that is, we often go back in our thoughts to previous problems to re-consider or re-analyze them. Critical thinkers are willing to pursue intellectual insights and truths in spite of difficulties, obstacles, and frustrations. They recognize the need to struggle with confusion and unsettled questions over an extended period of time in order to achieve deeper understanding and insight. They recognize that significant change requires patience and hard work. Important issues often require extended thought, research, struggle. Considering a new view takes time. Yet people are often impatient to "get on with it" when they most need to slow down and think carefully. People rarely define issues or problems clearly; concepts are often left vague; related issues are not sorted out, etc. When people don't understand a problem or situation, their reactions and solutions often compound the original problem. Students need to gain insight into the need for intellectual perseverance.

Application: Intellectual perseverance can be developed by reviewing and discussing the kinds of difficulties that were inherent in previous problems worked on, exploring why it is necessary to struggle with them over an extended period.

Studying the work of great inventors or thinkers through biography can also be of use, with students discussing why long-range commitment was necessary. In time, students will see the value in pursuing important ideas at length.

Texts discourage this trait by doing too much for students: breaking processes into proceduralized fragments and drilling the fragments. Texts try to remove all struggle from learning. Students should come to see mental struggle as crucial to learning by discovering its reward in genuine understanding. Texts often present knowledge and knowledge acquisition (for example, scientific conclusions) as simple ("this experiment proved"), rather than the result of much thought, work, dead ends, etc.

Students should have some experiences slowly reading difficult material. Prove to them that if they are careful and stick to it, examining it one word, phrase, and sentence at a time, they can master it. Such in-depth reading can be done as a class, sentence by sentence, with students interpreting and explaining as they go.

Students with hobbies, skills, or interests could discuss how they learned about them, their mistakes, failures, and frustrations along the way, and the tenacity their mastery required.

Raise difficult problems again and again over the course of the year. Design long-term projects for which students must persevere. Of course, it is important to work with students on skills of breaking down complex problems into simpler components, so that they will see how to attack problems systematically.

Students can discuss experiences they have had wherein they came to understand something that at first baffled them, or seemed hopelessly confusing and frustrating. *"What was it like to not understand or be able to do it? How did you come to understand it? What was that like? Was it worth it? Did it seem worth it at the time? What made you change your mind?"*

Texts will sometimes say of a problem that it is hard to solve, and leave it at that. This encourages an "Oh, that's very complicated. I'll never get it." attitude antithetical to the critical spirit. Life's problems are not divided into the simple and the hopeless. To help students develop the sense that they can begin to attack even complex problems, you could divide the class into groups and have them discuss various ways in which the problem could be approached, seeing if they can break the problem down into simpler components. It is important to devote considerable time to problem analysis, in order to develop student confidence in their ability to distinguish hard from easy problems and to recognize when a longer term commitment will be necessary. Students will not develop intellectual perseverance unless they develop confidence in their ability to analyze and approach problems with success. You should not overwhelm students with the task of *solving* problems so difficult that they have little hope of making progress, nevertheless, they should be expected to make some progress toward understanding and sorting out complexities.

Take a basic idea within a subject ("well-written," "justice," "culture," "life," "matter," etc.). Have students write their ideas on it and discuss them. Every month or so, have them add to, revise, or write another paper. At the end of the year, they can assess the changes in their understanding from repeated consideration over the course of the year, graphically illustrating their own progress and development achieved through perseverance.

For students to recognize the need for further study of an idea, they need to have some sense of how their present knowledge is limited. Presenting some problems that are beyond their knowledge can be useful, if the class can come to see what they would have to learn to solve them. In this context, students can successfully uncover what they don't know, thereby fostering intellectual humility as well as laying the foundation for intellectual perseverance.

Illustrate how getting answers is not the only form of progress, show students how having better, clearer questions is also progress. Point out progress made. Sympathize with students' natural frustration and discouragement.

Have students discuss the importance of sufficient thought regarding significant decisions and beliefs, and the difficulty of becoming rational and well-educated, fairminded people.

When study and research fail to settle key questions, due to the inadequacy of available resources, the class could write letters to appropriate faculty of one or two colleges. Have students describe their research and results and pose their unanswered questions. The teacher may have to explain the replies. Students can then reopen the issues for further, better-informed discussion.

Lesson plans in which the strategy is used

S-9 Developing Confidence in Reason

Principle: The rational person recognizes the power of reason and the value of disciplining thinking in accordance with rational standards. Virtually all of the progress that has been made in science and human knowledge testifies to this power, and so to the reasonability of having *confidence* in reason. To develop this faith is to come to see that ultimately one's own higher interests and those of humankind at large will be served best by giving the freest play to reason, by encouraging people to come to their own conclusions through a process of developing their own rational faculties. It is to believe that, with proper encouragement and cultivation, people can develop the ability to think for themselves, to form reasonable points of view, draw reasonable conclusions, think coherently and logically, persuade each other by reason and, ultimately, become reasonable persons, despite the deep-seated obstacles in the native character of the human mind and in society as we know it. It is to reject force and trickery as standard ways of changing another's mind. This confidence is essential to building a democracy in which people come to genuine rule, rather than being manipulated by the mass media, special interests, or by the inner prejudices, fears, and irrationalities that so easily and commonly tend to dominate human minds.

You should note that the act of faith we are recommending is not to be blind but should be tested in everyday experiences and academic work. In other words, we should have confidence in reason, because reason works. Confidence in reason does not deny the reality of intuition; rather, it provides a way of distinguishing intuition from prejudice.

At the heart of this principle is the desire to make sense of the world, and the expectation that sense can be made. Texts often don't make sense to students, sometimes because what they say doesn't make sense, more often because students don't have opportunities to make sense out of what they are told. Being continually called upon to "master" what seems nonsensical undermines the feeling that one can make sense of the world. Many students, rushed through mountains of material, give up on this early. ("If I try to make sense of this, I'll never finish. Trying to really understand just slows me down.")

Application: As a teacher, you can model confidence in reason in many ways. Every time you show your students that you can make rules, assignments, and classroom activities *intelligible* to them so that they can see that you are doing things for well-thought-out reasons, you help them to understand why confidence in reason is justified. Every time you help them solve a problem with the use of their own thinking or "think aloud" through a difficult problem in front of them, you encourage them to develop confidence in reason. Every time you encourage them to *question* the reasons behind rules, activities, and procedures, you help them to recognize that we should expect *reasonability* to be at the foundation of our lives. Every time you display a patient willingness to hear their reasons for their beliefs and actions you encourage confidence in reason. Every time you clarify a standard of good reasoning, helping them to grasp *why* this standard makes sense, you help them to develop confidence in reason.

One reason students have little faith in reason is that they don't see reason being used in their everyday lives. Power, authority, prestige, strength, intimidation, and pressure are often used instead of reason. Students develop a natural cynicism about reason which educators should help them to overcome.

Texts often make knowledge acquisition seem mysterious, as though scholars have some sort of mystical mental powers. Make the reasoning behind what they study clear, and students will feel that knowledge and reason are within their grasp.

Give students multiple opportunities to try to persuade each other and you. Insist that students who disagree *reason* with each other, rather than using ridicule, intimidation, peer pressure, etc.

By beginning study of a new topic by discussing what they know about it, students can begin to realize that their initial knowledge is worthwhile. By allowing students to tackle problems and tasks on their own before explaining what to do, teachers help students experience the power of their own minds. By then showing them a better way that scholars have developed, students can see its superior power for themselves. Thus, as they learn, they can feel their minds grow.

Have students compare and contrast the following concepts: intimidate, convince, persuade, trick, brainwash.

Lesson plans in which the strategy is used

S-10 Refining Generalizations and Avoiding Oversimplifications

Principle: It is natural to seek to simplify problems and experiences to make them easier to deal with. Everyone does this. However, the uncritical thinker often oversimplifies, and as a result misrepresents problems and experiences. What should be recognized as complex, intricate, ambiguous, or subtle is viewed as simple, elementary, clear, and obvious. For example, it is typically an oversimplification to view people or groups as *all good* or *all bad*, actions as *always right* or *always wrong*, one contributing factor as *the cause*, etc., and yet such beliefs are common. Critical thinkers try to find simplifying patterns and solutions, but not by misrepresentation or distortion. Making a distinction between useful simplifications and misleading oversimplifications is important to critical thinking.

One of the strongest tendencies of the egocentric, uncritical mind is to see things in terms of black and white, "all right" and "all wrong." Hence, beliefs which should be held with varying degrees of certainty are held as certain. Critical thinkers are sensitive to this problem. They understand the relationship of evidence to belief and so qualify their statements accordingly. The tentativeness of many of their beliefs is characterized by the appropriate use of such qualifiers as 'highly likely,' 'probably,' 'not very likely,' 'highly unlikely,' 'often,' 'usually,' 'seldom,' 'I doubt,' 'I suspect,' 'most,' 'many,' and 'some.'

Critical thinkers scrutinize generalizations, probe for possible exceptions, and then use appropriate qualifications. Critical thinkers are not only clear, but also *exact* or *precise*.

Application: Whenever students or texts oversimplify, the teacher can ask questions which raise the problem of complexity. For instance, if a student or text over-generalizes, the teacher can ask for counter-examples. If a text overlooks factors by stating one cause for a problem, situation, or event, the teacher can raise questions about other possible contributing factors. If different things are lumped together, the teacher can call attention to differences. (*"Is this situation 'just like' that one? What are some differences?"*) If interconnected or overlapping phenomena are too casually separated, the teacher can probe overlaps or connections. If only one point of view is expressed, though others are relevant, the teacher can play devil's advocate, bringing in other points of view.

Texts grossly oversimplify the concept of "characterization" by having students infer character traits from one action or speech (and thus leave students with a collections of unintegrated, fragmented, contradictory snap judgments, rather than a developed, consistent, complete understanding of characters). Students should analyze the whole character by considering the variety of attitudes, actions, and statements.

Texts often state such vague generalities as "People must work together to solve this problem." Such a statement glosses over complications which could be clarified in a discussion. *"Why don't people work together on this? How should they? Why? Why wouldn't this seemingly obvious solution work? So, what else must be done? How could these needs and interests be reconciled?"*

Among the most common forms of oversimplification found in social studies texts is that of vaguely expressed explanations. Students can better understand explanations and descriptions of historical events, and peoples' reactions to them, by considering offered explanations in depth. For example, a text says that citizens of a former colony resented the rule they lived under. Students could discuss questions like the following: *Why did they resent being ruled by others? What, exactly made them unhappy with their situation? How would we feel about being conquered and ruled? What consequences might arise from our being taken over? Why? How might we respond? Why? Why would a country want to rule another group? What would it get out of it? Why wouldn't they want to give it up? What do they say are their reasons for not giving it up? Why don't the people they rule accept those reasons? Was this group's treatment of that group consistent with those reasons?*

Another common form of oversimplification in history texts occurs when texts describe *"the"* reason or cause of present or historical situations. This treatment often serves texts' sociocentric bias when discussing the causes of wars in which the U.S. has been involved; the enemy bears total responsibility. Students have had a sufficient number of experiences with conflict to be able to see how sometimes both sides are partly to blame. By discussing these experiences, and drawing analogies, students can learn to avoid simple, pat, self-serving interpretations of events. *"Did the U.S. contribute to this situation? How? Why did they do this? What might they have done instead? What result might that have had? Was only one side to blame?"*

When discussing generalizations, the teacher could ask students for counter-examples. The class can then suggest and evaluate more accurate formulations of the claim. *"Is this always the case? Can you think of a time when an x wasn't a y? Given that example, how could we make the claim more accurate?"* ("Some-times ...." "When this is the case, that happens ...." "It seems that...." "When this *and* that are *both* true, then ....)

The teacher can encourage students to qualify their statements when they have insufficient evidence to be certain. By asking for the evidence on which student claims are based and encouraging students to recognize the possibility that alternative claims may be true, the teacher can help students develop the habits of saying "I'm not sure," and of using appropriate probability qualifiers.

Analogies and models (for example, in science) simplify the phenomena they represent. The class can examine ways such analogies and models break down. *"In what ways is this a poor analogy? How does this model break down? Why? What accounts for the differences? What does that tell us about our subject? Could the analogy or model be improved? How? Why is that better?"*

Lesson plans in which the strategy is used

S-11 Comparing Analogous Situations: Transferring Insights to New Contexts

Principle: An idea's power is limited by our capacity to see its application. Critical thinkers' ability to use ideas mindfully enhances their ability to transfer ideas critically. They practice using ideas and insights by appropriately applying them to new situations. This allows them to organize materials and experiences in different ways, to compare and contrast alternative labels, to integrate their understanding of different situations, and to find fruitful ways to conceptualize novel situations. Each new application of an idea enriches our understanding of both the idea applied and the situation to which it is applied. True education provides for more than one way to organize material. For example, history can be organized in our minds by geography, chronology, or by such phenomena as repeated patterns, common situations, analogous "stories", the dynamics of various kinds of change, and so on. The truly educated person is not trapped by one organizing principle, but can take knowledge apart and put it together many different ways. Each way of organizing knowledge has some benefit.

Application: Critical teaching, focussing more on basic concepts than on artificial organization of material, encourages students to apply what they have just learned to different but analogous contexts. Using similar information from different situations makes explanations clearer, less vague. For example, a conflict in literature might parallel a war or political conflict. Economic relations between nations could be compared to the economy of a household. *"How would that dynamic explain this situation?"*

When students master a new skill, or discover an insight, they can be encouraged to use it to analyze other situations. Combine the strategy with independent thought by asking students to name, recall, or find analogous situations.

Students can find analogies between historical events or beliefs and present day actions and claims. Any parallel situations can be compared, and insights into each applied to the other. *"Given what we know about our own civil war, it's causes and results, what it was like, what can we say about this other country's civil war?" "Does anything said here about the beginning of this country tell us anything about the beginning of our own country? Vice versa?"*

When students have learned a scientific law, concept, or principle, they can enrich their grasp of it by applying it to situations not mentioned in the text. *"Is air like a liquid in this way?"* By exploring student understanding in this way, teachers can also discover students' misunderstandings of what they just learned.

After an idea has been covered, it can be brought up again, when useful. For example, a passage mentions a U.S. soldier during the war with Mexico leading troops over desert on horseback. If students have discussed the principle that geography and technology affect history, they could be reminded of that insight, and discuss questions like the following: *How did the desert affect the cavalry march? Why? What other affects do deserts have on war? Have we talked about other deserts that were involved in war or war maneuvers? Compare deserts to other difficult terrain, like mountains. How would the desert have affected marching troops? What else could have affected such a march?*

Lesson plans in which the strategy is used

S-12 Developing One's Perspective: Creating or Exploring Beliefs, Arguments, or Theories

Principle: The world is not given to us sliced up into categories with pre-assigned labels on them. There are always many ways to "divide up" and so experience the world. How we do so is essential to our thinking and behavior. Uncritical thinkers assume that their perspective on things is the only correct one. Selfish critical thinkers manipulate the perspectives of others to gain advantage for themselves. Fairminded critical thinkers learn to recognize that their own way of thinking and that of all other perspectives are some combination of insight and error. They learn to develop their point of view through a critical analysis of their experience. They learn to question commonly accepted ways of understanding things and avoid uncritically accepting the viewpoints of their peer groups or society. They know what their perspectives are and can talk insightfully about them. To do this, they must create and explore their own beliefs, their own reasoning, and their own theories.

Application: Perspective is developed through extended thought, discussion, and writing. Students who are unsure what to think can be given time to reflect and come to tentative conclusions. Students who have definite conclusions about the subject at hand can consider ideas from other perspectives, answer questions about what they think, or reflect on new situations or problems. Students can compare what they say they believe with how they act.

Texts rarely call upon students to thoughtfully react to what they read. Teachers can raise basic and important questions about what students learn, having them discover and discuss underlying principles in their thought.

One-to-one Socratic questioning may facilitate development of perspective, especially for students who think they've exhausted their ideas. This strategy will also often coincide with evaluating actions and policies, arguments, or assumptions.

Students could explain how what they have learned has changed their thinking in some way. A written assignment could be used as an opportunity for a student to explore an idea in depth, and either come to conclusions, or clarify issues and concepts.

In general, we should look for opportunities to ask students what *they* believe, how *they* see things, what reasons seem most persuasive to *them*, what theory *they* think best explains what we are trying to explain, and so forth. We should look for occasions in which they can name and describe their own perspectives, philosophies, and ways of thinking.

Explore big questions, helping students integrate details from different lessons and try to come to grips with the world. *What things are most important in life? What's the difference between important and trivial? What are people like? What kinds of people are there? What's the difference between right and wrong? What is friendship?* During such discussions, raise points made during study, and have students relate their general ideas to specifics they have studied.

Lesson plans in which the strategy is used

S-13 Clarifying Issues, Conclusions, or Beliefs

Principle: The more completely, clearly, and accurately an issue or statement is formulated, the easier and more helpful the discussion of its settlement or verification. Given a clear statement of an issue, and prior to evaluating conclusions or solutions, it is important to recognize what is required to settle it. And before we can agree or disagree with a claim, we must understand it clearly. It makes no sense to say "I don't know what you mean, but I deny it, whatever it is." Critical thinkers recognize problematic claims, concepts, and standards of evaluation, making sure that understanding precedes judgment. They routinely distinguish facts from interpretations, opinions, judgments, or theories. They can then raise those questions most appropriate to understanding and evaluating each.

Application: Teachers should encourage students to slow down and reflect before coming to conclusions. When discussing an issue, the teacher can ask students first, *"Is the* issue clear? What do you need to know to settle it? What would someone who disagreed with you say?" Students should be encouraged to continually reformulate the issue in light of new information. They should be encouraged to see how the first statement of the issue or problem is rarely best (that is, most accurate, clear, and complete) and that they are in a better position to settle a question *after* they have developed as clear a formulation as possible.

When discussing an issue, teachers can have students discuss such questions as, *"Do we understand the issue? Do we know how to settle it? Have we stated it fairly? (Does our formulation assume one answer is correct? Would everyone involved accept this as a fair and accurate statement of the issue?)*

Are the words clear? Do we have to analyze any concepts? Do we know when the key words and phrases apply and don't apply? Do we clearly understand how they apply to this case?

Does this question ask something about facts? About the meanings of words? Are we evaluating anything? What? Why? What criteria should we use in the evaluation?

What facts are relevant? How can we get the evidence we need? How would the facts be gathered? What would researchers have to do to conduct such a study? What problems would they face? How could those obstacles be surmounted?"

When a statement is unclear, the class can discuss such questions as, *"How can we know whether or not this is true? What would it be like for this claim to be true? False? Do we clearly understand the difference? What evidence would count for it? Against it? Are any concepts (words or phrases) unclear? What does it assume? What does it imply? What does its opposite imply? Is there a clearer way to say this? Is there a more accurate way to say this? Can it be rephrased? Do the different ways of putting it say the same thing? Why would someone agree? Disagree?"*

This strategy provides a way of remodelling lessons that focus on "Fact/ Opinion," or which have vague passages of text.

To encourage students to distinguish fact from interpretation, the teacher could use questions like the following: *Does this description stick to the facts, or is reasoning or response included? Is this something that can be directly seen, or would you have to interpret what you saw to arrive at this statement? Is this how anyone would describe the situation, or would someone else see it differently? What alternative descriptions or explanations are there?* Students could then examine the assumptions, inferences, and theories underlying the alternatives.

Lesson plans in which the strategy is used

S-14 Clarifying and Analyzing the Meanings of Words or Phrases

Principle: Critical, independent thinking requires clarity of thought. A clear thinker understands concepts and knows what kind of evidence is required to justify applying a word or phrase to a situation. The ability to supply a definition is not proof of understanding. One must be able to supply clear, obvious examples and use the concept appropriately. In contrast, for an unclear thinker, words float through the mind unattached to clear, specific, concrete cases. Distinct concepts are confused. Often the only criterion for the application of a term is that the case in question "seems like" an example. Irrelevant associations are confused with what are necessary parts of the concept (e.g., "Love involves flowers and candlelight.") Unclear thinkers lack independence of thought because they lack the ability to analyze a concept, and so critique its use.

Application: There are a number of techniques the teacher can use for analyzing concepts. Rather than simply asking students what a word or phrase means, or asking them for a definition, the teacher can use one of the techniques mentioned below.

When introducing concepts, paraphrasing is often helpful for relating the new term (word or phrase) to ideas students already understand. The teacher can also supply a range of examples, allowing students to add to the list. The class should discuss the purposes the concepts serves. *Why are you learning this? When would it be useful to make this distinction? What does this concept tell us?*

When introducing or discussing a concept that is not within students' experience, the teacher can use analogies which relate the idea to one with which students are familiar. Students could then compare the concepts.

When discussing words or phrases with which students are familiar, we suggest that teachers have students discuss clear examples of the concept, examples of its opposite (or examples which are clearly not instances of the concept), and examples for which neither the word or its opposite are completely accurate (borderline cases). Have students compare the facts relevant to deciding when the term and its opposite apply. Students could also discuss the implications of the concept and why people make a distinction between it and its opposite. *"Give me examples of X and the opposite of X. Why is this an X? What is it about this that makes you call it an X? What are you saying about it when you call it that? Why would someone use this expression? Why would someone want to bring it to people's attention? What are the practical consequences of calling it that? How do we feel about or treat X's? Why?"* (Do the same for the opposite.) When discussing examples, always start with the clearest, most obvious, indisputable cases and opposite cases. Only when those have been examined at length, should discussion move to the more problematic, controversial, difficult, or borderline examples. *"Why is this case different from the others? Why do you kind of want to call it X? Why do you hesitate to call it X? What can we call this case?"*

When clarifying a concept expressed by a phrase rather than a single word, discuss cases in which the phrase applies, instead of merely discussing the individual words. For example, when clarifying the concept of a 'just law,' though a general discussion of 'justice' may be helpful, the more specific idea 'just law' should be discussed and contrasted with its opposite.

For concepts that commonly have a lot of irrelevant associations, the teacher can have students distinguish those associations which are logically related to the concept, from those which are not. Have the class brainstorm ideas associated with the term under discussion. *(What do you think of when you think of school?)* Then ask the students if they can imagine using the term for situations lacking this or that listed idea. *(If teachers and students gathered in a building to study, but there were no blackboard or desks, is it a school?)* Students may see that many of their associations are not part of the concept. They are left with a clearer understanding of what is relevant to the concept and will be less tempted to confuse mere association with it.

Whenever a text or discussion uses one term in more than one sense, the teacher can ask students to state how it is being used in each case or have students paraphrase sentences in which they occur. Then the teacher can ask students to generate examples in which one, both, or neither meaning of the term applies. For example, students could distinguish ordinary from scientific concepts of work and energy. The class could rephrase such seeming absurdities as "This solid table isn't solid," into "This table that I can't pass my hand through actually has lots of empty spaces in it."

When a text confuses two distinct concepts, students can clarify them. Students can distinguish concepts by discussing the different applications and implications of the concepts. *Can you think of an example of A that isn't B? What's the difference?* Students could rewrite passages, making them clearer. For example, a social studies text explains how 'consensus' means that everyone in the group has to agree to decisions. The teachers' notes then suggest discussion of an example wherein a group of children have to make a decision, so they vote, and the majority gets its way. The example, though intended to illustrate consensus, misses the point and confuses 'consensus' with 'majority rule.' The class could compare the two ideas, and so distinguish them. *"What did the text say 'consensus' means? What example does it give? Is this an example of everyone having to agree? What is the difference? How could the example be changed to illustrate the term?"*

Lesson plans in which the strategy is used

S-15 Developing Criteria for Evaluation: Clarifying Values and Standards

Principle: Critical thinkers realize that expressing mere preference does not substitute for evaluating something. Awareness of the process or components of evaluating facilitates thoughtful and fairminded evaluation. This process requires developing and using criteria or standards of evaluation, or making standards or criteria explicit. Critical thinkers are aware of the values on which they base their judgments. They have clarified them and understand *why* they are values.

When developing criteria, critical thinkers should understand the object and purpose of the evaluation, and what function the thing being evaluated is supposed to serve. Critical thinkers take into consideration different points of view when attempting to evaluate something.

Application: Whenever students are evaluating something — an object, action, policy, solution, belief — the teacher can ask students what they are evaluating, the purpose of the evaluation, and the criteria they used. With practice, students can see the importance of developing clear criteria and applying them consistently. When discussing criteria as a class or in groups, rational discussion, clarity, and fairmindedness are usually more important than reaching consensus.

The class could discuss questions like the following: *What are we evaluating? Why? Why do we need an X? What are X's for? Name or describe some good X's versus bad X's. Why are these good and those bad? What are the differences? Given these reasons or differences, can we generalize and list criteria? Can we describe what to look for when judging an X? What features does an X need to have? Why?*

Much of Language Arts instruction can be viewed as developing and clarifying criteria for evaluating writing. Students should continually evaluate written material and discuss their criteria. Specific points should be explained in terms of the values they support (such as clarity).

Students could relate the evaluation of governments to their perspectives on the purposes and functions of governments. During discussions in which they evaluate specific actions or policies of some government, they could relate their evaluations to this discussion of criteria and underlying values.

Lesson plans in which the strategy is used

S-16 Evaluating the Credibility of Sources of Information

Principle: Critical thinkers recognize the importance of using reliable sources of information when formulating conclusions. They give less weight to sources which either lack a track record of honesty, are not in a position to know, or have a vested interest in the issue. Critical thinkers recognize when there is more than one reasonable position to be taken on an issue; they compare alternative sources of information, noting areas of agreement; they analyze questions to determine whether or not the source is in a position to know; and they gather further information where sources disagree. They recognize obstacles to gathering accurate and pertinent information. They realize that preconception, for example, influences observation — that we often see only what we expect to see and fail to notice things we aren't looking for.

Application: When the class is discussing an issue about which people disagree, the teacher can encourage students to check a variety of sources representing *different points of view.* (Examining twenty sources representing the same point of view is worthless for teaching this principle.) This strategy can be used in history and news lessons.

The class can discuss the relevance of a source's past dependability, how to determine whether a source is in a position to know, and how motives should be taken into account when determining whether a source of information is credible. The teacher can ask the following questions: *Is this person in a position to know? What would someone need, to be in a position to know? Was this person there? Could he have directly seen or heard, or would he have to have* reasoned *to what he claims to know? What do we know about this person's expertise and experience? What experience would you need to have to be an expert? What must you have studied? What does he claim about this issue? Where did he get his information? Is there reason to doubt him? Has he been reliable in the past? Does he have anything to gain by convincing others? Who commissioned this report? Why?*

To more fully explore the idea of expertise with respect to a particular topic, the teacher could ask, *"What subjects, perspectives, theories, what kinds of details, what sorts of analyses would someone need knowledge of, in order to develop a complete and fairminded view of this subject?"* (For example, if the subject is a political conflict, an expert would need to know the historical background of the groups, their cultures, religions, and world views — including, for example, how each group sees itself and the others, — the geography of the area, the economic system or systems under which the groups live, etc.)

Finally, the teacher can use examples from the students' personal experience (for instance, trying to determine who started an argument) and encourage students to recognize the ways in which their own motivations can affect their interpretations and descriptions of events.

Lesson plans in which the strategy is used

S-17 Questioning Deeply: Raising and Pursuing Root or Significant Questions

Principle: Critical thinkers can pursue an issue in depth, covering germane aspects in an extended process of thought or discussion. When reading a passage, they look for issues and concepts underlying the claims expressed. They come to their own understanding of the details they learn, placing them in the larger framework of the subject and their overall perspective. They contemplate the significant issues and questions underlying subjects or problems studied. They can move between basic underlying ideas and specific details. When pursuing a line of thought, they are not continually dragged off the subject. They use important issues to organize their thought and are not bound by the organization given by another.

Application: Each of the various subject areas has been developed to clarify and settle questions peculiar to itself. (For example, history: How did the world come to be the way it is now?) The teacher can use such questions to organize and unify details covered in each subject. Perhaps more important are basic questions everyone faces about what people are like, the nature of right and wrong, how we know things, and so on. Both general and subject-specific basic questions should be repeatedly raised and used as a framework for organizing details.

Texts fail to develop this trait of pursuing root questions by presenting pre-formulated conclusions, categories, solutions, and ideals, by failing to raise crucial or thought-provoking issues (and so avoiding them), by suggesting a too-limited discussion of them, by mixing questions relevant to different issues or by pursuing their objectives in a confusing way. To rectify these problems, teachers need to provide opportunities for students to come to their own conclusions, construct their own categories, devise their own solutions, and formulate their own ideals. They need to raise thought-provoking issues, allow extended discussion of them and keep the discussion focussed, so that different issues are identified and appropriately addressed. The students, in turn, need to be clear about the objectives and to see themselves as accomplishing them in a fruitful way.

The class can begin exploration of an important topic, concept, or issue not discussed in any one place in their texts by looking it up in the table of contents, index, list of tables, etc. They can then divide up the task of reading and taking notes on the references. The class can then discuss their passages, and pose questions to guide further research using other resources, and share their findings. Each student could then write an essay pulling the ideas together.

Why do people go to war? What wars do you know about? What caused each? Why do people fight? Can we generalize from these cases?

What main concepts (distinctions, categories) are used in this subject? Why? Why is this distinction more important than that one?

When a class discusses rules, institutions, activities, or ideals, the teacher can facilitate a discussion of their purposes, importance, or value. Students should be encouraged to see institutions, for example, as a creation of people, designed to fulfill certain functions, not as something that is "just there." Thus, they will be in a better position, when they are adults, to see that it fulfills its goals. Or, for another example, ideals will be better understood as requiring specific kinds of actions, instead of being left as mere vague slogans, if the class examines their value.

When the text avoids important issues related to or underlying the object of study (such as moral implications), the teacher or students could raise them and discuss them at length. Students can go through the assigned material, and possibly other resources, using the chosen issue or issues to organize the details, for example, making a chart or issue map. Socratic questioning, it should be noted, typically raises root issues.

When a lesson does raise important questions but has too few and scattered questions, the teacher can pull out, rearrange, and add to the relevant questions, integrating them into an extended and focussed, rather than fragmented, discussion. Students can begin study with one or more significant questions and list relevant details as they read.

Lesson plans in which the strategy is used

S-18 Analyzing or Evaluating Arguments, Interpretations, Beliefs, or Theories

Principle: Rather than carelessly agreeing or disagreeing with a conclusion based on their preconceptions of what is true, critical thinkers use analytic tools to understand the reasoning behind it and determine its relative strengths and weaknesses. When analyzing arguments, critical thinkers recognize the importance of asking for reasons and considering alternative views. They are especially sensitive to possible strengths of arguments that they disagree with, recognizing the tendency of humans to ignore, oversimplify, distort, or otherwise unfairly dismiss them. Critical thinkers analyze questions and place conflicting arguments, interpretations, and theories in opposition to one another, as a means of highlighting key concepts, assumptions, implications, etc.

When giving or being given an interpretation, critical thinkers, recognizing the difference between evidence and interpretation, explore the assumptions on which it is based, and propose and evaluate alternative interpretations for their relative strength. Autonomous thinkers consider competing theories and develop their own theories.

Application: Often texts claim to have students analyze and evaluate arguments, when all they have them do is state preferences and locate factual claims, with very limited discussion. They fail to teach most techniques for analyzing and evaluating arguments. Texts that do address aspects of argument critique tend to teach such skills and insights in isolation, and fail to mention them when appropriate and useful. (See "Text Treatment of Critical Thinking and Argumentation," in the chapter, "Thinking Critically About Teaching: From Didactic to Critical Teaching".)

Instead of simply stating why they agree or disagree with a line of reasoning, students should be encouraged to place competing arguments, interpretations, or theories in opposition to one another. Ask, *"What reasons are given? What would someone who disagreed with this argument say?"* Students should then be encouraged to argue back and forth, and modify their positions in light of the strengths of others' positions.

Students can become better able to evaluate reasoning by familiarizing themselves with, and practicing, specific analytic techniques, such as making assumptions explicit and evaluating them; clarifying issues, conclusions, values, and words, developing criteria for evaluation; recognizing and pinpointing contradictions; distinguishing relevant from irrelevant facts; evaluating evidence; and exploring implications. (See the strategies addressing these skills.) After extended discussion, have students state their final positions. Encourage them to qualify their claims appropriately.

When learning scientific theories, students should be encouraged to describe or develop their own theories and compare them with those presented in their texts. Students can compare the relative explanatory and predictive powers of various theories, whenever possible testing predictions with experiments or research.

Lesson plans in which the strategy is used

S-19 Generating or Assessing Solutions

Principle: Critical problem-solvers use everything available to them to find the best solution they can. They evaluate solutions, not independently of, but in relation to one another (since 'best' implies a comparison). They take the time to formulate problems clearly, accurately, and fairly, rather than offering a sloppy, half-baked description and then immediately leaping to solutions. They examine the causes of the problem at length. They have reflected on such questions as, "What makes some solutions better than others? What does the solution to this problem require? What solutions have been tried for this and similar problems? With what results?"

But alternative solutions are often not given, they must be generated or thought-up. Critical thinkers must be creative thinkers as well, generating possible solutions in order to find the best one. Very often a problem persists, not because we can't tell which available solution is best but because the best solution has not yet been made available — no one has thought it up yet. Therefore, although critical thinkers use all available information relevant to their problems, including solutions others have tried in similar situations, they are flexible and imaginative, willing to try any good idea whether it has been done before or not.

Fairminded thinkers take into account the interests of everyone affected by the problem and proposed solutions. They are more committed to finding the best solution than to getting their way. They approach problems realistically.

Application: When presenting problem-solving lessons or activities, texts tend to provide lists of problem-solving steps which unnecessarily limit the process. For example, texts rarely encourage students to consider how others solved or tried to solve the same or a similar problem. They generally make "describing the problem" step one, without having students reformulate their descriptions after further examination. They do not suggest analysis of causes. Texts often break problem-solving into steps and have students memorize the steps. They then drill students on one or two steps. But students don't follow the process through. Thus, each step, practiced in isolation, has no meaning.

The best way to develop insight into problem-solving is to solve problems. If problems arise in the class — for example, if discussions degenerate into shouting matches — students should be assisted in developing and instituting their own solutions. If the first attempt fails or causes other problems, students should consider why and try again. Thus, they can learn the practical difficulties involved in discovering and implementing a workable solution.

We recommend first that the teacher have students state the problem, if that has not been done. Students should explore the causes at length, exploring and evaluating multiple perspectives. Encourage them to integrate the strong points within each view. As the process of exploring solutions proceeds, students may find it useful to reformulate the description of the problem.

Rather than simply asking students if a given solution is good, the teacher could encourage an extended discussion of such questions as, *"Does this solve the problem? How? What other solutions can you think of? What are their advantages and disadvantages? Are we missing any relevant facts? (Is there anything we need to find out before we can decide which solution is best?) What are the criteria for judging solutions in this case? (How will we know if a solution is a good one?) Why do people/have people behaved in the ways that cause the problem? Can you think of other cases of this problem or similar problems? How did the people involved try to solve them? What results did that have? Did they solve the problems? Could we use the same solution, or is our case different in an important way? How do the solutions compare with each other? Why? What are some bad ways of trying to solve the problem? What is wrong with them? Do any of these solutions ignore someone's legitimate concerns or needs? How could the various needs be incorporated? If this fact about the situation were different, would it change our choice of solutions? Why or why not?"*

Fiction often provides opportunities for analysis of problems and evaluation of solutions. Texts' treatments are often too brief, superficial, and unrealistic. They can be extended by having students clarify the problem and analyze solutions as described above.

History texts often provide opportunities for use of this strategy when they describe problems people or government attempted to solve, for instance, by passing new laws. Students can evaluate the text's statement of the problem and its causes, evaluate the solution tried, and propose and evaluate alternatives. Students should be encouraged to explore the beliefs underlying various choices of solutions.

For instance, ask, *"Why do these people favor this solution and those people that one? What does each side claim causes the problem? What does each perspective assume? What sort of evidence would support each perspective? What other perspectives can there be? Can the perspectives be reconciled? What is your perspective on this problem? Why?"*

Social studies texts provide innumerable opportunities for exploring crucial problems. *"What problems do we have in our country or part of the country? Why? Who is involved in this? Who contributes? How? Why? Who's affected? How? Why? What should be done? Why? Why not do it? What could go wrong? What do other people think should be done? Why? How can we find out more about the causes of this? How can we find out what different people want? Can the wants be reconciled? How? Why not? What compromises are in order?"*

What does this passage say was the problem? The cause? Explain the cause. What other explanations are there? Evaluate the explanations. What else was part of the cause? What was the solution tried? (Action, law, set of laws, policy, amendment, revolt, etc.) What were the effects? Who was affected? Did it have the desired effects? Undesirable effects? What should have been done differently, or what should we do now to rectify the problems that action caused? Do we need the law (policy, etc.) now?

Lesson plans in which the strategy is used

S-20 Analyzing or Evaluating Actions and Policies

Principle: Critical thinking involves more than analysis of reasoning; it includes analysis of behavior or policy and a recognition of the reasoning that that behavior or policy presupposes. When evaluating the behavior of themselves and others, critical thinkers are conscious of the standards they use, so that these, too, can become objects of evaluation. Critical thinkers examine the consequences of actions and recognize these as fundamental to the standards for assessing both behavior and policy.

Critical thinkers base their evaluations of behavior on assumptions to which they have rationally assented. They can articulate and rationally apply principles.

Application: The teacher can encourage students to raise ethical questions about actions and policies of themselves and others. Students can become more comfortable with the process of evaluating if they are given a number of opportunities to make and assess moral judgments *Why did x do this? What reasons were given? Were they the real reasons? Why do you think so? What are the probable consequences of these actions? How would you feel if someone acted this way toward you? Why? What reasons were your evaluations based on? Might someone else use a different standard to evaluate? Why? Do you think the action was fair, smart, etc.? Why or why not?*

Too often history texts fail to have students evaluate the behavior and policies about which they read. Texts often assume that people's stated reasons were their real reasons. Sometimes texts describe behavior inconsistent with the stated intentions, yet fail to have students discuss these inconsistencies. *"Why did that group or government say they took this action? What did they do? What result did they say they wanted? What results did it actually have? Who was helped? Hurt? Why? Is the stated reason consistent with that behavior? Was the reason they gave their real reason? Why do you think so?"*

Students should evaluate the behavior of important people of the past. Such evaluation can be enhanced by having interested students report on the long-term consequences of past actions and policies. Future citizens of a democracy need to develop their own sense of how leaders and countries should and shouldn't behave.

Students should also be called upon to generalize, to formulate principles of judgment. *What makes some actions right, others wrong? What rights do people have? How can I know when someone's rights are being violated? Why respect people's rights? Why be good? Should I live according to rules? If so, what rules? If not, how should I decide what to do? What policies should be established and why? What are governments supposed to do? What shouldn't they do?*

These generalizations can be further analyzed and tested by having students compare them to specific cases they have judged in previous lessons. *"Is this principle consistent with that judgment you made last week about (fictional character, historical or current event, etc.)?"*

Lesson plans in which the strategy is used

S-21 Reading Critically: Clarifying or Critiquing Texts

Principle: Critical thinkers read with a healthy skepticism. But they do not doubt or deny until they understand. They clarify before they judge. They expect intelligibility from what they read, and do not mindlessly accept nonsense. They realize that everyone is capable of making mistakes and being wrong, including authors of textbooks. They also realize that, since everyone has a point of view, everyone sometimes leaves out some relevant information. No two authors would write the same book or write from exactly the same perspective. Therefore, critical readers recognize that reading a book is reading one limited perspective on a subject and that more can be learned by considering other perspectives. Critical readers ask themselves questions as they read, wonder about the implications of, reasons for, examples of, and meaning and truth of the material. They do not approach written material as a collection of sentences, but as a whole, trying out various interpretations until one fits all of the work, rather than ignoring or distorting statements that don't fit their interpretation.

Application: Students should feel free to raise questions about materials they read. When a text is ambiguous, vague, or misleading, teachers can raise such questions as, *"What does this passage say? What does it imply? Assume? Is it clear? Explain it. Does it contradict anything you know or suspect to be true? How do you know? How could you find out? Does this fit in with your experience? In what way? Why or why not? What might someone who disagreed with it say? Does the text leave out relevant information? Does it favor one perspective? Which? Why do you suppose it was written this way? How could we rewrite this passage to make it clearer, fairer, or more accurate?"*

In Language Arts, rather than simply using recall questions at the end of fictional selections, have students describe the plot. Thus, students must pull out the main parts and understand cause and effect while being checked for basic comprehension and recall. Don't forget that students should continually evaluate what they read. *"How good is this selection? Why? Is it well written? Why or why not? Is it saying something important? What? How does it compare with other things we've read? Are some parts better than others? Which? Why?*

Students can evaluate unit, chapter, and section titles and headings in their texts. *"What is the main point in this passage? What details does it give? What ideas do those details support, elaborate on, justify? Is the heading accurate? Misleading? Could you suggest a better heading?"*

Often passages which attempt to instill belief in important U.S. ideals are too vague to give more than the vague impression that our ideals are important. Such passages typically say that the ideals are important or precious, that people from other countries wish they had them or come here to enjoy them, that we all have a responsibility to preserve them, and so on. Such passages could be reread slowly and deeply with much discussion.

The class could engage in deeper, critical reading by discussing questions like the following: *Why is this right important? How is this supposed to help people? Does not having this right hurt people? How? Why?*

Why would someone try to prevent people from voting or speaking out? How could they? Have you ever denied someone the right to speak or be heard? Why? Were you justified? Why or why not? What should you have done?

Why is this right precious? Why are these rights emphasized? Do you have other rights? Why doesn't the text (or Constitution) say that you have the right to eat pickles? What are the differences between that right and those mentioned?

Does everyone believe in this or want this? How do you know? Have you ever heard anyone say that tyranny is the best kind of government, or free speech is bad? Why?

Is there a basic idea behind all of these rights? Why does the text say people have this responsibility? How, exactly, does this help our country? Why do some people not do this? What does it require of you? And how do you do that? Is it easy or hard? What else does it mean you should do?

The teacher could make copies of passages from several sample texts which cover the same material and have students compare and critique them.

Students can discuss their interpretations of what they read. Small groups of students can compare their paraphrases and interpretations and write better ones.

Lesson plans in which the strategy is used

S-22 Listening Critically: The Art of Silent Dialogue

Principle: Critical thinkers realize that listening can be done passively and uncritically or actively and critically. They know that it is easy to misunderstand what is said by another and difficult to integrate another's thinking into our own. Compare speaking and listening. When we speak, we need only keep track of our own ideas, arranging them in some order, expressing thoughts with which we are intimately familiar: our own. But listening is more complex. We must take the words of another and translate them into ideas that make sense to us. We have not had the experiences of the speakers. We are not on the inside of their point of view. We can't anticipate, as they can themselves, where their thoughts are leading them. We must continually interpret what others say within the confines of our experiences. We must find a way to enter into their points of view, shift our minds to follow their trains of thought.

What all of this means is that we need to learn how to listen actively and critically. We need to recognize that listening is an art involving skills that we can develop only with time and practice. We need to learn, for example, that to listen and learn from what we are hearing, we need to learn to ask key questions that enable us to locate ourselves in the thought of another. We must practice asking questions like the following: "I'm not sure I understand you when you say ..., could you explain that further?" "Could you give me an example or illustration of this?" "Would you also say ...?" "Let me see if I understand you. What you are saying is .... Is that right?" "How do you respond to this objection?" Critical readers ask questions as they read and use those questions to orient themselves to what an author is saying. Critical listeners ask questions as they listen to orient themselves to what a speaker is saying: Why does she say that? What examples could I give to illustrate that point? What is the main point? How does this detail relate to the main point? That one? Is she using this word as I would, or somewhat differently? These highly skilled and activated processes are crucial to learning. We need to heighten student awareness of and practice in them as often as we can.

Application: The first and best way to teach critical listening is to model it. It is necessary that we actively and constructively listen to what students say, demonstrating the patience and skill necessary to understand them. We should not casually assume that we know what they mean. We should not pass by their expressions too quickly. Students rarely take seriously their own meanings. They rarely listen to themselves. They rarely realize the need to elaborate or exemplify their own thoughts. And we are often in a position to help them to do so with facilitating questions that result from close, enquiring listening.

Secondly, students rarely listen carefully to what other students have to say. They rarely take each other seriously. We can facilitate this process with questioning interventions. We can say things like: "Joel, did you follow what Diane said? Could you put what she said in your own words?" Or we can say, "Richard, could you give us an example from your own experience of what Jane has said? Has anything like that ever happened to you?"

The success of Socratic questioning and class discussion depends upon close and critical listening. Many assignments are understood or misunderstood through word of mouth. We need to take the occasion of making an assignment an occasion for testing and encouraging critical listening. In this way, we will get better work from students, because in learning how to listen critically to what we are asking them to do, they will gain a clearer grasp of what that is, and hence do a better job in doing it. Students often do an assignment poorly, because they never clearly understood it in the first place.

Students can describe discussions, videotapes, or movies in writing, then compare their versions in small groups, trying to accurately reconstruct what they heard. Whenever possible, they should watch the piece a second time to verify their accounts or settle conflicting accounts of what they saw and heard.

While watching a movie or video, students can be asked to take notes. Afterward, students can compare and discuss their notes. A teacher could periodically stop a movie or video and have students outline the main point, and raise critical questions.

Lesson plans in which the strategy is used

S-23 Making Interdisciplinary Connections

Principle: Although in some ways it is convenient to divide knowledge up into disciplines, the divisions are not absolute. Critical thinkers do not allow the somewhat arbitrary distinctions between academic subjects to control their thinking. When considering issues which transcend subjects, they bring relevant concepts, knowledge, and insights from many subjects to the analysis. They make use of insights into one subject to inform their understanding of other subjects. There are always connections between subjects (language and logic; history, geography, psychology, anthropology, physiology; politics, geography, science, ecology; math, science, economics). To understand, say, reasons for the American Revolution (historical question), insights from technology, geography, economics, and philosophy can be fruitfully applied.

Application: Reading and writing can and should be taught in conjunction with every subject. One way to teach reading during other subjects would be to have students who cannot answer questions about what they read skim their texts to find the answer. Teachers could also have students who misunderstood a sentence in their texts find it. Either the sentence was unclearly written, in which case, students could revise it, or the students didn't read carefully, in which case the class could discuss why the sentence does not mean what the students thought.

Any time another subject is relevant to the object of discussion, those insights can be used and integrated. Some teachers allot time for coverage of topics in different subjects so that the topic is examined from the perspective of several subjects (history, literature, art, music, science). Study of the news can combine with nearly every subject — language arts, social studies, math, geography, science, health, etc.

Socratic questioning can be used to make subject connections clear. The teacher can use discussion of students' issues and problems to show the importance of bringing insights from many subjects to bear.

The class could evaluate writing in their texts from a literary or composition standpoint. *"Given what you know about good writing, is this passage well written? Organized? Interesting? Why or why not? How can it be improved? Is the quote used evocative? To the point? How does it illustrate or enhance the point made?"*

Students can evaluate the psychological, sociological, or historical accuracy or sophistication of fiction and biography.

Lesson plans in which the strategy is used

S-24 Practicing Socratic Discussion: Clarifying and Questioning Beliefs, Theories, or Perspectives

Principle: Critical thinkers are nothing if not questioners. The ability to question and probe deeply, to get down to root ideas, to get beneath the mere appearance of things, is at the very heart of the activity. And, as questioners, they have many different kinds of questions and moves available and can follow up their questions appropriately. They can use questioning techniques, not to make others look stupid, but to learn what they think, helping them develop their ideas, or as a prelude to evaluating them. When confronted with a new idea, they want to understand it, to relate it to their experience, and to determine its implications, consequences, and value. They can fruitfully uncover the structure of their own and others' perspectives. Probing questions are the tools by which these goals are reached.

Furthermore, critical thinkers are comfortable being questioned. They don't become offended, confused, or intimidated. They welcome good questions as an opportunity to develop a line of thought.

Application: Students, then, should develop the ability to go beyond the basic what and why questions that are found in their native questioning impulses. To do this, they need to discover a variety of ways to frame questions which probe the logic of what they are reading, hearing, writing, or thinking. They need to learn how to probe for and question assumptions, judgments, inferences, apparent contradictions, or inconsistencies. They need to learn how to question the relevance of what is presented, the evidence for and against what is said, the way concepts are used, the implications of positions taken. Not only do we need to question students, we also need to have them question each other and themselves.

Classroom instruction and activities, therefore, should stimulate the student to question and help make the students comfortable when questioned, so that the questioning process is increasingly valued and mastered. Questioning should be introduced in such a way that students come to see it as an effective way to get at the heart of matters and to understand things from different points of view. It should not be used to embarrass or negate students. It should be part of an inquiry into issues of significance in an atmosphere of mutual support and cooperation. We therefore recommend that teachers cultivate a habit of wondering about the reasoning behind students' beliefs and translating their musings into questions.

The teacher should model Socratic questioning techniques and use them often. Any thought-provoking questions can start a Socratic discussion. To follow up responses, use questions like the following: *Why? If that is so, what follows? Are you assuming that...? How do you know that? Is the point that you are making that... or, ...? For example? Is this an example of what you mean..., or this,...? Can I summarize your point as...? What is your reason for saying that? What do you mean when using this word? Is it possible that...? Are there other ways of looking at it? How else could we view this matter?* (For more questions, see the section on Socratic discussion in the chapter, "Global Strategies: Beyond Subject Matter Teaching.")

Immediately after Socratic discussion, students can write for five minutes, summarizing the key points, raising new questions, adding analysis, examples, or clarification. Later these notes could be shared and discussion continued.

To develop students' abilities to use Socratic questioning, the teacher could present an idea or passage to students and have them brainstorm possible questions. For instance, they could think of questions to ask story or historical characters or a famous person or personal hero on a particular subject.

Pairs of students can practice questioning each other about issues raised in study, trading the roles of questioner and questioned. The teacher may provide lists of possible initial questions and perhaps some follow-up questions. Students could also be allowed to continue their discussions another day, after they've had time to think. As students practice Socratic questioning, see it modeled, and learn the language, skills, and insights of critical thinking, their mastery of questioning techniques will increase.

The direction and structure of a Socratic discussion can be made clearer by periodically summarizing and rephrasing the main points made or by distinguishing the perspectives expressed. *"We began with this question. Some of you said _____, others _____. These arguments were given .... Joan recommended that we distinguish X from Y. We've reached an impasse on X because we can't agree about two contradictory assumptions,_____ and _____. We decided we would need to find out _____. So let's take up Y."*

To practice exploring the idea of illuminating and probing Socratic questioning, students could read and evaluate different kinds of interviews, categorizing the questions asked. They could then list probing follow-up questions that weren't asked, and share and discuss their lists. *Why would you ask this? How could that be followed up? What would that tell you?*

S-25 Reasoning Dialogically: Comparing Perspectives, Interpretations, or Theories

Principle: Dialogical thinking refers to thinking that involves a dialogue or extended exchange between different points of view, cognitive domains, or frames of reference. Whenever we consider concepts or issues deeply, we naturally explore their connections to other ideas and issues within different domains or points of view. Critical thinkers need to be able to engage in fruitful, exploratory dialogue, proposing ideas, probing their roots, considering subject matter insights and evidence, testing ideas, and moving between various points of view. When we think, we often engage in dialogue, either inwardly or aloud with others. We need to integrate critical thinking skills into that dialogue so that it is as fruitful as possible. Socratic questioning is one form of dialogical thinking.

Application: By routinely raising root questions and root ideas in a classroom setting, multiple points of view get expressed and the thinking proceeds, not in a predictable or straightforward direction, but in a criss-crossing, back-and-forth movement. We continually encourage the students to explore how what they think about x relates to what they think about y and z. This necessarily requires that students' thinking moves back and forth between their own basic ideas and those being presented by the other students, between their own ideas and those expressed in a book or story, between their own thinking and their own experience, between ideas within one domain and those in another, in short, between any two perspectives. This dialogical process will sometimes become dialectical. Some ideas will clash or be inconsistent with others. *What would someone who disagreed say? Why? How could the first respond? Why? Etc.*

When texts give only one side of an issue or event, the teacher could have students discuss other views. *What did the other (character, group of people) think? Why? (Take specific statements from the text.) Would others see it this way? Would they use these words? How would they describe this? Why? What exactly do they disagree about? Why? What does X think is the cause? Y? Why do they differ?*

Students could list points from multiple perspectives for reference, then write dialogues of people arguing about the issues.

Texts approach teaching dialogical thinking by having students discuss perspectives other than that presented by their texts. Yet such discussion is simply tacked on; it is not integrated with the rest of the material. Thus, the ideas are merely juxtaposed, not synthesized. Rather than separate activities or discussions about different perspectives, the teacher can have students move back and forth between points of view. *"What do the environmentalists want? Why? Factory owners? Why? Workers? Why? Why do the environmentalists think the factory owners are wrong? How do the factory owners respond to that? ... What beliefs do the sides have in common? How would ecologists look at this dispute? Economists? Anthropologists?"*

S-26 Reasoning Dialectically: Evaluating Perspectives, Interpretations, or Theories

Principle: Dialectical thinking refers to dialogical thinking conducted in order to test the strengths and weaknesses of opposing points of view. Court trials and debates are dialectical in intention. They pit idea against idea, reasoning against counter-reasoning in order to get at the truth of a matter. As soon as we begin to explore ideas, we find that some clash or are inconsistent with others. If we are to integrate our thinking, we need to assess which of the conflicting ideas we will provisionally accept and which we shall provisionally reject, or which parts of the views are strong and which weak, or how the views can be reconciled. Students need to develop dialectical reasoning skills, so that their thinking not only moves comfortably between divergent points of view or lines of thought, but also makes some assessments in light of the relative strengths and weaknesses of the evidence or reasoning presented. Hence, when thinking dialectically, critical thinkers can use critical micro-skills appropriately.

Application: Dialectical thinking can be practiced whenever two conflicting points of view, arguments, or conclusions are under discussion. Stories and history lessons provide many opportunities. Dialectical exchange between students in science classes enables students to discover and appropriately amend their pre-conceptions about the physical world.

The teacher could have proponents of conflicting views argue their positions and have others evaluate them. A dialogical discussion could be taped for later analysis and evaluation. Or the teacher could inject evaluative questions into dia-logical discussion. *"Was that reason a good one? Why or why not? Does the other view have a good objection to that reason? What? And the answer to that objection?*

Does each side use language appropriately and consistently?

To what evidence does each side appeal? Is the evidence from both sides rele-vant? Questionable, or acceptable? Compare the sources each side cites for its evi-dence. Which is more trustworthy?

How can we know which of these conflicting assumptions is best? Is there a way of reconciling these views? The evidence?

What is this side right about? The other side? Which of these views is strongest? Why?"

Lesson plans in which the strategy is used

S-27 Comparing and Contrasting Ideals with Actual Practice

Principle: Self-improvement and social improvement are presupposed values of critical thinking. Critical thinking, therefore, requires an effort to see ourselves and others accurately. This requires recognizing gaps between ideals and practice. The fairminded thinker values truth and consistency and, therefore, works to minimize these gaps. The confusion of facts with ideals prevents us from moving closer to achieving our ideals. A critical education strives to highlight discrepancies between facts and ideals, and proposes and evaluates methods for minimizing them. This strategy is intimately connected with "developing intellectual good faith."

Application: Since, when discussing our society, many texts consistently confuse ideals with facts, the teacher can use them as objects of analysis. Ask, *"Is this a fact or an ideal? Are things always this way, or is this statement an expression of what people are trying to achieve? Are these ideals yours? Why or why not? How have people attempted to achieve this ideal? When did they not meet the ideal? Why? What problems did they have? Why? How can we better achieve these ideals?"* Students could rewrite misleading portions of text, making them more accurate.

Sometimes this strategy could take the form of *avoiding oversimplification.* For example, when considering the idea that we in this country are free to choose the work or jobs we want, the teacher could ask, *"Can people in this country choose any job they want? Always? What, besides choice, might affect what job someone has or gets? Would someone who looked like a bum be hired as a salesman? Does this mean they don't have this freedom? Why or why not? What if there aren't enough openings for some kind of work? How can this claim be made more accurate?"*

The teacher can facilitate a general discussion of the value of achieving consistency of thought and action. Ask, *"Have you ever thought something was true about yourself but acted in a way that was inconsistent with your ideal? Did you see yourself differently then? Did you make efforts to change the behavior? Can anyone think of ways to be more consistent? Why is it often hard to be honest about yourself and the groups you belong to? Is it worth the pain?"*

Sometimes texts foster this confusion in students by asking questions to which most people want to answer yes, for example: Do you like to help others? Do you listen to what other people have to say? Do you share things? Since none of us always adheres to our principles (though few like to admit it) you might consider rephrasing such questions. For example, ask, *"When have you enjoyed helping someone? When not? Why? Did you have to help that person? When is it hard to listen to what someone else has to say? Why? Have you ever not wanted to share something? Should you have? Why or why not? If you didn't share, why didn't you?"*

Such discussion can also explore the rationalizations people use. *What were you thinking? Why? Did you know you shouldn't, or did it seem OK at the time? Why?*

Obviously, the more realistic are our ideals, the closer we can come to achieving them. Therefore, any text's attempt to encourage unrealistic ideals can be remodelled. For example, rather than assuming that everyone should always do everything they can for everyone anytime, allow students to express a range of views on such virtues as generosity.

When discussing a departure from ideals or theory, have students analyze and evaluate it. Students could write an essay in which they focus on one such point. *"How is this supposed to work in theory? Why? What result is that supposed to have? Why is that considered good? How does this really work? Why? What incorrect assumption is made in the theory? What reasons are there for accepting this as it is? For trying to make it closer to the ideal? Is the way we actually do this justified? Why or why not? If it isn't justified, how can we correct it?"*

Students who are learning about capitalism could discuss how ads affect the workings of supply and demand. *"If ads get people to buy things for irrelevant reasons, or by distorting the facts, then is it true that people tend to buy the best products at the lowest prices? How does this affect manufacturers? What if it's cheaper and more profitable to make better ads than to make products? How does that affect the economy? Productions? How might it affect salaries?*

Lesson plans in which the strategy is used

S-28 Thinking Precisely About Thinking: Using Critical Vocabulary

Principle: An essential requirement of critical thinking is the ability to think about think-ing, to engage in what is sometimes called "metacognition". One possible definition of critical thinking is the art of thinking about your thinking while you're thinking in order to make your thinking better: more clear, more accurate, more fair. It is precisely at the level of "thinking about thinking" that most critical thinking stands in contrast to uncritical thinking. Critical thinkers can analyze thought — take it apart and put it together again. For the uncritical, thoughts are "just there". "I think what I think, don't ask me why." The analytical vocabulary in the English language (such terms as 'assume,' 'infer,' 'conclude,' 'criteria,' 'point of view,' 'rele-vance,' 'issue,' 'elaborate,' 'ambiguous,' 'objection,' 'support,' 'bias,' 'justify,' 'per-spective,' 'contradiction,' 'consistent', 'credibility,' 'evidence,' 'interpret,' 'distinguish') enables us to think more precisely about our thinking. We are in a better position to assess reasoning (our own, as well as that of others) when we can use analytic vocabulary with accuracy and ease.

Application: Since most language is acquired by hearing words used in context, teachers should try to make critical terms part of their working vocabulary.

When students are reasoning or discussing the reasoning of others, the teacher can encourage them to use critical vocabulary. New words are most easily learned and remembered when they are clearly useful.

When introducing a term, the teacher can speak in pairs of sentences: first, using the critical vocabulary, then, rephrasing the sentence without the new term, e.g., *"What facts are relevant to this issue? What facts must we consider in deciding this issue? What information do we need?"* The teacher can also rephrase students' state-ments to incorporate the vocabulary. *Do you mean that Jane is assuming that ...?*

When conducting discussions, participating students could be encouraged to explain the role of their remarks in the discussion: supporting a point, raising an objection, answering an objection, distinguishing concepts or issues, ques-tioning relevance, etc. *"Why were you raising that point here? Are you support-ing Fred's point or ...?"*

Students could look up and discuss sets of related critical vocabulary words, and discuss relationships among them, when each can be used, and for what purposes.

Lesson plans in which the strategy is used

S-29 Noting Significant Similarities and Differences

Principle: Critical thinkers strive to treat similar things similarly and different things differently. Uncritical thinkers, on the other hand, often miss significant similarities and differences. Things superficially similar are often significantly different. Things superficially different are often essentially the same. It is only by developing our observational and reasoning skills to a high point that we become sensitized to significant similarities and differences. As we develop this sensitivity, it influences how we experience, how we describe, how we categorize, and how we reason about things. We become more careful and discriminating in our use of words and phrases. We hesitate before we accept this or that analogy or comparison.

We recognize the purposes of the comparisons we make. We recognize that purposes govern the act of comparing and determine its scope and limits. The hierarchy of categories biologists, for instance, use to classify living things (with Kingdom as the most basic, all the way down to sub-species) reflects biological judgment regarding which kinds of similarities and differences between species are the most important *biologically*, that is, which distinctions shed the most light on how each organism is structured and lives. To the zoologist, the similarities whales have to horses is considered more important than their similarities to fish. The differences between whales and fish are considered more significant than differences between whales and horses. These distinctions suit the biologists' purposes.

Application: Texts often call on students to compare and contrast two or more things — objects, ideas, phenomena, etc. Yet these activities rarely have a serious purpose. Merely listing similarities and differences has little value in itself. Rather than encouraging students to make such lists, these activities should be proposed in a context which narrows the range of pertinent comparisons and requires some *use* be made of them in pursuit of some specific goal. For example, if comparing and contrasting two cultures, students should use their understanding to illuminate the relationship between them, perhaps to explain factors contributing to conflict or war. Thus, only those points which shed light on the particular problem need be mentioned, and each point has implications to be drawn out and integrated into a broader picture.

"What does this remind you of? Why? How is it similar? Different? How important are the differences? Why? What does it tell us about our topic? How useful is that comparison? Can anyone think of an even more useful comparison?"

Students can compare models to what they represent, and so evaluate them. *How much is the model like the real thing? Unlike it? What doesn't the model show? Why not? Could it? How or why not? What parts do they both have? Do they have analogous parts? Why or why not? How important are the missing or extra parts? How like the original thing is this part? How is this model helpful? In what ways is it misleading? What do we have to keep in mind when we look at this model? How good is this model? How could it be improved?*

When comparing characters from literature, rather than simply listing differences, students should analyze and *use* their comparisons. *Why are they different? (personality, lives, problems, current situations)* Don't let students over-generalize from differences. Texts have students make sweeping statements from one difference in attitude or action. Such differences may not reflect difference in character as much as differences in situation. Have students relate differences in characterization, to differences in perspective. Relate differences in feelings and behavior to differences in how characters see things. Relate all significant differences between characters to the theme.

Lesson plans in which the strategy is used

S-30 Examining or Evaluating Assumptions

Principle: We are in a better position to evaluate any reasoning or behavior when all of the elements of that reasoning or behavior are made explicit. We base both our reasoning and our behavior on beliefs we take for granted. We are often unaware of these assumptions. It is only by recognizing them that we can evaluate them. Critical thinkers have a passion for truth and for accepting the strongest reasoning. Thus, they have the intellectual courage to seek out and reject false assumptions. They realize that everyone makes some questionable assumptions. They are willing to question, and have others question, even their own most cherished assumptions. They consider alternative assumptions. They base their acceptance or rejection of assumptions on their rational scrutiny of them. They hold questionable assumptions with an appropriate degree of tentativeness. Independent thinkers evaluate assumptions for themselves, and do not simply accept the assumptions of others, even those assumptions made by everyone they know.

Application: Teachers should encourage students to make assumptions explicit as often as possible — assumptions made in what they read or hear and assumptions they make. Teachers should ask questions that elicit the implicit elements of students' claims. Although it is valuable practice to have students make good assumptions explicit, it is especially important when assumptions are questionable. The teacher might ask, *"If this was the evidence, and this the conclusion, what was assumed?"* or *If this is what he saw (heard, etc.), and this is what he concluded or thought, what did he assume? ("He saw red fruit and said 'Apples!' and ate it." "He assumed that all red fruits are apples." or "He assumed that, because it looked like an apple, it was good to eat.")*

There are no rules for determining when to have students evaluate assumptions. Students should feel free to question and discuss any assumptions they suspect are questionable or false. Students should also evaluate good assumptions. Doing so gives them a contrast with poor assumptions.

The following are some of the probing questions teachers may use when a class discusses the worth of an assumption: *Why do people (did this person) make this assumption? Have you ever made this assumption? What could be assumed instead? Is this belief true? Sometimes true? Seldom true? Always false? (Ask for examples.) Can you think of reasons for this belief? Against it? What, if anything, can we conclude about this assumption? What would we need to find out to be able to judge it? How would someone who makes this assumption act?*

Lesson plans in which the strategy is used

S-31 Distinguishing Relevant From Irrelevant Facts

Principle: Critical thinking requires sensitivity to the distinction between those facts that are relevant to an issue and those which are not. Critical thinkers focus their attention on relevant facts and do not let irrelevant considerations affect their conclusions. Furthermore, they recognize that a fact is only relevant or irrelevant in relation to an issue. Information relevant to one problem may not be relevant to another.

Application: When discussing an issue, solution to a problem, or when giving reasons for a conclusion, students can practice limiting their remarks to facts which are germane to that issue, problem, or conclusion. Often students assume that all information given has to be used to solve a problem. Life does not sort relevant from irrelevant information for us. Teachers can encourage students to make a case for the pertinence of their remarks, and help them see when their remarks are irrelevant. *"How would this fact affect our conclusion? If it were false, would we have to change our conclusion? Why or why not? What is the connection? Why does that matter? What issue are you addressing? Are you addressing* this *issue or raising a new one?"*

Students could read a chapter of text or story with one or more issues in mind and note relevant details. Students could then share and discuss their lists. Students can then discover that sometimes they must *argue* for the relevance of a particular fact to an issue.

Another technique for developing students' sensitivity to relevance is to change an issue slightly and have students compare what was relevant to the first issue to what is relevant to the second. ("What *really* happened?" versus "What does X *think* happened?" Or *"Can* you do this?" versus *"Should* you do it?" Or "Which one *is* best?" versus "Which do people *think* is best?" Or "Is this *legal?"* versus "Is this *right?"* versus "Is this *convenient?")*

Students who disagree about the relevance of a particular point to the issue discussed, should be encouraged to argue its potential relevance, and probe the beliefs underlying their disagreement. *Why do you think it's relevant? Why do you think it isn't? What is each side assuming? Do these assumptions make sense?*

Lesson plans in which the strategy is used

S-32 Making Plausible Inferences, Predictions, or Interpretations

Principle: Thinking critically involves the ability to reach sound conclusions based on observation and information. Critical thinkers distinguish their observations from their conclusions. They look beyond the facts, to see what those facts imply. They know what the concepts they use imply. They also distinguish cases in which they can only guess from cases in which they can safely conclude. Critical thinkers recognize their tendency to make inferences that support their own egocentric or sociocentric world views and are therefore especially careful to evaluate inferences they make when their interests or desires are involved. Remember, every interpretation is based on inference, and we interpret every situation we are in.

Application: Teachers can ask students to make inferences based on a wide variety of statements, actions, story titles and pictures, story characters' statements and actions, text statements, and their fellow students' statements and actions. They can then argue for their inferences or interpretations. Students should be encouraged to distinguish their observations from inferences, and sound inferences from unsound inferences, guesses, etc.

Sometimes texts will describe details yet fail to make or have students make plausible inferences from them. The class could discuss such passages. Or groups of students might suggest possible inferences which the class as a whole could then discuss and evaluate.

Teachers can have students give examples, from their experience, of making bad inferences, and encourage them to recognize situations in which they are most susceptible to uncritical thought. The class can discuss ways in which they can successfully minimize the effects of irrationality in their thought.

Science instruction all too often provides the "correct" inferences to be made from experiments or observations rather than having students propose their own. Sometimes science texts encourage poor inferences given the observation cited. Though the conclusion is correct, students should note that the experiment alone did not prove it and should discuss other evidence supporting it.

Students should interpret experiments, and argue for their interpretations. *What happened? What does that mean? Are there other ways to interpret our results? What? How can we tell which is best?*

Lesson plans in which the strategy is used

S-33 Evaluating Evidence and Alleged Facts

Principle: Critical thinkers can take their reasoning apart in order to examine and evaluate its components. They know on what evidence they base their conclusions. They realize that unstated, unknown reasons can be neither communicated nor critiqued. They can insightfully discuss evidence relevant to the issue or conclusions they consider. Not everything offered as evidence should be accepted. Evidence and factual claims should be scrutinized and evaluated. Evidence can be complete or incomplete, acceptable, questionable, or false.

Application: When asking students to come to conclusions, the teacher should ask for their reasons. *"How do you know? Why do you think so? What evidence do you have?"* etc. When the reasons students supply are incomplete, the teacher may want to ask a series of probing questions to elicit a fuller explanation of student reasoning. *"What other evidence do you have? How do you know your information is correct? What assumptions are you making? Do you have reason to think your assumptions are true?"* etc.

When discussing their interpretations of written material, students should routinely be asked to show specifically on what in the book or passage they base that interpretation. The sentence or passage can then be clarified and discussed and the student's interpretation better understood and evaluated.

"On what evidence is this conclusion based? Where did we get the evidence? Is the source reliable? How could we find out what other evidence exists? What evidence supports opposing views? Is the evidence sufficient or do we need more? Is

there reason to question this evidence? What makes it questionable? Acceptable? Does another view account for this evidence?"

Lesson plans in which the strategy is used

S-34 Recognizing Contradictions

Principle: Consistency is a fundamental — some would say the *defining* — ideal of critical thinkers. They strive to remove contradictions from their beliefs, and are wary of contradictions in others. As would-be fairminded thinkers they strive to judge like cases in a like manner.

Perhaps the most difficult form of consistency to achieve is that between word and deed. Self-serving double standards are one of the most common problems in human life. Children are in some sense aware of the importance of consistency ("Why don't I get to do what they get to do?"). They are frustrated by double standards, yet are given little help in getting insight into them and dealing with them.

Critical thinkers can pinpoint specifically where opposing arguments or views contradict each other, distinguishing the contradictions from compatible beliefs, thus focussing their analyses of conflicting views.

Application: When discussing conflicting lines of reasoning, inconsistent versions of the same story, or egocentric reasoning or behavior, the teacher can encourage students to bring out both views and practice recognizing contradictions. *"What does x say? What does y say? Could both views be true? Why or why not? If one is true, must the other be false? Where, exactly, do these views contradict each other? On what do they agree? (What happened, causes, values, how a principle applies, etc.)"*

Sometimes fiction illustrates contradictions between what people say and what they do. History texts often confuse stated reasons with reasons implied by behavior. They will often repeat the noble justification that, say, a particular group ruled another group for its own good, when they in fact exploited them and did irreparable harm. Students could discuss such examples. The teacher could use questions like the following: *What did they say? What did they do? Are the two consistent or contradictory? Why do you say so? What behavior would have been consistent with their words? What words would have been consistent with their behavior?*

When arguing opposing views, students should be encouraged to find points of agreement and specify points of dispute or contradiction. *"What is it about that view that you think is false? Do you accept this claim? That one? On what question or claim does your disagreement turn? What, exactly, is it in this view that you doubt or disagree with?"*

The class can explore possible ways to reconcile apparent contradictions. *"How could someone hold both of these views? How might someone argue that someone can believe both?"*

Lesson plans in which the strategy is used

S-35 Exploring Implications and Consequences

Principle: Critical thinkers can take statements, recognize their implications (i.e., if x is true, then y must also be true) and develop a fuller, more complete understanding of their meaning. They realize that to accept a statement one must also accept its implications. They can explore both implications and consequences at length. When considering beliefs that relate to actions or policies, critical thinkers assess the consequences of acting on those beliefs.

Application: The teacher can ask students to state the implications of material in student texts, especially when the text materials lack clarity. The process can help students better understand the meaning of a passage. *"What does this imply/mean? If this is true, what else must be true? What were, or would be, the consequences of this action, policy, solution? How do you know? Why wouldn't this happen instead? Are the consequences desirable? Why or why not?"*

The teacher can suggest, or have students suggest, changes in stories, and then ask students to state the implications of these changes and comment on how they affect the meaning of the story.

Teachers can have students explore the implications and consequences of their own beliefs. During dialogical exchanges, students can compare the implications of ideas from different perspectives and the consequences of accepting each perspective. *"How would someone who believes this act? What result would that have?"*

Lesson plans in which the strategy is used

Remodelling Language Arts Lessons

Introduction

Language arts, as a domain of learning, principally covers the study of literature and the arts of reading and writing. All three areas — literature, reading and writing — deal with the art of imagining, interpreting, and expressing *in language* how people *do live* and how they *might live* their lives. All three areas have to do with gaining command of language and expression. Of course, there is no command of language separate from command of thought and no command of thought without command of language.

Very few students will ever publish novels, poems, or short stories, but presumably all should develop insight into and learn the value of literature. Students should develop a sense of the art involved in writing a story and, hence, of putting experiences into words. At the heart of literature is the need we all have to make sense of our lives. This requires command of our own ideas, which requires command over the words in which we express them. Students must learn how to express themselves clearly, precisely, and accurately, which is to say, they must learn to *think* clearly, precisely, and accurately.

In words and ideas there is power — power to understand and describe, to take apart and put together, to create systems of beliefs and multiple conceptions of life. Literature displays this power, and skilled reading apprehends it. Unfortunately, most students leave school with little of this insight and skill. Few gain command of the language they use or even a sense of how to gain that command. To the extent that students have not achieved a command of the language in which they express themselves, they will struggle when called upon to interpret literature. They will find reading and writing frustrating and unrewarding. Because the foundations for such insights and skills are not typically laid in elementary education, it is difficult to develop them in student minds later on. It is necessary to build for insights and skills over an extended period of time, over years, not just months.

Present standard practice does not emphasize the sense-making function of language. Students do not approach the written word with an attitude that what they read should make sense to them. So, when they make a mistake, they fail to catch it. Many students have the idea that reading means starting at the first word and plowing on to the last period. They don't realize that good reading means pausing, checking your understanding, skimming back and re-reading what was unclear, reading some sentences twice, etc. The way reading is taught, students put all writing into two categories: readable without problems or struggle, and impossible to read, so give up. They don't learn that if something they read doesn't make sense, there are things they can do to crack the code.

Students have similar misconceptions about writing. "Writers begin at the first letter of the first word, and all the words (correctly spelled) come out in sentences (correctly punctuated), one after another until they are done." Texts tend to break writing down into meaningless directions — in an attempt to make writing easy — with the result that students think there is something wrong with them when they have trouble writing. "I don't know what to write" they moan, when faced with the intimidating blank page they must fill with perfect sentences. They don't realize that the first step in writing is often to forget spelling, grammar, and the rest, and scribble down everything you might say in any kind of order; organizing, revising, and crossing your t's come later.

Most of the time, they are asked to write when they have nothing to say and when "no one but the teacher is ever going to read it, anyway." Somehow, students don't require of themselves that their own writing make sense. ("Lincoln's mother died in infancy. He was born in a log cabin that he built with his own two hands.") Students rarely step back and ask themselves, "Does this make sense? Is this what I want to say? What am I saying?"

Unfortunately, for most students literature seems increasingly like a frill, something artificial, irrelevant, and bookish, apart from the important matters of life. Reading, except in its most elementary form, seems expendable as a means of learning. Writing often comes to be viewed as a painful bore and, when attempted, reduced to something approaching stream-of-consciousness verbalization.

The task of laying foundations for love of literature and language and for the command of language that that love presupposes needs to be clearly conceived and systematically addressed. It involves cultivating a new and different conception of literature, of reading, and of writing. It is a profound challenge. However, if we value students learning to think for themselves, we cannot ignore, we must meet, this challenge. If a basic goal of English classes is to instill a lifelong love of reading, we must seriously confront why most students end up with little or no interest in literature. We need to think seriously about the world in which they live: the music they listen to, the TV programs and movies they watch, the desires they pursue, the frustrations they experience, and the values that are embedded in their lives. We must design our instruction so that students systematically and critically confront how they are actually living their lives and how, if they can gain some insights and skills, they might live their lives. For example, we should help our students see through the superficiality of most popular TV programs in comparison to great works of literature.

Most teachers can probably enumerate the most common features and recurring themes of, say, students' favorite movies: danger, excitement, fun, romance, rock music, car chases, exploding planets, hideous creatures, mayhem, stereotypes, cardboard characters, and so on. The lyrics and values of most popular music are equally accessible, expressing as they do an exciting, fast-moving, sentimentalized, and superficial world of cool-looking, "dudes". Much student talk consists of slang. Though sometimes vivid, it is more often vague, imprecise, and superficial. Most quality literature seems dull to students in comparison.

Good English instruction must respect and challenge students' attitudes. Ignoring student preferences doesn't alter those preferences. Students must assess for themselves the relative worth of popular entertainment and quality works. Students need opportunities to scrutinize and evaluate the forms of entertainment they prefer. They need to assess the messages they receive from them, the conceptions of life they presuppose, and the values they manifest. As instruction is now designed, students typically ignore what they hear, read, and reiterate in school work. They may follow the teacher's request to explain why a particular story conveys an important insight, but for most this becomes a ritual performance for the teacher's benefit, having little influence on the students' actual beliefs and values.

Critical thinking can help students to refine their tastes and gain insights into language and literature, and we should encourage it with this end in mind. In any case, under no conditions should we try to force or order students to say what they don't believe. A well-reasoned, if wrong-headed, rejection of a "good" story is better than mindless praise of it. The problem is not that we don't expose students to important "content" in school; it is that we do not design instruction, on the whole, so that students must *think their way into and through* the content. To see this more clearly, we should make clear to ourselves the guiding ideals we want to underlie our instruction. We should then start to monitor our teaching to see whether these ideals are actually being cultivated by how we teach on a day to day basis.

The Ideal English Student

In addition to the need to enter sympathetically into the world of our students, appreciating how and why they think and act as they do, we must also have a clear conception of what changes we are hoping to cultivate. Consider language itself and the way in which an ideal student might approach it. We want students to be sensitive to language, striving to understand and use it thoughtfully, accurately, and clearly. We want them to become autonomous thinkers and so command rather than be commanded by language.

As Critical Reader

Critical readers approach stories as an opportunity to live imaginatively within another's world or experience, to consider someone else's view of things. They come to realize that the same story can legitimately be understood somewhat differently by different readers. They become interested in how others read a story. This experience is analogous to the recognition that the same situation can be understood differently by different people who bring a different point of view, different experiences, to the situation. Young children need many opportunities to read and interpret not only stories but their own experiences as well. They need to begin to talk to others about what this or that story, what this or that character, what this or that situation *"means"*.

Young readers must learn that a story does not explain itself, but must be "figured out". They must learn to try out different possible meanings. They must begin to listen to and consider what other students think about what a story or element of a story means. They must begin to learn the difference between passive, impressionistic reading and active, reflective reading. They must learn to begin to question, organize, interpret, and synthesize. They must not only begin to interpret, they must also begin to recognize their interpretations *as interpretations*, and to grasp the value of considering alternative interpretations.

Only as they come to recognize their interpretations as such, will they begin to see the need to test, revise, and refine their interpretations. Only then will they begin to make ideas their own, accepting what makes most sense, rejecting what is ill-thought-out, distorted, and false, fitting their new understanding into their existing frameworks of thought. The best way to do this is by discussions and assignments — including many small groups engaged in cooperative learning — in which students express and consider alternative interpretations.

Consider, for example, the classic story, *The Deer-Slayer*, by James Fenimore Cooper. It begins with the lines: "In upper New York state, along the Hudson and Mohawk rivers, the warlike Iroquois Indians were rampaging ... scalping, pillaging, massacring the white man who was trying to make a home in the wilderness that was part of America." As one reads on, one finds lines like: "mad to help any Indian .... Not one of them is a white man's friend", and "The Governor's raised the price on Indian scalps. Fifty pounds for each scalp you get." Through-out the story, one meets two kinds of Indians, good ones and bad ones. The "good" ones always work with and for the settlers. The bad ones are continually characterized as "savages" and "barbarians". They torture those they capture.

In this story, as well as others by Cooper *(The Last of the Mohicans* and *The Pathfinder)*, a foundation is laid for many self-serving myths about early American settlers and Native Americans. The foundation is laid for hundreds of Hollywood movies about cowboys and Indians and, in line with this same "good guys-bad guys" view of the world, hundreds of movies about cops and robbers, "Americans" and their evil enemies, etc.

In designing instruction, one might first have the class watch the movie "Last of the Mohicans" (available at most video stores), then read Xerox copies of the story as represented in an old classic comic book. These experiences could lead to many interesting small group discussions about how we classify and represent people, people we like and people we don't, our "enemies " and ourselves. Some library "research" assignments might be developed as part of this process. The "literature" and reading/writing elements of the curriculum could be integrated into the study of U.S. history, while the students were, simultaneously, learning to critically analyze and question movies and television programs.

In this process we would be moving the students back and forth between visual and print materials. We would continually work to help students see how they interpret and represent the world in the way they talk, write, and respond in their everyday lives. We would continually design activities so that students were alternately writing and talking about their interpretations of experiences in relationship to what they read and see (movies and videotapes) in and outside of class.

As Critical Writer

Command of reading and command of writing go hand-in-hand. All of the understanding, attitudes, and skills we have just explored have parallels in writing. Critical writers recognize the challenge of putting their ideas and experiences into words. They recognize that inwardly many of our ideas are a jumble, some supporting and some contradicting other ideas, some vague, some clear, some true, some false, some expressing insights, and some reflecting prejudices and mindless conformity. Because critical writers realize that they only partially understand and only partially command their own ideas and experiences, they recognize a double difficulty in making those ideas and experiences accessible to others.

As young readers, children need to begin to recognize they must *actively* reconstruct an author's meaning; as writers, they need to begin to recognize the parallel need to *actively* construct their own as well as the probable meanings given by their readers. In short, while writing, critical writers engage in parallel tasks to the ones they engage in while reading. Both are challenging; both organize, engage, and develop the mind; and both require the full and heightened involvement of critical and creative thought. The sooner we begin to cultivate these insights and skills by the activities that take place in our classes the better.

Students should read and respond to the writing of other students. When a student has written what seems perfectly clear to him or her, the mis-interpretations and misunderstandings other students experience vividly show the need to place oneself in the position of the audience when revising one's work. This need is driven home by the specific examples of problems readers have. Similarly, when students misinterpret what they read, the class should examine the sentence or paragraph and uncover the source of the mistake. Discuss (using principles of grammar and precise use of language) why *this* sentence could not have meant *that*. By working through such mistakes and seeing *why* they were mistakes, students deeply learn the principles of reading and writing and the need for clarity of thought and expression.

As Critical Listener

The most difficult condition in which to learn is in that of a listener. It is normal and natural for people to become passive when listening, to leave to the speaker the responsibility to express and clarify, to organize and exemplify, to develop and conclude. The art of becoming a critical listener is therefore the hardest and the last art that students develop. Of course, most students never develop this art. Most students remain passive and impressionistic in their listening throughout their lives.

Yet this need not be the case. If we introduce young students to the arts of critical reading and writing, we can also introduce them to the art of critical listening. Once again, each of the understandings, attitudes, and skills of reading and writing have parallels in listening. There is the same challenge to sort out, to analyze, and to consider possible interpretations, the same need to ask questions, to raise possible objections, to probe assumptions, and to trace implications. As listeners, we must follow the path of another person's thought. Listening is every bit as dialogical as reading and writing. Furthermore, we cannot go back over the words of the speaker as we can in reading, so there is all the more reason to emphasize the need for and the nature of active listening.

Furthermore, some students face a special problem in listening to a teacher, for if they listen so as to take seriously what is being said, they may appear to some of their peers to be playing up to the teacher, or foolish, if they seem to say a "wrong" or "dumb" thing. Student peer groups often create pressure to listen with casual indifference, even with passive disdain. To expect students to become active classroom listeners is, therefore, to expect them to rise above the domination of the peer group. This is very difficult for most students.

One of our most important responsibilities is to model active listening in front of our students, so that if a student says something, we demonstrate by our response that we are "actively" engaged in a thoughtful process of figuring out, or at least trying to figure out, what the student is saying. We should draw the students into this process:

Jill: I think a lot of the Indians were savages.

Teacher: I wonder what you mean by that, Jill. Could you tell us what you mean by the word 'savage'?

Jill: I'm not sure.

Teacher: Well, lets all look up the word 'savage' in our dictionaries and see if we can figure out together what it means to say of someone that they are "savage". (Students look up the word)

Teacher: What are some of the meanings you are finding?

Jack: One is "wild and un-cultivated".

Susan: Another is "cruel".

Frank: Here's another: "furious and ill-tempered".

Trish: It also says, "having a tribal life".

Teacher: Well, lets go back to Jill and see which of these she means. Jill, when you said that a lot of the Indians were savages, did you mean they were "cruel" or "ill-tempered" or merely that they had a "tribal life" rather than a non-tribal life.

Jill: I guess I meant that they were cruel.

Teacher: I see. I wonder if you think that more of the Indians were cruel than the settlers, or do you think that there were the same number of cruel people among the settlers?

Jill: I guess there were probably a lot of cruel settlers too.

Teacher: What do the rest of you think? Do you think that more of the Indians or more of the settlers were cruel? (Discussion continues for a time.)

Teacher: Well, there is considerable disagreement about this question. I wonder if we could find some dependable information about which of you is most accurate in your views. Do you think that would be hard or easy to find out?

To sum up, the ideal English student, as you can see, is quite like the ideal learner in other areas of learning; critical reading, writing, and listening are required in all subject areas. Yet the language arts are more central to education than perhaps any other area. Without command of one's native language, no significant learning can take place. Even other domains of learning must utilize this command. The ideal English student should therefore come close to being the ideal learner. While helping our students to gain command of reading, writing, and listening, we should see ourselves as laying the foundation for all thought and learning. The time to begin cultivating these ideals is as early as possible. The later we begin, the further away from the ideal we will end.

Ideal Instruction

Considering the ideal reader, writer, and listener paves the way for a brief overview of ideal instruction. In each case, we should use our understanding of the ideal as a model to move toward, as an organizer for our behavior, not as an empty or unrealistic dream. Reading, writing, and listening, as critical thinking activities, help to organize and develop learning. Each is based on a recognition that, if we actively probe and analyze, dialogue and digest, question and synthesize, we will begin to grasp and follow alternative schemes of meaning and belief. Each of us lives in a somewhat different world. Each of us has somewhat different ideas, goals, values, and experiences. Each of us constructs somewhat different meanings to live by. And we do this from the early days of our lives, not only when we grow up. In ideal instruction, we want students to discover and begin to understand different worlds so that they can better understand and develop their own. We want them to struggle to understand the meanings of others so they can better understand their own meanings. We want all students to begin this struggle, but each within the context of the stories and experiences that they are capable of understanding.

Unfortunately, most texts in the language arts do not have a unified approach to this goal. They are often a patchwork, as if constructed by a checklist mentality, as if each act of learning were independent of the one that precedes or follows it. Texts typically lack a global concept of literature, language, reading, writing, and listening. Even grammar is treated as a separate, unconnected set of rules and regulations.

This is not what we want, and this is not how we should design our instruction. Rather, we should look for opportunities to tie dimensions of language arts instruction together. There is no reason for treating any dimension of language arts instruction as unconnected to the rest. Thus far, we have talked about reading, writing, listening, and literature as ways of coming to terms with the constructing and organizing of meanings. We can now use this central concept to show how one can tie grammar to the rest of language arts instruction, for clearly grammar itself can be understood as an organized system for expressing meanings.

Each "subject" of each sentence, after all, represents a focus for the expression of meaning, something that we are thinking or talking about. Each "predicate" represents what is said about the subject. All adjectives and adverbs are ways of qualifying or rendering more precise the meanings we express in subjects and predicates. By the same token, each sentence we write has some sort of meaningful relationship to the sentences that precede and follow it. The same principle holds for the paragraphs we write. In each paragraph, there must be some unifying thing that we are talking about and something that we are saying about it.

To put this another way, at each level of language arts instruction, we should aim at helping the student gain insight into the idea that there is a "logic" to the language arts. That is, that all the elements of the language arts make sense, and make sense not only in relation to each other, but also in relation to our everyday experience of the world.

This is a key insight that builds upon the idea of constructing and organizing meanings; it makes even more clear how we can tie all of the language arts together. Basic grammar has a logic to it, and that logic can be understood. Individual words and phrases also have a logic to them and, therefore, they too can be understood. When we look into language use with a sense that there is an intelligible structure to be understood, our efforts are rewarded. Unfortunately, we face a special obstacle in accomplishing this purpose.

Typically, students treat the meanings of words as "subjective" and "mysterious." On this view, problems of meaning are settled by asking people for their personal definitions. What do *you* mean by 'love', 'hate', 'democracy', 'friendship', etc.? Each of us is then expected to come forward with a personal definition. *My* definition of love is this.... *My* definition of friendship is that ....

To persuade students that it is possible to use words precisely, we must demonstrate to them that all of the words in the language have established uses with established *implications* that they must learn to respect. For example, consider the words 'friend' and 'acquaintance'. If I call some people my friends, I imply that I know them well and am fond of them. If I call others acquaintances, I merely imply that I have met them, not that I know them well, not that I am necessarily fond of them. If I say that a country is democratic, I imply that the people rule that country. Each word in the language has established meanings which we must help students to learn to respect.

There is a parallel insight necessary for understanding how to arrange sentences in logical relationships to each other. Our language provides a wide variety of adverbial phrases that can make connecting our sentences together easier. Here, as above, students need to learn and respect this established logic.

Group I

Connectives	How they are used	Examples
besides what's more furthermore in addition	To add another thought.	Two postal cards are often more effective than one letter. *Besides*, they are cheaper.
for example for instance in other words	To add an illustration or explanation.	There is no such thing as an "unlucky number." *In other words*, this idea is pure superstition.

Group II

in fact as a matter of fact	To connect an idea with another one.	Last week I was ill. *In fact*, I had to stay in bed until Monday.
therefore consequently accordingly	To connect an idea with another one that follows from it.	The President vetoed the bill. *Consequently*, it never became a law.

Group III

of course to be sure though	To grant an exception or limitation.	He said he would study all day. I doubt it, *though.*
still however on the other hand nevertheless rather	To connect two contrasting ideas.	I like painting; *however*, I can't understand modern art.

Group IV

first next finally meanwhile later afterwards nearby eventually above beyond in front	To arrange ideas in order, time, or space.	*First*, drink some fruit juice. *Next*, have a bowl of soup. Then eat the meat. *Finally*, have some pie and coffee.
in short in brief to sum up in summary in conclusion	To sum up several ideas.	Scientists say that we should eat food that has all the proteins, fats, and vitamins we need. *In short*, they recommend a balanced diet.

110

Common Problems With Texts

A critical thinking approach to language arts instruction, with its emphasis on helping students understand the *logic* of what they study, can provide a strong unifying force in all of the basic dimensions of the language arts curriculum: reading, writing, language, grammar, and appreciation of literature. Unfortunately, it is rare to find this unifying theme in most language arts textbooks. As a result, the emphases in reading, writing, language, grammar, and literature do not "add-up" in the minds of students. They don't recognize the common denominator between reading and writing. They don't grasp how words in language have established uses and so can be used precisely or imprecisely, clearly or vaguely. Their lack of understanding of the logic of language in turn undermines their clarity of thought when reading and writing.

By the same token, grammar seems to students to be nothing more than an arbitrary set of rules. Typically, texts take a didactic approach. They introduce principles or concepts, then provide drills. Specific skills are often torn from their proper contexts and practiced merely for the sake of practice. Yet, without context, skills have little or no meaning. An occasional simple reiteration of basic purposes or ideas is insufficient. Students need to see for themselves when, how, and why each skill is used specifically as it is. For example, rather than *using* references when needed, texts "cover" "Using References" in one or two lessons. After reading about different kinds of reference books, students are asked questions like, "Where would you look to find out when Washington was born?" In contrast, consider how educated people use references. First, they must recognize that there is something they want or need to know. Then they make a reasonable guess as to where (in what kind of book) they might find it. They check listings, possibly skimming through several pages. If they don't find what they were looking for, they figure out another place to look. When they have found what they were looking for, they usually use the information in some way. The standard sort of drill doesn't really teach this process in a meaningful way.

Students rarely, if ever, evaluate what they read. Students do not explore their standards for evaluating written material, or distinguish for themselves when a written work is clear or unclear, engaging or dull, profound or superficial, realistic or unrealistic, and so on.

Texts occasionally have a short lesson or activity on describing plot, identifying theme, and finding the main point. But students are rarely, if ever, called upon to describe the plots of stories, for example. Yet these basic concepts are worthy of frequent discussion. Instead of describing the plots or distinguishing main points from details, most of the time, students are only required to recall random details from what they have read.

Asking Key Questions

Language and grammar

Keeping in mind the idea that language and grammar are, on the whole, logical, we should ask questions that help students discover this. What follows in the next paragraph is a variety of questions that ought to be raised in a variety of contexts. You would not, of course, raise them all at once. Some may be the basis of a series of cooperative learning activities in which student groups develop their own answers to one of these questions and report their answers, and how they came to these answers, to the class as a whole.

"What is a sentence? How is it different from a group of words? What is a paragraph? How is it different from a group of sentences? Why are some ways of using a word right and others wrong? What different kinds of sentences are there? When and how should each be used? Why follow the rules of grammar? How does punctuation help the reader? How does knowing about grammar help you to write? Read?"

Literature

Stories have their own logic. Events don't just happen. They make sense within the meanings and thinking of their authors. When we ask a question, there should be a method to it. The questions should lead students to discover how to come to terms with the logic of the story, at least to the meaning that they are giving to the story. In every case, we should have students support their answers by reference to passages in the story. It is not their particular answers that are of greatest importance, but rather how they support their answers with reasons and references to the story.

What happened? Why? What is the author trying to convey? Why is this important? What is the main character like? How do you know? How do their experiences relate to my experience or to those of people around me? How realistic are the characters? How consistent? If they aren't (realistic, consistent), why not? What conflicts occur in the story? What is the nature of this conflict? What relationship does it have to my life? What meaning does that conflict have for the character? For me? What does this work tell me about the people and everyday life around me? Can I identify with them? Should I? How does the view presented in this work relate to my view? To what extent do I accept the way this story represents people? Are they like the people I know? To what extent or in what way would I change it to make it more "lifelike"? How does it relate to ways of looking at things that I've found in other stories?

These categories of questions would need, of course, to be formulated in different ways to be intelligible to students at different grade levels. In many cases you would have to build up to them with particular preparatory activities. None of these questions are intended as ready-made for this or that classroom. They are intended merely to stimulate your thinking about the general kind of questions that, sooner or later, in one form or another, must be raised.

Persuasive writing

All people spend a good deal of their time trying to persuade others to accept or believe something or other. Young children often develop considerable skill in persuading their parents to allow them to do this or that or to buy this or that. Persuasive writing, like all persuasion, has a straightforward logic. In it, a writer attempts to get the readers to take on the writer's perspective on something. We, as readers, need to grasp what is being said and judge whether or not to accept it, whether or not it makes sense to accept it. Young children need to be introduced into the art of rational persuasion. They need to learn how to express themselves clearly (If we don't know what they are saying how can we be persuaded?). They need to learn how to back up what they are saying with good reasons, with evidence, with relevant examples and illustrations from their experience, and with intelligible explanations.

They also need to learn to respond to the persuasive appeals of others with basic critical thinking tools. Television ads, television programs, peer groups, and adults — all attempt to persuade them. Children need to begin to learn how to develop their own persuasive appeals at the same time that they begin to learn how to rationally assess the persuasive appeals of others. As always, we need to learn to continually model these processes for them as we find ways to engage them in small groups carrying these processes out for themselves. In general, we need to help children begin to think analytically and reasonably.

What, exactly, is the author trying to say? Why? How does the author support what he is saying with reasons, evidence, or experiences? What examples can I think of to further illuminate these ideas? What objections might be raised? What might the author say about my objections? What are the consequences of believing or doing as the author says? What kind of writing is this? How has the writer attempted to achieve his purpose? Have I good reason to accept what is being said? Doubt it? How could I check, or better evaluate, what is being said? What has been left out? Distorted? Where did the author get her evidence? How should I evaluate it? What has she left unexplained? What would she say about it? Of all the ideas or concepts, which are the most fundamental or basic? How does he use these ideas? How do these ideas relate to mine?

As always, these questions are meant to be merely suggestive, not necessarily to be the actual questions that you will ask this or that student. There are many possible reformulations of these questions which would render them more accessible, more understandable to young children. And, as always, children learn to be comfortable with analytic questions over time. We must be ever vigilant not to overwhelm them with more than they can take in at any given time.

Writing

Writing has a logic. Good substance poorly arranged loses most of its value. Whatever the principle of order chosen, thought must progress from somewhere to somewhere else. It must follow a definite direction, not ramble aimlessly. In the entire piece, as well as in each section and paragraph, ideally, each sentence should have a place of its own, and a place so plainly its own that it could not be shifted to another place without losing coherence. Children need to begin to discover that disorderly thinking produces disorderly writing and, conversely, orderly writing enhances orderly thinking.

We need to introduce children to the art of orderly, logical writing. We need to model this process for them. This can be done in a number of ways. We can work with the class as a whole writing a short paragraph, asking for suggestions from the class as to how we might begin. Then, once a sentence is on the board we might ask if the sentence is clear, how we might express it more precisely. Then, we can ask for suggestions for a follow-up sentence, for one that elaborates further on what is said in the first sentence. Then, once satisfied with the formulation of that sentence, we might ask for an example to illustrate the point made in the first two sentences. And so we might proceed, working with the class to develop the paragraph. In this way, students can observe minds at work in doing the labor of writing. A follow-up to this process might be to have the students work in groups, each group developing its own paragraph on a common main point. Then groups could choose a spokesperson to read their paragraph to the class as a whole and the class could then both get further experience in this process while gaining insight into how others think their way through a writing project. Over time we want students to become habituated to ask questions like those in the next paragraph.

What do I want to communicate? Why? What am I talking about? What do I want to say about it? How can I develop this point? Do I need an example here? What else do I want to say about it, and why? What else do I know or think about this? What am I sure of? What questions do I have? What must I qualify? How does this detail fit in? Would the reader accept this? What questions would the reader have? How can I answer those questions? If I word it this way, would the reader understand it the way I intended? How can I clarify my meaning? How could someone judge this idea? How can it be supported? How would others refute it? Which of those criticisms should I take into account? How should I change what I've said? Will the support seem to the reader to justify the conclusion? Should I change the conclusion, or beef up the support? What objections or problems would occur to the reader here? What do I want to say about them? Where am I getting my information? How would someone else interpret it? How can I adjust or support my interpretation? What implications do I want the reader to draw? How can I help the reader see that I mean this and not that? Which of all of the things I'm saying is the most important? How will the reader know which is most important? Have I assumed the reader knows something he may not know?

Conclusion

As a teacher of the language arts, it is essential that you develop for yourself a clear sense of the logic of language and of the unity of the language arts. If you model the insight that every dimension of language and literature makes sense, can be figured out, can be brought under our command, can be made useful to us, your students will be much more apt to make this same discovery for themselves. Remember, students are not used to unifying what they are studying. They are, rather, used to fragmented learning. They are used to forgetting, for everything to begin anew, for everything to be self-contained. On the whole, they are not now learning organization skills.

Furthermore, they are not used to clear and precise language usage. They are usually satisfied with any words that occur to them to say or write. They are unfamiliar with good writing. Disciplined thinking is something foreign to them. Therefore, don't expect the shift from a didactic approach ("The teacher tells us and we repeat it back") to a critical one ("We figure it out for ourselves and integrate it into our own thinking") to occur quickly and painlessly. Expect a slow transition. Expect the students to experience many frustrations along the way. Expect progress to come by degrees over an extended period of time. Commit yourself to the long view, to what Matthew Arnold called "the extreme slowness of things", and you will have the attitude necessary for success. Teaching in a critical manner with a critical spirit is a global transformation. Global transformations take a long time to achieve, but their effect is then often permanent. And that is what we want — students who learn to use language clearly and precisely for the rest of their lives, students who listen and read critically for the rest of their lives, students who become critical and creative persons for the rest of their lives.

Mystery Stories

by Betsy Stenklyft, Sargeant School,
Roseville, CA

Objectives of the remodelled lesson

The students will:
- brainstorm what the parts of a mystery story are
- using a matrix, students will analyze a short mystery story into its component parts based on their brainstormed list
- students will evaluate their original brainstormed list, and compare their analysis with the description in their texts

Original Lesson Plan

Abstract

Students read a two-page lesson entitled "Mysteries". The goal of this article is to inform the reader about mystery stories and the basic rules for writing them. Students then answer a series of questions designed to elicit the components of a mystery story.

Critique

I feel that this lesson is weak because it simply presents the information to the students. This lesson is used in isolation without the benefits of a mystery story, although reference is made to a previously read mystery story. I feel students will have difficulty understanding the article without prior discussion of the topic. I also feel that they will not feel any ownership of the material presented in the article.

Strategies used to remodel

S–9 developing confidence in reason
S–15 developing criteria for evaluation: clarifying values and standards
S–31 distinguishing relevant from irrelevant facts
S–17 questioning deeply: raising and pursuing root or significant questions

Remodelled Lesson Plan s–9

First, students will be given a conundrum to solve. After the solution is discovered, students will be asked to determine what kind of a story a conundrum is. If necessary, introduce 'mystery'. Then, students discuss what makes a conundrum a mystery. "Why is it different from a narrative? What components does it have that are unique to a mystery story?" After brainstorming is exhausted, students will then be asked to evaluate their list of ideas to determine which ideas are major components and which are not. "How can we tell the difference? Are all of these components *necessary* for a good mystery story? Why or why not?" **S–15**

Students will then be divided into several groups. Each group will write each of the components the group agreed upon as the heading on a matrix. The students then read the mystery story, "The Bloodhound Gang", and find parts of the story that will fit onto their matrix. (For example, students might write that Mrs. Finch, the housekeeper, "kept breaking things, and small items kept disappearing" under the heading "Suspects".) **S–31** Students will then be asked to determine whether their headings were helpful in classifying the different parts of a mystery story. "Were the components complete? Did you miss getting some important parts of the story onto the matrix because there was no heading for them?" If necessary, re-evaluate the original brainstormed list of the components and add to or delete or leave the same if the students so desire.

Finally, have students read the informational article entitled "Mysteries". "Do the component parts of a mystery story listed in the story match the components on our list? If not, which list is better? Why?" Have students evaluate each difference. **S–9**

editor's note: Rather than introducing this lesson with a conundrum, the teacher could begin by having students recall the mystery story they have read and compare it to other stories. "In what ways was that different from other kinds of stories? What kinds of stories are there? (Take each category) How can you tell if a story is this kind? Why are stories grouped this way?" **S–17**

Writing Haiku

by Mary Louise Ross, Christ Church
School, San Rafael, CA

Objectives of the remodelled lesson

The students will:
- explore the thoughts and feelings of another culture through critical reading of Haiku
- practice creative thinking and writing

Original Lesson Plan

Abstract

Students read several haiku poems which are written on the board and in their workbooks. The class is encouraged to discuss the pattern of haiku and to count the number of syllables in each line. The nature theme is established and the students are asked to develop specific ideas about winter. The seasons are assigned for the students' creative writing of haiku poems. The students are to write a rough draft and read the poems to the class. They are then to revise and write a final copy of their haiku poems.

from *English for Christian Schools 4: Writing and Grammar,* Teachers' Edition. Bob Jones University Press © 1985, pp. 32–3.

Critique

This lesson missed the opportunity to explore the cultural background of haiku poetry. The teacher is the main investigator and disseminator of information. It is the teacher's responsibility to research the facts and to give the information to the students. There is no attempt to contrast other poetic styles and little to guide the students' thought into creative imagination. Groundwork for the study of haiku is negligible with the exception of a previous lesson on synonyms. The students need to have an enriching, valuable personal experience of exploring the Japanese culture and thereby understanding the underlying purpose and background of haiku poetry.

Although the basic facts are introduced in the lesson on haiku, other factors need to be established, such as the quality of emotions and how the feelings may be expressed most effectively. These feelings may be explored through the thoughts of the Japanese authors.

Students are asked to write rough drafts after viewing several poems correctly written, a beginning poem with one line, and two poems with an incorrect number of syllables. After reading aloud the first poems, finishing the one poem, and correcting the last poems, students were assigned haiku poetry on the seasons. At this point, discussion on background the students need, would be appropriate. That is, not only synonyms, syllables, and such, but the emotions,

117

feelings, and thoughts of these would-be writers should be explored. The students would have a more complete understanding of not only the mechanics, but of their thoughts and feelings and how to best express them through haiku.

Strategies used to remodel

S–21 reading critically: clarifying or critiquing texts
S–17 questioning deeply: raising and pursuing root or significant questions
S–4 exploring thoughts underlying feelings and feelings underlying thoughts

Remodelled Lesson Plan *S–21*

Groundwork for the study of haiku poetry should begin with an understanding of the Japanese culture and the exploration of the underlying purposes of the poetry. Appreciation for another culture may be accomplished through the visit of a foreign exchange student, a film on current Japanese life, and a study of oriental art, especially with respect to nature. Students could research Haiku, Japan, and Japanese (and other Asian art) in dictionaries, art books, and encyclopedias, and read more examples of haiku in library books. This overview of Japanese culture should discourage stereotypes and heighten the students' understanding of the people, their daily lives, and their art. With this background, the empathy of the students will develop so that the exploration of thoughts underlying feelings will naturally flow into the creativeness of haiku. **S–17**

During the discussion of the poetry, questions should be asked about the authors and how they felt and thought when writing the poems, and why they chose to express their feelings with poetry. Some study of Japanese literature may benefit the students' understanding of the authors' feelings. A background in other nature poems would contrast and give insight into the depths of feelings and ideas expressed in poetry. **S–4**

Students could evaluate the poems they read. "What do you think of this poem? How does it make you feel? What do you suppose the author was thinking and feeling? Why was it written? Is it well written? Do you like some of these more than others? Which? Why?" **S–17**

After the students have discussed the culture, the feelings of the authors, and their own responses to the poetry, brainstorming sessions may bring out ideas about nature and an awareness of how other students may express their thoughts through haiku.

It is understood that the mechanics of haiku poetry have been taught during appropriate intervals. The instruction may fit in naturally in the discussion concerning other poetic forms and the teacher may draw attention to the number of syllables with questions about the students' comparison between the nature poetry and the haiku poems. During the brainstorming sessions, feelings may be identified through the use of colorful words and their synonyms. Descriptive phrases may be listed around a central idea and synonyms substituted to balance the poetry with the correct number of syllables.

Thus the students are well prepared to develop their rough drafts and then to revise and rewrite their haiku poems in an atmosphere loaded with expressed thoughts and rich cultural understanding.

Despite the detail with which we have delineated the strategies, they should not be translated into mechanistic, step-by-step procedures. Keep the goal of the well-educated, fairminded critical thinker continually in mind.

"The Quest for the North Pole"

by Nora Brice Karr, Los Angeles U.S.D.,
North Hollywood, CA

Objectives of the remodelled lesson

The students will:
- read, analyze, and assess the charge that Robert Peary was *not* the first to the North Pole
- discuss ethnocentricity with regard to racial prejudice
- clarify and evaluate claims in their text
- discuss Peary's possible egocentricity
- evaluate the evidence

Original Lesson Plan

Abstract

This selection details the efforts of an Afro-American, Professor Allen Counter, to discover and disseminate information on Matthew Hensen, an African-American explorer who was a member of the team that claims to be first to have reached the North Pole in 1909. Commander Robert Peary has commonly been given credit for this feat; however, Counter's evidence indicates that Hensen reached the 90° N latitude location about 45 minutes before Peary. Peary reportedly asked Hensen not to tell anyone and Hensen honored this wish until after Peary's death in 1920.

from *Treasures,* Goodman H.B.J. Reading Program, Level 12, Grade 6, 1989. pp. 106–115.

Critique

This lesson was chosen because the selection is rich in discussion material on prejudice, ethnocentric views of historical events, and the morality of Peary's accepting the many honors he received for being "first". However, the suggested questions in the text fail to probe these ideas or the controversy.

While some of the questions ask for information about the controversy, they do not go deep enough nor do they require critical reading or thinking. Thus, students are exposed to a challenge of a "hero's" account of events with no discussion of ethical implications.

Strategies used to remodel

S–2 developing insight into egocentricity or sociocentricity
S–34 recognizing contradictions
S–4 exploring thoughts underlying feelings and feelings underlying thoughts

S–16 evaluating the credibility of sources of information
S–33 evaluating evidence and alleged facts
S–30 examining or evaluating assumptions
S–7   developing intellectual good faith or integrity
S–20 analyzing or evaluating actions or policies
S–27 comparing and contrasting ideals with actual practice

Remodelled Lesson Plan s–2

Discussion could lead to the nature of the controversy. "What did Peary claim? What did Hensen say? Could both be true? Why or why not? Is there a sense in which both claims are true?" **S–34**

The question of Peary's possible egocentricity should be discussed. "Why might Peary ask Hensen not to tell? **S–2** What feelings might Peary have had? Why? What feelings might Hensen have had about Peary? Why might he feel that way?" **S–4**

"What evidence does Professor Counter provide to support his conclusion that Hensen was actually first? Where did he get his information? Is there reason to doubt it? Is there reason to believe it? Which position has more evidence? Where might you find more evidence? **S–16** Do you have reason to think his evidence is true? Why? False? Why? Is this evidence enough?" **S–33**

"Professor Counter thinks Hensen has been denied his place in history as a result of racial prejudice in the early 1900's. What facts would be relevant to his statement? Is he making a valid assumption? How could you find out? **S–30** Could a similar controversy occur in our times? Why or why not?

The book says that who actually arrived at the North Pole first is not as important as that both men get credit, for it was a team effort. Ask students: Does it matter who was first? Why or why not? What examples can you give of 'firsts'? Can you give similar examples of 'seconds'? Why or why not? How does our society treat 'firsts'? Why? If it doesn't matter which was first, then why would Peary want Hensen to lie? **S–7**

"In neither account are the four Eskimo guides who were also there mentioned by name. Why might that be?"

"What do you think the importance of teamwork is in such an undertaking? Who should receive credit? Who should receive the fame? Why? Which would be most important to you personally, the achievement or the fame? Why? What values were you using in your decision making?" **S–30**

editor's note: "If what we have read here is true, what do you think of Peary?" **S–20** What might the public response have been had Hensen and Peary told that Hensen was first? What does Counter think it would have been? Why? Why would Hensen agree to this?

Students could look up "North Pole" and "Peary" in encyclopedias, dictionaries, and other books. "Which version was given in each? Why?"

"What other myths have been passed down as historical fact? Why? How do untruths get to be believed by so many? Should children be taught myths as though they were true?" **S–27**

Parts of Speech

Objectives of the remodelled lesson

The students will:

* through Socratic discussion, exercise independent thought to discover the logic of sentence structure and parts of speech for themselves
* begin to recognize parts of speech by understanding their functions within sentences
* avoid the oversimplified view of nouns presented in their texts

Original Lesson Plan

Abstract

In this lesson, "Nouns", students use the "test questions", "Do you see the _____? Do you see two _____?" to identify nouns. They are told that any word which has singular and plural forms that can complete the test sentences is a noun. They are asked how they could test a word to see whether or not it is a noun; to give plurals for a list of singular nouns; to use singular nouns in the subject to complete sentences; to use plural nouns in the subject to complete sentences (first orally, then in writing). The other parts of speech lessons occur in later lessons spread throughout the text.

from *Exploring in English 4* by John S. Hand, et al. Laidlaw Brothers. © 1975. pp. 132–133, T76.

Critique

Texts teach the parts of speech in a fragmented, mechanical, and misleading way. Instead of building on the function of nouns within the sentence, this lesson reduces the distinction to a mechanical test that makes the definition of 'noun' too narrow to be generally useful. The other parts of speech lessons are scattered through the text. Every one or two units, students cover another part of speech. Unfortunately, this tends to add to the fragmented quality of the parts of speech lessons. Each part of speech is taught in isolation; their relationships aren't understood.

Texts teach part of speech as a feature of the word itself, whereas words *themselves* are not one or another type. Many words can serve as several parts of speech, according to their role in particular sentences.

This lesson emphasizes repetition over understanding, by simply having students repeat the test. Students need to learn to distinguish parts of speech, not memorize a rule. Giving them practice describing and using the test does not foster the ability to make the distinction, or understand the concepts 'noun' or 'parts of speech' in terms that make sense to the student. Again, it turns a skill of understanding into a mechanical skill.

The test itself is misleading, since not all nouns satisfy the conditions it sets. More importantly, part of speech is not a characteristic of words themselves, but of their *function within a sen-*

tence. Furthermore, by only pointing out those nouns which are in the subject, the lesson fosters the idea that nouns occur only in the subject.

Grammatical points and distinctions should be taught in such a way that their usefulness is apparent to the student. For example, when reading difficult sentences, grammatical analysis gives readers a way to begin to get a handle on meaning, and to clarify vague passages. (For example, by using the principles that pronouns always refer to some noun and that transitive verbs require objects, one can rewrite sentences to make them clearer and more explicit or to check one's understanding.)

This remodelled lesson provides an example of what we mean by fostering understanding of grammatical logic, rather than memorizing mechanical recognition processes. If students discover these grammatical distinctions for themselves, we increase their understanding and encourage them to think for themselves. Students can use their texts for reference.

Strategies used to remodel
S-29 noting significant similarities and differences
S-10 refining generalizations and avoiding oversimplifications

Remodelled Lesson Plan

Begin with students' dictionaries and texts as references. Have students look up a word and draw their attention to the part of speech notation, and explain that they are going to begin to learn the different ways words are used. This will help them become better readers and writers.

Using the dictionary (various words of the main parts of speech), the dictionary explanations of the parts of speech, and definitions and explanations in their texts, briefly introduce the main parts of speech to students.

The teacher could select a word that functions as more than one part of speech and write sentences using the word differently, for example, "Lock the door. Put the key in the lock." Students can characterize the differences between these uses of the same word, such as, 'bench,' 'board,' 'date'. Students can compare such word groups as 'think' and 'thought,' 'believe' and 'belief. **S-29**

When students have had sufficient practice, the class may compare the different parts of speech. Encourage students to test their generalizations by trying to find counter-examples, and, if necessary, revising their claims. In some cases their generalizations may be nearly always true. If so, this could be pointed out. If they make a serious mistake which they fail to correct, you may want to supply a counter-example. **S-10**

When students have had sufficient practice, the class may discuss what nouns have in common. Encourage them to test their generalizations by trying to find counter-examples, and, if necessary, revising their claims. In some cases, their generalizations may be nearly always true. If so, this could be pointed out. If they make a serious mistake which they fail to correct, you may want to supply a counter-example. (When the class has covered other parts of speech, you may want to have them repeat this discussion.)

Myths

by Virginia Reilly, St. Apollinaris School,
Napa, CA

Objectives of the remodelled lesson

The students will:
- deeply question the meaning of a particular myth
- discuss the literal meaning of the myth
- apply their understanding of the myth they have studied to myths of other cultures

Original Lesson Plan

Skills Unit 31 focuses on myth and legend recognition. The children are directed to read a story about why Ra-wen-io, maker of all things on earth, gave Rabbit long back legs and long ears and why he gave Owl a short neck and big eyes. Upon finishing the story, children are asked to answer factual questions about the story and to consider the definition of 'myth' and 'legend'. They are then asked to read a Hawaiian story about Pele and how she became goddess of volcanoes. Again factual questions are asked. In addition, children are asked to identify the story as myth or legend. The unit concludes with a lesson on legend identification.

Critique

I will focus on the myth aspect of the lesson. Even though many sixth graders would be unable to recite definitions of 'myth' and 'legend' and identify a given story as one or the other, they have long been acquainted with myths and legends. Certainly it is important that children have the language of literature and be able to recognize different forms of literature, but that is not enough. Skills Unit 31 has for its main task myth recognition, but it fails to consider the worthier task of myth and its relationship to reality, seen and unseen.

In the section titled "Introducing the Skill Lesson," the teacher is told the scope of the lesson and what to say and do.

> Read the title. Explain that in this lesson pupils will read about two very old types of literature — the myth and the legend. The lesson will help them understand the difference between the two and will help them recognize each when they read or hear such tales.

Such is the scope of the lesson. Not only does it fail to encourage critical thinking in the student, but it likewise discourages the teacher from thinking critically. Neither teacher nor student is called upon to become actively involved in this lesson; rather they are told to do trite, uninteresting tasks.

After reading the first myth, the children read the following in their text:

The story you have just read is an American Indian myth. A myth is a very old story handed down among people. It may be about some gods or goddesses. It often explains something about nature, such as why there is thunder and lightning.

The children have been *given* a definition of 'myth'; they are not encouraged to explore for themselves the meaning of myth, an exercise more valuable because it engages their curiosity and taps their desire to know and understand. The lesson continues, and children read another story about gods and goddesses, after which they are asked to identify the story as legend or myth, a task which children complete successfully as the definition of myth in the text uses the key words, gods and goddesses. Thus the lesson of myths is completed without ever having explored myth and its meaning.

Strategies used to remodel

S–17 questioning deeply: raising and pursuing root or significant questions
S–35 exploring implications and consequences
S–14 clarifying and analyzing the meanings of words or phrases
S–11 comparing analogous situations: transferring insights to new contexts
S–9 developing confidence in reason
S–23 making interdisciplinary connections

Remodelled Lesson Plan s–17

The remodelled lesson, by having students discuss root questions, would explore myth and its meaning. Instead of defining 'myth' for the children and having them apply that definition to stories they read, I would begin by telling them that they are going to read an Indian myth. A discussion of the Indian myth in particular and of myth in general would follow. "What part of the myth seems unbelievable? Does the myth deal with reality? What reality does the myth explain? What are the obvious, seen realities that the myth explains and the less obvious but unseen realities that the myth implies? **S–35** Why does the myth describe a creator and creatures? How is that relationship developed through the actions of Ra-wen-io, Rabbit, and Owl, and what is implied about their relationships? What is the point of this story? Do myths reveal reality as it is or as a society perceives it to be? Why do people tell myths? What do myths reveal about the tellers of myths and their beliefs?"

The lesson would be extended over a period of time during which myths from other cultures would be read, discussed, and compared. "How do the details of myths differ? Why do they differ? Are myths alike in any way? How? Why? How do myths compare to other kinds of stories? Why are myths an important part of the literature of many cultures?" **S–14**

The lesson would conclude with a written essay in which the children would be asked to compare and contrast two myths, one which had been discussed in class and one which they would read for the first time. **S–11**

editor's note: After exploring the deeper meanings of myths, students could critique the superficial explanation in their text. "What does the text say myths are about, or what they are for? What did we say? What aspects of myths or what meaning do myths have that your text fails to mention? Why?" **S–9**

125

Students could read myths from other cultures they have studied, and discuss them. "What were their myths like? What do they tell us about those people, their lives, their culture?" **S–23**

Students could also examine the personalities and characteristics of animals in myths, and compare them to their impressions of those animals and what zoologists know of their behavior. **S–23**

When the powerful tools of critical thinking are used merely at the service of egocentrism, sociocentrism, or ethnocentrism, then genuine communication and discussion end, and people relate to one another in fundamentally manipulative, even if intellectual, ways.

Subject and Predicate

Objectives of the remodelled lesson

The students will:
- through Socratic discussion, exercise independent thought to discover the logic of sentence structure and parts of speech for themselves

Original Lesson Plan

This lesson, "The Two Parts of a Sentence", starts with a chart that divides three simple sentences into subject and predicate. The discussion explains that the subject tells who or what the sentence is about, and the predicate tells what the subject does or is. After this clarification, the class does oral and written exercises dividing sentences into subject and predicate.

from *Exploring in English 4* by John S. Hand, et al. Laidlaw Brothers. © 1975. pp. 56–58, 132–133, T15, T76.

Critique

Our approach to grammar encourages students to recognize the underlying logic of grammar. This logic dovetails well with the writing skills needed to construct a grammatical sentence, a paragraph, or a well organized, logically progressive essay. These same skills also establish or reinforce the thought patterns necessary for critical thought. We believe, in other words, that well designed grammatical instruction can re-enforce critical thinking principles, and vice versa.

Dividing sentences into subject and predicate is an excellent starting point for analyzing sentence structure and parts of speech. Since the class examines whole sentences, they must observe the relationships between the subject and predicate to divide the sentences. This division also builds a foundation for later distinctions between parts of speech, because every word or phrase we add to the sentence modifies the subject, the predicate, or the sentence. Furthermore, division of sentences into subject and predicate can help students clarify and analyze sentences.

The main weakness in this lesson is that it doesn't allow students to work through the logic of the subject/predicate relationship for themselves. The lesson starts with a chart that breaks three simple sentences into two parts, clearly labeled subject and predicate. Students get the labels first, and then have those labels defined and illustrated. We recommend that this process be reversed. Students could first uncover the subject/predicate pattern, and then learn the appropriate labels.

The following lesson plan is a specific example of what we mean by fostering understanding of grammatical logic, rather than memorizing mechanical recognition processes. If students discover these grammatical distinctions for themselves, we increase their understanding and encourage them to think for themselves.

Strategies used to remodel

S–1 thinking independently

S–11 comparing analogous situations: transferring insights to new contexts

S–21 reading critically: clarifying or critiquing texts

Remodelled Lesson Plan

Before opening the book to this lesson, the class can conduct an exercise that not only uncovers the subject/predicate relationship, but also uses the focus of the sentence as the basic unit of grammar. The teacher could write a simple sentence on the board. A good first sentence would be a simple subject and intransitive verb such as, "Birds sing." To encourage analysis of the main sentence parts, the teacher could ask questions like these: Which word tells you what is being talked about? Which word tells what is being done? **S–1**

Have students divide a few more sentences, each one a little longer. If this process bogs down, the teacher could model the distinction for a few sentences until some students catch on. Keep questioning as you go, to stimulate clarification through dialogue. When the distinction has become clear, the class will be ready for the subject/predicate exercise in the text (pp. 104-105).

After working through the lesson in the text, return to the simple sentences on the board. Take the original example, "Birds sing". Ask students questions such as these: How can we make the sentence longer? What words can we add to this sentence? How can we make it give us more information? How can we make this sentence tell us more about the birds and their singing? What does this addition tell us about? What question does this answer? Which birds? What about their singing? Singing what? Singing how? How does adding these words change the meaning of the sentence? If students need help, give them some examples like, "We could say, 'Blue birds sing.' or 'Blue birds sing when they are happy.'" Show them how additional words make the sentence more precise, by excluding some possibilities.

Subject	*Predicate*
Birds	sing.
Blue birds	sing.
Three blue birds	sing.
Three blue birds	sing together.
Three blue birds	sing together on the roof.

As each word or phrase is added, ask questions like, "What does the new word tell us about? (The birds. The subject. It tells us what color the birds are.) What does the word 'three' tell us? (More about the birds. More about the subject. How many birds there are.) What word does the word 'together' explain, about the birds, or about their singing? (Sing. The predicate. It tells something about how they sang, what they were doing when they sang.) What does this phrase modify? (The predicate. Sing. It tells where the birds sang.)

If the class exhaustively expands a couple of the sentences in this manner, it will become clear to them that every word or phrase they add to the basic sentence modifies either the subject or the predicate. Every additional word or phrase makes the sentence more precise. This activity also sets the foundation for later lessons teaching specific parts of speech.

The teacher could strengthen student comprehension of the logic of grammar by comparing the logic of sentences to that of a well constructed paragraph or essay. The teacher could take an intelligible sentence and add a word that doesn't fit. Point out that the word doesn't belong. Every word has a place in the sentence. Every sentence has a place in a paragraph. *S-11*

Using Grammatical Analysis on Complex Sentences *S-21*

This section has students reducing a complex sentence to its essentials, and then adding the other pieces. Thus grammar is used to clarify statements and enhance reading ability.

Have students write and punctuate the Pledge of Allegiance. (Write variations in punctuation on the board. Compare them. Have students find a correct version.)

Using the correct version, identify or have students identify the subject, verb, and direct and indirect objects: *I pledge* (pledge what, and to whom?) *I pledge allegiance to the flag....* (and do *what* to the republic?) I pledge allegiance to the republic.... *for which it stands* (To what does 'it' refer?).... Students could find as many simple sentences in the pledge as they can, and share and discuss their rewrites.

Similar lessons can be repeated on material from texts, newspapers, or other readings.

Harriet Tubman and the Ante-Bellum South

by Anne Lehan, Waldo Rohnert
Elementary School, Rohnert Park, CA

Objectives of the remodelled lesson

The students will:
- analyze the concept 'leader' and develop criteria for evaluating leadership
- appreciate the qualities of Harriet Tubman, especially her ability to lead
- apply their criteria to Harriet, supporting their judgments with details
- understand Harriet's actions in the context of her times
- appreciate how the same subject can be written about in different styles and for different purposes
- appreciate the importance of musical lyrics and tempo as primary sources of information

Original Lesson Plan

Abstract

Students read, out loud, taking turns, "General Moses" by Dorothy Sterling in their *Freedom's Ground* basal reader. The text, written in a lively style, relates the details of Harriet's activities on the Underground Railroad and stresses her many qualities of leadership including her intelligence, her survival skills, and her courage. Quotes from unidentified slaves extolling her virtues are sprinkled throughout the reading selection.

Students respond in writing to the "Reflections" questions as the end of the selection:

1. *Why did the plantation owners offer rewards for the capture "dead or alive" of Harriet Tubman? What "property" of the plantation owners did they accuse her of stealing?*

2. *Moses in the Bible led his people out of slavery in Egypt. Why did people call Harriet Tubman "Moses"? In what ways was she like him?*

3. *Harriet Tubman was a real person. How did she become a legend?*

4. *Make a list of some problems and hardships Harriet Tubman and her people might have had on their way North. Then write an essay on this topic, using the items from your list.*

Discussion of student responses follows completion of writing.

Critique

This is a fairly standard reading lesson utilizing the basal and involving some student participation in the initial oral reading and in the responses read to the written assignment. A teacher gifted in Socratic questioning could enrich the "Reflection" responses with some critical involvement, but opportunities are slim given the nature of the questions which, as in #1, are much too literal or, as in #2, require an extensive background in Biblical expertise to be able to react intelligently. #3 has a literal answer given in the text. #4 has possibilities if the list is then categorized, but the essay part is preposterous, as many 5th graders (for whom the basal is written) cannot even write a unified paragraph.

Strategies used to remodel

S–23 making interdisciplinary connections
S–14 clarifying and analyzing the meanings of words or phrases
S–15 developing criteria for evaluation: clarifying values and standards
S–32 making plausible inferences, predictions, or interpretations
S–31 distinguishing relevant from irrelevant facts
S–18 analyzing or evaluating arguments, interpretations, beliefs, or theories
S–22 listening critically: the art of silent dialogue

Remodelled Lesson Plan S–23

This remodel has four parts: *1)* Introduction, *2)* Literary Reference, *3)* Historical Reference, and *4)* Musical Reference.

1) Introduction S–14

Have students brainstorm the concept 'leader' by clustering the word on the board. Say, "I am going to encircle the word 'leader'. What do you think of when you see that word?" Encourage all responses. Cluster the responses. Show you appreciation of their willingness to respond, thus creating a climate for critical thinking.

Now, divide the class into groups and ask each group to arrange the responses associated with 'leader' by listing the most important characteristics first.

On the board, arrive at a consensus from the groups. Phrase words as qualities and ask students how these words could be useful to them. Help them see these are standards by which we evaluate a leader. Introduce and define the word 'criterion(a)'. **S–15**

Ask each student to silently chose one person he or she feels is a leader and quick-write for five minutes. Students can then share their writing with the group. Each group chooses the best to read to the class. (This is a Bay Area Writing Project technique.)

2) Literary Reference

Have students open their readers to "General Moses" by Dorothy Sterling and say that we are about to read a story about a famous person who lived in the South before the Civil War. Her name was Harriet Tubman. Tell them that after reading the story, they will be using the criteria for 'leader' established by them and will evaluate whether or not they think Harriet was a good leader. They will be asked to support their judgment with details from the story.

Out loud, taking turns, students will read the story.

Using Socratic questioning techniques, the class will evaluate Harriet's leadership qualities. Reference will be made as to why others (slaves) considered her a leader but students must make their own judgment based on criteria and reading details. **S–32**

For homework, each student is to write a paragraph arguing that Harriet was (or was not) a leader. Specific details from the story as well as reference to criteria must be included in the argument. **S–31**

3) Historical Reference

The lesson begins by having each group read their homework, choosing the best, and then reading that selection to the class. When working in groups, each student should make a written evaluative comment on each paper read. **S–18**

Students then open their history texts to the page discussing Harriet's contribution to the abolitionist movement (class is presently studying events leading to Civil War). In *Our United States* by Joanne Buggey, Allyn and Bacon, Inc., 1983, one paragraph on page 210 refers to Harriet. The treatment in the history text is briefly compared to the basal reading selection — different styles, tones, purposes, lengths, etc.

The teacher then very briefly reviews Harriet's place in the historical context of ante-bellum South and events leading up to Civil War (the present focus of social studies).

4) Musical Reference

Words to two Negro spirituals are handed out: "Oh Freedom" and "Buked and Scorned". Students are asked to follow words while listening to Harry Belafonte sing these songs on an old 33 LP and discuss their meaning. "What are these songs saying? Why? What does that imply? How can they help us understand slavery and the Underground Railroad?" **S–22**

The teacher then asks: Why have spirituals collectively been called "sorrow songs"? Continue by asking what value these songs have today. Review the meaning of "primary source" and ask how the term applies to spirituals.

For homework, each student is to find a song from the 1980's he or she thinks reflects in lyrics and tempo concerns of life today. Each is to bring in a record or tape and be prepared to discuss the selection as a primary source the next day.

"The Fun They Had"

Objectives of the remodelled lesson

The students will:
- exercise independent thought by determining the story's main point for themselves
- practice fairmindedness by shifting to an unfamiliar perspective to clarify and contrast their concepts of and attitudes toward 'school', 'teacher', and 'book' with that of the characters
- use critical vocabulary such as 'infer', 'assume', 'perspective', and 'conclude'
- explore the influences that people's place in time and experience has on their perspectives

Original Lesson Plan

Abstract

This science-fiction story is about Margie and Tommy, two children living in the year 2155, who discover an old book about school in the 20ᵗʰ century. Although Margie finds the old ways strange, she is envious of the fun students used to have learning from human teachers instead of machines, and being with other children instead of alone at home.

The lesson begins with a discussion of what it means to be "old-fashioned". Students then read the story and make inferences from context clues. Among the inference questions, are ones which require students to figure out the meanings of invented terms. Other questions require students to agree or disagree with story characters' statements, relate their own feelings about events in the story, and locate details. After the story has been reread, students review with the teacher what schools of the past were like, answer questions about the story (distinguishing when answers are stated or implied), and debate whether schools of the future will be superior to present schools. Some activities focus on categorizing the story as science fiction.

from *Lanterns*, Marjorie Seddon Johnson, et al. American Book Co. 1977. pp. 24c–32b

Critique

The main strength of this lesson lies in using material which encourages students to enter another point of view. Also, some of the questions develop critical thought by requiring students to make inferences from story details. The text questions, however, miss the point of the story, and distract students from considering it. Several parts of the lesson are irrelevant or only distantly related to the point of the story (such as discussion of 'old fashioned', schools of the past, and the debate about schools of the future). The time saved by dropping these can be used to explore more pertinent points.

Confusions in the text

The discussion of the concept 'old-fashioned' is ill-timed at best. Even if that were the key concept of the story, discussing it at the beginning takes the punch out of the story. The lesson 'Concept', *"What is up-to-date now may seem old-fashioned in the future,"* misses the point. The story is less about old-fashioned-ness than about the irony of Margie's envying today's students (few of whom consider themselves lucky). It is a story about differences in perspective.

Some of the inference/conclusion questions and suggested answers are confused and misleading. For instance, when Margie has too hard a time with her geography, her parents call a repairman who examines the mechanical teacher and fixes it. One section has teachers ask, *"In 2155, when pupils don't learn what they are supposed to, who is blamed, the pupils or the teacher? (the teacher) How do you know? (The inspector is sent for to fix the teacher. Margie isn't scolded.)"* The inference that when students of the future do poorly in school, they are not held responsible, is absurd. Had nothing wrong been found with the machine, Margie would have been held responsible. The teacher was simply the first place to look.

As with many texts, critical vocabulary is misapplied. The text asks students how they can tell that the teacher is a machine, and answers that it is inferred, when, in fact, it is directly stated. Similarly, the answer to the question, *"Why do you think the inspector thinks Margie will do fine?"* is given explicitly in the story.

Missed opportunities

The text fails to take full advantage of the strengths of the story, and many of the suggested questions. First, it doesn't have students explore Margie's point of view, or compare it to their own. It doesn't have students analyze key concepts in the story, such as 'school', or 'good teacher'. The story also provides an opportunity for discussion of the relationship between experience, perspective, and use of language. The characters use a number of expressions, such as 'regular book', differently than we do. Such uses of language could be used to develop students' awareness of how different experiences lead to differences in what is considered 'regular', 'normal', 'funny', or 'weird'.

In many instances, students could learn or practice using critical vocabulary. The exercises which require students to distinguish whether a fact is stated or unstated, is a missed opportunity to have them practice using 'infer'. Students can also use critical vocabulary to make the reasoning involved in the inferences, and the beliefs of the characters more explicit.

Strategies used to remodel

S–25 reasoning dialogically: comparing perspectives, interpretations, or theories
S–1 exercising independent thought
S–4 exploring thoughts underlying feelings and feelings underlying thoughts
S–3 exercising fairmindedness
S–14 clarifying and analyzing the meanings of words or phrases
S–35 exploring implications and consequences
S–28 thinking precisely about thinking: using critical vocabulary
S–21 reading critically: clarifying or critiquing texts

Remodelled Lesson Plan s-25

When students have read the story through once, the teacher can begin the lesson by asking such questions as, "What is the story about? What is the author's point? What idea is he trying to get across? What is the point of view of the main character?" **S-1** When discussing Margie's perspective, use questions like the following: Why does Margie envy students of the past? What is she thinking about when she feels this way? **S-4** What facts does Margie think about when she thinks about schools of the past? What doesn't she consider? What concepts or ideas are important to her? Are they the same as what you find most important? How accurate is Margie's view? Defend your answer. Do you agree that you are luckier than Margie? Why or why not? What values do you have in common with her? Why do you value this? Continue this process of having students compare their own and Margie's assumptions, experiences, inferences, and values. "How could someone argue that Margie's school is better than our schools? Worse?" **S-3**

To further explore Margie's perspective, students could analyze words and phrases from the story, such as 'book', 'teacher', etc. Consider asking, "What is Margie's idea of a good teacher? What qualities should a teacher have? What surprised her about teachers of the past? Why? What are the advantages and disadvantages of human versus machine teachers? How did she feel about her teacher? Why? How is Margie's idea of what 'school' means different from yours? Alike? Does Margie really have 'school', or should it be called something else? Why or why not?" **S-14**

The class could also discuss differences between how the characters would talk about school and teachers, and their own expressions, for example, 'my teacher is broken' versus 'my teacher is sick', 'regular book', 'regular teacher', 'funny schools', 'have school today', 'go to school', etc. **S-14** "Why does the author suppose people would use these expressions?" Students could discuss why the children in the story use words and phrases differently than they do. **S-35**

The teacher using the inference questions provided in the text could have students practice using critical vocabulary. (For example, "Why did Margie *assume* that human teachers taught in children's homes? Was this fact stated or *implied*? Why did the repairman *conclude* that Margie would do better?")**S-28**

If using the "Comprehension Skills" section at the end, the teacher could ask students to support those answers not stated in the story, and explain their reasoning. **S-21**

"The Great Storm"

by Virginia Reilly, St. Apollinaris School,
Napa, CA

Objectives of the remodelled lesson

The students will:

- explore for themselves, and in-depth, characterization and main idea in a story
- find evidence for their statements from the story and present it first in class discussion and then in an essay
- explore figurative language and its evocative power

Original Lesson Plan

Abstract

"The Great Storm," an adaptation of Chapter 15 of *Abbie Burgess: Lighthouse Heroine*, recounts the story of young Abbie Burgess who is responsible for keeping the lighthouse operating and taking care of her four younger sisters and her sick mother while her father is on shore buying supplies. When a violent storm blows in, stranding her father on shore, Abbie's responsibilities become more serious. The ordinary tasks of keeping the lamps lit and taking care of her family become dangerous, yet Abbie persists in doing what must be done. She moves the family to safety in one of the stone towers when the wooden room below the tower washes away, and she keeps the lamps lit and the ice scraped off the lighthouse windows until the storm ends and her father returns.

The comprehension questions at the end of the story ask the children to think about the main idea, describe Abbie's character, answer factual questions about the plot, and imagine life on a lighthouse.

Star Flight, Scott, Foresman Reading. ©
1985, pp. 54–69.

Critique

Three strong points of "The Great Storm" — development of character, main idea, and use of figurative language — are ignored (as in the case of figurative language) or undermined (as in the case of character development and main idea).

Character Development

Question 4 of "Comprehension Check" asks the following:

Which of these words would you use to describe Abbie?

lazy	timid
fun loving	strong
determined	courageous
thoughtless	responsible

A question of this type discourages critical thinking and trivializes the idea of character. It teaches children that a person's character can be defined simplistically by two or three words without reference to thought or evidence. It does not probe the nature of character, nor how a character is revealed. Further, giving children a multiple choice question about character stifles any curiosity or logical thought process. It virtually tells them what to think by limiting the type and number of words to choose from and leaves no room for thoughtful exploration. All thought ends. The answer is given to them; there is no reason to think. Children are taught they do not have to think to arrive at a worthwhile conclusion, nor are they responsible for their views. Judgments are made quickly and superficially with no accountability for their reasonableness.

Main Idea

Question 1 of "Comprehension Check" asks the following:

Which of the following sayings best describes the main idea of this story?

a) A stitch in time saves nine.
b) Where there's a will there's a way.
c) Haste makes waste.

This question asks children to think about the main idea, yet its message is, *"Don't think!"* A discussion of the main idea is worthwhile and can generate enthusiasm and careful thought. But when children are given a multiple choice question, what kind of enthusiasm or interest can there be? They have already been given the answer. One of the three is correct, they are told. No serious thought is necessary. The answer is put before them so what kind of commitment to defend and explain the answer can there be when the answer is not really theirs? [This also inadvertently reinforces the false ideas that there is only one correct way to word a story's theme, and that one can understand a story's theme without exploration and struggle.]

Language

"The Great Storm" has many good examples of effective figurative language, a basic aspect of study of literature, yet no attention is drawn to the use of language. Strip the story of its personification, its similes, and its strong descriptive passages and the story loses much of its intensity and interest.

Strategies used to remodel

S–1 thinking independently
S–14 clarifying and analyzing the meanings of words or phrases
S–20 analyzing or evaluating actions or policies
S–24 practicing Socratic discussion: clarifying and questioning beliefs, theories, or perspectives
S–16 evaluating the credibility of sources of information
S–33 evaluating evidence and alleged facts
S–17 questioning deeply: raising and pursuing root or significant questions

Remodelled Lesson Plan

Character Development

Instead of listing adjectives and asking the children to limit Abbie's character by choosing the ones that best describe her, and before taking into account Abbie's character, I would ask the children to think about the idea of character.
S–1 "What is character? How does one reveal one's character? How do you

reveal your character? How do your friends reveal their character?" **S–14** After exploring the idea of character with the children, I would ask them to apply their understanding of character, their own and others, to Abbie. "How does Abbie reveal herself? What does she reveal about herself? Does the author tell us what Abbie is like, or do Abbie's actions reveal her character? Is one way of character development more effective? More honest? Why? Why does Abbie act the way she does? Do her actions have anything to do with her values: her mother, her sisters, the sailors at sea, duty?" **S–20** All responses to the above questions should be supported with evidence that is reasonable and has some base in reality, either the reality of the story or the reality of everyday life. **S–24**

2) Main Idea **S–1**

A similar remodel would be appropriate for a discussion of main idea. Rather than listing three truisms, one of which can double as the main idea, I would ask children to think about the meaning of the main idea of a story. "How do we know that something is the main idea? How does an author lead readers to the main idea? Do characters — their thoughts, words, action, and what befalls them — help to express the main idea? Is the main idea universal? Should it be universal? Is something true just because a story suggests it is true?" **S–16** I would then ask the children to explain what they think is the main idea of "The Great Storm" using evidence from the story. "What makes you say so? Does anyone think otherwise? Why? Why do you think that's the main point? What parts of the story make you think that? How do the events of the story support the main idea? Are they realistic? Does your experience or the work of another author contradict or support this theme?" **S–33**

3) Language **S–17**

I would ask the students, "What passages do you like? What makes some passages effective, others less so? Consider the following passage:

> She stepped into a pit of blackness that was terrifying. The wind screamed and buffeted her against the tower. Needles of ice pricked her cheeks. The ocean lapped viciously below the tower, as though it were a monster eager to swallow the house and towers. Knowing that each step could send her crashing off the tower, Abbie stepped cautiously. (p. 62)

"Why is the description of the storm important to the story? How does the author convince you that there is a violent storm? Does the language of the storm make Abbie's actions more serious, more real? What would happen to the story if the storm were less real, less violent? What words in this paragraph are used figuratively? Which words or phrases aren't meant as a literal, accurate description? (pit of darkness, wind screaming, needles of ice, etc.) Can an ocean be vicious? In what sense? '... as though it were a monster' Why say this? Why describe the scene this way? How would it seem if it had been written more literally and factually?"

This lesson would culminate in an essay assignment in which the children would be expected to explain the main idea, Abbie's character, or use of figurative language, by making reasonable generalizations supported by convincing evidence.

"The Cave"

Objectives of the remodelled lesson

The students will:
- practice dialogical thinking by comparing and synthesizing several perspectives on events in a story
- develop criteria for evaluating actions by analyzing values
- evaluate actions in the story
- develop insight into sociocentricity by comparing gang attitudes with attitudes of other groups
- use critical vocabulary ('assumption,' 'conclude,' 'interpret,' and 'perspective') to analyze characters' thoughts and feelings

Original Lesson Plan

Abstract

Students read a story about a boy named Charley, a member of the Jesse James gang. Charley meets George an artist "bum" who has carved statues in the walls of his cave home. Charley begins visiting George regularly. Meanwhile, the Jesse James gang needs a cave for a clubhouse. Charley finds a candidate and leads the gang to it. He goes inside to explore it, falls down a deep hole, wanders through caverns and tunnels and finally comes into George's cave. He agrees to keep the cave secret. The gang, suspicious because Charley had been gone too long, and had returned to them holding one of George's carvings, decides to explore Charlie's discovery themselves. One day, Charley comes to visit George and finds the statues destroyed, George gone, and the gang in possession of the cave. He fights the gang-leader Pat, but loses. The story ends with his decision to join a tougher gang and eventually seek revenge on his old gang. The story is told in flashback.

from *To Turn a Stone,* by Theodore Clymer and Helen Wardeberg. © 1973 Ginn and Company. pp. 14-31.

Critique

We chose this lesson because the story content is conducive to developing a variety of critical thinking skills and insights. The guilt felt by the main character, as well as the broad range of other emotions, are fruitful subjects for exploration. The question of Charley's guilt or innocence of the gang's treatment of George is intriguing since, though he *feels* guilty, the facts of the situation do not clearly support his self-imposed verdict. Charley's decision to get revenge is also ripe material for student evaluation.

Although Charley's guilt is by no means well established, the text seems to beg the issue. ("*What events would you blame Charley for?*") This is especially surprising since it sets the purpose for reading the story as "*to decide whether Charley was to blame for what happened.*" We recommend a more thorough discussion of the issues of his guilt and plan of revenge.

Although the text does make a step toward developing dialogical thought when it asks students to take other points of view, it doesn't give students the necessary guidance for recognizing the implications of seeing an issue from different points of view. This is a common problem with texts. They fail to have students integrate taking other perspectives with analysis and evaluation of reasoning. The student is left with separate, unreconciled views rather than an integrated more complete view — they don't "add up" the views.

The text also misses the opportunity to have students explore the important relationships between thought and feelings in this story. The main character experiences a wide range of emotions, and students could take advantage of this to discuss what his thoughts and assumptions were likely to have been, and whether they were reasonable or justified. Such discussion can develop students' insight into emotion and thought, and their critique. Students should develop the insight that feelings don't come from nowhere, or from situations alone, but are, rather, a result of how we *interpret* situations (often unconsciously).

The lesson can also be used to have students practice using critical thinking vocabulary.

Strategies used to remodel

S–1   exercising independent thought
S–15 developing criteria for evaluation: clarifying values and standards
S–25 reasoning dialogically: comparing perspectives, interpretations, or theories
S–12 developing one's perspective: creating or exploring beliefs, arguments, or theories
S–29 noting significant similarities and differences
S–20 analyzing or evaluating actions or policies
S–2   developing insight into egocentricity or sociocentricity
S–4   exploring thoughts underlying feelings and feelings underlying thoughts
S–34 recognizing contradictions
S–28 thinking precisely about thinking: using critical vocabulary

Remodelled Lesson Plan

Instead of asking students "*What events would you blame Charley for?*" the teacher can ask "Is Charlie to blame?" **S–1** (Or the teacher could have students critique the text's question.) The class could discuss relevant details, and make their standards of evaluation explicit. Students might also change story details to make their points about standards clearer. If so, encourage them to use 'If'. ("If Charlie had ....) Consider using questions like the following: What exactly did Charley blame himself for? Find places in the story where he says he did something wrong. Why does he think each is wrong? Was it intentionally wrong, a mistake, or what? What was wrong with what the gang did? Why was it wrong? Can you be blamed for someone else's actions? When? Why? Can you be blamed if you didn't know the result of your actions? Why or why not? When? Could Charley have prevented the destruction of the art-work? How? Why not? **S–15**

The exercise in which students describe the story from George's and Pat's perspectives could be integrated here with such questions as: Would George blame Charley? Why or why not? Why do you think so? Would Pat blame Charley? Why not? (Pat didn't think wrecking the statues was wrong.) What did Pat think of Charley's behavior? Why? What did *he* think Charley did wrong? (Keeping the cave a secret; fighting him) What did other members of the gang think? Why? **S-25** Whose perspective is closest to yours? Why? How is yours different? **S-12** Students could also describe the main characters from other characters' perspectives and compare those descriptions to their own conclusions about the characters. Questions like the following could encourage comparisons of characters' and students' perspectives: Who is to blame? (according to Charley, George, You, etc.) For what? Why? What do these beliefs imply about each character? What similarities and differences among the characters account for their judgments? **S-29** Did George have a right to the cave? Why or why not? More of a right than the gang? Why or why not?

If using the question from the original about Charley's plan of revenge, students could develop insight into how values generate criteria of evaluation by extending discussion. Possible questions include the following: Why does Charley think his plan is a good one? What does he value that leads him to make that plan? What do you think the results of his plan are likely to be? What do you think of his plan? Why? What values of yours lead you to this conclusion? What would be the likely results of acting on your values in this situation? Why do you think Charley doesn't hold these values? Should Charley seek revenge? Should he use another method of getting revenge instead? Why or why not? (Discuss at length.) **S-20**

Students could develop insight into sociocentricity through examination of Pat's attitudes, those of his gang, and Charley's experience breaking away from the gang, but retaining gang attitudes. Students could discuss why a group of children would follow another child, what beliefs and values they shared, what assumptions the gang makes, etc. "Why was Pat leader? What can we infer about the gang's values? Why? Why was Charley out of the gang?" They could compare gang values and assumptions with those of other groups such as friends, countries, etc. (Some common ideas follow: You are either in the group or out of the group. Being in the group has certain requirements. The group's desires are more important than the needs and wants of those not in the group. Our group is the most important; if the desires of two groups conflict, you should chose ours. Some members of the group are more important than others.) The class could discuss reasons for such assumptions, and evaluate the consequences of making them. Students could make their own group assumptions explicit, and perhaps evaluate them — assumptions about clothes, interests, possessions, speech and behavior in and out of class, etc. **S-2**

The class could go through the story and discuss how Charley felt at various points, relating his feelings to his thoughts. "What situation was he in when he felt that way? Were his feelings mixed? How did he see or interpret the situation? What did he think about the situation? What else did he think? Why did he feel that emotion then? What does this tell us about his assumptions? Personality? How else could he have seen this situation? If he had seen it that way, how would he have felt about it? How might he have acted? **S–4** Is his thinking consistent, or are there inconsistencies or contradictions? Does he notice them? Why or why not?" **S–34**

The teacher can modify questions used throughout the lesson to allow students practice using critical vocabulary. For example, rather than asking, *"What clues told you that George was an educated man?"* you could ask, "What can you *infer* about George? What *evidence* led you to that *inference?"* Other possibilities include the following: What *assumption* are you making? From Pat's *perspective*, what did Charley do wrong? Why did Charley *conclude* that the cave was George's? How did the gang members *interpret* Charley's behavior? **S–28**

"The Lonely Silence"

Objectives of the remodelled lesson

The students will:
- exercise independent thought by discussing the story's main theme
- evaluate the main character's actions
- explore the thoughts underlying the feelings of the main character as well as examine the assumptions that may contribute to those thoughts
- discuss the sociocentricity of the assumption that difference deserves ridicule
- develop insight into egocentricity by exploring the main character's rationalizations

Original Lesson Plan

Abstract

The focal point of this lesson is a story about a young girl whose parents are deaf-mutes. The girl, Bina, teased about her parents when younger, is ashamed of them and determined that her present friends won't learn about them. When she finds out that her mother is planning a party for her, she becomes angry and afraid, argues with her mother, and storms out of the house. Later, at the hospital where she is a candystriper, she sees a little boy, Carl, also deaf and dumb. He is scared because he doesn't know where his mother is, and no one else knows sign language. At first Bina tries to ignore him for fear of giving away her secret. Just before leaving for the day, she changes her mind and calms him down by signing to him. When the nurse is impressed by her and her parents, Bina realizes that she has been more handicapped by her fears than her parents have been by their deafness.

Students first discuss self-pity, and then read the story. The skills of prediction and characterization are emphasized.

from *Moments* by Marjorie Seddon Johnson, et al. ©1977 American Book Company. pp. 178c–191b.

Critique

We chose this lesson because it provides fruitful material for having students practice evaluating actions, and discussing an example of emotional conflict. Although the specific events are not applicable to most students, the theme of being disabled by false beliefs is. Students should learn to see the ways that their beliefs affect their actions, sometimes harmfully.

Although the text takes advantage of the story to ask a few thought-provoking questions, it doesn't go far enough in exploring what is going on inside Bina. The text also misses the opportunity to have students discuss the difficulty and importance of confronting difficult problems like Bina's; Bina's self-serving thoughts while she tried to ignore Carl; or the sociocentricity of the children's attitudes (for example, the assumption: Differences deserve ridicule). By more carefully exploring the main character's experience, students can develop crucial insight into such affective traits as intellectual perseverance, good faith, and courage.

Oversimplification

As is common in texts, this lesson drastically oversimplifies and distorts the concept of character. The wording of many questions and suggested answers lead one to believe Bina's very character undergoes several drastic changes. [*Why did Bina hesitate before ringing the bell?... What does this tell you about the kind of person Bina was? (considerate) In what way was Bina like the first-graders when she spoke sharply to her mother? (She was inconsiderate and cruel.) What does this tell you about how Bina and her mother differ in the way they approach problems? (Bina avoids problems; her mother wants to deal with them.) What could you tell about Bina after you read that she would not help Carl? (She thought about herself before she thought about others; she was being selfish.) What words could you use to describe Bina when she refused to help Carl? (selfish, uncaring, unkind) What words could you use to describe Bina after she helped Carl? (unselfish, compassionate, kind, caring)*] At the end of the story, she does not so much change from a selfish person to a compassionate one, as overcomes an emotional conflict which had prevented her from consistently displaying her consideration and compassion. By calling her selfish when she tries to ignore Carl, the text ignores the conflict (which is clear in the story), that she experiences. Though called uncaring, she cares deeply, and was obviously upset and torn.

The problem, in part, arises from the text's confusion between evaluating an *action* and evaluating a *person*. It is unfair to make absolute judgments about a person's character based solely on a few uncharacteristic actions in the worst of situations. Though her treatment of her mother during their argument and her initial refusal to help Carl were unkind, it is unfair to call *her* cruel, unkind, and selfish, especially considering how torn she was when her behavior was at its worst. In part, the problem with the questions is that, though many ask about her feelings, none are followed up with discussions of *why* she felt as she did. Nor does the text have students "add up" the various pieces of information about Bina to come to a fuller and fairer judgment.

Unrealistic Ideals

Most of the questions and suggested answers ignore the trauma Bina has carried, and the conflict she experiences. Though one question asks students whether sometimes people don't help others because they are afraid, rather than selfish, the rest of the questions and answers about Bina contain harsh judgments about her character at the points in the story where she is most torn by conflict. As usual, the message is, "If you *ever* behave selfishly, you are a horrible person."

The text's conclusions set up an unrealistic ideal by down-playing the difficulty of helping Carl, as though one could simply shrug off strong fear and longstanding shame in a moment. (Among the positive words used to describe her at the end of the story is the striking absence of the word 'brave'.) Students should not be misled into thinking that kindness and compassion are always easy, or learn to despise themselves for occasional brief lapses.

Strategies used to remodel

S–1   thinking independently
S–30 examining or evaluating assumptions
S–4   exploring thoughts underlying feelings and feelings underlying thoughts
S–20 analyzing or evaluating actions or policies

S–10 refining generalizations and avoiding oversimplifications
S–27 comparing and contrasting ideals with actual practice
S–3 exercising fairmindedness
S–2 developing insight into egocentricity or sociocentricity
S–35 exploring implications and consequences
S-6 developing intellectual courage

Remodelled Lesson Plan

The remodel contains suggestions for a more fairminded and less oversimplified discussion of Bina, a clearer discussion of the key concepts, and discussions of egocentricity and sociocentricity.

Promoting fairminded discussion

When students have read and retold the story, they can discuss the central theme. Ask, "What point do you think the author is trying to make? Why? Where is the theme clearest?" **S–1**

Discussion can be expanded, and questions from the original rephrased. When asking what Bina's feelings are at various points in the story, the teacher could follow up with questions like the following: What was she thinking? Why? What assumption did she make? Was it a good assumption? **S–30** Why did she make it? Were her thoughts and ideas relevant? **S–4**

If evaluating Bina's behavior, the "characterization" questions can be rephrased to focus more on the specific behavior, rather than global judgments about her. For instance, rather than asking *"What could you tell about Bina after you read that she would not help Carl?"* ask, "What did you think of Bina's behavior when she tried to ignore Carl? Why?" **S–20** At the end, the class could examine and evaluate Bina, taking into account all of the details of her behavior. "Overall, what do you think of Bina? What sort of person is she? Were these traits consistent? Why not?" **S–10**

"Why was it so hard for her to help Carl?" **S–27**

If the class compares characters and behavior, the text questions can be altered and followed up; for instance, the original question about Bina's abandonment of the argument with her mother, *"What does this tell you about how Bina and her mother differ in the way they approach problems?"* can be reworded to "How did Bina and her mother differ in their approach to this problem? **S–10** Why?" **S–4** In another instance, the text asks, *"How were Nancy's feelings toward Carl different from Bina's?"* We suggest the teacher ask for *similarities* as well as differences, **S–3** and probe the reasons for those similarities and differences. **S–4**

Egocentricity and sociocentricity **S–2**

The class can discuss the children who had teased Bina. "What assumption did the first-graders make when they teased Bina? What assumption did she make in her reaction to the teasing? What assumption did she make after she moved? Have you ever been teased, like Bina was? How does it make people feel? **S–3** What effect did it have on Bina? Why? **S–35** What does this tell us about this sort of teasing? Have you ever teased others? Did you hurt their feelings? Why do people tease? Do you approve of teasing? When is teasing wrong? When is it OK? How can you tell which is which?" **S–20**

An especially fruitful passage for discussion is the one in the hospital scene which describes her state of mind. Students can discuss her feelings and the thoughts behind them, the worth or relevance of her reasons, why she snapped at Nancy, and why she thought what she did. (Anger: *She had come here to run away from just this problem ....It just wasn't fair.* Fear of being near Carl. *... she had worked hard these last years to build a separate life .... Next week ... this boy would be gone .... they would treat her as though she were different.*) Students could relate the discussion to times when they had similar self-justifying thoughts. This discussion could be extended by having students discuss similar times when they, someone they know, or another character had a similar confusion of conflicting feelings. "How can she feel all of these different ways all at the same time?" **S–4**

"Why did she change her mind and decide to help Carl? Was it easy or hard to do? What about her fear and embarrassment?" **S–6**

"The Scapegoat"

Objectives of the remodelled lesson

The students will:
- engage in dialogical thinking by exploring several points of view expressed in a story
- pursue at length the root conflict of the main character between wanting to avoid trouble with her sister and disagreeing with her
- discuss various possible consequences of the main character's options
- generate and assess solutions to the problem in the story by comparing various characters' statements of the problem with their own and developing criteria for evaluation
- explore the sociocentric assumptions regarding outsiders and loyalty

Original Lesson Plan

Abstract

The lesson focuses on a story about the trouble which arises when the school band leader (Mr. Franks) appoints a talented newcomer, Nancy, solo clarinetist. Most of the band members resent the decision as a slight to Katheryn (formerly best clarinetist at school). Katheryn's twin sister Margaret, however, agrees with the decision, and is appalled to learn that band members are refusing to sell concert tickets in order to get back at Mr. Franks, though they display no resentment toward Nancy. Margaret, deciding that her twin has no desire to be fair about the issue, and wanting to avoid a breach, avoids discussing the problem with her. After Nancy fakes incompetence and tries to back out of her new position, the twins overhear Nancy playing a difficult piece beautifully. Katheryn changes her mind and tells the rest of the band they were wrong. Margaret tells the story.

When introducing the material, the teachers' notes ask questions which encourage students to think about what it's like to be a newcomer. For follow-up, it asks questions which require students to write diary entries for Nancy, discuss how the story might have been told by other characters, role play a discussion between the twins, make and justify inferences, and identify cause and effect.

from *Networks* by Marjorie Seddon
Johnson, et al. © 1977, American Book
Company. pp. 229c–242b.

Critique

We chose this lesson for its excellence, as much as its failings. The story contains fruitful material for lengthy student discussions about the ethical implications of story characters' actions, and solutions to conflicts. Text strengths lie in the choice of material and the questions which encourage students to view the central conflict from different points of view.

Confusions

Unfortunately, the title of the story is misused — there can be no scapegoat when no one has done anything wrong. Mr. Franks cannot be construed as bearing the blame for the wrongdoing of another, since there is no reason to believe that Nancy has done anything wrong. A scapegoat takes the blame for another's wrong action. Though the band members unjustly blame Mr. Franks, their mistake lies in claiming the action to have been wrong, not blaming the wrong person. This lesson, therefore, encourages a sloppy use of language. Students could discuss the discrepancy between the story and its title, and suggest other titles.

One suggested question misuses the term 'conclude'. *Why did Margaret conclude that Nancy had memorized the tune for the tryouts?* It is clear in the story that she wondered, possibly suspected, but did not feel she had sufficient evidence to draw such a conclusion. Other questions make this clear. The original question, if used, should be reworded or critiqued.

Some suggested answers also show confused thought. *"Was the scapegoat blamed unjustly? (Yes. 'Anyway, Mr. Franks isn't pushing you around.')"* The suggested answer doesn't prove the inference; it gives Margaret's perspective. The answer to how students know Margaret disagrees with the others is also misleading, since the citation it gives happens *after* we learn her opinion.

Point of view

The text uses, though fails to distinguish or adequately explore the connections between, two senses of 'point of view': perspectives on the situation versus the literary sense of the voice of selection. Most of the time is spent on the latter. The "identifying point of view" activity, which has students distinguish first person from third person sentences, should be dropped in favor of more extended discussion of the affect of the narrator's point of view on the reader.

The activities of writing Nancy's diary entries, role playing a discussion between the sisters, and discussing the effect of changing the point of view of the story could be extended and integrated into a deeper and more thorough discussion of the various perspectives expressed in the story.

Opportunities for fostering critical thought

Rather than pursuing Margaret's dilemma in depth, the text merely asks students to identify her reason for not discussing the situation with Katheryn, and describe how they would have behaved. A more detailed and extended discussion could require students to grapple with the many aspects and difficulties of conflicting loyalty, similar to many problems children face.

The text neglects exploration of the sociocentric principle of "favoring our own over a stranger". Though the band members don't directly mistreat Nancy, they are ruled by hidden sociocentricity which they try to rationalize. Students can gain useful insight into the irrationality and dishonesty of sociocentricity and false loyalty by discussing the characters' behavior and remarks.

Strategies used to remodel

S–21 reading critically: clarifying or critiquing texts
S–25 reasoning dialogically: comparing perspectives, interpretations, or theories
S–16 evaluating the credibility of sources of information
S–35 exploring implications and consequences
S–20 analyzing or evaluating actions or policies
S–15 developing criteria for evaluation: clarifying values and standards
S–19 generating or assessing solutions
S–2 developing insight into egocentricity or sociocentricity
S–6 developing intellectual courage
S–4 exploring thoughts underlying feelings and feelings underlying thoughts

Remodelled Lesson Plan

We have divided the remodel into the following sections: *1)* Introduction, *2)* Discussions of perspectives, *3)* The problem, and *4)* Sociocentricity.

1) Introduction

After students have read the story, have them retell it. The class could have a more detailed discussion of the idea of a scapegoat. After students have looked the word up, have them discuss criteria for determining when it would apply. Have them compare those to the situation in the story. "Who was blamed? Was the blame justified? Should someone else have been blamed instead? For what? Does the word fit this situation?" Students could then suggest better titles. **S-21**

When having students reread the story, the teacher could have them keep notes of the perspectives of the various characters: Margaret, Katheryn, Nancy, and Phyllis. Under the appropriate headings, students can record details expressing or reflecting each character's point of view.

2) Perspectives S-25

The class can then discuss and expand on each point of view. Questions such as the following could be used: What was this character's situation? How does it compare to that of the others? What does this character think? Feel? Do? Say? Why? What ideas guide this character? How does this character define the problem? What assumptions does she make? Why? What does she value? How do her values compare to those of the other characters?

Students could also compare the story to what it would be like if told from other points of view, and how that would have affected the reader, and speculate about why the author chose to write it as she did. "Since Phyllis felt *this* way, how would she have told the story? How would it have been different?" They could also discuss whether this was the best choice. **S-16**

3) The Problem

Students could explore the sisters' lack of communication in greater depth, and evaluate it. Students could mention as many pros and cons of their silence as they can think of, compare the sisters' attitudes and situations, suggest alternative behaviors, and discuss the consequences of each. The following original and new questions might be used: *What caused silence between Margaret and Katheryn?* (The original answer, citing Margaret's reluctance, is incomplete, since neither sister was anxious to talk.) *Why might Margaret want to avoid arguing with her sister?* Why might Katheryn have avoided discussion? How did their disagreement affect their relationship? What may have happened if they had talked? **S-35** (Encourage multiple responses, or have groups of students use the suggested role play activity, and have the class compare the results of the different groups.) What do you think is the best thing to do in this kind of situation? (Rather than asking students what they would have done.) Why? **S–20** Why did Phyllis say "Some twin you are!"? What does this tell us about Phyllis' values? Was this remark appropriate? Why or why not? Why is a situation like this difficult?

Consider asking the class to evaluate the different reactions of the various characters. First, if students have not already formulated their own statement of the problem, ask them to do so. Then ask, "Who is affected by this problem? What are the criteria for a good solution? What would a good solution require? **S–15** What solution does each character come up with? What values are assumed by each? How do these solutions compare? Do any meet the criteria of a good solution? Why or why not? What would?"**S–19**

4) Sociocentricity S–2

Students could discuss some of the characters' attitudes about letting an "outsider" and "newcomer" take the top clarinet spot in the band. Such a discussion could help students consider the unfairness of sociocentric attitudes, as well as bring a clearer sense of detail to what "group think" and "us versus them" means, how it manifests itself, and how people try to hide it. The class could discuss such questions as these: Who used the word 'outsider'? What does it mean? What attitudes and feeling does that word express? What does Katheryn mean by her speech toward the end of the story? Why does she think the children were being dishonest with themselves? What did Phyllis say was her reason for not agreeing with Mr. Franks? For saying that Katheryn was cheated? Why was she angry with Margaret? If Katheryn was right that the children weren't being honest with themselves, *why* weren't they? Why didn't they give their real reasons? Why did they feel as they did? Why is it often hard to disagree with others in your group? Was Margaret being disloyal? Were the others? How did Margaret probably feel when Phyllis said, "Some twin you are!"? Does being loyal to a group (or a twin) require always agreeing with and supporting the group's beliefs? Why or why not? **S–6**

The class could explore the thoughts underlying Margaret's feelings as they change during the story. Students could also discuss Katheryn's change of heart at length. Have them discuss her feelings and reasoning when she was upset with Mr. Franks, and her feelings and reasoning after she heard Nancy play at the end of the story. **S–4**

The Logic of Questions

Objectives of the remodelled lesson

The students will:
- practice clarifying questions by distinguishing various interpretations of the question, "Which breed of dog is best?"
- develop different sets of criteria for evaluating breeds of dog

Original Lesson Plan

Abstract

Each lesson in this unit presents rules describing the transformations of statements into one of four different kinds of questions. In the first lesson, students learn how a statement can be made into a question by a change in intonation, while leaving the word order unchanged. The second lesson introduces students to the transformation rules of yes-no questions, and how the tense and placement of 'be' affects this transformation. (For example, "The car has been sold." "Has the car been sold?") The next lesson introduces the transformations that produce wh- questions (who, what, how, when, why, and where). To affect this transformation, students come to see that some information in the statement is replaced by a question marker. ("Miriam is *upstairs.*" "*Where* is Miriam?") In the last lesson, students are introduced to echo questions. ("Fred left town." "Fred left town, didn't he?")

from *Language and How to Use it 6,* William Jenkins, Charlotte Huck, et al. ©1973, Scott, Foresman, & Co. pp. 213–220.

Critique

We question the usefulness of this level of transformational grammar to 6th grade students. The rules for transforming statements into questions are cumbersome, confusing, complex, and unnecessary. Teaching students transformation rules to memorize is less important than teaching insight into the meaning, significance, the *logic* of questions, their uses, and their relationship to statements.

We recommend that, if possible, these lessons on transformational grammar be dropped. If transformational grammar must be taught, then we suggest fostering independent thought by having students discover the transformations for themselves. Students already know how to transform statements into questions, they do it all the time. They could compare statements with their parallel questions and formulate rules which describe the differences between them.

More important and useful for the students than transformational grammar, is that they become aware of the *logic* of questions. Every question has a logic to it, in that each sets a specific task or set of tasks to be accomplished in order to settle it. There are different types of questions, each requiring different methods of settlement. How a question is settled is parallel to how the corresponding statement is verified. That is, to verify the statement "Cheetahs are an endangered species", one would need to do the same sorts of things as to settle the question, "Are cheetahs an endangered species?" To understand the question and its logic is to understand precisely what would have to be done to settle it.

To settle any question, we need to be aware of the kinds of tasks the question requires us to perform (or which any authority we may consult must have performed). We distinguish three such kinds of tasks: *1)* gathering facts, evidence, empirical information; *2)* evaluating; *3)* analyzing or clarifying concepts (words or phrases). Many questions are mixed, that is, they require two or all three kinds of tasks. Grasping the logic of a factual question requires sensitivity to what facts are relevant to the question, and how those facts can be gathered. Factual questions require sense-data for their settlement; some also require use of numbers (counting or measuring). If you can't gather the information yourself, you can use your analysis of the question to evaluate sources of the relevant information.

The second possible kind of task set by a question is evaluation, with the question asking us to judge which is better or worse, desirable or undesirable, right or wrong, healthy or unhealthy, good or bad, etc. It is important to notice that to ask for an evaluation is not to ask for mere opinion. It is true that some evaluative questions are only asking us for our personal preferences, as in the question, "Which flavor of ice cream is best?" I need only consult my own taste to settle it. The most problematic evaluative questions, however, do not ask for preference. Consider the question: Which ice cream is the creamiest? Here the question is not asking which ice cream I *think* is the creamiest, nor which *tastes* the creamiest, rather which ice cream *is* the creamiest. An evaluation is then made (for which facts must be gathered) of the various brands, with the criterion for the evaluation being their cream content. What we need to do to settle the question is to *examine* ice creams, not merely say which we like. Evaluation is not equivalent to expressing mere opinion. Furthermore, evaluative questions require facts.

The third possible task is analyzing concepts, in which we have to clarify vague or ambiguous words, phrases, or questions, or where the question is itself asking about the relationship between words or concepts. (For example, "Are bachelors ever married?" or "Do animals think?" The latter has a conceptual component insofar as what we include in and exclude from the category 'thinking' depends on the meaning we ascribe to the term.)

Questions are generally mixed, requiring some combination of clarification, evidence, and evaluation. For example, suppose someone was asked, "Which is the best car?" As it stands, the question is vague. It asks one of a number of more specific questions. In different contexts the question could be asking which car is my personal favorite; which gets the best mileage; which is safest; which, if used to drive clients around, would most help me make a sale. Upon deciding which question is meant, the reasoner would then decide what criteria would be appropriate for the evaluation. The criteria for evaluation in turn, tell the reasoner what kinds of facts to seek when actually examining or researching cars.

Similarly the question "Is the U. S. a true democracy?" requires all three types of tasks. First, the conceptual: What would have to be true of a form of government before we can call it a democracy? Must all citizens have power? Equal power? At what point would we say, "No, that country isn't a democracy," and call it something else instead? Such analysis sets up *criteria* for the evaluation. Once we know what, exactly, to look for, we can try to find the facts. Finally, we would have to decide whether or not the U.S. meets the criteria well enough to be judged a true democracy.

By discussing the requirements of various kinds of questions, students can become clearer, more accurate and precise thinkers. The value of a lesson on questions is that questions become the subject of *study*, rather than something to be answered before moving on. Students are forced to slow their thought down and examine it in detail.

Strategies used to remodel

S–13 clarifying issues, conclusions, or beliefs
S–28 thinking precisely about thinking: using critical vocabulary
S–14 clarifying and analyzing the meanings of words or phrases
S–15 developing criteria for evaluation: clarifying values and standards
S–31 distinguishing relevant from irrelevant facts

Remodelled Lesson Plan *s–13*

To keep to the transformational grammar objective, the teacher could put statements and questions on the board. "What are the differences between these and those? How can you tell when a sentence is a question? (When you read? When you listen?) How do these two kinds of sentences differ?" (Elicit transformational rules.)

To introduce students to the logic of questions, the teacher might begin by asking a question like: Which breed of dog is best? After students have discussed their answers, the teacher can begin to record some of the criteria presupposed in their answers. (Favorite, friendly, brave, pretty, etc.) Some students may ask what is meant by 'best,' or 'best for what?' If so, the teacher can proceed to the next paragraph without spending any more time on best breeds.

Students could then be asked a question like: Why did you give different answers? Point out to students that the question, as originally asked, is vague, and could be understood as asking any number of more specific questions. The teacher could then point out that students assumed an interpretation of the question. Students could explain what they think are the most important qualities for a dog to have. The teacher could also ask, "How could the question be clarified? How would you reformulate/reword the question to make clear what is meant? What more specific questions could be asked, instead?"

Individual students could be asked to reformulate the question so that it corresponds to the questions each answered. "What more specific question did Mary answer? David? Did they answer the same question?" (For example, the response, "German Shepherds, because they're brave and ferocious," answers the question, "What breed of dog makes a good guard dog?") The class could discuss what questions could help the questioner formulate a clearer question. (What do you mean by 'best breed?' Do you mean the friendliest, or best worker? Best breed for what purpose?)

When students have exhausted possible formulations, the teacher could focus on the phrase 'best breed,' or ask students to identify the unclear words. Point out that the phrase is evaluative and presupposes a *purpose* for making the evaluation, and *criteria* for evaluation. **S–28** Students could then take several reformulations and develop sets of criteria for each. **S–14** Point out that these are the criteria which can then be used to evaluate various breeds. **S–15** Here it is more important that students suggest criteria and give reasons, than that they give definitive lists of criteria.

Students are then in a position to discuss the kinds of *evidence* required by the new questions. Students could give examples of dogs that did and didn't meet one of the criteria. Or they could mention the kinds of evidence one would need to settle the various interpretations of the original question. They could discuss how the information could be gathered. (You would have to know how easy it is to train it to do this kind of thing; how each breed would act in this kind of situation; how much care it requires; its temperament.) Students could mention resource works wherein they might find relevant and reliable information, but they should not confuse how to *research* the answer with the *logic of the question,* (what we would have to do to find out for ourselves). The class could compare the evidence required by different specific questions, and so deepen their sense of the importance of clarity of expression. (If I want to know if a breed adjusts to living in an apartment, it does no good to learn that it's a good sheep-herder.) **S–31**

Students could gain further practice and insight by clarifying a variety of questions. The teacher could use questions like the following: Is the question clear? Do we know how to settle it? Do we know what each word means, and what they mean together in this combination? Is something being evaluated? What? Why? What criteria are appropriate? What kinds of facts would we need? Where would we have to go to get the evidence for ourselves? Are the facts easy or hard to get? Why? **S–13**

Any questions could be discussed. The class could discuss different kinds of questions from other textbooks. Here is a list of possible questions for analysis. We have broken them into categories, though they could be used in any order:

Empirical: How tall is Mary? Is popcorn heavy? How many miles is it from the Earth to the moon? Why does yeast make bread rise? What is the capital of New Jersey?

Evaluative: Is Sue a good baseball player? Is sugar good for you? Which skateboard is the best? (Each of these also requires facts.)

Conceptual: Is a whale a fish? Can a democracy be a dictatorship?

Mixed: Are Sarah and Tom friends? (If their relationship is borderline, the question will be more conceptual.) Is Jack happy? Was life a hundred years ago better or worse than life now?

"The Fountain Of Youth"

Objectives of the remodelled lesson

The students will:
- exercise independent thought by identifying and clarifying the main issues and ideas in a written selection about Ponce de León
- look at his actions, develop criteria for evaluating them, and evaluate them from different perspectives
- evaluate the author's reasoning about Ponce de León by examining his assumptions, and looking at the issues dialectically
- explore the differences between history, fiction, and historical fiction and develop the concept 'historical fiction' by analyzing and categorizing statements in the story

Original Lesson Plan

Abstract

Students read a piece of historical fiction about Ponce de León. It first describes his rule of Haiti (briefly) and Puerto Rico (in more detail). It then describes his unsuccessful search for the fountain of youth, discovery and naming of Florida, battle with Floridans, and death.

The questions focus on skills of characterization, and distinguishing fact from fiction in historical fiction. Students discuss the author's conclusions that Ponce de León was greedy, cruel, and unhappy.

from *Moments,* Marjorie Seddon Johnson, Roy A. Kress, et al. ©1977, American Book Company. pp. 178c–191b.

Critique

We chose this lesson for its thought provoking content, as a variation of "the fact/opinion" theme, and because it combines language arts with social studies.

Fact/Fiction

The text focuses on "the ability to distinguish fact from fiction", as a way to teach the characteristics of historical fiction. Like fact/opinion, the fact/fiction distinction is neither exhaustive nor exclusive. An evaluation or interpretation, though not fact, need not be fiction. In making a distinction between fact and fiction, the text equates fact with statements which "can be proven" and fiction with those which "cannot be proven". This is another, and quite different, distinction. Not every fact can be proven now. (What people said; how he first learned about the Fountain of Youth.) The lesson confuses three claims: evidence exists for this statement; this statement is true, this was the case; evidence *alone* confirms this statement.

As is usual with fact/opinion questions, in this selection, students are not in a position to know what can and can't be proven, what evidence exists, or what that evidence shows. It is even possible that the author's "facts" may be wrong. He may not have researched the subject well, or may be biased in his presentation. Given students' training in "the fact/opinion distinction", students may have difficulty distinguishing the facts of the ruler's life from the details used to enliven the selection. The text's treatment encourages impressionistic thinking. ("Well, it *sounds like* a fact.") It would be better to distinguish degrees of certainty, and means of possible verification, or to distinguish what the author probably thinks happened from mere literary embellishments and from interpretations and judgments.

Misconceptions

The text encourages the false view that historical accounts, as opposed to fiction, contain only facts, and no "opinions". Page 306 of the lesson plan has the question, *"Would you find opinions like this in a history book account of Ponce de León's governorship?"* An extension emphasizes that value judgments are not found in histories. Yet every historical account is written from a point of view, after evidence has been weighed, and each presupposes values. Every historian chooses which details to mention, how to portray them, and interprets their significance and meaning. An historical account which contains only factual information may still encourage one evaluation over another. For example, some facts may be stressed while others are downplayed or eliminated. The reader can be led to conclude that one side of a conflict is right and the other wrong, when it may not be that simple. Furthermore, historical accounts often make explicit evaluations of events and figures. One encyclopedia we consulted described Ponce de León as a protector of colonial settlers against harassing Indians. Students' history texts are full of judgment and interpretation.

Some inconsistencies regarding the governor's character arise in the lesson as a result of "the fact/opinion distinction" motivating many of the questions. Although students are sometimes encouraged to judge Ponce de León as "cruel, greedy, and selfish", and accept the judgment unquestioningly, at other times they are encouraged to place the judgment in the category of "author's opinion", and, therefore, arbitrary belief (or part of the "fiction"). Though not unquestionable, the claims admit of reasoned judgment, dialogical reasoning, and evaluation. At one point, students do have a limited discussion of the author's reasoning, and are asked whether they agree or disagree with the author. Yet they do not examine the issue, concepts, evidence, opposing evidence, or views in sufficient depth to make their conclusions more than impressionistic. Nor does the lesson encourage an in-depth consideration of the author's conclusion that the explorer was an unhappy man (the inevitable punishment for cruelty and greed).

Insufficient discussion and synthesis

The "Comprehension/Characterization" activity #2, at the end, fosters insight into point of view by having students write about the explorer from the point of view of a Spanish soldier, missionary, or Puerto Rican. This activity, however, is unintegrated with the rest of the lesson. Thus, any insights gained thereby are not synthesized with the rest of the discussions. Students do not develop a unified perspective from a dialogical consideration of this man. Similarly, though extension #1 has students research many sources, and note differences in their accounts, it lacks discussion regarding how different accounts could be reconciled or judged.

The "Concept" reads *"excessive greediness can lead to cruelty to others."* Given the author's emphasis, other main ideas seem more apt: "Money and power do not always bring happiness." or, "Even a powerful leader and capable explorer can be led on by the false promise of an enticing myth." In any case, students should discover the main point for themselves.

Strategies used to remodel

S–23 making interdisciplinary connections
S–1 thinking independently
S–5 developing intellectual humility and suspending judgment
S–2 developing insight into egocentricity or sociocentricity
S–25 reasoning dialogically: comparing perspectives, interpretations, or theories
S–20 analyzing or evaluating actions or policies
S–17 questioning deeply: raising and pursuing root or significant questions
S–30 examining or evaluating assumptions
S–18 analyzing or evaluating arguments, interpretations, beliefs, or theories
S–33 evaluating evidence and alleged facts
S–13 clarifying issues, conclusions, or beliefs
S–14 clarifying and analyzing the meanings of words or phrases

Remodelled Lesson Plan

We have divided this remodel into four sections. In the introduction, students find and begin to clarify the main point of the selection. The next section, "Exploring the author's reasoning," contains suggestions for in-depth discussion. We make suggestions for a unified (rather than scattered or "hit-and-run") discussion of the type of literature of the selection in the last section.

Introduction

The teacher may want to begin the lesson by asking if students have heard of the Fountain of Youth, and if so, what they know about the story. An introduction could also bring in any pertinent historical background students know. Research or history regarding European society and attitudes about the New World could be brought in as well. "What do you know about this time? What was happening? Why were Europeans here? What were relations between Europeans and Native Americans like?" **S–23**

When the selection has been read, have students retell the story in their own words. Have them distinguish the main points from the details. "What point is the author making? **S–1** Is it well made? What supports his point?" Have them analyze the main issues. (What kind of leader was he, good or cruel? Was he happy? Gullible? etc.) Have students identify and clarify the key concepts (possibilities include: 'greed,' 'oppressor,' 'cruel leader,' 'legitimate government,' 'unhappy life,' 'fool'). Have students describe what kinds of evidence would be required to justify using these words and their opposites.

The class could discuss the character's belief in the fountain: Was it reasonable for him to believe in the fountain of youth? Why did he believe in it? (All of the natives, from many places, believed in it. He wanted to believe in it.) Students could also mention other examples of leaders with mistaken beliefs. **S–5** The class could have an extended discussion of wishful thinking; how sometimes we believe only because we *want* to believe. Students can relate this problem to their own lives. **S–2**

Exploring the author's reasoning

Then, to unify discussion of the author's characterization, the teacher may ask, "What does the author think of the main character? Why? (The descriptions could be listed on the board.) How could we know whether the author's conclusions are justified?" Have them fill out the reasoning — not just pieces of it, but as a whole.

If evaluating Ponce de León as a ruler, students should consider both sides of the issue. Have students examine the author's point of view in depth. You could also ask, "What is left out? (A view favoring Ponce de León.) How would Ponce de León or those who approved of him respond?" *S–25* (His primary responsibility was to his King and Queen, and his men; the natives weren't Christian or civilized; he could take what he wanted because he was stronger.) "What, if anything, could justify his behavior? Was his appointment as governor justified? Why or why not?" *S–20* The letter writing and alternative sources exercises could be integrated into this discussion. *S–17* If so, students can discuss how the different accounts should be reconciled or evaluated. Have students compare the author's concepts and assumptions with concepts and assumptions of opposing views. *S–30* Have students discuss their own conclusions, and back them up with reasons. *S–18* Or, if they feel they are not in a position to come to a conclusion, have them describe the evidence they would need to be able to decide. *S–5* Such a discussion could lead into a discussion of the explorer's possible sociocentricity. *S–2*

Type of Literature: clarifying 'historical fiction' *S–17*

Rather than using scattered activities and questions to clarify the phrase (or concept) 'historical fiction,' the teacher may want to lead a more unified discussion. The teacher may point out that an author of historical fiction may do a lot of research, or little, and may even ignore what he knows in order to make the story more interesting. Students can distinguish parts of the selection that are clearly the author's additions from those that are clearly historical. Unclear cases could then be compared to those two groups and discussed. When discussing parts of the selection other than history, have students distinguish claims that probably reflect the author's beliefs and conclusions, from what the author merely added to enliven the selection, whether the added details affect their impression of the main character, and if so, how. *S–33*

Teachers using the text questions on fact versus fiction could rephrase and incorporate them. Rather than asking whether details can be proven, the teacher could ask, "Can anyone now know if this is true? How could we find out if this is true? (letters, ship's log, official documents, records, laws, proclamations, other first hand accounts, and physical evidence such as graves and abandoned living areas.) Would evidence alone tell us? Are we evaluating him? What criteria are appropriate? Why? Does the author mean for us to believe it happened just this way, or is this just to make the story more interesting?" *S–13*

The class could also distinguish historical fiction from history and from other types of fiction. Students could discuss examples they have read of each type of writing. (For example, their history texts may have literary embellishments such as conversations or fictional life stories.) They could then describe the features enabling them to categorize writings, and generalize about each type. *S-14*

If we simply present the teacher with pre-packaged finished lesson plans, designed by the critical thinking of someone else, someone who used a process that is not clearly understood by the teacher, then a major opportunity for the teacher to develop her own critical thinking skills, insights, and motivations will have been lost.

"Do Me a Favor"

Objectives of the remodelled lesson

The students will:
- isolate, clarify, and pursue root issues regarding the exchanging of favors
- clarify such concepts as 'favor', 'fairness', 'selfishness', and 'generosity' through Socratic questioning
- examine the assumptions of the main characters, and how they affect each characters' actions
- distinguish facts relevant and irrelevant to key issues
- evaluate the main characters' actions and attitudes
- compare plays to other forms of literature

Original Lesson Plan

Abstract

Students read a play about favors done and owed. Liza keeps a memo-book in which she records favors she does and receives. In the beginning of the play, she agrees to take a baby-sitting job for Karen, to whom she owes a favor. When her mother reminds her of a previous commitment, she demands that her brother, Hooker, baby-sit (*"Hooker, you have to baby-sit with Bobby Winters this afternoon."*), in return for a favor he owes her. Hooker had plans to hike to see the first day of an archeological dig with his friend Neil, but finally agrees to baby-sit. Then, when the girls' various commitments for the day are cancelled, they decide that, since Hooker didn't baby-sit, he should repay his favor to Liza by taking the girls on the hike. When Liza demands the favor, Hooker convinces Liza to stop using her book. The children agree that favors will no longer be "owed", but done for friendship's sake.

The teachers' text develops the "Concept" that *"People should do each other favors out of friendship and not because they would like a favor in return."* Many questions review the complex sets of causes and effects (favors returned because owed, plans changed because other plans changed, etc.) Others require discussion of the play format. The "Comprehension Skills" are cause and effect, prediction, and characterization.

from, *Lanterns*. Marjorie Seddon Johnson, et al. American Book Co. 1977. pp. 90c–105b.

Critique

We chose this lesson for its focus on favors and friendship and because the preachiness and degree of confusion are fairly typical of texts. The main issues raised in the play are important, and are problems within most students' experience. The lesson, however, suffers from two basic flaws: it oversimplifies complicated issues and contains a mish-mash of relevant and irrelevant questions.

Oversimplification

The play itself sets up a false dilemma (exemplified in the two main characters, Liza and Hooker) which the text questions do nothing to critique: Always agree to do favors without concern for inconvenience or being taken advantage of, or be selfish, petty, and dictatorial, demanding favor for favor, insisting on being paid back no matter what the circumstances. Students are led to the "Concept" quoted above, and led *to see that friendship may entail helping whenever necessary — without expecting anything in return.* The text treats this statement as equivalent to the "Concept," though expecting favors is not equivalent to doing favors in order to get favors. Throughout, both the play and teacher's notes unfairly push the idea that turning down a request is selfish. Besides violating students autonomy of thought, such treatment ignores a number of other reasonable positions.

In the text's view, any concern with being taken advantage of (continually doing favors, yet having your requests for favors repeatedly turned down, or wondering if your generosity is the sole glue in a relationship) is selfishness. The text (like Liza) takes the phrase 'expect a favor in return' too literally, by associating it with Liza and her memo-book. One can expect that, having done favors for another, one can reasonably expect gratitude and reciprocation, without keeping track of every favor, or demanding a one-for-one return. Students who have grappled with the problem of one-sidedness shouldn't be made to feel selfish. Students should have a chance to express a range of responses to such issues as, "When should I do favors for others? Do people ever owe each other favors?"

Putting the issue in all or nothing terms leads the text to ignore complications present, though unexplored, in the play. For example, when Liza asks Hooker to baby-sit, she asks him to give up a hike to the *first day* of an archeological dig — a special, once-in-a-lifetime opportunity. There are, after all, big favors and little favors. In this case, she may have been asking too much. Students could discuss details which might reasonably influence a judgment about what favors should be done or returned, and evaluate Liza's literal interpretations of such expressions as: I owe you one; any time you need a favor, etc.

Also, the text questions fail to have students distinguish Liza's views or record-keeping from her obnoxious manner. Her behavior is consistently dictatorial. She demands obedience, rather than asking for favors. (*"Hooker Forbes, you listen to me! ... Not so fast! ... We want to go to Indian Mounds, too .... You owe me a favor, Hooker Forbes. And I demand that you pay me back now. Right now."*) The idea that favors should be two-way is unfairly associated with her manner.

Students do not discuss the resolution. Liza gave up keeping her book after Hooker got Karen to admit that intention to repay a favor should be accepted as equivalent to having repaid it. Neither this idea nor its possible relevance (or irrelevance) to the agreement to forget about "owing favors" are addressed. Hence, confusions in the play are not sorted out by the text questions.

Some of the characterization questions oversimplify understanding and evaluation of characters. They ask students to infer qualities from only one action. Explaining a character requires using many details, and understanding the totality behind the details. (*"What was the difference between the way Liza felt and the way Hooker felt? Liza was angry. Hooker didn't care."* Here, the answers shed no light on the characters. *"Who is more thoughtful, Karen or Liza? (Karen) Why? (Karen came to explain the change in situation right away. Liza just ran off without explaining Hooker's involvement.)"* Here, students are encouraged to make an inference based on insufficient evidence.)

Unintegrated discussion

Rather than pursuing issues surrounding favors (and, perhaps, having a discussion about the play format), the text questions jump around. The numerous irrelevant, trivial questions take time away from exploration of the important, real issues. Such questions include the following: *What made Liza run into the kitchen?* (Rather than asking every possible question about cause and effect, the questioner should stick with those necessary to understanding the plot or the issues.) *Did you ever have two things to do at the same time? Do you ever make lists or write notes to help you remember things? Can you think of any occasions when you changed your plans and it forced someone else to change theirs? Why did Karen panic? Liza? Why does the fact that Liza and Karen are Junior Scouts prove they won't slow up Hooker and Neil? Have students discuss the skills learned in scouting.*

These questions are mixed with relevant questions. Students do not pursue the main issues in an integrated discussion, but occasionally touch on and then abandon the basic and related issues. Opinions on a number of issues are requested, but the ideas are not related to the main issues, nor are positions followed up. Questions don't search for reasons or underlying principles.

We suggest then, that the class more thoroughly, systematically, honestly, and fairmindedly explore the issues raised by the play.

Strategies used to remodel

S–17 questioning deeply: raising and pursuing root or significant questions
S–1 thinking independently
S–14 clarifying and analyzing the meanings of words or phrases
S–4 exploring thoughts underlying feelings and feelings underlying thoughts
S–31 distinguishing relevant from irrelevant facts
S–26 reasoning dialectically: evaluating perspectives, interpretations, or theories
S–7 developing intellectual good faith or integrity
S–10 refining generalizations and avoiding oversimplifications
S–20 analyzing or evaluating actions or policies
S–3 exercising fairmindedness
S–34 recognizing contradictions
S–21 reading critically: clarifying or critiquing texts
S–29 noting significant similarities and differences
S–35 exploring implications and consequences

Remodelled Lesson Plan S–17

> We have divided the remodel into the following sections: *1)* Introduction; *2)* Finding the main issues; *3)* Exploring the issues and avoiding oversimplification; and *4)* Discussion of the type of literature.

1) Introduction

Rather than beginning (as in the original) with a discussion of friendship, before reading the play, consider asking, "From the title, what is this piece about? **S–1** What is a favor? How do favors differ from orders, demands, obligations, etc.? **S–14** Why do people do favors? Does asking for or doing favors ever cause problems? What? Why?"

2) Finding the main issues S–1

Then, when the play has been read, have students recap the story. (Here, the teacher could use appropriate "cause and effect" questions from the original.) Use questions like the following to have students state the issues between, and basic positions of, the main characters: What is this play about? What point is the author trying to make? What issues are raised between the main characters? When does Liza get mad at Hooker? Why? What does her anger here tell us about her attitudes and beliefs? When does Hooker get mad at Liza? Why? What do his anger and annoyance tell us about his attitudes and beliefs? **S–4** What do you think are the most important issues raised in this play? **S–17**

When students reread the play, they can note details relevant to the main issues they formulated and the reasoning of the main characters. Students who want to focus on different issues could form groups to discuss the issues of their choice. Or students could write issues as headings, and list relevant details underneath. **S–31**

Who was being selfish?   **Were any favors owed?**   **Which requests were fair?**

3) Exploring the issues and avoiding oversimplification S–17

To help students focus on the factors relevant to understanding and evaluating positions taken in the play, have students use the details in the play and their own experiences to clarify the main concepts or ideas.

If the main claims or issues turn, for example, on the idea of the reasonableness of the various requests (or expectations) of the main characters, those concepts could be clarified. First, students could list all of the favors mentioned in the story. For each, ask whether it was a reasonable request or expectation. Have students explain their answers. Have them group the favors as reasonable, unreasonable, borderline, and disputed. (Students could also propose and categorize variations, for instance, "If Liza had asked nicely ...," "If Hooker wasn't doing anything ...," "I once ...," etc.) "What makes these unreasonable? Why is that relevant? What do the examples (in each group distinguished above) have in common? How do they differ? Why is this borderline? Why do we disagree about this case? What distinguishes (reasonable from unreasonable requests, generosity from selfishness, etc?" **S–14**

Or, if the issues students explore have to do with selfishness and generosity, have students similarly group the characters' reactions to requests made of them.

Such discussions could become dialectical if more than one view is expressed. If so, students could be paired or put in small groups for discussion, and main positions or points made could be shared with the rest of the class. **S–26**

Questions like the following can also be used, to help students relate the issues to their own experiences: Whom do people usually ask for favors? How do you feel about asking for favors? Doing favors? Always? Sometimes? Never? Have you ever been refused a favor? Why? Have you ever refused to do a favor? Why? Is it sometimes OK to not do somebody a favor? When? Why, or why not? **S–7** Have you ever felt that someone owed you a favor? That you owed someone? Why or why not? **S–10**

The class could describe and evaluate the actions or reasoning of the main characters at various points in the play. Use questions like the following: What do you think of Liza's (Hooker's) behavior in this scene? Why? What words apply to her behavior? Why? What, if anything, should she have done differently? (For each response, ask: If she *had* done this instead, what would you think of her behavior here?) **S–20** What reasons might she give in her defense? Why might she think this way? **S–3** Is this behavior consistent or inconsistent with the rest of her behavior? **S–34**

The teacher could also use the following questions from the text when appropriate: *Do you think Liza felt good about doing favors for people?* (or rephrase as "How do you think Liza felt about doing favors?") *Do you think that Hooker was being selfish or ungrateful in not wanting to pay back Liza's favor? Why did Liza promise to do Karen a favor? Why did Liza's brother refuse to baby-sit? What made Hooker say "Boy, you have to be careful what you say to her"? What kind of person do you think Hooker is? Why? What kind of a person would demand that a favor be paid back? Why did Liza put the memo pad in her pocket?* **S–17**

The class could also be asked whether they find the characters and their actions realistic. Have them support their claims. "In what ways is this character realistic? Unrealistic? Is this how people really are? In what ways? Why did the author make the characters like that?" **S–21**

4) Discussion of the type of literature S–17

The teacher could also have students discuss the type of literature this piece is, and the format of plays and compare plays to stories. Ask, "What kind of writing is this? How do you know? What do you know about plays? What do all plays have in common? Why?" **S–1** Have students compare plays to other forms of writing with questions like the following: How are plays different from stories? How did you know Liza's and Hooker's thoughts, attitudes, and feelings? How do you learn about these aspects of characters in stories? What are the differences between how stories and plays affect the reader? **S–29** When might it be best to write in the play format? Story format? **S–35** Discuss at length. The following questions from the original lesson could also be used: *Have you ever gone to a play and been given a program? What is usually listed in a program? Why do you think playwrights divide their plays into acts?*

Viewpoints

Objectives of the remodelled lesson

The students will:
- examine the assumptions underlying various interpretations and viewpoints
- think fairmindedly to gain insight into opposing viewpoints, to better understand and learn from them
- engage in dialogical discussions about particular points of view
- develop insight into egocentricity and intellectual good faith by discussing obstacles to fairmindedness

Original Lesson Plan

Abstract

This lesson on viewpoints has two parts. First, the teacher reads aloud a story entitled "The Blind Men and the Elephant," about six blind men who each feel a different part of an elephant, and come to different conclusions about it. Students are asked the following questions: *Why do people often feel that their opinions are the right ones? How can this attitude keep people from learning more about a subject? What advice would you give to an opinionated person? Do you think he would listen? How do you react to a person who won't listen to what you have to say? Do you always listen to what others have to say? Do you try to understand another person's viewpoint? Do you try to understand why he has a different point of view?*

An extension suggests six blindfolded students feel different parts of an object. Each writes two sentences describing it, which they read aloud. Then the teacher lists several incomplete sentences to encourage students to express different viewpoints, e.g., "*In my opinion, one way each one of us can contribute to a better world is ...*" The teacher points out that answers to questions like "*Which color sweater do you like best?*" are purely opinion, there is no right or wrong answer.

In the second part, students read a short piece of nonsensical verse in which a bat and a pup disagree about whether the world is upside-down or the bat merely sees it that way. Students then distinguish two meanings for the word 'viewpoint': Place from which one can look at something; attitude of mind. Next, students read and discuss a dialogue in which five different viewpoints about rain are expressed. Students are expected to recognize that the blind men's opinions about the elephant differed because each had different information; the people in the dialogue differed because each had different plans for the day. Students discuss three other subjects (school holiday, pet dog, bedtime) and say what they believe the viewpoints of different people would be. The teacher then leads students to see that when arguments occur, they should attempt to understand the viewpoints of all people concerned.

from *Language and How to Use It 4*
Andrew Schiller, et al. Scott, Foresman, and Co. © 1973 pp. 162–165.

Critique

Introduction

The subject of these lessons is valuable for teaching students to think critically by encouraging them to try to understand their own viewpoints and the viewpoints of others. The topic of viewpoints is very important, with implications for the academic and personal lives of the students.

Everyone has a unique perspective, or set of beliefs, parts of which are personal and unique to each individual, and parts of which are shared. No one is aware of all of his or her viewpoint, and few know how they acquired them. No viewpoint is complete and perfectly consistent, it can always be improved. Since every viewpoint has some inconsistencies and contradictions, people have a tendency to compartmentalize their viewpoints, so inconsistencies and contradictions rarely conflict. Many of people's contradictions are between the beliefs they espouse and those they act upon.

Beliefs have a logic. One's viewpoint is not a collection of separate beliefs, but is a system of beliefs. Each belief has a place in a viewpoint. Each presupposes some beliefs and implies others. Understanding a belief means understanding its assumptions and implications — the system of beliefs of which it is a part. Although we often disagree with viewpoints that we do not understand, we cannot justifiably do so. Before we can rationally disagree we must know what we disagree with. The viewpoints of others, even if we find we cannot wholly agree with them, probably have some merits, some strengths, that we could use to supplement, strengthen, and enrich our own. When trying to understand another viewpoint, we should try to understand *why* the other thinks differently.

The stories in these lessons do provide some insights into the subject, but in many ways they are inadequate. By failing to be more thorough, the text misses the opportunity to fully develop the idea of viewpoints and how they affect reasoning. They mainly focus on two reasons for differences in viewpoints: different information, as in the elephant story, and "personal reasons" (for example, different plans and intentions), as in the rainy day dialogue. These kinds of reasons superficially address the topic, and are not the best for developing key insights, confronting problems of clash of perspective, and finding strategies to deal with them. The lessons don't address connections between beliefs. Nowhere do they address *evaluating* beliefs or systems of beliefs, merely sharing and supporting them.

Elephant Story

The story of the elephant and the blind men makes a fair beginning, as it focuses on an important source of disagreement — different information (and stubbornness). However, unlike most cases of conflicting viewpoints, the story does not adequately exemplify the ways in which interest, prejudice, and viewpoint often affect the selection, identification, and interpretation of information, nor do the questions help focus on these tendencies. We tend to protect our viewpoints by only considering the strongest information in their support, while not seeing information which may weaken them. Conversely, regarding viewpoints to which we are opposed, we often look for their weakest support and ignore the strongest. Thus, we often do not have complete information because we do not *want* it, and fail to recognize alternative interpretations of it. Unlike most cases, which require weighing of interpretations, judging of credibility, and so on, the blind men need only put their facts together. Also, the situation of the blind men and the elephant is too unlike most situations involving lack of information; students are unlikely to transfer the insight to their lives.

The original questions in the teachers' notes (quoted in the abstract) call for yes-or-no answers from students. The way they are phrased encourages students to give the "good person" answer, rather than having students discuss times when, and reasons why, they often fail to live up to the ideals emphasized in the lesson. Thus, the lesson inadvertently encourages intellectual bad faith.

The discussions suggested in this lesson's extension could be improved. Discussion of the first three sentence fragments, (*In my opinion, one way each of us can contribute to a better world is .... Adults can learn something from children by .... When judging someone else, it is important to ....*) could expose the logic of the beliefs expressed, looking for compatibilities and inconsistencies between various answers.

The last three suggested statements (*If I were an umpire at a baseball game, my hardest job would be .... When I look at the summer sky I see .... The most attractive color for a sweater is ....*) are statements about the speaker and idiosyncratic. As the text points out, "*... many answers are purely opinion. There is no 'right' or 'wrong,' or 'better' or 'worse' judgment.*" Preference statements allow for little or no rational discussion or assessment. These lessons — and texts in general — neglect that most important and difficult area wherein there *are* right or wrong, better or worse judgments.

The subject of umpires' experiences could be used to illustrate conflicts arising from differing viewpoints (umpires as against players and fans of each team), leading students to explore the way in which points of view, purpose, and self interest can affect the responses of different people to umpires' calls. The others could be used to help students distinguish types of issues.

The teacher using these lessons should be careful of "the fact/opinion distinction" implicit in them.

Viewpoints

As with the elephant story, the discussion about the rainy afternoon fails to get at the root of the problem of clash of viewpoints since agreement is neither necessary nor of any significance. On the other hand, two of the subjects at the end of the lesson — the pet dog and bedtime — are better for our purposes, as they do illustrate vast differences in viewpoint in situations requiring agreement or resolution. This activity could more fruitfully foster critical insight (especially insight into the ways *interest* affects viewpoints and evaluation of other's views) by extending the discussion to greater length, encouraging students to incorporate others' perspectives, evaluate arguments, etc. Other situations involving differing viewpoints could also be discussed, but should include some amount of conflict and not merely casual disagreement.

The explanation section recommends that the teacher lead students to two generalizations about conflicting viewpoints: people disagree because of personal attitudes and because of incomplete information. Both of these do contribute to conflicting viewpoints, but the list oversimplifies the problem. A viewpoint will often influence which information we look for, which facts we will emphasize or down-play, accept or reject. Students could be encouraged to recognize the tendency to select evidence which supports their perspective, while discounting evidence which may weaken it. The subjects at the end of the lesson (pet dog, for example), can be used to illustrate this. The facts which a parent may consider in deciding whether to get a dog, may seem irrelevant to the child. Self-interest often interferes with a fair consideration of the other's point of view.

The text doesn't talk about what to do besides "*impartially weighing the viewpoints of all concerned.*" Again, this is fine, as far as it goes, but is insufficient. (What exactly does this mean, and how does one go about doing it?) The text gives no guidance or practice in impartially weighing viewpoints. Students do not assess information, or the ways information could be interpreted. Superficially, students are asked to consider different viewpoints (at the end) but instruction could be made more explicit by probing and evaluating the assumptions, reconciling differences, and looking for and using more complete information.

Strategies used to remodel

S-7　developing intellectual good faith or integrity
S-30　examining or evaluating assumptions
S-5　developing intellectual humility and suspending judgment
S-3　exercising fairmindedness
S-31　distinguishing relevant from irrelevant facts
S-28　thinking precisely about thinking: using critical vocabulary
S-22　listening critically: the art of silent dialogue
S-2　developing insight into egocentricity or sociocentricity
S-32　making plausible inferences, predictions, or interpretations

Remodelled Lesson Plan s-7

The remodelled lesson plan has been divided into three sections: *1)* focuses on problems with information, *2)* applies insights gained to students' lives and thought, *3)* considers actual or imagined situations of conflict arising from different points of view, examining and assessing assumptions which may underlie each perspective.

1) Information and differing viewpoints

After reading the first story, the teacher could supplement the questions from the original (in italics) with a few others: *Did any of the six blind men give an accurate description of an elephant? Why not? In what way was each man's description partly right?* What could the men have accurately said? What was each assuming? **S-30** *How could the men have helped one another to "see" the elephant? Why weren't they likely to do so?* Why did the men disagree? Do people often make assumptions similar to those made by the men in the story? Why? Students could also discuss times they thought they had the whole story, but after learning more, changed their conclusions about an event or situation. **S-5**

2) Applying insights

To encourage students to apply the above insights to their own lives and experiences, the teacher could have them tell about a time two people interpreted the same situation differently. "What were the interpretations? Why were they different? Can they be reconciled? How? Why not?" If necessary, provide an example like the following: One morning I come in, and am very unfriendly to everyone. What might you conclude? How could my behavior be interpreted? Discuss how different points of view affected conclusions. Have students make assumptions explicit. **S-30**

For an extension of the first lesson, the teacher can substitute different sentences for those in the book. It would be helpful if the class has already had discussions which brought out different perspectives or if there are school or class issues or problems to discuss. Evaluative statements, especially ethical judgments, provide for good topics. Students could also discuss the claims from an opposing view. **S-3** Students could point out specific points of agreement or disagreement. Have students find assumptions in the various points of view. **S-30** Students could also be asked to identify information supporting assumptions and viewpoints, as well as suggest information that may have been left out. **S-31** Students could write and share their responses and engage in extended discussion. The class could be split into discussion groups to maximize participation and allow students choice of issue. The teacher could have students record or take notes on their discussions for analysis later.

Using the recordings or notes, students could give complete statements of perspectives with which they disagree. **S-3** (This activity can be discussed later, and any difficulties students experienced shared.) Students can correct any misconceptions of their own ideas. They could then categorize the kinds of points of disagreement (contradictory factual claims, incompleteness of facts, questions of relevance, interpretation, values, relative importance of different values, preferences, problems with words or concepts). Some students may want to map out viewpoints showing the connections between different beliefs in a perspective. (These facts and this assumption led to this conclusion. That conclusion and this other belief led to this other conclusion ....) **S-28** Some students may find ways to reconcile some of the differences. If so, these could be discussed and evaluated. Students may want to speculate on some of the reasons for their disagreements. **S-22**

3) Conflicts and difficulties in listening S-2

Although many conflicts are obviously based on a lack of information, there are other bases for disagreement. It is not always easy to get both sides in a conflict to agree as to what is relevant to the conflict. For example, parents want their child to go to bed, but the child does not want to. For the parents to say, "You have school in the morning", may not seem relevant to the child. To foster insights into the children's egocentricity, the teacher could extend the last activity of the last lesson. Students might use role-playing to bring out parents', neighbors', and siblings' views on the subjects given. The class can describe the perspectives at length, again, comparing similarities and differences between different beliefs expressed, and discuss possible reasons for these differences. **S-22** ("What might a neighbor think about your dog? Why?") **S-32**

The discussion in the first lesson can be used here, supplemented with students' experiences in giving opposing views during this activity, and that in section 2. These questions have been taken from the explanation section #1 of the original (quoted in the abstract) and rephrased to foster independent thinking, intellectual good faith, and extend discussion. Why is it sometimes hard to listen? Why do people have different viewpoints? (Encourage multiple responses.) Why is it often hard to understand another's view? When have you found it the hardest to listen sympathetically to other viewpoints? Why? What was going on in your head? **S-7**

All the various strategies explained in the hand-book are couched in terms of behaviors. The principles express and describe a variety of behaviors of the 'ideal' critical thinker; they become applications to lessons when teachers canvass their lesson plans to find appropriate places where those behaviors can be fostered. The practice we recommend helps guard against teachers using these strategies as recipes or formulas, since in each case good judgment is required in the application process.

Introduction to Remodelling Social Studies Lessons

Introduction

Social studies is nothing more or less than the study of how humans live together as a group in such a way that their dealings with one another affect their common welfare. All of us, like it or not, engage in social study. We all, in our everyday lives, attend to, generalize, and reason about how we are living together in our respective groups. We pay special attention to the groups that are of immediate interest to us. But we develop concepts of other groups as well. We make judgments about the effect upon our welfare of groups behaving as they do. We make judgments about the effect of our group's behavior upon other groups. We gather evidence from experience, from books, and from the media that we use to justify conclusions we come to about our own groups, our own society, and about other groups, including that of other societies.

In point of fact, all children, as a result of thousands of hours of TV watching and thousands of interactions with others, internalize hundreds of judgments about people and groups, and about what is and is not appropriate social behavior, before they enter any school room. Piaget's studies of children, particularly his study for UNESCO, illustrate this point well. Consider the following excepts from his interviews of children of different ages from different nations. In them we have evidence that the everyday realities of children's lives typically have a more profound effect on what they learn about the nature of social behavior than what we think we are teaching them in the classroom:

> *Michael M.* (9 years, 6 months old): Have you heard of such people as foreigners? *Yes, the French, the Americans, the Russians, the English ....* Quite right. Are there differences between all these people? *Oh yes, they don't speak the same language.* And what else? *I don't know.* What do you think of the French, for instance? Do you like them or not? Try and tell me as much as possible. *The French are very serious, they don't worry about anything, an' it's dirty there.* And what do you think of the Russians? *They're bad, they're always wanting to make war.* And what's your opinion of the English? *I don't know ... they're nice ....* Now look, how did you come to know all you've told me? *I don't know ... I've heard it ... that's what people say.*

Maurice D. (8 years, 3 months old): If you didn't have any nationality and you were given a free choice of nationality, which would you choose? *Swiss nationality.* Why? *Because I was born in Switzerland.* Now look, do you think the French and the Swiss are equally nice, or the one nicer or less nice than the other? *The Swiss are nicer.* Why? *The French are always nasty.* Who is more intelligent, the Swiss or the French, or do you think they're just the same? *The Swiss are more intelligent.* Why? *Because they learn French quickly.* If I asked a French boy to choose any nationality he liked, what country do you think he'd choose? *He'd choose France.* Why? *Because he was born in France.* And what would he say about who's the nicer? Would he think the Swiss and the French equally nice or one better than the other? *He'd say the French are nicer.* Why? *Because he was born in France.* And who would he think more intelligent? *The French.* Why? *He'd say that the French want to learn quicker than the Swiss.* Now you and the French boy don't really give the same answer. Who do you think answered best? *I did.* Why? *Because Switzerland is always better.*

Marina T. (7 years, 9 months old): If you were born without any nationality and you were given a free choice, what nationality would you choose? *Italian.* Why? *Because it's my country. I like it better than Argentina where my father works, because Argentina isn't my country.* Are Italians just the same, or more, or less intelligent than the Argentinians? What do you think? *The Italians are more intelligent.* Why? *I can see the people I live with, they're Italians.* If I were to give a child from Argentina a free choice of nationality, what do you think he would choose? *He'd want to stay an Argentinian.* Why? *Because that's his country.* And if I were to ask him who is more intelligent, the Argentinians, or the Italians, what do you think he would answer? *He'd say Argentinians.* Why? *Because there wasn't any war.* Now who was really right in the choice he made and what he said, the Argentinian child, you, or both? *I was right.* Why? *Because I chose Italy.*

The fact, then, that children form much of their thinking about how humans live together in groups as a result of their own native egocentrism, buttressed by the sociocentrism of those around them in everyday life, is one major problem for instruction. But it is not the only problem. The other major problem lies in the fact that when highly intelligent and well educated scholars from different societies study how humans live together in groups they sometimes differ significantly in the conclusions they come to. Human social behavior can be studied, to put this another way, from different points of view. And the conclusions one comes to about human behavior in part depend on the point of view from the perspective of which one studies behavior. That is why there are different schools of thought in social studies.

We believe that these two major problems for social studies instruction entail an important general strategy for teaching. To combat the first problem it is essential that the bulk of activities focus on engaging the student's own thinking, so that the thinking that students actually use on social problems in their everyday lives are explicitly discovered by the students and, where appropriate, challenged. To combat the second major problem it is essential that students discover and enter into dialogue with more than one point of view, indeed with multiple points of view. These two needs come together if we turn progressively away from a didactic approach to teaching and focus progressively on a critical approach (See Chapter 8, "Thinking Critically About Teaching", for a fuller account).

The major problem to overcome in remodelling social studies units and lessons, then, is that of transforming *didactic* instruction within *one* point of view into *dialogical* instruction within *multiple* points of view. As teachers, we should see ourselves not as dispensers of absolute truth nor as proponents of uncritical "relativity", but as careful, reflective seekers after truth, as involved in a search in which we invite our students to participate. We continually need to remind ourselves that each person has a somewhat different point of view, that each point of view rests on assumptions about human nature, that thinking of one point of view as *the truth* limits our understanding of the very thing we want to grasp. Practice entering into and coming to understand divergent points of view, on the other hand, heightens our insight into the real problems of our lives.

Children, as we have already underscored, already face the kinds of issues studied in social studies and are engaged in developing views on questions like the following:

What does it mean to belong to a group? Does it matter if others do not approve of me? Is it worthwhile to be good? What is most important to me? How am I like and unlike others? Whom should I trust? Who are my friends and enemies? What are people like? What am I like? How do I fit in with others? What are my rights and responsibilities? What are others' rights and responsibilities?

We humans live in a world of human meanings. There is always more than one way to give meaning to our behavior. We create points of view, ideologies, religions, and philosophies that often conflict with each other. Children need to begin to understand the implications of these crucial insights: that all accounts of human behavior are expressed within a point of view; that no one account of what happened can possibly cover all the facts; that each account stresses some facts over others; that when an account is given (by a teacher, student, or textbook author), the point of view in which it is given should be identified and, where possible, alternative points of view considered; and finally, that points of view need to be critically analyzed and assessed. Of course, the introduction of children to these truths must take place slowly, concretely, and dialogically. We must be on the alert for occasions that facilitate student discoveries in this area. We must be patient and think in terms of their development of insights over a period of years.

Adults, as well as children, tend to assume the truth of their own unexamined points of view. People often unfairly discredit or misinterpret ideas based on assumptions differing from their own. To address social issues critically, students must continually evaluate their beliefs by contrasting them with opposing beliefs. From the beginning, social studies instruction should encourage dialogical thinking, that is, the fairminded discussion of a variety of points of view and their underlying beliefs. Of course, this emphasis on the diversity of human perspectives should not be covered in a way that implies that all points of view are equally valid. Rather, students should learn to value critical thinking skills as tools to help them distinguish truth from falsity, insight from prejudice, accurate conception from misconception.

Dialogical experience in which children begin to use critical vocabulary to sharpen their thinking and their sense of logic, is crucial. Words and phrases such as 'claims', 'assumes', 'implies', 'supports', 'is evidence for', 'is inconsistent with', 'is relevant to' should be carefully and progressively integrated into such discussions. We should begin to introduce students to the vocabulary of educated thinking as soon as possible, but we should start from simple, intuitive examples that come from their own experience.

Formulating their own views of historical events and social issues enables students to synthesize data from divergent sources and to grasp important ideas. Too often, students are asked to recall details with no synthesis, no organizing ideas, and no distinction between details and basic ideas or between facts and common U.S. interpretations of them. Students certainly need opportunities to explicitly learn basic principles of social analysis, but more importantly they need opportunities to *apply* them to real and imagined cases and to develop insight into social analysis.

As people, students have an undeniable right to develop their own social perspective — whether conservative or liberal, whether optimistic or pessimistic — but they should also learn over time to analyze their perspectives, to compare them accurately with other perspectives, and to scrutinize the facts they conceptualize and judge in the social domain with the same care required in any other domain of knowledge.

Students should, in other words, become as adept in using critical thinking principles in the social domain as we expect them to be in scientific domains of learning. We should begin as soon as possible to foster an attitude of applying sound standards of judgment to every area of learning and we should do so in concrete, engaging ways, so that students are continually engaged in activities that are disciplining their thinking and developing their insight into the standards by which they and we are assessing that thinking.

Traditional lessons cover several important subjects within social studies: politics, economics, history, anthropology, and geography. Critical education in social studies focuses on basic questions in each subject, and prepares students for their future economic, political, and social roles.

Some Common Problems with Social Studies Texts

- End-of-chapter questions often ask for recall of a random selection of details and key facts or ideas. Minor details are often given the same emphasis as important events and principles. Students come away with collections of sentences but little sense of how to distinguish major from minor points. The time and space given to specifics should reflect their importance.

- Often the answers to review questions are found in the text in bold or otherwise emphasized type. Thus, students need not even understand the question, let alone the answer, to complete their assignments.

- Time-lines, maps, charts and graphs are presented and read as mere drill rather than as aids to understanding deeper issues. Students do not learn to *read* them or *use* them. Students do not develop useful schemas of temporal or spatial relationships — time-lines and globes in their heads.

- Texts rarely have students extend insights to analogous situations in other times and places. Students do not learn to *use* insights or principles to understand specifics. They do not learn to recognize recurring patterns.

- Although texts treat diversity of opinion as necessary, beliefs are not presented as subject to examination or critique. Students are encouraged to accept that others have different beliefs but are not encouraged to understand why. Yet only by understanding *why* others think as they do, can students profit from considering other points of view. The text writers' emphasis on simple tolerance serves to end discussion, whereas students should learn to consider judgments as subject to rational assessment.

- Students are not encouraged to recognize and combat their own natural ethnocentricity. Texts encourage ethnocentricity in many ways. They often present U.S. ideals as uniquely ours when, in fact, every nation shares at least some of them. Although beliefs about the state of the world and about how to achieve ideals vary greatly, the U.S. version of these is often treated as universal or self-evident. Students should learn not to confuse their limited perspective with universal belief.

- Ethnocentricity is reflected in word choices that assume a U.S. or Western European perspective. For example, cultures are described as "isolated" rather than as "isolated from Europe". Christian missionaries are described as spreading or teaching "religion" rather than "Christianity". Cultures are evaluated as "modern" according to their similarity to ours. In addition, texts often assume, imply, or clearly state that most of the world would prefer to be just like us. The "American Way of Life" and policies, according to the world view implied in standard texts, is the pinnacle of human achievement and presents the best human life has to offer. That others might believe the same of their own cultures is rarely mentioned or considered.

- Texts often wantonly omit crucial concepts, relationships, and details. For example, in discussing the opening of trade relations between Japan and the U.S., one text failed to mention why the Japanese had cut off relations with the West. Another text passed over fossil fuels and atomic energy in two sentences.

• Most texts treat important subjects superficially. There seems to be more concern for the outward appearance of things and trivial details than for their underlying dynamics. Texts often cover different political systems by merely listing the titles of political offices. Most discussions of religion reflect the same superficiality. Texts emphasize names of deities, rituals, and practices. But beliefs are not explored in depth; the inner life is ignored, the personal dimension omitted. Geography texts are filled with such trivia as names of currencies, colors of flags, vegetation, and so on. Students do not learn important information about other countries. Important information that is covered is usually lost amidst the trivia and so soon forgotten.

• Many texts also tend to approach the heart of the matter and then stop short. Important topics are introduced, treated briefly, and dropped. History, for instance, is presented as merely a series of events. Texts often describe events briefly but seldom mention how people perceived them, why they accepted or resisted them, or what ideas and assumptions influenced them. Problems are dismissed with, "This problem is very complicated. People will have to work together to solve it." In effect, this tells students that when something is complicated, they shouldn't think about it or try to understand it. Students do not learn how to sort out the contributing factors or develop and assess specific solutions.

• Texts often encourage student passivity by providing all the answers. Students are not held accountable for providing significant answers on their own. Texts usually err by asking questions students should be able to answer on their own, and then immediately providing the answer. Once students understand the system, they know that they don't have to stop and think for themselves because the text will do it for them in the next sentence.

• After lengthy map skills units, students are asked to apply those skills to answer simple, pointless questions. ("Find the following cities:") Students practice reading maps in their texts for reasons provided by the texts. They are not required to determine for themselves what questions a map can answer, what sort of map is required for this or that problem, or how to find it. Map reading practice could be used to develop students' confidence in their abilities to reason and learn for themselves, but rarely is. Graphs and charts are treated similarly.

• Although the rich selections of appendices are convenient for the students, they discourage students from discovering where to find information on their own. In real life, problems are not solved by referring to a handy chart neatly labeled and put into a book of information on the subject. In fact few, if any, complex issues are resolved by perusing one book. Instead, we should teach students to decide what kind of information is necessary and how to get it. In addition, many of the appendices are neatly correlated, designed and labeled to answer precisely those questions asked in the text. Students therefore do not develop the strategies they need to transfer their knowledge to the issues, problems, and questions they will have as adults.

• Texts often emphasize the ideal or theoretical models of government, economic systems, and institutions without exploring real (hidden) sources of power and change. Texts rarely distinguish ideals from the way a system might really operate in a given situation. They often give people's *stated* reasons as the *real* reasons for their actions.

• Explanations are often abstract and lack detail or connection to that which they explain, leaving students with a vague understanding. Texts fail to address such questions as: *How* did this bring about that? What was going on in people's minds? Why? How did that relate to the rest of society? Why is this valued? Without context, the bits have little meaning and therefore, if remembered at all, serve no function and cannot be recalled for use.

Subject-Specific Problems

There are somewhat different problems which emerge in each of the areas of social studies. It is important to identify them.

175

History

- Although texts *mention* that to understand the present one must understand the past, they fail to *show* students the necessity of knowing historical background. They fail to illustrate *how* current situations, events, problems, conflicts, and so on can be better understood and addressed by those who understand how they came to be. "It is important to understand the past" becomes a vague slogan rather than a crucial insight which guides thought.

- Although texts refer to past problems, give the solutions attempted, and mention results, students don't evaluate them *as solutions.* They don't look at what others did about the same problem, nor do they analyze causes or evaluate solutions for themselves. We recommend that teachers ask, "To what extent and in what ways did this solve the problem? Fail to solve it? Create new problems?" Students should assess solutions people have tried and argue for their own solutions.

- When discussing causes and results of historical events, texts present the U.S. interpretation as though it were fact. They often treat historical judgment and interpretation as though they were facts on the order of dates. Thus, students gain little or no insight into historical reasoning, into how one reasonably decides that this caused that.

- When texts present negative information about the U.S., they don't encourage students to explore its consequences or implications. Students are not encouraged to refine their judgment by judging past actions and policies.

- Primary sources, when used or referred to at all, are not examined as sources of information or as explications of important attitudes and beliefs which shaped events. Their assessment is not discussed, nor are influences which shape that assessment. Texts fail to mention, for example, that most history was written by victors of wars and by the educated few. Much information about other points of view has been lost. Most selections from primary sources are trivial narratives.

Politics

- Traditional lessons stress that we should all be good citizens, but fail to explore what that entails (for example, the importance of assessing candidates and propositions before voting).

- Texts tend to make unfair comparisons, such as comparing the *ideal* of governments of the U.S. and its allies to the *real* Soviet government.

- Important ideals, such as freedom of speech, are taught as mere slogans. Students read, recall, and repeat vague justifications for ideals, rather than deepen their understanding of them and of the difficulty in achieving them. In effect, such ideas are taught as though they were facts on the order of the date a treaty was signed. Texts do not, for example, have students discuss the positive aspects of dissent such as the need to have a wide-ranging open market of ideas.

- Texts often confuse facts with ideals and genuine patriotism with show of patriotism or false patriotism. The first confusion discourages us from seeing ourselves, others, and the world accurately; we fail to see the gap between how we want to be and how we are. The second encourages us to reject constructive criticism. The concept of love of one's country is reduced to a pep rally.

Economics

- Texts assume our perspective on economics. They fail to explain how other systems work. Students are ill-prepared to understand the economies of other countries.

- Texts generally contrast *ideal* capitalism with *real* socialism. Students come away with the idea that what we have needs no improvement and with a set of overly negative stereotypes of others.

- Texts cover economic systems superficially, neglecting serious and in-depth coverage of *how* they are supposed to work (for example, in our system, people must make rational choices as consumers, employers, employees, and voters). Students are left with vague slogans rather than realistic understanding and the ability to *use* principles to understand issues, problems, and specific situations.

Anthropology

- Cultural differences are often reduced to holidays and foods rather than values, perspectives, habits, and more significant customs, giving students little more than a superficial impression of this field. Students fail to learn how much people (themselves included) are shaped by their cultures, that their culture is only one way of understanding or behaving, or how much hostility is generated by culture clashes. For example, what happens when someone from a culture wherein looking someone in the eye is rude meets someone from a culture wherein *avoiding* another's eye is rude? Each feels offended, becomes angry at the other who breaks the rules. Are "Germans cold", or do "Americans smile too much"? Texts overemphasize tolerance for food and clothing differences but often neglect developing insight into more important or problematic differences.

Geography

- Texts more often use maps to show such trivialities as travelers' and explorers' routes (At which of these three places did he land first? Second?) than to illuminate the history and culture of the place shown and the lives of the people who actually live there.

- Texts fail to explain *why* students should know specific details. For example, texts mention chief exports, but don't have students explore their implications or consequences: What does this tell us about this country? The people there? It's relationships with other countries? Environmental problems? Economic problems? International and domestic politics?

What ties many of these criticisms together and points to their correction is the understanding that study of each subject should teach students how to *reason* in that subject, and this requires that students learn how to synthesize their insights into each subject to better understand their world. The standard didactic approach, with its emphasis on giving students as much information as possible, neglects this crucial task. Even those texts which attempt to teach geographical or historical reasoning do so only occasionally, rather than systematically. By conceptualizing education primarily as passing data to students, texts present *products* of reasoning. A critical approach, emphasizing root questions and independent thought, on the other hand, helps students get a handle on the facts and ideas and offers students crucial tools for thinking through the problems they will face throughout their lives. Remember, it is not the number of facts that we give them that counts, it is the number of facts they understand and use.

Students need assignments that challenge their ability to assess actual social behavior. Such assignments will, of course, produce divergent conclusions by students depending on their present leanings. Student thinking, speaking, and writing should be graded not on some authoritative set of substantive answers, but rather on the quality of student thinking. This requires of course that we explicitly discuss with our students the precise qualities we are looking for in their work.

Over time, there should be, for example, many illustrations of sentences that are clear in contrast to sentences that are vague and ambiguous. There should be many illustrations and discussions of what it means to elaborate a point and illustrate it with examples. There should be many illustrations and discussions of what it means to support a point with reasons clearly stated. There should be many illustrations and discussions of what it means to collect evidence. There should be illustrations and discussions of what it means to question the source of information, what it means to try to determine whether what is said in a book is questionable or not.

There should be many illustrations and discussions of what it means to have a point of view and to see an event from this or that point of view.

These many illustrations and discussions should, over time, help students develop intellectual standards for their own thought and for assessing the thought of others. Many of these discussions may be based in other areas of the curriculum. For example, the same intellectual standards need to be developed in all areas: in language arts, in social studies, in math, and in science. The same intellectual standards are necessary whenever we read, write, speak, and listen. All students need to learn the importance of trying to be clear, precise, accurate, logical, relevant, practical, and so forth. (See the diagram on "Perfections and Imperfections of thought", Regarding a Definition of Critical Thinking", and the Glossary.) Each area or domain or study applies these standards with some individual variations, but there is much more in common than is different.

The problem now is that most students are not developing any intellectual standards. Doing well in school is learning how to perform for, how to please the teacher — that is what most students are coming to believe. We in the classroom need to teach in such a way that students do not draw this conclusion. We need to teach so that progressively over time the students become more and more clear about the standards they are using in their thinking. Students should be discovering that they have a mind and that it is possible to discipline it, just as it is possible to discipline the body. In both cases, they should come to understand what develops that fitness and what undermines it.

Some Recommendations for Action

Students in social studies, regardless of level, should be expected to begin to take responsibility for their own learning. This means that they must begin to develop the art of independent thinking and study and begin to cultivate intellectual and study skills. This includes elementary steps in learning to critique the text in use.

Discussions and activities should be designed or remodelled by the teacher to develop the students' use of critical reading, writing, speaking, and listening. Furthermore, students should begin to get a sense of the interconnecting fields of knowledge within social studies, and the wealth of connections between these fields and others, such as math, science, and language arts.

The students should not be expected to memorize a large quantity of unrelated facts, but rather to begin to think in terms of interconnected domains of human life and experience. This includes elementary forms of identifying and evaluating various viewpoints; gathering and organizing information for interpretation; distinguishing facts from ideals, interpretations, and judgments; recognizing relationships and patterns; and applying insights to current events and problems.

Students should repeatedly be encouraged to identify the perspective of their texts, imagine or research other perspectives, and compare and evaluate them. This means, among other things, that words like 'conservatism' and 'liberalism', the 'right' and 'left', must begin to become more than vague jargon; they must be progressively recognized as names of different ways of thinking about human nature and society.

Students need to begin to experience actually thinking within diverse political perspectives. No perspective, not even one called 'moderate', should be presented as *the* correct one. By the same token, we should be careful not to lead the students to believe that all perspectives are equally justified or that important insights are equally found in all points of view. Beware especially of the misleading idea that the truth always lies in the middle of two extremes. We should continually encourage and stimulate our students to think and never do their thinking for them. We should, above all, teach, not preach.

History

History lessons should show students how to reason, and actually engage them in reasoning historically. They should help them discover why historical reasoning is necessary to understanding the present and to making rational decisions regarding the future. To learn to reason historically, students must discuss issues dialogically, generating and assessing multiple interpretations of events they study. This requires students to distinguish facts from interpretations. It also requires that they develop a point of view of their own.

- Many crucial historical insights have analogies in students' lives which can be used to clarify historical events. For example, as with wars between nations, relatively few childhood conflicts are entirely caused by *one* side. Most result from an escalation of hostilities in which both sides participate.

- Dates are useful not so much as things-in-themselves, but as markers placing events in relation to each other and within a context (historical, political, anthropological, technological, etc.). To reason historically, we need to orient ourselves to events in relation to each other. So when you come across a particular date, you might ask the students to discuss in pairs what events came before and after it and to consider the significance of this sequence. They might consider the possible implications of different conceivable sequences. (Suppose dynamite had been invented 50 years earlier. What are some possible consequences of that?)

- What do we know about this time? What was happening in other parts of the world? What countries or empires were around? What technology existed? What didn't exist? What were things like then?

- Why is this date given in the text? What dates are the most significant according to the text? To us? To others? Notice that many dates significant to other groups, such as to Native Americans, are not mentioned. All dates that are mentioned result from a value judgment about the significance of that event.

All students should leave school with a time-line in their heads of basic eras and a few important dates, and with a deeply held and thoroughly understood conviction that all history is history from a point of view, and that one needs to understand how things came to be and why.

Economics

When reasoning economically, North Americans reason not only from a market economy perspective, but also as liberals, conservatives, optimists, or pessimists. Lessons on economics should stress not only how our system is supposed to work but also how liberals, conservatives, etc. tend to interpret the same facts differently. Students should begin to consider questions like the following: "What can I learn from conservative and liberal readings of these events? What facts support each interpretation?" They should also have an opportunity to imagine alternative economic systems and alternative incentives, other than money, to motivate human work. Students should begin to analyze and evaluate their own present and future participation in the economy by exploring reasoning and values underlying particular actions, and the consequences of those actions.

Some Key Questions in Subject Areas

Instruction for each subject should be designed to highlight the basic or root questions of that subject and help students learn to reason within each field. To help you move away from the didactic, memorization-oriented approach found in most texts, we have listed below some basic questions, to suggest what sort of background issues could be used to begin to unify and organize instruction and relate it to students' lives. We have made no attempt to provide a comprehensive list. Furthermore, we are not assuming that these questions can be asked as we have formulated them. You would probably have to re-express them in terms that take into account your students and the particular context in which you might introduce them. Consider the questions, therefore, as suggestive only. Some will be too sophisticated for your students in the form in which we have expressed them.

History

What is history? Can we record everything that happened in the past and put it into a book? If not, who selects what to include and exclude? According to whose value judgments? Do you have a history? Where do you record your history? Would your friends and your enemies write the same history of you? What can we learn from understanding that what gets written in history books is selected based on value judgments that historians make? Can you distinguish within this paragraph of your history book which sentences are expressing facts from those sentences that are giving you the historian's interpretation of those facts? From whose point of view is this chapter on the American Revolution written, from the British point of view, from the Indian (Native American) point of view, or from the revolutionaries' point of view? Based on the two different accounts we have looked at as to why the colonists revolted, which one do you think is more justified and why?

Anthropology

What is "culture"? Why do different cultures exist? What shapes culture? How do cultures change? How have you been influenced by our culture? By ideas in movies and TV? How does culture influence people? What assumptions underlie our culture? Others' cultures? To what extent are values universal? Which of our values are universal? To what extent do values vary between cultures? Within cultures? How can cultures be categorized? What are some key differences between cultures that have writing and those that don't? What are the implications and consequences of those differences? Is it possible to judge another culture? What standards might we use? How is your peer group like a culture? How are cultures like and unlike other kinds of groups — clubs, nations, groups of friends, families, generations?

Geography

How do people adapt to where they live? What kinds of geographical features influence people the most? How? How do people change their environment? What effects do different changes have? How can uses of land be evaluated? How can we distinguish geographical from cultural influences? (Are Swedes hardy as a result of their geography or as a result of their cultural values?) Which geographical features in our area are the most significant? Does our climate influence our motivation? How so? Would you be different if you had been raised in the desert? Explain how. Why is it important to know what products various countries export? What does that tell us about that country, its relationships to other countries, its problems, its strengths?

Politics

What kinds of governments are there? What is government for? What should governments do? What shouldn't they do? What is our government like? What are other governments like? How did they come to be that way? Who has the most power? Who *should* have power? What ways can power be used? How is our system designed to prevent abuse of power? To what extent is that design successful? What assumptions underlie various forms of government? What assumptions underlie ours? On what values are they theoretically based? What values are actually held? How is the design of this government supposed to achieve its ideals? To what extent should a country's political and economic interests determine its foreign relations? To what extent should such ideals as justice and self-determination influence foreign policy decisions? Take a particular policy and analyze the possible effects of vested interests. How can governments be evaluated? How much should governments do to solve political, social, or economic, problems?

Economics

What kinds of economic decisions do you make in your daily life? What kinds will you make in the future? On what should you base those decisions? How should you decide where your money goes? When you spend money, what are you telling manufacturers? How is a family like an economic system? What kinds of economies are there? In our economy, who makes what kinds of decisions? What values underlie our economy? What does our economic system assume about why people work? According to proponents of this economic system, who should receive the greatest rewards? Why? Who should receive less reward? How can economic systems be evaluated? What problems are there in our economy according to liberals? Conservatives? Socialists? What features of our economy are capitalistic? Socialistic? How does ideal capitalism, how does ideal socialism, work? In what ways do we depart from ideal capitalism? Are these departures justified? What kinds of things are most important to produce? Why? What kinds of things are less important? Why?

Unifying Social Studies Instruction

Although it makes sense to say that someone is reasoning historically, anthropologically, geographically, etc., it does not make the same sense to say that someone is reasoning socio-scientifically. There is no *one* way to put all of these fields together. Yet, understanding the interrelationships between each field and being able to integrate insights gained from each field is crucial to social studies. We must recognize the need for students to develop their own unique perspectives on social events and arrangements. This requires that questions regarding the interrelationships between the fields covered in social studies be frequently raised and that lessons be designed to require students to apply ideas from various fields to one topic or problem. Keep in mind the following questions:

• What are people like? How do people come to be the way they are? How does society shape the individual? How does the individual shape society?

• Why do people disagree? Where do people get their points of view? Where do I get my point of view?

• Are some people more important than others? From what point of view?

• How do people and groups of people solve problems? How can we evaluate solutions?

• What are our biggest problems? What has caused them? How should we approach them?

- What are the relationships between politics, economics, culture, psychology, history, and geography? How do each of these influence the rest? How does the economy of country X influence its political decisions? How does the geography of this area affect its economy? How is spending money like voting?

- How can governments, cultures, and economic systems be evaluated?

- Could you have totalitarian capitalism? Democratic communism?

In raising these questions beware the tendency to assume a "correct" answer based on our social conditioning as U.S. citizens, especially on issues dealing with socialism or communism. Remember, we, like all peoples, have biases and prejudices. Our own view of the world must be critically analyzed and questioned if our students are to become fairminded persons.

Try to keep in mind that it takes a long time to develop a person's *thinking*. Our thinking is connected with every other dimension of us. All of our students enter our classes with many "mindless" beliefs, ideas which they have unconsciously picked up from TV, movies, small talk, family background, and peer groups. Rarely have they been encouraged to think for themselves. Thinking their way through these beliefs takes time. We therefore need to proceed very patiently. We must accept small payoffs at first. We should expect many confusions to arise. We must not despair in our role as cultivators of independent critical thought. In time, students will develop new modes of thinking. In time they will become more clear, more accurate, more logical, more openminded — if only we stick to our commitment to nurture these abilities. The social studies provide us with an exciting opportunity, since they address issues central to our lives and well-being. Of course, it is not easy to shift the classroom from a didactic-memorization model, but, if we are willing to pay the price of definite commitment, it can be done. Over time, students can learn to live an "examined" life, one in which they come to terms with the social nature of their lives, if we will carefully and encouragingly cultivate it.

Rosa Parks

by Betty White, Valley Springs
Elementary School, Jackson, CA

Objectives of the remodelled lesson

The students will:
- explore the relationships between thoughts and feelings of people involved with Rosa Parks and the bus boycott
- evaluate actions and policies

Original Lesson Plan

Abstract

This page on Rosa Parks is one of a series entitled "Someone You Should Know". In this brief narrative, students read that she was physically tired from a hard day's work, and tired of unfair treatment, and so refused to stand and allow a white to sit on the crowded bus, thereby setting off the Montgomery bus strike and becoming known as "The Mother of the Modern Civil Rights Movement."

Students are helped to see the economics of the strike ("What if there had only been 25 blacks in Montgomery?"), and discuss why Ms. Parks is known as "The Mother of the Modern Civil Rights Movement", why blacks had not objected to riding in the back of the bus before, and how they feel about boycotts.

from *America Past and Present*, Dr. Joan Schreiber, William Stripen, Dr. John Patrick, Dr. Richard Remy, Dr. Geneva Gay, and Dr. Alan Hoffman. Scott Foresman and Company. p. 383.

Critique

This selection is part of a biographical report on Rosa Parks. This unit in the text deals with difficult challenges and choices of the modern era, from early 1900's to the present. In this selection, very few questions were asked so the students get a true picture of this situation in the 1950's. They are asked questions that they can answer directly from the text. The text seems to suggest that twenty-five thousand Blacks automatically went on strike because of her and her alone. The text also fails to recognize the emotional impact of the situation. Questions lacked the use of critical vocabulary.

editor's note: The text lacks historical context. The boycott (and her refusal) seem to have come from nowhere. One objective is to learn "how an 'ordinary' person can help change things for the better" which over-emphasizes her role. The lesson also implies that the boycott was successful (and worked well), though it says that the company didn't change, the Supreme Court stepped in. As a boycott, then, (as opposed to a protest) in a way, it failed.

The biggest problem with the standard treatment of the Civil Rights Movement is over-emphasis on laws like the bus law and little or nothing on worse forms of oppression such as denial of the right to vote.

Strategies used to remodel

S–20 analyzing or evaluating actions or policies
S–4 exploring thoughts underlying feelings and feelings underlying thoughts
S–28 thinking precisely about thinking: using critical vocabulary
S–17 questioning deeply: raising and pursuing root or significant questions
S–3 exercising fairmindedness
S–27 comparing and contrasting ideals with actual practice

Remodelled Lesson Plan

Have students read the first two paragraphs of the selection. Ask them, "Why would Rosa Parks have to give up her seat to a white person if the bus became full? Do you think this was fair? **S–20** How did she feel about having to give up her seat? Why? What do you suppose she thought about it? How do you suppose the white people felt when they took the seats of black people? What did they probably think about it? How would you feel taking Rosa Park's seat? Why? **S–4** How do practices like this one get started?"

Continue to read the selection.

"When Ms. Parks was arrested, what law do you think she broke? What *inconsistency* or double standard was she pointing out by not giving up her seat? **S–28** Have you ever experienced inconsistency in the way you have been treated because of your age? Why hadn't the Black people complained about this system before? How did 'walking' change the situation? **S–17** Was this fair to the bus company? **S–3** The Supreme Court decided that the bus company had been denying Black people equal rights and that they should be allowed to sit anywhere. Do you agree? Why or why not? Was that treatment 'unequal'? Why or why not? What does 'equal' mean in this context? Why is Rosa Parks called 'The Mother of the Modern Civil Rights Movement'? Recently, Caesar Chavez went on a hunger strike. How is this similar to Rosa Parks?"

editor's note: "Why does the text use the word 'ordinary'? In what sense was Ms. Parks ordinary? Was she extraordinary in any sense? Why do you suppose her case was the catalyst for the boycott? How could such a small action have such a huge consequences, and take on such meaning?" **S–17**

"Why did these rules and laws exist? Why would whites want them? Was this practice consistent with U.S. ideals? Why was it allowed for so long?" **S–27**

Students could also compare this protest with the struggle for the vote.

Schools in the People's Republic of China

by Nora Brice Karr, Los Angeles U.S.D.,
North Hollywood, CA

Objectives of the remodelled lesson

The students will:
- learn to recognize the ethnocentricity in their texts
- discuss how cultures teach their ideals in schools, and evaluate this practice
- critique oversimplifications in text

Original Lesson Plan

Abstract

The text discusses education in China since the 1949 Communist Revolution. It states that children were trained to serve the Communist cause. Revolutionary ideals were taught throughout the grades. Mao Tse-Tung's ideas and sayings were taught and four of his quotes are given as examples. Writing lessons were based on learning his sayings; a photo of Mao was found in each classroom.

The teacher's edition directs that students analyze the quotes from Chairman Mao for meaning and political message. This is to be accomplished by the following two questions: What meanings do they (quotes) convey? What meanings were they meant to convey?" [End of analysis.]

"Since Mao's death in 1976, his photo no longer adorns each schoolroom. New leadership has made changes but it may be some years before we know how schooling in China has changed because the Chinese government is strict about what foreign travelers may see and do in China", states this 1983 text.

from *Our World: Lands and Cultures*,
Grade 6, Scott Foresman Social Studies,
1983 pp. 223–226.

Critique

This lesson was chosen because of the importance of developing an understanding of one-fourth of the world's population. It is also useful as a timely tie-in with the study of current events and newspaper study.

The lesson suffers from sociocentric bias which is subtle and sophisticated, thus making it more difficult for students to detect. For example, there is a strong emphasis on the teaching of revolutionary communist ideals in schools with no reference to U.S. students learning the ideals of *its* revolutionary leaders. A point is made about Mao's photo in classrooms with no comment or question about seeing a picture of George Washington in U.S. classrooms.

The text misuses the word "believe" in the following excerpt. "They (Chinese people) believe their patient efforts are building a better future. They do not have the freedom to believe otherwise." No distinction is made here between what one, or a group might "believe" as opposed to what their external actions might appear. (**editor's note:** This claim is misleading and ominous, giving the impression that the government controls every thought in the minds of every citizen.)

End of lesson "Checking Up" questions can all be answered from the text (recall) with the exception of one unclear question which asks, "How do you think Chinese schoolchildren see themselves?" The lesson deals in superficial irrelevancies with little attempt to develop understanding of Chinese, U.S., or any other school system.

Strategies used to remodel

S–21 reading critically: clarifying or critiquing texts
S–3 exercising fairmindedness
S–20 analyzing or evaluating actions or policies
S–10 refining generalizations and avoiding oversimplifications
S–7 developing intellectual good faith or integrity

Remodelled Lesson Plan S–21

After reading the text telling about Mao's photo in schools, students could be asked about pictures in their own school experience. Why would schools hang these pictures? What do the people represent? Are they important? Why? Would a picture of Mao be the equivalent of a picture of George Washington? Why or why not? **S–3**

The texts' emphasis on Chinese students study of the beliefs of the Chinese revolutionary government could be discussed with the following questions. "Why would the government want children to learn what it believes in? Why do you think the book makes a big point of the children being taught communist beliefs? Do other countries teach students their governments' beliefs? How? Why? Can you give examples from your own experience? Is there something wrong with this practice? When would it be wrong? Why? (Students could discuss the Pledge of Allegiance.) **S–20**

Direct students' attention to "They believe …. They do not have the freedom to believe otherwise. "What does the word 'believe' mean? Can the author know what one billion people believe? Why or why not? **S–10**

"Would the emphasis on sharing taught in Chinese schools be emphasized in U.S. schools? Why or why not? Would this ideal of sharing support the desire of Chinese college students for more freedoms, or not? Why? How? How might these demonstrations reflect the education these students have received?"

editor's note: What does the text mean by "They do not have the freedom to believe otherwise"? How could this be? (Pursue at length: Could a government control citizens' beliefs? How? To what degree? In what ways?) Why does the text put this point this way (strongly and absolutely)? What could we say instead? What would be a more accurate description? **S–7** What attitude does the author have toward the Chinese government? Why? How do you know?

Maps and Globes

by Karen L. Wergedal, Wilder
Elenentary, Littleton, CO

Objectives of the remodelled lesson

The students will:
- think independently to compare the advantages and disadvantages of maps and globes
- explore the reasons for maps and the uses of maps as sources that help people interpret physical environments
- make predictions about the appropriate uses of different types of flat maps and globes; gather evidence; discuss findings; and draw conclusions regarding the advantages and disadvantages of flat maps and globes — their significant similarities and differences

Original Lesson Plan

Abstract

Have one student stand in front of the class. Demonstrate how other students can see only his or her face or back of head, depending on how the student is turned. Relate this to the globe (students can see only one hemisphere at a time). Have one student stand with back turned toward other students. Hold smiley face illustration, gorilla mask, or other appropriate prop next to the student's head. Relate this to the fact that students can see the whole world at once on a flat map.

Carefully cut and peel an orange so the skin comes off in one piece. If you can manage this tedious feat (it is possible), the skin will easily fold back into a globular shape. Discuss with students how this demonstrates the distortions on a flat map as compared to the globe (Mercator Projection). An old soccer ball can also be used for this demonstration.

Discuss with students the following facts: The student can see only one-half of the globe at a time, but can see the whole world on a map. On a globe, the relative sizes of the continents and oceans are accurate, but on a map, sizes become more distorted the farther north or south of the equator. Have students restate these comparisons in their own words.

from *Where and Why*, Supplemental text.
Nystrom. Grade 4.

Critique

Since there is no text, per se, and the objectives and activities are written in a "discovery" mode, at first glance, this lesson would appear to be a critical thinking lesson. In fact, it comes closer than some, with its combination of discovery and discussion. However, if we closely examine the suggested activities, we find them to be basically teacher-directed, focusing on four predetermined conclusions. They are as follows:

a) Students can see only one hemisphere at a time on a globe;

b) Students can see the whole world at once on a flat map;

c) A flat map has obvious distortions as compared to a globe; and,

d) Both a globe and a flat map have their advantages and disadvantages.

The objective implies the opportunity for experiences in critical thinking and then didactically directs that thinking.

editor's note: The original fails to have students discuss the practical *implications* of these differences for actual map and globe use. (Why is it sometimes better to see the whole world at once? etc.)

Strategies used to remodel

S–1 thinking independently
S–9 developing confidence in reason
S–29 noting significant similarities and differences

Remodelled Lesson Plan *s–1*

This remodel will be a truer discovery lesson. It requires specific questioning strategies on the part of the teacher, and critical thinking on the part of the student, as well as using their own background knowledge.

Students will be exposed to a wide array of sizes, shapes, and types of flat maps and globes. Then the students will be asked for their observations on the *a)* similarities and differences in maps, *b)* similarities and differences in globes, and *c)* the similarities and differences between flat maps and globes. These observations will be shared through a combination of brainstorming and Socratic discussion.

Students will brainstorm ideas about the purposes for maps, developing categories. Now the students will have adequate experience with flat maps and globes and their purposes, as well as some skill in observing, comparing and contrasting, and in sharing facts and opinions through both independent and/or small group research and class discussion.

Students will make predictions about the appropriate uses for different types of flat maps and globes, experience either guest cartographers, videos, or films, and or visit a cartographer and work-place to gather evidence, and through Socratic discussion in class, draw their final conclusions regarding the advantages and disadvantages of using flat maps and globes.

As a culminating activity, students could catalogue the flat maps and globes in their school, prepare a manual for map and globe use, including a list of the advantages and disadvantages of each as a tool to demonstrate the concept of maps as sources that help people interpret physical environments. Students will offer the catalogue for use in the school's media center for reference. **S–9**

editor's note: To help students explore the purposes for and uses of the maps and globes, the teacher could use questions like the following: If you wanted to understand where the U.S. and the U.S.S.R. are in relation to each other, which should you use? [I chose these two countries, because the most common flat maps are misleading in two ways: the U.S.S.R. is a fairly short hop over the North Pole; and, the two countries nearly meet at the Bering Straits.] If you wanted to get a sense of the relative sizes of two countries, which should you use? What would happen if you used the wrong one? *S–29*

The analytical vocabulary in the English language, with such terms as 'assume,' 'infer,' 'conclude,' 'criteria,' 'point of view,' 'relevance,' 'interpretation,' 'issue,' 'contradiction,' 'credibility,' 'evidence,' 'distinguish,' enables us to think more precisely about our thinking.

Consumer Concerns: Television Advertising

by Nora Brice Karr, Los Angeles U.S.D.,
North Hollywood, CA

Objectives of the remodelled lesson

The students will:
- critique text for evidence of bias
- discover importance of ads for TV industry
- explore effect of costs of ads on products
- evaluate commercials to develop criteria
- differentiate between relevant and irrelevant facts

Original Lesson Plan

Abstract

This two-page social studies lesson has a one-day recommended teaching time. The text states that, "... producers use advertising to give people information. This information can help people make wise decisions about how to spend their money ... helps people learn about the many choices available to them." It goes on to explain that the high costs of TV ads are due to the great care taken to produce high quality ads. It describes market research to determine what kind of products to advertise. It mentions that ads "persuade" and "encourage" consumers. The lesson states that the use of big cats in car commercials (such as cougars), "somehow make a car and the person driving it seem more powerful and more attractive."

The text states, "Some experts have figured out that four cents out of every dollar we spend go to pay for advertising the products we buy. Others point out that if it were not for the high prices advertisers paid to have their products shown on television, there would be no way to pay for regular television programs."

Activities suggested are: a chart of commercials during a favorite TV show; a market research poll of friends asking what they like in commercials; and planning an original commercial.

from *Our World: Lands and Culture , Grade 6,* Scott Foresman Social Studies, 1983, pp. 161–162.

Critique

This lesson was chosen because advertising is a "plumb" for critical thinking skills, yet, has *no* thinking skills incorporated into a subject which students experience daily. Nowhere in the text is there any *analysis* of TV ads. Neither insight into methods and tactics used to lure customers nor a discussion of advertisings' ability to create wants and artificial needs are included.

There is no dialogue suggested that would get students thinking about or discussing advertising methods, or what the high cost of ads means to consumers of the products. No analysis of assumptions is included; there is no attempt to develop critical insight.

In short, an everyday experience which helps shape one's opinions and, often, one's view of life is tossed out to students with utter disregard for evaluation, clarification, or refinement of generalizations, and in a grotesquely misleading way (ads are not designed to promote consumer wisdom).

Strategies used to remodel

S–22 listening critically: the art of silent dialogue
S–21 reading critically: clarifying or critiquing texts
S–28 thinking precisely about thinking: using critical vocabulary
S–25 reasoning dialogically: comparing perspectives, interpretations, or theories
S–15 developing criteria for evaluation: clarifying values and standards
S–13 clarifying issues, conclusions, or beliefs
S–10 refining generalizations and avoiding oversimplifications
S–34 recognizing contradictions

Remodelled Lesson Plan s–22 ────────

The author's point of view needs to be clarified. Possible questions would be: Are ads discussed in positive, negative, or neutral terms? What evidence can you cite to support your view? What attitude does this author convey? **S–21** Why might a person have this perspective? **S–28** Would another perspective be reasonable? Why or why not? **S–25**

Students need to develop criteria for evaluation of TV ads. "What are TV ads? What are good ads? Why? What are bad ads? Why? Can we generalize a list of criteria? What should we look for when judging an ad?" **S–15**

Using a specific commercial, the teacher can ask: Are the ideas clear? How can we know if this claim is true? What does this claim assume? Is the assumption reasonable? What does it imply? How? Does the ad misuse any concepts? How? What facts are relevant? Are relevant facts presented? Are there any irrelevant facts? Are these facts stated or implied? **S–13**

Students can compare the costs of a heavily advertised product with a similar non-advertised product (say, a generic). What is the cost difference? What factors might contribute to the difference? (The teacher must be certain to help students consider a variety of factors (quality, where the product is made, transportation costs, salaries where the product is made, etc.) so as not to mislead students.) **S–10**

Students could discuss the consequences of fewer TV ads. What might happen? Why? Could the opposite be true? How? **S–10** What might be the consequences of no commercials? Would that be desirable? Who could take opposite view? **S–25**

   editor's notes: The lesson could begin with a discussion about ads (What are they for? What do you think about them?), perhaps through writing. Then students could compare their ideas with the text. **S–21**

   Students could relate their analyses of ads and this lesson to the concept of the 'rational or wise consumer'. "Do commercials help people spend wisely? Give me an example of such an ad. What else can we say about ads? How does showing a cougar or singing a jingle give me information? **S–34**

   Compare product labels as well as prices.

   How would those who made the ads evaluate them? What do they value in ads? What criteria would *they* use? **S–25**

The Rise of Nations

by Theresa A. Barone, Covington Middle
School, Birmingham, MI

Objectives of the remodelled lesson

The students will:
- explain how France, Spain, and England became unified as individual nations
- identify and understand the different factors that contributed to a nation forming
- discuss the future implications of these nations and their relationships
- clarify the concept of nations rising by critiquing the simplified version of the text
- assume another point of view to help understand national pride
- compare different nations' origins

Original Lesson Plan

Abstract

This lesson describes how France, Spain and England emerged during the later part of the Middle Ages. The main idea is that strong rulers helped people think of themselves as part of a nation. The lesson briefly describes how William of Normandy united the English, how Princess Isabella and Prince Ferdinand united Spain, and how Joan of Arc helped save France from English rule, thereby uniting the French. The teaching suggestions ask students to recall that people at this time were living in small communities and had no feelings of nationality. During the Renaissance, people were becoming more interested in events outside their communities. Also, after reading about Joan of Arc, the students are asked to write a story in which they describe how Joan of Arc helped the French. As a reinforcement, they are asked to recall how Egypt was united (struggled against the Nile and had strong leaders).

from *The World Past and Present*,
Barbara Radner Reque, D. C. Heath
Social Studies, 1985, pp. 208–209.

Critique

This two-page lesson contains so much information that much of it is simplified. Although the main idea of rulers forming a nation is an important one, many other concepts need to be considered. The text simply omits the idea of people and their beliefs forming a unified country.

The lesson ties the past events to the emergence of these nations. The text wants the students to understand the relationship between the preceding events (life on a manor, crusades, the Renaissance) and the progression towards unity. However, the text does not mention the future implications of these unified states. The students are not asked to speculate about why these events are important and what this has to do with Europe today.

The text misses another important idea, that of point of view. The students have an opportunity to think about national pride and what a citizen in another nation might feel about the beginnings of their nation. Asking them to reflect on that idea might prove to be a valuable part of the lesson.

Finally, the reinforcement suggestion connecting ancient Egypt to the rising of modern Europe is confusing. Many factors contributed to Egypt's unity and to try and simplify this idea so it will fit with the lesson is absurd. Therefore, this part of the lesson will be omitted in the remodel.

editor's note: It may not be a bad idea to have students compare the emergence of these three nations with that of other countries they have studied *if* such a discussion avoids oversimplification.

Such an important and basic topic deserves more than brief treatment. It is worth spending more time to put the crucial conceptual understandings in place.

Strategies used to remodel

S–14 clarifying and analyzing the meanings of words or phrases
S–10 refining generalizations and avoiding oversimplifications
S–5 developing intellectual humility and suspending judgment
S–3 exercising fairmindedness
S–11 comparing analogous situations: transferring insights to new contexts
S–12 developing one's perspective: creating or exploring beliefs, arguments, or theories

Remodelled Lesson Plan

The lesson will begin as the text suggests, asking students to recall how people lived during this time and if they thought of themselves as part of a nation. It might be necessary to review the idea that people lived in their communities without needing to leave. Once the crusades and Renaissance came about, people were more interested in leaving their communities. However, before assigning the text, the students should discuss the concept of nationality and unity in a nation. Questions that might clarify these ideas include: What makes a nation a nation? What is the difference between a nation and a community? What is the difference between the U.S. and the U.S.S.R.? the U.S. and California? What keeps a nation united? **S–14**

Reading the text pages can follow, with a reminder to students to think about the concept of nationality while they read. After reading, ask the students to recap the main points. Discuss each nation one at a time, and ask how that nation was united. To avoid oversimplification, be sure to include: Was that individual the only one responsible for uniting the nation? What other people might help form a nation? What other factors might be considered? Do the people and their beliefs play a role? Why? Let them discover that although the text's version is important to understand, there are many ideas the text left out. **S–10** Did the text leave out relevant information about how these nations emerged? What kind of information? **S–5**

Asking students to imagine being an English, French, or Spanish citizen during this period in history could prove to be worthwhile as well as fun. For example: Write a newspaper editorial about Joan of Arc for an English paper or for a French paper. Describe Ferdinand and Isabella's wedding as if you were a Spanish citizen. The teacher should encourage the writing to be full of national pride. **S-3**

The ideas of nationality and unity should not be left without discussing the future. Ask the students to think about modern Europe and the foundation that was laid in the 1400's. Discuss if they can see any implications of the French and English relationships when their developments were so closely tied. Also ask about the Spanish and the Muslims and the Spanish kingdoms being united by a marriage. The relationships between each of these countries in the past might have some effect on their future. Also ask the students if a nation were being formed today, in Africa or the Middle East for example, what kinds of considerations should be made? Are there any important leaders? What are the views of the people? What about the surrounding nations? What could they learn from the past to help them in their struggle to become a nation? **S-11**

editor's note: The teacher could make the whole lesson an exploration of the concept 'nation'. Initial discussion (as above), then, while reading, note any points made regarding the concept. Students can compare the three stories of emerging nationhood. "What was different about these areas after they became nations? What had changed? What does it mean for a place to become a nation? **S-14**

What other countries' beginnings do you know about? When (roughly) did it become a nation? How? Why? How does that nation's beginnings compare with these three? Did it become a nation for the same reasons or from the same causes? When did New England colonists become "Americans"? Why? What effect did that have on the birth of our nation? **S-11**

Would any of the people of the time have resisted these changes? What might they have said?

Why did this happen then, and not before? **S-12**

Primary Sources and Perspectives

Objectives of the remodelled lesson

The students will:
- compare their accounts of an event
- generate criteria for evaluating reports
- apply those criteria by assessing the credibility of a primary source in their texts

Original Lesson Plan

Abstract

Students are asked to write a letter describing a recent class activity and then to note and compare differences in the reports. The teacher's notes suggest that this activity may be linked to Captain Cochrane's journey across Russia. Captain Cochrane wrote *Narrative of a Pedestrian's Journey Through Russia and Siberian Tartary,* based on his walk across Russia in 1820. The text quotes and paraphrases his observations about the physical terrain, the climate, the resources, the cities, and the people he met. He also wrote about the variety of ethnic groups he encountered as well as details about their customs and life-styles.

from *Europe, Africa, Asia, and Australia,* Kenneth S. Cooper. © 1984 by Silver Burdett Co. pp. 186–201.

Critique

Historical perspective

The concluding activity for this chapter, "Writing a Letter", has rich possibilities for fostering an understanding of historical perspective which transcends this particular episode and could tie together a whole set of related concepts, such as, bias, credibility, point of view, incomplete evidence, etc. Instead, after having students describe a group experience and exchange their descriptions, the text directs students merely to *note* differences. Thus, the text lays the groundwork for what could be a meaningful, in-depth understanding of historical perspective, but stops short of accomplishing those ends. Students do not discuss reasons for the differences, nor how different accounts could be reconciled or evaluated.

Evaluating source credibility

The questions on Captain Cochrane's account of his trip through Russia (pp. 187–8) toy with assessing historical perspective but are much too brief and superficial to teach students how or why they need to question such a report. The teacher should call attention to the *process* of evaluating reports so that it becomes a tool that can be used whenever appropriate.

Question d), "*Do people always give favorable accounts of what they see or do? (No. Even the captain was critical of many things.)*" is basically a rhetorical question which doesn't go deeply into evaluation. It completely skips over a whole range of reasons for bias in reporting and is essentially useless. Question e) at least asks, "Why or why not?" but again, does not seriously give students a working strategy for dealing with historical reports.

If the text's purpose is to consider primary sources, much more of the significant parts of the source must be quoted. Here we have only isolated fragments used to punctuate the text's narrative. The text pays lip-service to an important application of critical skills, but does almost nothing to actually develop them.

Strategies used to remodel

S–34 recognizing contradictions
S–15 developing criteria for evaluation: clarifying values and standards
S–10 refining generalizations and avoiding oversimplifications
S–1 thinking independently
S–16 evaluating the credibility of sources of information
S–11 comparing analogous situations: transferring insights to new contexts
S–22 listening critically: the art of silent dialogue

Remodelled Lesson Plan

Evaluating source credibility

You could have students write their letters as directed on p. 199. Then you might have them share their accounts in groups and note the differences. (These can be categorized by the students, for example, differences of fact, emphasis, interpretation, omission, etc.) Then, you might ask students, "Why are there different accounts of the same experience? Do these accounts contradict each other? Can they be reconciled? Can we say that some accounts are more accurate? Why?" **S–34** If disagreements arise, students could defend their positions, and explain opposing views. Encourage them to modify their positions in light of the strengths of opposing views.

Students should generalize about what makes some accounts better than others. Consider asking, "Which are right? How do you know? What are some of the criteria for deciding which accounts are best? **S–15** (accuracy, completeness, objectivity, fairness, etc.) Is it bad or good to have different accounts? How does your picture of the event change by reading several reports? How could a perspective be strengthened by incorporating others into it?" (Encourage students to take aspects of more than one point of view, and describe a more complete idea, and use qualifying terms, such as, most, probably, etc.) **S–10**

Applying source credibility criteria to historical reports

Next, review the account of Captain Cochrane's visit to Russia. You might ask, "What questions would you ask about Captain Cochrane's report to help assess its historical validity?" **S–1** You could suggest that they use the criteria previously developed in "Writing a Letter". Possible questions might be, "When did he write his report? As he travelled or after? Would this be important to know? Why or why not? What aspect of the report's truth would it affect? Have you ever tried to write down a sequence of events some time after they occurred? Give specific examples. What problems did you find? Did he leave some things out of his report? Why did he select the things he did report on from all the possibilities? What accounts might have been given about his trip by the people he met? Is there anything in the text that helps you infer what kind of a reputation for reliability Captain Cochrane might have had? Can you infer to whom he wrote? Was he paid in advance for his report? Would this affect what he said? How? What kind of background did Captain Cochrane have? Was he well educated? Had he travelled much, read much? Why could these questions be important to ask? Are there any other accounts that might support or undermine his observations? Can you think of other questions that might help you to detect or assess an author's point of view? (Was he paid for writing his report? By whom? How might this affect what he said? Was he the kind of person who liked everyone he met and thought everybody was friendly?)" *S-16* This line of questioning could generate a lengthy discussion leading to a critical understanding of how history is written and how it represents a certain perspective rather than absolute truth. It is also important for students to ask questions rather than always depending on the teacher to do it.

Applying source credibility criteria to personal accounts *S-11*

Another extension of this lesson could be made by drawing on students' experience. They could relate an event reported in the school or community newspaper, a T.V. story, someone's account of an accident, a fight, etc. Then students could assess the strength of the report using the criteria developed above. "What does our study of primary sources tell us about listening to people? If a friend complains to you about his or her parents, how might you respond? Why? *S-22* Should you always raise your critical questions aloud? When might you keep them to yourself? Why? (The teacher could mention application of these principles in courts of law.) They could also relate the above to other history or geography lessons, (for example, compare how American and British accounts of the Revolutionary War would differ). By this point, they should begin to generalize principles of critical assessment applicable to a variety of situations, producing fairly sophisticated critical insights that will help them have a better understanding of how reporters' perspectives influences their reports.

Famous People: Gandhi

Objectives of the remodelled lesson
The students will:
- clarify 'unjust laws' through Socratic questioning
- exercise independent thought when evaluating laws
- evaluate methods of changing unjust laws
- probe underlying ideas of the relationship of governments to their citizens and to other governments
- understand Gandhi's methods as a leader
- develop their perspectives regarding means of correcting injustice
- transfer ideas discussed when evaluating actions and arguments from current events

Original Lesson Plan

Abstract

Students read that Gandhi was a spiritual leader of millions of Indians, that he protested the unfair salt law, and lead other protests against the British. The lesson emphasizes his pacifism, willingness to go to jail, and results of his actions.

from *Our World,* Grade 6, Teacher's Edition, by JoAnn Cagemi. © 1983 by Holt, Rinehart and Winston, Inc. p. 265.

Critique

We chose this lesson for its thought provoking subject and common form. Many texts have special mini-lessons focussing on individuals, though, like this one, they often fail to explore the individuals' importance in sufficient depth. Such explorations could allow students to appreciate the power of a dedicated individual, and the relationship of the individual to society.

The charge of unjust laws has been the impetus for innumerable revolts, revolutions, social upheavals, and public debates. Exploring the concept, related concepts, and current or historical events gives students a chance to develop and apply their ideas about government, law, ethics, and citizenship. Extended discussion of this material produces more well-developed perspectives crucial to fairminded thought. The text fails to take full advantage of this opportunity by failing to encourage extended discussion, and by presenting conclusions, such as, "The salt law was unfair", without allowing students to discuss their justification. Independent thought is best fostered by refined judgment achieved through practice.

Strategies used to remodel
S–17 questioning deeply: raising and pursuing root or significant questions
S–24 practicing Socratic discussion: clarifying and questioning beliefs, theories, or perspectives
S–1 thinking independently

S–14 clarifying and analyzing the meanings of words or phrases
S–35 exploring implications and consequences
S–6 developing intellectual courage
S–8 developing intellectual perseverance
S–3 exercising fairmindedness
S–20 analyzing or evaluating actions or policies
S–11 comparing analogous situations: transferring insights to new contexts

Remodelled Lesson Plan S–17

After our suggested introductory discussion, *1)* Clarifying 'just law' versus 'unjust law', our remodel follows the two-part structure of the original: *2)* Responses to unjust laws, and *3)* Gandhi's significance. In section *4)* we suggest questions for additional discussions.

1) Clarifying 'just law' versus 'unjust law' S–24

When students have read the text and heard the background material, they could discuss the concepts 'fair' and 'unfair laws', or 'just' and 'unjust laws,' with questions like the following: What law was mentioned as an example of an unjust law? Is it unjust? **S–1** Why or why not? Can you give me examples of unjust laws? (Discuss each at length: Does everyone agree it is unjust? Why is it unjust?) Why did the British make the salt law? Students could reread the sentence, *"It was illegal to possess salt not purchased from the government."* Why would the British Government make such a law? Who would benefit? How? Why were the other laws we've discussed made? Then students might summarize the differences between just and unjust laws. **S–14** They could also discuss their assumptions about the purposes and limits of government. The teacher could probe student responses to earlier questions, eliciting assumptions, and basic concepts, etc.

2) Responses to unjust laws S–35

To better understand Gandhi's significance, students could compare possible reactions to unjust laws, and their consequences. Encourage them to include examples in their discussion. You may use questions like the following: What can people do when their laws are unjust here? Elsewhere? What have different people done? What happened next? Why? What was Gandhi's method? How was his approach different than most? You could remind students of relevant background material; for example, the boycott of British cloth. What was his purpose? Why did he think those actions would help the people of India? [Help students see the public relations difficulties, and loss of economic control he caused.]

Students could compare alternatives and their results, for both the individuals and countries. "Was Gandhi a criminal? Do people have the right to break unjust laws? Why or why not? When? Under what circumstances? (You may point out that Gandhi's protests were public and publicized, and that he accepted the penalties imposed on him.) **S–6** Would you be willing to go to prison for your beliefs? Why or why not?" **S–8**

3) Gandhi's significance

If using the part of the original lesson on Dr. King, the teacher may point out that similarities in method were no accident; King had been profoundly influenced by Gandhi. Students could discuss their impressions of Gandhi, and his role in history. What do you think of him? Why? Was he a great leader? In what way? (If students do not realize it, you may explain that he did not hold office; he influenced many people because he was loved and respected.) Why did he succeed in his goal to make Indians free? The class could also discuss other pacifists.

4) Other discussions

Students may want to discuss their ideas about Gandhi's belief in nonviolence, and so develop their perspective on means of social change: Is violence ever justified? Why or why not? Which works better, violence, or nonviolence, or neither? If discussing at length, have students consider multiple points of view. The teacher could have students rephrase each others' arguments. **S–3**

The passage could also be used to generate a discussion of the roles and responsibilities of governments, specifically colonial governments. Again, encourage students to discuss as many specific examples and events as possible. The following questions could be used: What would you call a government that has a lot of unjust laws? If a group of people governs another, does it have an obligation to be just and fair to those it rules? Why or why not? What are some principles of fairness or justice? Does one group of people have the right to rule over another group against their will, or should every group be allowed to rule themselves? Why? **S–20**

Students could also discuss the text statement: *"The British could no longer rule the Indians without their consent."* Ask, "What does this mean? Why couldn't they? If this is so, why do people ever tolerate unjust laws? What stops them from freeing themselves?" **S–35**

The class could also relate these ideas to international politics and U.S. foreign policy by discussing questions like the following: If a government has many unjust laws, should other governments do anything about it, or is it none of their business? Why? What, if anything, should be done? What might the people in the unjust government say? Would they think of themselves as unjust? Should we help governments that seem to us to be unjust? **S–20**

This lesson could also be related to current events, or to a newspaper lesson, by using the ideas discussed, and applying them to examples of governments which have been recently charged with injustice. Students could discuss the justification for the charges, come to their own conclusions, and engage in fairminded discussion. What law are these people [protesting, arguing about, etc.]? Why was it made? Why do some people object? Is it just? Why or why not? (Have students relate their conclusions to the criteria they discovered in section 1.) **S–11**

Countries of Eastern Europe

Objectives of the remodelled lesson
The students will:
* use map skills to draw conclusions and explore implications, thus exercising independent thought
* recognize the geo-political significance of the Bosporus
* transfer this insight to analogous configurations
* understand geo-political power struggles over the Bosporus from several points of view; exercising fairmindedness

Original Lesson Plan

Abstract

The lesson begins by identifying the countries of Eastern Europe along the Danube River. Geographical features such as the Carpathian and Balkan mountains, the Iron Gate, and the Hungarian Plain are indicated. Countries of the Black Sea are noted. The Bosporus strait is highlighted as a dividing point between Europe and Asia and as a water gateway to the Sea of Marmara, the Dardanelles and the Aegean and Mediterranean Seas. The importance of this water gateway is underlined. Student questions center on locating and identifying the countries and geographical features of Eastern Europe and explaining the interest of the Black Sea countries in controlling the Bosporus.

from *Europe, Africa, Asia, and Australia*
Kenneth S. Cooper. © 1984 by Silver
Burdett Co. pp. 186–201.

Critique

We chose this lesson because it presents some excellent opportunities to explore the implications of geography and could, if developed, provide a basis for understanding important geo-political tensions which have shaped and will continue to shape world history. The text stops short of examining those implications, however.

Pursuing implications and connections
One of the characteristics of critical thinkers is a propensity to probe the underlying structure of whatever they are studying. They ask questions such as: Why is this particular geographical feature highlighted? What is the larger context of this feature? How is it related to human activity? What is its history? What does the history tell me about its significance? How does this situation require understanding and synthesis of geography, technology, history, economics, and politics? Can I apply this insight to other situations? How do I know which other situations are similar? What features are alike? Different? How should I adjust for the differences?

If the lesson were taught as the original lesson plan suggested, the students would come away with a collection of memorized facts and only a minimal or superficial understanding of what they imply. Three out of four of the Checkup questions are factual recall. The fourth question asks, *"What is the Bosporus? The Dardanelles? Why are they important?"* The answer to the latter question, worded just as in the text, is, *"The Bosporus is important because it is the only way out of the Black Sea and because it makes it possible to cross a bridge to get from Europe to Asia. The Dardanelles is important because whoever holds it holds the water gateway to a large part of Eastern Europe."* The text does not make explicit the strategic considerations at work.

Fostering independent thought

Another characteristic of critical thinkers is the ability to think independently, to move away from slavish dependence on authorities (such as texts) to drawing their own conclusions and exercising the power of autonomous thinking. In this lesson, however, students are not encouraged to think independently and draw their own conclusions. If, as the text states, *"the map tells the story,"* why does the text immediately reiterate the story? The effect of such juxtaposition makes the map superfluous. In another instance the text states, *"It is easy to see the importance of this waterway."* This is followed by an elaboration of its importance: *"Whoever holds it holds the water gateway to a large portion of Eastern Europe."* The subject is then dropped and students are not encouraged to exercise their power of judgment independently. With the heavy emphasis on maps and map skills in this and previous grade levels, students should be ready to use those skills to independently predict and explore the implications of geography suggested in this lesson. Instead, students are asked only the most obvious questions under "Reading Maps". The only interpretation students are asked to do is superficial and leads to no meaningful synthesis. The expression 'control gate' is not clarified, leaving the idea vague in students' minds. 'Control' implies a possibility of power, which has political implications.

Transference and confidence in reason

Critical thinkers regularly seek to transfer new information and ideas to other contexts so as to link up their knowledge in meaningful patterns. This networking of ideas and information enhances memory as well as understanding. It is also an economical strategy which saves having to start from the ground up every time an analogous situation arises. Transfer maximizes the effort that has been expended in the first place to understand deeply.

This lesson fails to have students relate the conclusions about this particular geographical feature to others they have studied or read about. Rather than stressing general underlying principles inherent in geographical configurations, and having students transfer those principles to analogous situations, the text simply moves on to another subject. The Bosporus, therefore, is seen as unique rather than one of a type of significant areas.

Strategies used to remodel
S–9 developing confidence in reason
S–23 making interdisciplinary connections
S–35 exploring implications and consequences
S–3 exercising fairmindedness
S–11 comparing analogous situations: transferring insights to new contexts

Remodelled Lesson Plan s–9

1) Situating the Bosporus and exploring its political implications

You could begin this lesson by having the students study the map on pp. 466-7 of their texts. It would be useful to draw their attention to the Bosporus and ask them to use the scale of distance to figure out approximately the width and length of the strait. **S–23** Confirm the dimensions using the information to the teacher on p. 199. You might then compare the size of this geographical feature to something they are familiar with, or ask a student to make such a comparison. Then consider asking something like, "Why would the countries bordering the Black Sea be interested in the Bosporus?" It might be a good idea to focus on the transportation of supplies and trade goods. Next you might ask, "Do these countries have alternative ways of getting supplies or goods in and out of their countries? What are they? (air, overland) What are the advantages and disadvantages of each?" You could mention that the Soviet Union's other major sea-port is frozen in winter. In order to elicit that, in time of war, the country that controls an area can deny its enemies access to supplies, etc., you could ask, "If Turkey went to war with the Soviet Union, what use could they make of the Bosporus? Would this be a serious problem for the Soviet Union? In what way? What pressures might the Soviet Union or other Black Sea countries bring to bear on Turkey? What might they want from Turkey?" **S–35**

At this point, it would be easy to ask some more hypothetical questions which encourage students to synthesize ideas already discussed. The teacher could ask, "What if Turkey decided to close the Bosporus?" One idea would be to ask students to imagine that they represent one of the Black Sea countries, and submit a protest to Turkey carefully stating their reasons. **S–3** You could continue with other hypothetical questions such as, "What if Turkey decided to charge a high fee to ships using the Bosporus? What reasons might Turkey give for such an action? What might protesters give as their reasons for opposing it?" The teacher might give students the opportunity to pose hypothetical questions themselves to generate some of the conflicts possible in this particular geographical situation. **S–9** Solutions to the problems might be considered, if interest warrants.

2) Extending insights to analogous geographical features **S–11**

The lesson could then be extended by discussing analogous situations in other areas of the world. You might have students look for similar places on maps or globes, noting who owns each, and what other countries would have an interest in each, and why. (Suez and Panama Canals, Straits of Gibraltar, rivers, strategic mountain passes, etc.) Some students could research the histories of some of these, and report to the rest of the class. When a list has been made, you could use the following questions: Are, or have these areas been, the subject of contention? Why? What are some principles we learned about the Bosporus that might apply in these places as well? Why were you able to predict these tensions? **S–9**

Sojourner Truth

Objectives of the remodelled lesson

The students will:
- understand Sojourner Truth's message in "Ain't I a Woman" by exploring thoughts underlying feelings, clarifying issues and claims, making inferences, and integrating critical vocabulary
- appreciate her personal qualities
- evaluate arguments in "Ain't I a Woman," supplying evidence for conclusions
- identify society's double standards, inconsistency, racism, and sexism as revealed in "Ain't I a Woman"
- Socratically explore inconsistencies and double standards in personal thought and behavior
- recognize the speech's dramatic and expressive qualities

Original Lesson Plan

Abstract

Students read that Sojourner Truth gave a speech to the women's rights convention in Akron, Ohio. As men tried to shout her down, she went to the platform and said,

> That man over there says that women need to be helped into carriages and lifted over ditches, and to have the best place wherever. Nobody ever helps me into carriages or over mud puddles, or gives me any best place. And ain't I a woman? Look at me! I have ploughed and planted and gathered into barns and no man could head [do better than] me. And ain't I a woman? I could work as much and eat as much as a man — when I could get it — and bear the lash [whip] as well.
> And ain't I a woman? I have borne thirteen children and seen most all sold off to slavery, and when I cried out with my mother's grief, none but Jesus heard me. And ain't I a woman?...

Students are asked the following questions: **a.** *About what two groups of people was Sojourner Truth speaking?* (Blacks and women) **b.** *What work did she do that men did?* (Plowed, planted, and gathered crops) **c.** *What could she do equal to a man?* (Work, eat, and suffer punishment) **d.** *What special sadness did Sojourner Truth have to bear because she was a black woman?* (Her children were sold from her.) **e.** *Why did she keep repeating the phrase, "And ain't I a woman?"* (Answers will vary. Pupils may say to dramatize her speech, to emphasize women's abilities, to plead for women's rights.)

from *The United States and Its Neighbors,* Timothy M. Helmus, Val E. Arnsdorf, Edgar A Toppin, and Norman J. G. Pounds. © 1984 by Silver Burdett Co. pp. .142–143.

Critique

We chose this passage in part because it is representative of vignettes about famous people which are included within a lesson. This one, shorter than many, has little biographical information, though the text suggests Sojourner Truth as a subject for a biographical report. Too often texts gloss over stories of injustice and inhumanity; this piece is a laudable exception. Even this short segment presents opportunities for understanding Sojourner Truth as a remarkable individual with a powerful message and an effective way of dramatizing it. The text, however, misses all opportunities by choosing to dissect the excerpt principally in terms of its factual data. Most of the questions ask students to pull information out of the speech and repeat it. In emphasizing questions such as *"What work did she do that men did?"* (questions a–d), the text entirely misses the important message and social criticism of the speech. Questions such as this simply function to disassemble the speech into its parts and put them back together in chronological order. If supplementary biographical information were provided, the speech could more easily be considered on its own terms for the human qualities and important messages it expresses. In order to understand these things, students must do more than repeat information; they must infer meaning.

The text also fails to recognize the speech's dramatic and literary power, and its portrayal of Sojourner Truth as a passionate, courageous, multi-dimensional person. The text lists the recall questions under the heading, "Understanding Primary Sources." This is a useful skill, when *understanding* is achieved. Here, however, students are simply asked to *decode* a primary source. Oddly enough, the only question out of five (question **e**) that might lead to a significant understanding of one aspect of the speech, ignores its passion and energy. In the teacher's notes about the answer, no allusion is made to the anguish Sojourner Truth felt at the injustices directed toward herself and all African-American women of the time, or the inconsistency between belief in women's delicacy and treatment of African-American women. One of the important attributes of critical thinkers is the willingness to look at inconsistencies in their own thought, and discrepancies between their words and actions. Our thinking is often characterized by quite unconscious categories to which we apply different standards. That is, we treat our friends one way and family members another way, and we treat members of other racial, religious, ethnic, or social groups differently from members of our own. Critical thinkers search for these categories and inconsistencies in their own thinking and behavior, evaluate them, and adjust accordingly. The speech, "Ain't I a Woman," provides an excellent model which reveals these sorts of thinking patterns, decries the inequities they create, and invites self-examination in the name of justice.

Strategies used to remodel
S–4   exploring thoughts underlying feelings and feelings underlying thoughts
S–28 thinking precisely about thinking: using critical vocabulary
S–20 analyzing or evaluating actions or policies
S–27 comparing and contrasting ideals with actual practice
S–7   developing intellectual good faith or integrity
S–24 practicing Socratic discussion: clarifying and questioning beliefs, theories, or perspectives
S–13 clarifying issues, conclusions, or beliefs
S–32 making plausible inferences, predictions, or interpretations
S–18 analyzing or evaluating arguments, interpretations, beliefs, or theories
S–23 making interdisciplinary connections

Remodelled Lesson Plan _____

For our remodel, we have used the speech, "Ain't I a Woman," and have built a lesson around it emphasizing its message, what it tells us about Sojourner Truth as a person, its effectiveness as a dramatic piece, and one application students might make of it in their own lives. We have basically set aside the questions the textbook suggests.

1) The messages of "Ain't I a Woman"

In order to provide a context for understanding the excerpt from "Ain't I a Woman", the teacher could begin by assigning Sojourner Truth as a subject for a biographical report. After the presentation to the class, have students read the introduction and speech. You could then ask students what feelings they experienced as they read the speech. For example, "What did you think? What did you feel? Why? What do you think she was feeling as she spoke? How can you tell? Why did she feel this way?" **S–4**

You might guide this discussion to help students understand the theme of inconsistency or double standards in treatment of people based on race. Here are some sample questions: What words mean "saying one thing and doing something different"? (hypocrisy, inconsistency, double standard) What *inconsistency* or *double standard* was Sojourner Truth pointing out in her speech? (The treatment of white women vs. African-American women) What word do we use to describe when people are treated *inconsistently* because of the color of their skin? (Racism) Can you think of any other examples of this *double standard* of treatment based on race? **S–28** What's wrong with double standards or inconsistency in the treatment of people? **S–20** Have you ever experienced inconsistency in the way you were treated? How did you feel? Are we ever inconsistent in our treatment of others? How? **S–27** How do people feel when they are treated this way? Do we always know when we're applying double standards? What might help us to know? **S–7** What might the people she was talking about have said in answer to her? How was the double standard Sojourner Truth talked about hidden or disguised in words? What did the word 'woman' mean to the men she was talking to? What did it mean to her? **S–24**

When students seem ready, you could develop the speech's theme of women's role with questions such as: What image of women was she criticizing? **S–13** Do you think women then liked being thought of as helpless? Why or why not? Why might being thought of as helpless frustrate a person? What might be good about it? What does Sojourner Truth say about society's view of women? **S–32** (The romantic ideal of women was false.) What proof does she offer that these ideas are false? Was she right? **S–18** What did she want to change?

2) Sojourner Truth as a person **S–32**

The class could also discuss the following questions: What kind of woman was Sojourner Truth? How do you know? How strongly did she believe in what she was saying? How do you know? Do you understand how she felt about

207

these issues? Paraphrase her feelings. Paraphrase her message. Do you think the way she expressed herself helped her message or hindered it? Why?

3) "Ain't I a woman" as a dramatic, expressive piece S-23

A speech such as this provides an excellent opportunity for interdisciplinary work. The teacher could initiate a discussion of why the speech was (or wasn't) effective, from a poetic or dramatic point of view. Ask, "Was this a good speech? Why or why not? What do you think about the use of the word 'ain't'? Does it help her get her point across, or distract? Would the speech be improved by substituting 'Am I not?' How do her examples help her get her point across? Why doesn't she simply say that she doesn't get a cold if she sits in a draft, and doesn't care if her feet get wet, or that women aren't delicate? Why didn't she just say, "You keep talking about women, but you mean "white women," what about *all* women?" What effect would that have had? What effect did her words have?"

Columbus

Objectives of the remodelled lesson

The students will:
- practice using critical vocabulary, 'assumption,' 'inference,' 'contradiction'
- assess Columbus's reasoning by examining assumptions and implications, recognizing contradictions, and evaluating arguments
- clarify the words 'guess' and 'infer'
- engage in dialogical thinking, by exploring opposing arguments
- practice suspending judgment where evidence is inconclusive

Original Lesson Plan

Abstract

This is part of a lesson which details Columbus's preparations for his voyage to the New World. It includes his theories about geography and his purpose for the voyage. The lesson outlines the mistakes in Columbus's thinking as well as including objections from scholars of the time. To illustrate these errors, it quotes notes he made in the margins of a geography book. The bulk of the text describes Columbus's attempts to get financing from the rulers of Portugal, Spain, England and France, as well as specific preparations for the trip. It describes his ships and the sailing technology of the period. A segment from the end of the lesson speaks of the later voyages of Columbus, including setting up a base for Spanish expansion, and problems with the new colony. The text mentions that Columbus never accepted the idea that he had not reached the Indies.

from *Our United States,* Jo Anne
Buggey. © 1983 Follett. Allen & Bacon.
pp. 92–94, 98.

Critique

We selected this lesson because it provides an opportunity for students to develop some of the micro-skills of critical thinking, particularly making assumptions, inferences, and implications explicit. As they do so, students will learn and become skilled at using critical vocabulary. These skills will serve them well in many other areas of formal study and personal inquiry. Although our emphasis in this lesson is on micro-skills, there are also opportunities to reinforce more global critical thinking objectives, such as fairmindedness and intellectual humility.

This lesson contains some excellent material for analysis of reasoning. Although the subject is familiar, good supplementary information is provided. Nonetheless, the text fails to capitalize fully on the opportunity to use critical vocabulary and to explicitly examine Columbus's and others' reasoning. For example, the "Thinking Skill", p. 93, doesn't identify the source of Columbus's "wrong ideas" as wrong *assumptions*. The mental process of moving from assumptions to inferences to consequences is ignored. There is an attempt to show that Columbus's thinking was wrong, but little effort to show precisely in what respect it was wrong, why it was wrong, or how in some sense it was right. Vague, inaccurate words are used instead of the more precise critical terms. For example, the text uses the word 'guessed' instead of 'estimated', 'calculated', or 'inferred', thereby nonchalantly suggesting that Columbus's thinking is based on a whim, and may draw attention away from the real thinking that went into this venture. The teachers' notes on p. 93, propose asking for students' "opinions". Since opinion need not be based on fact or reason, it would be more worthwhile to ask for students' evaluations, and the reasons on which they are based.

Activity #3 under "Developing the Lesson" has students first copy the heading "Plans for the Voyage", then copy the main points. This activity is unimportant in this section and should be eliminated. Activity #4 has students learn details about the kinds of ships Columbus used. It seems appropriate only for interested students, but is not important for the whole class.

Strategies used to remodel

S–28 thinking precisely about thinking: using critical vocabulary
S–14 clarifying and analyzing the meanings of words or phrases
S–30 examining or evaluating assumptions
S–25 reasoning dialogically: comparing perspectives, interpretations, or theories
S–34 recognizing contradictions
S–18 analyzing or evaluating arguments, interpretations, beliefs, or theories
S–35 exploring implications and consequences
S–5 developing intellectual humility and suspending judgment

Remodelled Lesson Plan s–28 ─────────

We have organized our remodel into four parts, following the general sequence of the student text for parts 1, 2, and 3, and adding section 4. The parts are labeled: *1)* Identifying Columbus's assumptions and inferences, *2)* Evaluating Columbus's reasoning, *3)* Evaluating the consequences of Columbus's reasoning, and *4)* Applications and extensions.

1) Identifying Columbus's assumptions and inferences

This lesson offers an opportunity for development or reinforcement of critical vocabulary and a chance to situate these concepts in a familiar context. You might begin by saying that Columbus was not only an explorer, but a thinker as well. This lesson will deal not only with what Columbus did, but with what he thought. Then you could have students read "The Written Records of Columbus", identifying the notations as his conclusions about geography. The class could compare 'inference' to 'guess'. You could also ask, "What does 'guess' mean? If someone says, 'Guess what happened today?' what does she want you to do? Is she asking you to come to a conclusion based on evidence, or just say any idea that occurs to you? How can we describe Columbus's idea? Was it a wild guess? An intuitive guess? An educated guess? What word or phrase would be more accurate or specific?" **S–14**

Then you might continue by saying something like, "We don't have the text on which Columbus based his conclusions, but we can reason backwards to the *assumptions* he held about geography. What were his assumptions?" Students could read pp. 92-3 and list Columbus's possible assumptions and inferences.

Assumptions	*Inferences*
The Earth is a sphere.	You can travel either east or west to reach your destination.
Asia is extremely large. *or*	
Earth has not much more area than we are aware of.	Asia is not far west of Europe.
There is no land east of Asia and west of Europe. We are aware of all major land.	If you sail west, the first land you reach will be Asia.
Current technology is adequate for safe navigation of the ocean.	It is possible to make the voyage safely.

Then students could distinguish his mistaken assumptions and inferences from those that were correct. *S-30*

2) Evaluating Columbus's reasoning

We suggest that you read the background information on p. 92 to the class, and have them read "Columbus Seeks Help". You could now have students list the opposing assumptions and inferences. *S-25*

Opposing Assumptions	*Opposing Inferences*
The Earth is much larger than Columbus thinks.	The trip will take 3 years and cost too much money.
Navigation of the ocean is too difficult.	The trip can't be made safely.
What hasn't been done, can't be done.	Columbus can't do it.

Then students could note the contradictions between the views. For each pair of opposing views, you could ask, "What, exactly, do they disagree about? Where do they contradict each other?" *S-34* The class could also speculate about Columbus's reasons for rejecting the opposing views. You could point out that at this point his biggest mistake was his certainty despite the lack of sufficient evidence. Students could evaluate the relative reasonableness of the opposing views *at that time. S-18*

3) Evaluating the consequences of Columbus's reasoning

Then you might have students read the rest of the chapter. You could ask, "Were Columbus's mistakes serious? Why or why not? What were the likely consequences for Columbus of proceeding on the basis of faulty assumptions? What are the consequences generally? *S-35* How was Columbus surprised? How was he fortunate?" At this point you could have students read "The Third and Fourth Voyages". Then you might ask, "Which assumptions did Columbus revise? (Size of Asia and the ocean.) Which did he not revise? (Lack of land between Asia and Europe.)" Students could speculate about his reasons for maintaining his beliefs. If so, ask, "Can we be sure this is why? How could we find out? If we can't find out, how should our conclusion be stated?" **S–5**

4) Applications and extensions

The teacher could conclude this lesson with either a discussion or a written assignment as follows: Assess Christopher Columbus as a thinker. What were his strengths? Weaknesses? Was he a good critical thinker? Support your conclusions with specific examples. Would you have advised him to make his voyage based on the information available in 1492? Why or why not? What evidence might have led Columbus to revise his assumption that there was no major land mass between Asia and Europe? Should he have revised it given the evidence he had? Why or why not? **S–18**

An interesting corollary to this discussion of Columbus as a thinker might be to consider some of Columbus's personal qualities that helped and hindered him, such as, dogged persistence, enthusiasm, greed, courage, etc. Again, students should support their answers. This would be a good opportunity to illustrate how character traits influence thinking.

People and the Environment

Objectives of the remodelled lesson

The students will:
- understand some ways people have damaged the environment
- clarify the concept 'harmful changes to the environment'
- develop criteria for evaluating changes people have made to the environment
- practice dialogical reasoning by discussing environmental changes from multiple perspectives
- through Socratic discussion, explore how they affect the environment

Original Lesson Plan

Abstract

The lesson discusses the impact of people changing the natural environment in both the past and the present. Over-hunting has resulted in the extinction of some animals; burning and clearing forests (as well as unwise farming practices) have led to erosion; over-grazing has extended deserts; cities have reshaped the landscape. Strip mining has scarred the land, mineral and water supplies have been depleted; air, water and soil have been polluted by industry, modern transportation, and human wastes. The teachers' notes speak of the greenhouse effect, and advocate finding alternative forms of energy to fossil fuels. The term 'ecology' is defined and portrayed as a means for protecting the environment. Students are to list some ways the local environment is being protected. There is also a section on the polders of the Netherlands explaining what they are, why they were developed, at the same time showing a beneficial human change on the natural environment. Students are asked to focus on how and why people have changed the earth and how people are working to protect the environment. They are to rank these questions from least to most important.

from *Our World Today,* Jo Anne Buggey,
Follett Social Studies. Published by Allyn
and Bacon © 1983. pp. 108–115.

Critique

Exploring multiple perspectives in environmental issues

This lesson addresses an important topic, environmental change, but although it introduces some valuable concepts, the overall treatment is bland and incomplete. This type of presentation results in a superficial, overly simplistic understanding of the problems as well as a sense of personal distance from them. There is no attempt to promote individual responsibility for the environment.

One of the biggest problems of this lesson is the failure to consider a range of reasons for behavior which degrades the environment. For example, over-grazing is listed as a cause for the increase in size of the Sahara Desert, but there is no attempt to explain why the practice continues or why there is resistance to stopping it. In speaking of strip mining, water, air, and soil pollution, there is no hint of corporate, individual, or government opposition to efforts to regulate their activities, nor a consideration of their reasons for doing so.

The critical thinker needs to consider problems, particularly controversial ones, from a variety of points of view and frameworks of thinking. This sort of dialogical approach will reveal complexities, reasoning, needs, and concerns which might otherwise be ignored or dismissed. Consideration of a broad range of views will provide a more solid, realistic, and compassionate base from which decisions can be made. In this lesson we are not asking students to solve complex environmental issues and conflicts, but to consider that all sides have points of view from which their reasons flow. This can serve both as a base for future involvement in actual problem solving in this area, and as a model for critical thinking in other situations with multiple, competing points of view.

Exploring complexities in environmental issues

No mention is made of the cost of environmental clean-up, either to the offender or the general public. In fact, there is no specific mention of any particular agent or agency responsible for taking action to improve treatment of the environment. The captions under the paired pictures (before pollution and after clean-up) on p. 111, imply that the improvements just happened. *"Miners once stripped areas of Montana's landscape to get coal. After cleanup efforts the area looks hardly changed." "Past pollution made Lake Erie's waters unsafe for fishing or for swimming. The lake is now being cleaned up."* There is no discussion of the struggle involved in environmental improvement and the complex problems encountered in arriving at a solution.

Many textbooks tend to oversimplify both problems and solutions, giving students an unrealistic idea about how hard it is to solve problems, implicitly minimizing the world's need for good, persevering, fairminded thinkers. This weakness inadvertently fosters passivity, non-involvement, and the attitude that the problem will solve itself, or "someone" will "do something" about it. We think it is a counter-productive tendency which should be identified and corrected.

Both the teachers' notes and the students' text use the word 'carelessly' to describe how people have used the earth and its resources. This conveys an impression of innocence and unawareness, thereby minimizing the seriousness and urgency of the problem. On p. 112, one simple solution to the depletion of non-renewable resources is to *"find new mineral and water supplies. Settled areas may have to be abandoned as people search for new resources."* No other options are suggested or called for. This reinforces an underlying passiveness in approach. The discussion should address itself to what people must give up to achieve and maintain a clean environment.

Throughout the lesson, nuclear waste is not referred to as a pollution problem, nor is nuclear power named as an alternative source of energy. As these are very significant current environmental issues, they should be considered in some detail, from various viewpoints. Avoiding controversy stifles development of critical skills such as dialogical and dialectical reasoning and entering empathically into various views, recognizing contradictions, making assumptions explicit, etc.

Suggestions on text questions and activities

The key questions at the beginning of the lesson are good ones to consider. However, the suggested activity of having students vote to rank them in order of importance seems pointless. The follow-up on this at the end of the lesson calls for a re-vote, a discussion of why some answers were changed and a general re-ranking. The purpose of this is unclear and we would advise eliminating both activities. Other questions emphasize factual recall, such as those on p. 114, and ignore more substantive questions. Question 5 under "Checking Up" needs to be extended to include a consideration of who is taking responsibility for protecting the local environment, obstacles to the task, and the cost of the project.

Strategies used to remodel

S–8 developing intellectual perseverance
S–3 exercising fairmindedness
S–15 developing criteria for evaluation: clarifying values and standards
S–14 clarifying and analyzing the meanings of words or phrases
S–10 refining generalizations and avoiding oversimplifications
S–25 reasoning dialogically: comparing perspectives, interpretations, or theories
S–19 generating or assessing solutions
S–7 developing intellectual good faith or integrity
S–24 practicing Socratic discussion: clarifying and questioning beliefs, theories, or perspectives

Remodelled Lesson Plan *s–8*

Our remodel basically follows the sequence of the original lesson plan which can be divided into three parts: *1)* Introduction of the topic: harmful and beneficial changes to the environment, *2)* Dealing with environmental pollution, and *3)* Local environmental issues (suggested by question 5, p. 113). To each section, we have added elements which focus on bringing in dialogical questions to foster students' consideration of issues from differing perspectives, as well as encouraging a realistic look at the complexities of problem solving in this area. To section *1)* we have added consideration of why people continue harmful practices (their point of view). To section *2)* we have added a discussion of how clean-up actually happens, who does it, who opposes it, and why, as well as costs and a look at the nuclear waste question. Finally, we supplement section *3)* with suggestions for discussion of ways in which students can accept personal responsibility for caring for their environment.

1) Introduction of the topic

One way to begin the lesson might be to have students consider the key questions on p. 108. We would add these to the list. "How do people decide when an environmental effect is harmful? Why might they disagree? *S–3* What resistance is there to environmental regulation and why?" It would be useful to explore the concept 'harmful,' clarifying it in relationship to the environment, and emphasizing degrees of harm. Here are some questions you might use: What do we mean when we say something is harmful to the environment? Beneficial? What are some examples? Are some things more harmful to the environment than others? What are some examples? How can you judge how harmful they are? *S–15* Are some effects short-term? Long-term? *S–14* These questions will not be addressed in the text, but probably should be considered in discussions of material presented because they bring up crucial, practical aspects of the problems and they suggest the complexity and controversy inherent in environment management.

When students have read through the section on Polders and been provided with background information from the teachers' notes on pp. 108-9, you might ask, "Are all changes that humans make to the environment harmful?" Elicit specific examples of harmful and beneficial changes. You could emphasize that changes generally have mixed results; they are not all bad or all good. *S–10*

To engage students in dialogical reasoning you might discuss some advantages of changes that have been made to the environment, particularly from the point of view of those making the changes. For example, removal of forests provides additional farmland, strip mining provides industry with needed raw materials, etc. *S–3* As students read about overgrazing on p. 110, you could discuss why nomadic cultures continue the practice. As students compare the pictures on p. 111, consider asking, "Why might mine owners object to replanting?" A solid discussion of these points should prepare students for an understanding of why there is resistance to regulation of use of the environment. *S–25* A next move might be to consider reasons people oppose certain changes to the environment. "What are the harmful effects of some changes? The long-term effects? Aesthetic effects? How would one decide which interests should weigh most heavily? *S–15* What compromises might have to be made?" *S–19* Often there are local environmental debates which can serve as an additional focus for this discussion.

2) Dealing with environmental pollution *S–10*

There could also be specific mention of who takes responsibility for monitoring the environment. At this point you could have students compare the pictures of Lake Erie. Ask, "Who is bringing about the clean-up? Who is doing the clean-up? Paying for it?" You might mention government agencies (the EPA), private organizations (such as the Sierra Club), scientists, public opinion, and individuals active in environmental issues. In order to help your students see some of the complexities of environmental protection, you might emphasize that clean-up does not happen automatically and that there are cost considerations that enter into most resolutions of these problems.

After students read the remainder of the lesson (pp. 112-3) you could ask, "Why do people continue to pollute? What would it take to stop them? What are the implications of stopping? (higher taxes, lost jobs, more beautiful environment, preservation of a variety of species, better health) Is the government responsible for any pollution? Why? Give specific examples. What can be done to get people to stop polluting?" We suggest that you consider introducing the issue of nuclear waste if it doesn't come up. This is an important, current controversy and should not be ignored.

3) Local and individual environmental issues

You could conclude the lesson by doing the "Checking Up" questions, p.113. You might want to expand question #5 by adding, "Who is taking responsibility for protecting the environment in our area? Who is opposing it? What are some ways the environment in our area is being harmed? Who is going to do something about it?"

Interested students could investigate an area of local or personal concern, including consideration of the factors discussed in class, and present their findings to the class. If there is sufficient interest and consensus, the whole class could undertake such an investigation. This would logically lead to a consideration of ways students might join in implementing change, such as publicizing their findings in the local newspaper, writing to legislators, organizing litter pick-up activities, recycling, etc. This overall process should give students an understanding of the complexity of problem solving as well as a sense of personal investment and initiative in important issues.

Another way to encourage personal responsibility for caring for the environment might be to initiate a Socratic discussion of how students themselves affect their environment, considering such things as vandalism, litter, and careless consumption of resources. Here are some sample questions you could propose to your students: Do I affect my environment? How? Are there things I do without knowing it, which harm the environment? Do I use many resources? How? How does that affect the environment? What could I do to improve my environment? Are there any behaviors I need to change to help the environment? **S–7** What is my responsibility to others who share the environment? Can one person make a difference? How? Etc. **S–24**

Population Distribution

Objectives of the remodelled lesson

The students will:
- apply map skills to understanding population distribution, thereby exercising independent thought and develop confidence in their skills and reasoning abilities
- identify, and explore the implications of, the main factors which affect population distribution
- refine generalizations and correct textual oversimplifications about population distribution
- apply their new understandings by explaining specific concentrations of population

Original Lesson Plan

Abstract

This lesson focuses on world-wide population distribution. Students are asked to use a population map to determine which areas are heavily and sparsely populated. Reasons for these patterns are given: Arctic — too cold; Sahara desert — too hot, insufficient water; Amazon rain-forest and mountainous areas — unsuitable for farming. Population density is correlated with availability of level land, fertile soil, water for growing crops, and comfortable climate. Students are asked to use physical and climate maps to classify land forms and climates that support large populations. The teacher's notes suggest brief questions addressing the implications of crowding and speculations about future population patterns (domes on the ocean floor, space stations, etc.).

from *California: People of a Region,*
Level 4. © 1984 by McGraw Hill,
Webster Division. pp. 60–63.

Critique

General weaknesses

In this critique we first consider the global weaknesses of the original lesson, especially its tendency to oversimplify. Then we examine specific examples of those weaknesses from the text, noting important factors which have been omitted in explaining past population distribution trends. We critique the text's discussion of future population trends and conclude by suggesting improvements in the text's questions.

We chose this lesson because it offers an opportunity to apply heavily emphasized map skills to understanding population distribution. One failure of the lesson is that it does all the work for students, and thus does not require them to use what they already know from previous study, or to *use* their map reading skills. Students should experience the pleasure of independent thought and discovery. It will enliven the learning experience for students and give them a sense of purpose in studying as they move toward the goal of becoming autonomous learners and thinkers.

The lesson objectives focus on locating and listing, rather than on *understanding* and *interpreting* the data. Critical thinking must go beyond the simple accumulation of information to making it meaningful in a larger framework.

The most serious flaw in this lesson is that the student text situates the question of population distribution in the pre-modern technology era, giving a false and overly simplistic account of why people live where they do today. It emphasizes temperature, fertile soil, flat land, and availability of water as the principal factors of population distribution. It leaves out the role of modern technology in supporting large populations in areas which are not located in fertile, temperate agricultural zones. It does not account for the dynamics of the industrial/manufacturing age in population distribution: proximity to resources, availability of jobs, ease of transportation. Access to waterways, though not dealt with at all, is of vital importance in understanding population distribution, both historically and currently. Finally, the role of government administrative headquarters in attracting substantial populations is ignored.

Specific examples and omissions

The text implies that no large population centers exist in desert areas since food "*does not grow in the desert.*" How is one to account for cities such as Phoenix and Los Angeles? Although the text mentions mining and timber harvesting as activities which take place in mountainous areas, it leaves the impression that, since there is not much fertile land there, one could not expect to find large population centers there. Cities such as Amsterdam which base their large population on trading and transportation are not mentioned at all. The subsistence farming model is also inadequate to explain why a region such as the U.S. Mid-west, though ideal for food production, is lightly populated. Since less than 3% of the U.S. population is engaged in farming, good farming potential couldn't significantly affect population distribution.

In looking at future population trends, the text seems to ignore the movement of our economy toward an information/service emphasis. We are moving into that type of economy now, and it would be an interesting and useful thing for students to consider what changes they might expect in population patterns in the light of this new development. Although the notes to the teacher suggest that the implications of population growth for the future be discussed (p.62), they derail the discussion into exotic, futuristic "*solutions such as living in space stations, in enclosed domes, and on the ocean floor in 'bubbles of air'.*" What do people in Detroit who have lost auto production jobs do while waiting for this technology? It would seem more realistic and practical to confront population problems with resources and technology currently available. Furthermore, seeing economic shifts from agricultural to manufacturing to information will provide a useful framework for understanding a variety of social phenomena.

Critique of text questions

The "Concluding Questions" ask, "*Where do large cities get food? (transported from farm areas.)*" but do not follow up with a discussion of the implications. They do not correlate at all with the student text. Another question is, "*What happens when many people live in a small space? (Homes are smaller. More food and more goods, services, and jobs are needed.)*" This is an important issue to consider, but it seems to go far beyond the scope of the student text. We recommend dropping it in connection with this particular lesson.

In the Review section, questions 1-6 are a jumble of factual recall items which do not probe implications and have little coherence or contribution to understanding population distribution.

Question 7 reinforces the text's emphasis on suitability for subsistence farming as the main criterion for land that is "good for people to live on." We would use questions 8 and 9 at the beginning of the lesson to foster independent thought, rather than tacking them on after students have read the lesson. The text's placement of these questions in the review section makes them into factual recall items rather than the stimulus for independent, critical thought.

Strategies used to remodel

S–9   developing confidence in reason
S–1   thinking independently
S–35 exploring implications and consequences
S–10 refining generalizations and avoiding oversimplifications
S–21 reading critically: clarifying or critiquing texts
S–11 comparing analogous situations: transferring insights to new contexts

Remodelled Lesson Plan s–9

Our remodel concentrates on having students *use* maps and their own background knowledge to understand population distribution before they read the text. Then we look at the influence of types of economy and technology on population trends, considering what changes could occur in the future. The remodel is divided as follows: *1)* Where is world population concentrated and not concentrated? *2)* Climate, terrain, and other factors which influence population distribution. *3)* Read and critique text. *4)* Economic factors and population distribution, and *5)* Application.

1) Where is population concentrated? s–1

One way to begin, would be to direct the class to study the population maps on pp. 60-61. Then you might ask students for their observations on what the maps tell them about population distribution. We do not think you need to explain or interpret the information gathered at this point. It would probably be enough to ask students to briefly summarize what they can say about the distribution of earth's population by studying the maps.

Next, you could explain that with the help of a few additional maps students can use their reasoning skills and what they already know to understand why most people live crowded together rather than evenly spread out. They will need to use the physical map on pp. 48-49 and the climate map on pp. 52-53. If interested students would like more detailed maps, have them use an atlas or encyclopedia to supplement this lesson. Explain that after they have made use of the maps to answer some questions they will read the chapter to see if it correlates with their understanding of population distribution. You might suggest to them that they will probably come up with things the text doesn't mention, to reinforce their confidence in their abilities, independent of textual confirmation.

2) Climate, terrain, and other factors which influence population distribution

First, you might want to focus on the climate and population maps. You could ask, (Review question 9) *"What climate areas do most people live in?*

Why? How does climate affect human life? Why don't many people live in the Arctic? The Sahara? The Amazon jungle? **S–35** Can you think of or find any examples of large cities in any of these types of climate?" (Siberian cities, Phoenix, Los Angeles, Mombasa (Kenya)) For each example, consider discussing what makes it possible and desirable to have a large population there. For example, you could ask, "How does Los Angeles get enough water? Phoenix? Why do people live there?" One way to summarize this segment of the lesson would be to ask students to state what makes it possible to live in areas like deserts, jungles and the Arctic in this century. You may mention the cost of supporting large populations in inherently hostile climates, not only in terms of expense, but consumption of non-renewable resources. **S–10**

Next, you could have students look at the population map and the physical map. As they do this, you might ask, (Review question 8) *"What type of terrain do most people live on? Why?* What types of land forms do they generally avoid? Why? Is it possible to have large population centers in the mountains? What are some examples of cities in the mountains? **S–10** How do they get what they need to survive? What are the costs of living in mountainous terrain? **S–35** Why do people live there?"

A further possibility would be to direct students to look at their maps and list four or five large cities from anywhere around the world. Write the names on the board until you have fifteen or twenty. Then you could ask, "What do these cities have in common in terms of where they are situated?" **S–1** (Many will be on a navigable waterway. Some will be capital cities.) You might want to discuss why these are such important factors in attracting and supporting large populations. **S–35**

3) Read and critique text S–21

You could summarize this part of the lesson, emphasizing the types of climate and terrain most conducive to large population concentration, as well as exceptions to these "rules". Then you could have students read the text to confirm some of their observations and conclusions. Ask them to note anything they didn't include in their study that they find in the text, and anything they discussed that the text omits. You might make the point that texts are not always complete, and students themselves can go beyond what the text provides.

4) Economic factors and population distribution

As part of a transition to considering contemporary population trends, you may have the students look at all three types of maps. Focussing on the U.S., you could ask, "Are there any parts of our country which are good for food production, have enough water and are not heavily populated? **S–10** (Mid-west) Why aren't they? What is at work here?" You might want to point out to students that because of modern equipment a very few people can produce enough food for the whole country. You could add that economies have changed from the agricultural to a manufacturing/industrial type. This newer type of economy affects population distribution in its own way. Consider asking, "What kind of a location would be important for a textile mill, a steel mill, an automobile factory? (proximity to resources; good, cheap transportation) Why would people move to a town with a steel mill? (jobs) If the mill closes, what happens to the people? Will all of them stay there? What will determine where they go? *S–11*

Now you might discuss with students the observation that our economy seems to be in a period of change where heavy industrial production is being phased out or done abroad, and we are moving into an information processing/service type of economy. Discuss what kind of work people would do in this kind of an economy. (Computer industries, high-tech, finance, etc.) What kinds of population shifts might occur in this new type of economy? *S–1* You might mention that population is shifting south and west. You could follow that by asking students why they think this is happening. Remind students that change is sure to happen, and that they can understand why these changes in population distribution take place, if they consider what people need to live and what technology is capable of doing to assist them.

5) Application *S–11*

As a concluding assignment, the teacher could prepare a list of large cities from around the world. Each student could then select three, research relevant information about climate, terrain, proximity to waterways, resources, types of jobs available, seat of government, etc., and explain their size. It might be good to have them note any problems related to temperature, ease of importing food, water, etc. Then students could present their information and explanations either to the class as a whole or to each other in groups of four or five. Students could explore the implications of their findings.

The Soviet Union

Objectives of the remodelled lesson

The students will:
- exercise fairmindedness, when discussing the U.S.S.R.
- detect bias in the text, and ethnocentricity in their own thinking
- compare two concepts of the phrase 'political party'
- Socratically probe ideas underlying censorship
- evaluate Soviet foreign intervention

Original Lesson Plan

Abstract

These pages occur at the end of a chapter on the Soviet Union. The first passage discusses Lenin's importance to Soviets. The text mentions the Communist Party, describes elections, and discusses government control of books and newspapers. Students read an American girl's account of a Soviet school. The final passage discusses Soviet relations with other Communist countries. Students are asked to compare Soviet elections and schools with ours.

from *Europe, Africa, Asia, and Australia*
Kenneth S. Cooper. © 1984 by Silver
Burdett Co. pp. 229–231.

Critique

Sociocentrism in the text

We chose these passages because while they purport to deliver a balanced, "objective" picture of life in the Soviet Union, they maintain a strong sociocentric bias. The text's veneer of fairness makes the sociocentrism harder for a sixth-grader to identify and deal with. Curiously, the lesson errs not only in its anti-Soviet bias, but in its omission of legitimate and important criticisms of the Soviet Union. The resulting picture is unfairly negative and at the same time inappropriately innocuous.

The critical thinker strives to consider opposing ideologies and practices reasoning empathically within different frameworks. This multi-faceted approach should clearly reveal strengths and weaknesses in each position, and enable the student to evaluate each as fairly as possible. Each position should be as fully disclosed and open to scrutiny as possible, so that a fair evaluation can be made.

The need for fairmindedness

The section, "Lenin — the Official Hero", gives the impression that the people in the Soviet Union are unsophisticated and extreme in their adulation of Lenin. *"All nations honor heroes, but few countries in modern times go so far as the Soviets do to honor their official hero."* Several subtle things are at work here: the use of the word 'official' implies a forced, unspontaneous promotion of Lenin as hero; 'modern times' gives the impression that the Soviets are old-fashioned and unsophisticated; *"few countries ...go so far as the Soviets do ...."* reinforces a view of the Soviets as extremists. All of these things may, in fact, be true, but there is little acknowledgement that other countries do very much the same thing with their "heroes". The tendency to lionize heroes of the past should be seen as one common to most countries, not just the Soviet Union. Teacher's note b draws a parallel between Lenin and George Washington, but then derails the discussion into triviality by asking what monuments students might like to visit if they were to go to Washington D. C. It provides an opening for discussion of significant issues and then drifts off into banality, without ever having seriously probed similarities and differences. The text lacks depth of purpose here, and unfortunately this type of question is typical of many texts. Students are informed that a Soviet warned an American, *"You can joke about many things here but not about Lenin."* Students are asked why this was said. The given answer is, *"Because the Communist Party does not permit any criticism of Lenin or his ideas."* The answer is misleading, and, given the student text, a poor inference.

The text's discussion of "The Government and the Party" assumes that the concept 'political party' is the same for the U.S. and the U.S.S.R., and goes on to compare the operation of the Communist Party unfavorably with our system. (It is elitist, restrictive in membership, runs elections with no choice of candidates, and tolerates no opposition.) Here again, these things may be true, but they are viewed strictly from a U.S. perspective. Despite the instruction to the teacher on p. 230, there is no recognition that the *concept* may be understood differently by the Soviets, (thus altering the way it operates,) or that this problem comes up in a variety of contexts. A member of the Communist Party would be able to give reasons for preferring that system.

On p. 230, the text says, *"Pravda gives the news that the party thinks people ought to read."* We have no desire to take issue with that view, but would encourage recognition that our newspapers also print only the news they think *we* ought to read. The difference is more of degree than kind. By failing to recognize tendencies common to most countries, the text isolates the Soviets and subtly conveys the message that they are somehow essentially different from the rest of the world, and us in particular.

In the same section, "Books and Newspapers", favorable information is provided, yet almost every positive statement is followed by the qualifier, 'but'. Then the bad news is delivered. For example, *"The people in the Soviet Union read a great deal. But they are allowed to read only what is approved by the government." "More newspapers are printed in the Soviet Union than in the United States. But neither books nor newspapers print material against the Communists or the government."* Thus, what might be genuinely praiseworthy is generally sabotaged almost immediately. At the same time, the lesson fails to develop a sense of what is wrong with government control of reading material, leaving the criticism too abstract.

Soviet schools

The text provides some very interesting information about school in the Soviet Union from the perspective of an American girl who attended 6ᵗʰ grade there. Nevertheless, the image of a gray, regimented life is underscored without much consideration of positive aspects of Soviet schooling. The text's answers to the question, *"What is school like in the Soviet Union?"* are that it is held 6 days a week, students have to work very hard, they take at least 12 subjects, including English and they have a lot of homework. This emphasis will almost guarantee a negative response to the Enrichment Activity (p. 230) asking pupils to say whether they would like to attend a Soviet school. A more fairminded way to approach this would be to have the students discuss advantages and disadvantages of both educational systems and which gives a better education. The text quotes Laurie Hedrick's and her father's observations of the Soviet school: there were no interesting class discussions, no games, and a strong emphasis on drill. These negative comments are followed by the further remark that the Soviet school *"did seem to get results ...."* Here is a good opportunity for students to probe deeper, question the line of reasoning and examine the bias expressed. Another thing to consider is that most of these generalizations about school are based on a very small sample. It should also be noted that the educational system described as typical of the Soviet Union sounds very much like those of Western Europe and other Western aligned countries.

Omissions and failure to confront negative aspects of Soviet policies

The lesson concludes with a description of "The Soviet Union in the World". A sanitized version of Soviet aggression is presented here in an offhand manner. The invasion of Afghanistan is treated as follows: *"For example, in 1979, the Soviet Union sent armies into one of its southern neighbors, Afghanistan. This military action helped to support a government that was friendly to the Soviet Union."* No mention is made of resistance or opposition, struggle, or loss of life and loss of autonomy for Afghans. Only the phrase 'sent armies' gives a clue that this was an act of aggression. The same bland treatment of Soviet "influence" in eastern Europe completely ignores the military force and brutality with which Soviets enforced their will on resistant populations. Nor does the text mention that the United States engages in similar ventures. The picture is certainly incomplete and misleading. Here the text errs not so much in the direction of sociocentric negativism but in failure to confront issues fully and realistically.

Strategies used to remodel
S–3 exercising fairmindedness
S–2 developing insight into egocentricity or sociocentricity
S–21 reading critically: clarifying or critiquing texts
S–17 questioning deeply: raising and pursuing root or significant questions
S–12 developing one's perspective: creating or exploring beliefs, arguments, or theories

Remodelled Lesson Plan

Our remodel follows the sequence of the student text and can be divided into four major sections: *1)* Idealization of heroes, *2)* Comparison of aspects of Soviet and U.S. society, *3)* School in the Soviet Union, and *4)* Foreign relations.

1) Idealization of heroes

Before having the class read "Lenin — the Official Hero", you might assign a student (or small group of students) to rewrite the passage, substituting the name of a U.S. hero such as George Washington, for Lenin, and make other appropriate changes (e.g., 'U.S.' for 'Soviet Union'). **S–3** Then you could have those students read their version to the class. Ask the rest if the passage seems extraordinary in any way. If so, how? Then you could have them read the original section in their texts. You might ask the students if they can think of other nations' heroes whose names might be substituted in the same passage. Since the analogy is not perfect (for example, pictures of Lenin in living rooms), students should discuss whether any of the differences they noted are significant. You could point out that almost all nations and peoples honor their heroes in similar ways. The teacher's notes suggest asking the class why the U.S. writer's Soviet friend warned him not to joke about Lenin in the Soviet Union. It might be a good idea to point out that although there is no official edict forbidding joking about our heroes, we would be likely to react negatively to a Soviet visitor joking about Washington or Lincoln. The discussion could extend to a consideration of how and why heroes are idealized and how they become symbols for national pride and patriotism.

2) Comparison of aspects of Soviet and U. S. society

For the next section, "The Government and the Party", we suggest that you use the suggestions to the teacher for class discussion. When students have considered differences between the Communist Party and political parties in the U.S., you could ask them if the word 'party' means the same thing in both systems. "How might a Soviet explain the term? Is it fair to use our under-standing of the term as the only right one?" **S–2** Next, you might point out that the text is using a particular concept of elections (ours) as the standard of ref-erence. "Would a Soviet explain elections as the text does? What point of view is the text author taking?" **S–21** If possible, you could invite someone familiar with, and sympathetic to, the Soviet system to come and explain its operation and rationale, or have students write questions to the nearest Soviet con-sulate, and discuss the replies. Discussion could be expanded with exploration of multiple party systems, for example, in Europe. (Why might some people think that three or four parties are even better than two?)

The segment on "Books and Newspapers" could be used as a springboard for discussing how and why newspapers in general select a portion of the news for their readers. It should be pointed out that just as Pravda manages the news for its readership, U.S. (and other) newspapers use screening techniques for their ends. Consideration of bias in newspapers is a large topic and could com-prise a unit in itself, but some effort should be made to alert students to bias in their own cultural context as well as in that of the Soviet Union. **S–2**

Students could also discuss what is wrong with limiting people's access to written ideas. You might ask questions such as: Why would a government want to control what people read? What assumptions might underlie this policy? What fears would the government have? Are ideas dangerous? How? Can you think of any examples where ideas have led to changes in government? Do peo-ple need protection from ideas? Some people? All people? Why or why not? Does a person lose out by not having access to written ideas? How? Does a govern-ment lose out if its citizens don't have access to written ideas? Explain. **S–17**

3) School in the Soviet Union

Of more immediate interest to students is the next section on schooling in the Soviet Union. Have students read this section. As the students compare their subjects with those studied in the Soviet sixth grade (as in the text), you might have them discuss the significance of the differences and similarities they have noted. "Are there advantages to the Soviet system? Disadvantages? How might a Soviet student in the U.S. describe our schools?" *S-3* You could point out that the Soviet system is not unique to the Soviet Union, but is similar to those of many parts of the world, including Western Europe, Latin America and the Far East. If interest warrants, the discussion could extend to a consideration of purposes for schooling, how they differ from country to country and how they generate different systems. *S-17*

4) Foreign relations *S-12*

What does "sent armies" imply? Why would the Soviets send soldiers? Whom would they fight? Have students locate Afghanistan and other countries mentioned on maps or a globe. Why do you suppose the Soviet government especially wanted these countries to be "friendly" to it? What does it mean for countries to be friendly or unfriendly? Do you think it's right for a country to use force on another country to put a "friendly government" in power? Why or why not? Why would that country (U.S.S.R.) think it was OK? Has our country ever done anything like that?

As students answer the questions under "Checkup", you could encourage them to respond to questions 4 and 5 fairmindedly, using points brought up in class discussion. Otherwise, this could degenerate into a stereotypically negative portrayal of life in the Soviet Union. (The answers in the teacher's notes, p. 231, underscore this tendency to accentuate the negative and minimize the positive.) *S-3*

The Spanish-American War

Objectives of the remodelled lesson

The students will:

• clarify the concepts 'world leader,' and 'propaganda'
• clarify claims in their text
• discuss the role of sociocentricity in imperialism
• practice dialectical thinking when evaluating imperialistic actions, by evaluating arguments for and against it

Original Lesson Plan

Abstract

This selection contains most of the material from a chapter on imperialism. It points out that before the Civil War the U.S. was not very involved in foreign policy. It mentions some expansion into Alaska, and the Pacific islands (in order to support trade vessels, and acquire Naval bases) and the desire to spread Christianity and "our way of life". The chapter describes the revolt in and annexation of Hawaii. The rest of the passage focuses on the Spanish-American War, describing reasons for the Cuban revolt, the explosion of the Maine, and how those events affected American public opinion. It recounts some Philippine history, and Roosevelt's charge up San Juan Hill. The last section describes two main results of the war: the territories gained, and America's new role as a world power. It also continues a brief history of the Philippines until its independence.

The teachers' notes recommend a discussion of imperialism, examination of a time-line and a discussion of propaganda. The "Chapter Project" recommends two students be given an issue and asked to research and report on arguments from both sides. Detailed background information is provided for the Great White Fleet, inquiries into the causes of the explosion of the Maine, and the Philippine revolutionary, Emilio Aguinaldo.

from *The United States and Its Neighbors,* Timothy M. Helmus, Val E. Arnsdorf, Edgar A Toppin, and Norman J. G. Pounds. © 1984 by Silver Burdett Co. pp. 221–227.

Critique

We chose this excerpt because imperialism is an important aspect of U.S. and world history, and related ideas are at issue today. The text provides a fair amount of material relevant to evaluating policies of this period. It also provides, and suggests that the teacher discuss, an example where U.S. public opinion was swayed by propaganda, and so provides a clear example of uncritical response to media. Yet the text does not encourage synthesized, fairminded discussion of the material. The text has more the appearance of fairmindedness than its reality. Details are given, then discussion moves on. Students are not asked to put the pieces together and develop a unified view. Rather, they are left with a choppy collection of unsynthesized, unassessed facts and vague ideas. The text fails to have students *use* knowledge of history to understand the present world.

Imperialism

The suggested discussion of imperialism occurs too early, before enough details are covered to make reasonable evaluation possible. Students are not asked to evaluate specific actions described in the text. For instance, though the text mentions that Americans led a revolt against native Hawaiian leaders, that Congressmen wanted to annex Hawaii, and that the President disapproved of the way power had been seized, students are not asked for their evaluations of the different positions, or of the annexation that took place after the Spanish-American War broke out. The background material describes how the U.S. helped Philippine revolutionaries against Spain, and then, after the war, maintained control of the islands. Again, students are not asked for their reactions. Hence, their overall assessment of imperialism is unsynthesized with their conceptions of the details of imperialistic practices; the details have no place within a larger picture, no meaning.

The student text avoids describing how we acquired many of our territories; for example, "*we also controlled the Samoan Islands,*" and "*Soon Americans were starting large sugar plantations*" on Hawaii. A populated area does not change hands by itself. Neither the process nor the results of the changes are mentioned. Details are insufficient for evaluation.

More importantly, the questions on imperialism are incomplete and nearly one-sided. "*How do you feel about this policy?*" though neutral, merely asks for a "gut reaction", not for thoughtful conclusions. The other questions, "*What if the imperialistic country honestly feels it will make life better for the people in the country it is going to control?; We think we in the U. S. have a wonderful system of government. Do we have a responsibility to share it with other countries?*" both push positive conclusions about imperialism, and ignore other reasons people had for their actions. Though teachers are told to point out that, "*Quite often the territory and people who were 'expanded into' were not pleased and resisted,*" students are not asked to consider this point when making their judgments. Apart from this remark, and some of the background information on the Maine and Aguinaldo, points of view other than pro-U.S. are neglected. Students do not ask themselves how imperialism relates to such U.S. ideals as democracy and self-determination. The text doesn't raise the issue of how much good versus harm was done to indigenous peoples, thereby leaving out relevant details.

Propaganda

The discussion of propaganda is incomplete. The teachers' notes state, "*Using the Spanish-American War as an example, point out the effect of propaganda on public opinion. The sinking of the Maine ... was used to influence a public already outraged by the atrocity stories that had been appearing.*" The heading "Recognizing Propaganda" is misleading, since the passage points out propaganda's *effects*, not how to detect it. Such treatment is more likely to lead to a vague and impressionistic view that "propaganda is bad", than to the ability to detect and discount it. Students should clarify the concept 'propaganda', and discuss how to detect it and avoid its influence.

Other problems

The student text passage about the Maine is misleading. *"No one knows who blew it up"* assumes that people were responsible, whereas the teacher's background notes claim that it could have been an accident. Students could use the Maine example to explore how a nation of people can jump to unjustified conclusions based on insufficient evidence. The background material also suggests the effect of egocentric motives on the investigations of the incident, since investigators "found" what they wanted to find. Again, students don't use the material to develop critical insight into how desires can affect interpretations.

The chapter project comes closest to critical treatment of the material, by having students learn the pros and cons for various issues. Yet, it misses being an assignment in critical thought for several reasons: it recommends debate, rather than analysis and evaluation; students are not asked to respond to the points uncovered by their research; and, most importantly, the assignment has students find reasons Americans gave, rather than having them also learn what other people thought.

Questions about the time-line take the form of questions about causal relationships. Students then look at the time-line and note whether the events occurred in the right order and near each other. This inadvertently encourages the false idea that if one event follows another they are causally connected. This activity should be dropped. A better use of time-lines would be to compare other events and changes, and so better understand what else went on during the same time span.

Strategies used to remodel

S–20 analyzing or evaluating actions or policies
S–14 clarifying and analyzing the meanings of words or phrases
S–7 developing intellectual good faith or integrity
S–13 clarifying issues, conclusions, or beliefs
S–12 developing one's perspective: creating or exploring beliefs, arguments, or theories
S–25 reasoning dialogically: comparing perspectives, interpretations, or theories
S–5 developing intellectual humility and suspending judgment
S–2 developing insight into egocentricity or sociocentricity
S–6 developing intellectual courage
S–26 reasoning dialectically: evaluating perspectives, interpretations, or theories
S–28 thinking precisely about thinking: using critical vocabulary
S–3 exercising fairmindedness

Remodelled Lesson Plan s–20

After our introduction, section *1)* Clarifying 'world leader', our remodel follows the original lesson through sections *2)*, Early acquisitions, and *3)* The Spanish-American War. Unlike the original lesson, the evaluation of imperialism occurs last, in section 4.

Interested students could be assigned research projects about the histories (before and after this period) of some of the places discussed in the chapter, and could share their knowledge with the rest of the class, when relevant. The focus of such research could be the long-term results of this period.

1) Clarifying 'world leader' S–14

Either when beginning the lesson or later, students could discuss the concept, 'world leader'. You might ask, "What does the phrase imply? Why do some nations lead? What are the advantages and disadvantages of being a leading nation? What responsibilities does such a nation have? What responsibilities do its citizens have? **S-7** What responsibilities do other countries have to it?" Students could also compare the idea of a good leading country with a good leader (person).

2) Early acquisitions S-20

After students have read "Expansion into the Pacific", they could clarify the statement, *"It would be better, thought the merchants and sea captains, if these places were under American control."* You could ask, "Better than what? What are the alternatives? Why did they think this was better? Better for whom? **S-13** Was it bad for anyone? Why or why not? Do you agree with the merchants and sea captains? Why or why not?" **S-12**

When students have read through "Hawaii," you might ask, "What reason is given for expansion? What reason was given in the previous section? Given what the rest of the passage says, could there have been other reasons as well? Was it right for missionaries to go to Hawaii? Why or why not? Was it right for U.S. citizens to start big plantations? Why or why not? Does the text tell us how U.S. citizens came to own the land? Should the U.S. have annexed Hawaii then? What was different after the war started? Are the differences relevant to judging annexation? Does the text tell us what the native Hawaiians thought about these changes? What do you think they thought about them? **S-25** How could we find out? **S-5** Did the Americans have the right to revolt? Why or why not?"

3) The Spanish-American War

When students have read "Remember the Maine", extend discussion under "Recognizing Propaganda". Have students discuss why the term 'propaganda' applies here. (Some stories were untrue or exaggerated, the assumption that the Spanish were responsible for the loss of the Maine was unquestioned, and the anger it gave rise to was fueled and channeled into the desire for war.) The teacher could supplement the student text with the background material and the following questions: What, exactly, does "Remember the Maine" mean? How was it used? Why did it become a rallying cry? What effect do you think it had on U.S. citizens? How, besides going to war, could the U.S. have responded to the Maine incident? What can we learn from this story? How can we distinguish propaganda from fair reporting? What could U.S. citizens have done to avoid being unduly swayed by propaganda? Why did the different investigations have different findings? Is there a pattern here?" **S-2** (Discuss at length.)

When students have finished the excerpts (through "Results of the War") and have heard the background information on Aguinaldo, they could evaluate policy toward the Philippines, with questions like the following: Why did U.S. citizens enter the fight between Spain and the Philippines? What happened after the war? What did the people of the Philippines think about that? Do you think they realized that, once free of Spain, their land would be ruled by the U.S.? What reasons did U.S. citizens of the time have for controlling them? What were the reasons against it? What were the alternatives? What do you think U.S. citizens should have done? Why? **S–6**

4) Evaluating imperialism S–26

Such a discussion could naturally lead to an exploration and evaluation of imperialism. Students could list pros and cons, and evaluate their relative merits. If students have researched other countries' histories, and have not already given their reports, they could provide their reports before this discussion.

If this develops into an extended discussion, ask students to clarify their claims, develop their reasons, make assumptions explicit, analyze concepts, compare values, etc. "Of which actions we've studied do you approve? Disapprove? (Alaska, Samoa, revolt in Hawaii, war with Spain, annexation of Hawaii, protectorate of Cuba, rule of Philippines, etc.) Why? What, if anything, should have been done differently? On what does evaluation of imperialism depend? Our country's interest? What native people want? What we think is best for native people? If these factors conflict with each other, which is more important? Why? Is there another way "our way of life" could have been spread? Is one way better than the rest? Were the Americans interested in learning from native Hawaiians? Why not? Should they have been?" **S–2** Point out that most people assume that their way of life is best. Students could extend discussion by considering how (by what criteria) different ways of life could be evaluated, if at all.

Use of critical vocabulary could be fostered, as well as analytical skills practiced, with such questions as these: What *assumptions* are you making? Why do you think your *assumptions* are good? How could we know whether we were helping the indigenous people? What *criteria* could we use? What facts are *relevant?* Which facts do we have? How do you know? How could we get the facts we need? Were U.S. actions *consistent* with the reasons given? **S–28** As always, discourage closedmindedness, and have students restate opposing views whenever they have misunderstood or distorted them. If necessary, play devil's advocate for any position students ignore or down-play. **S–3** The teacher could have groups of students discuss their views on imperialism. Perhaps students who are unsure what to think could Socratically question strong proponents of different views. Such an exercise would be valuable questioning practice for the questioner, as well as helping the students being questioned develop their views or explain why they aren't sure. The Socratic questioners could then evaluate the ideas they've heard.

The class could compare this period with analogous periods they have studied.

How can we learn *why* people did what they did? Are people always honest about their motives? Is what people said, or the results of their actions a better indicator of their motives? **S–7**

How does what we have learned in this chapter help us understand the world today? What do we know about the Philippines, Cuba, etc. today? How did U.S. actions described in this chapter influence the present situation?

It should not be assumed that there is a universal standard for how fast teachers should proceed with the task of remodelling their lesson plans. A slow but steady evolutionary process is much more desirable than a rush job across the board.

Beliefs

Objectives of the remodelled lesson

The students will:
* clarify 'belief' and 'culturally shared beliefs' through Socratic questioning and analysis of their texts
* become aware of their culture by identifying manifestations of some culturally shared beliefs and probing their underlying structure by examining assumptions, implications, etc.
* develop self-awareness by making explicit processes by which they have arrived at some beliefs
* use fairmindedness to appreciate why members of another culture have different beliefs
* clarify their text's uses of the word 'belief'

Original Lesson Plan

Abstract

This chapter on beliefs is part of in a unit on culture. It emphasizes the following points: beliefs are one aspect of culture, beliefs grow out of values, beliefs affect other aspects of culture, cars are important in our culture, Aztec lack of understanding of and control over the environment led to belief in nature deities.

Students read a short passage about a space traveler who mistakes cars for monsters and discuss their feelings about cars, as an introduction to the importance of cars in our culture. Students survey television ads noting how many emphasize cars, and discuss some effects of valuing cars, such as drive-through restaurants. They are asked to put themselves in the Aztecs' place. They identify aspects of nature associated with gods from many cultures pictured in their texts. Students choose a category of culture, (language, technology, institutions) name beliefs relating to the category, and provide examples of the effects of those beliefs on the chosen aspect of culture.

from *Planet Earth,* James M. Oswald. ©
1976 by Houghton Mifflin. pp. T124–131.

Critique

Introduction

Since the problem of establishing rational beliefs and of up-rooting and eliminating irrational beliefs is at the heart of critical and fairminded thought, this is a particularly important lesson. Indeed, the problem of belief is so important it should serve as a background for many lesson plans and be a re-emergent theme in school as a whole. In any case, it is an ideal topic for a general Socratic discussion, which should help students begin to sort out a number of important distinctions and to organize their thinking across a variety of domains. In-depth discussion of culturally shared beliefs is also crucial to understanding the basic concept, 'culture', and to developing fairmindedness toward other cultures. Though the lesson has some potential for developing crucial insights, it is marred by confusion, superficiality, lack of insight into the effect of culture on the individual, and irrelevant and unintegrated passages and activities.

Confusion in the text

The text suffers from a confusion of the multiple meanings of 'belief'. At first, the text explains that beliefs have to do with values, for example, "Cars are important." The term retains this meaning through most of the lesson, (*"Out of their values grow many beliefs." "Show pictures of people working or demonstrating for a cause in which they believe."*) Then, without mentioning the change in meaning, the text uses the term in a much broader sense. When discussing the Aztec beliefs in gods of sun, rain, etc,. 'belief' means, "Anything someone thinks is true," e.g., "There is a sun god." (*"Many other humans have believed in gods and goddesses of air, water, sun and land."* *"Have students speculate about how Aztec beliefs in nature deities might affect the other categories of culture."*) This shift in meaning is ignored. At the end of the lesson, the meaning of 'belief' shifts back to that used at first. For instance, teachers are instructed to give such examples of "beliefs" as, *"One should say 'thank-you' when one is given something."* Since the term was explained in a narrow sense in the beginning of the lesson, attention should have been called to the later, broader sense. The problem can be corrected by having students distinguish the two senses of the term.

Though the topic is "beliefs as an aspect of culture," the lesson frequently cites examples of personal/individual beliefs that are not culturally shared (such as protest movements promoting certain beliefs). Examples of individuals' independent judgments shouldn't be juxtaposed with the idea of beliefs of our culture, without distinguishing these two sources of belief. Again, confused, unclear thought is fostered in the students. The class could make this distinction. To keep to the structure of the text, those beliefs which are an aspect of culture should be emphasized, the rest downplayed. Our remodel, however, takes this opportunity to explore beliefs in general.

The lesson emphasizes the idea that beliefs affect other aspects of culture. It overlooks the effect of other aspects of culture on beliefs, and so inadvertently confuses students. For instance, the text suggests that the belief that *"people should wear seat belts,"* shows an effect of beliefs on technology. Yet, in this case, danger inherent in the use of cars has led to the belief in the importance of seat belts. The cause and effect relationship is the opposite of what the text claims. The class could add a discussion of how culture affects beliefs, to the text discussion of how beliefs affect culture.

The discussion about how some beliefs lead to others is misleading. *"For example, someone who feels that the health of people is important may believe that all people have the right to inexpensive medical care.... (a belief that all should have medical care might cause a person to become a doctor or nurse who works with needy people in an impoverished area.)"* The text fails to point out that the conclusions reached were not based solely on the belief mentioned, but more on assumptions, or *systems of beliefs.* Also, the text fails to note that a number of alternatives could stem from a belief or set of beliefs.

Superficiality in the text

More seriously, however, the lesson ignores the crucial point of discussing beliefs as an aspect of culture. We have many of our beliefs simply because we were raised in our culture. We have internalized beliefs prevalent in our culture, for example, belief in the superiority of the two-party system. Although the lesson tries to encourage fairminded consideration of a different culture in its discussion of the Aztecs, it fails because it nearly suggests that each person *inde-*

pendently arrives at culturally shared beliefs. The teachers' text suggests that the teacher, "*Have students imagine what it would be like to live in the valley of Mexico in Aztec times. How would they feel when heavy rains caused floods? Would they think there might be some being that was causing the rain?*" "*The discussion of the Aztecs will help to build the idea that beliefs often develop out of events occurring in the natural system.*" The text never alludes to the idea that, when everyone around us believes something, we generally accept that belief, or that it often seems impossible to doubt or disbelieve it. This insight is crucial to developing understanding of and respect for other cultures, as well as the self-understanding the text tries to foster regarding culturally shared beliefs.

The importance of cars in our culture is a good introduction to cultural beliefs; it is true, easy to grasp, and has important implications. Yet, by itself it is insufficient; a superficial aspect of culture. The value is not basic, but arises from more fundamental values (independence, convenience, variety, speed, time, etc.). The lesson doesn't have students discuss other ways these values affect us. Students should spend substantial time making our culture's fundamental beliefs explicit, to be in a better position to assess them, and to better understand themselves.

The lesson also treats cars themselves superficially, merely as means of transportation, and so ignores the other aspects of our society's relationship to cars (status, image, etc.). Although the television survey is an excellent way of showing how we can recognize beliefs by looking behind words and behavior, better use could be made of it. The text uses it simply to make the point that cars are important in our culture. Students can practice analytic skills by examining ads for associated ideas, and so deepen their insight into their culture.

Irrelevant and unintegrated passages

As it stands, the space traveler story is an irrelevant, unintegrated introduction to the subject of cars. It is introduced as follows: "*Take a look at the way beliefs can affect just one part of people's lives.*" The story is then used simply to have students tell what the "monsters" really were, and then to describe their feelings about cars. Neither the story nor the discussion are relevant to the importance of cars in our culture. Use could be made of the story to develop the insight that there are things we have always known and which are obvious to us because we were raised in our culture, but those things would not be obvious to a stranger without our experiences. Such a use of the story could serve as an introduction to culture as a source of knowledge and beliefs, and so better serve the purposes of the original lesson.

The passage requiring students to tell which elements of nature were associated with pictured gods is trivial and irrelevant and should be dropped.

Strategies used to remodel
S–24 practicing Socratic discussion: clarifying and questioning beliefs, theories, or perspectives
S–17 questioning deeply: raising and pursuing root or significant questions
S–30 examining or evaluating assumptions
S–21 reading critically: clarifying or critiquing texts
S–35 exploring implications and consequences
S–3 exercising fairmindedness
S–11 comparing analogous situations: transferring insights to new contexts
S–14 clarifying and analyzing the meanings of words or phrases

Remodelled Lesson Plan

Our remodel includes *1)* an opening Socratic discussion about beliefs, followed by the three main parts of the original lesson. They are: *2)* Introducing 'culturally shared ideas', *3)* Exploring the importance of cars in our culture, *4)* Understanding another culture. We have added possible further discussion questions at the end, under section *5)*.

1) Socratic discussion of 'belief' S-24

You could begin the lesson by mentioning some of your beliefs, and having students volunteer theirs. You may then want to conduct a Socratic discussion of 'belief,' using these lead questions, and following up students' responses with probing questions: What is a belief? Do you have beliefs? Are there different kinds of beliefs? What are they? How do we come to have the beliefs that we have? Why are beliefs important? Are some beliefs more important than others? Why? Why do different people believe different things? Do our beliefs affect the way we act? How can we find out what someone believes? Do you always know what you believe? How can you find out what you believe? What is the difference between mere belief and something known?

2) Introducing 'culturally shared ideas' S-17

When, as in the original, students have read the little story and inferred the identity of the monsters, the story can be used to introduce the concept of 'culturally shared knowledge or ideas'. The teacher could ask, "Did the space traveler have a mistaken belief about cars? How do you know that cars aren't alive? When did you learn about cars? Why might a space traveler make that mistake? What can we infer about the traveler's home planet? (It doesn't have cars, at least, not like ours, or he would have recognized them.) How did you come to know about cars, what they are for, and what they are like?" Students may realize that they are familiar with cars, because they have grown up around them. Cars are a part of their culture. You could ask students to consider or write about what it would be like if they traveled to the space traveler's planet. They could discuss how things everyone was familiar with there would be new and confusing to them, and why they would likely have mistaken beliefs about what they saw.

3) Exploring the importance of cars in our culture S-17

When students have done the television survey and discussed the results, the teacher could use the following questions to make the purpose of the survey more explicit, and have students practice micro-skills and clarify their texts: Why does the text have you do the survey? What question does the survey answer? What answer does it give? Why did the text suggest that survey? What else could we do to answer the question? What assumptions is the text making? (Television ads reflect our culture. If something is shown in many ads, it is important to people in our culture.) Are the assumptions reasonable? *S-30* Why or why not? *S-21*

To develop insight into our culture, students could then discuss the meanings cars have in our culture in greater detail. You might ask, "Why do cars appear in so many commercials? What ideas are car commercials trying to get across? What ideas are associated with cars in the commercials? In the ads that had nothing to do with cars, but that had cars, why were cars shown in the ads? What ideas, images, or associations were the cars used to get across? Why? What culturally shared beliefs underlie the ads? (What do ads tell us about what cars mean to people in our culture? What do ads tell us about what cars mean to us?) Which of these beliefs do you share? Not share? Why? Why are cars important? What is important about cars? What are the differences between "cool" cars and "uncool" cars?" (Substitute the latest slang.)

To use the material on cars to probe some underlying values of our culture, the following questions could be used: Why are cars important to us? Could we do without cars? How? What would be the advantages and disadvantages of fewer cars or no cars in our culture? How would our culture have to change, in order for us to get along well without cars? **S–35** What does this tell us about what values we have? (independence, freedom, mobility, speed, convenience, being on time, doing lots of things, privacy, control, etc.) What else can we say about our culture and our reliance on cars? Imagine people who didn't like cars. Why might that person feel that way? **S–3** What values might that person have? What values wouldn't that person have? The class could also discuss the questions in the teacher's notes. Students may wish to compare their feelings about living in a place that had no cars, as in the original. They might be encouraged to probe the reasons for their different answers.

To further explore ideas in our culture, students could also discuss, or write about, other aspects of our culture influenced by the same values as those underlying values of cars, for example, clocks and watches, convenience foods and stores, clothing, separate family dwellings, express lines in grocery stores, clubs and social and political groups, etc. **S–11**

4) Understanding another culture

To apply the concept 'culturally shared belief' to another culture, students could read through the passage on the Aztecs, and discuss the following questions: Why would an Aztec child believe in those gods? **S–11** Why are you used to cars? When did you learn what cars are for? When do Aztec children come to believe in their gods? (Students may see that, when everyone around them believes in something, and those beliefs are continually expressed, assumed, or acted upon, children adopt those beliefs as their own, unreflectively.) Why do we say that the Aztec belief in nature gods is a part of their *culture*, rather than simply calling it a belief of the individual Aztecs?" **S–14**

5) Additional discussions **S–14**

To practice the micro-skill of distinguishing the different uses of 'belief', students could compare the following passages from the text: "*People feel some things are more important than others.... From this value may come such beliefs as — land should be owned by the group;" "The Aztecs did not know what caused floods or earthquakes.... The Aztecs were not the only humans who have felt this way about the natural system. Many other humans have believed in gods and goddesses of air, water, sun, and land."* To have students compare the different uses of the term 'belief,' you may ask, "What does the word 'belief' mean in the first passage? In the second? Give me examples of beliefs in the first sense. The second. How are the two meanings similar? Different? Paraphrase the passages, leaving out the word 'belief'." ("think is important" versus "think is true") *S-21*

To further develop students' ability to make clear distinctions, the teacher could have them sort the beliefs mentioned in the text into individual versus culturally shared beliefs. "Is this an individual's belief, or a culturally shared belief? How could we tell?"

Language

Objectives of the remodelled lesson

The students will:

• clarify the concepts, 'communication' and 'language,' and clarify the text's use of these words
• understand some advantages of verbal over non-verbal communication, supporting conclusions with evidence
• infer some advantages and disadvantages of using symbols
• understand language as a human system and situate particular languages within that system
• develop awareness of and tolerance for diversity in language (dialects, accents, archaic forms), thereby thinking fairmindedly
• engage in Socratic discussion to discover and develop their own thinking about language

Original Lesson Plan

Abstract

This lesson on language occurs in a unit on culture. In the first two paragraphs, students read that the previously blank page was changed by having words printed on it; that "human culture is printed on the natural system"; that human culture helps us meet our needs. The student text introduces the term 'communicate'. Students discuss gestures and symbols as forms of communication. The teachers' notes foster the insight that for communication to take place, both sender and receiver must understand the gestures and symbols. Advantages of maps and universal symbols are suggested. Human and animal communication are compared. The text mentions the use of "human language" to communicate facts, information, preferences, values, feelings, ideas, and beliefs (such as, "I think it's wrong to litter."). It also stresses how language enables us to speak of the past and the future, as well as how the written word helps us preserve human experience. Students name feelings of pictured people (happiness, fear, anger, etc.), discuss things they feel strongly about, and identify the needs that specific examples of communication help meet.

from *Planet Earth,* James M. Oswald. ©
1976 by Houghton Mifflin. pp. T80–87.

Critique

Focussing the goal

We chose this lesson because it deals with an important topic which seems to present some organizational and conceptual problems for the textbook writers. The lesson contains some important material and some good, creative suggestions for student activities. However, it suffers from lack of logical cohesion, fragmentation, and confusion in terminology. "The fact/opinion distinction" underlies this lesson. One of the main problems is that the lesson tries to combine and link up very tenuously related goals. The teacher's notes identify some of the goals as, *"Conceptualize <u>language</u>, by giving examples of the sounds, symbols, and gestures people use to communicate .... Demonstrate tolerance of diversity by investigating food preferences and pointing out that people's likes and dislikes vary."* If the authors felt the need to include a discussion on tolerance, why not use tolerance for other languages, dialects, accents, etc. as the focus? Another stated goal is, *"Demonstrate self-awareness by expressing her or his feelings in response to certain situations or objects."* Here again, the focus is deflected from language to feelings — quite another topic. The last listed goal, *"Cite evidence to support the hypothesis that humans use language to meet their needs."* seems like an attempt to unite the very fragmented preceding goals, but in fact only baffles the reader and trivializes the subject of language.

It is important for critical thinkers to be able to recognize systems of thinking within which they operate mentally, and to step back and examine how those systems operate, how they compare to similar systems, and what their role is in influencing thought and behavior. This lesson points in the right direction by inviting students to examine language as such a system, identifying its important features, comparing it to other systems of communication, etc. It shows weakness by not clearly delineating and distinguishing aspects of the system (conceptual problems) and by digressing from considering language *as a system* to discussing some of the *subjects* of language (food preferences, feelings). In the remodel, we hope to show how, by clarifying key concepts, eliminating extraneous material, and extending discussion through Socratic questioning, the lesson can be made to foster some of the goals of critical thinking.

Clarifying terms, correcting misconceptions, maintaining focus

Given the illogical mix of goals, it is not surprising that the first two paragraphs of the student text are confusing and directionless. At this stage it is enough to simply say that language is an important aspect of culture, and then directly address the topic of language itself. A second problem arises in that, although the text says that "language is human communication", it keeps using the redundancy 'human language', (by its definition, "human human communication"). We suggest using the distinction between verbal and non-verbal communication (mentioned in the last section of notes to the teacher), to help organize the lesson content in clear categories. Gesture, expression, and body language could then be seen as aspects of non-verbal communication, written and spoken language as aspects of verbal communication (language proper). Symbols could be discussed as a bridge between verbal and non-verbal communication. We advise dropping the parts of the lesson that wrest the focus away from language and center instead on feelings, preferences and needs. Instead, we suggest that you emphasize the range of possibilities of expression that language offers, thus keeping the attention on language. Although it is alluded to, the precision and efficiency of language in expressing oneself are not sufficiently clarified and stressed. The only differences between human and animal communication mentioned in the text are, *1)* people have more choice about how they can communicate something, *2)* people, unlike animals, can also talk about the past and future.

The lesson veers off course in another instance (p. 47) by asking students, *"Where do you get information about movies that are playing? About the weather? About holidays? etc."* This is now a lesson on reference skills rather than language.

The lesson fosters a common misconception about the relationship of language and symbol on p. 45. The text states, *"The symbols you probably know best are numbers and letters. Letters are put together to make words. And words are grouped together to make sentences. The sounds, gestures, and symbols that people use make up language.*" This scenario implies that language is constructed from letters and words, when, in fact, oral language preceded the written symbols by millennia. The primacy of oral expression is not only ignored, but implicitly denied.

Extending the lesson

The text wisely emphasizes that both sender and receiver must have a common system of communication to achieve mutual understanding. The student text then mentions that international symbols (such as those common at airports) are useful when people don't speak the same language. This is fine as far as it goes, but the possibility of learning other languages is never mentioned. There is excellent potential here to discuss different languages, how they are constructed, how they are not word for word structural equivalents of ours, how they reflect and enhance a particular culture, how they influence each other, etc. It would be an excellent opportunity to help students identify ethnocentric notions they hold about language, and to move beyond them. The question of tolerance would fit nicely here. It would also be an opportune moment to discuss regional or ethnic dialects; how they arose, how they meet the needs of their speakers, how they enrich the "standard" dialect, etc. A sense of various points of view and perspectives could be incorporated into this discussion, including a consideration of language prejudice and conflict.

On p. T85, students are directed to identify feelings and possible reasons for those feelings by looking at some pictures. This is a good way to illustrate how facial expression communicates, but there is no emphasis on how interpretation of such communication is very general. One cannot learn much from looking at expressions in pictures. This activity could be a good introduction to discussing the advantages of words to express more precisely and completely what we are thinking, feeling, experiencing.

An advantage of the written language that is hinted at but not made explicit, is in the section on Erasmus. All that is conveyed by the text is that written language extends forward into time. The implications of that very important fact are not explored at all. The notes to the teacher on p. T87 likewise introduce an important concept only to let it drop immediately. *"Language is not only a part of culture; in some ways it shapes culture."* How does it shape culture? Students will not understand this unless it is discussed and made clear and concrete.

Strategies used to remodel

S–24 practicing Socratic discussion: clarifying and questioning beliefs, theories, or perspectives
S–14 clarifying and analyzing the meanings of words or phrases
S–21 reading critically: clarifying or critiquing texts
S–32 making plausible inferences, predictions, or interpretations
S–5 developing intellectual humility and suspending judgment
S–10 refining generalizations and avoiding oversimplifications
S–23 making interdisciplinary connections
S–3 exercising fairmindedness

Remodelled Lesson Plan

The original lesson has three principal parts: *1)* Introduction of key vocabulary and concepts, *2)* Identification of some characteristics and advantages of human communication (language) and *3)* Consideration of some of the subjects language can talk about (food preferences, feelings) and how these capabilities help us meet our needs. Our remodel begins with an optional lead-in, a Socratic discussion of 'language'. Then incorporates the first two parts of the original, drops the third, and finally provides a section suggesting several alternatives for broadening and extending the lesson.

1) Optional Socratic discussion/lead-in S–24

One way to begin the study of language would be to initiate a Socratic discussion of the topic with questions such as: How did I learn my language? What is language like? Do animals have language? How is human language different from animal communication? What is language for? What makes language work? How do I know when it's working or not working? Why doesn't everyone speak the same language? Where did language come from? Can I think without language?" These and questions like them can be extended as interest warrants. The primary purpose of this type of introduction is to help students to see language as a whole, a system, and their own language as one of many manifestations of that system.

2) Introduction of key vocabulary and concepts

One possibility for beginning this phase of the lesson is to discuss the meaning of the term 'communication'. (p. 44, paragraph 3, "*the way we send and get messages.*") You might use the suggested activity on page T81, paragraphs 1 and 2, to emphasize the importance of comprehension in communication. You could help students to clarify further by asking, "Can animals *communicate?* How do they communicate? S–14 (If students don't mention them, share the examples of honey bees and dolphins on p. T87, or other examples you can provide.) In what ways do human beings communicate? About what do humans communicate? How does human communication differ from animal communication?" At this point, you could introduce the term 'language' and distinguish it from 'communication' by saying that it refers to spoken and written words. It is what we refer to as 'verbal communication'. The other ways of communicating are called 'non-verbal'. To have students clarify the way in which the text uses the word 'language', have them clarify in what way 'language' is used each time it occurs throughout the lesson. S–21

It would be appropriate to incorporate the activities suggested on p. T82, paragraph 4, here. (Identify the symbols on student text p. 45, name some other symbols they know, make up original symbols, discuss and improve on them, and note their limitations.) If you choose not to do this, you might ask, "In what circumstances would symbols be especially useful? What are some limitations symbols have?" Discuss the section on symbols by emphasizing that they are based on words and concepts. Have students read p. 45 and ask, "In our language, what do letters represent? What do words represent? What about sentences? Which do you suppose came first, symbols or spoken language? Explain your reasons." S–32 Emphasize that the symbols all represent the spoken language, which preceded them.

3) Characteristics and advantages of language

At this point, you might talk about some of the things language can do that non-verbal communication can't do as well. You could ask students what they think some of those advantages might be. As they read pp. 46–49 they could list the advantages on the board. (We suggest dropping all the information on feelings, food preferences, etc. on pp. T84–5.) An important insight that you might want to clarify is that the power to preserve ideas, discoveries, etc., helps subsequent generations to build on a broad knowledge base without having to "start from scratch". Another is emphasizing the range of possibilities of expression (nuance, precision) that language allows.

One way to do this might be to have students look at the pictures on pp. 48 and 49 and make up a sentence or two describing what they think the people are communicating. Have them read their interpretations to the class. You could then ask questions such as, "Did we all agree what the people were communicating? What were some of the differences in our interpretations? Why were there differences? How could we know which version was right? If we can't ask the people exactly what they meant, how sure can we be of our interpretation?" **S–5** The discussion should lead to the insight that although we can identify general feelings from gestures and facial expressions, we can't be sure of the details of the experience or the depth of the feeling being expressed. If the people in the pictures were able to speak to us, they could clarify what they meant much more precisely.

The range of expression language offers could be explored by having students write something like, "I love to swim." and "I hate to swim." on opposite sides of the blackboard, and then list a range of expressions in between. (I like to swim sometimes. I like to swim when the weather's warm. I'm afraid to swim in deep water. I don't like to swim often.) The purpose here is to illustrate the power of language to express nuance and a broad range of feeling. **S–10**

Another way to extend this discussion and to cultivate a global perspective about language (seeing it as a whole, a system) would be to consider with your students the fact that language changes. There are many ways to approach this idea in discussion. One might be to cite a brief passage from Shakespeare or the King James Bible (with some 'thee's' and 'thou's'). Or, have students list slang terms from old television shows, e.g., "Oh, golly." You could then ask, "Is this standard English? What's different about it? When was it written/recorded? Why don't we speak/write this way now? Will our language change in 100 years? What changes in our language are taking place now? Why does language change? Are changes good, bad, or neither?" **S–23**

4) Alternatives for broadening and extending the lesson

If interest and background warrant, the teacher could conclude the lesson with a discussion of attitudes toward language. You might begin by asking students to name some languages other than English. If there are any children in the class who speak other languages they will be a good resource as the discussion proceeds. Note that other languages are not word for word equivalents of English, but have their own structure. (If you are familiar with another language you could illustrate, say, differences in word order, by contrasting simple equivalents in English and the other language.) Note also that they meet the needs of their people just as our language meets ours. You might ask, "What might be important to an Eskimo that is not as important to us? What in our culture might not be important for an Eskimo to know? How do you think this would show up in languages? (Eskimos have many more words for 'snow' than we, because it is such an important part of their environment. We, on the other hand, have developed a computer vocabulary that reflects our interest in computers. Another example of culture influencing language is in Peru. Peruvians have many words for 'potato', reflecting the importance of potatoes as a food staple in that culture.) Another question might be, "How many students know someone who has learned a foreign language? How can a person learn another language? How long does it take? Is it hard? What would be some of the frustrations? Why would it be desirable to learn another language? What would be some problems of living in another country and not knowing the language?"

If you want to explore another aspect of language which invites a discussion of diversity and tolerance, you might consider the dialects that exist within a language. English is a good example because of its dialects in North America, Australia, New Zealand, Scotland, Malta, Jamaica, South Africa. "Why are there so many forms of a single language? Is one form better than another? Why or why not? What do we mean by 'standard English'? Does 'standard' mean better?" **S–5**

You might extend this discussion in several ways, encouraging students to see and develop tolerance for perspectives other than their own. Consider asking, "Have you ever heard someone speak English with an accent? Was it hard or easy to understand them? How did they learn their way of pronunciation? Would they think *you* had an accent? **S–3** Why are there differences in pronunciation? Is one form of English better than the others? Why or why not?"

The Constitution

Objectives of the remodelled lesson

The students will:
- learn some functions of the three branches of the U.S. government
- clarify claims in the text by exploring root issues regarding government and the distribution of power in our government
- compare ideals of the Constitution with actual practice
- through Socratic questioning, understand the reasons for and assumptions underlying rights guaranteed under the Bill of Rights
- develop their perspectives on human rights, and functions and limits of government
- transfer understanding of the Constitution to current events

Original Lesson Plan

Abstract

This chapter, "The Constitution of the United States", begins with a paragraph about the Articles of Confederation and why they failed. It then lists the leaders at the Constitutional Convention. The terms 'republic' and 'federal' are explained, and some of the powers of the national government listed. Separation of powers and the three branches of government are briefly explained. Students are asked to state which powers from a list belong to the states, and which to the federal government. Students are told about the Constitutional Convention debate between small and large states regarding how the number of representatives to Congress should be allotted, and how the issue was resolved. The term 'Amendments' is explained. Students are told that some states refused to approve the Constitution until the Bill of Rights was added. A three page Summary of the Constitution follows. Students are asked questions about the Bill of Rights.

from *The United States and Its Neighbors,* Timothy M. Helmus, Val E. Arnsdorf, Edgar A Toppin, and Norman J. G. Pounds. © 1984 by Silver Burdett Co. pp. 120–125.

Critique

Introduction

We chose this lesson for its emphasis on and summary of the Constitution, because understanding the Constitution is crucial to citizenship in a democracy. Students should explore the ideas underlying important aspects of our government: how it is supposed to work, why it was structured the way it was, how the structure is supposed to preserve citizens' rights, how it could fail to do so, and why some rights are both difficult and important to preserve. Critical education demands clear and well developed understanding of these points. When understanding is superficial or vague, hidden agendas and mere associations guide thought and behavior. Slogans substitute for reasons, prejudices for thought. Citizens become willing to accept the *appearance* of freedom, equality under the law, and democracy, rather than demanding their *realization.*

Summarizing the Constitution in language 5th graders can understand is an excellent idea, though some parts of the original could also be used. On the whole, the summary is good, though flawed by its incompleteness. For students to have enough details to understand the key concepts of the lesson, more of the specific duties of the branches of government should have been mentioned.

The greatest flaw with the lesson is its size and lack of depth; not nearly enough time is given to fostering understanding of this important document. This section is only part of a chapter which includes details of battles in the Revolutionary War. The relative importance of material should be reflected in the text space given to and time spent on it. Of the six chapter review questions, only one, a recall question, addresses the Constitution. Equal space is devoted to *"What do you think was the most important battle of the Revolutionary War? Explain."* Spending insufficient time on such important ideas leads the text to treat them superficially or vaguely. Students have little opportunity to understand key ideas fully, see the whole picture, appreciate reasons for important parts of the Constitution, or develop their perspectives on government, human relations, and how to preserve their rights.

Inadequate explanations

The lesson has too few questions, no extended discussion, and a number of the questions are trivial, or simple recall. Some of the suggested explanations and answers are sorely incomplete, confusing, or fail to answer the questions. For instance, the text answer to the question on why the right to a jury trial was considered important, is, *"It had been denied under British rule."* This answer is inadequate. Arson wasn't allowed under British rule, yet is not guaranteed under the Bill of Rights. The right to a trial by jury was included because the writers of the Constitution thought it was the best way to insure justice and prevent abuse by law. Students should consider why.

Important explanations are undeveloped. Questions about why the separation of powers and the Bill of Rights were included, for instance, fail to probe the reasons. The student text explains, *"The members of the Constitutional Convention wanted a government that would protect the people's rights, not take them away. So they divided the government's power into three parts, or branches. This is called separation of power."* Checkup question 4 (p. 120) asks, *"Why were powers divided among three branches of government?"* The suggested answer, by simply reiterating the abstract claim in the text, turns a thought-provoking question into a recall question. Students are encouraged to substitute reiteration for understanding; to accept an apparently unconnected answer as an adequate explanation. The text fails to explain *how* separation of powers protects people's rights.

The given answer to, *"Why was it necessary to add a Bill of Rights to the Constitution?"* is, *"because many states insisted that the people's rights as well as the rights of the government must be written down."* Again, the "answer" fails to answer the important questions: Why did people think rights should be written down? What is the advantage? Why write them into the Constitution? Does writing them into the Constitution guarantee they won't be violated? Crucial questions and connections are left unanswered. Students are not left with a clear understanding either of the connection between separation of powers and people's rights, or of the importance of the Bill of Rights.

Superficial treatment

Though the Constitution is the only thing covered in the "Skills Development," the subjects, separation of powers and checks and balances, should not be covered solely in multiple choice format. Such treatment discourages students from considering *why* these ideas are important, how they work, or how they can break down. Nor is the importance of specific rights addressed anywhere in the lesson. Students (following their texts) tend to understand freedom of speech, not in terms of the good of the society or the tendency of power to corrupt, but more as an issue of preference, "People should get to say whatever they *want*."

An activity, misleadingly called "Applying Current Events", simply has students collect pictures of government officials and buildings and display them under the headings "Executive Branch", etc., displaying a superficial understanding of the connection between the Constitution and current events.

Confusions

The student text, when discussing the Constitutional Convention, says, *"Other things were not so easy to decide. The delegates knew they wanted a Federal government. In such a government the power is divided between the national and the state governments. But how much power should go to the states? And how much to the national government? They solved this problem by writing just which powers the national government would have."* Suggesting that the problem of deciding how to allot power was solved by writing the powers down perpetuates sloppy, confused thought in the students, and makes the actual decisions reached seem arbitrary.

Another confusion occurs in a suggested activity. The text suggests students write a Constitution for their class *"stating the rules the class needs."* Constitutions are not lists of rules or laws, but rather definitions of offices, rights, and powers. By stating the activity in that form, the text inadvertently confuses students about the difference between a constitution and a body of laws.

Strategies used to remodel

S–21 reading critically: clarifying or critiquing texts
S–17 questioning deeply: raising and pursuing root or significant questions
S–27 comparing and contrasting ideals with actual practice
S–15 developing criteria for evaluation: clarifying values and standards
S–24 practicing Socratic discussion: clarifying and questioning beliefs, theories, or perspectives
S–13 clarifying issues, conclusions, or beliefs
S–12 developing one's perspective: creating or exploring beliefs, arguments, or theories
S–26 reasoning dialectically: evaluating perspectives, interpretations, or theories
S–11 comparing analogous situations: transferring insights to new contexts

Remodelled Lesson Plan

Following the three remodelled parts of the original lesson, [*1)* Introduction to the Constitution, *2)* Separation of powers and checks and balances, and *3)* The Bill of Rights], we have added discussions about Human rights issues in foreign policy and international politics *4)*, Probing the purposes and limits of government *(5)*, as well as some possible extensions*(6)*.

1) Introduction to the Constitution

When the passages about and summary of the Constitution have been read, to allow students a chance to get "the big picture", you may ask, "What is this document for? What is its purpose? What basic points does it cover?" **S-21** Students can skim their texts as they answer, or be asked to take notes as they read. (It defines the three branches of Federal Government, describes how offices are filled, lists duties of and limits on each branch.)

You might read the real Preamble to the students, and discuss it with them. You could then tell the students about some of the details left out of the text. Among the most important and easiest to understand are the following points: Congress passes Federal Laws, establishes Post Offices, secures authors' and inventors' rights to their writings and discoveries, must publish statements about how much money it spent, and must send laws to the President to sign. If he vetoes them, they can pass the law if two-thirds of both Houses agree. The President can recommend laws to Congress, and, with Senate approval, can appoint Supreme Court Justices and heads of the Departments (the teacher may want to list some of the departments). The Supreme Court decides cases that were tried in lower courts but which one side wants to appeal. State governments cannot enter into treaties. Amendments must be proposed by two-thirds either of Congress or of State Legislatures, and must be passed by three-fourth's of the States to become part of the Constitution. The class may want to discuss some of these points, such as, the difficulty of changing the Constitution, or why Presidential appointments need Senate approval. Students could reiterate the veto and override process, and discuss what protection it gives against abuse of power.

2) Separation of powers, and checks and balances S-17

Discussion of the previous point can lead into a discussion of the separation of powers, and checks and balances. To probe these ideas in greater depth than the text, thereby making the reasons for our system of government clearer, you could ask, "Have you ever been in a situation where some people had too much power, or abused their power? Why was that a problem? How could the problem be solved? How did the authors of the Constitution try to solve it? Why not give all of the power to one branch, say, the Executive? Why have each branch have some power over the others, rather than giving each branch complete control over its own duties? What does the text say in answer to this question? What does its answer mean? How could concentrating power lead to loss of people's rights? Make up an example which shows me how a system like this could prevent abuse of power. **S-21** This separation of powers, and system of checks and balances is the ideal. What could make it go wrong? (Using the checks and balances unfairly, or not using them at all.) Make up an example of how it could go wrong. Why would that be bad? What has to happen to make it work right? **S-27** What should we look for in our leaders? What sort of people should we elect? (For instance, when voting for President, voters should consider whom the candidate would appoint to important offices, or whether the candidate is a good judge of character. Perhaps members of Congress who abuse or fail to use checks on the President should be voted out.) **S-15**

The class could also relate some of the above ideas to a specific historical issue by discussing the text section, "Congress", why larger and smaller states disagreed, the arguments for both sides, and the solution. The students could also try to come up with alternative solutions to the problem of abuse of power, and compare their solutions with those in the Constitution.

3) The Bill of Rights S–24

Students may reread the Bill of Rights section in the summary. The teacher may also want to make the real Bill of Rights available, or have it read in class, and compared to the summary. Students could use the summary to generate a list of the rights covered. To foster in-depth understanding of the meaning and importance of the Bill of Rights, the teacher could conduct a Socratic discussion of each right, with questions like the following: What does this right mean? What does it say people should be allowed to do? How could it be violated or denied? S–13 How important is it? Why? Why would not having this right be bad? How would it hurt the individual? Society? Are there exceptions to this right? Should there be these exceptions? Why or why not?

The class could also discuss the underlying ideas and assumptions behind the Bill of Rights, especially the First Amendment rights. (The importance of following conscience, especially regarding political and religious beliefs; the idea that when people can discuss their ideas and consider all alternatives, the best ideas will prevail or compromise can be reached; people who do no wrong shouldn't have to be afraid of their government; even people who do wrong have rights; trials in which both sides argue before a jury of impartial citizens will best render justice; government has an obligation to be fair to citizens — not just do what it wants because it's strong; etc.) S–17

You might ask, "Why did some people want these rights written down? What are the advantages? Are there disadvantages? Are there important rights omitted? Should they be added to the Constitution? Why or why not?" Students could compare their answers to that given in the text.

For this activity, the teacher could split the class into groups, each of which could discuss one or two rights. One member of each group could then report to the rest of the class.

4) Human rights in other countries S–12

The class could also discuss these rights with respect to people all over the world, and so begin to forge their own perspectives on international politics, human nature, and the role of the U.S. as a world power. "Do you think everyone all over the world should have these rights? Why or why not?" (You may need to point out that not every country has these rights: In some countries you can be put in jail for disagreeing with your government leaders, even if you don't advocate violence; you can be taken by the police or soldiers, kept, tortured and even killed without ever having a trial; you can be arrested for practicing your religion, or not following the rules of the official religion; etc.) Students could then talk about what, if anything, our government should do about these countries, or the people in them. "How should we treat such countries? Should we give them aid, or withhold it? What kind? Should we tell them we want them to change, or is it none of our business? What if most of the people of the country voted for the leaders that do some of these things? If people want to escape these countries, should we let them move here and become citizens? Why do some Americans object to this idea?" Teachers familiar with the U.N. Declaration of Human Rights could mention it here. If students express different points of view, the teacher could conduct a dialectical exchange, by having students defend their views, clarify key concepts, explore assumptions, and note where the perspectives conflict. As always in such a discussion, encourage students to listen carefully to, and note strengths in, ideas with which they disagree. **S-26**

5) Purposes and limits of government *S-12*

The lesson could also be used for a discussion probing the purposes and limits of government, and deepen students' understanding of government and our Constitution. The Preamble could be reread to initiate discussion. The following questions could be used to develop an analogy with, say, student government, if the school or class has one: Why do we have student government? What does it do? Are you glad that there is student government? Why or why not? Why did the writers of the Constitution believe they had to start a government? Do you agree with them? Why or why not? What does government do for us? (The class could use a list of Federal Departments to generate some ideas.) How could we have these things without government, or why couldn't we have them without government? What is our government *not* supposed to do? Why? What do people not like about having a government? Why do most people think having a government is worth the disadvantages? **S-17**

6) Additional ideas *S-11*

The lesson could also be linked to a unit on the news. The class, or groups of students who could report to the class, could find newspaper articles about major bills being debated or passed, Supreme Court decisions, a Presidential nomination, or debates on foreign affairs. The class could outline both sides of the issue, pinpoint the relevant part of the Constitution, and discuss the implications of different possible outcomes. If the issue revolves around interpreting the Constitution, the class could discuss why there is no agreed upon interpretation. Students could also distinguish aspects of the issue involving the Constitution, from aspects which have become part of our government, but are not described in the Constitution.

Economic Systems

Objectives of the remodelled lesson

The students will:
- distinguish politics from economics, clarifying confusion in the text
- state advantages and disadvantages of different economic systems, avoiding stereotyping and oversimplification
- elaborate implications of various economic concepts
- identify basic assumptions behind each system
- in each system, distinguish ideals from facts
- practice dialectical reasoning and fairmindedness in arguing strengths and weaknesses of opposing economic systems

Original Lesson Plan

Abstract

The lesson defines 'economics' and then discusses the current dominant economic systems: capitalism, socialism, and communism. Elements of capitalism include the role of government and its relationship to the private entrepreneur, as well as the role of profit and competition. Consequences to workers and consumers are outlined. The text emphasizes that no system is "pure", there is overlap in all three. Likewise for socialism and communism, the elements of government ownership and control of production and resources are explained, along with consequences for consumers (little choice of goods, one price) and workers (set wage levels). Great Britain is cited as an example of a mixed economy, with elements of capitalism and socialism. Soviet communism is discussed with attention drawn to the gap between stated goals (no rich or poor) and actual practice. The text stresses the role of the government in regulating all aspects of the economy. A short digression on the Soviet political system follows. A chart showing the three systems on a continuum and another comparing features of the three systems are included at the end. Students are asked to describe how each system works, give an example of where each is practiced, compare them, and designate which system they prefer and why.

from *Our World Today,* Jo Anne Buggey,
Follett Social Studies. Published by Allyn
and Bacon © 1983. pp. 418–423.

Critique

Clarifying concepts

We chose this lesson because the important subject could provide a good basis for subsequent study and expanded understanding in later grades. Unfortunately, in some ways, the text actually lays the groundwork for prejudice and misunderstanding. One point about which the authors seem particularly confused is the relationship of communism to socialism. The text says, *"Communism is a special form of socialism,"* yet also says that there are three kinds of systems.

The text also perpetuates the common confusion between economics and political systems. Although elections, a political phenomenon, are not mentioned in the discussions of capitalism or socialism, they are discussed under communism, thus inappropriately fusing political elements into a consideration of an economic system. The effect is to discredit communism, the economic system, by criticizing political practices of the U.S.S.R.'s government.

The picture on p. 420, shows a crowd of people in a department store. The caption says, *"Under communism people have few choices when purchasing goods."* There is no way of getting to this conclusion by looking at the picture. How are students to *"discuss how this photograph helps explain the text"*? What they are in effect asked to do is make a negative judgment about communism with totally irrelevant evidence.

Ideals versus actual practice

The text confuses ideals with reality when discussing capitalism. For instance, on p. 418, the text states that businesses and industries compete by *"having lower prices or a better product or both."* This may be true in some cases, but often businesses merely *claim* to have a better product, when in fact the product is no better than a competitor's or in some cases is worse. The paragraph continues, *"Under capitalism a worker is free to work or not to work. Of course, those who do not work may not be able to buy the goods and services produced."* This is like saying that the workers are free to starve, when in fact the eating imperative may significantly affect their freedom to not work. Furthermore, there are many who want to work but cannot. Again, *"Workers are also free to choose the kind of work they want to do. No one tells them that they must take certain jobs."* While this is partly true, it is far from completely true. Workers are constrained by their opportunities for training and education, as well as by the shifting demand for certain types of labor, and many are not hired for reasons irrelevant to the job.

Sociocentrism and bias in the text

The lesson's treatment of socialism is somewhat more balanced, although much shorter than either capitalism or communism. Some general strengths and weaknesses are mentioned, albeit briefly. Students do not actually get a chance to explore specific advantages and disadvantages for the average citizen, such as free health care and heavy taxes.

The text's portrayal of communism, on the other hand, is one-sided and emphasizes the negative. The text is quick to point out that the communist ideal of eliminating social class distinctions *"has never been met in any of the communist countries."* The progress toward the ideal is not mentioned. The advantages of capitalism are touted while those of communism are either passed over lightly or altogether ignored. The disadvantages of capitalism are never made explicit. Although unions are mentioned, and the basis of worker/owner conflict laid, there is no follow-through and no detailed discussion of the sometimes violent struggle that has characterized this movement in the United States. Sweeping statements such as, *"Control by a communist govern-ment is complete."* serve to drive home the ominous message.

The larger problem in the lesson is sociocentricity. As it stands, the lesson does not encourage fairminded examination of each economic system for its strengths and weaknesses. Most people reading this lesson would not have the faintest idea why anyone would be anything but a capitalist.

Critical thinkers studying this material would want to understand, as fully and empathically as possible, why people support alternative economic systems. To do this, they would be willing to confront weaknesses in their own system, rather than seeing it as flawless. Likewise, they would be willing to view opposing systems from the perspective of their intelligent advocates, genuinely recognizing those systems' strengths as well as their weaknesses. This lesson gives students the impression that they have understood socialism and communism fairly, but it actually manipulates the material to inculcate an uncritical acceptance of capitalism and an uncritical rejection of socialism and communism.

Correcting misunderstanding and oversimplification

The text reiterates instructions to the teacher to emphasize the mixed nature of economic systems; that no country practices "pure" capitalism, socialism, or communism. This is a laudable move, but it is not sufficiently backed up in the text. The passage noting socialistic aspects of the U. S. economy is not connected with the idea that no country has a "pure" system. Where the text mentions the postal service and passenger rail service, it characterizes the government as an "owner", thus hiding the similarity to communist "government ownership of the means of production." Communist countries' divergence from communism is not mentioned.

Moreover, the text doesn't do an adequate job of explaining capitalism's strengths. The implications of capitalism are not explored either. Most claims about capitalism are left too abstract to be meaningful. Students should relate the dynamics of supply and demand to their own economic behavior.

The questions at the beginning of the lesson and in "Checking Up" are oriented toward simple recall, omit fair comparison and evaluation, and should be supplemented. Question #5, *"Which economic system do you prefer? Why?"* is guaranteed to produce the answer, "Capitalism", given the general orientation of the text. More detailed and in-depth evaluation should be substituted.

Strategies used to remodel
S–6　developing intellectual courage
S–14　clarifying and analyzing the meanings of words or phrases
S–35　exploring implications and consequences
S–30　examining or evaluating assumptions
S–7　developing intellectual good faith or integrity
S–25　reasoning dialogically: comparing perspectives, interpretations, or theories
S–27　comparing and contrasting ideals with actual practice
S–21　reading critically: clarifying or critiquing texts
S–2　developing insight into egocentricity or sociocentricity
S–3　exercising fairmindedness
S–10　refining generalizations and avoiding oversimplifications
S–26　reasoning dialectically: evaluating perspectives, interpretations, or theories

Remodelled Lesson Plan s–6

The remodel we have developed follows the order of the student text and adds an activity/assignment section at the end. It is organized as follows: *1)* Clarification of terms, *2)* Capitalism, *3)* Socialism, *4)* Communism, *5)* Suggestions for concluding activities.

1) Clarification of terms S–14

When the students have read the first paragraph in which economics is defined, it would be a good idea to have them distinguish it from politics or government. One way of doing this would be to ask the students what was covered in lessons on different forms of government. They could compare the subject with economics. The teacher could list the names of political systems and the names of economic systems. It is important to make students aware of these differences in order to sort out the confusion which occurs later in the lesson.

2) Capitalism

Then, students could read the section on capitalism. You might discuss its essential features and list them on the board. (Include individual ownership and control of money, property, and resources; profit; competition; freedom of workers.) You could extend the discussion of each feature and its implications for citizens. For example, in discussing competition, the class might mention that, associated with it, are usually winners and losers; there is sometimes a degree of risk; advertising is important; a variety of products may result; there are appealing incentives; ingenuity, creativity and novelty may be rewarded when profitable, and so on. When discussing 'profit', you could mention the pressures it puts on owners and their businesses or industries. "How have those pressures affected the workers? The product? The owners? Why are unions necessary? S–35 Why would owners be likely to resist unionization? What are the concerns of unions?" You could also point out that for capitalism to work as described, consumers have to be smart shoppers. Then you might ask, "What are the goals of capitalism? For owners? For workers? For consumers? Do these goals conflict? How does the system address the conflict? On what assumptions about people is this system based? What does this system assume about why people work and create? What evidence is relevant to settling the issue? S–30 What is your position? Why? What can make this system go wrong? Do you approve of the goals? Have they been achieved? To what extent?" S–27

Next, by way of summary, you might ask the students to mention some of the problems or disadvantages associated with capitalism. "What might be some ways of dealing with those problems? What are the advantages of capitalism? Why do people defend it?" S–25

Now you could direct students' attention to the fourth paragraph on p. 418. You might point out that the authors of the text are talking about some ideals of capitalism here and that if examined, a gap between ideals and facts will be discovered. You could ask questions such as these: Could you give an example of a product you use where you have a choice of several brands? Is one always clearly better or lower in price than the others? How do you know? What influenced you to buy it? How could we expand the text's explanation of how competition affects products? What happens if a worker decides not to work? When you don't have the money to buy food and housing, is not working a real option? If a worker is responsible for other people, is he or she "free" to choose not to work? Are workers always free to choose the kind of work they want to do? If you walked into IBM and asked for a job would you expect to be hired? Why not? Do people always have the opportunity for education or training for a job they want? What might stand in the way of their acquiring the necessary education? What happens to workers when their company closes down? Are they free to get whatever job they want? Why not? What other factors might make it hard to get the job you want? (racism, sexism, lack of "connections," etc.) **S-27**

Talk specifically about what the facts are (see critique) and why it is misleading to state ideals as if they were completely realized. You might mention that this is a common characteristic of many kinds of writing, including textbooks, and that readers should be alert of it. **S-21** The teacher could also ask, "Why would an author want to state ideals rather than facts? **S-2** What harm is there in stating ideals as though they were facts?" Continue discussion as interest warrants. **S-7**

3) Socialism

The class could now read the section on socialism. We suggest that you proceed in the same manner as with capitalism. You might list the essential features of socialism for clarity. Since the text does not, the teacher should include some of the benefits that socialism ideally provides, such as comprehensive health care, free education through university level, guaranteed employment, etc. **S-3** Ask, "What are some of the goals and ideals of socialism? What do you think of them? Have they been achieved? To what extent? Why or why not? (You might point out that there is not 100% employment in socialist economies.) What might be some implications of the features of socialism? How are the services, such as free medical care, paid for? What would life be like for a person living under socialism? How would it be different from capitalism? The same? **S-35** Where is socialism practiced? Why are there unions in socialist countries?" **S-27**

To establish an understanding of the relationship of political systems to economic systems, you might ask, "Can there be free elections in a socialist country?"

Then students should be ready for the teacher to share the background information on p. 418, emphasizing that no country has a pure version of any economic system. You could talk about some of the aspects of socialism in our economy. You might mention (or have students mention) Social Security, Medicare, etc. "Why are these 'socialist' in nature?" You might point out the last paragraph of the Capitalism section, emphasizing that the government controlled postal and passenger rail services in the U.S. are further examples of aspects of socialism in our economy. **S-10**

4) Communism

When students have read the section on communism, you could ask, "What are some goals of communism? What do you think of its goals? The text says that they have never been achieved. Why is this so? Is that true only for communism?" **S-3** Then you may want to discuss communism's essential features. You could ask, "What are some differences and similarities between communism and socialism?"

You could have students review the distinction between economics and government. Then you could consider with the students the third paragraph on p. 420. You might ask, "Is the text discussing economics or politics here? What political aspects does it bring into the discussion? What is the source of the confusion? Why do you suppose the author mixes in political considerations in this section? Was it done in the other sections? **S-2** Can we critique the chart on p. 420? (It is inaccurate to suggest that socialism is in the middle of a continuum between capitalism and communism. The degree of socialism could vary all the way from near complete government ownership to near private ownership. This simplistic representation defeats the text's own stated purpose of emphasizing mixed systems.)

You could ask the students to critique several other textual biases. You might point out that the sentence, *"Control by a communist government is complete."* is inaccurate. Ask, "How? Control of what? What impression does this sentence give? Is it fair? Why or why not?" Then you might want to discuss ways in which the government of a particular communist country does not control its citizens. (You may want to mention black market activities in the Soviet Union.) You could ask students, "Why do you suppose the author of this text made such a statement? How would you restate it more accurately? What are the authors guilty of here?" (bias)

You might continue by asking students to critique the picture and its caption on p. 420. "What does the picture show? Is the caption made clear by the picture? Why was it done this way? Is this another example of bias? Why or why not?" Or the teacher could have some students look at the picture and not the caption, others just the caption and try to guess what the picture could be, others could look at both. You could have students compare their impressions. To finish the section on communism, the class could discuss advantages and disadvantages, as for the other sections. **S-3**

5) Suggestions for concluding activities S-25

Several concluding activities could now tie the lesson together. One would be to have students role play defenders and critics of all three systems. They could compare the assumptions, basic concepts, and values of each.

A written assignment might be given as follows: "People who emigrate from the U.S.S.R. to the U.S. sometimes have difficulty adjusting to our economic system. Could you predict what some of those difficulties might be and why it could be hard for them to adapt?" (If desired, the assignment could be reversed for a U.S. citizen taking up residence in the Soviet Union.)

Another written assignment might be: Explain the goals of each of the economic systems studied. Compare them and then give your evaluation of each. Consider such things as fairness and whether the goals are easy or hard to achieve. Or students could write their analyses and assessments of the text. **S–26**

As a more extended project, students could find examples of each type of economic system. They could then determine what kinds of governments these countries have. They could also consider: Which have good relations with us? Poor? Can you see a pattern here? Why might capitalists and communists not trust each other?

> *Macro-practice is almost always more important than micro-drill. We need to be continually vigilant against the misguided tendency to fragment, atomize, mechanize, and proceduralize thinking.*

Looking Forward

Objectives of the remodelled lesson

The students will:
- identify some of their rights and responsibilities
- clarify claims in the text
- develop their perspectives on their lives and the future and compare them with that of the author, thus exercising independent thought
- pursue root questions regarding school, citizenship, and changes in the future
- evaluate how they spend their spare time
- discuss egocentricity as an obstacle to using spare time more effectively
- clarify 'thoughtful son/daughter,' 'thoughtful brother/sister,' 'good citizen,' 'role'
- develop awareness of their values and of ways they might affect the future
- practice dialectical thinking regarding changes they would like to see

Original Lesson Plan

Abstract

Students are informed that they have responsibilities and roles which will grow as they grow. The next four sections discuss four roles students have: as members of families, wherein students are asked to consider their responsibilities and what they learn from being family members; as students, wherein school is compared to a job; as people with spare time, wherein students are encouraged to use their spare time to improve themselves; and as citizens, wherein future responsibilities are discussed, and students are encouraged to begin being involved citizens now.

The next section briefly discusses technological changes since 1890 and suggests possible changes in the future. Two possible futures are then described; one negative, with people suffering from pollution, overpopulation, and starvation; one positive, with people enjoying healthy, active old age, no war, etc. Students then read a fable about a wise woman and a boy who tries to trick her. Since she always answers questions truthfully, he decides to hold a bird in his hands and ask her if it is dead or alive. If she says "dead", he will let it fly away; if she says "alive", he will kill it. The trick fails when she says, *"It is as you will, my child."* Students write about this statement.

from *The United States and Its Neighbors,* Timothy M. Helmus, Val E. Arnsdorf, Edgar A. Toppin, and Norman J. G. Pounds. © 1984 by Silver Burdett Co. pp. 460–465.

Critique

Introduction

We chose this epilogue for the important ideas covered regarding responsibilities, citizenship, and the future. We commend the authors for encouraging students to begin to work toward a better future now, and for raising some important issues. The lesson, however, does not go far enough. On the whole, rather than realistically addressing and pursuing important issues in depth, and encouraging students to develop their own ideas, the chapter suffers from vagueness, superficiality and terminal preachiness.

It does not encourage independent thought. Rather, it presents ideas without requiring much reflective response from students. Suggested questions are few, and discussion limited. Throughout, problems and some solutions are suggested, but students aren't encouraged to understand and explore the problems or their causes. Hence, students don't understand the importance of the clear, extended, fairminded thought required before reasonable action.

Vagueness

This lesson fails to connect vaguely expressed ideals to specific behaviors. For instance, in the section on citizenship, the student text says, *"You have to take those same ideas of freedom and equality to heart. You have to be willing to stand up for them."* The text then lists ways for students to be active citizens now, and *"make the United States and the world better."* These suggestions include: encouraging adults to vote, understanding important events so they will be ready to vote, complaining about any unfair treatment they experience as consumers, recycling, staying away from crime, becoming involved in scout, church, or community groups. Most items on the list are not related to the above general comments. The general comments are not anywhere clarified or made concrete or real, that is, how does one take ideas to heart or stand up for them? The most crucial or difficult concepts are left unanalyzed and vague. Without clarification, the ideals can become mere slogans with which all agree, but upon which few act. This practice fails to develop the intellectual courage and good faith needed to take ideals to heart.

The same problem occurs with the expressions *"build a better future"* and *"the future is in your hands."* The discussion neglects to raise such significant questions as, "What does 'better future' mean? Am I sure which changes really would be better? How much affect can I reasonably expect to have, and how? Why don't people already make these changes? What obstacles are there to such changes?" Such questions would bring the discussion from the level of abstract "Let's be good and wonderful" to specific discussion of what could be done, and what obstacles there are to doing them.

Superficiality

The section on school is especially disappointing. It describes students' present job thus, *"It is working hard in school .... following the rules of the school .... listening carefully to your teacher .... cooperating with other students .... coming to school every day unless you are sick."* The list of duties confines itself to mere outward behavior, completely overlooking the most important aspects. Education requires that students' attention be engaged, and that they *think* about what they learn. It also requires honesty: you shouldn't say you understand or agree, when you don't. Furthermore, critical education means listening to *everyone's* ideas and taking them seriously, not listening to the teacher alone.

The text discussion of the purpose of school is also flawed. It reads, *"You can learn a great deal about rights and responsibilities. And you can become prepared for a paying job later on that will be suited to your abilities and that you will enjoy."* The purpose of school is not confined to learning about rights and responsibilities and preparing for future careers. Absent from the passage are such ideas as satisfying curiosity, broadening perspectives, making sense of yourself and your world, profiting from the knowledge acquired by previous generations, developing judgment and refining notions of right and wrong, learning how to fit details into a complete picture, developing the ability to communicate effectively, deciding what to believe, and developing a sense of intellectual power and autonomy. The bland and incomplete picture presented does not motivate students to take school or education seriously.

The teacher's notes display superficial and confused ideas about critical thinking. For example, at the end of the lesson is the following suggested writing assignment, *"Do you agree or disagree that 'our country's future is in your hands'? What evidence can you give to support your opinion? How does your opinion affect how you live at the present time?"* The main question is poorly phrased, since it encourages full agreement or rejection. Complete agreement with the claim is unrealistic; complete disagreement, cynical and defeatist. To avoid oversimplification, the teacher could rephrase the question to ask students to what degree, and in what ways the future is in their hands.

Most of the suggested assignments cling to superficial, trivial, or cute ideas, rather than having students explore basic ideas. Among these suggestions are the following: *paraphrase J.F.K.'s words ("Now the trumpet summons us again — ... [a call to] struggle against the common enemies of man: tyranny, poverty, disease, and war itself."); build a model of a future community in space, underground, or underwater; write a one minute commercial that suggests ways in which people can build a better world; discuss the mechanics of solar energy.* More time should be spent on thoughtful discussion of basic questions.

Although separating different roles helps simplify ideas, to avoid oversimplification, students should also explore the connections between different roles or aspects of life. The following are among the possible points of connection and overlap: school and preparing to become voters; jobs and the desire for a better world; family, raising children, and the desire for better world; family and job; etc. Students have no chance to put their ideas together into a coherent whole.

Strategies used to remodel

S–12 developing one's perspective: creating or exploring beliefs, arguments, or theories
S–13 clarifying issues, conclusions, or beliefs
S–29 noting significant similarities and differences
S–14 clarifying and analyzing the meanings of words or phrases
S–21 reading critically: clarifying or critiquing texts
S–1 thinking independently
S–20 analyzing or evaluating actions or policies
S–6 developing intellectual courage
S–2 developing insight into egocentricity or sociocentricity
S–3 exercising fairmindedness
S–24 practicing Socratic discussion: clarifying and questioning beliefs, theories, or perspectives
S–28 thinking precisely about thinking: using critical vocabulary
S–19 generating or assessing solutions
S–7 developing intellectual good faith or integrity
S–10 refining generalizations and avoiding oversimplifications
S–17 questioning deeply: raising and pursuing root or significant questions

Remodelled Lesson Plan *s–12*

This chapter could be used as a summary of the year, a chance for students to synthesize and exchange ideas, and evaluate their knowledge and values. Our remodel follows their six part organization. We have added one part at the end.

1) Introduction

When the first section has been read, you might ask, "What does the author mean by the sentence '*Rights always involve responsibilities?*'" Ask for specific illustrative examples. You could extend the discussion of rights and responsibilities to our country. For each right mentioned in the text, you might ask what responsibility it implies and have students list other rights and responsibilities. (For example, the right to vote implies the responsibility to be an informed and fairminded voter.) Of each responsibility, consider asking, "How can you live up to it? What does it require?' **S–13** You could further extend discussion by asking, "Do you also have responsibilities to the rest of the world? As individuals? As citizens?" **S–12**

2) Families

When the class has read the second section, the teacher could ask what the analogy of the U.S. to family means; what similarities and differences there are; what other groups are also analogous to families; whether the analogies are good, (that is, whether the differences are significant,) and why or why not. **S–29**

Students could also discuss the differences between a thoughtful and thoughtless son or daughter, and brother or sister. If so, encourage students to mention *specific examples* of actions that fit in *each* category. **S–14** Students could relate this passage to the first, by discussing responsibilities implied by their rights as family members.

3) School

The following questions could be used to extend discussion of the passage about school: Why does the author think school is important? **S–21** Why do you think it is important? **S–1** What is school for? How can it help you in your personal life? As a citizen? What knowledge is required to enable you to vote wisely, as opposed to simply filling out a ballot? What does the author say a "job well done" at school means? What do you think it means? What do you have to do to do a good job in school? What should you avoid doing in order to do a good job as a student? **S–21** Is it easy or hard to do a good job at school? What aspects are easy? Hard? Students could develop self-awareness and awareness of others by comparing and discussing their answers.

What makes a job or career good to have? What would a bad job be like? What aspects of a job or career are most important? Least important? Why?

4) Spare time

When students have read the section on spare time, they could discuss how they spend theirs; whether they are satisfied with how they spend it; whether they think they should spend it differently, and if so, why they don't. **S-20** This topic could be extended with questions like the following: What other ways of spending your spare time would be productive? **S-1** Which do you think are most important? Which would you most enjoy? Would it be better to do something more important that you wouldn't enjoy, or less important that you would? Why? Would it be hard for you to change how you spend your spare time? Why or why not? What could help you change? Why do some people use their spare time to improve themselves or help others? Do you have an obligation to do so? Why do some people waste all of their spare time? Should you use all of your spare time to help others or improve yourself? Why or why not? If not, how do you decide how much you should spend in those ways?

5) Citizenship

When students have read the section on citizenship, you could use the following questions to help them to better understand the text, and clarify the concept, 'good citizen': What do *"take to heart"* and *"stand up for"* mean? What does it mean to take those ideas to heart, or to stand up for them? How can you tell if someone has taken them to heart? How would they act? Not act? When would someone have to stand up for them? How could someone stand up for them? Why would it be necessary? Would it be easy or hard? Why? In what kinds of situations could you stand up for these ideas now? Have you seen anyone do so? Was it hard for that person? **S-6** (Students could discuss such situations as a group of children treating someone unfairly, where no one stands up for justice. They could discuss why it happens, why it's hard to go against the crowd, and strategies for effectively doing so.) **S-2** Which suggestions in the text relate to these ideas? How?" **S-21**

To have students clarify the concept 'good citizen', consider asking questions like the following: What are the differences between good, bad, and indifferent citizens? What things are listed as ways of being good citizens? Are they important? Why? Are they necessary? If someone doesn't do these things, is he or she a bad citizen? What do bad citizens do? Are there other ways of being a good citizen? For each suggestion, you might ask how it helps the country. **S-14** Other questions could be added, such as the following: Which of all of these are the most important? Why? Which would be the most enjoyable? Hardest?"

6) The future

When the chapter is finished, consider asking, "What ideas here are the most important to the author? How can you tell? **S-21** Which do *you* think are the most important? **S-1** Which are the most interesting? Do you think that the two futures described are realistic? Why or why not? What other kinds of futures would be undesirable? Are there aspects of the second that you think are undesirable? Why or why not? Do you have an image of a better future? What is it like?"

To develop independent thought, students might brainstorm changes they would like to see. (Or, students could write for 10 minutes, and share their ideas.) You could then ask each student to rank them by their importance, or group them under such headings as "most important," "less important," "much less important," or "undesirable". **S–1** Have them share their groupings with the rest of the class. They may want to discuss their ideas at length. If so, you could allow students to try to convince each other of their different priorities. Have them distinguish ideas they share from those they do not, and note contradictions, examine assumptions, clarify key concepts, supply and question evidence, reconcile differences, and point out relative strengths and weaknesses. Students could then practice fairmindedness by arguing each others' positions. **S–3** Or students could be paired, with one student Socratically questioning another, to probe his beliefs neutrally. The students could then trade, and the other question the first. **S–24**

Students could also discuss whether it matters if everyone agrees about which problems or changes are the most important. Students could also use their sense of priorities to expand their self-knowledge if asked such questions as, "What do your rankings *imply* about your values? If you think that this is more important than that, what are you *assuming*? Etc." **S–28**

Students could also discuss the obstacles to changes. "What keeps people from making these changes? What would have to happen, or what could you do to bring them about? **S–19** Are there ways that you are now working against this change? How? **S–7** How could you stop?" Encourage students to be very specific, address their remarks to one desired change at a time, and give complete, rather than simple answers. You might provide questions like the following to help students extend their answers: How could you do that? What would you have to do before that could happen? What else would you have to do? And then? What could happen to prevent the change? Do some people disagree that your suggestion is a good one? If so, what could be done to convince them? What compromises would you be willing to make? **S–10**

7) Additional suggested activities **S–17**

Students should have a chance to discuss the passage as a whole, or pursue basic ideas in it, and relationships between the various topics. They could explore the concept, 'role'. To have them do so, you might ask, "What examples of roles were given in the text? What other examples can you think of? What roles do you think you might be taking on later? Which roles are chosen and which do you not have a choice about? When you take on a role, are there some aspects which you can decide how do to? Are there some about which you have no choice? Which roles do you look forward to taking on? Which not?

Why? Is there a way of changing how the role is fulfilled so that you wouldn't mind it? What are the relationships between roles (for example, between choosing a job and being a good citizen)? Would some choices of roles be incompatible? Would some roles help you fulfill others?" **S-10**

The discussions could be summed up with a written assignment. Students could write papers in which they describe what kind of life they want (family, work, where they want to live, what interests, skills, arts, or hobbies they want to develop, what public service they may want to do, what kinds of friends they want to have, etc.) Have them explain how they can begin to prepare for the life they envision, and the obstacles to doing so.

Or interested students who have had practice evaluating arguments could take one or more of the points read or discussed, and compare their points of view with that of the author or of another student. Have them give a summary of each point of view to be discussed, highlighting differences, presenting arguments for and against each, and giving reasons for their conclusions.

The reader should keep in mind the connection between the principles and applications, on the one hand, and the character traits of a fairminded critical thinker, on the other. Our aim, once again, is not a set of disjointed skills, but an integrated, committed, thinking person.

Spanish California

Objectives of the remodelled lesson

The students will:

- clarify the concepts 'to own land' and 'to claim land'
- examine the Spanish colonial period in California from multiple perspectives
- infer what the text does not make explicit
- recognize the role of ethnocentricity in Spaniards' treatment of California Indians
- recognize bias in the text
- draw their own conclusions after pursuing root issues about the Spanish period in California
- refine generalizations about the period by probing assumptions and implications, clarifying issues, and making use of critical vocabulary
- evaluate actions and policies of the people of the period
- Socratically examine the concept of 'ethnocentrism'

Original Lesson Plan

Abstract

This set of lessons is from a unit, "Europeans Come to California". We have selected two short passages from the chapter, "Europeans Explore California", and several other chapters from the unit.

The first passages discuss European claims to California. "Spanish Settlement in California" briefly describes the three forms of Spanish settlements: presidios, missions, and pueblos. It then focuses on the founding of the missions. "Life in Spanish California" focuses on life in the missions. It describes their slow start; gives a brief, "A Day at the Mission"; describes the physical layout of a typical mission; describes some of the hardships of Indian life at the missions; and describes presidios and pueblos, who lived in each, and what the residents did.

"Mexican California" explains how the missions were closed after the Mexican Revolution, how the lives of mission Indians changed, and describes life on Ranchos.

from *Our State: California*, Jo Anne
Buggey. © 1983, Follett. Allyn & Bacon,
Inc. pp. 177–8, 181–2, 184–193, T.E. 33–5.

Critique

The problem of ethnocentricity

We chose these lessons because their subject matter, the Spanish period in California, shows the initial meeting of two vastly different cultures, a basic concept in history. If students examine such periods of great change in depth, they will begin to develop the critical insights that actions and belief systems can be evaluated from a number of points of view, and that what is good in one framework is not necessarily so in another. They will see that when one culture subsumes another, both groups lose as well as gain. They will also have the opportunity to explore moral dimensions of historical events and decisions (an area texts tend to avoid). Students should begin to understand that texts themselves assume a point of view, and that authors write from within a particular perspective. The critical thinker should learn to identify and understand those perspectives.

It is crucial to avoid looking at such periods ethnocentrically — failing to consider actions from the perspectives of each culture. One of the problems that crops up in social studies texts is inadvertent ethnocentricity. The original lesson falls prey to it in that it is biased toward the Spanish. The ethnocentricity takes many forms, including choice of language, incomplete presentation of the Indian perspective, and an overly sympathetic portrayal of Spanish motives. Although many facts presented justify negative evaluation of the Spanish, such conclusions are avoided. Details and discussion are scattered. No basic ideas or unified concepts are stressed.

The text's word choice often presupposes a Spanish point of view. For instance, it uses 'religion' and 'Christianity' interchangeably. The claim that the priests wanted to 'teach religion' is misleading; they taught *their* religion, not religion in general. Likewise, the text uses the expression, 'life in California' rather than 'life in Spanish-controlled areas of California', again presupposing the Spanish view.

Dealing with negative implications

Although the text does not completely white-wash Spanish treatment of the Indians, it steers students away from evaluating certain aspects of the Spaniards' behavior. The text fails to use negative terms suggested by the details described. Given such facts as these, "Indians were locked up at night. When they tried to leave the missions, soldiers brought them back. They did the hard physical labor. They were ill-fed and ill-housed", one can conclude that they were badly treated slaves. By stopping short of naming this condition, the text discourages students from considering the implications of the situation or evaluating Spanish behavior. These facts sit juxtaposed with the belief that the Spanish wanted to help the Indians (the "correct answer" in the chapter review). A coherent point of view requires synthesis of all available facts. (A related problem here is the questionable generalization, since in different individuals, motives varied.)

Furthermore, when describing the harsh conditions in which the Indians lived, the text fails to put responsibility on the priests. They controlled housing, food, and work hours. They failed to provide for the Mission Indians. The facts about Mission life are described without reference to the priests. Also, by putting such claims as, "*The number of Indians in California got smaller and smaller*" in the passive voice, the fact seems simply to have "happened somehow" rather than having been caused directly or indirectly by the Spanish priests and soldiers.

Words versus deeds

The text repeatedly emphasizes the priests' *stated* reasons for founding the missions. Students read that Father Serra and others wanted to teach Christianity and the Spanish (or "better") way of life. Several times students are asked why the missions were started, and the text supplies those reasons. Students are discouraged from considering whether there may have been other reasons as well, such as free labor and setting the stage for Spanish rule, which would coincide better with actual Spanish treatment of the Indians. This repetition, over-simplification, and ethnocentricity foster a one-sided view of the period. The text also oversimplifies Indian problems after the closure of the missions. Though the text gives several reasons — lack of money to work the land, loss of land through force, and loss of knowledge of how to live off the land — the text answer, when students are asked why Indians had problems, is "lack of money", de-emphasizing negative effects of Spanish control. Again, even though the text points out that Mission Indians were even worse off after the missions closed, "the reason" for closing the missions was "to help the Indians".

European "superiority"

The text misses the opportunity to have students examine a basic assumption made by the Spanish, namely, the superiority of the European/Spanish/Christian way of life. Such cultural bias has often played a significant role in history. Nor does the text have students question the Europeans' belief that the "New World" was the rightful property of the first European country to claim and use it. It never recognizes the cultural specificity of such concepts as 'claim', 'deed', or 'owning land'. Neither does it have students consider these ideas from a Native American perspective. As a result, it never questions the Europeans' right to claim ownership of the land or subjugate its people.

The text also fails to have students explore in sufficient depth the differences between the Indian cultures, the lives of Mission Indians, and the Spanish ways. Extended discussion, use of imagination, pursuit of implications, and dialogical reasoning are crucial to an understanding of the changes forced on many Indians. Students have no chance to develop their own perspectives on the period.

Critique of text questions and activities

Rather than pursuing basic ideas in depth, text questions are scattered and time wasted on recall of such trivial facts as the following: *"Why did the rancheros brand their cattle? Why was it hard for Portolá to find Monterey Bay? The first Spanish explorer to find San Francisco Bay was (a) Serra (b) Cortes (c) Portolá. Scurvy is caused by …. The road that ran between the missions was called …. Drake claimed California for …."* The end of the unit "Thinking Skill" activity asks students to compare two pictures showing life in San Diego, California, and life in Boston, Massachusetts. They are to note differences and similarities. The answers focus on dress, road conditions and relative technological complexity.

In the chapter, "Europeans Explore California", students are directed to keep a list of the important events in the chapter and arrange them in chronological order. The teacher's answer key lists the arrival, discoveries, and claims of Cabrillo, Drake and Vizcaino. Students are not asked to distinguish important from unimportant information. The information is not related to key ideas such as, *"Why did the Spanish want to establish a settlement in Alta California"*, and, *"Why do you think the Spanish were not interested in settling California"* (though the text does ask these questions).

Strategies used to remodel

S–17 questioning deeply: raising and pursuing root or significant questions
S–14 clarifying and analyzing the meanings of words or phrases
S–28 thinking precisely about thinking: using critical vocabulary
S–25 reasoning dialogically: comparing perspectives, interpretations, or theories
S–12 developing one's perspective: creating or exploring beliefs, arguments, or theories
S–32 making plausible inferences, predictions, or interpretations
S–21 reading critically: clarifying or critiquing texts
S–2 developing insight into egocentricity or sociocentricity
S–5 developing intellectual humility and suspending judgment
S–20 analyzing or evaluating actions or policies

S–30 examining or evaluating assumptions
S–35 exploring implications and consequences
S–34 recognizing contradictions
S–26 reasoning dialectically: evaluating perspectives, interpretations, or theories
S–6 developing intellectual courage
S–11 comparing analogous situations: transferring insights to new contexts

Remodelled Lesson Plan s–17

Our remodel has six parts. The first three, *1)* Review and introduction, *2)* The meeting of two cultures, and *3)* Life in the missions, follow the original lesson. We have added a dialogical examination of the material from the first three sections in *4)* Evaluation of the period. We again follow the original lesson in section *5)* Results. We added section *6)* Supplementary discussions.

1) Review and introduction

At the beginning of this unit, so students will be better able to compare the cultures, you might have students review material on the Native Americans of South Coastal California, asking them to mention everything they remember, listing their ideas on the board, and having them skim that section of the text. Since the following ideas will be important in this unit, you might want to emphasize them: religious beliefs, use of the land, technology, and social organization. The teacher could keep lists of features of both cultures, on a large sheet of paper or the board. Students could add to the list throughout the unit.

Have the students read "Europeans Explore California". Here are some questions you might ask: How did Cabrillo "claim" the land? Drake? Why did they do this? What did 'owning land' and 'rights to land' mean to them? **S–14** What *assumptions* did they make? (the land was un-owned and their claiming it implied that other Europeans should accept their claim). **S–28** What did the Indians think about owning land? **S–25** Whose land was it? **S–12** (Students may discuss at length.)

2) The meeting of two cultures

Then, have students read, "The Spanish Settle in California". You could draw their attention to the passage on pp. 181–2, "*When Portolá returned to San Diego, he found the little colony near starvation …. The Spanish did not know how to live that way.*" Ask, "What did the Indians know that the Spanish didn't? What can we infer about the Indian culture? The Spanish culture?" **S–32**

To begin to have students identify the perspective of their text, you could have them compare the following sentences: *A mission is a settlement built around a church where local people are taught about religion.* (p. 181) *He went to Mexico to teach the Indians about Christianity.* (p. 182) You could ask, "What were the Indians taught? Is 'religion' the same as 'Christianity'? Did the Indians have a religion? Could the first sentence be made more accurate? How? **S–21** Why do you suppose the text was written this way?" **S–2** The class could also discuss the phrase 'better life' (p. 182). You might ask, "What does it mean? Why did Father Serra think his way of life was better? Would everyone agree?" Then you might want to draw student attention to the sentence, *"During the Spanish period, life in California centered around missions, Presidios, and Pueblos."* (p. 184) You could ask, "What does the sentence mean? Does 'life in California' refer to everybody living in California?" (It leaves out Native Americans who opposed, or were uninvolved with Spanish settlements.) Students could then be asked to rewrite the sentence to more accurately reflect the situation. **S–21**

Students could also discuss the sentence, *"Presidios were built to protect the settlers."* (p. 184) "To protect the settlers from whom? What can we infer from this?" (At least some Indians fought Spanish settlement.) **S–32**

3) Life in the missions

In the following chapter, "Life in Spanish California", when students have read "Life at the Missions", the following questions could be used: Why did the Indians come to the missions? Does the text answer this question? **S–5** When the text says, *"The priests needed the Indians to help them,"* what does it mean? What does this section tell us about the differences between the two cultures? If keeping lists about the two cultures, add these points, for example, the Spanish emphasis on schedules.

When students have read "A Day at the Mission", you could ask, "What does the sentence, *'When Father José unlocked the door, Older Sister hurried outside.'* imply? **S–32** Why was the door locked? Do you think that was right? Do you think that locking the Indians up at night was consistent with the reasons the text gives for the creation of the missions? Why or why not? **S–20** If you think it was consistent, what can you say the priests were assuming? **S–30** (If someone doesn't want your help, you may have to force them.) What does this section tell us about the differences between the two cultures?" If keeping lists, students could add these points. **S–17**

If students read, "What a Mission Looked Like", they could compare the dwellings of the two cultures and what the differences imply for each culture. (Labor requirements, permanence, complexity of settlement, materials required, etc.) This would give some purpose to reading the passage, by tying it in to the theme of the meeting between vastly different cultures. **S–35**

When students have read, "Indians and the Missions", the class could discuss questions like the following: Why weren't Indians allowed to leave? Who was responsible for the their conditions? Did the priests and soldiers treat them fairly? **S–20** What would you call their condition? What did the priests do for the Indians? What did the Indians do for the priests? Why did the number of Indians get smaller?

4) Evaluation of the period S–20

To integrate the preceding material, we suggest four discussion topics. First, to highlight the dialogical nature of the history of this period, we suggest that students refer to the lists of the characteristics of both cultures on the blackboard. Students could then discuss the advantages and disadvantages of each culture. You could say, "The Spanish thought their way of life was better; the Native Americans who resisted the Spanish thought *their* way of life was better. Nearly all people have this attitude about their own cultures. It is a common assumption. **S–2** (If students don't know it, you might introduce the term 'ethnocentric'.) What does it mean to say that one way of life is better than another? How could we evaluate two cultures?" (Discuss at length, if interest warrants.)

Next, the class could discuss the reasons behind the behavior of the Spanish and the Indians. "What reasons did Father Serra give for establishing missions? What other reasons were given in the text? Could there have been other reasons as well? Did all of the priests have the same reasons? Were the soldiers' reasons for being there the same as the priests'? How could we tell what their reasons were? What did the priests want from the Indians? Is what they wanted consistent with or the same as what they *said* they wanted, or is there a contradiction?" **S–34** At this point, the class could discuss reasons some Indians resisted Spanish settlement, and others were attracted to the missions and pueblos. **S–25**

Now the class should be ready to evaluate the text. You might ask, "What is the *point of view* of the text? Is it fair to both sides? Does the author's use of language reveal a *bias*? Give *examples*. Are there *ethnocentric assumptions* in the text? Which? Why do you say they are *ethnocentric*? Are there any groups the text ignores? Are any facts omitted? Are there ideas or *inferences* which are not made *explicit*? **S–28** What difference does it make if something is left out? What, if anything, can we conclude about the perspective of the authors?" **S–21**

Finally, students could evaluate the period as a whole. Here is a list of possible questions: What do you think of Spanish policy in California? Of what aspects do you approve? Disapprove? Why? Did the priests help the Indians? What, if anything, should the Spanish have done differently? Why? Did the Spanish have the right to do what they did? Why or why not? What do you think of the Indians' behavior toward the Spanish? Did the Indians help the Spanish? Why did some Indians join the missions? Should they have joined? Why or why not? Why did others fight the Spanish? Should they have fought? Why or why not? With which Indians do you agree — those who joined the Spanish, those who fought them, or those who did neither? Why? **S–12** What, if anything, should the Indians have done differently? What did the Indians learn from the Spanish? How did it affect them? Was the effect good, bad, neutral, or mixed? Why? What other things, if any, should they have learned? Why didn't they? What did the Spanish learn from the Indians? What could they have learned? Why didn't they? Should they have tried to learn more? Why or why not? Is it important for people to preserve their culture? Why or why not? Is there anything from the Indians' cultures you wish had been preserved, or incorporated into our culture? What difference does it make to the dominant culture if another is destroyed? Does it matter if a culture disappears? *S-26*

5) Results *S-35*

Before assigning the chapter, "Mexican California", the teacher could assign interested students an altered version of, "Use this Reading Skill". (p. 186) You might have the students distinguish what they consider to be the more important ideas from the less important ideas and write an alternative outline for the chapter. When the rest of the class has read and discussed the chapter, the class can compare the students' outlines with the text's chapter headings. *S-21*

When students have read the section, "Changes for the Indians", you might ask, "Which Indians does the text refer to? (Mission Indians) Was it right for the Mexican government to take the mission land? Why or why not? What happened to the mission Indians when they were freed from mission life? Why didn't they return to their old ways?" If necessary, you might have a student read aloud the passage from p. 182, *"The California Indians lived on what they could find. The Spanish did not know how to live that way."* Point out that if you are not raised to live off the land you lack the knowledge and skills necessary to survive. *S-21*

Have students read the rest of the chapter. You might ask what people are *not* discussed in the section, "Rise of the Ranchos"? (Indians who hadn't lived at the missions. Also, only some mission Indians found work on the ranchos. The chapter does not tell us what happened to the rest.) *S-5*

6) Supplementary discussions

Finally, you could conclude the unit with the following questions: Now that you have read the results of Spanish settlement of California, in what ways, if any, did the priests help the Indians? Were there things the priests should have done differently? The Indians? Students could discuss at length. *S-20*

If you would like to explore the general question of ethnocentricity in a Socratic discussion with your class, you might get started with questions such as the following: What identity do we as a class share? What nation and groups do we all belong to? What are some of the groups we don't belong to? When Americans have a disagreement with another country, do we think we're right? Does the other side think they're right? (Extend these questions to other groups.) Are we always right? Are others always wrong? Is it always a question of right and wrong? Is one group usually completely right or completely wrong? Why do people like to think they're right? How do people feel when another group assumes they are better? How can we overcome this tendency? How do people respond to those who question their own country's actions? Why? *S-6*

This unit will probably constitute the first example of the meeting of two cultures studied by your students. If not, consider having them compare this situation, the reactions of the people involved, and the results, to the other examples. If so, when other examples are studied in the future, it would be useful to have students make such comparisons. It is important to encourage students to integrate insights gained in this unit to subsequent analogous situations. *S-11*

The Middle Ages

Objectives of the remodelled lesson

The students will:
- Socratically consider some purposes for studying history
- identify and understand the underlying structure and assumptions of feudalism, using critical vocabulary appropriately and clarifying concepts
- examine feudalism from the perspectives of nobles and serfs, thus practicing dialogical thought
- identify diverse manifestations of unifying, basic ideas of feudalism in other Medieval institutions, transferring insights where appropriate, pursuing root questions, and examining fundamental assumptions
- discuss the implications of some of feudalism's basic ideas
- critique and clarify oversimplification and vagueness in the text

Original Lesson Plan

Abstract

The lesson begins by explaining the development and perspective of the terms 'modern' and 'Middle Ages' as used by historians, as well as pointing out the diversity of life in Europe during the period. The lesson focuses on the life of William the Conqueror, his boyhood, his claim to the throne of England, and the Battle of Hastings. The mechanics of feudalism are elaborated: vassalage, fiefs, and waging war without taxes. Reasons for frequent breakdowns of the system are noted. Details of daily living such as the construction of castles, life on a manor, and travel are included.

The text devotes significant space to describing the life of the serfs, attachment to the land, farming methods, other duties performed, surnames, and relationships to the lord. This is paralleled by a description of life in the cities for the middle class, including a description of some trades, the exchange of goods and services, and the structure and influence of guilds. The text details the system of apprentices, masters, and journeymen.

A section on Eleanor of Aquitaine follows, tracing her marriages and sphere of influence. The Crusades are briefly mentioned in connection with one of her husbands, Louis VII. The lesson concludes with a passage about monks and nuns, featuring Bernard of Clairvaux. After a brief biography, Bernard's daily routine at Citeaux is recounted by way of contrast to other Medieval life-styles previously considered. By the end of the lesson, students are expected to understand the terms 'modern' and 'Middle Ages', to explain how feudalism worked, to describe the ways guilds operated, and to restate the general vows monks and nuns took.

from *Europe, Africa, Asia, and Australia*
Kenneth S. Cooper. © 1984 Silver
Burdett Co. pp. 140–151.

Critique I

Overview of the study of history

Many of the social studies programs we have looked at heavily emphasize history. We chose this lesson as a representative of that type, hoping to provide an example of how a teacher of critical thinking might approach a history lesson. We have divided the critique into three parts, the remodel into nine. Lesson Plan I includes sections *1)* Introduction to the Middle Ages, terminology, and *2)* William the Conqueror. Lesson Plan II includes sections *3)* Feudalism: structure and basic features, *4)* Feudalism: underlying ideas and assumptions, *5)* City life, *6)* Guilds, and *7)* Eleanor of Aquitaine. Lesson Plan III includes sections *8)* Religion, and *9)* Feudalism compared to our system. We have tried to link the whole chapter together by relating each of the medieval institutions discussed to some of the basic ideas and fundamental assumptions of the time.

Although students are often told that it is important to study history and are even provided with some reasons for doing so, they are rarely given the opportunity to explore for themselves what history is, how they are involved in history and why it might be important to them. A Socratic discussion could serve this purpose.

In addition, critical thinkers need to understand how certain key assumptions and ideas gave rise to a variety of historical social institutions. Once understood, these ideas help tie together a great deal of information in meaningful ways. Without them, periods in history can seem like a hopeless jumble of data. Our primary focus in remodelling this unit is to highlight the powerful ideas underlying the facts, their influence on almost every Medieval social institution, and their relationship to our own ideas.

Establishing historical perspectives

This lesson has a number of strong points. The discussion of historical time perspective with regard to the word 'modern' is one of the best we have seen. It extends the idea of perspective in labeling time periods to the term 'Middle Ages' as well. That is, they were not "middle" to those living at that time. The introductory remarks on the Middle Ages note the variety of the culture in time, place, and social position and imply that only a fragment of the whole picture will be examined in this lesson. This is an important understanding for students to have, since the critical thinker relates parts to the whole in an effort to integrate material being studied.

The authors also do an excellent job of incorporating relevant and interesting anecdotal material, such as the origin of common family names in occupations or physical appearance, humorous episodes from William the Conqueror's life, daily life in a monastery, etc. There is a commendable effort to show aspects of Medieval life in both positive and negative light (life of the serfs, life in a city, Guild practices, broken promises, etc.) Nevertheless, the lesson could be improved by an explicit consideration of the concepts and ideas that gave rise to the peculiar social institutions and way of life characteristic of the Middle Ages. The text's emphasis is on the concrete, without a unifying framework to make sense of all the data. This is particularly important for students to have in this lesson, since this period is so different from their own. Without this foundation, students are likely to make hasty judgments and hold stereotypical views about the period. (Medieval practices are "weird", the Middle Ages were "dark ages".)

The next part of the critique, following the first remodel, will address the sections of the original relating to social structures.

Strategies used to remodel

S–24 practicing Socratic discussion: clarifying and questioning beliefs, theories, or perspectives

S–17 questioning deeply: raising and pursuing root or significant questions

Remodelled Lesson Plan I

1) Introduction to the Middle Ages, terminology

Before students begin this lesson on the Middle Ages, you might consider devoting some time to a Socratic discussion of history itself in order to give students some idea of what they are about and why it is important. Of course, you will need to adapt the discussion to the needs and experience of your particular class, but we offer some suggestions for getting started. "What is history? Is everything that happened part of history? Can everything that happened be put into a history book? Why not? If historians have to select some events to include and others to leave out, how do they do this? Is it likely that they will all agree? Is it possible for people observing and recording events to be biased or prejudiced? Could a historian be biased or prejudiced? How would you find out? If events, to be given meaning, have to be interpreted from some point of view, what is the point of view of the person who wrote our text? Do you have a history? Is there a way in which all people develop interpretations of the significant events in their own past? If there is more than one point of view that events can be considered from, could you think of someone in your life who interprets your past in a way different from you? Does it make any difference how your past is interpreted?" **S–24**

We suggest that you then proceed as directed through the text's introduction. You might point out on p. 142 that the text is just summarizing important events and periods (Charles Martel's victory, Charlemagne's reign). Much more information about these times is available, but the text authors have chosen to emphasize the later Middle Ages. [Interested students could research these times, perhaps through biographies, and report to the rest of the class. The class could then compare early to late Middle Ages.]

2) William the Conqueror **S–17**

Next, have students read the section about William the Conqueror. Then you might have them go back and refer to the text again to answer questions such as, "What words or phrases describe life at this time in Normandy? (warlike, fierce, dangerous, uncertain, full of intrigue and conflict, etc.) In such times why would a strong leader be valued? What part of this account implies how important such a leader was to the people? When a king or noble died, who usually took over? (relatives) When would the question of inheritance most likely be disputed? (When there was more than one relative of equal rank wanting the power.) How did the system work? Why did William think he could rule England? What do you think might have happened if William had been killed? Was there another to take his place? Why not? How is this different from our system?"

Here you could explain that there are other reasons a leader such as William was so important in the Middle Ages. They have to do with the way society was organized and the basic ideas behind that organization. This will give students a sense of what you want to stress throughout the chapter.

Critique II

Looking for underlying social structure and foundational ideas

A discussion of rigid hierarchical social classes will not make a great deal of sense to students unless they understand the basic assumptions behind such a system, as well as the chaotic environment in which rigid structure was an appealing, safe haven. The warlike nature of the Middle Ages can be better understood as one explores the implications of having a permanent "warrior class". If one sees personal relationship between leader and followers (complicated by questions of inheritance) as central to life in the Middle Ages, one can understand the betrayals and fragmentation of that society more clearly. We believe that these concepts can be taught in such a way that sixth graders will understand them. Studying history in this way will also help them to understand the dynamics of their own system and will demonstrate the power in examining the systems of thought underlying social structures.

The lesson, however, expresses its goals in terms of behaviors which tend toward the superficial. *("To give the meanings of modern and Middle Ages, to explain feudalism and to describe three ways of life during the Middle Ages: on the manor, in a city, and in a monastery or convent.")* The sections which "explain feudalism" discuss only the mechanics of it, not its basic ideas, how people at the time saw it, or why they accepted it. *"Feudalism is that system which granted fiefs for the service of knights. It divided the power to govern among a number of nobles. Each lord ruled his vassals just as he was ruled in turn by his lord."* etc.) The analogy of feudalism with a triangle, (p.144) although a possible starting point, is too simplistic by itself to explain what was really going on. It shows the ideal but not always the facts. Students should be encouraged to critique this model rather than just accepting it. Although texts often rely on oversimplified analogies, critical thinkers should test them to ascertain their strengths and weaknesses.

The final part of the critique, addressing religion and review, follows the second remodel.

Strategies used to remodel

S-10 refining generalizations and avoiding oversimplifications
S-30 examining or evaluating assumptions
S-32 making plausible inferences, predictions, or interpretations
S-17 questioning deeply: raising and pursuing root or significant questions
S-21 reading critically: clarifying or critiquing texts
S-35 exploring implications and consequences
S-25 reasoning dialogically: comparing perspectives, interpretations, or theories
S-14 clarifying and analyzing the meanings of words or phrases
S-28 thinking precisely about thinking: using critical vocabulary
S-11 comparing analogous situations: transferring insights to new contexts

Remodelled Lesson Plan II

3) Feudalism: basic structure

We suggest that you begin a discussion of feudalism by using the triangle image suggested in the text. You could point out that this was the ideal. If you choose to do so, you could tell students that when they finish reading and talking about this section you're going to ask them to revise the triangle image. You might want to have students read paragraph by paragraph, asking them to state key parts of the feudal system. In paragraph I, for example, note that land was acquired not with money, but by swearing loyalty. You could ask what this meant. (Promising a certain number of armed men with service to the king every year; not fighting for anyone else.) Emphasize that the oath was sworn to a person, not a nation or state. It could be useful to pursue the implications of this by asking, "What do you suppose happened if the leader died? (obligations were off; people could swear loyalty to someone else; they may often have sworn loyalty to the leader's heir) Was the sense of obligation to the new leader the same as to the original person? What if the heir was a weak leader? What may people have been tempted to do?" You might point out the shifting of allegiance in the Middle Ages, owing to personal ability to attract and keep followers, degree of protection offered, amount of land given, etc. You might draw student attention to where the text alludes to this and have them expand on it, exploring assumptions and implications. **S–10**

To deepen student understanding, you might explore the concept of 'promising service'. "On what assumptions does this practice rest? (that your word will be kept; that there will probably be fighting; that those involved are better off in these relationships) What are the consequences if someone breaks a promise? (no longer trusted; retaliation) If a vassal broke a promise to his lord, what do you suppose might have happened to the vassal? The lord? **S–30** When might a vassal have wanted to break his promise? (when he couldn't keep it, when he thought he could make a better agreement elsewhere, when he wanted to take more power) When might lords have broken their promises? What might have happened as a result?" **S–10**

Then, in order to explore the idea of fighting as an occupation, you could ask, "How did one get to be a knight in the Middle Ages? Was it easy or hard? Who could become knights? Why was it important for a knight to fight? (to get land/support, to fulfill promises, to keep skills sharp, win fame and glory) If knights' *"main purpose in life was fighting"*, what condition was a consistent part of medieval life? (war) **S–32** Interested students could do some research and construct their own time lines of all the wars in Western Europe between say, 1350 and 1450 to test the prediction. "How did wars then differ from now? (Discuss at length.) What did knights do when there wasn't a war to fight in? What generalizations can you make about having a warrior class?" (It exists for war, stimulates, encourages war, its identity is based on war.)

The class can then discuss the important features of feudalism mentioned in paragraph 3. (Money was not exchanged, but land was distributed in exchange for service, an army was ready to fight whenever called upon, you had to agree to go to war in order to possess land.) Paragraph 4 illustrates how the system was extended to lesser vassals all down the line. Here you might simply ask why it was important to own land. Students could discuss the alternatives to land ownership.

As you continue with the section on feudalism, after the first paragraph, you could ask, "How were disputes settled in the Middle Ages? How did the lord decide what judgment to make? Did law exist as it does now? What were the differences? Were judgments uniform in a country or language area? Do you understand another reason a lord was so powerful? (William the Conqueror) Why? What are the similarities and differences between being a leader now, and being a leader then? Between good leaders now and then? What were the advantages of a system such as feudalism? The disadvantages? How did it meet the needs of the time? How is it different from the system we live under? What ideas did they have that we don't? What ideas do we have that they didn't?" *S–17*

When students have read the next two paragraphs under Feudalism, you could ask, "What were some of the ways feudalism didn't work?" Then you might refer to the "ideal" image of feudalism as a triangle of power and ask students how they might revise it. (A number of separate triangles or one big triangle with a number of smaller ones inside, some triangles over-lapping, etc.) *S–10* "How is your design an improvement on the text's? Why did you make the changes you did?" *S–21*

Next, as students read the sections from the text on manors and lives of the serfs, you could say, "We have spent quite a bit of time talking about those at the higher levels of the social scale: kings, nobles, and knights. Yet, these people represented only a small minority of the population. Why do you think we spend more time on them?" Here you could mention that very widespread illiteracy was characteristic of most past civilizations and that generally only the elite were educated and left records of their times. "How does this affect our understanding of these times? (It is most often through their eyes, from their perspective, and focuses on themselves and their peers.) *S–35*

To analyze the concept 'serf', students could discuss such questions as these: Where were serfs on the hierarchy? What does 'attached to the land' mean? If serfs were *"just like the trees in a manor's forest"*, were their lives seen as being as valuable as, say, that of a Duke? Given their lowly status, what were serfs seen as good for? (labor) What words would describe what a serf was like from a noble's view? (weak minded, simple, in need of guidance, not to be trusted or given authority, etc.) How might they have seen the nobles? *S–25* How was a serf different from a slave? (not bought and sold) How were they like slaves? *S–14* Look at the names of some serfs in the text. To what do the names refer? (animals, physical appearance, personality traits, occupations) What were serfs identified with? For what were they valued? Do you think you could identify whether a person was a serf or a noble just from hearing his or her name? How?"

4) Feudalism: underlying ideas and implications **S-17**

The next section is crucial because it explores some of the basic assumptions underlying feudalism and other social structures of the Middle Ages (most often ignored in texts). It can also afford students the opportunity to engage in dialogical reasoning as they consider questions of social class from several points of view.

You might introduce this discussion by saying that an important thing to understand in any system is how it governs the relationship of one person to another. You might want to emphasize that social position in the Middle Ages almost always was determined by birth.

"From what you've read thus far, how would you describe the relation of one person to another in feudalism?" We advise that you introduce the term 'hierarchy' at this point, and have a student read a definition to the class. Others could rephrase the definition in their own words, or provide examples from their experience. Then you could ask, "What assumptions do you make about people when you organize them in a strict hierarchy such as feudalism? Are they equal or unequal? In what ways? What conclusions did leaders in the Middle Ages draw from these assumptions? **S-28** (The strong should make decisions for the weak; the strong should protect the weak; the weak should serve the strong, etc.) Think about what this system implies in terms of how many could be at the top of the hierarchy (few). The authority of the few was a natural corollary of their inherent superiority. The superior should govern the inferior. Who should be educated? Why? Who should dress well and have the best houses? Given these assumptions, why would it be important for people to be ranked, classed, and labeled? (So they and others would know how to relate to each other; what rules apply.) What might be some ways of identifying a person's social class simply by meeting them? (clothing, manner of speech, knowledge of rules of society, surnames, etc.) How easy do you think it was to move from one social class to another? How could it have been done? Why would this question probably not have occurred to most people living in the Middle Ages? Why was it in the interest of the wealthy, high classes to keep their numbers small? (When resources are limited, adding more people means less for each individual.) Why would serfs accept their place? What options did they have? What assumptions would they have made? What was more important to serfs than to people now? What ideas were less important?" **S-25**

5) Cities

After students read the section on "Living in cities", you could ask, "What word does the author repeat in describing life in cities? (crowded) Do you think that a person raised in the city then would emphasize 'crowded'? Remember that the period was warlike. What word might a person from the Middle Ages use to describe a city? (safe, protected, secure, efficient). Our perspective often affects how we judge something and causes us to notice things that are important to *u s* rather than to the original party. Do you think the serfs or the townspeople were better off? Support your choice with good reasons. What might have been some advantages of living in the city as a tradesman? Some disadvantages?" *S-17*

6) Guilds *S-11*

Ask students to look at the picture representing Medieval guilds. "What does the central figure remind you of? (king) What was the guild organization similar to? (political structure under feudalism) As you read the next section ask yourself how the word 'hierarchy' applies to guilds. How is the guild structure different from that we discussed under feudalism? *S-10* (one could progress; apprentice-ship was temporary) Why did guilds limit the number of apprentices? What's the problem with having *'too many people in their line of business'*? How did guilds limit members' freedom? How did guilds help their members? Why were guilds so powerful? What are the advantages and disadvantages of a monopoly?"

7) Eleanor of Aquitaine *S-10*

To tie in the next section, "A strong-willed woman", you could emphasize the implications and complexities that marriage alliances created with regard to land, power, and inheritance. It might be helpful to point out that this was typical of Medieval noble families and created endless conflicts and disputes over claims to rightful ownership and control of territory. Since the Crusades are alluded to in this section, you could mention that they were extremely important in introducing changes to the Medieval way of life, but that they are not discussed in depth here.

Critique III

The role of religion — omissions and superficiality

One of the most serious and puzzling omissions in the lesson is the role that religion, the Catholic Church, and religious ideas played in shaping almost every aspect of Medieval culture; basic assumptions about the purpose of human life and its relation to Deity, government, the calendar, and holidays. As presented, religion is just another manifestation of daily life — a benign practice rather than a powerful set of ideas. The discussion of Bernard of Clairvaux, although interesting in its detail, lacks a context within which to understand his life. Although it hints that he was protesting corrupt practices, (*"He picked Cîteaux because the monks there strictly followed the rules of a religious life. Bernard scorned those who took vows as monks but did not keep them strictly."*), it provides no background that would help students appreciate the significance of his life to the larger community.

The phrase, 'the Religious life', is vague. (*"Christianity was very powerful and many people led religious lives."*) What did it mean to lead a religious life in the Middle Ages? The text merely gives a daily schedule. The claim that religion was powerful is never elucidated. This is confusing and gives the (correct) impression that important ideas are being left out. Among the more significant shortcomings is the stunning omission of the role of God in religion. The word 'God' is never mentioned in the student text. Without some concept of humans' relationship to God and the church there is no basis for understanding why one would ever choose a life such as Bernard's. Had these religious assumptions been made clear, secular institutions such as feudalism and guilds could have been understood as reflections of those fundamental ideas; the reasons for their acceptance made clear. To leave them out of a discussion of the Middle Ages is incomprehensible. Without them, the Middle Ages cannot be adequately understood.

The one and one-half paragraphs devoted to the Crusades, another key development with far-reaching implications, is much too cursory, particularly when compared to the six paragraphs devoted to apprentices, though the textbook devotes more time to them in a later chapter. Students could read those references now. Again, without a grasp of fundamental ideas which organized life in the Middle Ages, it is hard to establish priorities for amount of coverage. The Checkup questions at the end of the chapter mirror the text's emphasis on nuts and bolts, rather than also exploring ideas and concepts which make sense of the many different aspects of Medieval life introduced in this lesson.

Strategies used to remodel

S–17 questioning deeply: raising and pursuing root or significant questions
S–32 making plausible inferences, predictions, or interpretations
S–27 comparing and contrasting ideals with actual practice
S–10 refining generalizations and avoiding oversimplifications
S–11 comparing analogous situations: transferring insights to new contexts
S–25 reasoning dialogically: comparing perspectives, interpretations, or theories

Remodelled Lesson Plan III

8) The religious life **S–17**

For the section entitled, "The religious life", you may want to do something similar to what was done for "Feudalism". It would be appropriate to tell students that religion was one of the most important aspects of life in the Middle Ages; that it affected every part of life, and that its *ideas* about the purpose of life, the relationship of God and humans, etc., really undergird the whole social structure, including feudalism. The text nowhere explains the meaning of *"Christianity was very powerful"* or the phrase 'a religious life'. If you have the background and resources, it would be advisable to supplement the lesson in this area. If not, you could proceed with the life of Bernard of Clairvaux. You might ask students what implications they draw from the lines, *"He picked Cîteaux because the monks there strictly followed the rules of a religious life. Bernard scorned those who took vows as monks but did not keep them strictly."* **S–32** (not all monks kept their vows) Why would this be important to him? Why would others not keep their vows? **S–27** Does that mean that the life described in the text was the way all monks lived? **S–10** How is hierarchy manifest in the religious life? **S–11** (vows, obedience to superior authority) Whom was Bernard trying to serve? Why? What ideas were at the core of his life?

9) Comparison of feudalism to other systems

Throughout, you may wish to compare Medieval values, assumptions, and practices with ours, and with other times and cultures. It is an excellent way of clarifying aspects of different systems, and encouraging students to look for basic, organizing ideas in any social structure, as well as providing a framework in which details will be better remembered. It also provides another opportunity for students to engage in dialogical thinking. The teacher could formalize this into a concluding activity where students are asked to explain the differences between feudalism's and capitalism's basic ideas, values and assumptions. **S–25**

7 Introduction to Remodelling Science Lessons

A critical approach to teaching science is concerned less with students accumulating undigested facts and scientific definitions and procedures, than with students learning to *think scientifically*. As students learn to think scientifically, they inevitably organize and internalize facts, learn terminology, and use scientific procedures. But they learn them deeply, because they are tied into ideas that they have thought through, and hence do not have to "re-learn" them again and again.

The biggest obstacle to science education is students' previous misconceptions. Although there are well-developed, defensible methods for settling many scientific questions, educators should recognize that students have developed their own ideas about the physical world. Merely presenting established methods to students does not usually affect their inner beliefs; they continue to exist in an unarticulated and therefore unchallenged form. Rather than transferring the knowledge they learn in school to new settings, students continue to use their pre-existing frameworks of belief. Students' own emerging egocentric conceptions about events in their immediate experience seem much more real and true to them than what they have superficially picked up in school.

For example, in one study, few college physics students could correctly answer the question, "What happens to a piece of paper thrown out of a moving car's window?" They reverted to a naive version of physics inconsistent with what they learned in school; they used Aristotelian rather than Newtonian physics. The *Proceedings of the International Seminar on Misconceptions in Science and Mathematics* offers another example. A student was presented with evidence about current flow that was incompatible with his articulated beliefs. In response to the instructor's demonstration, the student replied, "Maybe that's the case here, but if you come home with me you'll see it's different there."[1] This student's response graphically illustrates one way students retain their own beliefs: they simply juxtapose them with a new belief. Unless students practice expressing and defending their own beliefs, and listening critically to those of others, they will not critique their own beliefs and modify them in light of school learning. "As children discover they have different solutions, different methods, different frameworks, and they try to convince each other, or at least to understand each other, they revise their understanding in many small but important ways."[2]

Science texts suffer from serious flaws which give students false and misleading ideas about science. Students are not encouraged to develop real experiments; rather, they are told what is true and false and given demonstrations to perform. Typical science texts present the student, in other words, with the finished products of science. These texts present information and tell students what is so. They have students sort things into pre-developed categories, rather than stimulating students to discover and assess their own categories. Texts require students to practice the skills of measuring, graphing, and counting, often for no reason but mindless drill. Such activities merely reinforce the stereotype that scientists are people who run around counting and measuring and mixing bizarre liquids together for no recognizable reason.

Texts also introduce scientific concepts. But students must understand scientific concepts through ordinary language and ordinary concepts. After a unit on photosynthesis, a student who was asked, "Where do plants get their food?" replied, "From water, soil, and all over." The student misunderstood what the concept 'food' means for plants and missed the crucial idea that *plants make their own food.* He was using his previous (ordinary, human) concept of 'food'. Confusion often arises when scientific concepts that have another meaning in ordinary language (such as, 'work') are not distinguished in a way that highlights how purpose affects use of language. Students need to see that each concept is correct for its purpose.

Students are rarely called upon to understand the reasons for doing their experiments or for doing them in a particular way. Students have little opportunity to come to grips with the concept of 'the controlled experiment' or understand the reasons for the particular controls used. Furthermore, texts often fail to make the link between observation and conclusion explicit. Rarely do students have occasion to ask, "How did we get from *that* observation to *that* conclusion?" Scientific reasoning remains a mystery to students, whereas education in science should combat the common assumption that, "Only scientists and geniuses can understand science."

To learn from a science activity, students should understand its purpose. A critical approach to science education would allow students to ponder questions, propose solutions, and develop and conduct their own experiments. Although many of their experiments would fail, the attempt and failure provide a valuable learning experience which more accurately parallels what scientists do. When an experiment designed by students fails, those students are stimulated to amend their beliefs.

Many texts also treat the concept of "*the* scientific method" in a misleading way. Not all scientists do the same kinds of things — some experiment, others don't, some do field observations, others develop theories. Compare what chemists, theoretical physicists, zoologists, and paleontologists do. Furthermore, scientific thinking is not a matter of running through a set of steps one time. Rather it is a kind of thinking in which we continually move back and forth between questions we ask about the world and observations we make, and experiments we devise to test out various hypotheses, guesses, hunches, and models. We continually think in a hypothetical fashion: "If this idea of mine is true, then what will happen under these or those conditions? Let me see, suppose we try this. What does this result tell me? Why did this happen? If *this* is why, then *that* should happen when I ...."

We have to do a lot of critical thinking in the process, because we must ask clear and precise questions in order to devise experiments that can give us clear and precise answers. Typically the results of experiments — especially those devised by students — will be open to more than one interpretation. What one student thinks the experiment has shown often differs from what another student thinks. Here then is another opportunity to try to get students to be clear and precise in what they are saying. "Exactly how are these two different interpretations different? Do they agree at all? If so, where do they agree?"

As part of learning to think scientifically, clearly, and precisely, students need opportunities to transfer ideas to new contexts. This can be linked with the scientific goal of bringing different kinds of phenomena under one scientific law, and the process of clarifying our thinking through analogies. Students should seek connections, and assess explanations and models. "How do the concepts of gravity, mass, and air resistance explain the behavior of pebbles and airplanes, boulders and feathers?"

Finally, although scientific questions have only one correct answer, they may have a number of plausible answers only one of which is correct. It is more important for students to get into the habit of thinking scientifically than to get the correct answer through a rote process that they do not understand. The essential point is this: students should learn to do their own thinking about scientific questions from the start.

Once students give up on trying to do their own scientific thinking and start passively taking in what their textbooks tell them, the spirit of science, the scientific attitude and frame of mind, is lost. Never forget the importance of "I can figure this out for myself! I can find some way to *test* this!" as an essential scientific stance for students in relationship to how they think about themselves as *knowers*. If they reach the point of believing that knowledge is something in books that people smarter than them figured out, then they have lost the fundamental drive that ultimately distinguishes the educated from the uneducated person.

Unfortunately, this shift commonly occurs in the thinking of most students some time during elementary school. We need to teach science, and indeed all subjects, in such a way that this shift never occurs, so that the drive to figure out things for oneself does not die, but is continually fed and supported by day to day scientific thinking on our part.

From the outset we must design science activities so that students cannot mindlessly perform them. We should look for opportunities that call upon students to explain or make intelligible what they are doing and why it is necessary or significant. When students perform experiments, we should ask questions such as these:

- What exactly are you doing? Why? What results do you expect? Why? Have you designed any controls for this experiments? (Why do you have to use the same amount of liquid for both tests? Why do these have to be the same temperature? Size? What would happen if they weren't?) What might happen if we … instead?

When students make calculations or take measurements, we should ask questions like these:

- What are you measuring? Why? What will that tell you? What numbers do you need to record? In what units? Why? What equation are you using? Why? Which numbers go where in the equation? What does the answer tell you? What would a different answer mean?

When studying anatomy, students can apply what they learn by considering such questions as these:

- If this part of the body has this function, what would happen if it no longer functioned fully or at all? Why do you say so? What would that be like for the person? What if it functioned on "overdrive"? What other parts of the body would such breakdowns affect? Why?

When students use theoretical concepts in biology or zoology, for example, they could be asked to explain the purpose and significance of those concepts by answering questions like these:

- How important is this distinction? Let's look at our chart of categories of living things. Where on the chart is this distinction? Why? What distinction is more important? Why? Less important? Why? (Why is the distinction between vertebrates and invertebrates more important to zoologists than the distinction between warm-blooded and cold-blooded animals?)

- Did any categorizations surprise you or seem strange? Do zoologists group together animals that seem very different to you? Which? How can we find out why they are grouped this way?

In general, students should be asked to explain the justification for scientific claims.

- Why does your text say this? How did scientists find this out? How would that prove this conclusion? Could we explain these results another way? What? Then how could we tell which was right? What would we have to do? Why? What results would you expect if this were so, rather than that hypothesis?

Of course, all of the questions above need to be modified in the light of the grade level, the particular students, and the context. We must continually take into account precisely what questions in what form will stimulate their thinking. We want to make sure that we don't overwhelm them with questions they are not able to handle, for that will cause them to stop thinking as quickly as the straight didactic approach does.

In sum, whenever possible, students should be encouraged to express their ideas and try to convince each other to adopt them. Having to listen to their fellow students' ideas, to take those ideas seriously, and to try to find ways to test those ideas with observations and experiments are necessary experiences. Having to listen to their fellow students' objections will facilitate the process of self critique in a more fruitful way than if they are merely corrected by teachers who are typically taken as absolute authorities on "textbook" matters. Discussion with peers should be used to make reasoning from observation to conclusion explicit and help students learn how to state their own assumptions and recognize the assumptions of others.

Footnotes

[1] Hugh Helm & Joseph D. Novak, "A Framework for Conceptual Change with Special Reference to Misconceptions," *Proceedings of the International Seminar on Misconceptions in Science and Mathematics,* Cornell University, Ithaca, NY, June 20–22, 1983, p. 3.

[2] Jack Easley, "A Teacher Educator's Perspective on Students' and Teachers' Schemes: Or Teaching by Listening," *Proceedings of the Conference on Thinking, Harvard Graduate School of Education,* August, 1984, p. 8.

What Biome Do You Live In

Objectives of the remodelled lesson
The students will:
- through discussion, explore the concept 'biome,' the usefulness of distinguishing biomes, and historical implications of the concept

Original Lesson Plan

Abstract

Students use the high and low temperatures and the average annual amount of precipitation for their towns and a table to identify their biome. They then compare their towns with the description of their biome in the text, and explain differences.

from *Silver Burdett Science 6ᵗʰ Grade* by George G. Mallinson, Jacqueline Mallinson, William L. Smallwood, Catherine Valentino. ©1985 p. 101.

Critique

The lesson encourages independent thought by having students compare their area with the description, and speculate on reasons for any differences. We would extend this discussion. The lesson also offers an opportunity for interdisciplinary work by exploring the relationship between geography and history.

Strategies used to remodel
S–1 thinking independently
S–17 questioning deeply: raising and pursuing root or significant questions
S–23 making interdisciplinary connections

Remodelled Lesson Plan

The teacher, rather than immediately assigning this page, could first ask students how they could find out what biome they live in. "What do you need to know about an area? (Review the concept.) How could we find those things out?" **S–1**

When students have identified the biome, use the questions in the original lesson, extended with questions like the following: Why is that our biome? What is different here? Which differences are natural? Man-caused? If different places that have the same biome vary in these kinds of ways, why do we classify biomes? Does knowing which biome we belong to tell us anything? What? How can we use our knowledge about biomes? **S–17** Why do other places have our biome?

To have students make interdisciplinary connections, you could ask, "How does an area's biome affect the history of that place? Why? Identify the biomes of places we have studied in history. Would that history be different if that place had been tundra? Desert? How? Why?" **S–23**

The Human Skeleton

by Evelyn De La Paz Rios, Rice Elementary School, San Carlos, CA

Objectives of the remodelled lesson

The students will:
- make their preconceptions about the skeleton explicit by drawing it
- draw another skeleton after learning more about it, thereby examining, evaluating, and modifying their preconceptions

Standard Approach

The students' text has a brief discussion of the human skeleton with the names of the different bones.

Critique

Children in the elementary grades have certain ideas about the human body. Some of these ideas are correct and some are not. We must give children the opportunity to correct those which are incorrect by comparing what they do know with what they do not know and actively make their own modifications.

Strategies used to remodel

S–1 thinking independently
S–30 examining or evaluating assumptions
S–33 evaluating evidence and alleged facts

Remodelled Lesson Plan s–1

The students will be divided into partners and will take turns drawing each other's body outline as the person lies on the paper. After drawing the outlines, the students will exchange papers with their partners so that everyone will have an outline of his or her body. Without referring to a text book, each student will draw his or her skeleton in the outline. These drawings will hang in the room while the students gather information about their bodies, comparing it to other animals, machines, and artificial parts.

As students gather the information, they will record and map it out on a second body outline. By critiquing their initial ideas, the students will have a better understanding of the process of expanding their information base. **S–30**

289

The students will construct a model of a 5' skeleton using plaster of paris, old sheets, and cardboard tubes. The students will work in groups of 2, 3, or 4 to construct some part of the skeleton. After constructing the parts of the skeleton in proportion to the whole, they will assemble the skeleton.

With the modified knowledge about the human skeleton and the interest and humor engendered by making the models, students will be asked to write some creative response: a short comedy, a mystery, or perhaps a poem.

editor's note: What were you right about? How did you know those things? What were you wrong about? Why did you think that? How could you have been wrong? **S–33**

Follow up brainstorming sessions with discussion of the items listed — categorizing, evaluating, analyzing, comparing, ordering, etc.

Hair Keeps Animals Warm

Objectives of the remodelled lesson

The students will:
- discuss the importance of controlling variables when experimenting, by analyzing the experiment in their texts
- evaluate the model used by the text for its experiment design by discussing significant similarities and differences

Original Lesson Plan

Abstract

Students remove the labels from two tin cans. They glue cotton around one of them and fill both with the same amount of hot water. They predict the results and then measure and record the water temperature every five minutes for half an hour. The conclusion reads, *"Using the results from this experiment, explain how hair keeps an animal warm."* As an extension, they are to consider how sea mammals with little hair keep warm.

from *Silver Burdett Science 6,* George G. Mallinson, Jacqueline Mallinson, William L. Smallwood, Catherine Valentino. ©1985 p. 58.

Critique

This lesson affords the opportunity for students to critique their texts. It inadvertently encourages sloppy thinking in students. It does not answer the question it claims to. Though the title question is *"How does hair keep an animal warm?"* all that can be inferred from this experiment is that stuff similar to hair retains heat. It does nothing to explain *how*, it merely suggests *that* hair (or cotton) helps keep animals warm. Students are likely to answer the question with a restatement of what it asks, that is, "Hair keeps animals warm by keeping the heat in."

The lesson offers a number of opportunities for infusing critical thought. Students could explore and evaluate the analogy between the cans of warm water and animals. Critical vocabulary use can be reinforced. The extension about how sea mammals keep warm could be further extended with a discussion of people and reptiles.

Strategies used to remodel

S-21 reading critically: clarifying or critiquing texts
S-33 evaluating evidence and alleged facts
S-29 noting significant similarities and differences
S-10 refining generalizations and avoiding oversimplifications

Remodelled Lesson Plan s–21

Students could read the experiment, and discuss its design at length. For example, you might ask, "Why fill the cans from the same container? What could happen if you didn't? How would that affect the results? Why do both cans have to have the same amount? Why make a graph? Could the data be organized another way instead? Which is best for this kind of information? Why? How would you expect the experiment to turn out? Why? What kind of answer would you give to the question? What did the experiment show? Why? What did it claim to show? Are these the same or different? **S–33** Why? What is used in place of the animal? Its fur? How like and unlike are cans of warm water and cotton to animals and fur? Are the similarities relevant to the question the experiment poses? Are the differences? Assess this experiment." **S–29**

Finally, students could consider less hairy mammals and animals. "Does hair help keep all animals warm? Name some animals that have little or no hair. How do they keep warm?" **S–10**

Magnets

Objectives of the remodelled lesson

The students will:
- explore and clarify 'magnetism' through play and structured activities
- transfer what they learn about magnets to their understanding of the Earth

Original Lesson Plan

Abstract

The article containing the following suggestions emphasizes the importance of students' "playing" with magnets before the formal lesson begins. The author then suggests the following activities: students are given a variety of objects to test for attraction to magnets; students distinguish metals that are attracted from those that aren't; students devise tests which determine relative strengths of magnets; students make magnets; and students use magnets to find objects buried in sand.

from *Learning Magazine* Vol 15, #7
"Science — Discover the Wonder," by G. Douglas Paul pp. 44-45.

Critique

The first, third and fourth activities, as well as the introduction, encourage independent thought. It is unclear, however, whether or not students are to discuss their findings. The lesson does nothing to put the concept of magnetism into the larger picture of science. It misses the chance to discuss the purpose and applications of the object of study. Ships and airplanes use compasses, which rely on magnetism, to navigate. Magnetism is an important idea in astronomy.

Strategies used to remodel

S-1 thinking independently
S-11 comparing analogous situations: transferring insights to new contexts
S-23 making interdisciplinary connections
S-5 developing intellectual humility and suspending judgment

Remodelled Lesson Plan

This lesson could start with a discussion to find out what students already know about magnetism and its uses. Instead of giving students objects to test, students should be able to decide what to test and how to determine the attraction to the magnet. **S-1** This lesson does a good job when it transfers learning to the situation of making magnets, but it would do well to make this transfer explicit by asking students what more they have learned from *making* magnets, than from studying those already made.

Discuss a compass with students, explaining what it is used for. Let students play with compasses, or make them, and see how the magnet affects them. "Why does the compass needle usually point one way? Why does your magnet change that? What does that tell us about the Earth?" Students could be asked to describe or sketch the shapes of the magnetic field as discovered by noting where magnets attract and repel each other. They could look up drawings of the magnetic field around the Earth and compare the two. *S–11*

As an extension exercise, students could discuss why we use the expression 'magnetic personality' and what it means. The teacher could lead a discussion where the children try to puzzle this out. *S–23*

Finally, this lesson can be wrapped up by asking students to review what they have learned. They should be able to state what they now know and what they are uncertain of in the area of magnetism. "What kind of 'thing' is magnetism? Can we sense it? How do we know it's there? What do we know about it? What questions do you have about magnets and magnetism?" *S–5* Interested students could research magnets and report back to the class.

Polar Ice Caps Melt

Objectives of the remodelled lesson
The students will:
- design a model to explore the consequences of the melting of the polar ice caps
- evaluate their models by noting significant similarities and differences

Original Lesson Plan

Abstract

This lesson focuses on the question, *"If the polar ice caps melt, what would happen to the rest of the world?"* Students put sand, water, and a large chunk of ice in a large pan, and record periodic observations while the ice melts. They discuss the following questions: *In what way is the model similar to what happens on Earth? What kinds of errors occur when any model is used?*

from *Down to Earth* Arthur Wiebe, Sheryl Mercier, and Larry Ecklund editors. Fresno Pacific College, Project Aims. ©1984 p. 14.

Critique

This lesson provides an opportunity for model design and assessment, distinguishing relevant from irrelevant differences, differences in style of observations, and an exploration of a chain of causes and effects.

Strategies used to remodel
S-9 developing confidence in reason
S-1 thinking independently
S-31 distinguishing relevant from irrelevant facts
S-35 exploring implications and consequences
S-11 comparing analogous situations: transferring insights to new contexts
S-29 noting significant similarities and differences

Remodelled Lesson Plan S-9

You could begin by asking students what they think would happen if the polar ice caps melted. Guide them in designing a model to answer the question, with questions like the following: How could we find out, without it actually happening? How could we make a model we can watch? What could we do? Why? What could we use? Why? What would happen to the water? Where would it go? How could we make oceans and continents? *S–1*

During the course of the study, have students write down their observations (and times at which they made them). A student could put the observations in chronological order. Students could discuss their observations, and what they imply: What has happened? What did different students find? How can we compare these notes? (The class could use the notes to make a composite description, which would probably be more complete than that of any single student. Students could discuss differences between observations near the same time. Students could delete irrelevant observations.) *S–31* How is our model like what the real situation would be? Unlike it? What does that tell us about what would happen if the ice caps really melted? Follow up responses to elicit further effects. (Then what? What effect would *that* have?) Students could discuss affects on land, climate, people, and other forms of life. *S–35* The class could also discuss the question: What would happen if the ice caps grew? (Discuss at length.) *S–11*

The teacher could supplement the discussion of the worth of the model, with questions like the following: Why did we have to make a model to explore this question? In what ways was the model different from Earth? Which of these differences are relevant to our key question? How useful was the model? What might we have done, if we had the time and resources, to make the model more accurate? Why would that have been better? Do we need to have done that, or can we draw conclusions from our model? *S–29*

If students know about the ice ages, they could be brought into the discussion of this lesson. Students may be able to speculate about how scientists know the ice caps have changed sizes. "Given what we've learned about how the Earth would be affected by the melting of our ice caps, what could we expect scientists to find if ice caps had melted and grown a long time ago? If the ice caps used to be smaller (larger), what evidence would be left? How do scientists know how big the oceans used to be? If the oceans shrank (grew) what would coasts look like?" *S–11*

Making Models: The Atom

Objectives of the remodelled lesson

The students will:
- analyze the concept 'model' by discussing models they have seen and discussing the purposes of models
- develop criteria for evaluating models
- design and make models of an atom
- discuss the strengths and weaknesses of their models of atoms, noting significant similarities and differences

Original Lesson Plan

Abstract

Students examine pictures of models of atoms, are provided with materials, and are asked to make their own models of oxygen, carbon, or sodium atoms. They are asked if they can make the electrons revolve.

from *Concepts in Science 6ᵗʰ Grade* by Paul F. Brandwein, Elizabeth K. Cooper, Paul E. Blackwood, Elizabeth B. Hone. p. 293.

Critique

This lesson fragment offers an opportunity for students to discuss the purposes of models in general and the specific benefits of making models of atoms. Students can also practice assessing models, in light of those purposes. By examining their models at length and in great detail, students can develop their clarity of thought and expression, and review what they know about atoms.

Strategies used to remodel

S–29 noting significant similarities and differences
S–15 developing criteria for evaluation: clarifying values and standards
S–14 clarifying and analyzing the meanings of words or phrases
S–1 thinking independently
S–8 developing intellectual perseverance
S–10 refining generalizations and avoiding oversimplifications
S–31 distinguishing relevant from irrelevant facts
S–23 making interdisciplinary connections

Remodelled Lesson Plan S–29

The class could begin by discussing models in general and analyzing the concept. "What does 'model' mean? What models have you seen or made? Did they help you understand what they modeled? How? Why? How can you tell a good model from a poor model? What's an example of a good model? Why? A poor one? Why? **S–15** What differences were there between models you have seen and the things they modeled? (Ask this of several of the examples previously given.) Why make models? What purpose do they serve?" **S–14**

Tell students that they are going to make models of atoms. Have students discuss what they know about atoms, and ask, "How could models of atoms help us? How could we make a model of an atom?" You might ask them what parts they would need, and how they could put them together. **S–1** Students could make and evaluate various models of atoms and engage in an extended process of designing, making, discussing, and improving models of atoms. **S–8**

Students could be led in a discussion of the strengths and weaknesses of various models, with questions like the following: (Of each proposed model ask,) What parts does it have? What parts do atoms have? Does the model have any extra parts? Does it leave out parts? How is each part of this model like the part of the atom? (Continue for each part, including the connecters.) Unlike? (Encourage multiple responses.) Could this model be improved? How? How do these models help us? How could they mislead us? How can we avoid being misled? **S–10** Do these models help you understand atoms? How, or why not? Do any of these models suggest questions about atoms? What? Do the models help you find answers to those questions? Why or why not? Are the differences between the model and the atom relevant to the question you asked? Why or why not? **S–31** How could this model be improved? Why would that improve it?

The teacher could use the idea of models to clarify the concept 'analogy'. Have students recall analogies. Have them compare models and analogies. (A model is a thing, analogies are words. Both have similarities and differences to the originals. Both can be evaluated in terms of their purposes and whether relevant features are similar or different.) **S–23**

The Sun Heats the Earth

Objectives of the remodelled lesson

The students will:
- infer how surface temperature affects air temperature
- exercise independent thought by organizing their data on weather, and answering essay questions
- use insight into numbers to understand a scientific phenomenon

Original Lesson Plan

Abstract

"How Weather Begins" discusses solar energy and its relationship to the Earth's weather. This section explains how the warmth of the sun heats the atmosphere unevenly. One of the reasons for this is illustrated by an experiment in which students predict and observe which materials heat the most and least, and which lose heat the quickest and slowest. Another activity has the teacher shine a flashlight straight onto paper, then at an angle. Students compare the areas. The text relates the demonstration to the difference between summer and winter sunlight.

from *Silver Burdett Science 5th Grade*, George G. Mallinson, Jacqueline Mallinson, William L. Smallwood, Catherine Valentino. ©1985 pp. 260–261

Critique

The text confuses inferring and concluding, with remembering and sensing. Examples of this problem occur on teachers' notes on pp. 260, when students are asked to infer, conclude or figure out facts just mentioned in the text or described by students. For example, after discussing experiences of walking barefoot on hot and cool surfaces, students are to *conclude* that some of the surfaces were cooler than others. When you step from a hot surface to a cool one, you *sense* the latter is cooler; you do not conclude it.

The motivation exercise in the teachers' notes on p. 260, about walking barefoot, is not terribly motivating and is a poor introduction to the text. Although it *does* illustrate that some surface areas are warmer than others, it does not engage students in the way the experiment for this idea does. This experiment is a hands-on illustration of the preceding text and is thus more dynamic than the proposed motivation. Even if this option is not exercised, a more exciting motivation scenario could be explored.

The enrichment suggestion on p. 261 (wherein the teacher is supposed to demonstrate that light shown at an angle covers more area, and thus provides less energy per unit of space), falls short of fully illustrating the concept. Students need to consider the demonstration carefully and make its meaning explicit.

Strategies used to remodel

S–32 making plausible inferences, predictions, or interpretations
S–23 making interdisciplinary connections
S–1 thinking independently

Remodelled Lesson Plan

Rather than opening the chapter with a questionable inference (that palm trees imply tropical places), it would be better to ask students what weather is and what they know about it. You could substitute the experiment on how heat affects different surfaces for the "motivation," and ask students what surface temperatures might have to do with weather. "How is surface temperature related to air temperature?" **S–32**

The reasoning behind the enrichment activity for the different angles of sunlight could be made more explicit by eliciting or explaining that when the same amount of energy hits a smaller versus a larger area, the amount of energy per unit of area is greater. Here, students could be reminded of work with fractions. Write a fraction on the board, labeling the numerator 'amount of energy' and the denominator 'area'. Write a second fraction, labeled the same, but with a larger denominator. Thus, students can understand the idea mathematically, as well as verbally. **S–23**

Ask students if they can design other models to illustrate this concept. If they do not suggest any, suggest a few yourself (both adequate and inadequate) to check their understanding of the concept. For each model, ask if it does indeed show how the angle of sunlight affects the intensity of heat. Probe their answers; insist they not only answer but explain why or why not. (They may need two models: one for "Energy which arrives at an angle covers more space," another for "The same energy hitting more area provides less energy per area.") **S–1**

Animal Architects

by Brooke Bledsoe, Napa U.S.D., Napa, CA

Objectives of the remodelled lesson
The students will:
- use resource material to support a conclusion
- develop and give arguments
- assess the arguments given

Original Lesson Plan

I made the remark in class to my fifth grade students that "Birds are the best architects, and we have always studied them to learn how to create better designs for our own buildings." One of the students interjected that he had always thought beavers were the best architects.

Based on this impromptu difference of opinion, I assigned a discussion for the following Friday to take place between those who took the "birds" side versus those who took the "beavers" side.

They could bring in all the reference material they could gather, and I recommended that they meet as a group before they got started in order to organize what they needed and how they would proceed.

On Friday afternoon, we set the classroom up with a row of desks for the "birds" opposite a row of desks for the "beavers". Those who did not want to participate, or who were undecided, sat in a row at the end of the classroom between the two opposing sides. I challenged them to listen to the arguments and facts and to decide which side they thought presented the best arguments and which side they would finally agree with. They could form a third side or have individual opinions.

As the discussion progressed, I observed that the students had set a pattern of debate that was quite civilized, allowing alternate views to be voiced in the order in which they sat. It reminded me of the Presidential debates on television in which one candidate is allowed so much time to address a question and then the other takes a turn to answer the same question. I intervened here to encourage responses from any member of a team, out of seating order, to counter or challenge something said from the other side.

The "beavers" definitely out-argued the "birds". They were more logical, had stronger data, and used more quotes from authority. However, with my intervention, the question changed then to, "Were the beavers, perhaps, the better engineers, and the birds the better architects?"

301

I was very proud of the "undecided" group when I called time. They concluded that, although the "beavers" had made a much stronger case than the "birds", they really didn't prove the beavers were better architects, but rather that they build stronger houses. They also concluded that, since the beavers build only two types of houses, the variety of style and usefulness of the birds' nests, adapted to many environments, make the birds better *architects* and the beavers better *engineers*. My pride in the conclusions from my neutral group was due to their ability to see the difference between a stronger presentation, versus actual proof of the argument — a giant step towards critical thinking for ten-year-olds.

Critique

Other than curriculum content set out by the California Framework, I have pretty much left the textbooks and all workbooks behind in my mode of teaching. Thus, I am using my own logic to set forth methods to be used to teach the content prescribed. My plans and methods lack clarity and focus. Consequently, when using a situation that arises spontaneously, I need to progress in a logical order instead of shooting from the hip so much of the time. I feel as my clarity and focus crystallize, so will that of my students. The use of criteria and the clarification of vocabulary should be a starting point before sending the students to the reference materials.

Strategies used to remodel

S–26 reasoning dialectically: evaluating perspectives, interpretations, or theories
S–1 thinking independently
S–31 distinguishing relevant from irrelevant facts
S–34 recognizing contradictions
S–22 listening critically: the art of silent dialogue

Remodelled Lesson Plan S-26

I would use the same question: "Are birds better architects than beavers, or are beavers better architects than birds?" **S–1** Again, I would divide the children into the three groups described above: the "birds", the "beavers", and the "undecided". I would give them two days to meet and to gather reference material, but this time I would advise them that at any time during the debate they could change their minds. One could become undecided or one could change to the other side and back again if any doubt entered his or her mind. Through open-ended questioning from me, I would ask for clarification of 'architect' and 'engineer' and see what they would do with these terms. **S–31** I would choose a few comments from the two panels and ask if they really related to the argument, and I would select out any contradictions made by a side and hold them up for scrutiny. **S–34**

editor's note: The undecided students could also ask questions of the panelists. **S–22**

Parachutes and Other Falling Objects

Objectives of the remodelled lesson

The students will:
- design and test parachutes
- discuss characteristics which affect the descent rates of parachutes
- transfer insights about parachutes to falling objects in general and to falling objects on the moon
- hypothesize, test, and refine hypotheses regarding the descent rates of objects

Original Lesson Plan

Abstract

This lesson focuses on the key question, *"What is the rate of descent of your parachute?"* Students design, build, and test parachutes (twice each from three different heights), calculating the rates of descent in meters per second. They then discuss the following questions: *What things affect the rate of descent? Did the rate of your chute change from one height to another? Why? Select the five slowest rates of descent and the five fastest from the class chart. Have those students display and describe their parachutes. Were there similarities? What can you conclude? How would you modify your parachute to improve its performance?*

from *The Sky's the Limit* Arthur Wiebe
and Larry Ecklund editors. Fresno Pacific
College. Project Aims. © 1982 p. 13.

Critique

A major weakness of this lesson is its failure to connect why a parachute works to falling objects in general. It misses the opportunity to teach important science concepts such as gravity, wind resistance, and inertia. This trivializes the lesson by restricting it to measuring and recording data.

This lesson offers the opportunity to have students engage in extended scientific reasoning — posing questions, testing answers, posing new questions, and conducting further tests, all the while, assessing their original ideas and refining their initial generalizations. Headway can be made on the broadened topic without extended preparation, no measurements, and little recording of data.

303

Strategies used to remodel

S–8 developing intellectual perseverance
S–32 making plausible inferences, predictions, or interpretations
S–11 comparing analogous situations: transferring insights to new contexts
S–10 refining generalizations and avoiding oversimplifications
S–5 developing intellectual humility and suspending judgment
S–9 developing confidence in reason

Remodelled Lesson Plan *S–8*

Begin by asking if anyone knows what a parachute is and what it is for. Students should know that a parachute is designed to keep something from falling too quickly, that is, that it slows the rate of descent. "What affects the rate of descent of a parachute? How could we find out? How does a parachute work? Why does it work?"

Students could then design and test their parachutes. Students may repeat their tests on different days and/or in different places (windy vs. protected) and compare results. As in the original lesson, have them compare slow with fast parachutes and speculate on which differences affected the descent rate. They could compare parachutes of different materials, and those carrying different weights and shapes. Ask them, "What does this tell us? About air? Gravity? Objects? Why did we get the results we did? Why does the parachute fall slowly?" Students could then begin making generalizations and hypotheses, and designing experiments to test them. **S–32**

You could then broaden the original question to, "What affects the rate of fall of objects, and why?" **S–11** Students could practice making and refining generalizations. Suggest that they experiment with other kinds of falling objects such as paper planes, feathers, books, rocks, pillows, etc. Students need not measure, they could simply group objects in general categories of fast-falling, slow-falling, and in-between-speeds. After each test or each few tests, discuss results, eliciting complete explanations. "What were you testing for? (To see if weight, size, or density affects fall rate.) What did you do? (Dropped this and that from the same height at the same time and place.) Why? (If what we tested for affects fall rate, since they're the same in every way but this, then this should have fallen much more slowly than that.) What happened? (This fell much more slowly that that.) What does that mean? Could there be another explanation? Were there other differences between the two objects that could have accounted for the results? How do these latest finding compare with our earlier tests? What other questions could be asked? Is there anything else that you noticed that would explain the results? What else could you test for? Now what would you say affects descent rates? Why? What *doesn't* affect descent rates? Why?" **S–10**

The class could keep notes on the discussions, listing ideas, tests, and conclusions. The teacher could, perhaps during the summary, point out tests or hypothesis that failed or were proven wrong, but from which students learned something. **S–5** Students could use the class records to sort slow, medium, and fast falling objects, and write short passages comparing the three kinds of objects, trying to generalize from them, and speculating on the reasons for or principles behind the results. **S-9**

The material in this lesson could be related to botany with a discussion of different shaped seeds and seed containers, and how well they scatter seeds. Students could discuss objects falling on the moon. If necessary, first point out to students that the moon has less gravity, and less air. Students could compare how different objects (for example a rock versus a feather) would fall on the moon as opposed to Earth. **S-11**

Everyone learning to deepen her critical thinking skills and dispositions comes to insights over time. We certainly can enrich and enhance this process, even help it to move at a faster pace, but only in a qualified way. Time to assimilate and grow is essential.

Animals With Backbones

by JoAnne Rains, Clinton, South
Carolina

Objectives of the remodelled lesson

The students will:
- apply the concept of classification
- discuss animals with and without backbones and develop working definitions of vertebrate and invertebrate
- make other classifications within the vertebrates

Original Lesson Plan

Abstract

This chapter is called "Animals with Backbones". The concept of classification is taught at the beginning of the chapter, using some photographs that were not very clear. Students were asked, "How many animals can you name? Where would you see a lot of different animals? How could you group them?" The teacher's textbook suggests asking the student what 'classification' means and then relating the word to groupings, etc. The text shows a picture and tells the student, "All these animals are vertebrates." Then it names a group of invertebrates. The text continues telling facts.

from *Accent on Science,* Sund, Adams, Hackett, and Moyer. Charles B. Merrill Publishing Company, Columbus, Ohio, 1983. Grade 5.

Critique

I think that this lesson uses an illogical order. However, I do like the operational definitions followed by the use of the word several times in context.

The text misses several opportunities to use an inductive approach or discovery method of learning. The text asks, "If you go to a zoo, how would you find the birds?" Then it answers, "They are found in a section of the zoo called an aviary." This question does not lead the questioner in the proper direction. This question-and-answer sequence is followed by several similar sequences that bring in irrelevant material and are illogical in nature. The textbook is unclear in its reference to certain pictures. It provides misinformation concerning many of the illustrations. The questions always use a didactic approach in discussing vertebrate and invertebrate animals. The questions are overly simplistic for fifth grade students. For example, "How are you like a cat? How is a cat like a fish?"

Strategies used to remodel

S–1 thinking independently
S–29 noting significant similarities and differences
S–23 making interdisciplinary connections
S–32 making plausible inferences, predictions, or interpretations
S–17 questioning deeply: raising and pursuing root or significant questions

Remodelled Lesson Plan

I would begin this class with the students' text books closed. This lesson could be introduced with an inductive approach using the following activity. I might start by asking random students to change seats until I had all the girls on one side and all the boys on the other side of the room. Then I would ask, "What have I done as I changed your seating arrangement?" They should probably respond, "You have all the girls sitting together and all the boys sitting together." **S–1** Then I would introduce 'classification' for the first time. I might say, "That's great! Are you telling me that I have classified (divided) your class into two main groups that consist of boys and girls?" Then I would lead them into the idea of sub-groups by an exercise like the following. "Would all the blue-eyed girls stand up?" I would then allow the students to develop generalizations through discussion and questioning about the group as a whole and its various subgroups. These questions might be asked.

• How could we classify this whole group?

• How would you classify these persons who are standing up? What other groups do they belong to?

• What are some other ways that we can classify this group?

• What are some classifications that we find in real life?

If they have a problem getting started, I might give examples of dishes. Dishes can be classified into plates, cups, saucers, and bowls. Or that contact sports might be classified. "Can you tell me what other sports would fit into this classification?"

Using the text and supplementary materials, I would next examine pictures of vertebrates and invertebrates. I would guide them through questioning into their classifying the animals into the broad categories. After they have classified them, I would ask the following questions:

• How are these animals alike?

• What is there about *this* animal that kept you from putting it in this other group or classification? **S–29**

At this point I would develop the definition of 'vertebrate' and 'invertebrate'. I could say, "I will label this group 'vertebrates'." Then I would ask, "Why should they be called vertebrates?" Since they have already studied the human body, I hope that they would pick up on the connection of our backbone. After this connection has been made, I would write the word "invertebrate" on the board. Here a reference could be made to a recent language arts lesson on prefixes. **S–23** I would ask, "Do you recall from our reading lesson what the prefix 'in' means?" With that information and the information of what a vertebrate is, what might we infer about the word 'invertebrate'?" *S–32*

At this point, since the distinction between the vertebrates and invertebrates has been explored, I would spend the rest of the class period on vertebrates and deal with invertebrates in the next class period.

editor's note: Instead of the above initial activity, to have an introduction more relevant to the lesson, students could brainstorm a list of animals, and categorize them, while being introduced to 'classification'. (You may have to participate in the brainstorming and suggest things like frogs, eagles, and starfish, since students may be thinking of mammals only.) Students could also categorize the list into groups and sub-groups to develop a hierarchy of categories analogous (and probably remarkably similar) to scientists'. The teacher could then segue into the lesson by saying that scientists have some of their own categories. Then introduce the word 'vertebrates' and ask students if the word sounds or looks familiar. "Why is this such an important distinction to zoologists?" *S–17*

Measuring Calories

by Theresa A. Barone, Covington Middle
School, Birmingham, MI

Objectives of the remodelled lesson

The students will

- learn what 'calorie' means
- design and conduct experiments to determine calorie counts
- examine the reasons for the math they use
- develop ways of recording and presenting their data

Original Lesson Plan

Abstract

This teacher demonstration illustrates that a calorie is a unit of heat given off when a fuel, such as our food, is burned. The illustration of and directions for making a simple calorimeter are provided. A flask with a measured amount of water is placed on a ring stand or other support and the water temperature is recorded. Around the base of the flask, a protective shield from asbestos pads or aluminum foil is made. This shield prevents heat loss. The amount of heat given off in the experiment is calculated by determining how much the water temperature rises. It is suggested that the meat of a walnut or peanut be used as the heat source. The nut meat is lighted and placed under the flask of water in the shield. As soon as the nut is burned, take the water temperature again. The calorie content of the nut can then be calculated.

from *Inquire — A Handbook of
Classroom Ideas to Motivate the
Teaching of Intermediate Science,*
Educational Service Inc., 1976, p. 212.

Critique

The design of this demonstration allows for little or no student involvement. The students are not asked to think about any of the concepts involved, they are simply shown them. The lesson does not require the students to ask any questions about what a calorie is. The concept of calorie is also not related to any other concept, including food consumption or diet. Although the students are asked to calculate the calorie content of the nut, no mention of relating science to math is mentioned. Also when the students calculate the calories of a given food, the data should be put in a form useful to others. This lesson makes no mention of this important extension. Finally, a science lesson lends itself naturally to the discussion of variables and how to alter the experiment in order to minimize them: the concept of the controlled experiment. This lesson does not mention this idea either.

Strategies used to remodel

S–1 thinking independently
S–23 making interdisciplinary connections
S–35 exploring implications and consequences
S–33 evaluating evidence and alleged facts
S–5 developing intellectual humility and suspending judgment
S–27 comparing and contrasting ideals with actual practice

Remodelled Lesson Plan

This lesson will begin by asking students to put their prior knowledge to work. The students could begin by discussing what they already know about how people get energy and by looking up the definition of 'calorie'. Questions that can be asked might include: Where do people get energy? Can you get more energy and become healthier by eating huge amounts of food? What is used to measure the amount of energy in foods? Why is it important to consider calories when discussing proper nutrition? How are calorie counts made? **S–1**

Through the teacher's guidance it should be established that calorie counts of common foods are determined by actually burning food and measuring the heat energy the food gives off. Tell students that a calorimeter is an instrument that can measure the heat energy a food contains. Through discussion, ask the students to come up with the items they will need to make their own calorimeter. Begin by asking: How can we best test different foods? What will be the best materials to use that will give us the most accurate readings? What will we need to measure heat? How will the heat be measured? How will the heat be contained? What could throw off our results? What could effect the water temperature besides the burning food? What do we need to do to control these variables? How can we prevent these other things from messing up our results? **S–1**

Once the students have established all they need to set up their calorimeters, provide the materials for doing so. Allow them the opportunity to burn a variety of both foods and amounts.

After the data have been collected, discuss the importance of using the correct mathematical operations when arriving at their calorie counts, by having students discuss the equations at length. For example: What equation must we use? What number goes here? Why? How do we get this number? What do we do with that result? Did you add or subtract when measuring the difference in temperature? What would happen if you did not multiply the correct temperature change and the volume of water? **S–23**

Be sure to discuss the best way for recording their data and showing it so that others can learn from their experiments. How can we show our results? What are we showing? How should we arrange the data? What sort of graph can we use? What headings do we need? The data the students have collected is helpful when they discuss the implications for nutrition. Ask them how various foods counted. Which foods had higher or fewer calories? Why is this information valuable? **S–35** *editor's note:* Instead of designing their own experiments from scratch (If they have never designed an experiment or discussed experiment design before), students could study the original lesson's design, and develop the concept of controlled experiments by discussing features of the original (and alternatives). "What is this step for? Why is it necessary? What could we do instead?"

Students could look up the word 'calorie' in reference books (texts, dictionary, books about energy, etc.)

Students who tested the same food can compare their results, and see if they can explain any differences. "Why did you get different results for the same food? Should they be different? How different were they? Did you do exactly the same thing? *S–33* If those results are a bit off, could they all be just a bit off? What does that tell us?" *S–5* Point out to students that scientific experiments don't come out perfectly. (You might explain the notation ± and why it's used.) *S–27*

Insulation

Objectives of the remodelled lesson

The students will:
- develop experiments to settle the question, "Does water cool at different rates in different containers?"
- discover and clarify related questions that their experiments do not answer
- practice using the critical vocabulary: inference, conclusion, evidence, and relevance
- distinguish relevant from irrelevant information to the problem
- make inferences from their experiments and evaluate them
- explore practical applications of insulation

Original Lesson Plan

Abstract

This lesson asks, *"In which container (tin can or styrofoam cup) will the hot water retain its heat longer? Why?"* Students pour equal amounts of water at the same temperature into the containers. They record the highest temperatures, and the temperature every minute for fifteen minutes. They make line graphs, individually and together. Under discussion topics, teachers are asked to *"Encourage the students to draw conclusions about the relationship between the time it took the water to cool in one container compared to the other container."* The extension suggests that students could test several kinds of containers.

from *Introductory Investigations* Arthur Wiebe and Larry Ecklund editors. Fresno Pacific College Project Aims p. 10.

Critique

This lesson presents an experiment, rather than presenting a question and allowing students to design experiments, thereby failing to encourage students to engage in scientific reasoning. It also unnecessarily limits the containers used. Allowing students to propose and test different containers would help them broaden their understanding of which materials conduct heat and which insulate. Using only two materials prevents students from fruitfully attempting to make generalizations about insulation.

The lesson presents another opportunity for practicing critical thinking micro-skills by using critical vocabulary, distinguishing relevant from irrelevant evidence, and making and evaluating inferences. Furthermore, students could explore practical applications of insulation, thus applying the key concept to other situations (buildings, clothes, atmosphere).

Strategies used to remodel

S–9 developing confidence in reason
S–21 reading critically: clarifying or critiquing texts
S–1 thinking independently
S–13 clarifying issues, conclusions, or beliefs
S–19 generating or assessing solutions
S–17 questioning deeply: raising and pursuing root or significant questions
S–29 noting significant similarities and differences
S–10 refining generalizations and avoiding oversimplifications
S–35 exploring implications and consequences

Remodelled Lesson Plan **S–9**

A minor remodel of this lesson, would be to present the teachers' text to students, and have them explain why they are given those instructions. (Why does the temperature of the water have to be the same when the experiment starts? If it wasn't, how would that effect the results? Etc.) **S–21** Thus, students could begin to develop for themselves a sense of how to design a controlled test. The discussion could be reviewed when students are later asked to design other experiments.

Instead of setting up the experiment for students, engage them in a discussion of hot water cooling. You might ask, "What happens when water cools? Where does the heat go? How fast does hot water cool off? What affects the rate at which water cools off?" **S–1**

To help students think independently by designing experiments, use questions like the following: How can we find out what materials best retain heat? What kinds of containers should we test? What characteristics of the containers might affect cooling rate? (size, shape, material, thickness) How can we test each characteristic? **S–13** What units of measurement should we use? How can we make sure that the results are due *only* to what we are testing, and not influenced by other things? What, besides the container, could affect the cooling rate, or our measurements? How can we prevent that from affecting our results? What will we have to do? (All water should begin at the same temperature and containers should sit in the same temperature. If testing for shape, use two different shapes of the same size and material; if testing for material, use two different materials, of the same size and shape.) **S–19**

This discussion could also be used as an opportunity to teach the scientific method of hypothesis, controlled testing, observation, and inference, by providing these words during or after discussion.

Students could also themselves decide on good ways to record, organize, and report their observations though charts, graphs, or tables. ("What information will we need to record? What were we testing for? How can you organize the results and present them clearly? What headings will you need?" etc.) **S–1** Students could record cooling rates, or simply the time it took the water to reach room temperature. Students need to record times, temperatures, and a description of each container — its size, shape, and what it's made of. Students could also engage in qualitative observation by periodically feeling the outsides of the different containers. This data could be helpful to students when discussing the implications of their findings.

When students have completed their experiments, ask them what they observed, and what they conclude or infer. Have them explain their answers and reasoning as fully as possible. Extend the discussion by using questions like the following: What differences did you find between the containers? Why did you find those differences? What is it about the containers that accounts for those differences? *S–17* What containers gave similar results? Why? *S–29* The teacher could rephrase student responses using critical vocabulary, and encourage students to use such vocabulary as, observe, infer, evidence, relevant, conclusion, and assume.

The teacher could extend this lesson by having students design and conduct experiments to test new ideas they expressed in the above discussion. Thus, students develop a clearer, more complete, and less stereotyped idea of what scientists do. *S–10* Or students could merely pose and clarify unanswered questions. Perhaps interested students could conduct further tests and keep the rest of the class posted.

The class could then explore the importance of their experiments and findings in the direction of either science or practical application. To pursue the latter, consider asking the following questions: When is it useful to know what materials (shapes, sizes, etc.) hold heat? Let heat escape? ('Insulate' could be introduced, if not done before.) When do people need to know what materials insulate or conduct heat? Why? What other things do people keep in mind when choosing insulators or heat conductors? What other factors are relevant? (For example, why don't we wear styrofoam clothes to keep us warm?) Can you think of ways that nature insulates? How do those examples relate to your experiments? Are natural insulators like any of the materials you tested? Which? How? How are they different? *S–35*

Students could summarize their results by completing such sentences as, "Heat travels more quickly through materials that are .... Heat travels more slowly through materials that are ...." and by writing brief explanations why. *S–17*

Rubber Bands

Objectives of the remodelled lesson

The students will:
- engage in Socratic discussion about their observations of and speculations about rubber bands
- design and conduct tests about how much different rubber bands stretch and how far they shoot, thus exercising independent thought
- clarify the concept of 'stretch'
- apply their new insights to other stretchy and rubbery things

Original Lesson Plan

Abstract

The first lesson, "Rubber Band Stretch", focuses on the key question, *"How much does a rubber band stretch?"* Students suspend paper cups from different kinds of rubber bands attached to boards by means of tape and paper clips. They add pennies to the cups and measure how much the different rubber bands stretch. They graph their data and develop a formula relating stretch to mass. The extension has students compare rubber bands of different characteristics.

The second lesson, "Rubber Band Shoot", has students discuss the key question, *"How does a rubber band shoot?"* Students then stretch the rubber bands measured amounts, and let go. They graph their data and discuss the results. In the extensions, students compare the behavior of different rubber bands, and devise a formula combining stretch and shoot formulas.

from *Introductory Investigations*,
Fresno Pacific College — Project Aims.
Arthur Wiebe and Larry Ecklund,
editors pp. 33–35.

Critique

These lessons offer a number of exciting opportunities. Both lessons, however, put too much emphasis on measuring and recording. Students could make fuller observations, begin to develop a sense of what goes on when rubber bands stretch, and discuss the relationship of stretch to shoot qualitatively.

"Rubber Band Stretch" is unnecessarily confusing. Mass doesn't make rubber bands stretch, force does. Students should understand more clearly the reason for the design of this experiment. As given, the purpose of the test design is unclear. Nor does either lesson ask students to consider any application of what they have learned. No attempt is made to tie the information to other objects. Discussions of muscles, elastic, gum, and other stretchy things belong in this unit.

315

"Rubber Band Shoot" does not answer the question it purports to: *"How does a rubber band shoot?"* It succeeds in answering how *far* a rubber band shoots, and therefore confuses two distinct and very different questions.

Strategies used to remodel
S–24 practicing Socratic discussion: clarifying and questioning beliefs, theories, or perspectives
S–14 clarifying and analyzing the meanings of words or phrases
S–29 noting significant similarities and differences
S–13 clarifying issues, conclusions, or beliefs
S–33 evaluating evidence and alleged facts
S–1 thinking independently
S–11 comparing analogous situations: transferring insights to new contexts
S–21 reading critically: clarifying or critiquing text

Remodelled Lesson Plan

Before beginning the study of rubber bands, the teacher may want to lead students in a discussion regarding safety. Students could mention possible dangers and the best ways of avoiding them. We suggest an introductory lesson, since children love to play with rubber bands. This first lesson should be a chance for the children to manipulate and share observations about rubber bands. The teacher could record their findings and save them.

To begin the science unit, remind the class of their rubber band play. Ask them if they remember any of the ideas they mentioned. Discussion could be extended with questions like the following: What did you notice about rubber bands? (When necessary, elicit clarification.) What kind of rubber band was it? What, exactly, did you do? How did it look? Feel? Sound? Which of these things that you found, could we study? (Some students may want to explore ideas other than amount of stretch.) What differences did you find between rubber bands? Do you think the differences were related? How? Why? **S–24**

The class could discuss the idea of stretch and clarify it. What is stretch? What things stretch? How are all of these things alike? Different? **S–14** Are there different kinds of stretch? **S–29** How could we measure stretch? What might affect the measurements? What characteristics of rubber bands affect the amount of stretch? What kinds of rubber bands stretch the most? The least? How could we find out? What, exactly, should we measure? How? What do we need to record? How? Why?" **S–13**

At this point, the teacher could have students split into groups to design and conduct tests. The tests could then be discussed and evaluated. Students could then suggest and assess solutions to any problems they experienced while conducting or interpreting their tests. (For example, if students stretched a large and a small rubber band and simply measured the lengths, they wouldn't be able to distinguish later how much of the difference was due to stretchiness opposed to the original difference in length. Or different students may have gotten vastly different results, due to different amounts of force applied.) Such an experience would graphically illustrate the requirements of a well thought-out experiment. **S–33**

Or, the teacher could elicit design of a test similar to that in the book. "To stretch a rubber band, you need a force. To make accurate measurements, you need a way to control the force, so that results are due only to differences in the rubber bands, not to differences in force. What force can we use? If we pull, how can we be sure results won't vary because of different amounts of pull? We can't control or measure how much pull we use. Etc." Or students could analyze the original experiment. The teacher may want to have a wider variety of materials available than those mentioned in the original lesson.

Students could also decide on a reasonable method of presenting the data. **S-1** Some may also demonstrate or reproduce their experiments.

Students could write a paper describing their question, experiments, hypotheses, data, observations, inferences, assumptions and conclusions.

Ask if this experiment suggests any important issues or questions and how we might go about settling them. They might think of ways to apply what they've learned about stretch. The teacher could bring out the list of stretchy things made earlier in the lesson, and have students discuss the items in terms of what they learned about rubber bands. They could elucidate similarities to and differences from rubber bands and try to predict the effects the differences might have in a similar study. "What does it imply about muscles and exercises, fitted sheets, pants with elastic waists, and pennies in your pockets?" **S-11**

For the second lesson, you could ask students to share their questions about rubber band shooting. Each group or person selects one or more related questions and designs an experiment or study. Have students solve the questions of safety. Each study needs to address shooting method, means of observation, means of recording and presenting data.

Ask students to read the original lesson, and to do what they are asked in the lesson. Ask them the question, *"How does a rubber band shoot?"* If they answer with distances, ask them to consider their answer and decide what question they are really answering. **S-13** They should see, or you can point out, that distances answer the question "how *far* " not "*how*" rubber bands shoot. **S-21**

Discuss the relationship of stretch to shoot. "Were the stretchiest rubber bands the best shooters? Worst? Neither? Why do you think so? What were the best stretchers and shooters like?" It is interesting that the concept developed and measured in the first study became a variable in the second.

Relate rubber band "twanging" to musical instruments. What affects the sound the rubber bands make? What makes it hit a higher note? A lower note? Why? How is this like or unlike guitar strings and piano strings? (Interested students could research and report back to the class.) **S-11**

Relate rubber band behavior to rubber balls (what kinds bounce better?) and air filled balls (relate stretchiness to bounciness). **S-11**

> When texts teach skills and concepts, they describe how to use it (and when and why), but the practice is drill: Perform this operation on, or apply this distinction to, the items below. (Of the sentences below, rewrite those that are run-ons. What is X percent of Y? Put your results in the form of a bar graph using the following headings …. Locate N on the map on page 63.) Even when students can produce the correct results and repeat the explanations, they don't necessarily understand the functions and purposes of the skills and concepts, and so fail to use or apply them spontaneously when appropriate.

Remodelling Lessons in Other Subjects

Introduction

This chapter contains remodelled lessons from two strikingly different subjects demonstrating, among other things, that critical teaching strategies can be applied in all teaching situations. As always, we present these remodels not as perfect, but as plausible examples of how teachers can begin to reshape their instruction to encourage and cultivate critical thinking. As you read through them, you might consider how you might have critiqued and remodelled the original lessons. There are always a wide variety of ways in which we can exercise our independent thinking and decision-making while teaching for critical thinking. As critical thinkers we think for ourselves, thus our teaching reflects our uniqueness as persons. Our instruction is a creative as well as critical activity. Indeed we critique to create. We find fault only to improve. Critical thinking does not threaten; it excites us to think of new possibilities, new ways of encouraging our students to think for themselves, to become more responsible persons, and to put their own brain power into operation so that they can take control of their own learning. It is encouraging to see teachers in a variety of subjects remodelling and redesigning their own instruction. Within the next couple of years, exemplary remodels should be available for every subject and grade level.

Pre-Algebra

by John Taylor, Sonoma State
University, Rohnert Park, CA

Objectives of the remodelled lesson

The students will:
- be introduced to algebra in a form that seems reasonable
- exercise independent thought by making up word problems
- be able to define algebra and explain its function

Standard Approach

Students are given examples of basic algebraic equations and solve them step by step with the teacher. Then pupils will solve problems 1–4 at the end of the chapter and when all problems are completed, answers will be checked in the back of the text.

Critique

This lesson makes no attempt to explain the function of algebra as a simple extension of basic arithmetic, but rather jumps right into the methodology of solving algebraic equations. Though most students will be able (with some practice) to "solve for n", by not explaining the necessity of the algebraic equation with a step by step connection with the arithmetic style of problem solving, students will be left essentially in the dark. For a child, the jump to "4 – n = 2" is as confusing as quantum physics. I myself am a victim of this "leap of faith" method of teaching algebra and have only recently come to terms with my lack of understanding. By putting algebra in its proper context, it can be easily understood and mastered.

Strategies used to remodel

S-9 developing confidence in reason
S-11 comparing analogous situations: transferring insights to new contexts
S-19 generating or assessing solutions
S-17 questioning deeply: raising and pursuing root or significant questions

Remodelled Lesson Plan s-9

The teacher would begin the lesson with a simple arithmetic problem, such as 2 + 2 = ?, writing it as 2 + 2 = n. The teacher would then explain that 'n' means a number which we do not yet know, and that it comes in handy when we know some parts of a problem, but not others, for example, 2 + n = 4. The students will want to know how it is we could get the answer before knowing the first portion of the problem. Thus, the connection to word problems could be established with an example such as this: We need four people to play a certain game, but we only have 2 players. How many more people do we need?

$$2 + [\text{how many}] = 4?$$

$$2 + n = 4?$$

What do we need? What is the difference between all of what we need and what we already have?

As a follow up, the teacher could write "3 + n = 5" and ask the students to make up a story-problem using those numbers. **S-11** After some student word problems are discussed, the teacher would explain that algebra is the branch of mathematics that helps us solve problems from the inside out, as in the previous example. The students would then be given a word problem and asked to solve it using any method they like. **S-19** After assessing their solutions and discussing their methods, the teacher would offer an algebraic equation as an alternative, stressing the point that it may not be the only way to solve the problem, but probably the easiest and most efficient in most cases. **S-17**

"Father and Son"

by Kathlene Fries, Rancho Cordova, CA

Objectives of the remodelled lesson

The students will:
- critically listen to a song, exploring the meaning expressed in its lyrics
- evaluate and explore parent versus child perspectives in a disagreement
- make inferences and predictions for the lyrics
- generate possible solutions to a given problem

Standard Approach

> The students begin by listening to a record that goes with the music series. Melody and pattern are discussed, and notes are given for musical accompaniment. Students sing the song, look for patterns, and add the bells and rhythm instruments. Students then apply the melody to another set of lyrics, and note the same patterns.

Critique

The lesson plan, as it stands, allows for the listening to and the singing of a given piece of music. It also incorporates a bit of music theory in the form of patterns. Although this is a very appropriate way to teach music some of the time, I find it limiting because it does not allow time for the student to contemplate the meaning of the song. When I have written poetry or songs, I have always been driven by a need for expression. Music has been the means for much communication throughout history, and it would certainly be a travesty if the music education of the young did not include some critical listening and exploration of the meanings of some lyrics. I have found some music lyrics that are motivating for students to listen to, thus engaging them in critical listening. Although I feel that the listening to and singing of songs are important, I believe that the exploration of lyrics is vital to a well-rounded music education.

Strategies used to remodel

S–22 listening critically: the art of silent dialogue
S–32 making plausible inferences, predictions, or interpretations
S–19 generating or assessing solutions
S–17 questioning deeply: raising and pursuing root or significant questions

Remodelled Lesson Plan s-22

The class would receive a copy of the lyrics of the song "Father and Son" by Cat Stevens, with the speakers unidentified. The class would read the lyrics, and would discuss what is occurring. "There are two voices speaking in the song. What is the relation between the two, and how is this known?" When the class comes up with the parent/child idea, the students would be asked to identify the parent part of the song, and the child part of the song. When completed in their small groups, the class would listen to the tape of the song.

After listening to the song, the teacher could use questions like the following to guide discussion:

What is this song about? What is going on in this song? What are these people saying to each other? Why? Is the father listening to the son? Is the son listening to the father? What proof can you offer to support that? How old do you think the son is? Why? What is the perspective of the father? What reasons would he have to encourage the son to stay home? **S–32** If you were the son, would you stay? What would be your reasoning for your decision? How happy is the father, really? Is the son a part of that happiness? What will happen to his happiness if the son goes away? The son talks about "them" in the last section of the song. Who is he talking about? If you really wanted to do something that your parents did not want you to do, would you do it?

After this discussion, the eight groups of children would receive the following questions in a worksheet format. Each group would be responsible for answering four of the questions. While they worked in their groups, the students would hear the song again. Each group must write their answers, in preparation for sharing with the whole group. Each group would present one of their answers to the entire class. At the completion of the sharing, each child would choose a question to pursue for further thought in the form of a paragraph that would be due the next day.

Is the problem in this song just that the son wants to go away for a while, or is there a bigger problem between the two? What?

If you were a counselor, and you were called in to help these two people solve their problems, how would you go about getting to the root of their problem? How long would it take you to help them work it out? **S–19**

Is is okay for the son to disobey his father's wishes? How old should people be to question their parents' authority?

What will happen at the end of the dialogue? Give reasons to support your predictions. What kind of a relationship will the son have with his father if he chooses to go? **S–32**

Is there communication going on between these two people? Justify your answer with details from the song and by explaining what 'communication' means.

What kind of situation can you compare this to in your life? How are the two situations different and similar?

Do you always listen when your parents give you advice? Do you learn more from an experience if you heed someone else's advice, or when you make your own decisions and mistakes?

Is it true that "you will still be here tomorrow, but your dreams may not"? Can you think of some dreams that you now have that you have either carried with you for a long time, and will probably remain with you in the future, or dreams that seemed very important to you in the past, but have now been replaced by new dreams?

editor's note: Listen to the song first (for the whole experience as the artist intended it), then read the lyrics.

Relate the music and sound of the piece to its meaning. (What would this song be like as a heavy metal song?) (Compare many possibilities at length.) **S-17**

Thinking Critically About Teaching: From Didactic to Critical Teaching

John Dewey once asked a class he visited, "What would you find if you dug a hole in the earth?" Getting no response, he repeated the question: again he obtained nothing but silence. The teacher chided Dr. Dewey, "You're asking the wrong question." Turning to the class, she asked, "What is the state of the center of the earth?" The class replied in unison, "Igneous fusion."

To begin to teach critical thinking one must critique present educational practices and the beliefs underlying them and develop a new conception of knowledge and learning. Educators must ask themselves crucial questions about the nature of knowledge, learning, and the human mind. Educators should reflect on their own thought processes, their own experiences of learning, misunderstanding, confusion, and insight. They should recall and analyze their successes and failures when attempting to teach. They should examine the conceptions and assumptions implicit in their educational practices and self-consciously develop their own theories of education through analysis, evaluation, and reconstruction of their understanding of education and what it means to learn.

Most instructional practice in most academic institutions around the world presupposes a didactic theory of knowledge, learning, and literacy ill-suited to the development of critical minds and persons. After a superficial exposure to reading, writing, and arithmetic, schooling is typically fragmented thereafter into more or less technical domains, each with a large technical vocabulary and an extensive content or propositional base. Students memorize and reiterate domain-specific details. Teachers lecture and drill. Active integration of the students' daily non-academic experiences is rare. Little time is spent stimulating student questions. Students are expected to "receive" the knowledge "given" them. Students are not typically encouraged to doubt what they are told in the classroom or what is written in their texts. Students' personal points of view or philosophies of life are considered largely irrelevant to education. Classrooms with teachers talking and students listening are the rule. Ninety percent of teacher questions require no more thought than recall. Dense and typically speedy coverage of content is typically followed by content-specific testing. Interdisciplinary synthesis is ordinarily viewed as a personal responsibility of the student and is not routinely tested. Technical specialization is considered the natural goal of schooling and is correlated with getting a job. Few multi-logical issues or problems are discussed or assigned and even fewer teachers know how to conduct such discussions or assess student participation in them. Students are rarely expected to engage in dialogical or dialectical reasoning, and few teachers are proficient analysts of such reasoning. Knowledge is viewed as verified intra-disciplinary propositions and well-supported intra-disciplinary theories. There is little or no discussion of the nature of prejudice or bias, little or no discussion of metacognition, and little or no discussion of what a disciplined, self-directed mind or self-directed thought requires. The student is expected to develop into a literate, educated person through years of what is essentially content memorization and ritual performance.

The dominant pattern of academic instruction and learning is based on an uncritical theory of knowledge, learning, and literacy that is coming under increasing critique by theorists and researchers. Those who operate on the didactic theory in their instruction rarely formulate it explicitly. Some would deny that they hold it, even though their practice implies it. In any case, it is with the theory implicit in practice that we are concerned.

To illustrate, consider this letter from a teacher with a Master's degree in physics and mathematics, with 20 years of high school teaching experience in physics:

> After I started teaching, I realized that I had learned physics by rote and that I really did not understand all I knew about physics. My thinking students asked me questions for which I always had the standard textbook answers, but for the first time it made me start thinking for myself, and I realized that these canned answers were not justified by my own thinking and only confused my students who were showing some ability to think for themselves. To achieve my academic goals I had to memorize the thoughts of others, but I had never learned or been encouraged to learn to think for myself.

The extent and nature of "coverage" for most grade levels and subjects implies that bits and pieces of knowledge are easily attained, without any significant consideration of the basis for that knowledge. Speed coverage of content ignores the need of students to seriously consider content before accepting it. Most of us have experienced the difference between "intellectual" or merely verbal "knowledge" and true understanding — "Aha! So *that's* what that means!" Most teaching and most texts, designed to achieve the former kind of knowledge rather than the latter, are, in this sense, unrealistic. Students rarely grapple with content. As a result, standard practice tends to foster intellectual arrogance in students, particularly in those who have retentive memories and can repeat back what they have heard or read. Pretending to know is encouraged. Much standardized testing, which frames problems isolated from their real-life contexts and provides directions and hints regarding their correct solution, validates this pretense.

This has led Alan Schoenfeld, for example, to conclude that "most instruction in mathematics is, in a very real sense, deceptive and possibly fraudulent." In "Some Thoughts on Problem-Solving Research and Mathematics Education", (Mathematical Problem Solving: Issues in Research, Frank K. Lester and Joe Garofalo, editors, © 1982 Franklin Institute Press), he cites a number of examples, including the following:

> Much instruction on how to solve word problems is based on the "key word" algorithm, where the student makes his choice of the appropriate arithmetic operation by looking for syntactic cues in the problem statement. For example, the word 'left' in the problem "John had eight apples. He gave three to Mary. How many does John have left?" ... serves to tell the students that subtraction is the appropriate operation to perform. (p. 27)

In a widely used elementary text book series, 97 percent of the problems "solved" by the key-word method would yield (serendipitously?) the correct answer.

Students are drilled in the key-word algorithm so well that they will use subtraction, for example, in almost any problem containing the word 'left'. In the study from which this conclusion was drawn, problems were constructed in which the appropriate operations were addition, multiplication, and division. Each used the word 'left' conspicuously in its statement and a large percentage of the students subtracted. In fact, the situation was so extreme that many students chose to subtract in a problem that began "Mr. Left ..." (p. 27)

I taught a problem-solving course for junior and senior mathematics majors at Berkeley in 1976. These students had already seen some remarkably sophisticated mathematics. Linear algebra and differential equations were old hat. Topology, Fourier transforms, and measure theory were familiar to some. I gave them a straightforward theorem from plane geometry (required when I was in the tenth grade). Only two of eight students made any progress on it, some of them by using arc length integrals to measure the circumference of a circle. (Schoenfeld, 1979). Out of the context of normal course work these students could not do elementary mathematics. (pp. 28–29)

In sum, all too often we focus on a narrow collection of well-defined tasks and train students to execute those tasks in a routine, if not algorithmic fashion. Then we test the students on tasks that are very close to the ones they have been taught. If they succeed on those problems we and they congratulate each other on the fact that they have learned some powerful mathematical techniques. In fact, they may be able to use such techniques mechanically while lacking some rudimentary thinking skills. To allow them and ourselves to believe that they "understand" the mathematics is deceptive and fraudulent. (p. 29)

This approach to learning in math is too often paralleled in the other subject areas. Grammar texts, for example, present skills and distinctions, then drill students in their use. Thus, students, not genuinely understanding the material, do not spontaneously recognize situations calling for the skills and distinctions covered. Such "knowledge" is generally useless to them. They fail to grasp the uses of, the reasoning behind, and the meaning of the knowledge presented to them. In the rush to keep up, they turn their minds off. Since they are not expected to make sense of the bits they take in, they cease expecting what they learn, hear, read, or do to make sense to them.

Most teachers made it through their college classes mainly by "learning the standard textbook answers" and were neither given an opportunity nor encouraged to determine whether what the text or the professor said was "justified by their own thinking".

Predictable results follow. Students, on the whole, do not learn how to work by or think for themselves. They do not learn how to gather, analyze, synthesize, and assess information. They do not learn how to recognize and define problems for themselves. They do not learn how to analyze the diverse logic of the questions and problems they face and hence how to adjust their thinking to those problems. They do not learn how to enter sympathetically into the thinking of others, nor how to deal rationally with conflicting points of view. They do not learn to become critical readers, writers, speakers, or listeners. They do not learn to use their native languages clearly, precisely, or persuasively. They do not, therefore, become "literate" in the proper sense of the word. Neither do they gain much in the way of genuine knowledge, since, for the most part, they could not explain the basis for what they believe. They would be hard pressed to explain, for example, which of their beliefs were based on rational assent and which on simple conformity to what they have been told. They have little sense as to how they might critically analyze their own experience or identify national or group bias in their own thinking. They are much more apt to learn on the basis of irrational than rational modes of thought. They lack the traits of mind of a genuinely educated person: intellectual humility, courage, integrity, perseverance, and confidence in reason.

If this is a reasonable characterization of a broad scholastic effect, then instruction based on a didactic theory of knowledge, learning, and literacy is the fundamental determining cause. Administrators and teachers need to explicitly grasp the differences between instruction based on two very different sets of assumptions, the first deeply buried in the hearts and minds of most educators, parents, and administrators; the second emerging only now as the research base for a critical theory progressively expands. We express the basic difference as follows: "Knowledge can be 'given' to one who, upon receiving it, knows it", compared to, "Knowledge must be created and, in a sense, rediscovered by each knower."

Only if we see the contrast between these views clearly, will we be empowered to move from the former conception to the latter. Now let us set out the two opposing theories systematically in terms of specific contrasting assumptions and practices.

Two Conflicting Theories of Knowledge, Learning, and Literacy: The Didactic and the Critical

The Scholastically Dominant Theory of Knowledge, Learning and Literacy assumes:

1) That the fundamental need of students is to be taught more or less directly *what* to think, not *how* to think. (That students will learn *how* to think if only they know *what* to think.) • Thus, students are *given* or told details, definitions, explanation, rules, guidelines, and reasons to learn.

2) That knowledge is independent of the thinking that generates, organizes, and applies it. • Thus, students are said to know when they can repeat what has been covered. Students are given the finished products of others' thoughts.

3) That educated, literate people are fundamentally repositories of content analogous to an encyclopedia or a data bank, directly comparing situations in the world with "facts" that they carry about fully formed as a result of an absorptive process. That an educated, literate person is fundamentally a true believer, that is, a possessor of truth, and therefore claims much knowledge. • Thus, texts, assignments, lectures, discussions, and tests are detail-oriented and content-dense.

The Emerging Critical Theory of Knowledge, Learning, and Literacy assumes:

1) That the fundamental need of students is to be taught *how*, not *what*, to think. • Thus, significant content should be taught by raising live issues that stimulate students to gather, analyze and assess that content.

2) That all knowledge or content is generated, organized, applied, analyzed, synthesized, and assessed by thinking; that gaining knowledge is unintelligible without engagement in such thinking. (It is *not* assumed that one can think without something, some content, to think about.) • Thus, students should be given opportunities to puzzle their way through to knowledge and explore its justification, as part of the process of learning.

3) That an educated, literate person is fundamentally a repository of strategies, principles, concepts, and insights embedded in processes of thought rather than atomic facts. Experiences analyzed and organized by critical thought, not facts picked up one-by-one, characterize the educated person. Much of what is "known" is constructed by the thinker *as needed* from context to context, not *prefabricated* in sets of true statements about the world. That an educated, literate person is fundamentally a seeker and questioner rather than a true believer, and is therefore cautious in claiming knowledge. • Thus, classroom activities should consist of questions and problems for students to discuss and discover how to solve. Teachers should model insightful consideration of questions and problems, and facilitate fruitful discussions.

4) That knowledge, truth, and understanding can be transmitted from one person to another by verbal statements in the form of lectures or didactic writing. • Thus, for example, social studies texts present principles of geography and historical explanations. Questions at the end of the chapter are framed in identical language and can be answered by repeating the texts. "The correct answer" is often in bold type or otherwise emphasized.

4) That knowledge and truth can rarely, and insight never, be transmitted from one person to another by the transmitter's verbal statements alone. That one person cannot directly give another what he or she has learned; one can only facilitate the conditions under which people learn for themselves by figuring out or thinking things through. • Thus, students offer their own ideas, and explore ideas given in the texts, providing their own examples and reasons. Students come to conclusions by practicing reasoning historically, geographically, scientifically, etc.

5) That students do not need to be taught skills of listening in order to learn from others; they only need to learn to pay attention, which requires self-discipline or will power. Students should therefore be able to listen on command by the teacher. • Thus, students are told to listen carefully and are tested on their abilities to remember and to follow directions.

5) That students need to be taught how to listen critically, an active and skilled process that can be learned by degrees with various levels of proficiency. Learning what others mean by what they say requires questioning, trying on, and testing; hence, engaging in public or private debates with them. • Thus, teachers would continually model active critical listening, asking probing and insightful questions of the speaker.

6) That the basic skills of reading and writing can be taught without emphasis on higher-order critical thinking skills. • Thus, reading texts provide comprehension questions requiring recall of random details. Occasionally, "main point," "plot," and "theme" lessons cover these concepts. Literal comprehension is distinguished from "extras" such as inferring, evaluating, and thinking beyond. Only after basic literal comprehension has been established is the deeper meaning probed.

6) That the basic skills of reading and writing are inferential skills that require critical thinking, that students who cannot read and write critically are defective readers and writers, and that critical reading and writing involve dialogical processes in which probing critical questions are raised and answered. (What is the fundamental issue? What reasons, what evidence is relevant? Is this authority credible? Are these reasons adequate? Is this evidence accurate and sufficient? Does this contradict that? Does this conclusion follow? Should another point of view be considered?) • Thus, teachers should routinely require students to *explain* what they have read, to reconstruct the ideas, and to evaluate written material. Students should construct and compare interpretations, reasoning their way to the most plausible interpretations. Discussion moves back and forth between what was said and what it means.

7) That students who have no questions typically are learning well, while students with many questions are experiencing difficulty in learning; that doubt and questioning weaken belief.

7) That students who have no questions typically are not learning, while those who have pointed and specific questions are. Doubt and questioning, by deepening understanding, strengthen belief by putting it on more solid ground. • Thus, teachers can evaluate their teaching by asking themselves: Are my students asking better questions — insightful questions, questions which extend and apply what they have learned? ("Is that why...?" Does this mean that ...?" "Then what if ...?")

329

8) That quiet classes with little student talk are typically reflective of students learning, while classes with much student talk are typically disadvantaged in learning.

9) That knowledge and truth can typically be learned best by being broken down into elements and the elements into subelements, each taught sequentially and atomistically. Knowledge is additive. • Thus, texts provide basic definitions and masses of details, but have little back-and-forth movement between them. They break knowledge into pieces, each of which is to be mastered one-by-one: subjects are taught separately. Each aspect is further broken down: each part of speech is covered separately; social studies texts are organized chronologically, geographically, etc.

10) That people can gain significant knowledge without seeking or valuing it, and hence that education can take place without a significant transformation of values for the learner. • Thus, for example, texts tend to inform students of the importance of studying the subject or topic covered, rather than proving it by showing its immediate usefulness.

11) That understanding the mind and how it functions, its epistemological health and pathology, are not important or necessary parts of learning. To learn the basic subject matter of the schools, one need not focus on such matters, except perhaps with certain disadvantaged learners.

12) That ignorance is a vacuum or simple lack, and that student prejudices, biases, misconceptions, and ignorance are automatically replaced by the knowledge given them. • Thus, little if any attention is given to students' beliefs. Material is presented from the point of view of the authority, the one who knows.

8) That quiet classes with little student talk are typically classes with little learning, while student talk, focused on live issues, is a sign of learning (provided students learn dialogical and dialectical skills).

9) That knowledge and truth are heavily systemic and holistic and can be learned only by continual synthesis, movement back and forth between wholes and parts, tentative graspings of a whole guiding us in understanding its parts, periodic focus on the parts (in relation to each other) shedding light upon the whole, and that the *wholes* that we learn have important relations to other wholes as well as to their own parts and hence need to be frequently canvassed in learning any whole. (This assumption implies that we cannot achieve in-depth learning in any given domain of knowledge unless we grasp its relation to *other* domains of knowledge.) • Thus, education should be organized around issues, problems, and basic concepts which are pursued and explored through all relevant subjects. Teachers should routinely require students to relate knowledge from various fields. Students should compare analogous events or situations, propose examples, and apply new concepts to other situations.

10) That people gain only the knowledge that they seek and value. All other learning is superficial and transitory. All genuine education transforms the basic values of the person educated, resulting in persons becoming life-long learners and rational persons. • Thus, instruction poses problems meaningful to students, requiring them to use the tools of each academic domain.

11) That understanding the mind and how it functions, its health and pathology, are important, are necessary parts of learning. To learn the basic subject matter of the schools in depth requires that we see how we as thinkers and learners process that subject matter.

12) That prejudices, biases, and misconceptions are built up through actively constructed inferences embedded in experience and must be broken down through a similar process, hence, that students must reason their way out of them. • Thus, students need many opportunities to express their views, however biased and prejudiced, in a non-threatening environment, to argue their way out of their internalized misconceptions. Teachers should cultivate in themselves a genuine curiosity about how students look at things, why they think as they do, and the structure of students' thought. The educational process starts where the students are, and walks them through to insight.

13) That students need not understand the rational ground or deeper logic of what they learn in order to absorb knowledge. Extensive but superficial learning can later be deepened. • Thus, for example, historical and scientific explanations are presented to students as given, not as having been reasoned to. In language arts, skills and distinctions are rarely explicitly linked to such basic concepts as 'good writing' or 'clear expression'.

13) That rational assent is essential for all genuine learning; that an in-depth understanding of basic concepts and principles is essential for rational assent to non-foundational concepts and facts. That in-depth understanding of root concepts and principles should organize learning within and across subject matter domains. • Thus, students are encouraged to discover how the details relate to basic concepts. Details are traced back to the foundational purposes, concepts, and insights.

14) That it is more important to cover a great deal of knowledge or information superficially than a small amount in depth. That only after the facts are understood, can students discuss their meaning; that higher order thinking can and should only be practiced by students who have "mastered" the material. That thought-provoking discussions are for the gifted and advanced, only.

14) That it is more important to cover a small amount of knowledge or information in-depth (deeply probing its foundation, meaning, and worth) than a great deal of knowledge superficially. That the "slowest," as well as the brightest, students can and must probe the significance and justification of what they learn.

15) That the roles of teacher and learner are distinct and should not be blurred.

15) That we learn best by teaching or explaining to others what we know. Students need many opportunities to teach what they know and formulate their understandings in different ways, and to respond to diverse questions from other learners.

16) That the teacher should correct the learners' ignorance by telling them what they don't know and correcting their mistakes.

16) That students need to learn to distinguish for themselves what they know from what they don't know. Students should recognize that they do not genuinely know or comprehend what they have merely memorized. Self-directed learning requires recognition of ignorance. • Thus, teachers respond to mistakes and confusion by probing with questions, allowing students to correct themselves and each other. Teachers routinely allow students the opportunity to supply their own ideas on a subject before reading their texts.

17) That the teacher has the fundamental responsibility for student learning. • Thus, teachers and texts provide knowledge, questions, and drill.

17) That students should have increasing responsibility for their own learning. Students should see that only they can learn for themselves and actively and willingly engage themselves in the process. • Thus, the teacher provides opportunities for students to decide what they need to know and helps them develop strategies for finding or figuring it out.

18) That students will automatically transfer what they learn in didactically taught courses to relevant real-life situations. • Thus, for example, students are told to perform a given skill on a given group of items. The text will *tell* students when, how, and why to use that skill.

18) That most of what students memorize in didactically taught courses is either forgotten or inert, and that the most significant transfer requires in-depth learning which focuses on experiences meaningful to the student. Transfer must be directly taught.

19) That the personal experience of the student has no essential role to play in education.

19) That the personal experience of the student is essential to all schooling at all levels and in all subjects, that it is a crucial part of the content to be processed (applied, analyzed, synthesized, and assessed) by the students.

20) That students who can correctly answer questions, provide definitions, and apply formulae while taking tests have proven their knowledge or understanding of those details. Since the didactic approach tends to assume, for example, that knowing a word is knowing its definition (and an example), didactic instruction tends to overemphasize definitions. By merely supplementing definitions with assignments that say "Which of these twelve items are X?", students do not come to see the usefulness of the concept and fail to use it spontaneously when appropriate.

20) That students can often provide correct answers, repeat definitions, and apply formulae while yet not understanding those questions, definitions, or formulae. That proof of knowledge and understanding are found in the students' ability to explain in their own words, with examples, the meaning and significance of the knowledge, why it is so, to *spontaneously* use it when appropriate.

21) That learning is essentially a private monological process in which learners can proceed more or less directly to established truth, under the guidance of an expert in such truth. The authoritative answers that teachers have are the fundamental standards for assessing students' learning.

21) That learning is essentially a public, communal dialogical and dialectical process in which learners can only proceed indirectly to truth, with much zigging and zagging, backtracking, misconception, self-contradiction, and frustration along the way. Not authoritative answers, but authoritative standards are the criteria for engagement in the communal, dialogical process of enquiry.

Common Problems with Texts

When one examines textbooks from the perspective of the critical theory of knowledge, one is in a better position to restructure how one uses them. The single biggest problem, from this perspective, is that texts, primarily presupposing a didactic view of knowledge, are not designed to allow students to process or integrate what they "cover".

The object behind many lesson plans seems to be to expose students to a wide variety of unassessed "facts," on the assumption that, since this constitutes new information for them, it is good in itself. We, however, feel that school time is too precious to spend any sizeable portion of it covering *random* facts. The world, after all, is filled with an infinite number of facts. No one can learn more than an infinitesimal portion of them. Random fact-collecting is therefore pointless. True, we need facts and information, but there is no reason why we cannot gain facts *as part of the process* of learning how to think, as part of broader cognitive-affective objectives. Problem-solving or exploring basic ideas or issues are effective ways to find and use facts and to discover why facts interest us in the first place. We ought not to overburden students' minds with facts that they cannot put to use in their thinking. If we don't apprehend the relevance and significance of facts, we tend to forget them rather quickly. We encourage the reader therefore to develop a skeptical eye for lesson plans, activities, and questions that fall into the category of trivial pursuit or "fact-for-fact's-sake". Keep a wastebasket handy.

Often, though the lesson as a whole covers significant material, parts of it are trivial. The student's text provides insignificant details, and the teacher's edition suggests trivial activities which interrupt discussion of significant material. As a rule, texts fail to properly distinguish the trivial from the significant. Useless details and basic concepts receive equal time. End-of-chapter review questions especially confuse major with minor points. Structuring instruction around basic ideas and issues highlights crucial details.

Beyond the lessons and activities that need to be abandoned for their triviality, there are also lesson plans and activities that drill students — reading or filling out graphs, time-lines, and charts, generalizing, categorizing, researching, experimenting, problem-solving, and comparing. Such lessons turn skills of thought and crucial insights into mechanical procedures, or vague slogans. Students practice the skills for practice itself, seldom in a context in which the skill promotes understanding; thus, students fail to learn when to apply this or that procedure and so need to be told when to use it. The application of the skill is often merely memorized (and so easily forgotten), rather than understood. Students look for "indicator words", verbal cues, and shortcuts, rather than recognizing the logic of situations requiring use of the skill. Thus they can use the skill *only on request*, that is, when given directions to do so. They do not learn to recognize contexts in which the skill is needed. Students read maps, charts, graphs, etc., at the most basic level, rattling off facts; they do not discuss the meaning, significance, or implications of what they find. They copy charts and graphs, or formats for them, fill in graphs and time-lines, but do not then *use* them as helpful displays to organize information. The purposes of skills, the contexts within which they are needed, and the reasons for applying them in certain ways, should be discussed or discovered by students. Students should interpret the details they find and then explore their implications or significance.

This integration should be viewed, not as slowing down, but as deepening the understanding of the material. We should view the critical thinking that students practice as providing them with powerful concepts which they can use in a host of circumstances thereafter, and as laying the foundation for the "I-can-figure-things-out-for-myself" attitude essential for education. Standard practice and testing methods, whenever possible, should be replaced with those requiring skill, insight, and information. They should be presented to students with minimal direction given beforehand and minimal guidance given only when students are hopelessly bogged down.

Standard Treatment of Critical Thinking, Reasoning, and Argumentation

Finally, we recommend that the teacher keep an eye out for texts, questions, and activities that claim to emphasize or teach critical thinking, logic, reasoning, or argumentation. Often what is taught, or the way it is taught, discourages clear and fairminded thought.

Texts generally lack an integrated theory of critical thinking or the critical person. Lessons fail to clarify the relationship of specific critical skills and insights to the concept of the critical thinker. Critical thinking should not be conceived merely as a set of discrete skills and ideas, but should be unified and grounded in a consistent, complete, and accurate theory of thought and reason. This theory should be related to the practical problem of deciding what to believe, question, or reject, understood in terms of the distinction between the reasonable and the unreasonable person. Particular distinctions and insights should be connected to that theory, and specific skills should be placed within it. A unified conception of reasoning includes a unified conception of poor reasoning. Thus, each flaw in reasoning should be understood in terms of the underlying principles of good reasoning such as consistency, completeness, clarity, and relevance, as well as being tied into a well developed conception of why we reason poorly and why we are often influenced by poor reasoning.

The following problems are among the most common:

- Instruction in critical thinking should be integrated into the rest of the subjects whenever useful, rather than appearing occasionally in separate lessons. Instead of consistently using such terms as conclusion, inference, assumption, interpretation, and reasons whenever they are applicable, texts often restrict their use to too narrow contexts. Aspects of critical thinking are generally tacked on — taught in separate lessons and taught as drill, rather than brought in whenever relevant. Lacking a complete and explicit theory of reasoning and the rational person, text writers limit the use of critical skills and insights, failing to bring them in when interpretation, exploration, organization, analysis, synthesis, or evaluation are discussed or most needed.

- Some texts give checklists for evaluating reasoning. They rarely mention looking at or evaluating the argument as a whole. Students are asked to spot strengths and weaknesses in arguments but are given little guidance in figuring out how the points add up. Critical thinking lessons in texts have an overall lack of context when discussing arguments or conclusions. They use snippets rather than complete arguments, and ignore the larger context of the issue itself. Texts often seem to assume that students' final conclusions can be based solely on the analysis and evaluation of one argument. Critical insight should lead to clearer and richer understanding, more rationally informed beliefs about the issue — not merely a critique of a particular argument.

- A common misconception found in texts is the problem of vagueness. Texts typically misunderstand the nature of the problem. Usually texts mistakenly claim that some words are "vague" because "people have their own definitions". The cure is to provide your own definition. We, on the other hand, claim that words themselves are not vague. Sentences are vague (in some contexts). A particular word or phrase within a vague statement may be the culprit requiring clarification *in the context of that issue* — the word itself is not vague in and of itself (nor are the words making up the phrase) but only in some contexts. Definitions, since they are worded abstractly, rarely usefully clarify a word used vaguely. We recommend discussions like those mentioned in the strategy "clarifying and analyzing the meanings of words or phrases" and "clarifying issues, conclusions, or beliefs".

- Many texts emphasize micro-skills. Yet they seldom attempt to teach critical vocabulary to students. Perhaps this is fortunate, since they often misuse the vocabulary of critical thinking or logic. Many texts use the words 'infer' or 'conclude' when requiring students to recall, describe, or guess. Micro-skills (like many other skills) are treated as independent items, rather than as tools which assist understanding. "Analysis of arguments" too often consists of "separating fact from opinion" or simply agreeing or disagreeing, rather than clarifying or evaluating arguments.

- Teachers' notes often suggest debates. Yet traditional debate, with its emphasis on winning and lack of emphasis on rationality or fairminded understanding of the opposition, with its formal structure and artificial limits, rarely provides for the serious, honest, fairminded analysis and evaluation of ideas and arguments we want to foster. If afterward students merely vote on the issue, they need not rationally evaluate the views or justify their evaluations. Ultimately, such activities may encourage treatment of questions calling for reasoned judgment as though they were questions of preference. Debates can be useful if students are required to sympathetically consider both sides of an issue, not just defend their side, and to assess arguments for their rational persuasiveness rather than for mere cleverness.

- Many texts tend to simply ask students to agree or disagree with conclusions. They fail to require that students show they understand or have rationally evaluated what they agree or disagree with. Discussion is limited. Micro-skills are rarely practiced or orchestrated in these contexts which most require them. Argument evaluation is further oversimplified, since only two choices are presented: agreement or disagreement. Students are not asked "To what extent do you agree with this claim, or with what part of it?"

"Fact/Opinion," "Emotive Language," Value, and Bias

By far, the most all-pervasive, confused, and distorted ideas about critical thinking are found in the manner in which students are encouraged to "distinguish fact from opinion," and in the treatment of "emotive language", values, and bias. Texts generally set up or presuppose a false dichotomy with facts, rationality, and critical thinking on one side and values, emotions, opinions, bias, and irrationality on the other.

Texts give one or more of the following explanations of "the fact/opinion distinction": Facts are true; can be proven; are the most reliable source of information. Opinions are what someone thinks is true; are not necessarily true for everyone; are disputed; are judgments. Opinions are not necessarily either right or wrong. Often opinion is treated as equivalent to bias; *any* writing which expresses opinion, feeling, or judgment is labeled biased.

Among our criticisms of the uses of "the fact/opinion distinction" are the following: *1)* Students are usually asked to judge the truth of claims they are not in a position to know; *2)* the way the distinction is drawn in examples and exercises promotes uncritical thought, for example, the distinction often unhelpfully lumps together significantly different types of claims; *3)* often neither category is presented so as to allow for rational assessment. (Facts are presented as true, and therefore need no debate; opinions are just opinions, so there is no "truth of the matter". Texts generally speak of exchanging opinions, but rarely of assessing them.)

When asked to make this "distinction", students are typically given two or more statements. They are asked to read them and determine into which of the two categories each fits. Since the statements lack context, their truth or *reasonableness* typically cannot be rationally judged. Hence, as a rule, students are forced to make their judgments on a superficial basis. In place of some reasoned assessment, students are given "indicators of fact". For example, statements judged to be facts are those which contain numbers, or observations, or are phrased in "neutral" language. Statements judged to be opinions are those which contain such expressions as, 'I think', 'good', 'worst', 'should', 'I like', or any evaluative term.

Since facts are defined as true, in effect, texts typically teach students to accept any statement with numbers, descriptions, etc., in it. Fact/opinion exercises typically teach students that every statement that "sounds like a fact" is *true* and *should be accepted*. Claims which seem factual are not open to question. Students are rarely in a position to know whether or not the claim is true, but, since they need only look at the form of the statement and not its content, they can "get the right answers" to the exercises.

Students are often told that history is fact. (The evaluations and interpretations that appear in students' history books are forgotten.) Thus, if they read that a certain condition caused a historical event, they are in effect encouraged to believe it is fact and therefore true. But causes of historical events must be reasoned to. They are not written on the events for all to see. The interpretation, inextricably part of any historical account, is ignored.

This "distinction" between fact and opinion has no single, clear purpose. Sometimes text writers seem to intend to teach students to distinguish acceptable from questionable claims, and at other times, statements which are empirically verifiable from those which are not (that is, whether evidence or observation alone verifies the claim). In effect, many texts confuse these two distinctions by shifting from one to the other. Given the way texts usually teach the distinction, the claim, "I think there are four chairs in that room", would be categorized as opinion, since it begins with "I think", (an opinion indicator) and, since the speaker is unsure, the claim cannot be counted as true. Yet, by the second sense of the distinction, the claim is factual — that is, we need only look in the room and count chairs to verify it. It requires no interpretation, analysis, evaluation, judgment; it expresses no preference.

Texts virtually never address claims that are certainly true, but are not empirical, for example: "Murder is wrong." or "A diet of potato chips and ice cream is bad for you." Students following the "indicator word" method of drawing the distinction, are forced to call these claims opinion. They are then forced to say that, although they agree with them, they may not be true for everybody; the opposite opinion is just as valid; no objective support can be marshalled for them or objective criteria or standards used to evaluate them. Students who look at the contents of the claims would call them "facts", because they are unquestionably true. These students would miss the distinction between these claims and claims that can be tested by experiment or observation.

The distinction between fact and opinion is often drawn in such other guises as the distinction between accurate and biased or slanted accounts, news and editorials, history and historical fiction, knowledge and information, and belief and value. Thus, on the criterion above, a passage, selection, article or book which contains nothing but "facts" could not possibly be biased or untrustworthy. Yet in reality, a "purely factual" account could well be biased. What the writer claims as facts could simply be false, or without basis — that is, I could simply say it without verifying it. (When I claim that there are four chairs in that room, I may have pulled that number out of the sky.) Crucial facts which could influence one's interpretation of the given facts could have been left out. Interpretations or inferences can be implied.

The distinction, as typically covered, lumps together too many completely different kinds of statements. Among the "opinions" we found were the following: "I detest that TV show." "Youth is not just a time, it is an age." "Jon is my best student." "Most children in Gail's class do not like her." Thus, expressions of preference, evocative statements, evaluations, and descriptions of people's attitudes are put in the same category, given the same status.

Many of the distinctions covered in a confused way could be covered so as to foster critical thinking. Unfortunately, as texts are presently written, this end is seldom achieved. We recommend that students distinguish acceptable from questionable claims and evidence from interpretation, and that the teacher use the applications such as those given in the strategy "clarifying issues, conclusions, or beliefs".

Texts often seem to assume that evaluation and emotion are antithetical to reason, always irrational or a-rational; that all beliefs, except belief in facts, are irrational or mere whims. Values (like emotions) are "just there"; they cannot be analyzed, clarified, assessed, or restructured. Judging another's opinions amounts to checking them against your own, rather than openmindedly considering their support. Evaluative terms are often described as "emotive language" and are linked to the concepts of opinion and bias. Students are cautioned to look out for such terms and to not allow their beliefs to be influenced by them. We recommend these points be replaced with the more pertinent distinction of *rationally justified* use of evaluative terms from *unjustified* use, or *supported* from *unsupported* use of evaluative language, and that students analyze and assess values and discuss standards or criteria. Students can then share their views regarding the status of such claims and the significance of their disagreements. Students should be encouraged, not to abandon evaluative language, but to use it appropriately, when its use is justified; not to discount it, but to assess it. They should learn to analyze terms and determine what kinds of facts are required to back them up; set reasonable standards and apply them fairmindedly.

Texts are correct in distinguishing communications that attempt to influence belief from other kinds of writing and speech (as a basic distinction of critical thinking), but then they fail. They lump together what should be made separate: attempts to persuade, convince, or influence *by reason*, from other attempts to influence (such as by force, repetition, or irrelevant association). Not all appeals to emotion are equivalent; they can be relevant or irrelevant, well-supported or unsupported.

According to texts, bias occurs when a writer or speaker expresses a feeling on a topic. However developed the explanations of bias are, students' practice invariably consists of examining single sentences and underlining words that "show bias", that is, "emotive" or evaluative words. Students do not evaluate passages for bias. Students do not distinguish contexts in which writers' conclusions and evaluations are appropriately expressed from when they are not, or when the feelings or opinions have rational grounds from when they reflect mere whim, impression, or prejudice, or when evaluations are *supported* from when they are merely *asserted.* Nor do students discuss *how* they should take bias into consideration — for example, by considering other views. The practical effect of the standard approach is to teach students to notice when someone uses evaluative terms, and then measure that use against their own beliefs. We suggest that instead, students consider questions like the following: What is wrong with bias? Why? How can I detect it? How does that fit in with the ideal of the fairminded critical thinker? What should I do when I realize the author is biased? What does the text mean by warning me against being "unduly influenced" by bias?

> "Be aware of the hidden curriculum in all schools. If teachers ask only factual questions that test memory and recall, students assume that this is the most important aspect of learning. If principals spend more time focusing on administrative concerns, discipline, or standardized test scores, teachers also assume these aspects of school are the most important." *Greensboro Handbook*

10 Remodelling the Curriculum

C urricula can play a significant role in school life. Directed by a district's curriculum, instruction must meet the educational goals and objectives stated in the curriculum. It is crucial, therefore, that its articulation and interpretation are compatible with critical thinking. A curriculum heavily loaded with detail, for example, may restrict the teacher's freedom to emphasize critical thinking by requiring large amounts of information to be covered quickly and superficially. Curriculum may also draw attention away from critical thinking by emphasizing goals, activities, and instruction contrary to critical thought or by being linked to tests that focus on recall. Some curricula mention critical thinking in vague, superficial, or narrow ways, creating confusion and mis-instruction. One of the most significant problems is the neglect of the essential role of critical thinking in the student's acquisition of knowledge. Rarely is the concept of knowledge analyzed. Instead, articulation assumes that all educators know what knowledge is and how it differs from opinion, belief, or prejudice. Any attempt to make critical thinking a significant part of the educational life of students must involve a restructuring of the curriculum, making explicit the philosophy of knowledge and learning that underlay its writing and direct its implementation. This chapter offers suggestions for analyzing, evaluating, and remodelling curricula to emphasize education based on principles of critical thought, coherently integrated into a rich philosophy of education.

Curriculum: What is it?

Written curricula can and do appear in a variety of forms. The *Oxford English Dictionary* defines curriculum as: "A course; specifically a regular course of study or training, as at a school or university." Some curricula written in this narrow sense list the particular courses students are to study, detailing the content of these courses, and perhaps even including course outlines. Curricula of this type are often restrictive and often rely heavily on a memorization/recall method of instruction, severely limiting teacher freedom, creativity, and individuality.

Most curricula are more complete than this, broader in scope, addressing much more than content and outline. Generally, curricula are best thought of as a conception, written or presupposed in practice, of what to teach and how to teach it. More complete curricula contain, therefore, all or most of the following elements, each of which is a possible source of problems: philosophy, goals, standards, curriculum and instructional objectives, assessment, and instructional examples. Let us first consider each element in order, from general to specific.

Philosophy: A theory or logical analysis of the principles underlying education, knowledge, teaching, and learning, including assumptions about educational purposes and practices intended to influence or direct all subsequent curriculum formulations and applications.

Commentary: There are two major problems to watch out for here: 1) either the philosophy articulated is too vaguely expressed to be more than a set of empty platitudes, or 2) it is so narrowly expressed that it forces many teachers to accede to an approach that they do not and should not accept. The philosophy should provide a defensible analysis of the principles underlying education, knowledge, teaching, and learning which is open to alternative teaching styles, respects the individual differences between teachers, and is sufficiently clear and specific to have clear-cut implications for teaching and learning.

Goals: Usually an abstract statement of expected student attainment as a result of education.

Commentary: Goals should be written as unambiguously as possible. For critical thinking to be a significant element in the whole, some articulation of it must be visible throughout the goal statements.

Standards: A broad statement of expected student achievement on completion of a year's study within a specific subject area.

Commentary: If critical thinking is to play a significant role in instruction, then critical thinking standards must be explicit throughout. This is virtually never done.

Curriculum Objectives: A more specific statement of learning achievement shown by the student in any subject after completing the unit of study.

Instructional Objectives: Descriptions of minimal student achievement that should be demonstrated at the completion of one or more lessons.

Commentary: In both curriculum and instructional objectives, care must be taken not to imply lower order behavioral responses as the goal. These objectives should focus on the depth of student understanding, not, for example, on their ability merely to reproduce "correct" responses on recall oriented tests and assignments.

Assessment: Description of how student progress toward these goals, standards, and objectives is to be assessed; often used to assess teacher efficacy; rarely expressed, but implied by the Instructional Objectives.

Commentary: Again, care must be taken not to put the emphasis on lower order and multiple choice testing.

Instructional Examples: Curriculum may end with examples of instruction appropriate to the attainment of these goals, standards, and objectives.

Commentary: If the curriculum contains model instructional examples, they should explicitly display methods that encourage independent and critical thought.

The Importance of Philosophy of Education to Curriculum Construction

All curricula reflect some philosophy of education; however, often this philosophy is not expressed, but uncritically assumed. Whether expressed or assumed, some philosophy is, *without exception*, the basis of any formulation of educational purposes, goals, and objectives. It determines, one way or another, the nature of educational practice. It is clear that most curriculum writers do not consider the statement of philosophy to be a significant element, since they are often satisfied with a vague, platitudinous treatment. Some curricula include under "Philosophy" statements that are not, properly speaking, definitive of a philosophical perspective. In these cases, what is called "philosophy" is nothing more than a broad and general educational objective. Failure to make assumed philosophy explicit often leads to the development of curricula based on unacceptable or questionable educational assumptions which would be rejected if openly stated.

Sometimes the expressed philosophy is inconsistent with the methods of instruction or assessment. In these cases, the goals are often vaguely defined, obscuring the contradiction between curriculum objectives, instructional examples, and philosophy. For example, an educational "Philosophy" might emphasize the importance of autonomous and critical thought, while assessment focuses on testing which requires only recall and robotic practice of skills. Curriculum needs, then, an articulated theory of education, knowledge, teaching, and learning that guides all subsequent articulations of goals, objectives, and instructional examples. At the same time, the philosophy should not rule out alternative teaching styles, except those incompatible with independence of thought and other fundamental educational values (truth, fairmindedness, empathy, rationality, self-criticism).

Knowing and Thinking: A Model Philosophical Statement

Of fundamental and critical importance in any discussion of educational philosophy is the conception of knowledge and learning guiding the formulation of the curriculum. Since we can roughly understand curriculum as a course of study which has knowledge as its objective, those involved in both curriculum development and teaching should be clear about their answers to such questions as these: "What is knowledge? How do humans acquire knowledge? How are students best taught so they acquire genuine knowledge?" These questions may seem to have obvious answers or to be irrelevant to practical problems of instruction, but they are not. Indeed, one fundamental obstacle to educational reform is a set of misconceptions about knowledge embedded in teaching practice.

One persistent unexpressed misconception is that knowledge consists of bits and pieces of information to be implanted in the student's mind by the teacher and materials. Knowledge is unwittingly considered to be a thing that can be put into students' heads as some object might be put into their hands. Didactic instruction becomes dominant, and instruction is reduced to giving students information (principles, values, facts, etc.) to accept as true and commit to memory. Memorization and recall then become the fundamental modes of thought, and students study to reproduce the "correct answers" given to them by the teacher or text. Curriculum based on this misconception of knowledge confuses the mere appearance of knowledge with genuine knowledge. A parrot or tape recorder, let us not forget, is not a knower. Many who verbally reject rote learning unwittingly continue to encourage it simply because they fail to examine the philosophy underlying their instruction. Some practitioners also unknowingly undermine whatever effort they exert to break out of this mold by continually assessing student progress in ways that encourage memorization and recall rather than depth of understanding.

A particularly significant misconception in this model is that if one has the "stuff" of knowledge, one will automatically reason well. The power of reasoning, in this view, naturally follows the acquisition of information, and need not, indeed cannot, precede or accompany it. Students are expected to get the information first, and then through it, start to think. Unfortunately, because of the amount of information taken to be essential, the time for thought is put off later and later. Furthermore, students who passively and uncritically accept information, do not go on to think critically once they learn to parrot it. The habits of learning they established in getting information transfer to subsequent learning. Information parrots become parrots of thinking.

Content dense curricula often create fragmented and un-engaging instruction. Subjects become isolated units having little or no relation to each other, and are often defined in terms of a long list of fragmented specifics. Students rarely see how parts relate to the whole, or to their lives outside school. As a result, both teacher and student come to think of knowledge as bits of information grouped under the general heading of one or another subject. Under the heading "science," for example, are many subheadings: biology, astronomy, physiology, chemistry, physics, geology, and so on, with each subheading containing the bits of information that constitute that field.

The conception of knowledge and learning presupposed in the didactic paradigm of memorization and recall is deceptive. It produces the illusion and confidence of knowledge without the substance, without the comprehension and understanding essential to any valid claim to knowledge. Remember, though people claim to know many things, a claim to know does not, in and of itself, certify actual knowledge. To claim knowledge is to imply not only that the thing claimed is true, but also that the knower understands the claim and the reasons for making it. The strength of one's conviction does not attest to its truth. There is often conviction in prejudice, certitude in gossip, rumor, and hearsay, confidence in unjustified authority, and blind faith in tradition. Students must grasp the difference between belief and knowledge. Blind memorization blurs that distinction.

Consider how a person moves from believing a rumor to ascertaining its truth, from believing the claim of some authority to verifying, and thus knowing, its truth. This shift from believing to knowing requires the active engagement of thought; it requires looking for and assessing reasons for and against. The person who has moved from belief to knowledge understands the claim and the reason for it. This person can justify it. Knowledge exists only in minds that have comprehended and justified it through thought. Knowledge is something we must think our way to, not something we can simply be given. Knowledge is produced by thought, analyzed by thought, comprehended by thought, organized by thought, evaluated, refined, maintained, and transformed by thought. Knowledge can be acquired *only* through thought. The educational philosophy underlying educational goals, standards, and objectives should be based on an accurate and full conception of the dependence of knowledge on thought.

This conception of knowledge, that it exists only in and through critical thought, should pervade the whole of the curriculum. All of the disciplines — mathematics, chemistry, biology, geography, sociology, history, philosophy, literature, composition, and so on — are modes of thought. Remember, we *know* mathematics, not to the extent that we can recite mathematical formulas and apply them upon request, but only to the extent that we can *think mathematically*. We know science, not to the extent that we can recall information from our science textbooks and have gone through a series of actions described in a lab manual, but only to the extent that we can *think scientifically.* We understand sociology, history, and philosophy only to the extent that we can think sociologically, historically, and philosophically. We understand and can truly hold such values as freedom of speech and thought, tolerance for honest differences and plurality, and civic responsibility only to the extent that we have honestly examined the reasons for them and the practical consequences of holding them. When we teach courses in such a way that students pass without thinking their way into the knowledge that these subjects make possible, students leave without any more knowledge than they had initially. When we sacrifice thought to gain coverage, make no mistake, we *sacrifice knowledge at the same time.* The issue is not "Shall we sacrifice knowledge to spend time on thought?", but "Shall we continue to sacrifice both knowledge and thought for the mere appearance of learning, for inert, confused learning?"

As an illustrative example, consider history. In history classes, students expect to be given names, events, dates, places, and explanations to repeat on papers and tests. Teachers typically tell students what events occurred, their causes, their results, and their significance. When asked, students can say that understanding the past is important to understanding the present, but they do not take this seriously. They see no useful application of what they study in history classes, and so are frequently bored. History seems to them a dull drudgery, with no real purpose or significance, except to those who need to know it: teachers.

Consider history taught as a mode of thought. Viewed from the paradigm of a critical education, blindly memorized content ceases to be the focal point. The *logic* of historical thought — that is, learning to think historically *by* thinking historically — becomes the focal point. Students learn the content of history, in other words, while learning to think historically. They learn by experience that history is not a simple recounting of past events, but also an interpretation of these events from a point of view. In recognizing that each historian writes from a point of view, students can begin to identify and thus assess the points of view leading to various interpretations and propose their own interpretations based on alternative points of view. They can learn that historical accounts are not necessarily a matter of simple "true or false". The student of history has to assess the gain and loss of alternative conflicting accounts. To begin to recognize this fundamental logic of historical thought, students could explore the significance of their own personal history and the relationship of their past to their present. They could begin to see that their past and the way they interpret it significantly influences their perception of their present and anticipation of their future. Understanding their own interpretations and constructions of personal history becomes an important tool for understanding the present. From here it is a short step to recognizing the importance of cultural, national, and world history in understanding the present, as well as understanding the news as a mode of historical thinking. They learn, in short, to think historically. They not only gain historical information and insights, but also acquire skills, abilities, and values.

Knowledge, Skills, and Values: The Philosophical Statement Continued

Knowledge is a tool we use for many purposes: to explain, illuminate, answer, clarify, settle, solve, inform, perform, and accomplish. Divorced from its use, from the skills entailed by getting and using it, knowledge is empty. Indeed, one does not really know something if one does not understand its verification or purpose. To come to know anything, then, requires one to acquire the skills embodied in it. Schooling based on a didactic, lecture-drill-test, paradigm assumes that in giving students bits of information, they have, or will get, the skills embodied in the knowledge. This is much too optimistic, for students frequently see no sense to, nor use for, the information they accumulate. Furthermore, not learning information in the context of its use, they have no sense of how to use it. This lack cannot be made up for by mere reiteration of those uses.

Also entailed by knowledge is the notion of value. No one learns what they do not in some sense value. Knowledge has value because of its use. We value what it allows us to accomplish. Consider, for example, the things that students *do* value, how quickly they learn these things, how much they know about them, and how well they retain and use what they really come to know. A list would include sports, both professional and personal (skate-boarding, bicycling, etc.), music, television and movies, cars, fashions and styles, arcade games, and so on. Taking any one of these, say skate-boarding, it is easy to see the connection between knowledge, skills, and values. Students who value skate-boarding spend much time and energy learning the differences between available wheels, trucks, and boards, the advantages and disadvantages of each, the kind of riding best suited to each, and how well these components work together. They then use this knowledge to assemble a board adequate to the kind of riding they prefer. Difficulties do not dampen their enthusiasm to learn. Contrast this with someone who does not value skate-boarding, but who must, for some reason, learn the same information about wheels, trucks, and boards. Although we can, with some difficulty, get the uninterested student to memorize some of the same information as the interested student, the difference in the level of understanding and retention between the two is large. We could say that those who simply memorize the information do not really know about skate-boarding, but have only transitory — and typically confused — information. They do not value the information they have about skate-boarding because they do not value skate-boarding. They ineptly apply it. They confuse it. They distort it. They forget it.

Many skills and values gained by learning a body of knowledge have application beyond that body of knowledge. Many skills and values can be transferred to a wide variety of domains of thought. An education emphasizing critical thinking fosters transfer by stimulating students to use their own thinking to come to conclusions and solutions, to defend positions on issues, to consider a wide variety of points of view, to analyze concepts, theories, and explanations, to clarify issues and conclusions, to evaluate the credibility of authorities, to raise and pursue root questions, to solve non-routine problems, to try out ideas in new contexts, to explore interdisciplinary connections, to evaluate arguments, interpretations, and beliefs, to generate novel ideas, to question and discuss each other's views, to compare perspectives and theories, to compare ideals with actual practice, to examine assumptions, to distinguish relevant from irrelevant facts, to assess evidence, to explore implications and consequences, and to come to terms with contradictions, paradoxes, and inconsistencies. These intellectual skills and abilities cut across traditional disciplinary boundaries. They apply equally well to science as to language, to mathematics as to social studies, and have relevance to and significance in non-academic spheres of student life as well. To gain knowledge through critical thinking is to empower the student as a thinker, learner, and doer.

A Moment For Reflection

At this point, we recommend that the readers spend a few minutes reviewing the last two sections with the following question in mind: *"How does this expression of philosophy of education compare to those I have read in the curriculum statements I have seen?"* Most importantly, compare the above philosophy of education, the interrelation of knowledge, critical thinking, and values, to the sketchy objectives that often pass for a philosophy of education in standard curriculum.

Curriculum: Formulations and Reformulations

The problem with most of the goals and objectives of many curricula is that they are deeply vague and ambiguous. Lacking specificity, they are subject to many, even conflicting, interpretations and implementations. Ambiguous goals and objectives are often interpreted in ways that result in lecture and testing for retention of information, rather than in ways that emphasize principles of critical thought.

Another problem is that, although many of these goals and objectives complement each other, curricula present them as though they were separate and disconnected. A serious attempt to achieve any of the major goals involves linking goals with the other goals complementary to them. Otherwise, the result is superficial coverage of multiple topics. If nothing else, combining multiple but complementary goals and objectives saves time. Fortunately, whenever we approach our objectives deeply, we accomplish multiple goals simultaneously. By moving from the surface to depth, students learn more content skills, and see their value. They learn more, not because they "cover" more, but because they forget less and are able to *generate* more, that is, they see the implications of what they learn. This emphasis on depth of learning is sometimes called "high content".

A Model Case

What follows are examples of suggestions for curriculum development taken from the *Cooperative County Course of Study: Guide to a Balanced, Comprehensive, Curriculum, 1984–1987*, assembled and published by the California County Superintendents Association and the California State Steering Committee for Curriculum Development and Publications. (Published by Office of the Alameda Superintendent of Schools, California, 1984. Kay Pacheco, project director.) This document provides some excellent suggestions for curriculum development and some well thought-out examples of instructional techniques. However, it lacks an over-arching philosophy of education and creates an unwitting vacillation between didactic and critical modes of instruction. At times it emphasizes rote learning, at others, deeper, more critical discussion of the material. There are also ambiguities and vaguenesses in it, contributing to potential confusion regarding the goals and objectives. Examples below illustrate how these problems can lead to confusion in instruction. A remodelled curriculum that eliminates much of the vagueness and ambiguity of the original follows each cited example. Questions and comments follow, to elucidate the kinds of problems inherent in the original curriculum. This serves as a model for the kind of questioning that could be done when evaluating curricula. We do not comment on all of the objectives listed under the goals.

English Language Arts/Reading

This section is divided into six areas, each with a goal for the area, several objectives for reaching that goal, and sample learner behaviors corresponding to the various grade levels. The six areas and their stated goals are:

(Original Curriculum)
Listening and Speaking: To develop listening and speaking skill.
Reading: Develop reading skill.
Writing: Develop writing skill.

Vocabulary/Grammar: Develop appropriate use of words.

Literature, Media, and Subjects: Respond critically and creatively to appropriate literature, media, and subjects.

Study and Locational Skills: Use study and locational skills for independent living.

Under the first goal are five objectives students are to reach to have accomplished the goal. Contained in parentheses for each objective are the learner behaviors for students at the secondary school level.

Original Curriculum

Goal 1: To develop listening and speaking skills

Objectives:	*Learner Behaviors:*
1.1 To express facts and information received from listening.	Rates the value of information gained from each member of a panel.
1.2 To express personal and imaginative responses from listening.	Critiques the effectiveness of a media presentation.
1.3 To present ideas and information orally for various settings and purposes.	Uses facts and challenges opinions in a debate.
1.4 To gather information by listening and questioning.	Interviews and researches a person and writes an article.
1.5 To develop interpersonal communication skills.	Understands the rules and procedures of formal groups, such as parliamentary procedure.

These goals are very vague, ambiguous, and, if not further explained, superficial. Each can, and will, be construed in any number of ways, based on the teacher's background, operant educational philosophy, and past practice.

Several questions come to mind regarding both the goal and objectives stated in the original curriculum. For example, Objective 1.1 of the original refers to the gathering of facts, and the accompanying "Learner Behaviors" speaks of rating those facts. What *exactly* do both of these mean? Should any statement claimed to be factual be taken as factual? Not at all. How, then, is fact to be distinguished from purported fact? Do all facts stated in a conversation have relevance to the issue under discussion? Not necessarily, but how is relevance to be decided? Is there a difference between facts and conclusions drawn from the facts? Quite, but how are the two distinguishable? Is a conclusion drawn from facts always a reasonable or justifiable conclusion? No, not always, but how are conclusions to be assessed? By the agreement or disagreement with students' own beliefs, prejudices, and preferences? We hope not. By the strength of the conviction of the speaker? Never. By the charismatic persuasiveness or forceful personality of the speaker? By no means. Curriculum that does not address these questions, or that ambiguously mentions them, is very likely to lead to instruction that confuses facts with purported facts, that fails to distinguish facts from conclusions, and that promotes an unreasonable acceptance or rejection of conclusions drawn from facts.

Consider how this goal and its objectives might be reworded to explicitly emphasize critical thinking. We can do so by remembering that knowledge must be actively constructed, not passively acquired, and by understanding in what sense active listening is a mode of critical thinking.

Reading, writing, and listening presuppose a range of similar skills, abilities, and values. Passive, uncritical reading, writing, speaking, and listening have common failings. They fail to recognize the problems for thought that each ability involves. In each case, for example, we need to organize ideas, consider logical relationships, reflect upon experiences, and use imagination. If I am speaking to you, I have to decide what to say and how to say it. To do this, I need to clarify my own thoughts, provide elaborations and illustrations, give reasons and explanations, and consider implications and consequences. I need to evaluate and rank my ideas, emphasizing the main points and ordering the rest. I need to anticipate questions or problems you might have. I need to consider your point of view and background. I even need to assess your interest in what I am saying to determine how long or how far to pursue a line of thought.

If I am listening to you, I need to be prepared to raise questions to you or to myself as I actively attempt to make sense of what you are saying. These questions reflect critical thinking skills, and might include the following:

What is she getting at?
What is her purpose?
Do I need any further elaboration of any point made?
Do I see how the various points fit together?
How does what she is saying fit into my experience?
Do I understand why she is saying what she is saying?
Do I follow the implications?
Do I agree or disagree?
Should I pursue or drop the conversation?
Should I take this seriously or let it go in one ear and out the other?

Remodelled Curriculum

Goal 1.0: To develop critical listening and speaking skills

Objectives	*Learner Behaviors:*
1.1 In listening, to distinguish between a fact and a purported fact, between facts and conclusions; to critically assess conclusions. In speaking, to use facts and conclusions drawn from facts, using critical thinking principles whenever appropriate.	Questions the facts and conclusions drawn from the facts given by members of a panel, or in debate; indicates the basis for questioning.
1.2 To express well thought-out responses from listening, using critical thinking principles whenever appropriate.	Students insightfully discuss the degree to which a situation comedy realistically approaches the problems of everyday life, asking themselves: What is the problem, how is it approached and handled, how would this problem be handled in real life?
1.3 To distinguish between opinions and judgments of varying strengths, as in a rationally defensible opinion and an irrational or indefensible opinion, using critical thinking principles whenever appropriate.	Uses facts and defensible opinions to challenge less defensible opinions in class discussion or debate. Demonstrates reasoned judgment by supporting things said with good reasons.

The remodelled curriculum makes it clearer that a listener is not a passive receptor of information, but participates in the conversation, striving to understand and to clarify, to question, probe, and test, to grapple with ideas and claims. Not only do students better understand the topic discussed and retain the information, they also acquire valuable intellectual skills. As students use these skills, they better appreciate their value, making it more likely that they continue to use them in other contexts. Speaking, also, ceases to be concerned with confidence only, but is seen as a primary method of expressing one's thoughts, ideas, and beliefs to another. Students not only recognize the importance of knowing how to express oneself *intelligibly* (grammar, syntax, vocabulary, etc.), but also *intelligently*, appreciating the connection between thought and language, that the thought itself is as important as its expression. Indeed, if one's thoughts are unclear, vague, contradictory, or confused, the expression of them will likewise be unclear, etc. Students should know how to formulate, assess, and express their thoughts and ideas clearly and accurately. This is more clearly the focus of the remodelled curriculum than the original.

History/Social Studies

The History/Social Science curriculum in the *Cooperative County Course of Study* is superficial and vague, creating potential misunderstanding and mis-learning. Critical thinking standards are not explicit in either the Instructional Objectives or Learner Behaviors. Lower order behavioral responses and a superficial understanding of history and social science are inadvertently encouraged.

The problem with vaguely stated objectives and Learner Behaviors is their likely interpretation, given the dominant mode of instruction in today's schooling. The didactic paradigm of instruction is still the operant paradigm in most instructional settings. Teachers who were themselves didactically taught are likely to teach didactically. This tendency can be reduced only by bringing principles of critical thought to the fore in philosophical statements, subject-matter curriculum, and instructional examples.

Selected objectives and Learner Behaviors from the first goal are reproduced below. Comments follow, as well as a remodelled goal, objectives, and behaviors.

Original Curriculum

Goal 1.0: To acquire knowledge drawn from history, social science, and the humanities

Objectives	*Learner Behaviors*
1.1 To understand the past and present of American, Western, and non-Western civilizations.	Recommends solutions to contemporary economic problems based on the historic ideas, traditions, and institutions of the United States.
1.3 To know the democratic functions of local, state, and national government.	Lists the positive and negative aspects of a specific lobby, and supports one group by citing appropriate facts and figures.
1.4 To know the historical development of issues and concerns of major cultures.	Compares the United States position on disarmament to the U.S.S.R. position as related to political, geographic, and economic factors.

Objective 1.1 is very vague. It is given some specificity in the Learner Behavior which focuses on ideas, traditions, and institutions of the American past. However, the Learner Behavior is intended only as one example of what could be done with the objective. In what other ways are we to "understand the past"? This is not clear. It is susceptible to many and divergent interpretations, increasing the potential for shallow coverage.

The words 'to understand' in objectives 1.1, and 'to know' in objectives 1.3 and 1.4, are also vague and ambiguous. Is there a difference between knowing and understanding? We do not think there is. However, how might these two phrases be interpreted given the dominant mode of instruction in schools? In Bloom's taxonomy, 'knowledge' is synonymous with recall. Objective 1.3 might be interpreted something like this: "To be able to list the different branches and departments of government, and to describe the structure and purpose of each." Little more than memorization is required to fulfill this objective. The learner behavior becomes, literally, *listing* "positive and negative aspects of a specific lobby". This same criticism applies to Objective 1.4 and its accompanying Learner Behavior. A comparison of the Soviet and American position on disarmament may likewise become a list: "We think this, they think that." Simple lists do not require any understanding of the historical development of the positions, the assumptions underlying them, or the implications following from them. The list itself might not be fair, since citizens of the U.S. tend to think of their weapons as *defensive,* and Soviet weapons as *offensive.* Neither is any assessment of the two positions likely to be fair, without significant sympathetic role-playing of the Soviet point of view.

An important objective not included anywhere in this curriculum is insight into the notion that history is written from a point of view. The U.S. has a history, but accounts of this history vary with the point of view of the writer. A history of the U.S. written from the perspective of white male settlers will be very different from one reflecting the perspective of Native Americans, African-Americans, women, immigrants, or the British. Not only should students read historical accounts, they should also be sensitive to differences in perspective, be able to identify the perspective from which any historical report is written, assess this perspective, and, if necessary, rewrite it more objectively.

Remodelled Curriculum

Goal 1.0: To understand the meaning and significance of history, social science, and the humanities, and to acquire information drawn from them

Objectives	*Learner Behaviors*
1.1 To learn to think historically; to understand that historical accounts are interpretations of events; and to see how the past has shaped the present and how the present is shaping the future.	Rewrites historical accounts from a perspective other than the one from which it was written; assesses differing perspectives, and looks for relevant information that might have been left out of an account.
1.2 To understand the democratic functions of and purposes for the various branches and departments of local, state, and national government.	To defend, in writing or orally, the necessity of a branch or department of local, state, or national government to preserving democracy and individual rights; to argue against the necessity of one.
1.3 To understand the historical development of major issues and concerns of major cultures.	Compares, contrasts, and evaluates the United States and Soviet positions on disarmament, historically, politically, geographically, and economically, retaining a sensitivity to their tendency to favor the position of their own country.

Science

The science curriculum in the *Cooperative County Course of Study* is generally well done. The section reproduced below is representative of the rest of the science curriculum. At times, it tends to waiver between didactic and critical modes of instruction, but does, overall, emphasize and promote independent, critical thought. Students devise experiments to test for various results, and do not merely follow step-by-step instruction on how to set up and conduct tests. They use precise terminology and data in expressing experimental conclusions. They locate, examine, and assess contradictions and discrepancies, and defend a conclusion. They formulate principles about the interdependence of organisms and the implications for survival. The emphasis is on original work, discovery, application, and critical evaluation. Students apply what they learn. They learn to think scientifically, and so better learn science.

Original Curriculum

Goal 2.0: To develop and apply rational and creative thinking processes

Objectives	Learner Behaviors:
2.1 To develop the ability to organize and generate data.	Organizes data on the basis of a continuous variable and uses an accepted classification system to order or identify objects or phenomena.
2.2 To develop the ability to apply and evaluate data and generate theories.	Examines data from different sources for discrepancies and contradictions and defends a conclusion.
2.3 To use data-gathering and theory building processes in problem solving.	Tests a hypothesis by designing an experiment, collecting and recording data, and applies the results to an appropriate theory.
2.4 To demonstrate scientific information through the use of models, diagrams, and displays.	Conducts an original experiment to answer one unresolved scientific question.

Although these objectives and learner behaviors are desirable, there are some potential problems with this section. The science curriculum seems to assume a philosophy of knowledge and learning different from the rest of the curriculum. In the science curriculum the philosophy is more critical than didactic, emphasizing the connection between knowledge, skills, and value. It tends to encourage student discovery, application of knowledge, precision in method and terminology, evaluation of information, and original experimentation. This philosophy, however, is not explicit. Although it may have been assumed by the writers of this section, the possibility for didactic implementation is increased by the failure to explicitly state it.

This, however, is not the only problem with this section. The *Cooperative County Course of Study* science curriculum also has a lengthy list of content to be covered. How are teachers likely to cover this content given the dominant, unexpressed philosophy of education? Given that this dominant philosophy is didactic, instruction may tend toward the easier and quicker lecture-memorization approach. Content may be seen as an end in itself, that students having these bits of information know science. Although a more defensible and better philosophy may be assumed in the science curriculum, failure to state it explicitly may result in instruction contrary to it.

Conclusion

Curriculum can provide continuity, consistency, and focus in teaching. There must be, for example, some consistency in instruction and content between different sections of the same subject and level. Curriculum provides this consistency. Students must also be similarly prepared to move from one grade level to the next, one grade picking up where the last ended. This continuity is also provided by the curriculum. All too often, however, the focus is blurred. Curricula are often vaguely and ambiguously written, with heavy emphasis on the specification of content to be covered. One significant reason for this is the absence of a clear and defensible philosophy of education.

The philosophy of education must be explicitly stated to avoid several problems. First, it must be explicit to ensure that the conception of knowledge and learning guiding curriculum development is reasonable and realistic. If we believe that knowledge is best conceived as bits of information, and that learning is the ability to reiterate these bits of information, then we should state it openly. If, on the other hand, deficiencies of the didactic conception are verbally acknowledged, the implications of this admission should be followed up. The philosophy of knowledge, learning, and teaching must be in harmony with practice.

Second, the relation between knowledge, skills, and values must be explicit to ensure that conflicting conceptions of knowledge and learning do not creep in. Interestingly, in the *Cooperative County Course of Study*, discovery, application, precision, and critical evaluation have heaviest emphasis in the science curriculum. But, independent, critical thought is equally valuable and necessary in all subject areas. There appear to be two conceptions of knowledge and learning in this curriculum. The first is more didactic, and tacitly implied in all curriculum areas but science. The second is richer, and appears principally in the science section. Lacking explicit articulation, this conflict or contradiction is ignored. Remember, educational practice arises from some conception of knowledge, teaching, and learning. The dominant mode of instruction today is, as it has been for generations, didactic. Research has refuted this superficial approach, but we have not yet broken down the habits that instantiate it. We must now begin to write curricula so that we come to terms with a conception of knowledge, teaching, and learning that takes full cognizance of the intrinsically "thought-filled" nature of each.

> *Teachers need time to reflect upon and discuss ideas, they need opportunities to try out and practice new strategies, to begin to change their own attitudes and behaviors in order to change those of their students, to observe themselves and their colleagues — and then they need more time to reflect upon and internalize these concepts.*

11 Remodelling: A Foundation for Staff Development

T he basic idea behind lesson plan remodelling as a strategy for staff development in critical thinking is simple. Every practicing teacher works daily with lesson plans of one kind or another. To remodel lesson plans is to critique one or more lesson plans and to formulate one or more new lesson plans based on that critical process. It is well done when the remodeller understands the strategies and principles used in producing the critique and remodel, when the strategies are well-thought-out, and when the remodel clearly follows from the critique. The idea behind our particular approach to staff development in lesson plan remodelling is also simple. A group of teachers or a staff development leader with a reasonable number of exemplary remodels and explanatory principles can design practice sessions that enable teachers to begin to develop new teaching skills as a result of experience in lesson remodelling.

When teachers have clearly contrasting "befores" and "afters", lucid and specific critiques, a set of principles clearly explained and illustrated, and a coherent unifying concept, they can increase their own skills in this process. One learns how to remodel lesson plans to incorporate critical thinking only through practice. The more one does it the better one gets, especially when one has examples of the process to serve as models.

Of course, a lesson remodelling strategy for critical thinking in-service is not tied to any particular handbook of examples, but it is easy to see the advantages of having such a handbook, assuming it is well-executed. Some teachers lack a clear concept of critical thinking. Some stereotype it as negative, judgmental thinking. Some have only vague notions, such as "good thinking", or "logical thinking", with little sense of how such ideals are achieved. Others think of it simply in terms of a laundry list of atomistic skills and so cannot see how these skills need to be orchestrated or integrated, or how they can be misused. Teachers rarely have a clear sense of the relationship between the component micro-skills, the basic, general concept of critical thinking, and the obstacles to using it fully.

353

It is theoretically possible but, practically speaking, unlikely that most teachers will sort this out for themselves as a task in abstract theorizing. In the first place, most teachers have little patience with abstract theory and little experience in developing it. In the second place, few school districts could give them the time to do so, even if they were qualified and motivated enough themselves. But sorting out the basic concept is not the only problem. Someone must also break down that concept into "principles", translate the "principles" to applications, and implement them in specific lessons.

On the other hand, if we simply give teachers prepackaged, finished lesson plans designed by someone else, using a process unclear to them, then we have lost a major opportunity for the teachers to develop their own critical thinking skills, insights, and motivations. Furthermore, teachers who cannot use basic critical thinking principles to critique and remodel their own lesson plans probably won't be able to implement someone else's effectively. Providing teachers with the scaffolding for carrying out the process for themselves and examples of its use opens the door for continuing development of critical skills and insights. It begins a process which gives the teacher more and more expertise and success in critiquing and remodelling the day-to-day practice of teaching.

Lesson plan remodelling can become a powerful tool in critical thinking staff development for other reasons as well. It is action-oriented and puts an immediate emphasis on close examination and critical assessment of what is taught on a day-to-day basis. It makes the problem of critical thinking infusion more manageable by paring it down to the critique of particular lesson plans and the progressive infusion of particular principles. Lesson plan remodelling is developmental in that, over time, more and more lesson plans are remodelled, and what has been remodelled can be remodelled again; more strategies can be systematically infused as the teacher masters them. It provides a means of cooperative learning for teachers. Its results can be collected and shared, at both the site and district levels, so teachers can learn from and be encouraged by what other teachers do. The dissemination of plausible remodels provides recognition for motivated teachers. Lesson plan remodelling forges a unity between staff development, curriculum development, and student development. It avoids recipe solutions to critical thinking instruction. And, finally, properly conceptualized and implemented, it unites cognitive and affective goals and integrates the curriculum.

Of course, the remodelling approach is no panacea. It will not work for the deeply complacent or cynical, or for those who do not put a high value on students' learning to think for themselves. It will not work for those who lack a strong command of critical thinking skills and self-esteem. It will not work for those who are "burned out" or have given up on change. Finally, it will not work for those who want a quick and easy solution based on recipes and formulas. The remodelling approach is a long-term solution that transforms teaching by degrees as teachers' critical insights and skills develop and mature. Teachers who can develop the art of critiquing their lesson plans and using their critiques to remodel them more and more effectively, will progressively *1)* refine and develop their own critical thinking skills and insights; *2)* re-shape the actual or "living" curriculum (what is in fact taught); and *3)* develop their teaching skills.

The approach to lesson remodelling developed by the Center for Critical Thinking and Moral Critique depends on the publication of handbooks such as this one which illustrate the remodelling process, unifying well-thought-out critical thinking theory with practical application. They explain critical thinking by translating general theory into specific teaching strategies. The strategies are multiple, allowing teachers to infuse more strategies as they understand more dimensions of critical thought. This is especially important since the skill at, and insight into, critical thought varies.

This approach, it should be noted, respects the autonomy and professionality of teachers. They choose which strategies to use in a particular situation and control the rate and style of integration. It is a flexible approach, maximizing the teacher's creativity and insight. The teacher can apply the strategies to any kind of material: textbook lessons, the teacher's own lessons or units, discussion outside of formal lessons, etc.

In teaching for critical thinking in the strong sense, we are committed to teaching in such a way that children, as soon and as completely as possible, learn to become responsible for their own thinking. This requires them to learn how to take command of their thinking, which requires them to learn how to notice and think about their own thinking, and the thinking of others. Consequently, we help children talk about their thinking in order to be mindful and directive in it. We want them to study their own minds and how they operate. We want them to gain tools by which they can probe deeply into and take command of their own mental processes. Finally, we want them to gain this mentally skilled self-control to become more honest with themselves and more fair to others, not only to "do better" in school. We want them to develop mental skills and processes in an ethically responsible way. This is not a "good-boy/bad-boy" approach to thinking, for people must think their own way to the ethical insights that underlie fairmindedness. We are careful not to judge the content of the students' thinking. Rather, we facilitate a process whereby the students' own insights can be developed.

The global objectives of critical thinking-based instruction are intimately linked to specific objectives. Precisely because we want students to learn how to think for themselves in an ethically responsible way we use the strategies we do: we help them gain insight into their tendency to think in narrowly self-serving ways (egocentricity); encourage them to empathize with the perspectives of others; to suspend or withhold judgment when they lack sufficient evidence to justify making a judgment; to clarify issues and concepts; to evaluate sources, solutions, and actions; to notice when they make assumptions, how they make inferences and where they use, or ought to use, evidence; to consider the implications of their ideas; to identify contradictions or inconsistencies in their thinking; to consider the qualifications or lack of qualifications in their generalizations; and do all of these things in encouraging, supportive, non-judgmental ways. The same principles of education hold for staff development.

Beginning to Infuse Critical Thinking

Let us now consider how to incorporate these general understandings into in-service design. Learning the art of lesson plan remodelling can be separated into five tasks. Each can be the focus of some stage of in-service activity:

1) *Clarifying the global concept* — How is the fairminded critical thinker unlike the self-serving critical thinker and the uncritical thinker? What is it to think critically? Why think critically?

2) *Understanding component principles* underlying the component critical thinking values, processes, and skills — What are the basic values that (strong sense) critical thinking presupposes? What are the micro-skills of critical thinking? What are its macro-processes? What do critical thinkers do? Why? What do they avoid doing? Why?

3) *Seeing ways to use the various component strategies in the classroom* — When can each aspect of critical thought be fostered? When is each most needed? Which contexts most require each dimension? What questions or activities foster it?

355

4) *Getting experience in lesson plan critique* — What are the strengths and weaknesses of this lesson? What critical principles, concepts, or strategies apply to it? What important concepts, insights, and issues underlie this lesson? Are they adequately emphasized and explained? What use would the well-educated person make of this material? Will that usefulness be clear to the students? Will this material, presented in this way, make sense and seem justified to the students?

5) *Getting experience in lesson plan remodelling* — How can I take full advantage of the strengths of this lesson? How can this material best be used to foster critical insights? Which questions or activities should I drop, use, alter, or expand upon? What should I add to it? How can I best promote genuine and deep understanding of this material?

Let us emphasize at the outset that these goals or understandings are interrelated and that achieving any or all of them is a matter of degree. We therefore warn against trying to achieve "complete" understanding of any one of them before proceeding to the others. Furthermore, we emphasize that understanding should be viewed practically or pragmatically. One does not learn about critical thinking by memorizing a definition or set of distinctions. The teacher's mind must be actively engaged at each point in the process — concepts, principles, applications, critiques, and remodels. At each level, "hands-on" activities should immediately follow any introduction of explanatory or illustrative material. When, for example, teachers read a handbook formulation of one of the principles, they should then have a chance to brainstorm applications of it, or an opportunity to formulate another principle. When they read the critique of one lesson plan, they should have an opportunity to remodel it or to critique another. When they read a complete remodel set — original lesson plan, critique, and remodel — they should have a chance to critique their own, individually or in groups. This back-and-forth movement between example and practice should characterize the staff development process overall. These practice sessions should not be rushed, and the products of that practice should be collected and shared with the group as a whole. Teachers need to see that they are fruitfully engaged in this process; dissemination of its products demonstrates this fruitfulness. Staff development participants should understand that initial practice is not the same as final product, that what is remodelled today by critical thought can be re-remodelled tomorrow and improved progressively thereafter as experience, skills, and insights grow.

Teachers should be asked early on to formulate what critical thinking means to them. You can examine some teacher formulations in the chapter, "What Critical Thinking Means to Me". However, do not spend too much time on the general formulations of what critical thinking is before moving to particular principles and strategies. The reason for this is simple. People tend to have trouble assimilating general concepts unless they are clarified through concrete examples. Furthermore, we want teachers to develop an operational view of critical thinking, to understand it as particular intellectual behaviors derivative of basic insights, commitments, and principles. Critical thinking is not a set of high-sounding platitudes, but a very real and practical way to think things out and to act upon that thought. Therefore, we want teachers to make realistic translations from the general to the specific as soon as possible and to periodically revise their formulations of the global concept in light of their work on the details. Teachers should move back and forth between general formulations of critical thinking and specific strategies in specific lessons. We want teachers to see how acceptance of the general concept of critical thinking translates into clear and practical critical thinking teaching and learning strategies, and to use those strategies to help students develop as rational and fairminded thinkers.

For this reason, all the various strategies explained in the handbook are couched in terms of behaviors. The principles express and describe a variety of behaviors of the "ideal" critical thinker; they become applications to lessons when teachers canvass their lesson plans for places where each can be fostered. The practice we recommend helps guard against teachers using these strategies as recipes or formulas, since good judgment is always required to apply them.

Some Staff Development Design Possibilities

1) Clarifying the global concept

After a brief exposition or explanation of the global concept of critical thinking, teachers might be asked to reflect individually (for, say, 10 minutes) on people they have known who are basically uncritical thinkers, those who are basically selfish critical thinkers, and those who are basically fairminded critical thinkers. After they have had time to think of meaningful personal examples, divide them into small groups to share and discuss their reflections.

Or one could have them think of dimensions of their own lives in which they are most uncritical, selfishly critical, and fairminded, and provide specific examples of each.

2) Understanding component teaching strategies that parallel the component critical thinking values, processes, and skills

Each teacher could choose one strategy to read and think about for approximately 10 minutes and then explain it to another teacher, without reading from the handbook. The other teacher can ask questions about the strategy. Once one has finished explaining his or her strategy, roles are reversed. Following this, pairs could link up with other pairs and explain their strategies to each other. At the end, each teacher should have a basic understanding of four strategies.

3) Seeing how the various component strategies can be used in classroom settings

Teachers could reflect for about 10 minutes on how the strategies that they chose might be used in a number of classroom activities or assignments. They could then share their examples with other teachers.

4) Getting experience in lesson plan critique

Teachers can bring one lesson, activity, or assignment to the in-service session. This lesson, or one provided by the in-service leader, can be used to practice critique. Critiques can then be shared, evaluated, and improved.

5) Getting experience in lesson plan remodelling

Teachers can then remodel the lessons which they have critiqued and share, evaluate, and revise the results.

Other in-service activities include the following:

- Copy a remodel, eliminating strategy references. Groups of teachers could mark strategies on it; share, discuss, and defend their versions. Remember, ours is not "the right answer". In cases where participants disagree with, or do not understand why we cited the strategies we did, they could try to figure out why.

- Over the course of a year, the whole group can work on at least one remodel for each participant.

- Participants could each choose several strategies and explain their interrelationships, mention cases in which they are equivalent, or how they could be used together. (For example, refining generalizations could be seen as evaluating the assumption that all x's are y's.)

- To become more reflective about their teaching, teachers could keep a teaching log or journal, making entries as often as possible, using prompts such as these: What was the best question I asked today? Why? What was the most effective strategy I used today? Was it appropriate? Why or why not? What could I do to improve that strategy? What did I actively do today to help create the atmosphere that will help students to become critical thinkers? How and why was it effective? What is the best evidence of clear, precise, accurate reasoning I saw in a student today? What factors contributed to that reasoning? Did the other students realize the clarity of the idea? Why or why not? What was the most glaring evidence of irrationality or poor thinking I saw today in a student? What factors contributed to that reasoning? How could I (and did I) help the student to clarify his or her own thoughts? (From *The Greensboro Plan*)

The processes we have described thus far presuppose motivation on the part of the teacher to implement changes. Unfortunately, many teachers lack this motivation. We must address this directly. This can be done by focusing attention on the insights that underlie each strategy. We need to foster discussion of them so that it becomes clear to teachers not only *that* critical thinking requires this or that kind of activity but *why*, that is, what desirable consequences it brings about. If, for example, teachers do not see why thinking for themselves is important for the well-being and success of their students, they will not take the trouble to implement activities that foster it, even if they know what these activities are.

To meet this motivational need, we have formulated "principles" to suggest important insights. For example, consider the brief introduction which is provided in the Strategy chapter for the strategy "exercising fairmindedness":

Principle: To think critically about issues, we must be able to consider the strengths and weaknesses of opposing points of view; to imaginatively put ourselves in the place of others in order to genuinely understand them; to overcome our egocentric tendency to identify truth with our immediate perceptions or long-standing thought or belief. This trait correlates with the ability to reconstruct accurately the viewpoints and reasoning of others and to reason from premises, assumptions, and ideas other than our own. This trait also correlates with the willingness to remember occasions when we were wrong in the past, despite an intense conviction that we were right, and the ability to imagine our being similarly deceived in a case at hand. Critical thinkers realize the unfairness of judging unfamiliar ideas until they fully understand them.

The world consists of many societies and peoples with many different points of view and ways of thinking. To develop as reasonable persons, we need to enter into and think within the frameworks and ideas of different peoples and societies. We cannot truly understand the world if we think about it only from *one* viewpoint, as North Americans, as Italians, or as Soviets.

Furthermore, critical thinkers recognize that their behavior affects others, and so consider their behavior from the perspective of those others.

Teachers reflecting on this principle in the light of their own experience should be able to give their own reasons why fairmindedness is important. They might reflect upon the personal problems and frustrations they faced when others — spouses or friends, for example — did not or would not empathically enter their point of view. Or they might reflect on their frustration as children when their parents, siblings, or schoolmates did not take their point of view seriously. Through examples of this sort, constructed by the teachers themselves, insight into the need for an intellectual sense of justice can be developed.

Once teachers have the insight, they are ready to discuss the variety of ways that students can practice thinking fairmindedly. As always, we want to be quite specific here, so that teachers understand the kinds of behaviors they are fostering. The handbooks provide a start in the application section following the principle. For more of our examples, one can look up one or more remodelled lesson plans in which the strategy was used, referenced under each. Remember, it is more important for teachers to think up their own examples and applications than to rely on the handbook examples, which are intended as illustrative only.

Lesson plan remodelling as a strategy for staff and curriculum development is not a simple, one-shot approach. It requires patience and commitment. But it genuinely develops the critical thinking of teachers and puts them in a position to understand and help structure the inner workings of the curriculum. While doing so, it builds confidence, self-respect, and professionality. With such an approach, enthusiasm for critical thinking strategies will grow over time. It deserves serious consideration as the main thrust of a staff development program. If a staff becomes proficient at critiquing and remodelling lesson plans, it can, by redirecting the focus of its energy, critique and "remodel" any other aspect of school life and activity. In this way, the staff can become increasingly less dependent on direction or supervision from above and increasingly more activated by self-direction from within. Responsible, constructive critical thinking, developed through lesson plan remodelling, promotes this transformation.

Besides devising in-service days that help teachers develop skills in remodelling their lessons, it is important to orchestrate a process that facilitates critical thinking infusion on a long-term, evolutionary basis. As you consider the "big picture", remember the following principles:

✔ *Involve the widest possible spectrum of people* in discussing, articulating, and implementing the effort to infuse critical thinking. This includes teachers, administrators, board members, and parents.

✔ *Provide incentives to those who move forward in the implementation process.* Focus attention on those who make special efforts. Do not embarrass or draw attention to those who do not.

✔ *Recognize that many small changes are often necessary before larger changes can take place.*

✔ *Do not rush implementation.* A slow but steady progress with continual monitoring and adjusting of efforts is best. Provide for refocusing on the long-term goal and on ways of making the progress visible and explicit.

✔ *Work continually to institutionalize the changes made* as the understanding of critical thinking grows, making sure that the goals and strategies being used are deeply embedded in school-wide and district-wide statements and articulations. Foster discussion on how progress in critical thinking instruction can be made permanent and continuous.

✔ *Honor individual differences among teachers.* Maximize the opportunities for teachers to pursue critical thinking strategies in keeping with their own educational philosophy. Enforcing conformity is incompatible with the spirit of critical thinking.

It's especially important to have a sound long-term plan for staff development in critical thinking. The plan of the Greensboro City Schools is especially noteworthy for many reasons. *1)* It does not compromise depth and quality for short-term attractiveness. *2)* It allows for individual variations between teachers at different stages of their development as critical thinkers. *3)* It provides a range of incentives to teachers. *4)* It can be used with a variety of staff development strategies. *5)* It is based on a broad philosophical grasp of the nature of education, integrated into realistic pedagogy. *6)* It is long-term, providing for evolution over an extended period of time. Infusing critical thinking into the curriculum cannot be done overnight. It takes a commitment that evolves over years. The Greensboro plan is in tune with this inescapable truth.

Consider these features of the Greensboro plan for infusing reasoning and writing into instruction:

A good staff development program should be realistic in its assessment of time. Teachers need time to reflect upon and discuss ideas, they need opportunities to try out and practice new strategies, to begin to change their own attitudes and behaviors in order to change those of their students, to observe themselves and their colleagues — and then they need more time to reflect upon and internalize concepts.

Furthermore, we think that teachers need to see *modeled* the teacher attitudes and behaviors that we want them to take back to the classroom. We ask teachers to participate in Socratic discussion, we ask teachers to write, and we employ the discovery method in our workshops. We do *not* imply that we have "the answer" to the problem of how to get students to think, and we seldom lecture.

In planning and giving workshops, we follow these basic guidelines. Workshop leaders:

1. model for teachers the behaviors they wish them to learn and internalize. These teaching behaviors include getting the participants actively involved, calling upon and using prior experiences and knowledge of the participants, and letting the participants process and deal with ideas rather than just lecturing to them.

2. use the discovery method, allowing teachers to explore and to internalize ideas and giving time for discussion, dissension, and elaboration.

3. include writing in their plans — we internalize what we can process in our own words.

Here is what Greensboro said about the remodelling approach:

After studying and analyzing a number of approaches and materials, this nucleus recommends Richard Paul's approach to infusing critical thinking into the school curriculum (which has a number of advantages).

1. It avoids the pitfalls of pre-packaged materials, which often give directions which the teacher follows without understanding why or even what the process is that she or he is following. Pre-packaged materials thus do not provide an opportunity for the teacher to gain knowledge in how to teach for and about thinking, nor do they provide opportunity for the teacher to gain insight and reflection into his or her own teaching.

2. It does not ask teachers to develop a new curriculum or a continuum of skills, both of which are time-consuming and of questionable productivity. The major factor in the productivity of a curriculum guide is how it is used, and too many guides traditionally remain on the shelf, unused by the teacher.

3. It is practical and manageable. Teachers do not need to feel overwhelmed in their attempts to change an entire curriculum, nor does it need impractical expenditures on materials or adoption of new textbooks. Rather, the teacher is able to exercise his or her professional judgment in deciding where, when, at what rate, and how his or her lesson plans can be infused with more critical thinking.

4. It infuses critical thinking into the curriculum rather than treating is as a separate subject, an "add on" to an already crowded curriculum.

5. It recognizes the complexity of the thinking process, and rather than merely listing discreet skills, it focuses on both affective strategies and cognitive strategies.

This focus on affective and cognitive strategies may seem confusing at first, but the distinction is quite valid. Paul's approach recognizes that a major part of good thinking is a person's affective (or emotional) approach, in other words, attitudes or dispositions. Although a student may become very skilled in specific skills, such as making an inference or examining assumptions, he or she will not be a good thinker without displaying affective strategies such as exercising independent judgment and fairmindedness or suspending judgment until sufficient evidence has been collected. Likewise, Paul also emphasizes such behavior and attitudes as intellectual humility, perseverance, and faith in reason, all of which are necessary for good thinking.

Paul's approach also gives specific ways to remodel lesson plans so that the teacher can stress these affective and cognitive skills. Thirty-one specific strategies are examined and numerous examples of how to remodel lesson plans using these strategies are presented. These concrete suggestions range from ways to engage students in Socratic dialogue to how to restructure questions asked to students.

A critical factor in this approach is the way that a teacher presents material, asks questions, and provides opportunities for students to take more and more responsibility on themselves for thinking and learning. The teacher's aim is to create an environment that fosters and nurtures student thinking.

This nucleus recommends that this approach be disseminated through the faculty in two ways. First, a series of workshops will familiarize teachers with the handbooks. Secondly, nucleus teachers will work with small numbers of teachers (two or three) using peer collaboration, coaching, and cooperation to remodel and infuse critical thinking into lesson plans.

Since no two districts are alike, just as no two teachers are alike, any plan must be adjusted to the particular needs of a particular district. Nevertheless, all teachers assess their lessons in some fashion or other, and getting into the habit of using critical thought to assess their instruction cannot but improve it. The key is to find an on-going process to encourage and reward such instructional critique.

12 The Greensboro Plan: A Sample Staff Development Plan

by Janet L. Williamson

Greensboro, North Carolina is a city of medium size nestled in the rolling hills of the Piedmont, near the Appalachian Mountains. The school system enrolls approximately 21,000 students and employs 1,389 classroom teachers. Students in the Greensboro city schools come from diverse economic and balanced racial backgrounds. Forty-six percent of the students are White. Fifty-four per cent of the student population is minority; 52% is Black and 2% is Asian, Hispanic, or Native American. Every socio-economic range from the upper middle class to those who live below the poverty line is well-represented in the city schools. However, almost 28% of the student population has a family income low enough for them to receive either free or discounted lunches. Although our school system is a relatively small one, Greensboro has recently implemented a program that is beginning successfully to infuse critical thinking and writing skills into the K-12 curriculum.

The Reasoning and Writing Project, which was proposed by Associate Superintendent, Dr. Sammie Parrish, began in the spring of 1986, when the school board approved the project and affirmed as a priority the infusion of thinking and writing into the K-12 curriculum. Dr. Parrish hired two facilitators, Kim V. DeVaney, who had experience as an elementary school teacher and director of computer education and myself, Janet L. Williamson, a high school English teacher, who had recently returned from a leave of absence during which I completed my doctorate with a special emphasis on critical thinking.

Kim and I are teachers on special assignment, relieved of our regular classroom duties in order to facilitate the project. We stress this fact: we are facilitators, not directors; we are teachers, not administrators. The project is primarily teacher directed and implemented. In fact, this tenet of teacher empowerment is one of the major principles of the project, as is the strong emphasis on and commitment to a philosophical and theoretical basis of the program.

We began the program with some basic beliefs and ideas. We combined reasoning and writing because we think that there is an interdependence between the two processes and that writing is an excellent tool for making ideas clear and explicit. We also believe that no simple or quick solutions would bring about a meaningful change in the complex set of human attitudes and behaviors that comprise thinking. Accordingly, we began the project at two demonstration sites where we could slowly develop a strategic plan for the program. A small group of fourteen volunteers formed the nucleus with whom we primarily worked during the first semester of the project.

Even though I had studied under Dr. Robert H. Ennis, worked as a research assistant with the Illinois Critical Thinking Project, and written my dissertation on infusing critical thinking skills into an English curriculum, we did not develop our theoretical approach to the program quickly or easily. I was aware that if this project were going to be truly teacher-directed, my role would be to guide the nucleus teachers in reading widely and diversely about critical thinking, in considering how to infuse thinking instruction into the curriculum, and in becoming familiar with and comparing different approaches to critical thinking. My role would not be, however, to dictate the philosophy or strategies of the program.

This first stage in implementing a critical thinking program, where teachers read, study, and gather information, is absolutely vital. It is not necessary, of course, for a facilitator to have a graduate degree specializing in critical thinking in order to institute a sound program, but it is necessary for at least a small group of people to become educated, in the strongest sense of the word, about critical thinking and to develop a consistent and sound theory or philosophy based on that knowledge — by reading (and rereading), questioning, developing a common vocabulary of critical thinking terms and the knowledge of how to use them, taking university or college courses in thinking, seeking out local consultants such as professors, and attending seminars and conferences.

In the beginning stages of our program, we found out that the importance of a consistent and sound theoretical basis is not empty educational jargon. We found inconsistencies in our stated beliefs and our interactions with our students and in our administrators' stated beliefs and their interaction with teachers. For example, as teachers we sometimes proclaim that we want independent thinkers and then give students only activity sheets to practice their "thinking skills;" we declare that we want good problem solving and decision-making to transfer into all aspects of life and then tend to avoid controversial or "sensitive" topics; we bemoan the lack of student thinking and then structure our classrooms so the "guessing what is in the teacher's mind" is the prevailing rule. We also noted a tendency of some principals to espouse the idea that teachers are professionals and then declare that their faculty prefer structured activities rather than dealing with theory or complex ideas. Although most administrators state that learning to process information is more important than memorizing it, a few have acted as if the emphasis on critical thinking is "just a fad." One of the biggest contradictions we have encountered has been the opinion of both teachers and administrators that "we're already doing a good job of this (teaching for thinking)," yet they also say that students are not good thinkers.

While recognizing these contradictions is important, it does not in and of itself solve the problem. In the spirit of peer coaching and collegiality, we are trying to establish an atmosphere that will allow us to point out such contradictions to each other. As our theories and concepts become more internalized and completely understood, such contradictions in thought and action become less frequent. In all truthfulness, however, such contradictions still plague us and probably will for quite a while.

We encountered, however, other problems that proved easier to solve. I vastly underestimated the amount of time that we would need for an introductory workshop, and our first workshops failed to give teachers the background they needed; we now structure our workshops for days, not hours. There was an initial suggestion from the central office that we use *Tactics for Thinking*. as a basis, or at least a starting point, for our program. To the credit of central office administration, although they may have questioned whether we should use an already existing program, they certainly did not mandate that we use any particular approach. As we collected evaluations of our program from our teachers, neighboring school systems, and outside consultants, however, there seemed to be a general consensus that developing our own program, rather than adopting a pre-packaged one, has been the correct choice.

Finally, teachers became confused with the array of materials, activities, and approaches. They questioned the value of developing and internalizing a concept of critical thinking and asked for specifics — activities they could use immediately in the classroom. This problem, however, worked itself out as teachers reflected on the complexity of critical thinking and how it can be fostered. We began to note and collect instances such as the following: a high school instructor, after participating in a workshop that stressed how a teacher can use Socratic questioning in the classroom, commented that students who had previously been giving unsatisfactory answers were now beginning to give insightful and creative ones. Not only had she discovered that the quality of the student's response is in part determined by the quality of the teacher's questions, she was finding new and innovative ways to question her students. Another teacher, after having seen how the slowest reading group in her fourth grade class responded to questions that asked them to think and reflect, commented that she couldn't believe how responsive and expressive the children were. I can think of no nucleus teacher who would now advocate focusing on classroom activities rather than on a consistent and reflective approach to critical thinking.

As the nucleus teachers read and studied the field, they outlined and wrote the tenets that underscore the program. These tenets include the belief that real and lasting change takes place, not by writing a new curriculum guide, having teachers attend a one day inspirational workshop at the beginning of each new year, adopting new textbooks that emphasize more skills, or buying pre-packaged programs and activity books for thinking. Rather, change takes place when attitudes and priorities are carefully and reflectively reconsidered, when an atmosphere is established that encourages independent thinking for both teachers and students, and when we recognize the complex interdependence between thinking and writing.

The nucleus teachers at the two demonstration schools decided that change in the teaching of thinking skills can best take place by remodelling lesson plans, not by creating new ones, and they wrote a position paper adopting Richard Paul's *Critical Thinking Handbook*. This approach, they wrote, is practical and manageable. It allows the teacher to exercise professional judgment and provides opportunity for teachers to gain insight into their own teaching. In addition, it recognizes the complexity of the thinking process and does not merely list discrete skills.

The primary-level teachers decided to focus upon language development as the basis for critical thinking. Their rationale was that language is the basis for both thinking and writing, that students must master language sufficiently to be able to use it as a tool in thinking and writing, and that this emphasis is underdeveloped in many early classrooms. This group of teachers worked on increasing teacher knowledge and awareness of language development as well as developing and collecting materials, techniques and ideas for bulletin boards for classroom use.

By second semester, the project had expanded to two high schools. This year, the second year of the program, we have expanded to sixteen new schools, including all six middle schools. Kim and I have conducted workshops for all new nucleus teachers as well as for interested central office and school-based administrators. Also, this year, at three of the four original demonstration sites, workshops have been conducted or planned that are led by the original nucleus teachers for their colleagues.

It is certainly to the credit of the school board and the central administration that we have had an adequate budget on which to operate. As I have mentioned, Kim and I are full-time facilitators of the program. Substitutes have been hired to cover classes when teachers worked on the project during school hours. We were able to send teachers to conferences led by Richard Paul and we were able to bring in Professor Paul for a very successful two-day workshop.

Our teachers work individually and in pairs, and in small and large groups at various times during the day. A number of teachers have video-taped themselves and their classes in action, providing an opportunity to view and reflect on ways that they and their colleagues could infuse more thinking opportunities into the curriculum.

Essentially, we have worked on three facets in the program: *1)* workshops that provide baseline information, *2)* follow-up that includes demonstration teaching by facilitators, individual study, collegial sharing of ideas, peer coaching, individual and group remodelling of lesson plans, teachers writing about their experiences both for their personal learning and for publication, team planning of lessons, peer observation, and *3)* dissemination of materials in our growing professional library.

We are expanding slowly and only on a volunteer basis. Currently, we have approximately seventy nucleus teachers working in twenty schools. By the end of next year, 1988-1989, we plan to have a nucleus group in each of the schools in the system. Plans for the future should include two factions: ways for the nucleus groups to continue to expand their professional growth and knowledge of critical thinking and an expansion of the program to include more teachers. We plan to continue to build on the essential strengths of the program — the empowerment of teachers to make decisions, the thorough theoretical underpinnings of the program, and the slow and deliberate design and implementation plan.

Our teachers generally seem enthusiastic and committed. In anonymous written evaluations of the program, they have given it overwhelming support. One teacher stated:

> It is the most worthwhile project the central office has ever offered ....Because
> - it wasn't forced on me.
> - it wasn't touted as the greatest thing since sliced bread.
> - it was not a one-shot deal that was supposed to make everything all better.
> - it was not already conceived and planned down to the last minute by someone who had never been in a classroom or who hadn't been in one for X years.
> It was, instead,
> - led by professionals who were still very close to the classroom.
> - designed by us.
> - a volunteer group of classroom teachers who had time to reflect and read and talk after each session, and who had continuing support and information from the leaders, not just orders and instructions.

Short Range and Long Range Goals

Developing and sustaining a good critical thinking program is a long-range enterprise that takes a number of years. Accordingly, we have developed both long-range and short-range goals. Truthfully, we began the program with some confusion and hesitancy about our goals; we developed many of these goals as the program progressed and we continue to redefine our priorities.

Short range goals include:
- Staff development and workshops for all teachers, for school based administrators, and for central office administrators.
- Development of a professional library with materials and resources which teachers have identified as useful.

- Adoption of an elementary writing process model which can be used by all teachers.
- Adoption of a secondary writing model which can be used by teachers in all disciplines.
- Establishment of demonstration schools and demonstration classrooms.
- Development and encouragement of peer observations and peer coaching.
- Establishment of a network for communicating and sharing with other school systems.
- Adoption of instruments that encourage self-reflection and analysis of teaching.
- Adoption of processes and instruments for evaluating the project.
- Growth in knowledge and mastery of a number of programs and approaches to critical thinking as well as an expanded, common vocabulary of critical thinking terms.
- Participation of teachers in a number of experiences of remodelling lessons and sharing these remodelled lessons with colleagues.

Long range goals include:
- Development of a concept of critical thinking that allows for individual perceptions as well as for the differences between technical thinking and thinking dialectically.
- Development of ways to help students transfer good thinking from discipline to discipline and from school work to out-of-school experiences.
- Development of insight into our own thinking, including our biases and a consideration of contradictions in our espoused objectives and our behavior.
- Development of a supportive atmosphere that fosters good thinking for teacher, administrators, and students.

> *One does not learn about critical thinking by memorizing a definition or set of distinctions.*

13 What Critical Thinking Means to Me: The Views of Teachers

C ritical thinking is a process through which one solves problems and makes decisions. It is a process that can be improved through practice, though never perfected. It involves self-discipline and structure. Sometimes it can make your head hurt, but sometimes it comes naturally. I believe for critical thinking to be its most successful, it must be intertwined with creative thinking.

Kathryn Haines
Grade 5

Thinking critically gives me an organized way of questioning what I hear and read in a manner that goes beyond the surface or literal thought. It assists me in structuring my own thoughts such that I gain greater insight into how I feel and appreciation for the thoughts of others, even those with which I disagree. It further enables me to be less judgmental in a negative way and to be more willing to take risks.

Patricia Wiseman
Grade 3

Critical thinking is being able *and* willing to examine all sides of an issue or topic, having first clarified it; supporting or refuting it with either facts or reasoned judgment; and in this light, exploring the consequences or effects of any decision or action it is possible to take.

Kim V. DeVaney
Facilitator, WATTS

All of us think, but critical thinking has to do with becoming more aware of *how* we think and finding ways to facilitate clear, reasoned, logical, and better-informed thinking. Only when our thoughts are backed with reason and logic, and are based on a process of careful examination of ideas and evidence, do they become critical and lead us in the direction of finding what is true. In order to do this, it seems of major importance to maintain an open-minded willingness

367

to look at other points of view. In addition, we can utilize various skills which will enable us to become more proficient at thinking for ourselves.

Nancy Johnson
Kindergarten

Critical thinking is a necessary access to a happy and full life. It provides me the opportunity to analyze and evaluate my thoughts, beliefs, ideas, reasons, and feelings as well as those of other individuals. Utilizing this process, it helps me to understand and respect others as total persons. It helps me in instructing my students and in my personal life. Critical thinking extends beyond the classroom setting and has proven to be valid in life other than the school world.

Veronica Richmond
Grade 6

Critical thinking is the ability to analyze and evaluate feelings and ideas in an independent, fairminded, rational manner. If action is needed on these feelings or ideas, this evaluation motivates meaningfully positive and useful actions. Applying critical thinking to everyday situations and classroom situations is much like Christian growth. If we habitually evaluate our feelings and ideas based on a reasonable criteria, we will become less likely to be easily offended and more likely to promote a positive approach as a solution to a problem. Critical thinking, like Christian growth, promotes confidence, creativity, and personal growth.

Carolyn Tarpley
Middle School
Reading

Critical thinking is a blend of many things, of which I shall discuss three: independent thinking; clear thinking; and organized Socratic questioning.

As for the first characteristic mentioned above, a critical thinker is an independent thinker. He doesn't just accept something as true or believe it because he was taught it as a child. He analyzes it, breaking it down into its elements; he checks on the author of the information and delves into his or her background; he questions the material and evaluates it; and then he makes up his own mind about its validity. In other words, he thinks independently.

A second criterion of critical thinking is clarity. If a person is not a clear thinker, he can't be a critical thinker. I can't say that I agree or disagree with you if I can't understand you. A critical thinker has to get very particular, because people are inclined to throw words around. For example, they misuse the word 'selfish.' A person might say: "You're selfish, but *I'm* motivated!" A selfish person is one who systematically *ignores* the rights of others and pursues his own desires. An unselfish one is a person who systematically *considers* the rights of others while he pursues his own desires. Thus, clarity is important. We have to be clear about the meanings of words.

The most important aspect of critical thinking is its spirit of Socratic questioning. However, it is important to have the questioning organized in one's mind and to know in general the underlying goals of the discussion. If you want students to retain the content of your lesson, you must organize it and help them to see that ideas are connected. Some ideas are derived from basic ideas. We need to help students to organize their thinking around basic ideas and to question. To be a good questioner, you must be a wonderer — wonder aloud about meaning and truth. For example, "I wonder what Jack means." "I wonder what this word means?" "I wonder if anyone can think of an example?" "Does this make sense?" "I wonder how true that is?" "Can anyone think of an experience when that was true?" The critical thinker must have the ability to probe deeply, to get down to basic ideas, to get beneath the mere appearance of things. We need to get into the very spirit, the "wonderment" of the situation being discussed. The students need to feel, "My teacher really wonders; and really wants to know what we think." We should wonder aloud. A good way to stimulate thinking is to use a variety of types of questions. We can ask questions to get the students to elaborate, to explain, to give reasons, to cite evidence, to identify their points of view, to focus on central ideas, and to raise problems. Socratic questioning is certainly vital to critical thinking.

Thus, critical thinking is a blend of many characteristics, especially independent thinking, clear thinking, and Socratic questioning. We all need to strive to be better critical thinkers.

Holly Touchstone
Middle School
Language Arts

Critical thinking is wondering about that which is not obvious, questioning in a precise manner to find the essence of truth, and evaluating with an open mind.

As a middle school teacher, critical thinking is a way to find out from where my students are coming (a way of being withit). Because of this "withitness" produced by bringing critical thinking into the classroom, student motivation will be produced. This motivation fed by fostering critical thinking will produce a more productive thinker in society.

Thus, for me, critical thinking is a spirit I can infuse into society by teaching my students to wonder, question, and evaluate in search of truth while keeping an open mind.

Malinda McCuiston
Middle School
Language Arts, Reading

Critical thinking means thinking clearly about issues, problems, or ideas, and questioning or emphasizing those that are important to the "thinker." As a teacher, I hope to develop Socratic questioning so that my students will feel comfortable discussing why they believe their thoughts to be valid. I hope that they will develop language skills to communicate with others and that they will be open to ideas and beliefs of others.

Jessie Smith
Grade 1

The spirit of critical thinking is a concept that truly excites me. I feel the strategies of critical thinking, implemented appropriately in my classroom, can enable me to become a more effective teacher. By combining this thinking process with my sometimes overused emotions and intuitive power, I can critically examine issues in my classroom as well as in my personal life. I feel it is of grave importance for us as educators to provide a variety of opportunities for our students to think critically by drawing conclusions, clarifying ideas, evaluating assumptions, drawing inferences, and giving reasons and examples to support ideas. Also, Socratic dialogue is an effective means of enabling the students to discover ideas, contradictions, implications, etc., instead of being told answers and ideas given by the teacher. Critical thinking is an excellent tool for the teacher to help the students learn how to think rather than just what to think. Hopefully critical thinking will help me be a more effective teacher as well as excite my students.

Beth Sands
Middle School
Language Arts

Critical thinking is what education should be. It is the way I wish I had been taught. Although I left school with a wealth of facts, I had never learned how to connect them or to use them. I loved learning but thought that being learned meant amassing data. No one ever taught me how to contrast and compare, analyze and dissect. I believed that all teachers knew everything, all printed material was true and authority was always right. It took me years to undo the habits of "good behavior" in school. I want to save my students the wasted time, the frustration, the doubts that I encountered during and after my school years. And teaching and using critical thinking is the way to do that.

Nancy Poueymirou
High School
Language Arts

For me, critical thinking is a combination of learning and applying a data base of learning to evaluate and interrelate concepts from diverse academic disciplines. Critical thinking is understanding that knowledge, wisdom, and education are not divided into math, science, English, etc. It is the fairness of tolerance combined with a strong sense of ethics and morals. It is the fun of feeling your mind expand as you accomplish intellectual challenges that attain your own standards. It is the zest of life.

Joan Simons
High School
Biology

Both as teacher and individual, I find critical thinking skills essential elements of a full and enjoyable life. With the ability to think critically, one can both appreciate and cope with all aspects of life and learning. When dealing with problems, from the most mundane to the most complex, the ability to think critically eliminates confusion, dispels irrational emotion, and enables one to arrive at an appropriate conclusion. At the same time, as we ponder the beauty and creativity of our environment, we are free to "wonder" and enjoy the complexity around us, rather than be perplexed or intimidated by it, because we have the mental capability to understand it. To live is to be ever curious, ever learning, ever investigating. Critical thinking enables us to do this more fully and pleasurably.

Mary Lou Holoman
High School
Language Arts

A critical thinker never loses the joy of learning, never experiences the sadness of not caring or not wondering about the world. The essence of the truly educated person is that of being able to question, inquire, doubt, conclude, innovate. And beyond that, to spread that enthusiasm to those around him, obscuring the lines that divide teacher and student, enabling them to travel together, each learning from the other.

Jane Davis-Seaver
Grade 3

Critical thinking is a means of focusing energy to learn. The learning may be academic (proscribed by an institutional curriculum or self-directed) or non-academic (determined by emotional need). It provides a systematic organization for gathering information, analyzing that information, and evaluating it to reach reasonable, acceptable conclusions for yourself.

Blair Stetson
Elementary
Academically Gifted

Critical thinking is the ability to reason in a clear and unbiased way. It is necessary to consider concepts or problems from another's point of view and under varying circumstances in order to make reasoned judgments. Awareness of one's own reasoning processes enables one to become a more fairminded and objective thinker.

Karen Marks
Elementary
Academically Gifted

Critical thinking is questioning, analyzing, and making thoughtful judgments about questions, ideas, issues or concepts. It refines thoughts to more specific or definite meanings. The critical thinker must be an active listener who does not simply accept what he/she hears or reads on face value without questioning, but looks for deeper meaning. Critical thinking also involves evaluating the ideas explored or problems addressed and better prepares a student to be able to think about the world around him or her.

Becky Hampton
Grade 6

Critical thinking has given me a broader means of evaluating my daily lesson plans. It has helped me better understand the thinking principles of each student I teach. It has also enabled me to practice strategies in lesson planning and to become a more effective classroom teacher.

Pearl Norris Booker
Grade 2

Critical thinking provides me the opportunity to broaden the thinking process of my students. It can be used to have the students to reason and to think about different ideas of a problem or a given situation.

Portia Staton
Grade 3

Critical thinking is a process that takes all the ideas, questions and problems that we are faced with each day and enables us to come up with solutions. It is the process by which we are able to search for evidence that support already existing answers, or better yet, to come up with new solutions to problems. Through critical thinking, one begins to realize that many times there is more than one solution whereupon decisions can be made. To me, critical thinking has helped and will continue to help me understand myself and the world around me.

Debbie Wall
Grade 4

Critical thinking is a skill that involves the expansion of thoughts and the art of questioning. This skill must be developed over a period of time. It is a way of organizing your thoughts in a logical sequence. Knowledge is gained through this process.

Carolyn Smith
Grade 5

Critical thinking is questioning, analyzing and evaluating oral or written ideas. A critical thinker is disciplined, self-directed, and rational in problem solving. Reaching conclusions of your own rather than accepting everything as it is presented, is internalizing critical thinking.

Denise Clark
Grade 2

To think critically, one must analyze and probe concepts or ideas through reasoning. It makes one an *active* reasoner, not a *passive* accepter of ideas (or facts). It turns one into a doer, an evaluater, or re-evaluater. Critical thinking occurs everywhere, is applicable everywhere and while it can be tedious, need not be, because as one thinks critically, new ideas are formed, conclusions are drawn, new knowledge is acquired.

Janell Prester
Grade 3

Critical thinking means to think through and analyze a concept or idea. You are able to back up your reasoning and think through an idea in a manner which allows an over-all focus. If a person is a critical thinker, a yes-no answer is too brief. An answer to a problem or idea must have an explanation and reasoning backing it.

Donna Phillips
Grade 4

Critical thinking is a tool that teachers can use to offer a new dimension of education to their students: that of thinking about, questioning and exploring the concepts in the curriculum. When critical thinking is an integral part of the teaching-learning process, children learn to apply thinking skills throughout the curriculum as well as in their daily lives. Socratic dialogue fosters critical thinking and motivates the teacher and learner to share and analyze experiences and knowledge. Critical thinking involves the child in the learning process and makes education more meaningful to the individual, thus facilitating learning.

Andrea Allen
Grade 1

The most important part of critical thinking, to me, is *discovery*. We discover a deeper level of thinking. We discover the reasons for ideas instead of just accepting ideas. We are motivated by action, interaction, and involvement. We discover we have the ability to expand our thoughts to include all aspects and perspectives of our beliefs.

Mandy Ryan
Grade 5

Critical thinking, to me, is the process of analyzing new and old information to arrive at solutions. It's the process of learning to question information that you may have taken for granted. It's being independent. Critical thinking is letting people think for themselves and make judgments for themselves.

Leigh Ledet
Grade 4

Critical thinking is the process of taking the knowledge you have gained through past experience or education and re-evaluating conclusions on a certain situation or problem. Because students must evaluate the reasons for their beliefs, they become actively involved in learning through the teacher's use of Socratic questioning. Allowing students to clarify their reasons through the writing process further stimulates the students to become critical thinkers. The ultimate goal for students to understand in using critical thinking is to become active thinkers for themselves.

Robin Thompson
Middle School
Language Arts

Critical thinking, to me, is to be open-ended in my thoughts. It is like opening a door which leads to many other doors through which ideas may evolve, move about, change, and come to rest. It is like a breath of freshness in which one can gain new insight over long-established opinions. It stimulates and generates endless new possibilities.

Eutha M. Godfrey
Grades 2-3

Critical thinking is thinking that demonstrates an extension of an idea or concern beyond the obvious. A critical thinker's values are significant to his learning.

Frances Jackson
Grade 2

To me, critical thinking means independence. It gives me a tool which lets me explore my own mind extending beyond basic recall to a higher level of reasoning. I then feel more in touch with myself and my own inner feelings. This results in my becoming a better decision-maker.

Jean Edwards
Grade 5

Critical thinking is the process of working your mind through different channels. It is the process of thinking logically. Critical thinking is analyzing your thoughts through questions. It is the process of seeing that your ideas and concepts may not be the same as another's. It is opening your mind to those who have different views and looking at their views.

Cathy L. Smith
Grade 3

Critical thinking is to question in-depth at every possible angle or point of view, to look at someone else's point of view without making hasty judgments. Critical thinking is to logically and fairly re-orient your own personal point of view, if necessary. To think critically, you are self-directed in your thinking process, as well as disciplined.

Mary Duke
Grade 1

Critical thinking is the vehicle by which I encourage students to become active participants in the learning process. I allow more time for and become more aware of the need for students to express ideas verbally and in written form to clarify ideas in their own minds. I recognize the importance of developing skills for analyzing and evaluating. Ultimately, once students become comfortable using critical thinking skills, they assume greater responsibility for their learning.

Dora McGill
Grade 6

Critical thinking is clear, precise thinking. I believe that all human actions and expressions involve in some way, thinking. For example, I believe that feelings, emotions and intuitions are much the results of earlier thought (reactions) to stimuli. I think that this, in one way, explains the variations of emotional responses in some people to similar stimuli. Thus, I believe that critical thinking not only has the potential to clarify new and former conscious thoughts but also to effect/change likely (future) emotive and intuitive reactions/responses.

More concrete and less theoretical outcomes of critical thinking may be more relevant to me as an educator. Better questioning skills on the part of the students and the teacher are an obvious outcome. There seem to be several positive outcomes of better questioning: more opportunity for in-depth understanding of content, a natural (built-in) process for accessing the effectiveness of lessons, and more opportunity for student participation, self-assessment, and direction are three apparent outcomes. There are, of course, many other outcomes of developing better questioning skills, and from the other skills of critical thinking.

I simply believe that critical thinking improves the overall integrity of the individual and the collective group, class, school, community, etc.

Richard Tuck
High School
Art

I perceive critical thinking in teaching as a tool for my learning. As I attempt to develop the critical thinker, I will become more aware of the students' thoughts, values, and needs. I must learn from what students offer, and develop acceptance and sensitivity to the individual. The knowledge I gain from the student will determine what I utilize as strategies or principles of critical thinking.

> Loretta Jennings
> Grade 1

Critical thinking is the ability to look at a problem or issue with a spirit of openmindedness and to take that problem and analyze or evaluate it based on the facts or good "educated" hypotheses. Critical thinking is being flexible enough to suspend one's bias towards an issue in order to study all sides to formulate an opinion or evaluation.

> Mark Moore
> Grade 4

Critical thinking to me involves mental conversations and dialogues with myself. I try first to establish the facts. Then I try to search for criteria to examine my "facts." The next question is whether or not there are distortions and irrelevancies. I have to examine whether I have a personal bias which has led me to select only certain facts and leave others out.

I then try to mentally list facts and arguments on both sides of a question and, finally, draw logical questions and conclusions.

> Barbara Neller
> Middle School
> Social Studies

Critical thinking is a systematic, logical approach to life in which an individual, using this method, truly learns and understands a concept rather than imitates or mimics. Knowledge and intellectual growth are achieved by a variety of strategies which include examining a variety of viewpoints, making assumptions based on viable evidence and forming well thought out conclusions.

> Jane S. Thorne
> High School
> Math

Critical thinking allows students to become active participants in their learning. Socratic dialogue stimulates communication between teacher and students, thus creating an atmosphere where everyone is encouraged to become risk-takers. A teacher needs to become a model of critical thinking for the students. Through this interaction, content can be analyzed, synthesized, and evaluated with thinking.

> Carol Thanos
> Grade 6

Critical thinking is the complex process of exploring an issue, concept, term or experience which requires verbal as well as non-verbal involvement from the participant. It involves listing ideas related to the subject, so that the person involved could objectively examine the relationship of the ideas thought of. It demands the person involved in the process to investigate the certain issue, concept, or process from varied vantage points, in order that intuitions, assumptions, and conclusions are presented with reasoned opinions or experienced evidences. Critical thinking is a task that involves the participant's in-depth assessment of his or her body of knowledge, experience and emotions on the subject in question.

> Ariel Collins
> High School
> Language Arts

Critical thinking is thinking that is clear, fairminded, and directed. It is not sloppy or self-serving thinking, but deep and probing thought aimed at finding the truth. It is skillful thinking aimed at genuine understanding, not superficial head-shaking. It is *the* tool used by and descriptive of an educated person whose mantra would be "veritas."

Helen Cook
Middle School
Science

Critical thinking is a process of questioning and seeking truth and clarity. It is a continual endeavor as one is constantly exposed to new knowledge which must be reconciled with prior conclusions. As one's body of knowledge grows, it is all the more important to be able to critically consider and determine *what is truth.*

Critical thinking demands certain prerequisites: openmindedness, willingness to withhold snap judgments, commitment to explore new ideas. The development of such qualities empowers me to participate in the various facets of critical thinking, e.g., clarifying ideas, engaging in Socratic discussions. These skills are not nearly so difficult as achieving the mind-set which must precede them. Only a *commitment* to question and persevere and honestly pursue truth will supply the impetus necessary to delve beneath the surface of issues and concepts. Yet this predisposition is difficult to achieve, because it necessitates taking risks, making mistakes, being wrong and being corrected — activities very threatening to our safe ego boundaries.

Only in transcending these ego boundaries does growth occur and genuine learning transpire. Critical thinking is comprised of a sense of wonderment, daring and determination. It is undergirded by a value of truth and personal growth. It is the continual learning process of the individual.

Deborah Norton
High School
Social Studies

The definition of critical thinking that I now hold is one that explains some things that I have felt for some time. I am convinced that everything that I know, that is a part of my education, I have figured out or found for myself. I have had close to twenty years of formal, didactic education, but I could tell you very little about anything that was presented to me in lecture through all those classes, except perhaps some trivia. In college, I did my real learning through the writing that I did, either from research or from contemplation. I have felt that this was true, but a lot of my own teaching has continued to be didactic and students have learned to be very accepting and non-questioning and to *expect* to be told what the right answer is, what someone else has decided the right answer is. I hope that I can change that now. I now feel that it is imperative that my students learn to be critical thinkers, and I hope that I can model that belief and, through all my activities in class, lead them in that direction. We all need to be open-minded, to realize that there are often many sides to a problem, many points of view and that there are strategies and techniques for analyzing, making decisions, and making learning our own. I want to be, and I want my students to be, questioning, open-minded, fairminded, synthesizing individuals — in other words, critical thinkers.

Liza Burton
High School
Language Arts

> *We learn how to learn by learning, think by thinking, judge by judging, analyze by anlyzing; not by reading, hearing, and reproducing principles guiding these activities, but by using those principles. There is no point in trying to think for our students.*

14 Regarding a Definition of Critical Thinking

Many people who feel that they don't know what critical thinking is, or means, request a definition. When they realize there is no *one* definition of critical thinking given by all theorists, many people feel frustrated and confused. "Even the experts can't agree about what they're talking about. How can I teach it if *I* don't know what it is, and no one else can tell me?" This reaction, though understandable, is somewhat mistaken. Although theorists provide a variety of definitions, they do not necessarily reject each others' definitions. They feel that their own definitions most usefully convey the basic concept, highlighting what they take to be its most crucial aspects, but they do not necessarily hold that other definitions are "wrong" or worthless. Novices, on the other hand, often get caught up in the wording of definitions and do not probe into them to see how compatible their meanings are. The various proposed definitions, when examined, are in fact much more similar than they are different.

Furthermore, because of the complexity of critical thinking, its relationship to an unlimited number of behaviors in an unlimited number of situations, its conceptual interdependence with other concepts (such as the critical person, the reasonable person, the critical society, a critical theory of knowledge, learning, literacy, and rationality, not to mention the opposites of these concepts), it is important not to put too much weight on any one definition. A variety of useful definitions have been formulated by distinguished theoreticians, and we should value these diverse formulations as helping to make important features of critical thought more apparent.

Harvey Siegel, for example, has defined critical thinking as "thinking appropriately moved by reasons". This definition helps us remember that our minds are often *inappropriately* moved by forces other than reason: by desires, fears, social rewards and punishments, etc. It points out the connection between critical thinking and the classic philosophical ideal of rationality. Yet, clearly, the ideal of rationality is itself open to multiple explications. Similar points can be made about Robert Ennis' and Matthew Lipman's definitions.

Robert Ennis defines critical thinking as "rational reflective thinking concerned with what to do or believe." This definition usefully calls attention to the wide role that critical thinking plays in everyday life, for, since all behavior is based on what we believe, all human action is based upon what we in some sense *decide* to do. However, like Siegel's definition, it assumes that the reader has a clear concept of rationality and of the conditions under which a decision can be said to be a "reflective" one. There is also a possible ambiguity in Ennis' use of 'reflective'. As a person internalizes critical standards — sensitivity to reasons, evidence, relevance, consistency, and so forth — the application of these standards to action becomes more automatic, less a matter of conscious effort and, hence, less a matter of overt "reflection" (assuming that Ennis means to imply by 'reflection' a special consciousness or deliberateness).

Matthew Lipman defines critical thinking as "skillful, responsible thinking that is conducive to judgment because it relies on criteria, is self-correcting, and is sensitive to context." This definition is useful insofar as one has a clear sense of the difference between responsible and irresponsible thinking, as well as what to encompass in the appropriate self-correction of thought, the appropriate use of criteria, and appropriate sensitivity to context. Of course, it would not be difficult to find instances of thinking that were self-correcting, used criteria, and responded to context *in one sense* but nevertheless were *uncritical* in some other sense. For example, one's particular criteria might be uncritically chosen or the manner of responding to context might be critically deficient in a variety of ways.

We make these points not to underestimate the usefulness of these definitions but to point out limitations in the process of definition itself when dealing with a complex concept such as critical thinking. Rather than working solely with one definition of critical thinking, it is more desirable to retain a host of definitions, and this for two reasons: *1)* in order to maintain insight into the various dimensions of critical thinking that alternative definitions highlight, and *2)* to help oneself escape the limitations of any given definition. In this spirit, we will present a number of definitions which we have formulated. Before reading these definitions, you might review the array of teachers' formulations in the chapter "What Critical Thinking Means to Me". You will find that virtually all the teachers' definitions are compatible with each other, even though they are all formulated individually. Or consider the following list of definitions.

Critical Thinking is:

a) skilled thinking which meets epistemological demands irrespective of the vested interests or ideological commitments of the thinker;

b) skilled thinking characterized by empathy into diverse opposing points of view and devotion to truth as against self-interest;

c) skilled thinking that is consistent in the application of intellectual standards, holding oneself to the same rigorous standards of evidence and proof to which one holds one's antagonists;

d) skilled thinking that demonstrates the commitment to entertain all viewpoints sympathetically and to assess them with the same intellectual standards, without reference to one's own feelings or vested interests, or the feelings or vested interests of one's friends, community or nation;

e) the art of thinking about your thinking while you're thinking so as to make your thinking more clear, precise, accurate, relevant, consistent, and fair;

f) the art of constructive skepticism;

g) the art of identifying and removing bias, prejudice, and one-sidedness of thought;

378

h)   the art of self-directed, in-depth, rational learning;

i)   thinking that rationally certifies what we know and makes clear wherein we are ignorant;

j)   the art of thinking for one's self with clarity, accuracy, insight, commitment, and fairness.

A Definition of Critical Thinking

We can now give a definition of critical thinking that helps tie together what has been said so far, a definition that highlights three crucial dimensions of critical thought:

1) the perfections of thought
2) the elements of thought
3) the domains of thought

The Definition:

> Critical thinking is disciplined, self-directed thinking which exemplifies the perfections of thinking appropriate to a particular mode or domain of thought. It comes in two forms. If disciplined to serve the interests of a particular individual or group, to the exclusion of other relevant persons and groups, it is sophistic or *weak sense critical thinking*. If disciplined to take into account the interests of diverse persons or groups, it is fairminded or *strong sense critical thinking*.

Critical thinkers use their command of the elements of thought to adjust their thinking to the logical demands of a type or mode of thought. As they come to habitually think critically in the strong sense, they develop special traits of mind: intellectual humility, intellectual courage, intellectual perseverance, intellectual integrity, and confidence in reason. Sophistic or weak sense critical thinkers develop these traits only narrowly in accordance with egocentric and sociocentric commitments.

Now we shall explain what we mean by the *perfections* and *imperfections* of thought, the *elements* of thought, the *domains* of thought, and *traits of mind*. In each case we will comment briefly on the significance of these dimensions. We will then relate these dimensions to the process of helping students to come to terms, not only with the logic of their own thought, but with the logic of the disciplines they study, as well.

The Perfections and Imperfections of Thought

clarity _____ vs _____ unclarity

precision_____ vs _____ imprecision

specificity _____ vs _____ vagueness

accuracy_____ vs _____ inaccuracy

relevance _____ vs _____ irrelevance

consistency _____ vs _____ inconsistency

logical _____ vs _____ illogical

depth _____ vs _____ superficiality

completeness _____ vs _____ incompleteness

significance _____ vs _____ triviality

fairness_____ vs _____ bias or one-sidedness

adequacy (for purpose) _____ vs _____ inadequacy

379

Each of the above are general canons for thought; they represent legitimate concerns irrespective of the discipline or domain of thought. To develop one's mind and discipline one's thinking with respect to these standards requires extensive practice and long-term cultivation. Of course achieving these standards is a relative matter and often they have to be adjusted to a particular domain of thought. Being *precise* while doing mathematics is not the same as being precise while writing a poem or describing an experience. Furthermore, there is one perfection of thought that may be periodically incompatible with the others, and that is *adequacy to purpose*.

Because the social world is often irrational and unjust, because people are often manipulated to act against their interests, because skilled thought is often used to serve vested interest, those whose main purpose is to forward their selfish interests, often skillfully violate the common standards for good thinking. Successful propaganda, successful political debate, successful defense of a group's interests, successful deception of one's enemy often requires the violation or selective application of many of the above standards. The perfecting of one's thought as an instrument for success in a world based on power and advantage differs from the perfecting of one's thought for the apprehension and defense of fair-minded truth. To develop one's critical thinking skills merely to the level of adequacy for social success is to develop those skills in a lower or *weaker* sense.

It is important to underscore the commonality of this weaker sense of critical thinking for it is dominant in the everyday world. Virtually all social groups disapprove of members who make the case for their competitors or enemies, however justified that case may be. Skillful thinking is commonly a tool in the struggle for power and advantage, not an angelic force that transcends this struggle. It is only when the struggle becomes mutually destructive and it becomes advantageous for all to go beyond the onesidedness of each social group, that a social ground can be laid for fairmindedness of thought. No society yet in existence cultivates fairness of thought generally in its citizens.

The Elements of Thought

Both sophistic and fairminded critical thinking are skilled in comparison with uncritical thinking. The uncritical thinker is often unclear, imprecise, vague, illogical, unreflective, superficial, inconsistent, inaccurate, or trivial. To avoid these imperfections requires some command of the elements of thought. These include an understanding of and an ability to formulate, analyze, and assess:

1) The problem or question at issue
2) The purpose or goal of the thinking
3) The frame of reference or points of view involved
4) Assumptions made
5) Central concepts and ideas involved
6) Principles or theories used
7) Evidence, data, or reasons advanced
8) Interpretations and claims made
9) Inferences, reasoning, and lines of formulated thought
10) Implications and consequences which follow

Focusing on the nature and interrelationships of the elements of thought illuminates the logic of any particular instance of reasoning or of any domain of knowledge. For example, *at least one question is at issue in every instance of reasoning*. Can the student identify and precisely express those problems or questions, distinguishing the differences between them?

All human reasoning is oriented to serve some purpose or goal. Can students clearly express their purpose or goal and adjust their thinking to serve it? Can students analyze and critique their purpose or goal? Do students recognize the point of view or frame of reference in which they are thinking? Do they consider alternative points of view?

All reasoning must start somewhere and proceed in some direction. Can students identify what they are assuming or taking for granted in their reasoning? Can they follow out the implications and consequences of their reasoning? Can they identify contradictions in their thought?

All reasoning uses some ideas or concepts and not others. Can students identify and analyze the most fundamental concepts in their reasoning? Can they determine, for example, whether they are using a term in keeping with established usage or modifying that usage?

Most reasoning relies on principles or theories to make sense of what one is reasoning about. Can students identify the principles or theories they are using? Can they clarify them, question them, consider alternatives, apply them precisely?

Most reasoning is based on some experiences, evidence, or data which are interpreted and used as the basis of inferences. Can students identify the experiences, evidence, or data they are using or basing their reasoning upon? Can they identify their inferences? Can they rationally argue in favor of their inferences? Can they formulate and consider possible objections to their inferences?

Finally, as we have already emphasized, *all disciplines have a logic.* Can students discuss the logic of the disciplines they are studying? Can they identify their fundamental goals or purposes? The kind of questions they attempt to answer? Their basic concepts or ideas? Their basic assumptions? Their basic theories or principles? The sort of data, evidence, or experiences they focus upon? Whether there is fundamentally one or multiple conflicting schools of thought within the discipline? When students cannot answer these questions about a subject field, they cannot think critically within it. They have no idea how to begin to compare one field to any other, nor therefore how to correct or qualify the results of one field in light of the results of another.

Traits of Mind

There are, we believe, at least seven interdependent traits of mind we need to cultivate if we want students to become critical thinkers in the strong sense. They are:

a) *Intellectual Humility:* Awareness of the limits of one's knowledge, including sensitivity to circumstances in which one's native egocentrism is likely to function self-deceptively; sensitivity to bias and prejudice in, and limitations of one's viewpoint.

b) *Intellectual Courage:* The willingness to face and assess fairly ideas, beliefs, or viewpoints to which one has not given a serious hearing, regardless of one's strong negative reactions to them.

c) *Intellectual Empathy:* Recognizing the need to imaginatively put oneself in the place of others to genuinely understand them.

d) *Intellectual Good Faith (Integrity):* Recognition of the need to be true to one's own thinking, to be consistent in the intellectual standards one applies, to hold oneself to the same rigorous standards of evidence and proof to which one holds one's antagonists.

e) *Intellectual Perseverance:* Willingness to pursue intellectual insights and truths despite difficulties, obstacles, and frustrations.

f) *Faith in Reason:* Confidence that in the long run one's own higher interests and those of humankind at large will be served best by giving the freest play to reason, by encouraging people to come to their own conclusions by developing their own rational faculties.

g) *Intellectual Sense of Justice:* Willingness to entertain all viewpoints sympathetically and to assess them with the same intellectual standards, without reference to one's own feelings or vested interests, or the feelings or vested interests of one's friends, community, or nation.

These intellectual traits are interdependent. Each is best developed while developing the others as well. Consider intellectual humility. To become aware of the limits of our knowledge, we need the *courage* to face our own prejudices and ignorance. To discover our own prejudices, we must *empathize* with and reason within points of view we are hostile toward. To do so, we must typically *persevere* over a period of time, for reasoning within a point of view against which we are biased is difficult. We will not make that effort unless we have the *faith in reason* to believe we will not be deceived by whatever is false or misleading in the opposing viewpoint, and an *intellectual sense of justice*. We must recognize an intellectual *responsibility* to be fair to views we oppose. We must feel *obliged* to hear them in their strongest form to ensure that we are not condemning them out of ignorance or bias on our part. At this point we come full circle back to where we began: the need for *intellectual humility*.

These traits are applicable to *all* domains or modes of knowledge, not merely to some. Like the perfections and elements of thought, with which they are intimately intertwined, they are universally relevant. Of course, those reasoning to achieve selfish ends often betray intellectual standards to gain success. Schooling today neglects this deep-seated problem of selfish thought. Though most students enter and leave school as essentially uncritical thinkers, some develop a range of critical thinking skills to advance selfish ends. Yet the difference between selfish and fairminded thought rarely becomes a significant issue in instruction. Before going further, therefore, something more should be said about the nature of selfish thought.

Selfish Critical Thinking, Prejudice, and Human Desire

Human action is grounded in human motives and human motives are typically grounded in human desire and perceived interest. Getting what we want and what advances our prestige, wealth, and power naturally structures and shapes how we understand the situations and circumstances of our daily lives. We routinely categorize, make assumptions, interpret, and infer from within a viewpoint which we use to advance our personal ends and desires. We are, in a word, naturally prejudiced in our own favor. We reflexively and spontaneously gravitate to the slant on things that justifies or gratifies our desires. It is not enough to be taught to be ethical, honest, kind, generous, thoughtful, concerned with others, and respectful of human rights. The human mind easily construes situations so it can conceive of selfish desire as self-defense, cruelty as discipline, domination as love, intolerance as conviction, evil as good.

The mere conscious will to do good does not remove prejudices which shape our perceptions or eliminate the on-going drive to form them. To minimize our egocentric drives, we must develop critical thinking in a special direction. We need, not only intellectual skills, but intellectual character as well. Indeed we must develop and refine our intellectual skills *as* we develop and refine our intellectual character, to embed the skills in our character and shape our character through the skills.

People not only *can*, but often *do* create the illusion of moral character in a variety of ways. For instance we systematically confuse group mores with universal moral standards. When people act in accordance with the injunctions and taboos of their groups they naturally feel righteous. They receive much praise in moral terms. They may even be treated as moral leaders, if they act in a striking or moving fashion. For this reason, people often cannot distinguish moral from religious conformity or demagoguery from genuine moral integrity.

Genuine moral integrity requires intellectual character, for *bona fide* moral decisions require thoughtful discrimination between what is ethically justified and what is merely socially approved. Group norms are typically articulated in the language of morality and a socialized person inwardly experiences shame or guilt for violating a social taboo. In other words, what we often take to be the inner voice of conscience is merely the internalized voice of social authority — the voice of our mother and father, our teachers and other "superiors" speaking within us.

Another common way we systematically create the illusion of morality is through egocentrically structured self-deception, the shaping and justification of self-serving perceptions and viewpoints. When engaged in such spontaneous thought we systematically confuse our viewpoint with reality itself. We do not experience ourselves as selecting among a range of possible perceptions; quite the contrary, it seems to us that we are simply observing things as they are. What is really egocentric intellectual arrogance we experience as righteous moral judgment. This leads us to see those who disagree with us as fools, dissemblers, or worse.

Since our inner voice tells us our motives are pure and we see things as they really are, those who set themselves against us, or threaten to impede our plans, seem the manifestation of evil. If they use violence to advance their ends, we experience their action as aggressive, as blind to human rights and simple justice. But if we use it, it is justifiable self-defense, restoring law and order, protecting right and justice.

Self-announced prejudice almost never exists. Prejudice almost always exists in obscured, rationalized, socially validated, functional forms. It enables people to sleep peacefully at night even while flagrantly abusing the rights of others. It enables people to get more of what they want, or to get it more easily. It is often sanctioned with a superabundance of pomp and ceremony. It often appears as the very will of God. Unless we recognize these powerful tendencies toward selfish thought in our social institutions, in what appear to be lofty actions, we will not face squarely the problem of education.

Education, properly conceived, cultivates knowledge through higher order thinking, a process which simultaneously cultivates traits of mind intrinsic to the standards and values presupposed by fairmindedness. Unless we take the tendency toward selfish thinking seriously, we are apt to contribute to students' critical thinking only in the narrow-minded sense.

The Spirit of Critical Thinking

To tie all of the above together, consider how the concept of critical thinking can be unpacked. The term 'critical', as we use it, does not mean thinking which is negative or finds fault, but rather thinking which evaluates reasons and brings thought and action in line with our evaluations, our best sense of what is true. The ideal of the critical thinker could be roughly expressed in the phrase 'reasonable person'. Our use of the term 'critical' is intended to highlight the intellectual *autonomy* of the critical thinker. That is, as a critical thinker, I do not simply accept conclusions (uncritically). I evaluate or critique reasons. My critique enables me to distinguish poor from strong reasoning. To do so to the greatest extent possible, I make use of a number of identifiable and learnable skills. I analyze and evaluate reasons and evidence; make assumptions explicit and evaluate them; reject unwarranted inferences or "leaps of logic"; use the best and most complete evidence available to me; make relevant distinctions; clarify; avoid inconsistency and contradiction; reconcile apparent contradictions; and distinguish what I know from what I merely suspect to be true.

The uncritical thinker, on the other hand, doesn't reflect on or evaluate reasons for a particular set of beliefs. By simply agreeing or disagreeing, the uncritical thinker accepts or rejects conclusions, often without understanding them, and often on the basis of egocentric attachment or unassessed desire. Lacking skills to analyze and evaluate, this person allows irrelevant reasons to influence conclusions, doesn't notice assumptions and therefore fails to evaluate them, accepts any inference that "sounds good"; is unconcerned with the strength and completeness of evidence, can't sort out ideas, confuses different concepts, is an unclear thinker, is oblivious to contradictions, and feels certain, even when not in a position to know. The classic uncritical thinker says, "I've made up my mind! Don't confuse me with the facts." Yet, critical thinking is more than evaluation of simple lines of thought.

As I evaluate beliefs by evaluating the evidence or reasoning that supports them (that is, the "arguments" for them), I notice certain things. I learn that sometimes I must go beyond evaluating small lines of reasoning. To understand an issue, I may have to think about it for a long time, weigh many reasons, and clarify basic ideas. I see that evaluating a particular line of thought often forces me to re-evaluate another. A conclusion about one case forces me to come to a certain conclusion about another. I find that often my evaluation of someone's thinking pivots around the meaning of a concept, which I must clarify. Such clarification affects my understanding of other issues. I notice previously hidden relationships between beliefs about different issues. I see that some beliefs and ideas are more fundamental than others. As I think my way through my beliefs, I find I must orchestrate the skills I have learned into a longer series of moves. As I strive for consistency and understanding, I discover opposing sets of basic assumptions which underlie those conclusions. I find that, to make my beliefs reasonable, I must evaluate not individual beliefs but, rather, large sets of beliefs. Analysis of an issue requires more work, a more extended process, than that required for a short line of reasoning. I must learn to use my skills, not in separate little moves but together, coordinated into a long sequence of thought.

Sometimes, two apparently equally strong arguments or lines of reasoning about the same issue come to contradictory conclusions. That is, when I listen to one side, the case seems strong. Yet when I listen to the other side, that case seems equally strong. Since they contradict each other, they cannot both be right. Sometimes it seems that the two sides are talking about different situations or speaking different languages, even living in different "worlds". I find that the skills which enable me to evaluate a short bit of reasoning do not offer much help here.

Suppose I decide to question two people who hold contradictory conclusions on an issue. They may use concepts or terms differently, disagree about what terms apply to what situations and what inferences can then be made, or state the issue differently. I may find that the differences in their conclusions rest, not so much on a particular piece of evidence or on one inference, as much as on vastly different perspectives, different ways of seeing the world, or different conceptions of such basic ideas as, say, human nature. As their conclusions arise from different perspectives, each, to the other, seems deluded, prejudiced, or naive. How am I to decide who is right? My evaluations of their inferences, uses of terms, evidence, etc. also depend on perspective. In a sense, I discover that *I have a perspective.*

I could simply agree with the one whose overall perspective is most like my own. But how do I know I'm right? If I'm sincerely interested in evaluating beliefs, should I not also consider things from other perspectives?

As I reflect on this discovery, I may also realize that my perspective has changed. Perhaps I recall learning a new idea or even a system of thought that changed the way I see myself and the world around me in fundamental ways, which even changed my life. I may remember how pervasive this change was — how I began to interpret a whole range of situations differently, continually used a new word, concept, or phrase, paid attention to previously ignored facts. I realize that I now have a new choice regarding the issue under scrutiny.

I could simply accept the view that most closely resembles my own. But I realize that I cannot reasonably reject the other perspective unless I understand it. To do so would be to say, "I don't know what you think, but whatever it is, it's false." The other perspective, however strange it seems to me now, may have something both important and true, which I have overlooked and without which my understanding is incomplete. Thinking along these lines, I open my mind to the possibility of change of perspective. I make sure that I don't subtly ignore or dismiss these new ideas; I realize I can make my point of view richer, so it encompasses more. As I think within another perspective, I begin to see ways in which it is right. It points out complicating factors I had previously ignored, makes useful distinctions I had missed, offers plausible interpretations of events I had never considered, and so on. I become able to move between various perspectives, freed from the limitations of my earlier thought.

One of the most important stages in my development as a thinker, then, is a clear recognition that I have a perspective, one that I must work on and change as I learn and grow. To do this, I can't be inflexibly attached to any particular beliefs. I strive for a consistent "big picture". I approach other perspectives differently. I ask how I can reconcile the points of view. I use principles and insights flexibly and do not approach analysis as a mechanical, "step one, step two" process. I pursue new ideas in depth, trying to understand the perspectives from which they come. I am willing to say, "This view sounds new and different; I don't yet understand it. There's more to this idea than I realized; I can't just dismiss it."

Looked at another way, suppose I'm rethinking my stand on an issue. I re-examine my evidence. Yet, I cannot evaluate my evidence for its completeness unless I consider evidence cited by those who disagree with me. Similarly, I find I can discover my basic assumptions by considering alternative assumptions, alternative perspectives. I can examine my own interpretation of situations and principles by considering alternative interpretations. I learn to use fairmindedness to clarify, enhance, and improve my perspective.

A narrowminded critical thinker, lacking this insight, says not, "This is how *I* see it," but, "This is how *it is*." While working on pieces of reasoning, separate arguments, and individual beliefs, this person tends to overlook the development of perspective as such. Such thinking consists of separate or fragmented ideas and the examination of beliefs one at a time without appreciation for connections between them. While conscious and reflective about particular conclusions, this type of thinker is unreflective about his or her own point of view, how it affects his or her evaluations of reasoning, and how it is limited. When confronted with alternative perspectives or points of view, this person assesses them by their degree of agreement with his or her own view. Such an individual is given to sweeping acceptance or sweeping rejection of points of view and is tyrannized by the words he or she uses. Rather than trying to understand why others think as they do, such people dismiss new ideas, assuming the objectivity and correctness of their own beliefs and responses.

As I strive to think fairmindedly, I discover resistance to questioning my beliefs and considering those of others. I find a conflict between my desire to be fairminded and my desire to feel sure of what I think. It sometimes seems a lot easier to avoid the confusion, frustration, and embarrassment that I feel when re-assessing my beliefs. Simply trying to ignore these feelings doesn't make them go away. I realize that unless I directly address these obstacles to fairminded critical thought, I tend to seek its appearance rather than its reality, that I tend to accept rhetoric rather than fact, that without noticing it, I hide my own hypocrisy, even from myself.

By contrast, the critical thinker who lacks this insight, though a good arguer, is not a truly reasonable person. Giving good-sounding reasons, this person can find and explain flaws in

385

opposing views and has well-thought-out ideas, but this thinker never subjects his or her own ideas to scrutiny. Though giving lip service to fairmindedness and describing views opposed to his or her own, this thinker doesn't truly understand or seriously consider them. One who often uses reasoning to get his or her way, cover up hidden motives, or make others look stupid or deluded is merely using skills to reinforce his or her own views and desires, without subjecting them to scrutiny. Such people are not truly reasonable. By cutting themselves off from honestly assessing their own perspectives or seriously considering other perspectives, these people are not using their mental capacities to their fullest extent.

To sum up, the fully reasonable person, the kind of critical thinker we want to foster, contrasts with at least two other kinds of thinkers. The first kind has few intellectual skills of any kind and tends to be naive, easily confused, manipulated, and controlled, and therefore easily defeated or taken in. The second has skills, but only of a restricted type, which enable pursuit of narrow, selfish interests and effective manipulation of the naive and unsuspecting. The first we call "uncritical thinkers" and the second "weak sense", or selfish, critical thinkers. What we aim at, therefore, are "strong sense" critical thinkers, those who use the fullest powers of their minds in the service of sincere, fairminded understanding and evaluation of their beliefs.

Glossary: An Educator's Guide to Critical Thinking Terms and Concepts

accurate: Free from errors, mistakes, or distortion. *Correct* connotes little more than absence of error; *accurate* implies a positive exercise of one to obtain conformity with fact or truth; *exact* stresses perfect conformity to fact, truth, or some standard; *precise* suggests minute accuracy of detail. Accuracy is an important goal in critical thinking, though it is almost always a matter of degree. It is also important to recognize that making mistakes is an essential part of learning and that it is far better that students make their own mistakes, than that they parrot the thinking of the text or teacher. It should also be recognized that some distortion usually results whenever we think within a point of view or frame of reference. Students should think with this awareness in mind, with some sense of the limitations of their own, the text's, the teacher's, the subject's perspective. See *perfections of thought.*

ambiguous: A sentence having two or more possible meanings. Sensitivity to ambiguity and vagueness in writing and speech is essential to good thinking. *A continual effort to be clear and precise in language usage is fundamental to education.* Ambiguity is a problem more of sentences than of individual words. Furthermore, not every sentence that can be construed in more than one way is problematic and deserving of analysis. Many sentences are clearly intended one way; any other construal is obviously absurd and not meant. For example, "Make me a sandwich." is never seriously intended to request metamorphic change. It is a poor example for teaching genuine insight into critical thinking. For an example of a problematic ambiguity, consider the statement, "Welfare is corrupt." Among the possible meanings of this sentence are the following: Those who administer welfare programs take bribes to administer welfare policy unfairly; Welfare policies are written in such a way that much of the money goes to people who don't deserve it rather than to those who do; A government that gives money to people who haven't earned it corrupts both the giver and the recipient. If two people are arguing about whether or not welfare is corrupt, but interpret the claim differently, they can make little or no progress; they aren't arguing about the same point. Evidence and considerations relevant to one interpretation may be irrelevant to others.

analyze: To break up a whole into its parts, to examine in detail so as to determine the nature of, to look more deeply into an issue or situation. *All learning presupposes some analysis of what we are learning,* if only by categorizing or labelling things in one way rather than another. Students should continually be asked to analyze their ideas, claims, experiences, interpretations, judgments, and theories and those they hear and read. See *elements of thought.*

argue: There are two meanings of this word that need to be distinguished: *1)* to argue in the sense of *to fight* or to emotionally disagree; and *2)* to give reasons for or against a proposal or proposition. In emphasizing critical thinking, we continually try to get our students to move from the first sense of the word to the second; that is, we try to get them to see the importance of *giving reasons* to support their views without getting their egos involved in what they are saying. This is a fundamental problem in human life. To argue in the critical thinking sense is to use logic and reason, and to bring forth facts to support or refute a point. It is done in a spirit of cooperation and good will.

argument: A reason or reasons offered for or against something, the offering of such reasons. This term refers to a discussion in which there is disagreement and suggests the use of logic and bringing forth of facts to support or refute a point. See *argue.*

to assume: To take for granted or to presuppose. Critical thinkers can and do make their assumptions explicit, assess them, and correct them. Assumptions can vary from the mundane to the problematic: I heard a scratch at the door. I got up to let the cat in. I *assumed* that only the cat makes that noise, and that he makes it only when he wants to be let in. Someone speaks gruffly to me. I feel guilty and hurt. I assume he is angry *at me,* that he is only angry at me when I do something bad, and that if he's angry at me, he dislikes me. *Notice that people often equate making assumptions with making false assumptions.* When people say, "Don't assume", this is what they mean. In fact, we cannot avoid making assumptions and some are justifiable. (For instance, we have assumed that people who buy this book can read English.) Rather than saying "Never assume", we say, "Be aware of and careful about the assumptions you make, and be ready to examine and critique them." See *assumption, elements of thought.*

assumption: A statement accepted or supposed as true without proof or demonstration; an unstated premise or belief. *All human thought and experience is based on assumptions.* Our thought must begin with something we take to be true in a particular context. We are typically unaware of what we assume and therefore rarely question our assumptions. Much of what is wrong with human thought can be found in the uncritical or unexamined assumptions that underlie it. For example, we often experience the world in such a way as to assume that we are observing things just as they are, as though we were seeing the world without the filter of a point of view. People we disagree with, of course, we recognize as *having a point of view.* One of the key dispositions of critical thinking is the on-going sense that as humans we always think within a perspective, that we virtually never experience things totally and absolutistically. There is a connection, therefore, between thinking so as to be *aware of our assumptions* and being *intellectually humble*.

authority: *1)* The power or supposed right to give commands, enforce obedience, take action, or make final decisions. *2)* A person with much knowledge and expertise in a field, hence reliable. Critical thinkers recognize that ultimate authority rests with reason and evidence, since it is only on the assumption that purported experts have the backing of reason and evidence that they rightfully gain authority. Much instruction discourages critical thinking by encouraging students to believe that whatever the text or teacher says is true. As a result, students do not learn how to assess authority. See *knowledge*.

bias: A mental leaning or inclination. We must clearly distinguish two different senses of the word 'bias'. One is neutral, the other negative. In the neutral sense we are referring simply to the fact that, *because of one's point of view, one notices some things rather than others*, emphasizes some points rather than others, and thinks in one direction rather than others. This is not in itself a criticism because *thinking within a point of view is unavoidable*. In the negative sense, we are implying *blindness or irrational resistance to weaknesses within one's own point of view* or to the strength or insight within a point of view one opposes. Fairminded critical thinkers try to be aware of their bias (in sense one) and try hard to avoid bias (in sense two). Many people confuse these two senses. Many confuse bias with emotion or with evaluation, perceiving any expression of emotion or any use of evaluative words to be biased (sense two). Evaluative words that can be justified by reason and evidence are not biased in the negative sense. See *criteria, evaluation, judgment, opinion*.

clarify: To make easier to understand, to free from confusion or ambiguity, to remove obscurities. *Clarity* is a fundamental perfection of thought and *clarification* a fundamental aim in critical thinking. Students often do not see why it is important to write and speak clearly, why it is important to *say what you mean and mean what you say*. The key to clarification is *concrete, specific* examples. See *accurate, ambiguous, logic of language, vague*.

concept: An idea or thought, especially a generalized idea of a thing or of a class of things. Humans think within concepts or ideas. *We can never achieve command over our thoughts unless we learn how to achieve command over our concepts or ideas.* Thus we must learn how to identify the concepts or ideas we are using, contrast them with alternative concepts or ideas, and clarify what we include and exclude by means of them. For example, most people say they believe strongly in democracy, but few can clarify with examples what that word does and does not imply. *Most people confuse the meaning of words with cultural associations*, with the result that 'democracy' means to people whatever *we* do in running *our* government — any country that is different is undemocratic. We must distinguish the concepts implicit in the English language from the psychological associations surrounding that concept in a given social group or culture. The failure to develop this ability is a major cause of uncritical thought and selfish critical thought. See *logic of language*.

conclude/conclusion: To decide by reasoning, to infer, to deduce; the last step in a reasoning process; a judgment, decision, or belief formed after investigation or reasoning. All beliefs, decisions, or actions are based on human thought, but rarely as the result of conscious reasoning or deliberation. *All that we believe is*, one way or another, *based on conclusions* that we have come to during our lifetime. Yet, we rarely monitor our thought processes, we don't critically assess the conclusions we come to, to determine whether we have sufficient grounds or reasons for accepting them. People seldom recognize when they have come to a conclusion. They confuse their conclusions with evidence, and so cannot assess the reasoning that took them from evidence to conclusion. Recognizing that *human life is inferential*, that we continually come to conclusions about ourselves and the things and persons around us, is essential to thinking critically and reflectively.

consistency: To think, act, or speak in agreement with what has already been thought, done, or expressed; to have intellectual or moral integrity. Human life and thought is filled with inconsistency, hypocrisy, and contradiction. We often say one thing and do another, judge ourselves and our friends by one standard and our antagonists by another, lean over backwards to justify what we want or negate what does not serve our interests. Similarly, we often confuse desires with needs, treating our desires as equivalent to needs, putting what we want above the basic needs of others. *Logical and moral consistency are fundamental values of fairminded critical thinking.* Social conditioning and native egocentrism often obscure social contradictions, inconsistency, and hypocrisy. See *personal contradiction, social contradiction, intellectual integrity, human nature.*

contradict/contradiction: To assert the opposite of; to be contrary to, go against; a statement in opposition to another; a condition in which things tend to be contrary to each other; inconsistency; discrepancy; a person or thing containing or composed of contradictory elements. See *personal contradiction, social contradiction.*

criterion (criteria, pl): A standard, rule, or test by which something can be judged or measured. Human life, thought, and action are based on human values. The standards by which we determine whether those values are achieved in any situation represent criteria. Critical thinking depends upon making explicit the standards or criteria for rational or justifiable thinking and behavior. See *evaluation.*

critical listening: A mode of monitoring how we are listening so as to maximize our accurate understanding of what another person is saying. By understanding the logic of human communication — that *everything spoken expresses point of view*, uses some ideas and not others, has implications, etc. — critical thinkers can listen so as to enter sympathetically and analytically into the perspective of others. See *critical speaking, critical reading, critical writing, elements of thought, intellectual empathy.*

critical person: One who has mastered a range of intellectual skills and abilities. If that person generally uses those skills to advance his or her own selfish interests, that person is a critical thinker only in a weak or qualified sense. If that person generally uses those skills fairmindedly, entering empathically into the points of view of others, he or she is a critical thinker in the strong or fullest sense. See *critical thinking.*

critical reading: Critical reading is an active, intellectually engaged process in which the reader participates in an inner dialogue with the writer. Most people read uncritically and so miss some part of what is expressed while distorting other parts. A critical reader realizes the way in which *reading, by its very nature, means entering into a point of view other than our own*, the point of view of the writer. A critical reader actively looks for assumptions, key concepts and ideas, reasons and justifications, supporting examples, parallel experiences, implications and consequences, and any other structural features of the written text, to interpret and assess it accurately and fairly. See *elements of thought.*

critical society: A society which rewards adherence to the values of critical thinking and hence *does not use indoctrination and inculcation as basic modes of learning* (rewards reflective questioning, intellectual independence, and reasoned dissent). Socrates is not the only thinker to imagine a society in which independent critical thought became embodied in the concrete day-to-day lives of individuals; William Graham Sumner, North America's distinguished anthropologist, explicitly formulated the ideal:

> The critical habit of thought, if usual in a society, will pervade all its mores, because it is a way of taking up the problems of life. Men educated in it cannot be stampeded by stump orators and are never deceived by dithyrambic oratory. They are slow to believe. They can hold things as possible or probable in all degrees, without certainty and without pain. They can wait for evidence and weigh evidence, uninfluenced by the emphasis or confidence with which assertions are made on one side or the other. They can resist appeals to their dearest prejudices and all kinds of cajolery. Education in the critical faculty is the only education of which it can be truly said that it makes good citizens. (*Folkways*, 1906)

Until critical habits of thought pervade our society, however, there will be a tendency for schools as social institutions to transmit the prevailing world view more or less uncritically, to transmit it as reality, not as a picture of reality. Education for critical thinking, then, requires that the school or classroom become a microcosm of a critical society. See *didactic instruction, dialogical instruction, intellectual virtues, knowledge.*

critical thinking: *1)* Disciplined, self-directed thinking which exemplifies the perfections of thinking appropriate to a particular mode or domain of thinking. *2)* Thinking that displays mastery of intellectual skills and abilities. *3)* The art of thinking about your thinking while you are thinking in order to make your thinking better: more clear, more accurate, or more defensible. Critical thinking can be distinguished into two forms: "selfish" or "sophistic", on the one hand, and "fairminded", on the other. In thinking critically we use our command of the elements of thinking to adjust our thinking successfully to the logical demands of a type or mode of thinking. See *critical person, critical society, critical reading, critical listening, critical writing, perfections of thought, elements of thought, domains of thought, intellectual virtues.*

critical writing: To express ourselves in language requires that we arrange our ideas in some relationships to each other. When accuracy and truth are at issue, then we must understand what our thesis is, how we can support it, how we can elaborate it to make it intelligible to others, what objections can be raised to it from other points of view, what the limitations are to our point of view, and so forth. *Disciplined writing requires disciplined thinking; disciplined thinking is achieved through disciplined writing.* See *critical listening, critical reading, logic of language.*

critique: An objective judging, analysis, or evaluation of something. The purpose of critique is the same as the purpose of critical thinking: to appreciate strengths as well as weaknesses, virtues as well as failings. *Critical thinkers critique in order to redesign, remodel, and make better.*

cultural association: Undisciplined thinking often reflects associations, personal and cultural, absorbed or uncritically formed. If a person who was cruel to me as a child had a particular tone of voice, I may find myself disliking a person who has the same tone of voice. Media advertising juxtaposes and joins logically unrelated things to influence our buying habits. Raised in a particular country or within a particular group within it, we form any number of mental links which, if they remain unexamined, unduly influence our thinking. See *concept, critical society.*

cultural assumption: Unassessed (often implicit) belief adopted by virtue of upbringing in a society. Raised in a society, we unconsciously take on its point of view, values, beliefs, and practices. At the root of each of these are many kinds of assumptions. Not knowing that we perceive, conceive, think, and experience within assumptions we have taken in, we take ourselves to be perceiving "things as they are", not "things as they appear from a cultural vantage point". Becoming aware of our cultural assumptions so that we might critically examine them is a crucial dimension of critical thinking. It is, however, a dimension almost totally absent from schooling. Lip service to this ideal is common enough; a realistic emphasis is virtually unheard of. See *ethnocentricity, prejudice, social contradiction.*

data: Facts, figures, or information from which conclusions can be inferred, or upon which interpretations or theories can be based. As critical thinkers we must make certain to distinguish hard data from the inferences or conclusions we draw from them.

dialectical thinking: Dialogical thinking (thinking within more than one perspective) conducted to test the strengths and weaknesses of opposing points of view. (Court trials and debates are, in a sense, dialectical.) When thinking dialectically, reasoners pit two or more opposing points of view in competition with each other, developing each by providing support, raising objections, countering those objections, raising further objections, and so on. Dialectical thinking or discussion can be conducted so as to "win" by defeating the positions one disagrees with — using critical insight to support one's own view and point out flaws in other views (associated with critical thinking in the restricted or weak sense), or fairmindedly, by conceding points that don't stand up to critique, trying to integrate or incorporate strong points found in other views, and using critical insight to develop a fuller and more accurate view (associated with critical thinking in the fuller or strong sense). See *monological problems.*

dialogical instruction: Instruction that fosters dialogical or dialectic thinking. Thus, when considering a question, the class brings all relevant subjects to bear and considers the perspectives of groups whose views are not canvassed in their texts — for example, "What did King George think of the *Declaration of Independence*, the Revolutionary War, the Continental Congress, Jefferson and Washington, etc.?" or, "How would an economist analyze this situation? A historian? A psychologist? A geographer?" See *critical society, didactic instruction, higher order learning, lower order learning, Socratic questioning, knowledge.*

dialogical thinking: Thinking that involves a dialogue or extended exchange between different points of view or frames of reference. Students learn best in dialogical situations, in circumstances in which they continually express their views to others and try to fit other's views into their own. See *Socratic questioning, monological thinking, multilogical thinking, dialectical thinking.*

didactic instruction: Teaching by telling. In didactic instruction, the teacher directly tells the student what to believe and think about a subject. The student's task is to remember what the teacher said and reproduce it on demand. In its most common form, this mode of teaching falsely assumes that one can directly give a person knowledge without that person having to think his or her way to it. It falsely assumes that knowledge can be separated from understanding and justification. It confuses the ability to *state* a principle with *understanding* it, the ability to *supply* a definition with *knowing* a new word, and the act of *saying* that something is important with *recognizing* its importance. See *critical society, knowledge.*

domains of thought: Thinking can be oriented or structured with different issues or purposes in view. *Thinking varies in accordance with purpose and issue.* Critical thinkers learn to discipline their thinking to take into account the nature of the issue or domain. We see this most clearly when we consider the difference between issues and thinking within different academic disciplines or subject areas. Hence, mathematical thinking is quite different from, say, historical thinking. Mathematics and history, we can say then, represent different domains of thought. See the *logic of questions.*

egocentricity: A tendency to view everything in relationship to oneself; to confuse immediate perception (how things *seem*) with reality. One's desires, values, and beliefs (seeming to be self-evidently correct or superior to those of others) are often uncritically used as the norm of all judgment and experience. Egocentricity is one of the fundamental impediments to critical thinking. As one learns to think critically in a strong sense, one learns to become more rational, and less egocentric. See *human nature, strong sense critical thinker, ethnocentrism, sociocentrism, personal contradiction.*

elements of thought: All thought has a universal set of elements, each of which can be monitored for possible problems: Are we clear about our *purpose or goal?* about the *problem or question at issue?* about our *point of view or frame of reference?* about our *assumptions?* about the *claims* we are making? about the *reasons or evidence* upon which we are basing our claims? about our *inferences and line of reasoning?* about the *implications and consequences* that follow from our reasoning? Critical thinkers develop skills of identifying and assessing these elements in their thinking and in the thinking of others.

emotion: A feeling aroused to the point of awareness, often a strong feeling or state of excitement. When our egocentric emotions or feelings get involved, when we are excited by infantile anger, fear, jealousy, etc., our objectivity often decreases. Critical thinkers need to be able to monitor their egocentric feelings and use their rational passions to reason themselves into feelings appropriate to the situation as it really is, rather than to how it seems to their infantile ego. Emotions and feelings themselves are not irrational; however, it is common for people to feel strongly when their ego is stimulated.

One way to understand the goal of strong sense critical thinking is as the attempt to develop rational feelings and emotions at the expense of irrational, egocentric ones. See *rational passions, intellectual virtues.*

empirical: Relying or based on experiment, observation, or experience rather than on theory or meaning. *It is important to continually distinguish those considerations based on experiment, observation, or experience from those based on the meaning of a word or concept or the implications of a theory.* One common form of uncritical or selfish critical thinking involves distorting facts or experience in order to preserve a preconceived meaning or theory. For example, a conservative may distort the facts that support a liberal perspective to prevent empirical evidence from counting against a theory of the world that he or she holds rigidly. Indeed, within all perspectives and belief systems many will distort the facts before they will admit to a weakness in their favorite theory or belief. See *data, fact, evidence.*

empirical implication: That which follows from a situation or fact, not due to the logic of language, but from experience or scientific law. The redness of the coil on the stove empirically implies dangerous heat.

ethnocentricity: A tendency to view one's own race or culture as central, based on the deep-seated belief that one's own group is superior to all others. Ethnocentrism is a form of egocentrism extended from the self to the group. Much uncritical or selfish critical thinking is either egocentric or ethnocentric in nature. ('Ethnocentrism' and 'sociocentrism' are used synonymously, for the most part, though 'sociocentricity' is broader, relating to *any* group, including, for example, sociocentricity regarding one's profession.) The "cure" for ethnocentrism or sociocentrism is empathic thought within the perspective of opposing groups and cultures. Such empathic thought is rarely cultivated in the societies and schools of today. Instead, many people develop an empty rhetoric of tolerance, saying that others have different beliefs and ways, but without seriously considering those beliefs and ways, what they mean to those others, and their reasons for maintaining them.

evaluation: To judge or determine the worth or quality of. *Evaluation has a logic and should be carefully distinguished from mere subjective preference.* The elements of its logic may be put in the form of questions which may be asked whenever an evaluation is to be carried out: *1)* Are we clear about *what precisely we are evaluating?*; *2)* Are we clear about *our purpose?* Is our purpose legitimate?; *3)* Given our purpose, what are the *relevant criteria or standards* for evaluation?; *4)* Do we have *sufficient information* about that which we are evaluating? Is that *information relevant to the purpose?*; and *5)* Have we *applied our criteria accurately and fairly to the facts* as we know them? Uncritical thinkers often treat evaluation as mere preference or treat their evaluative judgments as direct observations not admitting of error.

evidence: The data on which a judgment or conclusion might be based or by which proof or probability might be established. Critical thinkers distinguish the evidence or raw data upon which they base their interpretations or conclusions from the inferences and assumptions that connect data to conclusions. Uncritical thinkers treat their conclusions as something given to them in experience, as something they directly observe in the world. As a result, they find it difficult to see why anyone might disagree with their conclusions. After all, the truth of their views is, they believe, right there for everyone to see! Such people find it difficult or even impossible to describe the evidence or experience without coloring that description with their interpretation.

explicit: Clearly stated and leaving nothing implied; *explicit* is applied to that which is so clearly stated or distinctly set forth that there should be no doubt as to the meaning; *exact and precise* in this connection both suggest that which is strictly defined, accurately stated, or made unmistakably clear; *definite* implies precise limitations as to the nature, character, meaning, etc. of something; *specific* implies the pointing up of details or the particularizing of references. Critical thinking often requires the ability to be explicit, exact, definite, and specific. Most students cannot make what is *implicit* in their thinking *explicit*. This deficiency hampers their ability to monitor and assess their thinking.

fact: What actually happened, what is true; verifiable by empirical means; distinguished from interpretation, inference, judgment, or conclusion; the raw data. There are distinct senses of the word 'factual': "True" (as opposed to "claimed to be true"); and "empirical" (as opposed to conceptual or evaluative). You may make many "factual claims" in one sense, that is, claims which can be verified or disproven by observation or empirical study, but I must evaluate those claims to determine if they are true. People often confuse these two senses, even to the point of accepting as true, statements which merely "seem factual", for example, "29.23 % of Americans suffer from depression." Before I accept this as true, I should assess it. I should ask such questions as "How do you know? How *could* this be known? Did you merely ask people if they were depressed and extrapolate those results? How exactly did you arrive at this figure?" Purported facts should be assessed for their accuracy, completeness, and relevance to the issue. Sources of purported facts should be assessed for their qualifications, track records, and impartiality. Education which stresses retention and repetition of factual claims stunts students' desire and ability to assess alleged facts, leaving them open to manipulation. Activities in which students are asked to "distinguish fact from opinion" often confuse these two senses. They encourage students to *accept as true* statements which merely "look like" facts. See *intellectual humility, knowledge.*

fair: Treating both or all sides alike without reference to one's own feelings or interests; *just* implies adherence to a standard of rightness or lawfulness without reference to one's own inclinations; *impartial* and *unbiased* both imply freedom from prejudice for or against any side; *dispassionate* implies the absence of passion or strong emotion, hence, connotes cool, disinterested judgment; *objective* implies a viewing of persons or things without reference to oneself, one's interests, etc.

faith: *1)* Unquestioning belief in anything. *2)* Confidence, trust, or reliance. A critical thinker does not accept faith in the first sense, for every belief is reached on the basis of some thinking, which may or may not be justified. Even in religion one believes in one religion rather than another, and in doing so implies that there are good reasons for accepting one rather than another. A Christian, for example, believes that there are good reasons for not being an atheist, and Christians often attempt to persuade non-Christians to change their beliefs. In some sense, then, everyone has confidence in the capacity of his or her own mind to judge rightly on the basis of good reasons, and does not believe simply on the basis of blind faith.

fallacy/fallacious: An error in reasoning; flaw or defect in argument; an argument which doesn't conform to rules of good reasoning (especially one that appears to be sound). Containing or based on a fallacy; deceptive in appearance or meaning; misleading; delusive.

higher order learning: Learning through exploring the foundations, justification, implications, and value of a fact, principle, skill, or concept. *Learning so as to deeply understand.* One can learn in keeping with the rational capacities of the human mind or in keeping with its irrational propensities, cultivating the capacity of the human mind to discipline and direct its thought through commitment to intellectual standards, or one can learn through mere association. Education for critical thought produces higher order learning by helping students actively think their way to conclusions; discuss their thinking with other students and the teacher; entertain a variety of points of view; analyze concepts, theories, and explanations in their own terms; actively question the meaning and implications of what they learn; compare what they learn to what they have experienced; take what they read and write seriously; solve non-routine problems; examine assumptions; and gather and assess evidence. Students should learn each subject by engaging in thought within that subject. They should learn history by thinking historically, mathematics by thinking mathematically, etc. See *dialogical instruction, lower order learning, critical society, knowledge, principle, domains of thought.*

human nature: The common qualities of all human beings. People have both a primary and a secondary nature. Our primary nature is spontaneous, egocentric, and strongly prone to irrational belief formation. It is the basis for our instinctual thought. People need no training to believe what they want to believe: what serves their immediate interests, what preserves their sense of personal comfort and righteousness, what minimizes their sense of inconsistency, and what presupposes their own correctness. People need no special training to believe what those around them believe: what their parents and friends believe, what is taught to them by religious and school authorities, what is repeated often by the media, and what is commonly believed in the nation in which they are raised. People need no training to think that those who disagree with them are wrong and probably prejudiced. People need no training to assume that their own most fundamental beliefs are self-evidently true or easily justified by evidence. People naturally and spontaneously identify with their own beliefs. They experience most disagreement as personal attack. The resulting defensiveness interferes with their capacity to empathize with or enter into other points of view.

On the other hand, *people need extensive and systematic practice to develop their secondary nature, their implicit capacity to function as rational persons.* They need extensive and systematic practice to recognize the tendencies they have to form irrational beliefs. They need extensive practice to develop a dislike of inconsistency, a love of clarity, a passion to seek reasons and evidence and to be fair to points of view other than their own. People need extensive practice to recognize that they indeed have a point of view, that they live inferentially, that they do not have a direct pipeline to reality, that it is perfectly possible to have an overwhelming inner sense of the correctness of one's views and still be wrong. See *intellectual virtues.*

idea: Anything existing in the mind as an object of knowledge or thought; *concept* refers to generalized idea of a class of objects, based on knowledge of particular instances of the class;

conception, often equivalent to concept, specifically refers to something conceived in the mind or imagined; *thought* refers to any idea, whether or not expressed, that occurs to the mind in reasoning or contemplation; *notion* implies vagueness or incomplete intention; *impression* also implies vagueness of an idea provoked by some external stimulus. Critical thinkers are aware of what ideas they are using in their thinking, where those ideas came from, and how to assess them. See *clarify, concept, logic, logic of language.*

imply/implication: A claim or truth which follows from other claims or truths. One of the most important skills of critical thinking is the ability to distinguish between what is actually implied by a statement or situation from what may be carelessly inferred by people. Critical thinkers try to *monitor their inferences to keep them in line with what is actually implied* by what they know. When speaking, critical thinkers *try to use words that imply only what they can legitimately justify.* They recognize that there are established word usages which generate established implications. To say of an act that it is murder, for example, is to imply that it is intentional and unjustified. See *clarify, precision, logic of language, critical listening, critical reading, elements of thought.*

infer/inference: An inference is a step of the mind, an intellectual act by which one concludes that something is so in light of something else's being so, or seeming to be so. If you come at me with a knife in your hand, I would probably infer that you mean to do me harm. Inferences can be strong or weak, justified or unjustified. Inferences are based upon assumptions. See *imply/implication.*

insight: The ability to see and clearly and deeply understand the inner nature of things. Instruction for critical thinking fosters insight rather than mere performance; it cultivates the achievement of deeper knowledge and understanding through insight. *Thinking one's way into and through a subject leads to insights* as one synthesizes what one is learning, relating one subject to other subjects and all subjects to personal experience. Rarely is insight formulated as a goal in present curricula and texts. See *dialogical instruction, higher order learning, lower order learning, didactic instruction, intellectual humility.*

intellectual autonomy: Having rational control of ones beliefs, values, and inferences. The ideal of critical thinking is to learn to think for oneself, to gain command over one's thought processes. Intellectual autonomy does not entail willfulness, stubbornness, or rebellion. It entails a commitment to analyzing and evaluating beliefs on the basis of reason and evidence, to question when it is rational to question, to believe when it is rational to believe, and to conform when it is rational to conform. See *know, knowledge.*

(intellectual) confidence or faith in reason: Confidence that in the long run *one's own higher interests and those of humankind at large will best be served by giving the freest play to reason* — by encouraging people to come to their own conclusions through a process of developing their own rational faculties; faith that (with proper encouragement and cultivation) people can learn to think for themselves, form rational viewpoints, draw reasonable conclusions, think coherently and logically, persuade each other by reason, and become reasonable, despite the deep-seated obstacles in the native character of the human mind and in society. Confidence in reason is developed through experiences in which one reasons one's way to insight, solves problems through reason, uses reason to persuade, is persuaded by reason. Confidence in reason is undermined when one is expected to perform tasks without understanding why, to repeat statements without having verified or justified them, to accept beliefs on the sole basis of authority or social pressure.

intellectual courage: The willingness to face and fairly assess ideas, beliefs, or viewpoints to which we have not given a serious hearing, regardless of our strong negative reactions to them. This courage arises from the recognition that *ideas considered dangerous or absurd are sometimes rationally justified* (in whole or in part), and that *conclusions or beliefs espoused by those around us or inculcated in us are sometimes false or misleading.* To determine for ourselves which is which, we must not passively and uncritically "accept" what we have "learned". Intellectual courage comes into play here, because inevitably we will come to see some truth in some ideas considered dangerous and absurd and some distortion or falsity in some ideas strongly held in our social group. It takes courage to be true to our own thinking in such circumstances. Examining cherished beliefs is difficult, and the penalties for non-conformity are often severe.

intellectual empathy: Understanding the need to imaginatively put oneself in the place of others to genuinely understand them. We must recognize our egocentric tendency to identify truth with our immediate perceptions or longstanding beliefs. Intellectual empathy correlates with the ability to accurately reconstruct the viewpoints and reasoning of others and to *reason from premises, assumptions, and ideas other than our own.* This trait also requires that we remember occasions when we were wrong, despite an intense conviction that we were right, and consider that we might be similarly deceived in a case at hand.

intellectual humility: Awareness of the limits of one's knowledge, including sensitivity to circumstances in which one's native egocentrism is likely to function self-deceptively; sensitivity to bias and prejudice in, and limitations of one's viewpoint. Intellectual humility is based on the recognition that *no one should claim more than he or she actually knows.* It does not imply spinelessness or submissiveness. It implies the lack of intellectual pretentiousness, boastfulness, or conceit, combined with insight into the strengths or weaknesses of the logical foundations of one's beliefs.

intellectual integrity: Recognition of the need to be true to one's own thinking, to be consistent in the intellectual standards one applies, to hold oneself to the same rigorous standards of evidence and proof to which one holds one's antagonists, to practice what one advocates for others, and to honestly admit discrepancies and inconsistencies in one's own thought and action. This trait develops best in a supportive atmosphere in which people feel secure and free enough to honestly acknowledge their inconsistencies, and can develop and share realistic ways of ameliorating them. It requires honest acknowledgment of the difficulties of achieving greater consistency.

intellectual perseverance: Willingness and consciousness of the need to pursue intellectual insights and truths despite difficulties, obstacles, and frustrations; firm adherence to rational principles despite irrational opposition of others; a sense of the need to struggle with confusion and unsettled questions over an extended period of time in order to achieve deeper understanding or insight. This trait is undermined when teachers and others continually provide the answers, do students' thinking for them or substitute easy tricks, algorithms, and short cuts for careful, independent thought.

intellectual sense of justice: Willingness and consciousness of the need to entertain all viewpoints sympathetically and to assess them with the same intellectual standards, without reference to one's own feelings or vested interests, or the feelings or vested interests of one's friends, community, or nation; implies adherence to intellectual standards without reference to one's own advantage or the advantage of one's group.

intellectual virtues: The traits of mind and character necessary for right action and thinking; the traits of mind and character essential for fairminded rationality; the traits that distinguish the narrowminded, self-serving critical thinker from the openminded, truth-seeking critical thinker. These *intellectual traits are interdependent*. Each is best developed while developing the others as well. They cannot be imposed from without; they must be cultivated by encouragement and example. People can come to deeply understand and accept these principles by analyzing their experiences of them: learning from an unfamiliar perspective, discovering you don't know as much as you thought, and so on. They include: intellectual sense of justice, intellectual perseverance, intellectual integrity, intellectual humility, intellectual empathy, intellectual courage, (intellectual) confidence in reason, and intellectual autonomy.

interpret/interpretation: To give one's own conception of, to place in the context of one's own experience, perspective, point of view, or philosophy. Interpretations should be distinguished from the facts, the evidence, the situation. (I may interpret someone's silence as an expression of hostility toward me. Such an interpretation may or may not be correct. I may have projected my patterns of motivation and behavior onto that person, or I may have accurately noticed this pattern in the other.) The best interpretations take the most evidence into account. Critical thinkers recognize their interpretations, distinguish them from evidence, consider alternative interpretations, and reconsider their interpretations in the light of new evidence. *All learning involves personal interpretation, since whatever we learn we must integrate into our own thinking and action.* What we learn must be given a meaning by us, must be meaningful to us, and hence involves interpretive acts on our part. Didactic instruction, in attempting to directly implant knowledge in students' minds, typically ignores the role of personal interpretation in learning.

intuition: The direct knowing or learning of something without the conscious use of reasoning. We sometimes seem to know or learn things without recognizing how we came to that knowledge. When this occurs, we experience an inner sense that what we believe is true. The problem is that sometimes we are correct (and have genuinely experienced an intuition) and sometimes we are incorrect (having fallen victim to one of our prejudices). A critical thinker does not blindly accept that what he or she thinks or believes but cannot account for is necessarily true. A critical thinker realizes how easily we confuse intuitions and prejudices. Critical thinkers may follow their inner sense that something is so, but only with a healthy sense of intellectual humility.

There is a second sense of 'intuition' that is important for critical thinking, and that is the meaning suggested in the following sentence: "To develop your critical thinking abilities, it is important to develop your critical thinking *intuitions.*" This sense of the word is connected to the fact that we can learn concepts at various levels of depth. If we learn nothing more than an abstract definition for a word and do not learn how to apply it effectively in a wide variety of situations, one might say that we end up with no *intuitive* basis for applying it. We lack the insight into how, when, and why it applies. Helping students to develop critical thinking intuitions is helping them gain the practical insights necessary for a ready and swift application of concepts to cases in a large array of circumstances. We want critical thinking to be "intuitive" to our students, ready and available for immediate translation into their everyday thought and experience.

irrational/irrationality: *1)* Lacking the power to reason. *2)* Contrary to reason or logic. *3)* Senseless, absurd. Uncritical thinkers have failed to develop the ability or power to reason well. Their beliefs and practices, then, are often contrary to reason and logic, and are sometimes senseless or absurd. It is important to recognize, however, that in societies with irrational beliefs and practices, it is not clear whether challenging those beliefs and practices — and therefore possibly endangering oneself — is rational or irrational. Furthermore, suppose one's vested interests are best advanced by adopting beliefs and practices that are contrary to reason. Is it then rational to follow reason and negate one's vested interests or follow one's interests and ignore reason? These very real dilemmas of everyday life represent on-going problems for critical thinkers. Selfish critical thinkers, of course, face no dilemma here because of their consistent commitment to advance their narrow vested interests. Fairminded critical thinkers make these decisions self-consciously and honestly assess the results.

irrational learning: All rational learning presupposes rational assent. And, though we sometimes forget it, not all learning is automatically or even commonly rational. *Much that we learn in everyday life is quite distinctively irrational.* It is quite possible — and indeed the bulk of human learning is unfortunately of this character — *to come to believe any number of things without knowing how or why.* It is quite possible, in other words, to believe for irrational reasons: because those around us believe, because we are rewarded for believing, because we are afraid to disbelieve, because our vested interest is served by belief, because we are more comfortable with belief, or because we have ego identified ourselves, our image, or our personal being with belief. In all of these cases, our beliefs are without rational grounding, without good reason and evidence, without the foundation a rational person demands. We become rational, on the other hand, to the extent that our beliefs and actions are grounded in good reasons and evidence; to the extent that we recognize and critique our own irrationality; to the extent that we are not moved by bad reasons and a multiplicity of irrational motives, fears, and desires; to the extent that we have cultivated a passion for clarity, accuracy, and fairmindedness. These global skills, passions, and dispositions, integrated into behavior and thought, characterize the rational, the educated, and the critical person. See *higher and lower order learning, knowledge, didactic instruction.*

judgment: *1)* The act of judging or deciding. *2)* Understanding and good sense. A person has good judgment when they typically judge and decide on the basis of understanding and good sense. Whenever we form a belief or opinion, make a decision, or act, we do so on the basis of implicit or explicit judgments. All thought presupposes making judgments concerning what is so and what is not so, what is true and what is not. To cultivate people's ability to think critically is to foster their judgment, to help them to develop the habit of judging on the basis of reason, evidence, logic, and good sense. Good judgment is developed, not by merely learning about principles of good judgment, but by frequent practice judging and assessing judgments.

justify/justification: The act of showing a belief, opinion, action, or policy to be in accord with reason and evidence, to be ethically acceptable, or both. Education should foster reasonability in students. This requires that both teachers and students develop the disposition to ask for and give justifications for beliefs, opinions, actions, and policies. Asking for a justification should not, then, be viewed as an insult or attack, but rather as a normal act of a rational person. Didactic modes of teaching that do not encourage students to question the justification for what is asserted fail to develop a thoughtful environment conducive to education.

know: To have a clear perception or understanding of, to be sure of, to have a firm mental grasp of; *information* applies to data that are gathered in any way, as by reading, observation, hearsay, etc. and does not necessarily connote validity; *knowledge* applies to any body of facts gathered by study, observation, etc. and to the ideas inferred from these facts, and connotes an *understanding* of what is known. Critical thinkers need to distinguish knowledge from opinion and belief. See *knowledge*.

knowledge: The act of having a clear and justifiable grasp of what is so or of how to do something. Knowledge is based on understanding or skill, which in turn are based on thought, study, and experience. 'Thoughtless knowledge' is a contradiction. 'Blind knowledge' is a contradiction. 'Unjustifiable knowledge' is a contradiction. Knowledge implies justifiable belief or skilled action. Hence, when students blindly memorize and are tested for recall, they are not being tested for knowledge. *Knowledge is continually confused with recall in present-day schooling.* This confusion is a deep-seated impediment to the integration of critical thinking into schooling. *Genuine knowledge is inseparable from thinking minds.* We often wrongly talk of knowledge as though it could be divorced from thinking, as though it could be gathered up by one person and given to another in the form of a collection of sentences to remember. When we talk in this way, we forget that *knowledge*, by its very nature, *depends on thought.* Knowledge is produced by thought, analyzed by thought, comprehended by thought, organized, evaluated, maintained, and transformed by thought. Knowledge can be *acquired only* through thought. Knowledge exists, properly speaking, only in minds that have comprehended and justified it through thought. Knowledge is not to be confused with belief nor with symbolic representation of belief. Humans easily and frequently believe things that are false or believe things to be true without knowing them to be so. A book contains knowledge only in a derivative sense, only because minds can thoughtfully read it and through that process gain knowledge.

logic: *1)* Correct reasoning or the study of correct reasoning and its foundations. *2)* The relationships between propositions (supports, assumes, implies, contradicts, counts against, is relevant to, ...). *3)* The system of principles, concepts, and assumptions that underlie any discipline, activity, or practice. *4)* The set of rational considerations that bear upon the truth or justification of any belief or set of beliefs. *5)* The set of rational considerations that bear upon the settlement of any question or set of questions. The word 'logic' covers a range of related concerns all bearing upon the question of rational justification and explanation. *All human thought and behavior is to some extent based on logic* rather than instinct. Humans try to figure things out using ideas, meanings, and thought. Such intellectual behavior inevitably involves "logic" or considerations of a logical sort: some sense of what is relevant and irrelevant, of what supports and what counts against a belief, of what we should and should not assume, of what we should and should not claim, of what we do and do not know, of what is and is not implied, of what does and does not contradict, of what we should or should not do or believe. *Concepts have a logic* in that we can investigate the conditions under which they do and do not apply, of what is relevant or irrelevant to them, of what they do or don't imply, etc. *Questions have a logic* in that we can investigate the conditions under which they can be settled. *Disciplines have a logic* in that they have purposes and a set of logical structures that bear upon those purposes: assumptions, concepts, issues, data, theories, claims, implications, consequences, etc. The concept of logic is a seminal notion in critical thinking. Unfortunately, it takes a considerable length of time before most people become comfortable with its multiple uses. In part, this is due to people's failure to monitor their own thinking in keeping with the standards of reason and logic. This is not to deny, of course, that logic is involved in all human thinking. It is rather to say that the logic we use is often implicit, unexpressed, and sometimes contradictory. See *knowledge, higher and lower order learning, the logic of a discipline, the logic of language, the logic of questions.*

the logic of a discipline: The notion that every technical term has logical relationships with other technical terms, that some terms are logically more basic than others, and that every discipline relies on concepts, assumptions, and theories, makes claims, gives reasons and evidence, avoids contradictions and inconsistencies, has implications and consequences, etc. Though all students study disciplines, most are ignorant of the logic of the disciplines they study. This severely limits their ability to grasp the discipline as a whole, to think independently within it, to compare and contrast it with other disciplines, and to apply it outside the context of academic assignments. Typically now, students do not look for seminal terms as they study an area. They do not strive to translate technical terms into analogies and ordinary words they understand or distinguish technical from ordinary uses of terms. They do not look for the basic assumptions of the disciplines they study. Indeed, on the whole, they do not know what assumptions are nor why it is important to examine them. What they have in their heads exists like so many BB's in a bag. Whether one thought supports or follows from another, whether one thought elaborates another, exemplifies, presupposes, or contradicts another, are matters students have not learned to think about. They have not learned to use thought to understand thought, which is another way of saying that they have not learned how to use thought to gain knowledge. *Instruction for critical thinking cultivates the students' ability to make explicit the logic of what they study.* This emphasis gives depth and breath to study and learning. It lies at the heart of the differences between lower order and higher order learning. See *knowledge.*

the logic of language: For a language to exist and be learnable by persons from a variety of cultures, it is necessary that *words have definite uses and defined concepts that transcend* *particular cultures.* The English language, for example, is learned by many peoples of the world unfamiliar with English or North American cultures. Critical thinkers must learn to use their native language with precision, in keeping with educated usage. Unfortunately, many students do not understand the significant relationship between precision in language usage and precision in thought. Consider, for example, how most students relate to their native language. If one questions them about the meanings of words, their account is typically incoherent. They often say that people have their own meanings for all the words they use, not noticing that, were this true, we could not understand each other. Students speak and write in vague sentences because they have no rational criteria for choosing words — they simply write whatever words pop into their heads. They do not realize that every language has a highly refined logic one must learn in order to express oneself precisely. They do not realize that even words similar in meaning typically have different implications. Consider, for example, the words explain, expound, explicate, elucidate, interpret, and construe. *Explain* implies the process of making clear and intelligible something not understood or known. *Expound* implies a systematic and thorough explanation, often by an expert. *Explicate* implies a scholarly analysis developed in detail. *Elucidate* implies a shedding of light upon by clear and specific illustration or explanation. *Interpre t* implies the bringing out of meanings not immediately apparent. *Construe* implies a particular interpretation of something whose meaning is ambiguous. See *clarify, concept.*

the logic of questions: The range of rational considerations that bear upon the settlement of a given question or group of questions. A critical thinker is adept at analyzing questions to determine what, precisely, a question asks and how to go about rationally settling it. A critical thinker recognizes that different kinds of questions often call for different modes of thinking, different kinds of considerations, and different procedures and techniques. Uncritical thinkers often confuse distinct questions and use considerations irrelevant to an issue while ignoring relevant ones.

lower order learning: Learning by rote memorization, association, and drill. There are a variety of forms of lower order learning in the schools which we can identify by understanding the relative *lack of logic informing them.* Paradigmatically, lower order learning is learning by sheer association or rote. Hence students come to think of history class, for example, as a place where you hear names, dates, places, events, and outcomes; where you try to remember them and state them on tests. Math comes to be thought of as numbers, symbols, and formulas — mysterious things you mechanically manipulate as the teacher told you in order to get the right answer. Literature is often thought of as uninteresting stories to remember along with what the teacher said is important about them. Consequently, students leave with a jumble of undigested fragments, scraps left over after they have forgotten most of what they stored in their short-term memories for tests. Virtually never do they grasp the logic of what they learn. Rarely do they relate what they learn to their own experience or critique each by means of the other. Rarely do they try to test what they learn in everyday life. Rarely do they ask "Why is this so? How does this relate to what I already know? How does this relate to what I am learning in other classes?" To put the point in a nutshell, very few students think of what they are learning as worthy of being arranged logically in their minds or have the slightest idea of how to do so. See *didactic instruction, monological and multilogical problems and thinking.*

monological (one-dimensional) problems: Problems that can be solved by reasoning exclusively within one point of view or frame of reference. For example, consider the following problems: *1)* Ten full crates of walnuts weigh 410 pounds, whereas an empty crate weighs 10 pounds. How much do the walnuts alone weigh?; and *2)* In how many days of the week does the third letter of the day's name immediately follow the first letter of the day's name in the alphabet? I call these problems and the means by which they are solved "monological". They are settled within one frame of reference with a definite set of logical moves. When the right set of moves is performed, the problem is settled. The answer or solution proposed can be shown by standards implicit in the frame of reference to be the "right" answer or solution. *Most important human problems are multilogical rather than monological,* nonatomic problems inextricably joined to other problems, with some conceptual messiness to them and very often with important values lurking in the background. When the problems have an empirical dimension, that dimension tends to have a controversial scope. In multilogical problems, it is often arguable how some facts should be considered and interpreted, and how their significance should be determined. When they have a conceptual dimension, there tend to be arguably different ways to pin the concepts down. Though life presents us with predominantly multilogical problems, schooling today over-emphasizes monological problems. Worse, and more frequently, present instructional practices treat multilogical problems as though they were monological. The posing of multilogical problems, and their consideration from multiple points of view, play an important role in the cultivation of critical thinking and higher order learning.

monological (one-dimensional) thinking: Thinking that is conducted exclusively within one point of view or frame of reference: figuring our how much this $67.49 pair of shoes with a 25% discount will cost me; learning what signing this contract obliges me to do; finding out when Kennedy was elected President. A person can think monologically whether or not the question is genuinely monological. (For example, if one considers the question, "Who caused the Civil War?" only from a Northerner's perspective, one is thinking monologically about a multilogical question.) The strong sense critical thinker avoids monological thinking when the question is multi-logical. Moreover, higher order learning requires multi-logical thought, even when the problem is monological (for example, learning a concept in chemistry), since students must explore and assess their original beliefs to develop insight into new ideas.

multilogical (multi-dimensional) problems: Problems that can be analyzed and approached from more than one, often from conflicting, points of view or frames of reference. For example, many ecological problems have a variety of dimensions to them: historical, social, economic, biological, chemical, moral, political, etc. A person comfortable thinking about multilogical problems is comfortable thinking within multiple perspectives, in engaging in dialogical and dialectical thinking, in practicing intellectual empathy, in thinking across disciplines and domains. See *monological problems, the logic of questions, the logic of disciplines, intellectual empathy, dialogical instruction.*

multilogical thinking: Thinking that sympathetically enters, considers, and reasons within multiple points of view. See *multilogical problems, dialectical thinking, dialogical instruction.*

national bias: Prejudice in favor of one's country, it's beliefs, traditions, practices, image, and world view; a form of sociocentrism or ethnocentrism. It is natural, if not inevitable, for people to be favorably disposed toward the beliefs, traditions, practices, and world view within which they were raised. Unfortunately, this favorable inclination commonly becomes a form of prejudice: a more or less rigid, irrational ego-identification which significantly distorts one's view of one's own nation and the world at large. It is manifested in a tendency to mindlessly take the side of one's own government, to uncritically accept governmental accounts of the nature of disputes with other nations, to uncritically exaggerate the virtues of one's own nation while playing down the virtues of "enemy" nations. National bias is reflected in the press and media coverage of every nation of the world. Events are included or excluded according to what appears significant within the dominant world view of the nation, and are shaped into stories to validate that view. Though constructed to fit into a particular view of the world, the stories in the news are presented as neutral, objective accounts, and uncritically accepted as such because people tend to uncritically assume that their own view of things is the way things really are. To become responsible critically thinking citizens and fairminded people, students must practice identifying national bias in the news and in their texts, and to broaden their perspective beyond that of uncritical nationalism. See *ethnocentrism, sociocentrism, bias, prejudice, world view, intellectual empathy, critical society, dialogical instruction, knowledge.*

opinion: A belief, typically one open to dispute. Sheer unreasoned opinion should be distinguished from reasoned judgment — beliefs formed on the basis of careful reasoning. See *evaluation, judgment, justify, know, knowledge, reasoned judgment.*

the perfections of thought: Thinking, as an attempt to understand the world as it is, has a natural excellence or fitness to it. This excellence is manifest in its *clarity, precision, specificity, accuracy, relevance, consistency, logicalness, depth, completeness, significance, fairness, and adequacy.* These perfections are general canons for thought; they represent legitimate concerns irrespective of the discipline or domain of thought. To develop one's mind and discipline one's thinking with respect to these standards *requires extensive practice and long-term cultivation.* Of course, achieving these standards is a relative matter and varies somewhat among domains of thought. Being *precise* while doing mathematics is not the same as being precise while writing a poem, describing an experience, or explaining a historical event. Furthermore, one perfection of thought may be periodically incompatible with the others: adequacy to purpose. Time and resources sufficient to thoroughly analyze a question or problem is all too often an unaffordable luxury. Also, since the social world is often irrational and unjust, because people are often manipulated to act against their interests, and because skilled thought often serves vested interest, thought adequate to these manipulative purposes may require *skilled violation of the common standards for good thinking.* Skilled propaganda, skilled political debate, skilled defense of a group's interests, skilled deception of one's enemy may require the violation or selective application of any of the above standards. Perfecting one's thought as an instrument for success in a world based on power and advantage differs from perfecting one's thought for the apprehension and defense of fairminded truth. *To develop one's critical thinking skills merely to the level of adequacy for social success is to develop those skills in a lower or <u>weaker</u> sense.*

personal contradiction: An inconsistency in one's personal life, wherein one says one thing and does another, or uses a double standard, judging oneself and one's friends by an easier standard than that used for people one doesn't like; typically a form of hypocrisy accompanied by self-deception. Most personal contradictions remain unconscious. People too often ignore the difficulty of becoming intellectually and morally consistent, preferring instead to merely admonish others. Personal contradictions are more likely to be discovered, analyzed, and reduced in an atmosphere in which they can be openly admitted and realistically considered without excessive penalty. See *egocentricity, intellectual integrity.*

perspective (point of view): Human thought is relational and selective. It is impossible to understand any person, event, or phenomenon from every vantage point simultaneously. Our purposes often control how we see things. Critical thinking requires that this fact be taken into account when analyzing and assessing thinking. This is not to say that human thought is incapable of truth and objectivity, but only that human truth, objectivity, and insight is virtually always limited and partial, virtually never total and absolute. The hard sciences are themselves a good example of this point, since qualitative realities are systematically ignored in favor of quantifiable realities.

precision: The quality of being accurate, definite, and exact. The standards and modes of precision vary according to subject and context. See *the logic of language, elements of thought.*

prejudice: A judgment, belief, opinion, point of view — favorable or unfavorable — formed before the facts are known, resistant to evidence and reason, or in disregard of facts which contradict it. Self-announced prejudice is rare. Prejudice almost always exists in obscured, rationalized, socially validated, functional forms. It enables people to sleep peacefully at night even while flagrantly abusing the rights of others. It enables people to get more of what they want, or to get it more easily. It is often sanctioned with a superabundance of pomp and self-righteousness. Unless we recognize these powerful tendencies toward selfish thought in our social institutions, even in what appear to be lofty actions and moralistic rhetoric, we will not face squarely the problem of prejudice in human thought and action. Uncritical and selfishly critical thought are often prejudiced. Most instruction in schools today, because students do not think their way to what they accept as true, tends to give students prejudices rather than knowledge. For example, partly as a result of schooling, people often accept as authorities those who liberally sprinkle their statements with numbers and intellectual-sounding language, however irrational or unjust their positions. This prejudice toward psuedo-authority impedes rational assessment. See *insight, knowledge.*

premise: A proposition upon which an argument is based or from which a conclusion is drawn. A starting point of reasoning. For example, one might say, in commenting on someone's reasoning, "You seem to be reasoning from the premise that everyone is selfish in everything they do. *Do* you hold this belief?"

principle: A fundamental truth, law, doctrine, value, or commitment, upon which others are based. Rules, which are more specific, and often superficial and arbitrary, are based on principles. Rules are more algorithmic; they needn't be understood to be followed. Principles must be understood to be appropriately applied or followed. Principles go to the heart of the matter. Critical thinking is dependent on principles, not rules and procedures. Critical thinking is principled, not procedural, thinking. Principles cannot be truly grasped through didactic instruction; they must be practiced and applied to be internalized. See *higher order learning, lower order learning, judgment.*

problem: A question, matter, situation, or person that is perplexing or difficult to figure out, handle, or resolve. Problems, like questions, can be divided into many types. Each has a (particular) logic. See *logic of questions, monological problems, multilogical problems.*

problem-solving: Whenever a problem cannot be solved formulaically or robotically, critical thinking is required: first, to determine the nature and dimensions of the problem, and then, in the light of the first, to determine the considerations, points of view, concepts, theories, data, and reasoning relevant to its solution. Extensive practice in independent problem-solving is essential to developing critical thought. Problem-solving is rarely best approached procedurally or as a series of rigidly followed steps. For example, problem-solving schemas typically begin, "State the problem." Rarely can problems be precisely and fairly stated prior to analysis, gathering of evidence, and dialogical or dialectical thought wherein several provisional descriptions of the problem are proposed, assessed, and revised.

proof (prove): Evidence or reasoning so strong or certain as to demonstrate the truth or acceptability of a conclusion beyond a reasonable doubt. How strong evidence or reasoning have to be to demonstrate what they purport to prove varies from context to context, depending on the significance of the conclusion or the seriousness of the implications following from it. See *domain of thought.*

rational/rationality: That which conforms to principles of good reasoning, is sensible, shows good judgment, is consistent, logical, complete, and relevant. Rationality is a summary term like 'virtue' or 'goodness'. It is manifested in an unlimited number of ways and depends on a host of principles. There is some ambiguity in it, depending on whether one considers only the logicalness and effectiveness by which one pursues one's ends, or whether it includes the assessment of ends themselves. There is also ambiguity in whether one considers selfish ends to be rational, even when they conflict with what is just. Does a rational person have to be just or only skilled in pursuing his or her interests? Is it rational to be rational in an irrational world? See *perfections of thought, irrational/irrationality, logic, intellectual virtues, weak sense critical thinking, strong sense critical thinking.*

rational emotions/passions: R. S. Peters has explained the significance of the affective side of reason and critical thought in his defense of the necessity of "rational passions":

> There is, for instance, the hatred of contradictions and inconsistencies, together with the love of clarity and hatred of confusion without which words could not be held to relatively constant meanings and testable rules and generalizations stated. A reasonable man cannot, without some special explanation, slap his sides with delight or express indifference if he is told that what he says is confused, incoherent, and perhaps riddled with contradictions.
>
> Reason is the antithesis of arbitrariness. In its operation it is supported by the appropriate passions which are mainly negative in character — the hatred of irrelevance, special pleading, and arbitrary fiat. The more developed emotion of indignation is aroused when some excess of arbitrariness is perpetuated in a situation where people's interests and claims are at stake. The positive side of this is the passion for fairness and impartial consideration of claims ....
>
> A man who is prepared to reason must feel strongly that he must follow the arguments and decide things in terms of where they lead. He must have a sense of the giveness of the impersonality of such considerations. In so far as thoughts about persons enter his head they should

be tinged with the respect which is due to another who, like himself, may have a point of view which is worth considering, who may have a glimmering of the truth which has so far eluded himself. A person who proceeds in this way, who is influenced by such passions, is what we call a reasonable man.

rational self: Our character and nature to the extent that we seek to base our beliefs and actions on good reasoning and evidence. Who we are, what our true character is, or our predominant qualities are, is always somewhat or even greatly different from who we *think* we are. Human egocentrism and accompanying self-deception often stand in the way of our gaining more insight into ourselves. We can develop a rational self, become a person who gains significant insight into what our true character is, only by reducing our egocentrism and self-deception. Critical thinking is essential to this process.

rational society: See *critical society.*

reasoned judgment: Any belief or conclusion reached on the basis of careful thought and reflection, distinguished from mere or unreasoned opinion on the one hand, and from sheer fact on the other. Few people have a clear sense of which of their beliefs are based on reasoned judgment and which on mere opinion. Moral or ethical questions, for example, are questions requiring reasoned judgment. One way of conceiving of subject-matter education is as developing students' ability to engage in reasoned judgment in accordance with the standards of each subject.

reasoning: The mental processes of those who reason; especially the drawing of conclusions or inferences from observations, facts, or hypotheses; the evidence or arguments used in this procedure. A critical thinker tries to develop the capacity to transform thought into reasoning at will, or rather, the ability to make his or her inferences explicit, along with the assumptions or premises upon which those inferences are based. Reasoning is a form of explicit inferring, usually involving multiple steps. When students write a persuasive paper, for example, we want them to be clear about their reasoning.

reciprocity: The act of entering empathically into the point of view or line of reasoning of others; learning to think as others do and by that means sympathetically assessing that thinking. (Reciprocity requires creative imagination as well as intellectual skill and a commitment to fairmindedness.)

relevant: Bearing upon or relating to the matter at hand; *relevant* implies close logical relationship with, and importance to, the matter under consideration; *germane* implies such close natural connection as to be highly appropriate or fit; *pertinent* implies an immediate and direct bearing on the matter at hand (a pertinent suggestion); *apposite* applies to that which is both relevant and happily suitable or appropriate; *applicable* refers to that which can be brought to bear upon a particular matter or problem. Students often have problems sticking to an issue and distinguishing information that bears upon a problem from information that does not. Merely reminding students to limit themselves to relevant considerations fails to solve this problem. The usual way of teaching students the term 'relevant' is to mention only clear-cut cases of relevance and irrelevance. Consequently, students do not learn that not everything that *seems* relevant is, or that some things which *do not seem* relevant are. Sensitivity to (ability to judge) relevance can only be developed with continual practice —

practice distinguishing relevant from irrelevant data, evaluating or judging relevance, arguing for and against the relevance of facts and considerations.

self-deception: Deceiving one's self about one's true motivations, character, identity, etc. One possible definition of the human species is "The Self-Deceiving Animal". Self-deception is a fundamental problem in human life and the cause of much human suffering. Overcoming self-deception through self-critical thinking is a fundamental goal of strong sense critical thinking. See *egocentric, rational self, personal contradiction, social contradiction, intellectual virtues.*

social contradiction: An inconsistency between what a society preaches and what it practices. In every society there is some degree of inconsistency between its image of itself and its actual character. Social contradiction typically correlates with human self-deception on the social or cultural level. Critical thinking is essential for the recognition of inconsistencies, and recognition is essential for reform and eventual integrity.

sociocentricity: The assumption that one's own social group is inherently and self-evidently superior to all others. When a group or society sees itself as superior, and so considers its views as correct or as the only reasonable or justifiable views, and all its actions as justified, there is a tendency to presuppose this superiority in all of its thinking and thus, to think closedmindedly. All dissent and doubt are considered disloyal and rejected without consideration. Few people recognize the sociocentric nature of much of their thought.

Socratic questioning: A mode of questioning that deeply probes the meaning, justification, or logical strength of a claim, position, or line of reasoning. Socratic questioning can be carried out in a variety of ways and adapted to many levels of ability and understanding. See *elements of thought, dialogical instruction, knowledge.*

specify/specific: To mention, describe, or define in detail; limiting or limited; specifying or specified; precise; definite. Student thinking, speech, and writing tend to be vague, abstract, and ambiguous rather than specific, concrete, and clear. Learning how to state one's views specifically is essential to learning how to think clearly, precisely, and accurately. See *perfections of thought.*

strong sense critical thinker: One who is predominantly characterized by the following traits: *1)* an ability to question deeply one's own framework of thought; *2)* an ability to reconstruct sympathetically and imaginatively the strongest versions of points of view and frameworks of thought opposed to one's own; and *3)* an ability to reason dialectically (multilogically) in such a way as to determine when one's own point of view is at its weakest and when an opposing point of view is at its strongest. Strong sense critical thinkers are not routinely blinded by their own points of view. They know they have points of view and therefore recognize on what framework of assumptions and ideas their own thinking is based. They realize the necessity of putting their own assumptions and ideas to the test of the strongest objections that can be leveled against them. Teaching for critical thinking in the strong sense is teaching so that students explicate, understand, and critique their own deepest prejudices, biases, and misconceptions, thereby discovering and contesting their own egocentric and sociocentric tendencies. Only if we contest our inevitable egocentric and sociocentric habits of thought, can we hope to think in a genuinely rational fashion.

Only dialogical thinking about basic issues that genuinely matter to the individual provides the kind of practice and skill essential to strong sense critical thinking.

Students need to develop all critical thinking skills in dialogical settings to achieve ethically rational development, that is, genuine fairmindedness. If critical thinking is taught simply as atomic skills separate from the empathic practice of entering into points of view that students are fearful of or hostile toward, they will simply find additional means of rationalizing prejudices and preconceptions, or convincing people that their point of view is the correct one. They will be transformed from vulgar to sophisticated (but not to strong sense) critical thinkers.

teach: The basic inclusive word for the imparting of knowledge or skills. It usually connotes some individual attention to the learner; *instruct* implies systematized teaching, usually in some particular subject; *educate* stresses the development of latent faculties and powers by formal, systematic teaching, especially in institutions of higher learning; *train* implies the development of a particular faculty or skill or instruction toward a particular occupation, as by methodical discipline, exercise, etc. See *knowledge*.

theory: A systematic statement of principles involved in a subject; a formulation of apparent relationships or underlying principles of certain observed phenomena which has been verified to some degree. Often without realizing it, we form theories that help us make sense of the people, events, and problems in our lives. Critical thinkers put their theories to the test of experience and give due consideration to the theories of others. Critical thinkers do not take their theories to be facts.

think: The general word meaning to exercise the mental faculties so as to form ideas, arrive at conclusions, etc.; *reason* implies a logical sequence of thought, starting with what is known or assumed and advancing to a definite conclusion through the inferences drawn; *reflect* implies a turning of one's thoughts back on a subject and connotes deep or quiet continued thought; *speculate* implies a reasoning on the basis of incomplete or uncertain evidence and therefore stresses the conjectural character of the opinions formed; *deliberate* implies careful and thorough consideration of a matter in order to arrive at a conclusion. Though everyone thinks, few people think critically. We don't need instruction to think; we think spontaneously. We need instruction to learn how to discipline and direct our thinking on the basis of sound intellectual standards. See *elements of thought, perfections of thought.*

truth: Conformity to knowledge, fact, actuality, or logic: a statement proven to be or accepted as true, not false or erroneous. Most people uncritically assume their views to be correct and true. Most people, in other words, assume themselves to possess the truth. Critical thinking is essential to avoid this, if for no other reason.

uncritical person: One who has not developed intellectual skills (naive, conformist, easily manipulated, dogmatic, easily confused, unclear, closedminded, narrowminded, careless in word choice, inconsistent, unable to distinguish evidence from interpretation). Uncriticalness is a fundamental problem in human life, for when we are uncritical we nevertheless think of ourselves as critical. The first step in becoming a critical thinker consists in recognizing that we are uncritical. Teaching for insight into uncriticalness is an important part of teaching for criticalness.

vague: Not clearly, precisely, or definitely expressed or stated; not sharp, certain, or precise in thought, feeling, or expression. Vagueness of thought and expression is a major obstacle to the development of critical thinking. We cannot begin to test our beliefs until we recognize clearly what they are. We cannot disagree with what someone says until we are clear about what they mean. Students need much practice in transforming vague thoughts into clear ones. See *ambiguous, clarify, concept, logic, logic of questions, logic of language.*

verbal implication: That which follows, according to the logic of the language. If I say, for example, that someone used flattery on me, I *imply* that the compliments were insincere and given only to make me feel positively toward that person, to manipulate me against my reason or interest for some end. *See imply, infer, empirical implication, elements of thought.*

weak sense critical thinkers: 1) Those who do not hold themselves or those with whom they ego-identify to the same intellectual standards to which they hold "opponents". 2) Those who have not learned how to reason empathically within points of view or frames of reference with which they disagree. 3) Those who tend to think monologically. 4) Those who do not genuinely accept, though they may verbally espouse, the values of critical thinking. 5) Those who use the intellectual skills of critical thinking selectively and self-deceptively to foster and serve their vested interests (at the expense of truth); able to identify flaws in the reasoning of others and refute them; able to shore up their own beliefs with reasons.

world view: All human action takes place within a way of looking at and interpreting the world. As schooling now stands, very little is done to help students to grasp how they are viewing the world and how those views determine the character of their experience, their interpretations, their conclusions about events and persons, etc. In teaching for critical thinking in a strong sense, we make the discovery of one's own world view and the experience of other people's world views a fundamental priority. See *bias, interpret.*

Recommended Readings in Critical Thinking

The General Case for Critical Thinking

Bailin, Sharon. *Achieving Extraordinary Ends: An Essay of Creativity.* Kluwer-Academic Publishers, Norwell, MA, 1988.

Baron, Joan and Robert Sternberg. *Teaching Thinking Skills: Theory and Practice.* W. H. Freeman Co., New York, NY, 1987.

Blair, J. Anthony and Ralph H. Johnson, eds. *Informal Logic (First International Symposium).* Edgepress, Point Reyes, CA, 1980.

Glaser, Edward M. *An Experiment in the Development of Critical Thinking.* AMS Press, New York, NY, reprint of 1941 edition.

Mill, John Stuart. *On Liberty.* AHM Publishing Corp., Arlington Heights, IL., 1947.

Resnick, Lauren. *Education and Learning to Think.* National Academy Press, Washington, D.C., 1987.

Scheffler, Israel. *Reason and Teaching.* Hackett Publishing, Indianapolis, IN, 1973.

Siegel, Harvey. *Educating Reason: Rationality, Critical Thinking, & Education.* Routledge Chapman & Hall, Inc., New York, NY, 1988.

Sumner, William G. *Folkways.* Ayer Co., Publishing, Salem, NH, 1979.

Toulmin, Stephen E. *The Uses of Argument.* Cambridge University Press, New York, NY, 1958.

Critical Thinking Pedagogy

Brookfield, Stephen D. *Developing Critical Thinkers.* Jossey-Bass, San Francisco, CA, 1987.

Costa, Arthur L. *Developing Minds: A Resource Book for Teaching Thinking.* A.S.C.D., Alexandria, VA, 1985.

D'Angelo, Edward. *The Teaching of Critical Thinking.* B. R. Grüner, N. V., Amsterdam, 1971.

Goodlad, John. *A Place Called School.* McGraw-Hill, New York, 1984.

Lipman, Matthew. *Ethical Inquiry.* Institute for the Advancement of Philosophy for Children, Upper Montclair, N.J., 1977.

Lipman, Matthew. *Harry Stottlemeier's Discovery.* Institute for the Advancement of Philosophy for Children, Upper Montclair, N.J., 1982.

Lipman, Matthew. *Lisa.* Institute for the Advancement of Philosophy for Children, Upper Montclair, N.J., 1976.

Lipman, Matthew. *Mark.* Institute for the Advancement of Philosophy for Children, Upper Monclair, N.J., 1980.

Lipman, Matthew, Ann M. Sharp, and Frederick S. Oscanyan. *Philosophical Inquiry.* University Press of America, Lanham, Maryland, 1979.

Lipman, Matthew, and Ann M. Sharp. *Philosophy in the Classroom.* 2ⁿᵈ edition, Temple University Press, Philadelphia, PA, 1980.

Lipman, Matthew. *Social Inquiry.* Institute for the Advancement of Philosophy for Children, Upper Montclair, N.J., 1980.

Meyers, Chet. *Teaching Students to Think Critically: A Guide for Faculty in all Disciplines.* Jossey-Bass, San Francisco, CA, 1986.

Paul, Richard W., et al. *Critical Thinking Handbook: K–3. A Guide to Remodelling Lesson Plans in Language Arts, Social Studies, and Science.* The Center for Critical Thinking and Moral Critique, Rohnert Park, CA, 1987.

Paul, Richard W., et al. *Critical Thinking Handbook: 4ᵗʰ–6ᵗʰ. A Guide to Remodelling Lesson Plans in Language Arts, Social Studies, and Science.* The Center for Critical Thinking and Moral Critique, Rohnert Park, CA, 1987.

Paul, Richard W., et al. *Critical Thinking Handbook: 6ᵗʰ–9ᵗʰ A Guide to Remodelling Lesson Plans in Language Arts, Social Studies, and Science.* The Center for Critical Thinking and Moral Critique, Rohnert Park, CA, 1989.

Paul, Richard W., et al. *Critical Thinking Handbook: High School. A Guide for Redesigning Instruction.* The Center for Critical Thinking and Moral Critique, Rohnert Park, CA, 1989.

Raths, Louis. *Teaching for Thinking: Theories, Strategies, and Activities for the Classroom.* 2ⁿᵈ edition, Teachers College Press, New York, NY, 1986.

Ruggiero, Vincent. *Thinking Across the Curriculum.* Harper & Row, New York, NY, 1988.

Ruggiero, Vincent. *Art of Thinking.* 2ⁿᵈ edition, Harper & Row, New York, NY, 1988.

Sizer, Theodore R. *Horace's Compormise: The Dilemma of the American High School.* Houghton Mifflin, Boston, 1984.

College Textbooks (Not Focused on a Specific Discipline)

Barker, Evelyn M. *Everyday Reasoning.* Prentice-Hall, Englewood Cliffs, NJ, 1981.

Barry, Vincent E., and Joel Rudinow. *Invitation to Critical Thinking.* 2ⁿᵈ edition, Holt, Rinehart & Winston, New York, NY, 1990.

Brown, Neil and Stuart Keely. *Asking the Right Questions: A Guide to Critical Thinking.* 2ⁿᵈ edition, Prentice-Hall, Englewood Cliffs, NJ, 1986.

Capaldi, Nicholas. *The Art of Deception.* 2ⁿᵈ edition, Prometheus Books, Buffalo, New York, 1979.

Cederblom, Jerry. *Critical Reasoning.* 2ⁿᵈ edition, Wadsworth Publishing Co., Belmont, CA, 1986.

Chaffee, John. *Thinking Critically.* 2ⁿᵈ edition, Houghton Mifflin, Boston, MA, 1988.

Damer, T. Edward. *Attacking Faulty Reasoning.* 2ⁿᵈ edition, Wadsworth Publishing Co., Belmont, CA, 1987.

Engel, Morris. *Analyzing Informal Fallacies.* Prentice-Hall, Englewood Cliffs, NJ, 1980.

Engel, Morris. *With Good Reason: An Introduction to Informal Fallacies.* 3ʳᵈ edition, St. Martin's Press, New York, NY, 1986.

Fahnestock, Jeanne and Marie Secor. *Rhetoric of Argument.* McGraw-Hill Book Co., New York, NY, 1982.

Fisher, Alec. *The Logic of Real Arguments.* Cambridge University Press, New York, NY, 1988.

Govier, Trudy. *A Practical Study of Argument.* 2ⁿᵈ edition, Wadsworth Publishing Co., Belmont, CA, 1988.

Hitchcock, David. *Critical Thinking: A Guide to Evaluating Information.* Methuan Publications, Toronto, Canada, 1983.

Hoagland, John. *Critical Thinking.* Vale Press, Newport News, VA, 1984.

Johnson, Ralph H. and J. A. Blair. *Logical Self-Defense.* 2ⁿᵈ edition, McGraw-Hill, New York, NY, 1983.

Kahane, Howard. *Logic and Contemporary Rhetoric.* 5ᵗʰ edition, Wadsworth Publishing Co., Belmont, CA, 1988.

Meiland, Jack W. *College Thinking: How to Get the Best Out of College.* New American Library, New York, NY, 1981.

Michalos, Alex C. *Improving Your Reasoning.* Prentice-Hall, Englewood Cliffs, NJ, 1986.

Miller, Robert K. *Informed Argument.* 2ⁿᵈ edition, Harcourt, Brace, Jovanovich, San Diego, CA, 1989.

Missimer, Connie. *Good Arguments: An Introduction to Critical Thinking.* 2ⁿᵈ edition, Prentice-Hall, Englewood Cliffs, NJ, 1986.

Moore, Brooke N. *Critical Thinking: Evaluating Claims and Arguments in Everyday Life.* 2ⁿᵈ edition, Mayfield Publishing Co., Palo Alto, CA, 1989.

Moore, Edgar. *Creative and Critical Reasoning.* 2ⁿᵈ edition, Houghton Mifflin, Boston, MA, 1984.

Nickerson, Raymond S. *Reflections on Reasoning.* L. Erlbaum, Assoc., Hillsdale, NJ, 1986.

Ruggiero, Vincent. *Moral Imperative.* Mayfield Publishing, Palo Alto, CA, 1984.

Scriven, Michael. *Reasoning.* McGraw-Hill Book Co., New York, NY, 1976.

Seech, Zachary. *Logic in Everyday Life: Practical Reasoning Skills.* Wadsworth Publishing Co., Belmont, CA, 1988.

Shor, Ira. *Critical Teaching & Everyday Life.* University of Chicago Press, Chicago, IL, 1987.

Toulmin, Stephen E., Richard Rieke, and Alan Janik. *An Introduction to Reasoning.* Macmillan Publishing Co., New York, NY, 1979.

Weddle, Perry. *Argument: A Guide to Critical Thinking.* McGraw-Hill, New York, NY, 1978.

Wilson, John. *Thinking with Concepts.* 4ᵗʰ edition, Cambridge University Press, New York, NY, 1987.

Science and Critical Thinking

Giere, Ronald N. *Understanding Scientific Reasoning.* Holt, Rinehart, and Winston, New York, NY, 1979. (Out of print.)

Radner, Daisie and Radner, Michael. *Science and Unreason*. Wadsworth, Publishing Co., Belmont, CA, 1982.

Mathematics and Critical Thinking

Schoenfeld, Alan. *Mathematical Problem Solving*. Academic Press, Orlando, FL, 1985.

Language Arts and Critical Thinking

Adler, Mortimer. *How to Read a Book*. Simon and Schuster, New York, NY, 1972.

Horton, Susan. *Thinking Through Writing*. Johns Hopkins, Baltimore, MD, 1982.

Kytle, Ray. *Clear Thinking for Composition*. 5ᵗʰ edition, McGraw-Hill Book Co., New York, NY, 1987.

Mayfield, Marlys. *Thinking for Yourself: Developing Critical Thinking Skills Through Writing*. Wadsworth Publishing Co., Belmont, CA, 1987.

Rosenberg, Vivian. *Reading, Writing, and Thinking: Critical Connections*. McGraw-Hill Book Co., New York, NY, 1989.

Scull, Sharon. *Critical Reading and Writing for Advanced ESL Students*. Prentice-Hall, Englewood Cliffs, NJ, 1987.

Critical Thinking and the Media

Lazere, Donald. *American Media & Mass Culture*. University of California Press, Berkeley, CA, 1987.

Also of Interest

Baker, Paul J., and Louis Anderson. *Social Problems: A Critical Thinking Approach*. Wadsworth Publishing Co., Belmont, CA, 1987.

Bloom, Benjamin. *Taxonomy of Educational Objectives*. David McKay Co., Inc., New York, 1956.

Goffman, Erving. *Presentation of Self in Everyday Life*. Doubleday & Co., New York, NY, 1959.

Lappé, Francis Moore. *Rediscovering America's Values*. Ballantine Books, New York, NY, 1989.

Siegel, Harvey. *Relativism Refuted*. Kluwer-Academic Publishers, Norwell, MA, 1987.

Tavris, Carol. *Anger: The Misunderstood Emotion*. Simon & Schuster, New York, NY, 1987.

Wilson, Barrie. *The Anatomy of Argument*. University Press of America, Lanham, Maryland, 1980.

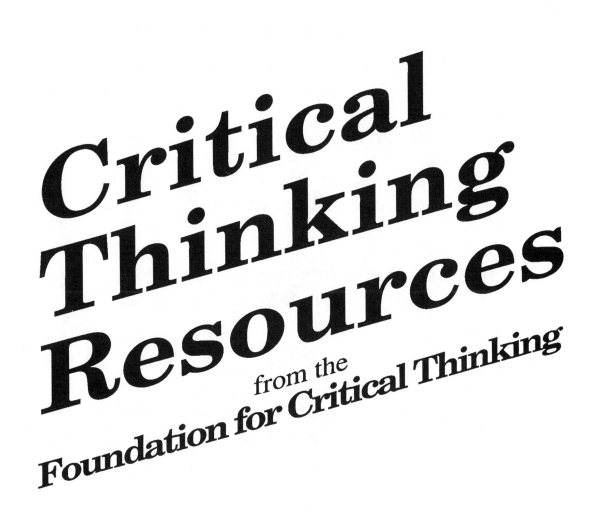

Critical Thinking Resources

from the

Foundation for Critical Thinking

 Grade Level Handbooks

 Hundreds of audio and video tapes by distinguished educators

 Annual Conferences

 A Critical Thinking Clearing House

 The Latest Theory and Research

 **Staff Development**

Critical Thinking Strategies

What every teacher needs to know!

What do I do when . . .

. . . my students do not learn how to work by, or think for, themselves?

. . . they don't know how to reason well enough to master a subject?

How do I . . .

. . . teach "content" when my students don't read, write, speak, or listen critically?

Solution!

✔ *How-to-do-it handbooks help you the teacher, alone or with others, to use critical thinking as a powerful tool for teaching and learning.*

✔ *Devised and designed by one of the best known and respected authorities on critical thinking, Richard Paul.*

✔ *Acclaimed by teachers and leading educators, such as Art Costa, Sandra Black, Bob Swartz.*

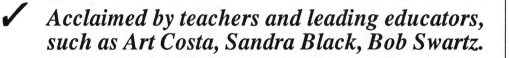

Critical Thinking Strategies
Handbooks K-3, 4-6, 6-9, High School

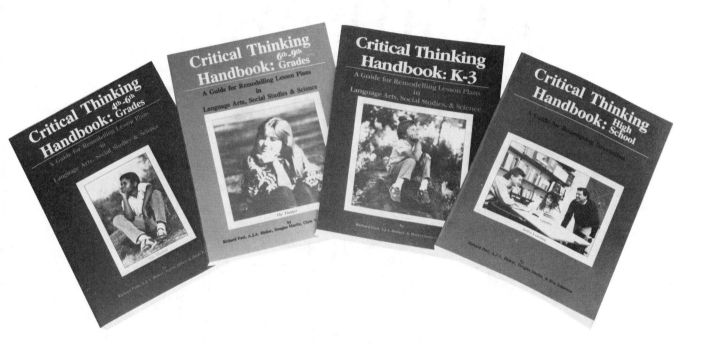

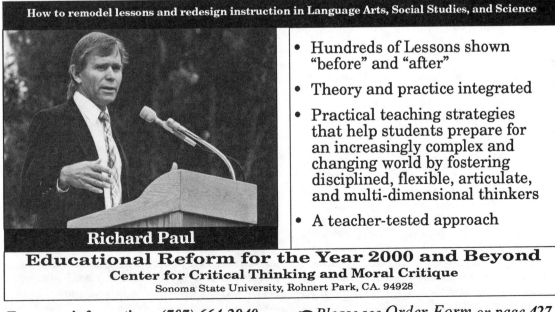

How to remodel lessons and redesign instruction in Language Arts, Social Studies, and Science

Richard Paul

- Hundreds of Lessons shown "before" and "after"

- Theory and practice integrated

- Practical teaching strategies that help students prepare for an increasingly complex and changing world by fostering disciplined, flexible, articulate, and multi-dimensional thinkers

- A teacher-tested approach

Educational Reform for the Year 2000 and Beyond
Center for Critical Thinking and Moral Critique
Sonoma State University, Rohnert Park, CA. 94928

For more information: **(707) 664-2940**   ☞ *Please see Order Form on page 427*

Richard Paul has written over forty articles on critical thinking in the last five years, yet ready access to them has been hampered by the variety of publications in which they have appeared. This anthology collects together the major essays of Richard Paul on critical thinking, including a number of important unpublished ones. As a collection, it makes a powerful case for critical thinking as essential not only for academic but for political, social, and personal life as well. Paul inevitably canvases critical thinking from a broad perspective. He views it historically, socially, psychologically, ethically, philosophically, and pedagogically. While seeing clearly its universal application across domains of knowledge and learning, he also sees the need for working out the details of that universality in specific contexts and domains. Bringing his major papers together enables the reader to grasp something of the breadth and depth of the role thinking plays in human life and knowledge, and of why reform of education grounded in critical thinking is essential to the future of humankind. It enables the reader to see why critical thinking must be cultivated from the earliest years of children's lives and why this must be understood as a long term commitment.

Paul's writings on critical thinking model the processes that all thinking must undergo as it develops. They overlap and criss-cross each other in many different ways. Reflective readers will find themselves coming at the same ground from a number of different vantage points.

As the table of contents indicates, this volume includes essays and papers that integrate the theory and practice of critical thinking and critical thinking instruction. It will be of special interest, therefore, to educators concerned with classroom practice.

Critical Thinking

Table of Contents

☛ *Please see Order Form on page 427*

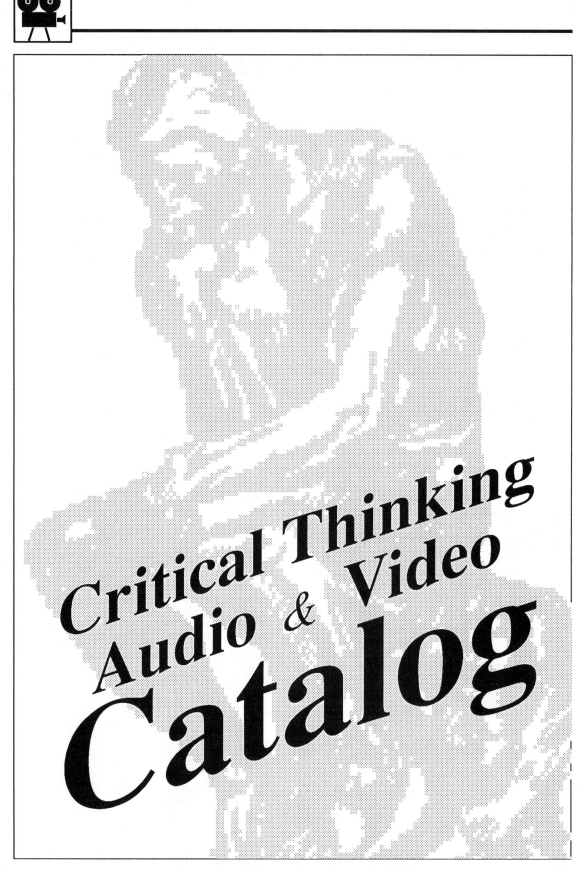

Critical Thinking Audio & Video Catalog

☛ *Please see Order Form on page* ***427***

With many distinguished educators:

Richard Paul

Carol Tavris

David Perkins

Robert Ennis

☛ *Please see Order Form on page 427*

The Best of Theory and Practice

Art Costa

Dianne Romain

John Chaffee

Vincent Ryan Ruggiero

☛ *Please see* Order Form *on page* **427**

From Kindergarten through Graduate School

Jan Talbot

Ralph Johnson

J. Anthony Blair

Linda Phillips

☛ *Please see* Order Form *on page* **427**

Critical Thinking Forum
on VHS Tape!

❑

from the
Center for Critical Thinking and Moral Critique
a series of eight Resource Programs produced for PBS Adult Learning Service

Part I: Why Critical Thinking?

Critical Thinking and the Human Emotions — Most instruction is designed without an adequate understanding of the profound role of human emotions and passions in learning. In this program, Carol Tavris, distinguished social psychologist and author of *Anger: The Misunderstood Emotions,* engages in a lively discussion on the relation of disciplined thought to emotions and passions. Many of the traditional views of reason and emotion are critiqued in this session, and the implications for education emerge vividly.

Critical Thinking and Mathematical Problem Solving — Surely it's not possible to pass a math class without doing much disciplined thinking. Not so! argues Alan Schoenfeld, distinguished math educator from the University of California. Most students do not learn to think mathematically precisely because of the domination of didactic lecture, standard algorithmic practice and one-dimensional testing that characterizes most math classes. When independent critical thinking is the heart of class activity, Schoenfeld says, genuine mathematical thinking emerges for the first time.

Infusing Critical Thinking into Community College Instruction — For critical thinking to become a significant force in student learning, it is essential that it permeate instruction across the disciplines. Unfortunately, students do not arrive on campus with developed critical thinking abilities and most professors are up in the air as to how they can cover essential content and also foster critical thinking. In this program, faculty development leaders from five diverse community colleges discuss their strategies for making critical thinking central to instruction.

Infusing Critical Thinking into Instruction at Four Year Colleges and Universities — Though four year colleges and universities tend to draw students with higher test scores and grade point averages than those entering community colleges, it does not follow that those students have developed critical thinking skills and abilities adequate to university learning. Five faculty development leaders from diverse colleges and universities discuss the problem of infusing critical thinking into instruction.

☛ *Please see Order Form on page 427*

Critical Thinking Forum
on VHS Tape!

❏

from the
Center for Critical Thinking and Moral Critique
a series of eight Resource Programs produced for PBS Adult Learning Service

Part II: How to Infuse Critical Thinking K–12

Critical Thinking: The Thinking that Masters the Content —
This program investigates why traditional didactic instruction inevitably fails and why critical thinking is essential to in-depth learning. Three dimensions of thought are emphasized: 1) fine-textured thinking such as identifying evidence and reasons, probing for assumptions, drawing careful conclusions, and noticing inconsistencies; 2) skills such as reasoning within multiple points of view and reading, writing, speaking, and listening critically; and 3) affective skills so students develop traits such as fairmindedness, intellectual courage, humility, and persistence.

Transforming Critical Thinking Principles into Teaching Strategies —
Critical thinking is based not on rules but on principles that can be learned by any willing teacher and transformed into a variety of teaching and learning strategies. In this program, a variety of grade-levels and subject matter illustrations are used to illustrate how critical thinking principles that are integrated into modes of teaching become modes of learning as well.

Remodelling Lessons and Redesigning Instruction to Infuse Critical Thinking — In this program, the teacher becomes the focus as Richard Paul explains how, by learning to think critically about their own instruction, teachers can remodel their lessons and redesign their instruction. Virtually every traditional lesson or unit can be remodelled in a variety of ways to infuse critical thinking. When it is, passive students become actively engaged. The teacher's monologue becomes a classroom dialogue. And content becomes something understood, mastered, and used — not just something memorized today and forgotten tomorrow.

The Greensboro Plan: Long-Term Critical Thinking Staff Development in an Urban Multi-Racial School District — In its third year of a long-term staff development program to infuse critical thinking, two teachers become full-time classroom consultants to encourage teachers to think critically about their own instruction. The aim is to remodel lessons and redesign instruction in order to infuse reasoning, writing, and critical thinking pervasively. Slowly but progressively, a new atmosphere is developing that encourages independent thinking for both teachers and students. This volunteer program, growing in support from both teachers and administrators, is a model for districts willing to work for long-term, substantial, educational reform.

☞ *Please see Order Form on page 427*

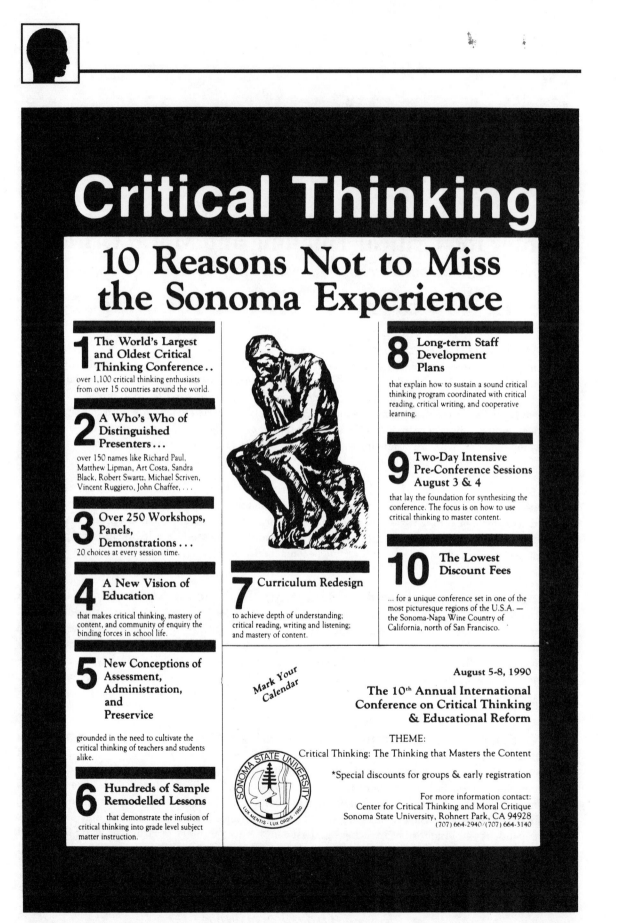

Critical Thinking

10 Reasons Not to Miss the Sonoma Experience

1 The World's Largest and Oldest Critical Thinking Conference..
over 1,100 critical thinking enthusiasts from over 15 countries around the world.

2 A Who's Who of Distinguished Presenters...
over 150 names like Richard Paul, Matthew Lipman, Art Costa, Sandra Black, Robert Swartz, Michael Scriven, Vincent Ruggiero, John Chaffee, . . .

3 Over 250 Workshops, Panels, Demonstrations...
20 choices at every session time.

4 A New Vision of Education
that makes critical thinking, mastery of content, and community of enquiry the binding forces in school life.

5 New Conceptions of Assessment, Administration, and Preservice
grounded in the need to cultivate the critical thinking of teachers and students alike.

6 Hundreds of Sample Remodelled Lessons
that demonstrate the infusion of critical thinking into grade level subject matter instruction.

7 Curriculum Redesign
to achieve depth of understanding; critical reading, writing and listening; and mastery of content.

8 Long-term Staff Development Plans
that explain how to sustain a sound critical thinking program coordinated with critical reading, critical writing, and cooperative learning.

9 Two-Day Intensive Pre-Conference Sessions August 3 & 4
that lay the foundation for synthesizing the conference. The focus is on how to use critical thinking to master content.

10 The Lowest Discount Fees
... for a unique conference set in one of the most picturesque regions of the U.S.A. — the Sonoma-Napa Wine Country of California, north of San Francisco.

Mark Your Calendar

August 5-8, 1990

The 10th Annual International Conference on Critical Thinking & Educational Reform

THEME:
Critical Thinking: The Thinking that Masters the Content

*Special discounts for groups & early registration

For more information contact:
Center for Critical Thinking and Moral Critique
Sonoma State University, Rohnert Park, CA 94928
(707) 664-2940 / (707) 664-3140

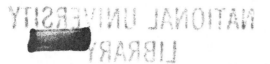

Order Form

Please send me free information on:

The Annual Critical Thinking Conference ....☐

The Audio & Video Tape Collection ....☐

Other (Specify) _____ ☐

I would like to order the following:

Books

Critical Thinking: What Every Person Needs to Survive
in a Rapidly Changing World (700 pp.) ....☐ $19.95 _____

Critical Thinking Handbook: K–3 (322 pp.) ....☐ $18.00 _____

Critical Thinking Handbook: 4–6 (316 pp.) ....☐ $18.00 _____

Critical Thinking Handbook: 6–9 (320 pp.) ....☐ $18.00 _____

Critical Thinking Handbook: High School (416 pp.) ....☐ $18.00 _____

The Greensboro Plan for Critical Thinking Staff Development (212 pp.) ......☐ $8.95 _____

Discount Available for Bulk Orders

VHS Tapes

Critical Thinking Forum 1990: Parts I and II ....☐ $650 _____
All eight programs delivered as available in Spring/Fall 1990

Part I: Why Critical Thinking? ....☐ $375 _____
Four programs delivered as available in Spring 1990

Part II: How to Infuse Critical Thinking K–12 ....☐ $375 _____
Four programs delivered as available in Fall 1990

Purchase by Individual Program *(please check those you wish to order)*

Critical Thinking and the Human Emotions ....☐ $125 _____

Critical Thinking and Mathematical Problem Solving ....☐ $125 _____

Infusing Critical Thinking into Community College Instruction ....☐ $125 _____

Infusing Critical Thinking into Instruction at Four Year Colleges/Universities ....☐ $125 _____

Critical Thinking: The Thinking that Masters the Content ....☐ $125 _____

Transforming Critical Thinking Principles into Teaching Strategies ....☐ $125 _____

Remodeling Lessons & Redesigning Instruction to Infuse Critical Thinking ....☐ $125 _____

The Greensboro Plan: Long Term Critical Thinking Staff Development ....☐ $125 _____

Shipping: $3.50 for the first tape or book, $1.00 for each additional item
  Foreign Orders: $7.50 for the first tape or book, $2.00 for each additional item   Shipping $ _____

California orders 6.25% tax $ _____

Total $ _____

Make Check or Purchase Order Payable to: Foundation for Critical Thinking *(U.S. currency only)*
Send order to: Center for Critical Thinking and Moral Critique
        Sonoma State University, Rohnert Park, CA 94928   (707)664-2940

Ship to:

Name: _____

Address: _____

_____Phone: _____

Help Us "Remodel" this Handbook

In the spirit of good critical thinking, we want your assessment of this handbook and ideas for its improvement. Your ideas might be rewarded with a scholarship to the next International Conference on Critical Thinking!

Evaluation:

Here's what I found most useful about the handbook:

_____

_____

_____

_____

This is what I think is in need of change:

_____

_____

_____

_____

Here are my ideas for improving the handbook:

_____

_____

_____

Send evaluation to: Center For Critical Thinking; Sonoma State University; Rohnert Park, CA 94928.